D1453450

Italy's Eighteenth Century

Italy's Eighteenth Century

GENDER AND CULTURE
IN THE AGE OF THE GRAND TOUR

EDITED BY

*Paula Findlen, Wendy Wassyng Roworth,
and Catherine M. Sama*

Chapters 1, 2, 4, and 11 were translated by Matthew Sneider

STANFORD UNIVERSITY PRESS
STANFORD, CALIFORNIA

This book is dedicated to our sisters Sharon, Susan, Emily, and Leslie
and to sisterhood past, present, and future

Stanford University Press
Stanford, California

©2009 by the Board of Trustees of the Leland Stanford Junior University.
All rights reserved.

This book has been published with the assistance of the University of Rhode Island Center
for the Humanities and the School of Humanities and Science, Stanford University.

No part of this book may be reproduced or transmitted in any form or by any means, elec-
tronic or mechanical, including photocopying and recording, or in any information storage
or retrieval system without the prior written permission of Stanford University Press.

Printed in the United States of America on acid-free, archival-quality paper

Library of Congress Cataloging-in-Publication Data

Italy's eighteenth century : gender and culture in the age of the grand tour / edited by Paula
Findlen, Wendy Wassyng Roworth, and Catherine M. Sama.
      p. cm.
   Includes bibliographical references and index.
   ISBN 978-0-8047-5904-5 (cloth : alk. paper)
   1. Italy—Intellectual life—18th century. 2. Women—Italy—Intellectual life—18th century. 3. Sex role—Italy—History—18th century. 4. Italy—Social life and customs—18th
century. I. Findlen, Paula. II. Roworth, Wendy Wassyng. III. Sama, Catherine M.
   DG447.I865 2009
   945'.07—dc22
                        2008020030

Typeset by Bruce Lundquist in 10.5/14 Adobe Garamond

Contents

Illustrations

Acknowledgments

This book developed from the conference *Italy's Eighteenth Century: Gender and Culture During the Age of the Grand Tour*, held at the Getty Research Institute and William Andrews Clark Memorial Library, co-sponsored with the UCLA Center for 17th- and 18th-Century Studies in 2002. Louis Marchesano, collections curator of prints and drawings at the Getty Research Institute, co-organized the conference with Paula Findlen. Thomas Crow, director of the Getty Research Institute, Gail Feigenbaum, associate director of programs at the Getty, and Peter H. Reill, director of the UCLA Center for 17th- and 18th-Century Studies, all helped to make this a provocative and enjoyable event. We thank the staff of both institutions for making the event go so smoothly. Chloe Chard, Massimo Ciavolella, Carole Paul, and Geoffrey Simcox, who all participated in the conference, stimulated discussion that led to the idea of publishing the papers. More recently, Carole Paul served as the external reviewer for this manuscript and offered sage advice on its final composition.

We express our gratitude to them and to other colleagues, family, and friends who provided inspiration, encouragement, and support throughout the development of this interdisciplinary project. We would also like to thank Meredith Kunz for assistance with editing, Matthew Sneider for his translations of Italian essays, and Brian Brege for the index. Many institutions lent support, including the University of Rhode Island Center for the Humanities, Stanford University, the American Academy in Rome, the British School at Rome, the Getty Research Institute, the American Council for Learned Societies, the American Philosophical Society, and the Center for Advanced Study in the Behavioral Sciences. They offered material support for the completion of this project and sabbatical leave for two of the three editors.

The essays in this volume present original research by international scholars in fields ranging from the history of science, art, and music to literature, travel writing, and gender studies. Some were presented in earlier versions at the conference; other, new essays were included to broaden the scope of our theme. We would like to acknowledge the patience, cooperation, and generosity of all the authors who contributed essays to the book. Their enthusiasm for this project has made it a pleasure to complete.

We are especially appreciative of the care with which Stanford University Press has seen this project into print. Norris Pope, Emily-Jane Cohen, Judith Hibbard, and Tom Finnegan have all been a pleasure to work with. We thank them for their enthusiasm and understanding of the pleasures and importance of collaborative research.

During the course of this collaborative project, the editors learned a great deal from each other and the other authors about the women and men in these essays: their lives and loves, their successes and losses, and their contributions to letters, arts, and sciences in eighteenth-century Italy. As we prepared this volume, we experienced some joyous and some painful personal events of our own—the birth of a child, the serious illness of a brother, the death of a beloved sister. Without the love and compassion of our families and friends, bringing our work to fruition would not have been possible.

Providence, Rhode Island, and Stanford, California
August 2008

Italy's Eighteenth Century

Gender and Culture in Eighteenth-Century Italy

PAULA FINDLEN

> What you say about the Italians is what all foreigners
> say, what must strike them at first sight. But you must
> probe more deeply to judge this country.
>
> —Germaine de Staël, *Corinne, or Italy* (1807)[1]

Touring Italy, Again

"The voyage to Italy is the most interesting of all possible voyages," declared the abbé Gabriel-François Coyer after his trip of 1763.[2] Italy had long captured the imagination of foreigners, but it did so to an unprecedented degree during the eighteenth century, when Grand Tourists arrived in ever-growing numbers. They came primarily to view the tangible remains of Italy's glorious past—its art, architecture, great libraries and museums, and especially its antiquities—and to sample certain elements of its present that they found in the theaters, opera houses, coffeehouses, casinos, and salons. "One comes to Italy to look at buildings, statues, pictures, people," wrote Hester Lynch Thrale Piozzi in 1789.[3] In an era in which travel was a necessary part of a gentleman's education and increasingly a possibility for a handful of adventurous women, firsthand experience of Italy became an

Many thanks to Martha Feldman, Marta Cavazza, Carole Paul, and especially my coeditors, Catherine Sama and Wendy Wassyng Roworth, for generously sharing their knowledge of eighteenth-century Italy with me. Their comments and bibliographic suggestions have substantially improved the introduction as a reflection of a multidisciplinary conversation about the state of this field.

essential prerequisite to any claim to be a citizen of the world. "A man who has not been to Italy," declared Samuel Johnson in 1776, "is always conscious of an inferiority from his not having seen what it is expected a man should see."[4]

Two years after Coyer completed his voyage, twenty-five-year-old James Boswell explained to Rousseau why he lingered in the southernmost parts of Europe: "My desire to know the world made me resolve to intrigue a little while in Italy," he confessed.[5] The very month that Boswell penned this letter, Tobias Smollett found himself in Florence shunning the very thing that his fellow Scotsman craved: "the intolerable caprices and dangerous resentment of an Italian virago."[6] He haunted the Uffizi and dreamed of visiting it daily in another life in which he would reside permanently in Florence. When Smollett arrived in Rome, he avoided the common practice of hiring an antiquarian, furnishing himself instead with maps, guidebooks, and an unschooled Roman servant so that he could see the city for himself rather than claim any pretension of connoisseurship in the hands of a professional and learned guide (*cicerone*). It was experience rather than knowledge that he sought to acquire. By contrast, Boswell happily reported to Rousseau from Rome: "I have almost finished my tour of Italy . . . and I believe that I have acquired taste to a certain degree."[7]

While these representative travelers may not have agreed uniformly about how Italy would be the culmination of their education, they nonetheless concurred on the fundamental role of an Italian experience for eighteenth-century Britons and Europeans. In between their trips, for example, lay the imaginary journey of Ann Radcliffe's English travelers, whose wanderings in Naples, set in "about the year 1764," were the pretext for telling her melodramatic tale of love, family, honor, and Roman Catholic iniquity in *The Italian* (1796).[8] The year 1764 was also the first time that the antiquarian Edward Gibbon laid eyes on the Eternal City. His three-month encounter with Rome famously inspired the writing of *The Decline and Fall of the Roman Empire* (1776–1783). Gibbon was hardly alone in the desire to produce something tangible from his Italian experience. The astronomer Jérôme de Lalande, whose year in Italy commenced in August 1765, transformed his experience into a bestselling guidebook, *Voyage d'un françois en Italie* (1769), so lengthy, detailed, and definitive that Napoleon's advisors used it as a blueprint for pillaging the scientific and artistic treasures of the Italian peninsula almost thirty years later. Germaine de Staël carried the updated edition of Lalande's book with her during a trip which inspired the writing of her melancholic bestseller *Corinne or Italy* (1807; Figure I.1). An allegorical and highly nostalgic portrait of Italy as a "learned lady" for foreigners to love, her novel immortalized one of the crucial images of Italy in the eighteenth century.[9]

As even a casual perusal of eighteenth-century travel literature reveals, there were many ways to tour Italy.[10] Two years after the appearance of Lalande's bestselling Baedeker for the enlightened public, Charles Burney highlighted the value of a musical Grand Tour in *The Present State of Music in France and Italy* (1771), presenting Italy as a feast for the ears as well as the eyes. The landscape of Roman ruins, Renaissance palaces, and Baroque galleries and churches also revealed a wealth of contemporary vocal and instrumental talent. Burney took his readers to the opera houses and into homes where learned *conversazione* gave way to musical performance. In Bologna, he visited the retired castrato Carlo Broschi (1705–1782), better known to his fans as Farinelli, and first laid eyes on the improviser Maria

Figure I.1 Elisabeth Vigée-Lebrun, *Madame de Staël as Corinne*, 1808. Erich Lessing/ Art Resource.

Maddalena Morelli (1727–1800), celebrated under her Arcadian name as Corilla Olimpica, in Florence where he sang tenor to her accompaniment on violin. [11] He very much wanted his readers to *hear* Italy just as Lady Anne Miller, also on the Grand Tour in 1770, sought to create an artistic guidebook that went beyond simple enumeration of paintings—mere catalogues without any hint of knowledge or taste that transformed such a list into an experience of connoisseurship. She promised readers of her *Letters from Italy* (1776) that she would describe "even to tediousness" absolutely everything she saw. [12]

The Grand Tour has played such an important role in the study of eighteenth-century Italy that it is virtually impossible to discuss the Italian peninsula during this period without some allusion to the significance of foreigners in shaping perceptions of Italian society, especially after the Treaty of Aix-la-Chapelle in 1748 which inaugurated a half-century of peace after several decades of intermittent warfare, making it far easier to travel. Their writings, published and unpublished, created an indelible image of Italy as an early modern tourists' paradise, a terrain of exploration and self-discovery that quickly established a sort of humdrum routine as successive waves of travelers followed in the footsteps of their predecessors, marching to the tune of the latest guidebooks and rarely deviating from this well-trodden path. [13] This Italy was an itinerary rather than a living, breathing entity; it existed to confirm assumptions and prejudices rather than to overturn them, and it outlined a history of a region that its inhabitants would—and did—write differently.

When the London-based Italian teacher and journalist Giuseppe Baretti (1719–1789) published his acerbic rebuttal to the stereotypical images of Italy in the writings of Grand Tourists in 1768, he aptly summed up the character of the oblivious visitor, describing him as someone who "saw little, inquired less, and reflected not at all." Baretti echoed the commonly held view among Italians that few foreigners really understood anything of the history, culture, and customs of the land they visited, preferring an imaginary Italy to the actual one since it was a more effective mirror of their own preoccupations. Foreigners, he observed, were less apt to comprehend the differences between the Italian states, preferring to transform this long and complicated set of relations and linguistic, cultural, and political differences into a unitary whole. "But it is so hard to say any thing universal of Italy," he warned his readers. [14] Such misperceptions were compounded by a strong sense of cultural superiority on the part of many Grand Tourists that Baretti hoped to dispel. He not only recounted the misbehavior and ignorance of English youth abroad but also sought to correct exaggerated accounts of the political turpitude, religious decadence, laxity of morals, and lack of ambition that allegedly flourished in the warm Mediterranean climate. Certainly Italy was different, but that did not necessarily make it inferior to the lands north of the Alps which, after all, drew so much inspiration from this part of the world.[15]

Not all foreigners who passed judgment on Italy were quite so transitory or ill-informed. In an era in which the Austrian Hapsburgs and the Spanish Bourbons ruled most of Italy, save for the Papal States and the republics of Genoa, Venice, and Lucca, and when the English and French saw the Italian peninsula as critical to maintaining their own presence in the Mediterranean through trade and diplomacy, there were many reasons to linger awhile in the Italian peninsula. Each of these four major European powers considered its attachment to Italy to be an important component of any claim to be the presumptive heir of the ancient Roman empire. Growing numbers of foreigners resident in the principal Italian cities—British consuls such as Joseph Smith in Venice, Sir Horace Mann in Florence, and Sir William Hamilton and his flamboyant wife Emma in Naples; antiquaries such as Johann Joachim Winckelmann and James Byres in Rome; and an international colony of artists, dealers, connoisseurs, and ciceroni that included such luminaries as painters Anton Raphael Mengs (1728–1779), Gavin Hamilton (1723–1798), and Angelica Kauffman (1741–1807), sculptors Christopher Hewetson (ca. 1739–1799) and Bertel Thorwaldsen (1770–1844), and artist, dealer, and banker Thomas Jenkins (1722–1798) as well as formal institutions such as the French Academy (founded in 1666 and installed in the Palazzo Mancini in 1725)[16]—helped to shape the most urbane aspects of Italian society and culture, especially in the second half of the eighteenth century. Their writings, artworks, and activities contributed to the image of Italy as a foreigners' paradise, and they profited directly from tourists and visiting artists through sales of artworks and antiquities, by serving as guides and providing art training. They advertised their knowledge of this region as the antidote to ignorance and inexperience.

As early as 1740, the well-traveled Lady Mary Wortley Montagu, at the beginning of her own lengthy residence in northern Italy, poked fun at the young English dandies who lounged around the Venetian coffeehouses, elegantly dressed in the latest fashions, sipping coffee and chocolate, spooning sorbets, discussing their latest affairs, and learning no Italian.[17] She would have found Boswell's unrestrained sexual tourism the epitome of the boorish behavior of the British abroad, though she initially came to Italy in search of her own thwarted *affaire du coeur* with the young Venetian Francesco Algarotti (1712–1764). Disappointed in love, Wortley Montagu found other reasons to remain. Having arrived in Italy carrying her considerable library in tow, she proclaimed it to be the ideal environment in which a thinking woman could flourish, better in every respect than the British Isles. "The character of a learned lady is far from being ridiculous in this country," she informed her daughter in 1753, "the greatest Familys being proud of having produce'd female writers and a Milanese Lady being now proffessor of Mathematics in the University of Bologna."[18] It was the presence of learned women such as the mathematician Maria Gaetana Agnesi (1718–1799)—appointed professor in absentia in 1749 since she never actually left Milan for Bologna[19]—that made Wortley Montagu confident of her chosen land of expatriation. When the French poet Anne-Marie Fiquet du Boccage met her in Venice in the summer of 1757, Lady Mary was sufficiently enamored of the Italy of Benedict XIV to show her visitor a portrait of the pope which she kept in her palace, while professing her utter disdain for Roman Catholicism.[20]

Upon completing her tour of Italy, Madame du Boccage wondered why the French did not correspond more frequently with the numerous talented Italian scholars and poets whom she met.[21] Britons and northern Europeans found Italy a different place, in part because they expected it to be quite unfamiliar. For them, Italy was both a utopia and a dystopia, a place of dreams and aspirations that offered endless opportunities to reinvent one's identity but also a location from which one could return home truly appreciative of the superiority of a world that was not defined and constrained by its past. There was an undeniable stink in the Venetian lagoons and Roman marshes, a sense of indolence in the Florentine galleries, a lingering Spanish decadence to the splendors of Naples that could not be denied—or at least this was what many visitors perceived. Italy had faded so that other places might flourish. "The inhabitants of this country were once the triumphant lords and conquerors of the world; but at present the softer arts prevail," observed Thomas Nugent in 1749.[22] Visitors looked everywhere for signs of this waning of Italy. They found it partly in the mustiness of its relics (talismans of previous eras of great political and artistic regimes) and partly in the perceived corruption of Italian morals that seemed to express itself most clearly in the unusual behavior and occupations of some of its most prominent men and women. What Mary Wortley Montagu considered an

Italian virtue—the flourishing of learned and aristocratic women who proclaimed their independence from traditional customs and beliefs—others equally perceived to be a sign of Italy's corruption. Was Italy a place where women became men, and men became women? The Marquis de Sade, who fled to Italy in July 1775 to avoid prosecution for a litany of sexual transgressions, was quite sure that there was "a great penchant for betraying one's sex" throughout the Italian peninsula.[23] He linked the image of Italy as a world turned upside down to his understanding of its decline since the Renaissance. Trapped in the mausoleum of history and culture, the Italians inevitably could not progress as a civilization.

Were we only to follow the path trodden by the likes of Boswell, Gibbon, Lalande, Sade, the intrepid Lady Mary and earnest Lady Anne, the dashing Madame de Staël, and their fellow travelers, we might be left with this impression. The Grand Tour produced a rich and diverse array of documentation—diaries, guidebooks, novels, portraits, sketches, curios, and even buildings—that offers us a glimpse of a vibrant artistic, antiquarian, musical, and literary culture, a world of people constantly on the verge of self-illumination and grand historical reflection in response to their environment. Some of the most interesting, colorful, and important figures of the eighteenth century traveled to, were inspired by, and passed judgment on the history and contemporary fate of Italy. As a result of this torrent of words and images, it is all too easy to see the fruits of their encounter, both trivial and profound, as the sum total of Italy's contribution to the age of Enlightenment and Revolution, and to see the Italian peninsula only through their eyes.

Seductive as the narrative of the Grand Tour may be, it inevitably limits our vision of the past. Italian society and culture in the eighteenth century was far more than simply a tourists' playground and artists' haven. This point, of course, is hardly novel but worth revisiting in light of the persistence of certain stereotypes. Rather than simply revisiting the caricatures of Italian society perpetuated by the accounts of Grand Tourists, we should analyze them in relationship to documents internal to this culture. If the eighteenth century, as many scholars have suggested, was the period in which the Italian peninsula developed new, stronger, and more diverse connections to many other parts of Europe, then one of the goals of studying this century should be an exploration of the dialogue between foreign and indigenous views of Italy.[24] As Ilaria Bignamini observes, Italians were "fully-fledged actors on the scene of the Grand Tour."[25] They not only shaped this cultural activity by guiding foreigners through their cities, painting their portraits, and supplying them with real and faked antiquities and lessons in Italian history and culture but also sought to realize their own vision of bringing Italy into the modern era.

This volume, originating from a conference held at the Getty Research Institute and the William Andrews Clark Library of UCLA in conjunction with a Getty Center exhibit in 2002 on Italy and the Grand Tour, presents some of the recent work by Italian and North American scholars on eighteenth-century Italy. Our goal is to examine selected aspects of the social and cultural life of the Italian peninsula, both in its own terms and in relation to foreign observations of this region. What were some of the distinctive features of Italy in the eighteenth century? Why did they emerge, and how did they operate in practice? To what extent did these elements of Italian society and culture shape discussions of Italy abroad? Implicitly, while engaging in a dialogue with the scholarship focused on those two classic images of the eighteenth century—the Enlightenment and the Grand Tour—we have tried to indicate the possibilities of another history that expands our understanding of this fascinating period.[26]

We have focused on the relationship between gender and culture for several reasons. As a great deal of recent scholarship has shown, the eighteenth century was an especially important moment for the reassessment of traditional roles of men and women.[27] It was also a critical period in the emergence of a new understanding of sexual behavior and affective relations.[28] Recent work on eighteenth-century Italy has begun to explore these issues, highlighting the Italian peninsula's distinctive contributions to public debates about marriage, sexuality, and the place of women in society.[29] Scholarship on *cicisbei*, castrati, and the sexual behavior and artistic proclivities of Grand Tourists in Italy has begun to develop an account of attitudes toward male sexuality.[30] This volume explores the theme of gender and culture across disciplines; it seeks to create a conversation among scholars in the fields of history, literature, philosophy, art history, and music regarding perceptions of gender in the eighteenth century.

Other Visions of Italy

Far from being trapped irrevocably in its past, Italy was a region undergoing profound political, social, and economic transformation at a level it had not experienced since the end of the Renaissance. At the beginning of the eighteenth century the configuration of the Italian peninsula reflected the outcome of the political struggles of the sixteenth century. The Spanish were the dominant foreign power, ruling Lombardy, the Kingdom of Naples, Sicily, and Sardinia. The Papal States controlled much of central Italy while the Republic of Venice retained its independence and a foothold in the Adriatic, and the Republic of Genoa, closely allied with the Spanish, retained some measure of its political independence and commercial interests in the Mediterranean, including control of Corsica until 1768. A handful of smaller states—far fewer in number by the eighteenth century than at the height of the Renaissance—continued to be governed by hereditary princes, most famously the Medici in Florence, the Gonzaga in Mantua, the Este in Modena, the Farnese in Parma, and the House of Savoy in Piedmont, whose territory and influence grew as others reached the point of obsolescence.[31] Tiny Lucca retained its place as Italy's other long-lived republic while the dukes of Guastalla maintained their autonomy from their Gonzaga cousins in Mantua. With important exceptions, Italy had become a largely aristocratic and agrarian society. Italian cities were still lively places to live in and to visit, full of conversation and cosmopolitan civility, but the vast commercial enterprises and glittering court culture that had brought many of them to prominence in the late Middle Ages and the Renaissance no longer were their defining features.

The first half of the eighteenth century saw the collapse of a number of the political arrangements that had governed the Italian states for almost two centuries. The death of Charles II of Spain in 1700 triggered the War of Spanish Succession (1700–1713) between the Austrian Hapsburgs and the French Bourbons. Many regions found themselves pawns once again in an international game of war and diplomacy. In 1707 the Hapsburgs gained control of the Kingdom of Naples which they subsequently ceded to the Bourbons in 1734.[32] The House of Savoy gained temporary possession of Sicily in 1713—it would later become a Hapsburg (1720) and finally a Bourbon territory (1734)—followed by their acquisition of Sardinia in 1718. Formerly Spanish Lombardy became Austrian in 1713, though the Hapsburg right of possession would continue to be periodically contested until the end of the War of Austrian Succession (1740–1748). In between these events, many prominent ruling families found themselves on the verge of extinction. The marquisate of Mantua, ruled by the Gonzaga since 1328, became a Hapsburg possession in 1707. The death of the last Farnese duke, Antonio, in 1731 precipitated a struggle between the Bourbons and Hapsburgs for control of the duchy. The last surviving male member of the Medici family, the gluttonous and ailing Gian Gastone, died in 1737. Tuscany welcomed a foreign ruler, Duke Francis Stephen of Lorraine, whose marriage to Maria Theresa paved the way for his succession as emperor in 1745; his third son, Peter Leopold, succeeded him as grand duke in 1765. Like Lombardy, Tuscany was now a Hapsburg possession though not directly subject to its rule.

The uneasy relationship between older and newer visions of Italy might best be observed by considering the aspirations of Elisabetta Farnese (1692–1766), who certainly rivaled the Hapsburg emperor Charles VI (ruled 1711–1740) and his daughter, the empress Maria Theresa (ruled 1740–1780), in the influence she exercised on the political reconfiguration of Italy. The second wife of Philip V and last descendant of the ruling family of Parma, Elisabetta Farnese became queen of Spain in 1714 (Figure I.2). Initially under the influence of cardinal Giulio Alberoni (1664–1752), she aspired to oust the Hapsburgs from Italy in order to reunify many of its disparate parts under a Bourbon-Farnese dynasty. While failing to recover Lombardy and Sardinia for Spain, she nonetheless succeeded in placing her eldest son, Charles, on the Neapolitan throne in 1734 and restored the duchy of Parma and Piacenza (expanded to include Guastalla) to her family's possession under his younger brother Philip in 1748.[33] When she retired from the Spanish court upon the death of her husband in 1746, an English pamphlet begrudgingly admired "the Queen's boundless Ambition" and "extraordinary Passion for governing" by declaring her "Mistress of all *Italy*."[34] Its anonymous author recommended to the new king Ferdinand VI that he either shut his stepmother up in a convent or send her to Siberia to prevent her from undermining his rule. The Spanish queen was exactly the sort of powerful female figure who inspired tales of Italy as a land of literary and political Amazons where men were content to be ruled by women. Elisabetta Farnese embodied the failed struggle to claim Italy for an Italian princely lineage in the face of its reconquest and ultimately political marginalization by various foreign powers.

Farnese's bold plan to reinvent the map of Italy found no immediate successors. The most important indigenous ruler within Italy, the papacy, was on the verge of reversing its longstanding reputation as an ecclesiastic office from which many of Italy's ruling families had realized their ambitions since the fifteenth century. The place of religion in Italian society changed dramatically in the course of the eighteenth century, beginning with a substantial reduction in the temporal powers of the papacy. Failed efforts to capture the Republic of San Marino and to gain Parma and Piacenza for the papacy

Figure I.2 Louis Michel van Loo, *Portrait of Elisabetta Farnese, Queen of Spain, Second Wife of Philip V*, ca. 1745 (oil on canvas, 107 x 84 cm). Réunion des Musées Nationaux/ Art Resource.

in the 1730s clarified the secondary status of the Papal States in the carving up of the Italian peninsula. The papacy ceased to vie for new territory. Equally telling, it did not play a decisive role in the diplomatic negotiations among those who harbored such aspirations.[35] Instead, it carved out a new role for itself as the guardian of an immense cultural patrimony, inaugurating what Christopher Johns has aptly described as "Settecento papal arts programs."[36] Under Clement XII (1730–1740)—who restored the papacy to financial solvency, in part by reviving the public lottery—ambitious building and public works projects embellished the façade of Rome, continuing the work of his distinguished predecessor Clement XI (1700–1721). At the same time, the papacy focused its attention on scholarly projects designed to write a more complete and scientific history of Roman Catholicism and its doctrines with the new tools of modern scholarship. Benedict XIV (1740–

1758), another pope inspired by the foundational work of Clement XI, made significant efforts to reform longstanding ecclesiastical rituals and institutions. Like many popes of the eighteenth century, he saw Rome as a city of faith, knowledge, and culture.

Despite this bold new vision of a reinvigorated Catholicism, the eighteenth-century papacy found itself facing a number of challenges, both within and without. The century that began with Clement XI's condemnation of Jansenism in 1713 and Clement XII's condemnation of freemasonry in 1738 ended with the suppression of the Society of Jesus in 1773 during the papacy of Clement XIV (1769–1775) and the forced exile of Pius VI (1775–1799) from Rome at the hands of Napoleon's army. They declared Rome a republic on 13 February 1798 and escorted the pope to Siena a week later. He died a prisoner in the citadel of Valence the following year, having been immortalized in Sade's *Juliette* (1798) as the willing audience for a long history of ecclesiastic debauchery and depravity which Juliette recites as a prelude to a papal orgy.

The transformation of religious values in the age of Enlightenment affected many aspects of Italian society. Throughout the century, the papacy and its supporters grappled with the shape of enlightened Catholicism.[37] This question resonated throughout Catholic Europe but played an especially crucial role in the intellectual life of the Papal States and surrounding territories. Just how modern should Italy become? What did modernity mean in a region rich with history, tradition, and faith? The tensions between traditional values and novel ideas threatened to divide, if not actually shatter, Ludovico Antonio Muratori's (1672–1750) vision of an Italian Republic of Letters. The kind of intellectual experimentation, cultural innovation, and programs for social, juridical, and economic reform that we associate with the Enlightenment played no small role in shaping Italy's eighteenth century. Whether it was in the opera house, the salon, the academy, the gallery, or the pages of journals such as *Il Caffè*, conversations revolved around the possibilities for change. These innovations too caught the attention of the more discerning visitors who perceived the Italian cities as making distinctive contributions to learning, the arts, and public life. For example, many of the most famous and popular sites in Rome, including the Spanish Steps, the Trevi Fountain, the Piazza del Popolo, and the Villa Borghese, were designed, built, or renovated during the eighteenth century. While strongly immersed in the past, eighteenth-century Italians were painfully conscious of the present they inhabited and eager to stake their place in this world.

The Italian states generally did not exhibit the military strength, economic vitality, and colonial ambitions of their British and northern European counterparts, but they were hardly a closed and stagnant world, unable or unwilling to keep up with the times. Some of the most interesting and sustained efforts at political and economic reform in the second half of the eighteenth century occurred in Piedmont, Lombardy, and Tuscany while regions such as the Papal States, the Kingdom of Naples, and the Republic of Venice also attempted to transform traditional social structures to respond to the new circumstances in which they found themselves. As Franco Venturi demonstrated in his monumental studies of the eighteenth-century *illuministi*, Italy fully participated in the project of Enlightenment.[38] With the noteworthy exception of scholarship on figures such as Giambattista Vico (1668–1744) and Cesare Beccaria (1738–1794), we still know little about Italian contributions to this European-wide efflorescence of new ideas, projects, and institutions since studies of the Italian Enlightenment do not feature prominently in general surveys of this subject.

Many of the most passionate Italian advocates for modernity did not simply advocate change at home but based their ideas on reading foreign books, corresponding with foreign scholars, and experiences culled from traveling in Britain and northern Europe—a kind of reverse Grand Tour. Writers such as Algarotti, Baretti, the poet and dramatist Pietro Metastasio (1696–1782), the playwright Carlo Goldoni (1707–1793), and the adventurer Giacomo Casanova (1725–1798), musicians such as Farinelli and Giuseppe Domenico Scarlatti (1685–1757), and painters such as Rosalba Carriera (1675–1757), Giovanni Battista Tiepolo (1696–1770), and Antonio Canaletto (1697–1768) acted as cultural brokers in cities such as London, Paris, Madrid, Vienna, Dresden, and Potsdam. Inhabiting both worlds, they represented Italy abroad and also brought news of these other parts of the world to Italy.[39] The ongoing dialogue between the Italian peninsula and the rest of Europe played a significant role in the cosmopolitan character of its eighteenth century.

The eighteenth century may well be the least studied period of Italian history. Lying between the Renaissance and the Risorgimento, it has often been perceived as a political and cultural low point in the history of this region. The general consensus of the broader community of eighteenth-century scholars has implicitly reinforced this vision by suggesting that Italy did not shape this century as actively as northern European counterparts such as France, England, and Germany.[40] Save for a handful of passionate devotees of the writings of prominent figures such as Goldoni, who commanded a European-wide audience, literary scholars have generally preferred to study any period but the eighteenth century.[41] Art historians working on the eighteenth century have also lamented the degree to which the history of Italian painting, sculpture, and architecture has been neglected except for the work of artists such as Canaletto, Giovanni Paolo Panini (1692–1765), Pompeo Batoni (1708–1787), and Giambattista Piranesi (1720–1778), who contributed directly to the visual production of the Grand Tour.[42] The case of music stands apart since the eighteenth century was the great age of opera. Italian musicians, librettists, and singers played a crucial role in shaping musical taste and the culture of public performance at this time.[43] However, since scholars in other fields rarely read the work of music historians, this aspect of Italy's eighteenth century has not been integrated into a more general social and cultural history. The same might also be said of the history of science, whose scholarship has produced a number of important studies of the intellectual preoccupations of eighteenth-century Italy, its scientific academies, and its most interesting practitioners that certainly demonstrate the importance of Italy to furthering our understanding of eighteenth-century science in general.[44]

Since the 1950s, a small group of Anglo-American historians have begun to outline a history of this period. Their work has explored specific aspects of politics, economy, and culture in the Italian states of the eighteenth century, introducing English-speaking readers to the possibilities of what Eric Cochrane evocatively labeled the "forgotten centuries" and engaging in a dialogue with the considerably richer historiography of this period written by Italian and French scholars. We are still in the initial stages of developing a more comprehensive account of this neglected period of Italian history.[45] Unfortunately, the majority of the excellent work by many European, especially Italian, scholars on this period has not yet found its way into English.[46] Until this occurs, accounts of the eighteenth century will remain impoverished.

As Baretti observed, Italy was not a nation in this period but a collection of states whose diversity of political and economic arrangements was matched only by their linguistic and cultural regionalism. Not every city celebrated its learned philosophical women in the manner of the university town of Bologna or shrouded them in the piety of enlightened Catholicism to the degree that one sees in Milan. The Papal States and the Kingdom of Naples far surpassed other Italian states in the number of castrati that they created and celebrated, and in the quantity of antiquarians who haunted the archeological digs, galleries, and libraries in search of new insights into the past. The prominence of women artists, poets, translators, *salonnières*, and journalists in Venice was indeed one of its distinctive characteristics, just as that peculiar Italian phenomenon of formally assigning male companions to aristocratic wives—*cicisbeismo*—reputedly originated in Genoa, where women supposedly had far greater social freedoms at the beginning of the eighteenth century than did their counterparts in many other Italian cities.[47] Naples was the only state that produced a few female revolutionaries at the end of the century—most notably the journalist Eleonora Fonseca Pimentel (1752–1799)[48]—while Rome was quite decidedly a city of antiquarians, abbés, poets, and salonnières who fought over far less momentous issues than the promise of political independence.

Despite these differences, there are ways in which Italy was also a cultural unity that transcended its pronounced regionalism. To some degree, foreigners were correct in perceiving connections between the various Italian states and their peoples. This promise of a larger Italy, for example, lay at the heart of Gian Vincenzo Gravina and Giovan Maria Crescimbeni's founding of the Accademia degli Arcadi in 1690, not simply as a Roman institution but as a literary community for the Italian peninsula, inspired by the ghostly presence of the recently deceased Queen Christina of Sweden, who played such a prominent role in Roman academy and salon life in the late seventeenth century after abdicating her throne and converting to Catholicism. By the mid eighteenth century, there were colonies up and down the peninsula, numbering fifty-six by 1761. Being an Arcadian became a kind of cultural capital among poets and other aspiring writers.[49] More critically, Muratori's famous sketch of an Italian Republic of Letters at the beginning of the century sought to raise the standards of scholarly conversation among his contemporaries by outlining plans for reviving the arts and sciences. It informed subsequent projects such as the Venetian *Giornale de' letterati d'Italia* (1710–1740) and the Swiss *Bibliothèque italique* (founded in 1728), which sought to foster intellectual community across political boundaries, bringing the news of Italy to their readers.[50] Even while the Italian peninsula suffered under the burdens of foreign rule, its leading citizens aspired to create a better, stronger Italy and left behind numerous traces of these projects and dreams.

Neither the Hapsburgs nor the Bourbons fully succeeded in their quest to make the Italian peninsula their own. As the century wore on and the world outside of Italy changed, they too found their presence in Italy under assault. With the arrival of the French army in Piedmont in the spring of 1796, virtually all the political arrangements that defined Italy for much of the century dissolved within the next two years; those which remained were under considerable strain. While none of the Italian states experienced a full-fledged revolution that radically challenged the very structures underpinning their society, reverberations of the French Revolution echoed throughout the peninsula.[51] French observers of the Italian scene had already suggested that many leading citizens of the Italian states were sympathetic to the goal of overthrowing the Old Regime. Napoleon fueled their fantasies of an independent Italian nation while making no promises about its eventual existence. Between 1797 and 1798 Lombardy, the Papal States, and the Kingdom of Naples all became part of Napoleon's empire while other states sued for peace. The Republic of Venice, whose leading citizens gave up their ancient rights and privileges upon the arrival of Napoleon's troops in the lagoon in May 1797, ended with hardly a whimper, only to find itself subject to Austrian rule after the Treaty of Campoformio (17 October 1797).[52] While the French ruled Italy for a briefer period than either the Hapsburgs or the Bourbons, their own efforts to reinvent their nation and, under Napoleon, transform it into an empire left a powerful impression upon their Italian subjects. Mastering Italy was an essential component of the French claim to be the new Roman empire of the eighteenth century. The Grand Tourists of the preceding century as much as Napoleon's political rivals helped to foster this great ambition.

Napoleon may rightfully be described as the first person to make the "Italian nation" a political entity.[53] Prior to his arrival in the Italian peninsula, "Italy" denoted a geographic region defined by the ancient Romans, a literary ideal promoted by writers such as Petrarch, Machiavelli, and Francesco Guicciardini, and a sector of the Republic of Letters devoted to increasing the reputation of Italian contributions to the arts, letters, and sciences abroad while advocating for reforms at home. The "Italians" as a people, however, inhabited the pages of virtually every travel book written about Italy in the eighteenth century. For some, they were an annoying obstacle in the pursuit of a pristine experience of a landscape, its art, and its ruins. As Alexander Drummond wrote disparagingly of Italy in 1754, "In this country there is enough to see without being fooled by the Italians."[54] Other visitors actively tried to anatomize the people they encountered. The Italians were increasingly present in works of history and political theory written by such notables as Montesquieu, Gibbon, and Jean Charles Léonard de Sismondi, who described them as a people whose distinctive characteristics and customs explained their historical greatness and contemporary obsolescence. Who, then, were the Italians?

Gender Trouble in Eighteenth-Century Italy

Marveling at the strange reports he heard from visiting Englishmen about the social customs of Italians at midcentury, Baretti ironically queried: "Or are the men and women in Italy of a different species from those of other countries?"[55] Perceptions of gender played an especially important role in constructing an image of the Italians in the age of the Grand Tour. The fascination with—as well as fear of—sexual ambiguity lay at the heart of understanding Italy's alleged cultural difference. Many travelers observed that Italy was full of exceptional women who did not abide by the rules of society as many northern Europeans understood them. "Italy has produced more learned women than any part of Europe," observed Lady Sydney Morgan upon hearing of the death of the classicist and Greek professor Clotilde Tambroni (1758–1817), echoing the opinion of virtually every traveler in the eighteenth century.[56]

When Charles Burney arrived in Bologna in August 1770, for example, he made sure to meet Italy's most famous woman professor and university graduate, the physicist Laura Bassi (1711–1778), to complement his visit with Farinelli. After a demonstration of her electrical experiments, a subject in which he deemed himself an amateur enthusiast, Burney wrote admiringly that she has "fairly earned her title of *Dottoressa*."[57] Bassi's thesis defense, university degree, and professorship in 1732—like the 1705 admission of the painter Rosalba Carriera to the Accademia di San Luca as a regular member, despite rules barring women's admission; the controversial crowning of Corilla Olimpica as poet laureate on the steps of the Capitoline in 1776; and Maria Dalle Donne's (1778–1842) receipt of a medical degree from Bologna in 1799—represented the most visible moment of Italy's well-publicized celebration of its women.

For travelers in search of learned women, virtually every city offered up one or two female prodigies. In 1738 the French lawyer and politician Charles de Brosses recorded his surprise at finding the poet Francesca Manzoni (1710–1743) immersed in the Latin books of the Biblioteca Ambrosiana in Milan, and his pleasure at meeting some of the most talented women of Italy, including the formidable salonnière Clelia Grillo Borromeo (1684–1777), the mathematician Agnesi, and the physicist Bassi. In the early decades of the eighteenth century, the prominent role of women in the intellectual and cultural life of the Italian cities was a great novelty for foreigners. Having heard stories of the university women and female academicians and artists of Italy, they came prepared to pass judgment on them in person. Quite a few made the pilgrimage to Padua to find the statue of Elena Lucrezia Cornaro Piscopia (1646–1684), who had graduated from the university there in 1678 with a degree in philosophy.[58] They also admired her portrait in the very library in which Manzoni studied and wrote and, traveling south, collected impressions of learned Italian women like curios for their cabinets. De Brosses' famous description of Agnesi—"more stupendous than the Duomo of Milan"[59]—captures the essence of the foreign fascination with Italian women. Like the churches, galleries, and Roman ruins, they were monuments to be admired and critiqued.

Following the highly publicized debate of the Accademia dei Ricovrati of Padua in 1723 regarding whether women should be educated, numerous responses to this question indicated just how central an issue women's learning was to understanding their place in society. Discerning the nature of woman was a cultural preoccupation of the educated elite of the Italian peninsula.[60] Establishing a genealogy of Italy's learned women reinforced the idea that the Italian peninsula had historically produced more literate and cultured women than any other region of Europe. The Venetian writer Luisa Bergalli (1703–1779), for example, collected and published the work of 248 female poets of the thirteenth through eighteenth centuries in her *Componimenti poetici delle più illustri rimatrici d'ogni secolo* (1726). Sympathetic readers told her that there were many more for her to celebrate. By 1728, for example, seventy-four women had been admitted to Arcadia.[61] When the Venetian playwright Pietro Chiari described his epoch as "The Century of Women" in 1783, he captured the incessant fascination with educated, independent-minded, and socially unconventional women that characterized the eighteenth century.[62]

Not everyone thought that Italy's learned women were quite as advertised. In 1764 Giuseppe Baretti informed readers of his periodical, *La frusta letteraria*, that while he disagreed with those who felt that Italy had produced no noteworthy women of learning, he nonetheless felt that "the female sex is not generally educated by us with all that care which she ought to be and with which she is educated in other parts of Europe."[63] Others

concurred with his assessment that learning was largely an aristocratic privilege in this society. After visiting Bologna in 1784, the Italian city which
claimed to celebrate learned women more than any other by producing such
luminaries as the physicist Bassi and the anatomist-artist Anna Morandi
Manzolini (1714–1774) and admitting many others to its academies, Hester
Lynch Thrale Piozzi, recently remarried to the Brescian singer and composer Gabriele Piozzi, perceptively observed: "Here is no struggle for female
education as with us. . . . A Lady in Italy is *sure* of applause, so she takes
little pains to obtain it."[64] To her eyes, the celebration of women's learning
was yet another means of foreclosing the real discussion regarding the possibility of educating all women. A contemporary of Mary Wollstonecraft, she
viewed the Italian tradition more as a vestige of the past than a harbinger
of the future.

What Lynch Piozzi could not see, however, were the very real struggles for
knowledge that propelled many of the women immortalized in the portrait
gallery of the Bologna Academy of Sciences, or inscribed into the membership of the Accademia degli Arcadi in Rome and the Accademia dei Ricovrati in Padua, into the public eye. Not every learned woman was, in fact,
aristocratic. Corilla Olimpica was of relatively modest social origins as the
daughter of a violinist, though her Neapolitan patron, Faustina Pignatelli,
celebrated for her mathematical acumen and philosophical learning, could
not have been more highly placed. The acclaimed Roman poet Faustina
Maratti Zappi (1680–1745) and the anatomist Morandi Manzolini were
daughters of painters; Laura Bassi was a lawyer's daughter, Clotilde Tambroni the daughter of a cook, and Agnesi the eldest daughter of a Milanese
silk merchant; Maria Dalle Donne was the daughter of peasants from the
Bolognese countryside. The Venetian journalist Elisabetta Caminer Turra
(1751–1796) grew up surrounded by print because publishing was her father's
trade; both she and Rosalba Carriera, daughter of a clerk and a lacemaker,
emerged from the professional and artisanal culture of La Serenissima. Angelica Kauffman, the foreign centerpiece of the Roman artistic community,
also learned her trade from an artist father.[65] While the salons and academies that admitted and fêted women were largely aristocratic, the women
who studied and taught in the universities, like the female artists of this
period, belong to the middling classes. Like the saintly women canonized
by the Roman Catholic Church in the course of the eighteenth century, the
learned women of this period increasingly did not come from the highest
level of society.

Nonetheless, Lynch Piozzi was quite correct to state that none of these individual cases forced Italian society to rethink the education and status of women in general. Casanova, whose *Lana caprina* (1772) argued force-fully for the equality of the sexes—one of the few Italian texts to do so in the eighteenth century—and wryly suggested that women enjoyed greater sexual pleasures, nonetheless confessed in his autobiographic memoirs that he would rather remain a man:

> After all this examination, I ask myself if I would consent to be born again as a woman and, curiosity aside, I answer no. I have enough other pleasures as a man which I could not have as a woman, and which make me prefer my sex to the other.[66]

Casanova enjoyed trying to understand women. To some degree, he was sympathetic to the goals of a select few who had begun to advocate that women should not only be celebrated as prodigies—surpassing the limits of their sex—but educated more broadly. But nothing he observed made him want to assume their position in society, save in the kind of masked ball that made Sade wonder about the Italian penchant for transgressing one's sex.

The Italian peninsula's fascination with its female poets, artists, journal-ists, and philosophers was, in the end, a celebration of their uniqueness. The imaginary community of *pastorelle* and *filosofesse*, female Arcadians and phi-losophers, was exactly that: a construction of an ideal in which to deposit the actual accomplishments of a handful of women in various Italian cities to create the myth of the learned lady. Similarly, the fame of a few women painters did not make the arts a comfortable home for women aspiring to exercise their talents, as both Carriera and Kauffman discovered in their efforts to find the right audience for their paintings. The iconic status of these women reaffirmed their function in society. Madame du Boccage sar-donically commented during her stay in Naples that all the women she met fashioned themselves as either Minerva or Venus, making learning a kind of endless performance. She particularly admired Maria Angela Ardinghelli (1728–1825), well known for her translations of the scientific work of the experimental physiologist Stephen Hales, for eschewing this sort of vain display and excessive flattery.[67] Boccage shrewdly remarked that the men who praised women rarely meant it sincerely, while other women responded by being highly critical of those members of their own sex who aspired to display their talent.

For the inhabitants of the Italian cities, women of talent and learning were civic monuments, organic expressions of the qualities that made each city individually great. This strong sense of regionalism contrasted markedly with foreign attitudes toward the same phenomenon. For visitors, Bergalli and Carriera in Venice, Caminer Turra in Venice and later Vicenza; Bassi, Morandi Manzolini, Tambroni, and Dalle Donne in Bologna; Agnesi, Manzoni, and Grillo Borromeo in Milan; Corilla Olimpica in Florence and later Rome; and Ardinghelli and Pignatelli in Naples were, much like Staël's fictional Corinne, expressions of the essence of the Italian character. The Piedmontese writer Baretti sternly rebuked his English readers for leaping to such ridiculous conclusions about the minds and morals of Italian women when he wrote that "the character of a numerous nation does not depend on a few individuals."[68]

Foreign women who contributed actively to the cultural life of the Italian peninsula were also incorporated into this vision of Italy. Kauffman was indeed an expression of Italy's artistic spirit, just as Emma Hamilton's (ca. 1765–1815) wildly popular "attitudes," a kind of *tableau vivant,* made her a living antiquity whose performance in Naples perfectly complemented a tour of the recently discovered ruins of Pompeii and Herculaneum and the royal archeological museum. The French artist Elisabeth Vigée-Lebrun was so struck by Hamilton's place in Neapolitan society when she visited in 1790 that she painted her as the image of southern Italy (Figure I.3). Staël would later incorporate elements of Hamilton's dramatic performances into her description of Corinne. Like the Anglo-Venetian Giustiniana Wynne (1732–1791), whose unhappy love affair with Andrea Memmo has recently been transformed into a popular book, Corinne was indeed half-English in a Mediterranean land, a combination of the qualities of Corilla Olimpica and Lady Hamilton and equally destined for tragedy.[69]

Of course, there were other images of Italian women in circulation that regarded not their minds but their bodies. As Grand Tourists traveled from one city to another, they tried to assess the differences in social behavior they observed in each location. In which city did women circulate most freely? Some argued for Venice, others for Bologna, Florence, Milan, or Genoa. Were they truly constrained by their piety? No one really thought so. Attempts to understand social conventions among the Italian patricians quickly devolved into stereotypes of Catholic priggishness and sexual promiscuity. "Before marriage their women are nuns," declared Thomas Watkins in 1792, "and after it libertines."[70] Boswell predictably took this kind of com-

Figure I.3 Emma Hamilton portrayed in front of an erupting Vesuvius. Elisabeth Vigée-Lebrun, *Lady Hamilton as a "Bacchante,"* 1790–1791. © Walker Art Gallery, National Museums Liverpool.

ment one step further by considering how the behavior of Italian women epitomized "the corruption of Italy." He wrote to Rousseau that the reason he wished to stay in Italy was because "the women are so debauched that they are hardly to be considered moral agents, but as inferior beings."[71]

Samuel Sharp, the English traveler who most incited Baretti's wrath, agreed with Boswell. His experiences of Venice, Naples, and Florence in 1765–66 incited a loathing for Italian social customs so bilious that he wrote at length about the bold behavior of women and its effect on men. It was in Venice that he first observed married women rowing up and down the Grand Canal in their gondolas, accompanied not by their husbands but by at least one cicisbeo. By the time he arrived in Naples in November 1765, he condemned this system of male companionship as an "abominable and infernal fashion" which ruined marriages (Figure I.4). Six months later in Florence, he considered himself fully apprised of how this peculiar social custom worked, writing that Florentine ladies took three cicisbei, one to uphold her dignity, another to act as a servant, and a third to be a lover.[72] He attributed these practices to a peculiarly Italian inability to distinguish between moral and immoral behavior. Baretti acerbically responded that if Sharp's book were ever translated into Italian, his fellow Italians would appoint an exorcist to cure him of these misconceptions.

Also the subject of widespread commentary within Italy, cicisbeismo was the social custom that most fascinated foreigners. As early as 1696, a Sienese broadside *Il cicisbeo tormentato* made this figure an icon of the male condition; many plays in the mideighteenth century, most notably the work of Goldoni, feature the cicisbeo as a stock figure of Italian comedy.[73] As Roberto Bizzocchi points out, cicisbeismo was not as exclusively Italian as this commentary might have us believe. Muratori, for example, felt it

Figure I.4 Pietro Longhi, *The Visit*, 1746. The Metropolitan Museum of Art, Frederick C. Hewitt Fund, 1912 (14.32.2). Image © The Metropolitan Museum of Art.

was a legacy of French customs introduced into Italy in the late seventeenth century.[74] Its categorization as an Italian vice, however, says a great deal about how relations between the sexes were perceived from the outside, especially by Protestants visiting a Catholic country. Were the number and names of cicisbei written into some marriage contracts? The German traveler Johann Georg Keyssler certainly thought so, since he (and others) cited a Spinola marriage contract that he heard about during his travels of 1729–30, which excluded the possibility of a wife taking or her husband becoming a cicisbeo, as a sign that this practice was in decline. He found the custom far less distasteful than many Englishmen, writing that while a Genoese woman might have as many as five, they "all pass under the denomination of *Platonic* lovers."[75] De Brosses emphasized that taking a cicisbeo was a matter of honor rather than dishonor in the family. Lalande also considered Sharp incredibly naïve in believing that cicisbeismo had anything to do with passion.

Baretti also shared this opinion. He argued that cicisbeismo was not a function of loveless marriages and misplaced lust but a sophisticated form of friendship and kinship, a service to a family as much as a relationship with an individual. He defined the etymology of cicisbeo as "whisperer" rather than "adulterer." Emphasizing these other aspects of male companionship, he sought to downplay the escalating critique of Italian masculinity which presented the cicisbeo as an enslaved male.[76] This image of an emasculated, effeminate Italy filled the pages of books about the Grand Tour. Invoking the other name of the cicisbeo, Boswell wrote to Rousseau from Lucca: "A *cavaliere servente* is a being whom I regard as illustrating the last stage of human degradation. A lover without love, a soldier without pay, a being who is more a drudge than a *valet de chambre*, who does continual duty, and enjoys only appearances!" Sade more pragmatically lamented that the presence of so many attentive men made it harder for others to get to know Italian women because they had already chosen a "second husband," though Boswell does not seem to have had any problem overcoming this barrier.[77]

Women travelers were less censorious of cicisbeismo, as were men such as Sir Horace Mann, who resided for many years in Florence and participated in these customs, even introducing a new kind of double chair in his conversazioni which he described to Horace Walpole in 1744 as *cicisbeatoii*.[78] Wortley Montagu first observed the custom in Genoa in August 1718, long before she took up residence in Italy. She marveled at "the Custom of Tetis beys," telling her sister that in its earliest incarnation women could choose as many as eight or ten, even though the fashion nowadays was to have only one:

> Upon my Word, nothing but my own Eyes could have convinc'd [me] there were any such upon Earth. The fashion begun here and is now receiv'd all over Italy, where the Husbands are not such terrible Creatures as we represent them.[79]

To her eyes, cicisbeismo revealed the advantages of a social system controlled by women, since it was entirely the question of a woman's choice that captured her imagination, the very antithesis of the seraglio of the Sublime Porte she had just left behind at the conclusion of her husband's embassy in Constantinople. Lady Anne Miller, more restrained in her outlook than the flamboyant Lady Mary, instead saw cicisbeismo as the definition of a good, companionate marriage. She recalled her pleasure at seeing an aging couple at a caffè in Piazza San Marco who had spent forty years together, "and with the most steady constancy had loved each other, till age and disease were conducting them hand in hand together to the grave." Thrale Piozzi made light of the custom when she chose an eighty-year-old cleric as her cicisbeo—but she did not see this practice as a sign of moral depravity.[80]

Criticism of cicisbeismo was simply part of a broader condemnation of Italian men in general—and it is quite striking that none of this commentary condemned the female equivalent, the *cicisbea*, who appears frequently in Sir Horace Mann's description of Florentine social life. What had become of the tradition of the proud Romans, whose virility was imitated in the stances taken by British and French sitters for Pompeo Batoni's portraits? (Figure I.5). In the opinion of many travelers, Italy was a land of Amazons precisely because its men were so enervated and emasculated. After describing an encounter with Bassi in October 1763 to a female correspondent, Coyer remarked: "What do you say of this Masculine Sappho? Her husband perhaps would have been humiliated to have such a learned wife if he himself had not been learned."[81] The delicate equilibrium between the sexes was under assault, and it was the women rather than the men who seemed to carry the day. Cicisbeismo was a phenomenon utterly unrelated to the presence of learned women since it was an aristocratic social practice, but it nonetheless confirmed what many visitors suspected: the Italian upper classes must be dominated by a new kind of Amazon. Staël captured this sentiment well when she had Corinne's Scottish lover, Lord Oswald Nelvil,

Figure I.5 Anonymous gentleman on the Grand Tour. Pompeo Batoni, *Portrait of a Young Man*, ca. 1760–1765 (oil on canvas, 246.7 x 175.9 cm). Metropolitan Museum of Art/Art Resource.

declare: "In Italy, the men are worth much less than the women, for they have the women's faults as well as their own."[82]

The images of men that emerged from the Italy of the Grand Tour did little to dispel this view. The prattling cicerone leading tourists around the ruins satirized in the caricatures of Pier Leone Ghezzi (1674–1755) (Figure I.6), the versifying abbé who inhabited the academy and the salon, and the solicitous cicisbeo who brought his lady chocolate and a dressing gown in the morning and waited upon her in the opera box at night were all representations of men of culture rather than action, a far cry from the image of the Renaissance *condottiere* of centuries past.[83] Among the many dubious etymologies of the word *cicisbeo* was a definition suggesting possible Greek origins: *cicys sbeo*. A force extinguished, in other words, effeminate.[84] Visitors could not help but conclude that there was something . . . lacking . . . in the Italian male.

The preoccupation with what Italian men were *not* in the eighteenth century reached its culmination in the assessment of the castrato. As Roger Freitas and Martha Feldman discuss in this volume, the castrato was the musical counterpart of the cicisbeo. A man made womanish and gawky in his appearance, with the voice of a young boy, he was a striking figure on the public stage. In the fall of 1775, the Marquis de Sade attended the opera of *Perseus and Andromeda* in Florence. There was absolutely nothing that pleased him about the performance. What especially horrified him was the voice and appearance of a castrato. "It was the first time that I saw this species of half-men in a theater," he wrote the anonymous female recipient of his letters. He described his repulsion upon hearing "a small, clear voice, much higher than a woman's emerge from a rather large, fatty,

Figure I.6 Two Roman antiquarians examining a coin. Arthur Pond (after Pier Leone Ghezzi), *Due famosi antiquari*, 1739. Fine Arts Museum of San Francisco, Achenbach Foundation for Graphic Arts, 1963.30.17290.

and somewhat ill-formed body of a man." [85] For Sade the castrato was one of the clear signs of the moral decline of Italy at the end of the eighteenth century. He could not believe that any woman would love them, despite reports of the long retired Farinelli's great celebrity. (His body was recently exhumed in July 2006 from the Certosa cemetery in Bologna to examine what remains of his anatomy and physiology.)

The celebrity of the castrato fully complemented the longstanding perception of the Italian peninsula as a region that openly tolerated, if not actively promoted, homosexuality. If travel was a transformative experience, would Grand Tourists return from Italy with characteristics of the other sex? *The Entertaining Travels and Adventures of Mademoiselle de Richelieu*, published around 1740, described an imaginary voyage of a cross-dressing Frenchwoman Alithea, who gave herself "the Appearance of a Man" in order to travel. In Italy she and her cross-dressing companion enjoy the attention of both male and female admirers. The response to cross-dressing women travelers indicates how readily foreigners believed Italy to be a land in which the differences between the sexes simply dissolved. Italian women find the French women attractive because they are so feminine, while men find the women's boyishness equally appealing, due to "that abominable Goust to which the *Italian* Men are, I am told, addicted." [86] By the time they reach Rome, Alithea's fondest desire is to seduce another woman. At the end of the decade, John Cleland would translate the physician Giovanni Bianchi's account of the life of the Roman servant Caterina Vizzani, who died for her Sapphic proclivities. Like Sade, he became a moralist in the presence of the Italians, harshly censoring them for neither condemning Vizzani's behavior nor finding the cause of her unnatural desires. [87]

The fear that women might return from Italy somewhat male—*viragos*, in the term of the day—was fairly minimal since so few women traveled. Those who did were, by and large, an unconventional group to begin with. Concerns about the effect of the Grand Tour on men, however, were rampant. Would a lengthy stay in Italy make a man half-woman, as many thought the rakish Lord John Hervey and, later, the members of the Society of Dilettanti had become? Moralists warned that this was the inevitable result of such a journey south. By the 1760s the British had a term for the Italianate Englishman: the *macaroni* (Figure I.7). A foppish young gentleman with preposterous hair, fancy clothes, and an imported air, he spent entirely too much time at the opera in Covent Garden, where, "enervated and emasculated by the Softness of the *Italian* Musick," as John Dennis wrote in 1711, he ceased to care for women. In June 1770 the *Oxford Magazine* defined the macaroni as "neither male nor female, a thing of neuter gender." [88] He was the foreign equivalent of the castrato.

Robert Hitchcock's play, *The Macaroni* (1773), immortalized this vision of the effect of Italy on Englishmen in the character of Jack Epicene. Recently returned from Venice, his dress is so outlandish that a friend declares: "you make such large advances to the feminine gender, that in a little time 'twill be difficult to tell to which sex you belong." Epicene reflects the failure of the Englishman abroad to resist the vices of other nations. He returns home still willing to marry for the sake of his family but tells

Figure I.7 The English *macaroni*, lately returned from Italy. Philip Dawe, *Pantheon Macaroni [A Real Character at the Late Masquerade]*, printed for John Bowles, 1773 (mezzotint). BM Sat 5221. British Museum, London.

his fiancée that she should take a cicisbeo so that he might return to his beloved Italy. His friends finally force him to concede his error, confessing "that a Macaroni is the most insignificant—insipid—useless—contemptible being—in the whole creation" and repudiating his "degenerate, exotic effeminacy." [89]

The English obsession with the alleged homosexuality of the Italians—more a reflection of their own anxieties about sexuality than an actual understanding of the different social norms of the two regions of Europe[90]—gave them a readymade explanation for their own moral failings. If Englishmen did not always behave like honorable men, it was not due to any intrinsic flaw in the national character but a result of pernicious foreign influence. Italy had seduced and corrupted them. It lured them to the Mediterranean and followed them home across the Channel. With the publication of Montesquieu's influential *Spirits of the Laws* (1748), a theory emerged to explain the source of this corruption. Montesquieu and a number of his contemporaries believed that climate played a determinative role in the nature of a people. Cold, northern countries were relatively free of vice while warm, southern ones overflowed with a criminal degree of passion. Montesquieu specifically invoked the experience of going to the opera in England and Italy as his best example. The same music, he wrote, that so incited the Italians received a more measured reception in the north. [91] The Italians, he suggested, were naturally enslaved by their passions and therefore sexually degenerate.

Baretti strongly objected to this sweeping characterization of the Italians. He reminded his readers that the Italians were not, *pace* Boswell, a savage race incapable of understanding what had been said about them. Invoking a cosmopolitan Italian readership who consumed the books and essays of all the great London wits and French *philosophes*, he conjured up their laughter at such preposterous generalizations. How could anyone who had lived in Turin, Milan, Bologna, and Florence in the winter truly believe that the climate of northern and central Italy was significantly more temperate than many parts of northern Europe? Italy was not quite the Mediterranean seraglio Montesquieu envisioned from his travels, and the Italians were not "a womanish race of people, only fit for fiddling and singing, because they are born under too warm a sun." Baretti had his own criticisms of his fellow Italians, but he sought to reclaim their national character by arguing that foreigners viewed Italy like a bad connoisseur who claims but fails to understand a painting. "They travel to see things, and not men." [92]

The pastorelle, filosofesse, cicisbei, castrati, ciceroni, and even the macaroni were all there to be seen in eighteenth-century Italy, and they are the subject of the chapters that follow. The fact that such individuals *did* exist and such customs *were* primarily Italian, in some general sense, raises the question of how local practices and foreign perceptions interacted. If the examination of gender, as Joan Scott famously wrote, is about understanding a system of relations between men and women as well as the crafting of male and female roles in society, then the kind of "gender trouble" observed in Italy in the eighteenth century offers us an important window into understanding some crucial facts of this society.[93] Perhaps one of the reasons the Italian peninsula did not produce a Mary Wollstonecraft or an Olympe de Gouges, women we associate with the origins of modern feminism, was because the society of eighteenth-century Italy had given women a role, albeit limited and largely ceremonial, in its leading educational and cultural institutions. Aristocratic women had choices beyond marriage, and talented daughters of professionals and artisans could aspire to some degree of public recognition, perhaps even to an artistic, literary, or scientific career. Cicisbei did not simply serve women but also fostered their own social position through networks of friendship and kinship. Castrati existed to fulfill a specific musical vocation that had the approval of the Roman Catholic Church. Despite mounting criticism of these practices in the late eighteenth century, they nonetheless lingered into the nineteenth century, no longer active features of a society under reconstruction in the age of the Risorgimento but vestiges of its early modern past.

PART ONE

Gender and Public Life

ONE

Cicisbei

Italian Morality and European Values in the Eighteenth Century

ROBERTO BIZZOCCHI

Sismondi and the Cicisbei

In J. C. L. Sismondo Sismondi's portrait of the moral decline of the Italian conscience in the final chapters of his *Histoire des républiques* (*Storia*) (1807–1818)—a decline that he attributed to the loss of political and religious freedoms in the sixteenth century—a great deal of space is reserved for the figure of the cicisbeo, the cavalier servente who openly kept company with a married noblewoman, not only in public but also in private. Since the cicisbeo is a figure most commonly associated with the eighteenth century (think, for example, of the "*giovin signore* [young gentleman]" in the famous poem "Il Giorno" by Giuseppe Parini, 1763), it is all the more interesting that Sismondi speaks of him at the beginning of his chapter on the seventeenth century. It is almost as though the topic pressed upon him with urgency in light of the end of political independence and the

---

This chapter is an updated and expanded version of an earlier article published in Italian: "Cicisbei. La morale italiana," *Storica* 9 (1997), pp. 63–90. Translated by Matthew Sneider.

affirmation of the Counter Reformation. He marvels at the scarce interest dedicated to the theme by other writers:

> No one has numbered among the public calamities of Italy what is per-
> haps the most general reason for the private troubles of all Italian families;
> the offense, I say, made to the sacred bond of matrimony by another open
> bond, regarded as honorable, which foreigners always witness in Italy with
> equal stupor, without understanding the reason—the *cicisbei* or the *cavalieri*
> *serventi.*

The cicisbei remain the protagonists in the successive pages on Italian corruption, from which I can cite here only a few phrases: "no husband regarded his consort any longer as a faithful companion and partner for life . . . no father dared assure himself that the children of his marriage were his." In this manner "the institution of all the ridiculous duties of the *cicisbei*" was "the most efficacious means of calming agitated spirits recently reduced to servitude." Sismondi even claims that "not because certain women had lovers, but rather because a woman could no longer show herself in public without a lover, Italians ceased to be men."[1]

The final section of Sismondi's *Histoire* is a fundamental text for Italian culture and the image of modern Italy. On the one hand, the *Histoire* was at the center of attention for and the focus of debates of the nineteenth century's greatest intellectuals, beginning with Alessandro Manzoni, who in 1819 wrote *Osservazioni sulla morale cattolica* to refute the text. On the other hand, Sismondi's invocation of this kind of male behavior revived with greater authority this image of relations between the sexes in Italy that had previously been popularized by a long series of tales, reliable or otherwise, and through judgments, often very negative and contemptuous, reported over the course of the eighteenth century by foreign travelers who came into contact with Italians during their Grand Tours. On cicisbei Sismondi seems particularly to echo the pages of the Englishman Samuel Sharp, whose words were so ferocious as to immediately provoke a resentful response by Italian writer Giuseppe Baretti.[2]

Cicisbei are an interesting subject for two reasons: first, for the reality of the social phenomenon that they represent, and second, for the national stereotype which was constructed around them. The present chapter deals to a greater degree with the latter issue, but it also seeks to shed some light on the former, although the documentary research here is still in its beginning stages.

Scholars and Cicisbei

A bibliography on the topic of cicisbeismo is not lacking. This bibliography, however, dates primarily to the period between the end of the nineteenth century and the beginning of the twentieth; it is composed almost entirely of works by positivist scholars of Italian literature. I note this last fact to clarify the intellectual attitude that marks the greater part of our body of knowledge on the topic: an attitude which mixes, in a manner characteristic of such scholars, moralism and spicy anecdote, erudition and frivolity. It is an attitude in which the most crucial of questions is ever present, sometimes below the surface and sometimes, amusingly, quite in the open: did they do it or didn't they?

That certain responses to this question have been offered which contradict Sismondi is not terribly important. On the other hand it is worth noting that almost all scholars of cicisbei follow Sismondi, perhaps unconsciously, in his sociological characterization of the phenomenon. I take Luigi Valmaggi as an example of the general tendency. Valmaggi was a cautious follower, regarding the crucial curiosity, of the idea of *omnia munda mundis*; he was the author of a 1927 book which reprised and reordered the scholarship of recent decades, allowing him to review broadly the eighteenth-century literary sources.[3] The cicisbeismo which emerges from Valmaggi's book is an (innocent) peculiarity of the eighteenth-century Italian nobility, an unexplained *unicum* in the history of human civilization. Apart from its innocence, the relevant point is that the specialized studies confirm, in an entirely different historiographic context, the gist of Sismondi's description: his political and moral dramatization of cicisbeismo in relation to servitude and the Counter Reformation would not even be conceivable without enclosing and isolating its usage to Italy, in the early modern period and in the ruling class.

In times and in the hands of spirits much closer to ourselves, the theme of cicisbei has been the object of three analyses which have a scholarly acuity lacking in those of the early twentieth century. Luciano Guerci has the merit of having gathered and interpreted eighteenth-century treatises (which Valmaggi must have judged less amusing than the poems and the accounts of travelers) and, above all, of having connected the gallantry of the cavalieri serventi to the "sociability" of conversations and salons.[4] Romano Canosa has placed the custom in the context of the sexual repression promoted by Catholic moralists, in his opinion substantially victorious in imposing chastity in every nonconjugal relationship between men and women.[5] Finally, Marzio Barbagli has dedicated to husbands and cicisbei a brief but dense paragraph in his important book on the family where, following a famous page of Cesare Beccaria, he relates "gallantry" and cicisbeismo to the absence of "freedom in marriage"—the ability to choose one's spouse. In this sense, cicisbeismo was a practice which offered a controlled outlet for impulses of physical attraction, friendship, and "sympathy."[6]

When one examines the historical sociology of marital or extramarital relations between the sexes, the cavalier servente ceases to be the ridiculous marionette of erudite literati or the tragic puppet of Sismondi. He remains, however, a human specimen specific to eighteenth-century Italian nobility. Barbagli, who like Guerci and Canosa,[7] shares this conviction with his predecessors, makes the objection which occurs spontaneously at this point: if the cicisbeo is related to the absence of freedom in marriage—a fact widespread also outside of Italy—why does the custom appear characteristic of the *Italian* aristocracies? I propose to reformulate the very premise of this question.

Contracts and Cicisbei

An important component of this image of cicisbeismo as a peculiarly Italian custom is the prevailing conviction that it had the character of a legally regulated institution. In fact, Barbagli argues that the usage was legally fixed: "The cicisbeo was chosen jointly by wife and husband and was sometimes provided for in the nuptial contracts."[8] This affirmation is not accompanied by reference to any evidence. In reality it is an opinion repeated many times before Barbagli, whose proof, however, remains rather vague.

In his book on Parini, Cesare Cantù asserts that "in nuptial contracts it was stipulated that a *cavalier servente* be given to the lady, and a specific individual was sometimes even named." This assertion is accompanied by a note, however, which speaks of a sonnet by Parini in praise of a woman who does *not* have a cicisbeo.[9] Giosue Carducci, also speaking of Parini, repeats the thesis of the "*cavalier servente* stipulated and even designated by the nuptial contracts," adding that "when the Marquis Spinola, in mid-eighteenth century Genoa, acted in a contrary fashion—stipulating his refusal of any *servente*—it appeared singular and inconvenient."[10] Note that this is an accord regarding the absence, and not the presence, of the cicisbeo. In any event, Carducci depends for this information on Achille Neri, one of the positivist literati to whom I made reference above, who in his turn depends on the legal historian Carlo Gabba, who depends on still others—a mechanism of Chinese boxes in which reference to any specific notarial act seems to have been lost.[11]

A notarial act marked with a place, a date (Rome, September 17, 1793), and a notary's name (Felci), appears and is also partially published in a *zibaldone*, an anecdotal book written around the time of Neri's study. The author, David Silvagni, reports for several pages on the patrimonial agreements contained in the nuptial contract between don Paluzzo Altieri and donna Marianna di Sassonia where—he comments—"there was not the usual promise to grant to the bride . . . a *cavalier servente* of her liking, as was the usage and as we have read in the contract of a Visconti woman married into the house of the Marsciano counts."[12] Silvagni, however, shows us nothing of this Visconti-Marsciano contract.

Among the authoritative scholars of our own day, Paolo Ungari, in his fundamental book on the family law, has explicitly dealt with the problem of legal formalization:

> Leaving aside the possibility of documenting pacts regarding the cicisbeo in nuptial contracts, which are attested by many, the series of accessory stipulations . . . , all of which clearly preordain an independent social and sentimental life, are interesting and very easy to document.

The "accessory stipulations" are those which regarded the "treatment" of the wife—allowance, servants, carriage, box at the opera, and so on. Ungari exhibits notarial formulas regarding this treatment. But he can adduce not one nuptial contract which includes agreement over a cicisbeo, despite the caricatured representation of a contract's stipulation in Vittorio Alfieri's satirical comedy *Il divorzio*.[13]

In his book on eighteenth-century Venice, the French historian Jean Georgelin, on the trail of an unsubstantiated reference by Philippe Monnier, also went in search of notarial stipulations of agreement on cicisbei: "The anecdote—he concludes—had the success that one might imagine. But the examination of thousands upon thousands of noble marriage contracts obliges us to deny it: *we have not found even one which mentions it*."[14] I can declare the same thing—for what my tens of contracts, added to the thousands, are worth—regarding the Tuscan contracts which I have read.

In conclusion, even if we cannot argue that the phenomenon of legal stipulation never existed, we can regard it as being much less pervasive than many studies on cicisbeismo imply. Until contrary proof comes to light, it will be correct to regard cicisbeismo as more a common practice than a legal institution.

Compari and Cicisbei

The fact that cicisbeismo may not have been a matter of law and contracts reveals some interesting dimensions of this social practice. The less one insists on the institutionalized role and the crystallized artificiality of the relationship of *cicisbeato*, the more we may consider it within the overall *reality* of relations between the sexes and therefore contextualize it in an environment rather far from the literary satire of Parini's giovin signore.

The existence of recognized and overt ties between men and women, ties which are independent of and prior to—but also contemporary with and parallel to—the engagement and marriage of one or both of the parties with another person, has been attested among the populations of various parts of Italy and Europe for centuries, almost up to the eve of the sexual freedom of our own time. The most obvious of these ties is godparenthood—the bond of spiritual family relations and familiar intimacy which is created between godfather and godmother and between these two and the godchild and parents. We do not need Boccaccio's slyness (novellas VII, 3 and 10; novella X, 4) to imagine opportunities for adulterous sex in the relative freedom of encounter conceded to godfathers and godmothers.

But for our purposes this sacramental and technically circumscribed family relation is less interesting than a generic and widespread usage which clearly has some relation to baptism—as demonstrated by its most common name, godparenthood of San Giovanni (*comparatico di San Giovanni*), and the importance of the feast of San Giovanni on June 24—which nevertheless has as its principal function the creation of a couple. This couple is generally, but not exclusively, composed of a male and a female and in fact is almost always a young man and a young woman.

Numerous variants of this usage exist. The most dramatic is the presence of a girl pretending to be a mother who baptizes a doll. We find an example of the former in the following description from Barile in Basilicata in 1889:

> On the feast of San Giovanni . . . a great number of boys and girls move
> from the village. . . . the girls carry dolls wrapped in swaddling clothes in

their arms. When they arrive at the clearing of San Pietro the girls take turns choosing the godfather and the godmother, and they ask them to baptize their newborns. So in every little group the girl-mother places her little one sweetly on the ground and the two little godparents, holding each other by the hand, jump over it three times, holding their feet together, while pronouncing the following formula. . . . *Pupe de San Giuanne / battezzame sti panne / Sti panne so bbattezzate / tutte compare sime chiamate* (Babes of San Giovanni / We baptize these bundles / These bundles are baptized / Now we are all godparents).

In many similar cases, though not necessarily in this case, the relations of godparenthood created by these rituals last "for life."[15]

The other principal variant of comparatico di San Giovanni seems to be situated in a decidedly more adult sphere. Let me give an example:

In Sardinia there is a special relation of godparenthood called godparent-hood of San Giovanni. Its ties do not last longer than one year. It is generally created between married persons, without leaving space for suppositions or suspicions regarding the parties to the contract, and it concludes in the following manner. . . . On the feast of San Giovanni the godfather and the god-mother take [a vase] and, followed by many people in attendance, they move toward the church. Once there, one of the two throws the vase against the door and the entire crowd eats an herb omelet together. Thereafter each person, placing his or her hands on those of the male or female near to them, sings out over and over: *compare e comare di San Giovanni* (godfathers and godmothers of San Giovanni). Once this has been done, there are many hours of dancing which bring the festival to an end.[16]

Agnès Fine, author of a notable book on spiritual family relations which includes diverse cases of godparenthood of San Giovanni, or its equivalent, in Mediterranean Europe (Italy, Spain, Portugal, Albania, and Dalmatia), gathered from a Corsican peasant a typology dating to the 1930s. It mixes certain characteristics of the preceding two examples, because it focuses on young but unmarried adults and is not limited to one year. Consequently "it often happened that a real friendship grew up and survived the marriage of one or the other. At public dances, for example, the godfather invited the godmother to have the first dance without her husband taking offense." The old peasant explains:

They were thought of as brother and sister. It wasn't a little ceremony that you would forget overnight. For their lives, they were faithful to it . . . it was a sort of vow. *That* [sexual relations] wasn't a part of it. What's more,

> I believe that here in the region there has never been a marriage between *cummà e cumpà de San Ghjuani* [godmother and godfather of San Giovanni]! They were like brother and sister.[17]

Just like certain late-nineteenth-century literary critics and many contemporary ethnographers, the Corsican peasant expresses a presumption of chastity which was not at all shared by the bishops who dealt with godparenthood of San Giovanni. Evidence for Italy, sporadic in the Middle Ages but abundant beginning in the Tridentine era, is found in the series of ethnographic investigations which Cleto Corrain and Pierluigi Zampini carried out on diocesan synods. Faced with the preponderant number of documents for central, southern, and peninsular Italy, the authors at first denied that the phenomenon existed in northern Italy but then changed their minds when they encountered clear evidence in a 1571 synod of Carpi in the duchy of Modena.[18] At any rate, all the synods thunder against false and sacrilegious godparenthood, a pretext—as the 1692 synod of Bitonto (Bari) declares—"with which [the false godfather and godmother] fool the world and indulge more freely their lust" or—according to the 1651 synod of Gerace (Reggio Calabria)—"these, having obtained license to frequent each other, commit very sinful crimes under the cover of an honest name."[19]

There are traces of a popular belief in the suspension of prohibitions during the feast of San Giovanni, because from June 23 to June 25 the Lord causes the saint to sleep (*"Godete, non temete, Giovanni dorme"* [Enjoy yourselves, don't fear, Giovanni is asleep]). In an interesting article inspired by the theories of Lévi-Strauss, Salvatore D'Onofrio has explained this belief as a ritualization of the sexual charge in godparenthood, seen as incestuous and therefore dangerous for sexual reciprocity.[20]

In short, godparenthood of San Giovanni seems to represent a sort of relationship between the sexes which was alternative to and at the same time supplementary to marriage. The reference to spiritual family relations tied to baptism (and therefore prohibition of marriage), whether fictitiously imparted to a doll or recalled by the saint and by the day, is the essential characteristic. Godfather and godmother are linked by a strong intimacy. It is stronger, according to some evidence, than the relationship between brother and sister which the Corsican peasant evokes. By definition, however, it is and must remain nonconjugal in nature.

If godparenthood, therefore, serves certain functions (choice, freedom, variety, "sympathy") which do not necessarily belong to the state of matrimony, it is not surprising that Agnès Fine poses the problem in terms corresponding to our questions about cicisbeismo:

> The relationship of friendship was clearly distinguished from the conjugal relationship. It is well known that marriage alliance in the rural world depended strictly on family strategies and that one married according to the size of the dowry, the number of brothers and sisters, and one's own place among them. Without a doubt, one did not expect marriage to permit the expression of sentiments of "sympathy." Did godparenthood of San Giovanni play this role?[21]

Certain elements do exist which help us to bridge the gulf that seems to divide the refined eighteenth-century *damerino* (little gentleman) from the rural populations of a European history of very *longue durée*—above all, the chivalrous culture of courtly love of which godparenthood and cicisbeismo, as relationships which were in principle platonic, are both examples. It was this intellectual affiliation of cicisbeismo that Giuseppe Baretti emphasized in the already cited polemic with the Englishman Samuel Sharp, and it was not difficult for the erudite Neri to uncover certain pertinent citations from the erotic treatises of the Renaissance.[22] But the reference is also true for godparenthood. In societies like those of the Occident, in which relations between the sexes stretch from reciprocal reclusion to conjugal sexuality, friendship between men and women must resemble the relationship between brother and sister. As Fine argues, taking up the thesis of other scholars, it is precisely that rite of intersexual fraternity which lies at the origin of courtly love.[23]

Within the bounds of courtly love, which were truly a little evanescent, the connection between godfathers and cicisbei is based on the support of at least one more precise analogy. Its sign is the practice, repeatedly seen in the popular world, of leaving to chance—fictitiously or not—the coupling of godfathers and godmothers, in this case generally for a certain period of time, typically for one year. The custom of drawing names from two series of tickets, one for males and one for females, described by Pitré for San Giovanni in Sicily, finds its parallel in Carnival feasts of the Iberian Peninsula and in a game for the evening of Epiphany in the province of Cuneo.[24] But the most interesting case is that of *valentinage*, studied with particular attention to France by Arnold van Gennep. Valentinage derives from the belief, of medieval origin and widespread throughout Europe, in the coupling of birds on February 14. It involves linking, by means of a random drawing of names, a young man and young woman who are thereby required or authorized to maintain for a year—until the next Saint Valentine's Day—a relationship of gallantry, with little gifts, invitations, accompaniments to parties. Although the valentines are not subjected, not even symbolically, to the nuptial prohibition of the godparents of San Giovanni, their link is also quite distinct from normal forms of engagement.[25]

Van Gennep has demonstrated that valentinage existed both in rural villages and in courtly and aristocratic circles in England and France. And it is here that one might identify a correspondence between extramatrimonial ties in the popular world and cicisbeismo in aristocratic circles, thanks to two pieces of evidence that Valmaggi, although refusing to accept them, had the merit of bringing to light. The first is evidence for an Italian and noble valentinage found in the *Ceremoniale* book of the court of Turin in an entry dated February 14, 1677. In this case as well, the valentines were randomly extracted and the couples were required for one year to engage in the customary forms of tenuous courting. The second piece of evidence more precisely links the world of the cicisbei to the sphere of popular gallantry. This was a game played by the Neapolitan aristocracy which consisted of a kind of mischievous drawing of names, accordingly valid for one evening alone (the last of the year), described by Ferdinando Galiani in his *Oration on the Occasion of the Random Drawing of Cicisbei and Cicisbee* (1759).[26]

Galiani's report is especially interesting because it combines the idea of a random drawing of names with a precise reference to cicisbeismo. Name drawing invokes the custom of valentinage and more generally the juvenile and popular sphere of the dynamic of nonconjugal relationships between the sexes. By linking cicisbeismo with valentinage, Galiani strips the cavalier servente of his uniqueness, a view which makes his role unrepeatable and without comparison precisely because it is rigidly contained in an overly elaborated etiquette.

The strongest connection between godparents and cicisbei may perhaps be found in a practice which identifies their commonalities. I am referring to the custom according to which the lady and her cicisbeo held children at baptism, standing before the altar as a couple like a godmother and a godfather. The extent of the practice must still be verified, but it is attested to with certainty in the case of the noblewoman of Lucca Luisa Palma Mansi, whose private diary I will discuss below.[27]

Nonetheless, there naturally remains a very important difference between cicisbeismo and those other kinds of relationships which can be linked, more or less closely, to the godparenthood of San Giovanni. The service of the cavaliere allowed a continuity and freedom of attendance, also attendance in private, which appears unimaginable even in the long-lasting and intimate "friendship" evoked in the testimony of the Corsican peasant, given that the definition of honor in peasant society was far more concerned with sexual behavior and therefore a woman's virtue.[28] But this is not enough, in my opinion, to deny that the two phenomena belong to one whole: the channeling of extraconjugal drives. The distance which separates them can, in fact, be bridged by considering the variable function of the sense of honor among the different social classes in Italy.

Other Cicisbei

If we must not exclude from our horizon the sphere of popular godparenthood, it will be all the more worthwhile to explore the social world of the European nobility, in which marriage was at least equally determined by economic calculations, and where the sense of honor was less centered on sexual behavior than in rural villages.

Recall Sismondi's summary judgment of cicisbeismo as a custom "which foreigners always witness in Italy with equal stupor." The astonishment of those travelers inspired in them an abundant series of remarks and judgments, many times taken up by Valmaggi and his predecessors, which make relations between the sexes among the eighteenth-century Italian nobility a gallery of prodigies of nature (or rather against nature). This is not surprising; we always attribute to those different from ourselves that which appears blameworthy or ridiculous.

Rather than dwell on these foolish remarks, I prefer to examine the writings of an observer who was not negatively predisposed: the enlightened philosophe Charles Dupaty, who traveled in Italy in 1785. Rather than writing the usual colorful descriptions, Dupaty poses questions that signal his desire to understand what he has witnessed:

> Cicisbeismo merits close attention. It is said that in no place is it as in vogue as in Genoa. What is a *cicisbeo* in appearance? What is he in reality? In what manner does a woman take a *cicisbeo*? In what manner does a man wish to be a *cicisbeo*? What do the husbands think? Is the *cicisbeo* the lieutenant of a husband? To what extent is he so? What is the origin of this usage? For what reason does it persist or change? What influence does it have on customs? Can traces or similarities be found in the customs of other peoples?

In one sense, the response is disappointing since Dupaty never really completes his research; on the point that we are seeking to clarify, however, it is revealing: "These are questions which are difficult to resolve. In short, the *cicisbeo* in Genoa is more or less the same as the *ami de la maison* (friend of the house) in Paris."[29]

Dupaty suggests a comparison which, if it is not terribly profitable for research on the ami de la maison, yields good results for probing the idea of the *petit-maître*. Leaving aside the background of the term, the *petit-maître* of the eighteenth century was a fashionable *damerino*. Like Parini's giovin signore, he professed a superficial interest in the new enlightened ideas. He was frivolous, cynical, and libertine in matters of love. The literature which turns on this personage—in one way or another a large part of the century's erotic literature in France—offers a continual illustration of the theme of marriage as a contractual condition, marriage which was sentimentally indifferent from the outset or which became so over time, marriage which was more or less tranquilly compatible with an amorous extraconjugal life, better if light-hearted and varied. "Where the wife is, the husband does not go; and where the husband may be found, the wife avoids going: one fears getting a bad reputation." This was the observation which Pierre-Jacques Brillon, as early as 1700, made in his *Théophraste moderne, ou nouveaux caractères sur les moeurs*.[30] In short, as Bernard-Joseph Saurin reaffirmed later from the male point of view in a 1760 comedy entitled *Les moeurs du temps*, "One marries one woman, one lives with another, and one loves no one but one's self."[31]

Moreover, since we are discussing national stereotypes, we should note that it would be paradoxical if France were to lack a significant archetype of erotic amorality. A well-consolidated tradition about the French obviously designates them as masters in this field. In Italy the "great freedom of commerce between the one and the other sex" was ascribed—as by Muratori in the *Annali* of 1707—to the "fatal legacy of their teachings and examples."[32] As for cicisbei in particular, the idea—of which we also find a trace in Dupaty—that Genoa (near France) was their cradle is an indication of the existence of a theory (almost always neglected or distorted) that was quite different from the explanation which emphasized the purely Italian character of the custom.

We find this theory expressed with great clarity in a *Dialogo* of Paolo Mattia Doria, the old and conservative Doria, "in which—as the title declares—examining the reason why dancing women never tire, is painted the portrait of an Italian *petit maître*, affected admirer of the maxims and customs of the French *petits maîtres* and cicisbei." In Doria's dialogue, the description made by the "Italian *petit maître*" Leandro to the "old family man" Pancrazio of the relations among the husband, the wife, and the cicisbeo is preceded by a preamble in which adoption of the custom is openly explained as an imitation of the fashions of "Paris, the city which has introduced good taste to all Europe."[33]

In reality, apart from the case made for the prestige of the Parisian model, the correspondence between petits maîtres and cicisbei is not as perfect as Doria would have it. But the partial divergence may perhaps be explained by the ideology of total freedom which is characteristic of French erotic experimentation. Although cicisbeismo was not a static or regimented custom, the strenuous and uncompromising philosophical coherence of French libertinism rejected even those few rules which the practices of the cavalier servente required.

A French nobleman traveling in England in 1784 noted, as a characteristic trait of social life in that country, the intimacy in the married lives of aristocratic couples in contrast to his own homeland. Horace Walpole contrasted the lives of English couples with the custom of the cavalieri serventi of Florence.[34] The prospect of a British cicisbeo figured as the quintessence of the absurd in the *Corinne ou l'Italie* of Madame de Staël. If we follow the conclusions of Randolph Trumbach's lovely book on the English aristocratic family of the eighteenth century, it may be true that conjugal affection developed there a good half century in advance of other countries, in particular Italy. And it is also true that the eighteenth century is for England the century of the sentimental comedy. The difference is nonetheless only chronological, unless one wishes to dismiss as mere imitation—of the French model, let it be understood, and not of the Italian model—the erotic light-heartedness of the comedy of manners in this period.

It will suffice here to cite as an example the high point and a recognized masterpiece of that theatrical genre, *The Way of the World* (1700) by William Congreve. In a famous and celebrated scene (the fifth scene of the fourth act) the protagonist who bears the name of Millamant (French for "thousand lovers") dictates to her future husband Mirabell the conditions of their coming life together:

> Trifles, as liberty to pay and receive visits to and from whom I please; to write and receive letters without interrogatories or wry faces on your part . . .

to have my closet inviolate; to be sole empress of my tea-table, which you must never presume to approach without first asking leave; and lastly, wherever I am, you shall always knock at the door before you come in.

Faced with the perplexity of the ex-libertine Mirabell, Millamant reaffirms the evidence of the English version of matrimony according to the *moeurs du temps*:

Let us never visit together, nor go to a play together, but let us be very strange and well bred: let us be as strange as if we had been married a great while, and as well bred as if we were not married at all.[35]

Rather than weigh down the reference to a classic text such as *The Way of the World* with too many citations, I limit myself to noting that in the introduction which Italian anglicist Nicoletta Neri provides for her annotated edition of the original text, one finds a review of other examples in English theater—from other epochs as well—comparable to the marriage pact between Mirabell and Millamant. This review shows us that the consequences of free commerce between married ladies and cicisbei, consequences always denounced as the most scandalous, were also a literary theme in England. Here are the demands of a soon-to-be bride in Philip Massinger's *The City Madam* (1632): "I'll have the state conveyed / into my hands. . . . And, when I have children, if it be enquired / by a stranger, whose they are, they shall still echo / My Lady Plenty's, the husband never thought on."[36] It would be difficult to find clearer proof of the fact that the Englishman Sharp, perhaps the most brutal proponent of that idea of the illegitimacy of noble offspring—which we have also seen in Sismondi—went to Italy already disposed to find it.

The attribution of a controversial custom to bad foreign influences is also found in Spain. There, in the early eighteenth century, the lady's cavalier servente was called *estrecho* or *chichisveo* or *cortejo*. Only over the course of the century did the name cortejo prevail and it, moreover, was sometimes joined by that of *petimetre*—clearly modeled on the French. But Carmen Martín Gaite, author of a book based on a wide array of evidence in which the cortejo plays a large part, has demonstrated that, prior to and independent of being imported from abroad, this figure addressed a need which arose from the configurations of marriage in the Spanish aristocracy of the seventeenth and eighteenth centuries.

This interesting book gives us a new and revealing element regarding the analogies between aristocratic and popular customs of love. The author recalls a game of her own childhood and of that of her mother:

> The game was called *echar los estrechos* and the way it worked was that on the last day of the year, we girlfriends put some slips of paper with our names in a bag, and slips of paper with the names of boys that we knew or wanted to know in another bag. And we held a drawing to make couples.[37]

Martín Gaite's theory that echar los estrechos is an example of a wider genre is also fully confirmed for Spain—aside from the information about valentines and Galiani's oration which we pointed out above—by evidence from the minister Campomanes on the tradition "de echar Compadres y Comadres" (of drawing godfathers and godmothers, presumably adults) for the new year and, for the nobility, by the long explanation given by a doña Paula to Giuseppe Baretti about the extraction of the *años* and of the estrechos on the last day of the year and the eve of Epiphany respectively. Doña Paula herself is very clear about the opportunities for great and easy intimacy reserved to the noble cicisbeo: the año or estrecho

> of a lady acquires the right to stay in her company with greater attendance than normal. He enters her house at any hour: he eats with her when he so desires without a specific invitation; he courts her; and, finally, he is in some manner incorporated into her family. . . . In this way, the ladies are sure of always having constant visits to their houses and escorts out.

For the Spanish cavalieri serventi, moreover, we have evidence of great interest, evidence furnishing a living embodiment of the typology of male and female behavior described generally so many times.

There are two autobiographical diaries kept by the Spanish writer Nicolás Fernández de Moratín and by his son, the comedy writer Leandro, at the end of the eighteenth century and in the first years of the nineteenth, which also contain valuable information about their friendships with women. They are intimate writings containing annotations for their own use, generally in abbreviated form, often in Latin, always skeletal. Let us say that plotted on a graph representing degrees of distortion, they are furthest from the tales of a chatty traveler, ill-disposed and ignorant of the language of the country. In other words, they come as close to representing firsthand experience as any source we might uncover.

The elder Moratín's diary has been used to conduct a study of the role of the cortejo. Nicolás was the cortejo of a certain O. over the course of

1778 and of a certain N. in the following year. His telegraphic notes fill with many precise facts the many empty pigeonholes of the exercise of serving: today together to the circus, today together to the bullfight, another day a gift. There are also a few little statistics, compiled by the interested party: "*diciembre 1778. A casa de O' veinticinco veces*" (December 1778. To O's house twenty-five times). But the truly precious thing which this text offers us is evidence of the fact that, for all its ritualization, the relationship between the cicisbeo and the lady was nothing strange, unique, or unnatural. Rather, it belonged to the varied dynamic of relations between a man and a woman, the components of which it shares: desire, caprice, conflict, boredom, and so on; even jealous rivalry, when a little officer of the garrison begins to frequent the *belle*. I shall not forget an essential component, and since in this specific case—as far as it is possible to believe Nicolás when he talks to himself—I have satisfied my curiosity, I do not wish to prevent my reader from doing likewise: "*18 mayo de 1778. Sofá, futui optime.*"[38]

Cicisbei in the Theater of the World

To restate the results of the preceding analysis, insofar as cicisbeismo can be given a fixed role, this phenomenon also occurred outside the eighteenth-century Italian nobility. Now we may return to the discussion of Italy to explore some new aspects of the complexity of this custom.

As I have already mentioned, until now studies of cicisbeismo have greatly favored analysis of literary works, more or less consciously constructed as such, over nonliterary sources about cicisbei. I have thus far highlighted the limitations of these literary works, but creative literature is not entirely misleading. Beyond the picturesque anecdotes of travelers and the sermons of the treatise writers and the satirical poets, we have at our disposal the acute, extraordinarily penetrating vision of cicisbeismo found in the theater of Carlo Goldoni.[39] Of course, when dealing with an author who declared on all occasions his desire to do nothing more than give voice to truth and to bring the world in its natural form onto the stage, it will be necessary to exercise the most scrupulous care.[40] But here the purpose is not to reconstitute specific situations or personages, or even to take a few lines of dialogue as representative of real episodes. Rather, the goal is to assess the image of cicisbeismo which is vitally portrayed in Goldoni's moral program in which he advocated prudence, economy, judgment, and, more specifically, a reasoned view of matrimony and conversation between the sexes.

Given the inevitable tensions and ambiguities existing within such a program, Goldoni's cavalier servente could easily appear as a professional marionette, rigid, specialized, and stereotyped to the highest degree. It is therefore significant that Goldoni, in general, chooses to go beyond simply replicating the stereotype of the cicisbeo. Perhaps the most conventional image occurs in his comedy explicitly dedicated to and expressly given the title of *Il cavaliere e la dama*. Here, for understandable reasons, the plot centers on the story of a service which is more than moral, indeed a service which is stoic to the point of heroism (and hence contradictory in the manner of Goldoni). The more Goldoni heightens this contrast, the more artificial the representation of the libertine married couple seems—a couple for other reasons odious—especially when they are engaged in a four-way conversation (i. 10) with the wife's cavalier servente and the husband's cicisbea.

But the clearest proof that cicisbeismo in Goldoni's theater of the world is not just a scripted role lies precisely in the fact that it proliferates in his work outside of the eponymous comedy, and with more convincing subtleties. Cicisbeismo interacts there with other aspects of life, such as age, status, type of family, and relations within family. It always appears as a fruit of conversation, of sociability, of attendance between men and women, at least married women. Consequently cicisbeismo manifests itself in a range of representations diverse enough to allow comparison with the multiple manifestations of the heterosexual eros.

Above all else, as Goldoni informed the French readers of his *Mémoires*, there were at least two views of cicisbeismo current among the Italian aristocracies that defined its essential role in describing different kinds of marriages:

> In Italy there are husbands who tolerate the *cavalieri serventi* of their wives and indeed are their friends and confidants; but there are also jealous husbands who look with contempt on these singular beings, second masters in ill-matched marriages.[41]

In his comedies and reflections on Italian society, Goldoni explored other typologies of cicisbei, beyond those of *Il cavaliere e la dama*. In these plays there are also cicisbei who are tolerated through weakness or convenience, or who are rejected, or even menacingly liquidated, and not only in the bourgeois environment of the Pantaloni (*L'uomo prudente*, i. 3, 12 etc.) or the rustic environment of Cancian (*I rusteghi*, ii. 13; iii. 2) but also by the noble Roberto who trembles in *La dama prudente* and to whom the citation from the *Mémoires* refers. Moreover, there are cicisbee who are the objects of a wife's jealousy, as occurs throughout *La moglie saggia* and in *Il festino*. The classic example of the cuckolded male finds its counterpart in Goldoni's frustrated wives in search of their husband's attention.

By moving beyond the uniform and stereotypical representation of the ciscisbeo, Goldoni's depiction clearly sketches a possible history in relationships of cicisbeato, in addition to portraying the jealousy—or lack thereof—of husbands and wives. Two exceptionally fine examples will suffice. The first is the masterful touch given to the sketch of relations between the countess and the doctor, her "old *cicisbeo*," in the *Famiglia dell'antiquario* (i. 11; ii. 15–16): a rapid archaeological tour of the ruins of erotic attraction, or at least reciprocal compatibility, between a man and a woman who grow older in habitual rudeness or tolerance like two ill-matched spouses. The second—truly an example of the refined moral understanding of Goldoni—is the portrait of the ill-married lady of *La villeggiatura*, donna Lavinia, whose behavior is the antithesis of the libertinism of the many cynical and capricious cicisbee. Lavinia is seriously in love with her servant Paoluccio. She waits two years with passionate fidelity for his return from a stay in Paris, where, unfortunately—and to her dismay—he learned inconstancy in love.

The extremely rich gallery of cicisbeato relations presented by Goldoni constitutes by itself sufficient evidence that cicisbeismo was a real experience of men and women, and not simply an illusion of rigid masks. The reformer of Italian theater himself could hardly fall into the trap, like so many distracted travelers, of representing erotic life in Italy as a new *Commedia dell'Arte*.

Cicisbei in Flesh and Blood

In contrast to the stereotypical images presented by other literati and many travelers, the complex and nonpolemical representation of cicisbei by Goldoni is confirmed by the nonliterary sources on cicisbei which have thus far come to light. I will discuss the most important of these sources here, warning the reader that such sources are not easily found and that this investigation is still in its early stages. In order to fully write a social history of this subject, it will be necessary to greatly increase the available documentation and to deepen its analysis.[42]

The source which in a certain sense is most complete, but which for other reasons is disconcerting and even a little enigmatic, is a *Relation de l'état de Gênes* drawn up in 1737 by the French envoy Jacques de Campredon.[43] Campredon was not the usual gossipy and irresponsible traveler; he was in Genoa to serve the interests of his government with the aim of promoting the influence of France over Corsica. His *Relation* had the practical and important purpose of informing his foreign minister of the local situation. The detailed prosopography of the roughly 130 patricians at the head of the oligarchic republic of Genoa, which forms the nucleus of his report, therefore could not be too casually fantastical. The fact which interests us is that each of the biographical sketches of those men in power identifies not the wife (although many are clearly married) but the lady to whom the man is cavalier servente. This has the result of revealing, by means of multiple interweavings, the existence of a vast and all-inclusive network of *cicisbeali* relations which connected the entire urban aristocracy.

Campredon's reports on individual members of the Genoese ruling families, upon which it is impossible to dwell at length, sometimes deal with the more intimate aspect of the pairings. Given the context of the *Relation*, however, he obviously placed particular emphasis on their public and social aspect. The identification of the cicisbee clearly points to the possibility of conditioning the political choices of Genoese patricians by means of feminine influence. Beyond this contingent goal, however, it also suggests with clarity in more than one case (when Campredon declares that one person is "*lié à la famille au moyen de sa sigisbée*," tied to the family through his cicisbea) that these recognizable extraconjugal ties served to create or reinforce social, even more than political, relations in the circle of the oligarchy. Within the cavalier servente's function of accompanying a lady in public, which we have already encountered many times, an element of "sociability" is by definition incorporated. This sociable aspect increased opportunities for social encounters; it acted to mediate and balance urban social life. That element, specifically as regarded pacification of factional conflict, had already been underlined for Genoa in 1718 in a private letter of the English noblewoman Mary Wortley Montagu.[44] Twenty years later the *Relation* offers the exceptional description of a holistic interweaving of similar relations for an entire city, and therefore a complete duplication of relations with respect to marriage alliances, despite the fact that Campredon demonstrates a very clear disinterest in matrimonial bonds, therefore underestimating their importance.

An image in some sense opposed to this "functionalist" approach, in which the cicisbeato created a kind of moral equilibrium, emerges—as one might expect—from legal sources. Until now the most fruitful of these sources for an investigation of cicisbei have been the papers of certain magistracies of the Republic of Venice which were responsible for the control of the private lives of the patricians; these materials form the basis of a noteworthy book by Luca De Biase.[45] The magistrates naturally intervened in family life when faced with the emergence of moral or patrimonial disorder. This led De Biase to point to the cicisbeato as a practice subversive of the traditional order of the ancien regime family, leaving aside the fact that the cicisbeato was, above all, a prop for that order because it acted as a controlled outlet for desires for certain kinds of encounters, providing social opportunities for women, and fulfilling erotic urges which were thus channeled—largely with success, though not without exceptions—in a manner compatible with the absence of freedom in the choice of spouses.

The most penetrating and concrete representations of the relationships tied to the custom of cicisbei are preserved for us by private and very intimate writings such as letters and diaries. Researching this kind of material in the eighteenth-century collections of Italian archives is an immense undertaking. For now I limit myself to two references.

The great Enlightenment figure of Milan, Pietro Verri, and his three brothers had—some more and some less—a very active erotic life. Their correspondence, which is partially published and partially in the process of publication, and of extraordinary interest also for private matters, contains references to more than one cicisbeale relationship captured in the quotidian affairs of daily life. The overall lesson one learns from this correspondence is the profound intermixing of the custom with the totality of life's experience, erotic but not only erotic, for the men and women they knew. Predictably, their letters confirm the privileged role of the aristocratic cavalier servente in the circulation of women in social life. They also amply attest to the fact that the custom, far from constructing artificial relations inhuman for their rigid vacuity or monstrous for their profound corruption, could naturally encompass—with greater richness than an arranged marriage—the entire range of the most diverse exchanges between a man and a woman. To point to at least one specific document, let me refer to a letter in which Pietro, on August 22, 1767, recounts to his brother Alessandro the first phases of his relationship—which would be long, tormented, and mercurial until its cooling and rupture—with Maddalena Isimbardi (sister of Cesare Beccaria).

He insists explicitly on the fact that his "service" to the lady was developing not as an adventure classifiable as libertine gallantry, but as a profound, amorous passion.[46]

The other reference appears in the diary of a noblewoman of Lucca between the late eighteenth and the early nineteenth centuries, which I have already had occasion to cite.[47] This diary finally presents us with a female voice on the question. The *Memoires ou Notices de Louise Palma Mansi*—written in French for practice and also because of her natural adoption of the principal language of eighteenth-century sociability—is a daily and detailed chronicle of her very intense social life. Palma Mansi conducted herself brilliantly, exhibiting a constitution which could not be tired by "conversations" in salons, parties, and balls, performances of music, opera, and theater, trips to country residences, and various holidays. In this life Luisa had the company of at least three cicisbei who partially overlapped with each other, as was absolutely expected and accepted in the practice of this social custom. Although her diary is somewhat more reticent than the letters of the Verri brothers about the degree and the type of intimacy in their relations, it nonetheless does not hide the different degrees of sentiment which she felt toward each one. Indeed, while Lorenzo Trenta and especially his younger brother Cesare seem to have been essentially Luisa's companions in society, there was clearly something more between her and Costantino de Nobili, so much so that their relationship ended brusquely and in the wake of an unmistakable fit of jealousy on her part. As for the husband Lelio Mansi, a man—by contrast to the cicisbei—twenty years older than Luisa, he appears to have accepted the situation graciously, and yet without fulfilling the caricature of the ridiculously submissive cuckold. Throughout the *Memoires*, he appears as a figure not at all absent from the life of his wife, sometimes as a participant in her social diversions, and always discreetly visible on the affective horizon of the woman. Upon his death in 1807, Luisa interrupted her diary for five years and took it up again in a noticeably different tone.

Stendhal and the Cicisbei

Just as the evidence presented in this chapter contradicts the stereotype of cicisbeismo as exclusively Italian and aristocratic, the materials brought to light by looking beyond literary sources also help to correct the stereotype of the cicisbeo which culminated in the work of Sismondi, who portrayed the custom as an abyss of tragicomic and almost mechanical corruption. In all its aspects, however, the elaboration of the stereotype as a stereotype is itself an interesting historical theme. Although it is not possible to treat this subject in depth here, it is enough to point to the fact that it is part of a long tradition which, from the epoch of the conflict between Reformation and Counter Reformation, painted the Italian character as cynical ("Machiavellian") and immoral. Catholicism and the overwhelming cultural and political influence of the papacy clearly had a decisive role in negatively conditioning many foreign (and also many Italian) judgments during the era of the Grand Tour. They were, for example, an integral part of Samuel Sharp's contemptuous opinion, cited above. And it must nonetheless necessarily be recognized that Catholic and papist Italy with its castrati presented at least one other usage—this almost entirely its own—which was morally indefensible and which perhaps overly influenced the general image of the country.[48]

Despite protestations to the contrary, it remains a fact that other peoples of Europe, including Protestant peoples, knew or had known a practice of married life which allowed the open existence of a third figure, the woman's male companion. The growing affirmation of the affectionate and domestic model of married and family life made that figure inopportune and unacceptable. The precocity of that affirmation in certain areas, especially in England, must have intensified the impatience of the British when they observed the survival of this practice in Italy. In reality, it was not an exception but a delayed ending to a custom that had been—and still was—prevalent in many parts of Western Europe.[49]

Between the end of the eighteenth century and the beginning of the nineteenth, the new family model also began to spread throughout Italy and the custom of the cicisbeo began to decline. The simultaneity of events has fed the fortune of an anecdote according to which it was the arrival of the French, and in particular the hostility of the wife of Viceroy Eugène de Beauharnais, which put an end to the custom. Put this way, the explanation is insufficient and ingenuous. But it is nonetheless true that the Napoleonic occupation of Italy brought with it a bourgeois conception of the family. While it suppressed certain privileges and injustices which lay at the foundation of the ancient regime marriage of interest, it also promoted suppression of any libertine light-heartedness and demanded a new level of seriousness about the nature of the conjugal bond and its related duties.[50] The reading of Luisa Palma Mansi's *Memoires* is revealing on the crisis, which she witnessed with acumen and irritation after the fall of the oligarchic republic of Lucca in 1799. Faced with the new style of sociability imposed by the French generals, in which gallantry no longer obeyed the exclusive caste rules and no longer maintained the delicate social balance of cicisbeale service, the old aristocratic sociability floundered.

For all these reasons, it seems appropriate to conclude by evoking, among those foreigners greatly interested in Italy, the name of Stendhal, who was a Napoleonic Frenchman worthy of being compared to Sismondi as a fabricator of stereotypes on the character of Italians. Stendhal paid his tribute to the mask of the cicisbeo in no less a place than the beginning of the *Charterhouse of Parma*, where he invoked the topos of the cicisbeo's identification in the marriage contract. Even so it was Stendhal who substantially and vividly fueled an exaltation of the Italian eros by offering a view which was diametrically opposed to its condemnation by Sismondi. Stendhal's image focused not on hypocrisy and effeminacy but on passion and burning truth. By frequently comparing the Italian approach to love with his unfavorable views on the social vanity of love in France, Stendhal created what we might describe as almost an extreme dramatization of the old theme of the petit-maître. Stendhal resolved any contradiction once and for all with a characteristic comment in *Promenades dans Rome*: "Love took immediate control of the custom of the *cicisbei* or *cavalieri serventi*."[51] We could well adopt this phrase as the most satisfactory definition of the phenomenon, and as a classic and famous confirmation of what I have written to this point.

It remains only to note that Stendhal in *Promenades* speaks quite deliberately of love and cicisbei in a section dedicated principally to brigandage. If Sismondi, gathering together an already lengthy if somewhat sympathetic and paternalistic tradition of deploring Italian decadence, constructed an idol opposed to liberal Protestant ideology, the idol of hypocrisy, Stendhal undertook a similar operation in relationship to the program of order and control that lay at the heart of the Napoleonic state, giving rise to the other illustrious story: the trope of the violent Italian outlaw.

In both stories—let it be clearly understood—what counted and what counts still is the common and precise identification of something unresolved in the morality of Italians, whether for the lack of the Reformation or the short duration of Napoleonic rule. Sismondi and Stendhal rightly agreed when they pointed to a specific difficulty in harmonizing the individual, society, and the state in the history of Italy. But as for the connection with private life, Sismondi erred in negatively emphasizing the theme of sexual corruption; trading stereotype for stereotype, Stendhal proposed one which was perhaps less implausible: passionate and uncontrolled individualism. It seems that normalcy for Italy is still destined to be out of reach. But the cicisbei are not to blame. The peculiarity of Italy is not hidden in the alcoves where eighteenth-century men and women conducted their erotic lives.

The Temple of Female Glory

*Female Self-Affirmation in the
Roman Salon of the Grand Tour*

M A R I A   P I A   D O N A T O

The eighteenth century was a period in which women played an extraordinary role as cultural protagonists throughout Europe, and one of the central expressions of this new level of activity was the salon.[1] The object of this chapter is to offer a panorama of this female practice in Rome through examination of case studies, in order to investigate the role of women in cultural change. In a city where the Counter Reformation had consolidated a certain hierarchy of knowledge, a certain method of recruiting elites, and a precise ideal of society, the salon, in the second half of the eighteenth century, became at once the symptom of and the vehicle for change.

In particular, during the age of the Grand Tour the Roman salon became a locus of self-affirmation through deployment of diverse female strategies. Various factors made this possible. In the first place, the secularization of European society profoundly changed the view that Europe had of Rome; the city became the capital of a neoclassical culture whose pervasive influence on Europe as a whole dramatically affected traditional cultural practices. The difficulties faced by the institutions of the universal church

---

Translated by Matthew Sneider.

were matched by the erosion, in Rome, of the reciprocity between cultural institutions and social structures. The reciprocal ties between nobility and *curia* were not as close as they formerly had been, new intellectual classes were in the process of emerging, and ecclesiastical control over social life had weakened. In a word, lay society had escaped from ecclesiastical hegemony and Rome became a different kind of city, open to new cultural influences.[2]

Women were an important part of this dynamic. They made their presence known in Roman society in several ways. Female self-affirmation could occur within the ideology of nobility, an ideology which was traditional but not unchangeable, or by means of politics. In both of these arenas, women used their social status and the power of their family connections to establish their position within the city's elite. Another, and not contradictory, path was to pursue the pleasures of the imagination.[3] By participating in intellectual debate, women became actors in the articulation of a new public sphere; by inserting themselves into the circuits of knowledge, women contributed to their modification. The salon was the meeting point of female aspirations and the aspirations of emerging intellectual classes; it imitated the Parisian model within the diverse social conditions and intellectual dynamics peculiar to Roman society.[4] More generally, the tensions which ran through Roman society were reflected in this emerging social and cultural institution. The salon became a central locus for the evolution of female intellectual figures in the Papal States.

Salons and the "Conversation of Ladies"

For the many travelers on the Grand Tour who arrived in Rome from all over Europe in the second half of the eighteenth century, the salons held by women of the aristocracy and the urban bourgeoisie were one of the attractions—"the principal resource of foreigners and the principal amusement in a city in which there is no spectacle except in a very small part of the year."[5] In the pope's city as in all great cities, as the English diplomat Louis Dutens affirmed, "there are societies suitable for all tastes and all states. . . . there are always many houses open in the evening, where one converses and where one games if one desires; here one finds people of spirit; the nobility is polite and obliging."[6] In Rome, international capital of neoclassicism, the salon was the place where "the first nobility of both sexes [meet together] and those foreigners who come to see Rome are presented," and where, as one foreigner who never left Rome, Johann Joachim Winckelmann, wrote, "life is spent between jocundity and sentiment."[7]

It was not always like this—indeed, quite the opposite. The Counter Reformation noticeably reduced the spaces for and the possible range of female culture by imposing an ideal of segregation, although women maintained a decisive role in the complex "games" of prelates' careers.[8] At the end of the seventeenth century, when Spain's hold on the peninsula weakened and the political and cultural hegemony of France caused its models and intellectual fashions to filter through (notwithstanding the tense relations between Paris and the Holy See), the first—episodic—female literary salons appeared.[9] But the *précieuse* tradition was channeled above all into the academy of Arcadia.[10] The "conversation of ladies" clashed with the competition posed by other forms of male and ecclesiastical sociability and with the neo-Tridentine project of moralizing the church and the court.[11]

Only in the mideighteenth century, with the beginning of the "crisis of trust" between the Roman Catholic Church and Europe, and with the weakening of the neo-Tridentine impetus, did the growing flux of travelers attenuate ecclesiastical control over social and cultural life. Quite different from the devout pilgrims of earlier centuries, these travelers cast a secular eye on Rome and imposed new habits.[12] Ambassadors began to hold evening parties on a regular basis in which guests conversed, theatrical productions were mounted, music and impromptu poetry was heard.[13] But noble Capitolines did not hesitate to make the salon their own, transforming it into a social practice which allowed them to be more visible both locally and, through the echo of their activities in various descriptions of the Grand Tour, abroad. The management of the evening parties, which took place in family residences, was delegated—even if not exclusively—to women who consequently adopted a freer and more light-hearted style of life, following a model of relations between the sexes which made women the civilizers of customs.

A sort of salon system was already codified in the papal city in the 1760s. Two Frenchmen, the erudite Jerôme Richard and the astronomer Jerôme de La Lande, gave a detailed description of it. There were the *conversazioni di prima sera* held right after sunset by cardinals, according to ancient custom,[14] or hosted by bourgeois ladies and by *mezze dame*—"ladies who are not of the first nobility . . . but to whose houses cardinals and persons of first rank nonetheless sometimes go"[15] together with cultured travelers, literati, antiquarians, and artists. Later in the night there followed the *conversazioni di seconda serata* of the principal noble families: "those which last a part of the night in winter and until dawn in summer . . . held by the princesses and ladies of Rome . . . where one can play card games, during which refreshments are served."[16] The most brilliant seem to have been those of the Barberini and Doria princesses and of the marquises Bolognetti and Patrizi. Among the greatest noble houses, however, some preferred *conversations particulières* which were composed exclusively of friends, intimate acquaintances, and famous foreigners—conversations like those of Vittoria Corsini Odescalchi, Livia Borghese Altieri, or Margherita Gentili Boccapaduli, "who knew the sciences and received lettered men."[17] All travelers noted this multipolar system, whether they praised its brilliance or lamented its formality and its slight intellectual interest.

On the one hand, this system reproduced the political and cultural polycentrism of the court of Rome surrounded by the courts of cardinals and secular princes; on the other hand, it mirrored the stratification of Roman society in which nobility was a complex of ancient feudality, urban patriciate, "papal" noble families, and foreign cadet branches rooted in the city,[18] and in which the civil class of officers and professionals often imitated the comportment of the nobility (both lay and ecclesiastical). The salon, however, was not an inert practice. In a city in which the nobility formed a relatively open system, characterized by numerous opportunities to ascend the social ladder into the ranks of the nobility, holding a salon made it possible to intervene in its internal hierarchy. It is, for example, unnecessary to emphasize how important it was, in the symbolic system of honors, to receive a person of royal blood. The Landgrave of Hesse Kassel in 1777 and the King of Sweden in 1784 were two truly important guests at the conversation held by Giuliana Falconieri Santacroce. In 1793 the presence of Sofia Albertina of Sweden in her salon sealed the role that, over many years of careful management of her social life, the beautiful princess had made for herself and for the Santacroce, a family of titled Roman nobility for three centuries which, however, was neither among the richest nor among those risen to the highest honor of the pontificate.[19] Through the success of her salon, they established a reputation that transcended the limits of their wealth.

It would also, perhaps, be useful to think of the salon as an important aspect of the search for visibility and a new cultural identity in the context of the slow but sure divestment of the Roman nobility from curial careers, which began in the second half of the eighteenth century—but I must leave this hypothesis for future investigations. There is no doubt, however, that the need for places in which to receive travelers—and above all female travelers—was acutely felt in an exclusively male court where the papal palaces were inaccessible to women. Hence the pope himself was forced to designate certain Roman ladies to court the most illustrious *touristes* and to organize suitable entertainments; he therefore reinvented a sort of symbolic "female nepotism." Already Ippolita Boncompagni Ludovisi, wife of Abbondio Rezzonico—nephew of Clement XIII and Senator of Rome— was always surrounded by "a very large company, a distinction attached to her quality as niece of the ruling pope,"[20] a fact all the more significant since the pope limited public entertainments even during Carnival. Pius VI (1775–1799) delegated this "diplomatic" activity to the young and gracious Costanza Falconieri, married in 1781 to his nephew Luigi Braschi Onesti. In the palace on Piazza Navona (a palace constructed by the papal uncle for his family of petty *marchigiana* nobility, reviving a little the splendors of seventeenth-century nepotism) she held a salon which was semiofficial in character. The salon, harshly criticized by ecclesiastics and conservatives who saw it as an execrable novelty and even the root of all evils,[21] ended up receiving official sanction and establishing itself in the social life of Rome, so much so that by the end of the eighteenth century the custom of holding *conversazione damasista* was truly universal.[22]

Observing Rome through Its Salons

For women who used the salon to give luster to their families, self-affirmation coincided with familial aspirations according to a noble ideology that was as traditional as it was flexible. In Rome, moreover, this ideology manifested itself in relation to the peculiar nature of the ecclesiastical monarchy; this is true even if the alliance between the nobility and the curia was beginning to erode. The Milanese Count Alessandro Verri, who arrived in Rome in 1767 after having played a central role in the Enlightenment journal *Il Caffè* and after having traveled in France and England, was introduced to its society and offered a valuable commentary on it in his letters of the time. He reported to his brother Pietro that the attitudes of Roman noblewomen imitated those of the ecclesiastical hierarchy.

> I begin to sample . . . the many princesses and the infinite red successors of the apostles. This is true for the Duchess of Bracciano, who strives more to have a caustic and piquant spirit than to win over foreigners with the only attraction—cordial politeness—which she does not know. She has paid me

certain attentions, perhaps because she believes that I count for something in my country or at the court, and the mere suspicion counts a great deal in this empire of opinion. And yet she is not frequented by foreigners, because she is a woman occupied with aims and second aims, eternal aims; she is a slanderer, a politician, and a sphinx; everything in her sphere has that feminine ecclesiastical character which is so in fashion here. This curia abounds with these duchesses and princesses who lack only red berettas or *tané* hose—they truly seem monsters. What is the use of being a woman if you are not tender and cordial? They seem so many female popes (*papesse*). The same is true for the Princess Altieri who receives cardinals in her house at all hours, whence it sometimes appears that she is holding a synod. Thus does she sacrifice herself to count for something.[23]

In this description, Verri perceptively noted how Capitoline noblewomen used their salons, above all, to stay in contact with the highest church officials and to influence court business. From his male and intellectual point of view, he saw this choice as a sacrifice, or rather an affirmation of power which ran contrary to the proper role of women in society. Women, long secluded, placed themselves overbearingly at the center of the new practice of sociability. Verri felt that this prevented intellectual discussion: "I find a great difference between the women of Italy and France," he told his brother. "The Frenchwoman is a tranquil and tender being, who stays in one corner of the room and exercises the most urbane hospitality: she only rarely leads the conversation but is for the most part the fulcrum and the preserver of decent sociability. In Italy she is the venerated idol, she is the center of all thoughts, she wants to be preeminent and is the tyrant of, rather than a partner in, the conversation. Here Roman ladies have . . . a masculine and sometimes even impertinent tone. . . . their involvement in politics ruins all society."[24]

The interference of Roman ladies in the affairs of the Holy See and the cumbersome presence of the ecclesiastical hierarchy in their salons was a characteristic noted by all foreigners. They also observed the role of salonnières in diplomacy. Wrote Giuseppe Gorani, an impoverished Milanese nobleman and a future *girondin*:

If the mistress of the house does not game, she takes possession of some eminence or of some minister and converses with him for as long as the circle lasts. Personages covered with dignities do likewise and these conversations are so serious and so silent that one might hear the buzzing of a fly.[25]

Others noted that the interference of women in politics translated, above all, into partisanship for one or another of the European powers. According to de La Lande:

> There is much freedom [in the conversations] when speaking of the affairs of Rome and even more when speaking of those of foreign countries; everyone there is occupied with politics and takes the part of France or England, of Austria or Prussia, of the Molinists or the Jansenists.[26]

Already in 1757 the French ambassador, the Duc de Choiseul, described the conversations as places in which the system of "national" factions ingrained in the supranational dimension of the Roman court exercised a strong influence. In the dispatch of diplomatic affairs, the salons of this or that princess were often annexes of antechambers of members of the College of Cardinals. Agnese Colonna Borghese, for example, was said to be "an excessively intriguing woman, dangerous and false," who used "all her artifices for . . . intrigues of interest" and exercised a strong influence on her cardinal relatives.[27] She

> is to be found in conversation at her own house every evening; here she games and here are always present her uncle the cardinal, her relative *monsignor* Colonna di Sonnino, other cardinals, diverse ladies and gentlemen; and when her mother, the widow of the *connétable*, is at her house, the Cardinal Alessandro Albani, her close friend and confidant, is also often present.[28]

Choiseul considered the house of Giulia Albani Chigi, a woman famous for her social and political aspirations, to be a "school of intrigues and cruelty" essentially in support of the house of Austria to which both families were tied and of which Cardinal Alessandro Albani was the Protector. He also noted that Vittoria Corsini Odescalchi, princess of Bracciano, harbored "a ridiculous aversion for the French" despite her "spirit and *savoir vivre.*"[29] Numerous salons were regarded as the branch offices of the ambassadors of foreign powers, and travelers tended to frequent them in hope of meeting certain figures in each setting. Giuliana Falconieri Santacroce, for example, was never absent from the evening parties of the Cardinal de Bernis, nor from those of the Spanish ambassador Nicolas de Azara, and these two always returned the favor. Hence Santacroce became, so to speak, a fashionable point of reference for the Bourbon party in Rome, at a moment when this faction identified itself with opposition to the Jesuits and, later, with the French Revolution.[30] In a certain sense, the presence of so many travelers offered women of the most important aristocratic families the opportunity to win back, by means of the salon, a role in the court of Rome. They did not directly interfere in the careers of prelates of the higher rank (as was the case before the antinepotism moralization of the *zelanti* at the end of the seventeenth century, beginning most clearly under Innocent XI but having its symbolic beginning in Alexander VII's decision not to receive Donna Olimpia at the Vatican). In the multipolar system of the eighteenth century, in which the equilibrium between the European powers was constantly shifting, women and their salons offered a space for representation, information, and mediation which their relatives the cardinals—but not only them, as we have seen—might use.

Leisure and Culture in the Salon

The salon was a social game whose stakes were achievement of some measure of success in the city's symbolic hierarchy and participation in its power structure. At the same time, we must not forget that the salon was also a center of amusement and pleasure. As sexual segregation weakened and social habits became secularized in the Rome of the Grand Tour, the salon could be a space of freedom, the antidote to "the poison of boredom" and to the constrictions of life as a wife and a mother.[31] Friendship, courting, and love took place there—more or less codified in cicisbeismo[32]—as did dancing, card playing, and chess. The salon, moreover, was the place where a woman could pursue the pleasures of the imagination. It was an important cultural institution in the Eternal City. From this vantage point, the fact that Rome was ever more the center of an international movement in artistic and literary endeavors made it a natural locus for the growth of a lively salon society. Imitating the Parisian model, women who had long been denied access to such cultural activities received foreign savants, travelers, and artists—not to mention more cultured and literate Roman nobles in search of fame—and participated in the circuits of intellectual exchange.

The most successful Roman salonnières were accorded enormous respect among their male counterparts. "After three, she receives friends and foreigners who frequent her as the only European in Rome," wrote Alessandro Verri in 1767, describing the cosmopolitanism of Margherita Sparapani Gentili Boccapaduli,[33] who was for forty years the leading spirit of one of the most vivacious salons in the capital. The marquise's story is, in many respects, singular. Born in 1735, the sole family heir after her father died without producing any male offspring, she enjoyed the lavish attentions of two generations of relatives and received a liberal education. "I was educated with the greatest caresses and indulgence," she later recalled.

> This was contrary to the opinion of my mother, a rather severe woman of character. Nonetheless, I received from my great-uncles everything that the caprice of my age desired. . . . I rode with my uncle the colonel, who took me with him dressed like a little officer. . . . my mother wanted me to learn Latin but I, little given to study in general, appealed to my uncles that the language might be changed from Latin to French, and this was done.

Margherita's loving great-uncles, one a cardinal and the other an officer in the army, named her universal heir of the Gentili house.[34] In 1754 she married a young man from the best Capitoline nobility, Giuseppe Boccapaduli. In 1760, however, he was placed under legal interdict because of the sorry state of his finances and forced to return to his parents, whereupon Margherita enjoyed the freedom of the married state without its inconveniences since the couple formally separated and would never again live together. Above all, she could dispose of her own time and money (upon the death of her mother in 1779, she also inherited the entire patrimony of the Sparapani) to cultivate her interests and pleasures. Among these were frequenting fashionable evening parties and hosting, in her turn, a cultured conversation. It was in this way that Verri met the marquise and was struck by the qualities which she expressed in her salon: "an ingenuous character, but nonetheless with great experience of the world, a great facility of customs, a background of very bizarre good humor, an exquisite taste in all things."[35] From this was born an amorous association which would last all their lives.

Verri's description of Gentili Boccapaduli's salon gives us a detailed understanding of its activities and *habitués*.

> Most times we are: I myself, the prince (Lante), and a common friend, a French painter and great gentleman. We sing, we play music, we dance, we read, and we work. She sings. . . . the painter plays the flute well, the marquise plays the *tiorba savojarda*; when I add my violin we make a rural and clamorous orchestra. She is presently reading *Miss Clarissa Harlow*.[36]

This intimate circle of friends alternated with a larger literary conversation in Gentili Boccapaduli's salon to which nobles, travelers, intellectuals, and naturally Alessandro (who, moreover, came to live in an apartment in his beloved's palace) were invited. The relationship between Margherita and Alessandro went beyond the limits of social convention and was decisive for the noblewoman's intellectual evolution. But their amorous friendship did not shirk the rites of the salon; indeed it contributed directly to its structure and content. One of the other protagonists of late-eighteenth-century Roman culture, the abbot Giovanni Cristofano Amaduzzi—Arcadian and editor of the Roman journal *Efemeridi letterarie*—summed up in a few lines the merits and the circumstances which made the marquise's salon so pleasurable:

> The marquise is courted assiduously by *cavaliere* Alessandro Verri, hence he is the attraction for the other Milanese who now frequent her. Fortunately, despite the five decades of her age which are attributed to her, she has kept some vestiges of beauty; these she reinforces with brio and with grace, and adds moreover the merits of an ingenious culture, the attraction of a museum of natural history and the even more potent attraction of offering dinner; she is at the same time an heiress and very rich: hence what marvel is it that she still has admirers? . . . Father Jacquier is also of her group and he himself is an object of attraction.[37]

The habitual presence of famous savants such as the physicist and mathematician François Jacquier—member of the order of the Minims and commentator on Newton—was one reason for interest in the salon in Via Arcione. No traveler failed to emphasize the intellectual significance of her guests in praising the merits of the marquise; was it not through the wise choice of participants in a conversation that a lady might affirm her role as the arbiter of taste and the judge of merit? The guides to late-eighteenth-century Rome frequently recalled the virtues of Margherita and her "French" conversation[38] and legitimated her path to self-affirmation in the eyes of Roman society.[39]

Disposing freely of her goods, the marquise Gentili Boccapaduli also used her salon to pursue her own interests. Her guests were often involved in private theatrical representations, some of which were composed by her friends, whose merits and defects were then discussed.[40] She cultivated the natural sciences (she possessed, moreover, a good collection of *naturalia*); astronomical observations and experiments "on light, with the solar microscope, with the pneumatic machine, etc.,"[41] were made at her house. Noted for her culture and her generosity, the marquise became the dedicatory of all kinds of works, from the antiquarian to the poetic.[42] The salon was fundamental to her intellectual and emotional development, a fact which she herself evoked in describing the evolution of her interests:

> The readings of my youth were frivolous. I read all of the most celebrated French novels, the comedies and tragedies of *Volter* [sic], Racine, *Cornelio*

[Corneille] and others, various histories, travels. At a more mature age I undertook other readings, but all for entertainment and not—as I should have—for instruction. Hence I always remained ignorant and if some little dusting of knowledge adhered to me, it was the effect of having had the pleasure of frequenting educated and learned persons from whom I was able to take an idea or two—by listening to their conversation and especially by questioning the learned Father Jacquier, Monsignor Stoi [Stay, a famous Latinist], the Abbot Serassi, the Abbot Taruffi, and the very learned Alessandro Verri. To these friends alone I owe those few ideas I have, in addition to having frequented many foreign travelers. I must confess that I have always been full of curiosity but equally averse to applying myself with constancy. . . . I have a curious head: I love literature and I respect the sciences and the arts, but I have not applied myself to anything. Natural history . . . has always interested and amused me without serious application.[43]

In these few lines, Gentili Boccapaduli summed up her image as a salonnière. Rejecting the model of the *femme savante*, she affirmed a freer and more casual approach to the pleasures of the mind and the senses that relied upon interpersonal exchange in places where fashion and culture were mixed together. She alluded to the various intellectuals who constantly frequented her salon; each represented an interest, from the sciences to ancient and modern letters—a body of knowledge to which women could have access in the protected space of the salon. But none of them inspired her to cultivate expertise. Rather it was the entirety of knowledge, and conversations about it, that she pursued with great pleasure.

Women and the Emergence of a New Roman Sociability

Margherita Gentili Boccapaduli undoubtedly profited from favorable and fortuitous circumstances; nonetheless we can consider her at least in part representative of new possibilities to which elite Roman women in the age of the Grand Tour had access. To gauge the evolution in the ideal of female education and in cultural habits that occurred over the course of a few decades, one may compare, in Alessandro Verri's letters to his brother Pietro, Margherita with her mother, Constanza Giorio Sparapani, or with her mother-in-law, Maria Laura dal Pozzo Boccapaduli. Verri's portrait of Costanza is positive, but he did not hesitate to report her limits: "She has a very good head; she has a natural and indescribable talent. Having read little, having seen nothing other than Rome, she sometimes says and thinks things which are great and true. . . . Add to this poor woman seventy-two years and scruples; and yet the foundation of her soul is ancient Quirino, true and real."[44] More critically, he found her mother-in-law Laura (who disapproved of Verri because "he believes in nothing; has English beliefs") "old and unenlightened," "a Spanish thinker."[45] Neither of them had the curiosity or education of the younger generation of salonnières.

Further research needs to be done to paint a more comprehensive portrait of Roman salonnières. But the circumstances observed in Gentili Boccapaduli's salon find confirmation in the stories of two other women: a Roman of bourgeois origin (a *mezza dama*) and a Swiss painter resident in Rome. These two examples shed light on diverse aspects of salon life and illuminate the manner in which the convergence between female aspirations and cultural dynamics was brought about in late-eighteenth-century Rome.

The path taken by Maria Cuccovilla Pizzelli had many points in common with that of the Marquise Boccapaduli, beginning with the habitués of her salon. She was also born in 1735, the daughter and the wife of lawyers. She first studied music (which in addition to being a traditional element of female instruction was often, in Rome, a sign of distinction and a means of cultivating the company of persons of rank[46]) and then, thanks to her intellectual vivacity, was able to study modern and ancient languages, the sciences, and ancient history. Pizzelli studied Greek with the poet and Jesuit scholar Raimondo Cunich, who celebrated their friendship and the merits of his pupil in epigrams which animated her conversazione and which made the round of other Roman salons.[47] The dissolution of the Society of Jesus in 1773 turned out to be an advantage for the rise of Pizzelli's salon; in the difficult situation in which they found themselves afterwards, many former Jesuits, in search of appropriate sociability and affective ties, exercised their skills for a female public. "Upon the suppression of the Society of Jesus many stars began to shine in society which had until that moment shone only in the cloister," noted Giovanni Gherardo De Rossi, banker, playwright, art critic, and later director of the academy of the arts in Portugal.[48]

Learned former Jesuits and other ecclesiastics remained such a constant presence in Pizzelli's life that they made their pupil a model of the enlightened Catholic concord between "philosophical culture and Christian modesty." Pizzelli, contemporaries noted, "formed in this manner a splendid *apologia* of her sex."[49] However, Maria's desire to cultivate her own cultural identity led her to make her house into a meeting place for intellectuals of all sorts. Visitors observed the intellectual heterogeneity of her salon. "I spoke

a great deal with Cunich, the poet, about Villoisons's Homer, with Gara-
toni, the Barberini librarian, and with Monsignor Stay," noted in his diary
Friedrich Münter, antiquarian and philologist but also emissary to Rome
of the radical Masonic sect of the Illuminati.[50] In the evening parties on
the Via dei Fornari, for example, the Dane heard the future cardinal Giulio
della Somaglia make his comparisons between ancient and modern Rome.
Not insignificant at this level of society, Pizzelli's house was frequented by
cultured aristocrats, both Roman and foreign, and its fame passed beyond
the confines of Rome.[51]

Pizzelli exercised the central role in her salon, playing a variety of different
roles: according to De Rossi, she adapted herself "in company to the taste of
each person, always showing satisfaction and pleasure."[52] Gorani, with his
caustic irony, described Pizzelli as a pedant "surrounded by her wise court"[53]
and furnished a useful clue regarding what this meant when he compared
her to Madame de Tencin, making the French model the clear source of her
inspiration. A more poetic portrait of this Roman lady compared her with
Madame Lambert as well as Madame de Tencin, rhapsodizing that she was
"erudite without arrogance, humble without smallness, her spirit distinguished for its solidity, for its exquisite fineness and its aptitude, she united
grace with naiveté, spirit with naturalness, ease with justice, a noble decorum with lovability."[54] Pizzelli strove to cultivate the virtues of the perfect
guide in sociability; one French visitor described her as a "cultivated spirit,
[with] good sense, sweet taste, modesty, goodness in her heart." Her house
was known as "the rendezvous of the most beautiful spirits in Rome. One
discusses everything there without affectation and with a tolerance worthy
of she who is the host."[55] Identifying the "lively desire to cultivate her spirit"
with her salon, Maria carved out a role for herself in literary life:

> The profound reflections with which she sprinkled her conversation with
> learned men; the penetration with which she revealed the most delicate char-
> acteristics of works of intellect and the just criticism with which, in seeking
> elucidation for her doubts, she revealed their most hidden defects, made her
> the oracle of those who aspired to the rank of author.[56]

A number of the most noteworthy writers of the end of the century con-
gregated in Pizzelli's home, knowing it to be fertile ground in which to cultivate an audience for their work. The great tragedian Vittorio Alfieri, after
having left his native Piedmont to dedicate himself independently to letters,
followed his beloved Luisa Stolberg d'Albany to Rome and took advantage

of Maria's salon to read his unedited tragedy *Virginia* in 1782. Electrified by having heard the work of Alfieri in Via dei Fornari, Vincenzo Monti (at the time secretary of Luigi Braschi Onesti and already known in Arcadia for his talent) declaimed his *Aristodemo* in various conversazioni before putting it on stage at the Teatro della Valle.[57] De Rossi also debuted as a comedy writer in his friend's house. In this fashion, Pizzelli's salon became the private testing ground for a variety of public performances.

Indeed, Pizzelli's salon helped to shape a Roman audience that was rather receptive to literary works, which circulated freely there without the hindrance of censorship and the difficulties of the theater business. Recalling his evenings in the salons of Rome, Alfieri reflected in these terms in his *Vita*:

> On many occasions I read all these tragedies a little at a time to various companies, always mixed of men and women, of literates and idiots, of people who were sensible to diverse feelings and of louts. In reading my productions I sought (in truth) advantage no less than praise. . . . every time 12 or 15 individuals, mixed as I mentioned, gather together, the collective spirit which is formed in this varied company will be rather near and similar to a public audience at the theater.

The tragedian admitted that he benefited from his contact with the salons and the heterogeneous audience they created for his work, recalling with pleasure the response of both his male and female listeners: "nor will I deny that no few excellent suggestions were given me after those various readings, by literate men, by men of the world, and, especially as regards feelings, by various women."[58]

By means of the salon, women became the embodiment of a *general* public, very different from the old republic of letters, gifted with judgment without having any specialized competences. These mechanisms of articulation of the bourgeois public sphere were common in many locations in eighteenth-century Europe; nonetheless I would argue that the Roman salons, despite their lack of the kind of philosophical brilliance found in other capital cities, had a truly important role in the papal city, where, as one participant put it, "a friar from the choir-stalls presides over the kingdom of poetic imagination,"[59] that is, where the control over publishing was in the hands of the ecclesiastical authorities and the public commercial arenas were limited. In a city in which the scholarly community for centuries was identified with ecclesiastics, the public of the salons was a lay public precisely because it was characterized by the presence of women. Hence, those who aspired to affirm themselves as authors outside of the traditional career patterns (that is, in substance, the ecclesiastical career) frequented them assiduously. "In Rome a person who did not wear the habit of an abbot and who wished to become involved in literature, was at that time a strange thing . . . I endeavored to study to overcome the prejudice that existed against my dress"; in this way did the comedian De Rossi recall the time of his literary debut in the salons after having become one of the principal authors of comedies in Rome and the master of a genre, like the *favola*, made for the cultured worldliness of the conversation.[60]

Salonnières and Women Artists: Reciprocal Benefits

Like Margherita Boccapaduli, Maria Pizzelli identified herself in the dialogic dimension of the conversazione, keeping the "modest" role of listener and placing herself at the service of the authors who frequented her salon. At the same time, her salon was frequented by other women, younger than she, who chose another way. On the occasion of the *Accademia poetica* organized by Maria's friends after her death in 1808, Enrica Dionigi, Adelaide Lucangeli, and Maria Fulvia Bertocchi proclaimed themselves her pupils and emulators. The first two were poetesses, according to a rather traditional Arcadian model, and the third, while she earned her living as an instructor of noble girls, sought to craft an identity as the author of popularizing texts of sacred and profane history and as a theatrical playwright.[61] Unlike Boccapaduli and Pizzelli, they presented their own writings to society rather than simply facilitating the talents of others.

Even prior to the appearance of this younger generation of salonnières, forms of female sociability like the salon were very important for women who made a profession of their talents, whether they frequented salons of other women (perhaps higher in class and in wealth) or promoted salons of their own. The role of foreigners in Roman salon life was decisive in these other developments. Indeed, the colony of foreign artists had always been large in Rome, but in the second half of the eighteenth century the neoclassical ideology of the arts expanded its significance for society in general. The attenuated distinctions of class and nationality increasingly privileged the status of artists as creators of culture: in the *communis patria* artists were highly important protagonists in intellectual sociability and contributed to creation of a new—also female—image of talent.[62]

The leading spirit of one of the most important salons in Rome at the end of the eighteenth century was a foreigner, an artist, and a woman. Angelica Kauffman, born in 1741, was a contemporary of Boccapaduli and Pizzelli. The Swiss-Austrian painter (who received the education necessary to develop her precocious talent) first stayed in Rome for several months in 1763 and again from April 1764 to July 1765 after a visit to Naples. She came under the influence of Winckelmann, who was already famous as a connoisseur of antiquities, and in May 1765 Angelica was accepted into the Accademia di San Luca. A very famous artist, she established herself definitively in Rome in 1782 after having lived in London (where she opened her apartment-atelier to admirers, clients, and colleagues) and after having contracted a marriage of convenience with the Venetian Antonio Zucchi. Their Roman house—in which Angelica enjoyed the freedom which her status as a foreigner, but not a stranger to the artistic and intellectual environment of Rome, guaranteed her—became the preferred meeting place for antiquarians and theorists of the arts, artists, and amateurs.[63]

Kauffman's friend, admirer, and habitué, Giovanni Gherardo De Rossi, described her salon as the meeting place of some of the most influential personages in the cosmopolitan environment of neoclassical Rome:

> In the morning she sat down either to draw or to paint . . . and then passed the evening in the company of the most cultured men, and particularly those most knowledgeable in the arts: the *consiglier* Reiffestein, the famous landscape artist Hackert, the celebrated engraver Volpato, the then abbot and now Cardinal Spina, and other men of merit, who over the course of her life were replaced by other no less respectable subjects, formed at that time the foundation of her society, to which was added every man of letters and every cultured traveler who might be found in Rome.[64]

The salon of Via Sistina was not only frequented by her fellow painters but was opened to participants in all of the arts, according to a neoclassical canon of intellectual refinement which this type of sociability helped to define. "Persons of letters, or persons distinguished for some talent, received from her the most affectionate reception and, since the passion for music was not extinguished in her heart, she delighted in listening to those who professed it with excellence," observed De Rossi.[65] Goethe found in her salon a well-mannered society and an attentive audience for his Roman works.[66]

A woman celebrated throughout Europe, and an arbiter of female taste in painting sought after by queens and princesses, Angelica gladly received other women who made a profession of their talents and who came to

Rome for the rich and noble international public gathered together there.[67] Such women explicitly sought Kauffman's protection and friendship, and she responded by painting a number of the leading female authors of late eighteenth-century Italy (see Figure 6.3). According to De Rossi:

> when at different times the two renowned extemporaneous poetesses—Fortunata Fantastici and Teresa Bandettini—came to Rome, they desired to know Angelica, and were very dear to her; hence she wished to paint the portraits of each and to each made a gift of her work. I recall having heard both the one and the other of these able women improvise in Kauffman's house, and neither sang better than in those moments: and indeed their inspiration had to heat up and catch fire in a place which might almost be called a temple of female glory.[68]

For these literary women, the salon held by another woman offered social and cultural legitimization of their activities and a guarantee of their honor since the salon was, by its nature, sexually mixed and therefore (despite the ferocious criticisms of the conservatives) morally protected.

Kauffman was the most well-known foreign woman in Rome between the eighteenth and nineteenth centuries to create a salon that acted as a bridge between different worlds—linked by neoclassical culture, even if divided by gender, by class, by wealth, by nationality.[69] Other foreign women enriched Roman salon life with their presence. As we have seen, the way was also open for Roman patrician women by this time, and a number of them moved easily between the salons created by educated Roman women and those inspired by cultured foreigners. To recall another example which connects two generations of women, let us cite an habituée of the Pizzelli and Kauffman houses, Marianna Candidi Dionigi. She was born in 1753 and, after having studied music with Neapolitan masters Giovanni Paisiello and Domenico Cimarosa, she learned Latin and Greek from Raimondo Cunich, as did her older friend Maria Pizzelli; she was then introduced to the figurative arts and affirmed herself as a painter. Candidi Dionigi became a member of the Accademia di San Luca and maintained, in her turn, until her death in 1826 a salon in her house on the Via del Corso which became the meeting place of many literati and artists.[70] Other women would sponsor salons with analogous features throughout the nineteenth century.

·   ·   ·

The salon in eighteenth-century Rome, therefore, was sometimes a point of convergence between diverse female strategies of self-affirmation, whether the search for greater freedom, social distinction, and education or the affirmation of status as intellectuals and artists. Within the salon, mechanisms of gender reciprocity worked across generations and also across classes. The guarantee that the noble habituées of salons offered to artists of humble origins was repaid by what we might call the "intellectual guarantee" of female freedom.

As the examples discussed above illustrate, the arts and literature, music, and the theater were the dominant occupations of the Roman salons, according to a canon of female education which privileged refinement of taste, tempering of morality, and simple amusement. The salon differed from other customary forms of sociability in the Rome of the popes, such as the conversations of the cardinals, learned academies, or circles linked to the professions because it did not focus on the sacred sciences and, more generally, the kind of erudition which helped aspiring clerics and scholars promote their careers and increase their prestige within the curia. Insertion of women into the Roman cultural circuit helped modify its content and its internal hierarchy. By the end of the eighteenth century, women played a fundamental role in Roman public life in ways that they had not done at the century's beginning; they created a greater space in which secular conversations about culture could occur and, in turn, created opportunities for themselves to become active participants in this new definition of culture. The salon was the primary venue for this transformation.

It is clear that women were not the only public interested in these pleasures of the imagination. They were only a part of an expanding lay audience, eager for sensations and ideas although ideologically cautious. But they were not only passive recipients of the secularization which was overtaking culture in Rome. By shaping specific forms of sociability, women promoted this process. The salon was a very important space of circulation for specific intellectual products and for diverse literary and musical genres. As the former Jesuit scholar Juan Andrés noted in his discussion of Maria Pizzelli's gatherings, the salons constituted an important point of reference in unification of taste and in propagation of a neoclassical culture which was no longer identified with ecclesiastical culture.[71] The salon, moreover, was frequented by intellectuals who were seeking to define their own social profile outside of ecclesiastical institutions (or by those who were expelled from those institutions, like the former Jesuits[72]). It is not possible to discuss in greater detail here the sociology of the Roman intellectual classes[73]; one can only note how men of nonnoble birth, animated by a strong sense of their own identities (like the extemporaneous poet Francesco Gianni "of plebian lineage, noble in heart / contemptuous of chance, eager for glory"[74]), found in the salon a precious resource, in terms both concrete and symbolic, and found new forms of patronage through the offices of the Roman salonnières. The salon was not the only space of legitimization, however. Quite the contrary—in a social and cultural dynamic of which the salon was the first manifestation, between the eighteenth and nineteenth centuries opportunities for diversion and intellectual refinement accessible to women multiplied. These were the literary academies, the theater, and the balls, the art expositions and the visits to the ateliers of artists, musical concerts and trips to archeological sites, natural curiosities, and the spectacles of science, not to mention the emergence of the Masonic lodges.[75] It was also possible in the academies, and in particular in the literary world of Arcadia, to display talent and receive applause. Is it a matter of chance that the salon and the academy became the two environments characterized by the presence of women?

If women, by means of the salon, gave legitimacy to a type of (male) intellectual who had difficulty conforming to the rules governing ecclesiastical cultural institutions, then these intellectuals returned the favor by redefining pedagogical and moral ideals *for women*. The ideal became that of a gentlewoman who increasingly knew how to "divide her time well among the noble task of educating her children, the cultivation of her spirit, the pleasant exercise of music, and the pleasures of gentle society"[76]; that of a woman who was "loveable, without the first flower of youth, witty without the ordinary folly which generally accompanies vivacity in the fair sex, as capricious as necessary to preserve delightful pleasure"[77]; a woman to whom it is possible to dedicate poems, sentimental romances, tragedies and comedies, journals of fashion—indeed a metonymic figure of the public and the market. In this redefinition salon sociability was no longer considered a "necessary evil" as it was for the précieuses at the end of the seventeenth century,[78] but rather the means and the end of a female education which permitted and even reinforced associations between women and the male intellectuals whom they patronized, to the benefit of all society.[79] In the eyes of certain advocates of this new form of sociability, the frequenting of the two sexes in the salon, the "reciprocal scientific and literary communication between the two sexes," accelerated the progress of society and stripped the man of his "natural fierceness and coarseness."[80] Such an ideal was quite far from the traditional argument for segregation of the sexes, although it emerged from the kind of enlightened Catholicism then popular in the Italian peninsula that compared Roman cultural life favorably in relationship to the excesses of the French salons philosophiques from which "the knowledge of the excellent Roman ladies not only is distinguished, because it lacks pomp and disgusting pedantry, but still more because it is not fed on the pernicious reading of those infected books, which contain maxims directly opposed to the true Catholic religion and to the probity of customs."[81] In this respect, Roman salons were quite different from their Parisian counterparts since their secularism emerged as a complement to, rather than an adversary of, ongoing traditions of clerical intellectual life in the Eternal City.

In the midst of the French Revolution, the voices in Rome which revisited the polemic over study for women also tuned themselves to this note, recalling the unique legacy of women in the second half of the eighteenth century. I am not certain if a woman is concealed beneath the pseudonym Rosa Califronia, but in the *Breve difesa dei diritti delle donne* (1794) she defends the superiority of women in their aptitude for study and, to defend her thesis, furnishes a catalogue of "illustrious women" currently living in Rome: musicians, artists of every branch, scholars, teachers, and also noble and patrician women celebrated for their salons.[82] Ultimately there was no great difference between them; they all sought self-affirmation and defined a new position for women's access to culture. By the end of the eighteenth century, Rome was a city filled with talented women whose contributions were widely recognized beyond the papal city. The emergence of the Roman salons played a crucial role in effecting this transformation.

THREE

Giustina Renier Michiel and Conflicting Ideas of Gender in Late Eighteenth-Century Venice

SUSAN DALTON

"Giustina Renier Michiel experienced the immense pain of witnessing the fall of the Republic of San Marco. Fall? Let us say this no more. The overly aged Republic died because it had to die."[1] Such were the words of Mario Vianello-Chiodo writing more than sixty years ago about Renier Michiel and her experience with the end of the Venetian Republic in 1797. Renier Michiel was both a participant in the final century of this republic and a witness to its demise. Despite its reduced state after the loss of Crete and many other parts of its empire to the Ottomans in the seventeenth century, and notwithstanding its internal divisions, the Venice that she knew was nonetheless still a vibrant cultural center, known for its theater and journalism. It was also an integral stop on the Grand Tour, famous not only for its theaters and gambling halls but also for its unique character, built as it was on the lagoon.[2]

Women were active participants in this community, as authors, painters, and salon hosts. Rosalba Carriera, Luisa Bergalli Gozzi, Giustiniana Wynne di Rosenberg, and Isabella Teotochi Albrizzi were all renowned women of the eighteenth-century *Serenissima*, and yet we still do not know very much about them. In most cases, we are familiar with the basic biographical details, thanks in large part to literary scholars and the biographers of famous women who have kept their stories alive. During the nineteenth century, Oscar Greco, Agostino Verona, and Luigi Carrer, for example, wrote about Italian women, including Giustina Renier Michiel, as did writers at the beginning of the twentieth century such as Ginevra Canonici Fachini, Carlo Villani, Vittorio Turri, and Giulio Natali.[3] Recently scholars have shown renewed interest in the women of eighteenth-century Venice; thanks to their efforts, we are now beginning to understand enough about their lives and activities to say something more general about gender and culture in the Venetian Republic.[4]

Giustina Renier Michiel's story was both unique and typical of women of her social standing. Renier Michiel was a member of a prestigious patrician family linked to the world of letters through her position as salon hostess and author. Like her, other women who hosted literary salons in Venice also socialized and collaborated with the century's best-known men of letters. To cite two examples, Caterina Dolfin Tron (1736–1793) was a close friend of Carlo and Gasparo Gozzi, as was Isabella Teotochi Albrizzi (1760–1836) of Ugo Foscolo, Ippolito Pindemonte, and Antonio Canova. Also like Renier Michiel, both of these women ended their first marriages and had ties to the world of politics. Albrizzi's second husband, Giuseppe Albrizzi, was a Venetian state inquisitor, while Dolfin Tron, in a notable misalliance—the pairing of individuals of different social status—married one of the most powerful men of the latter half of the century, future procurator Andrea Tron.[5] Of course, Renier Michiel's experience was also distinctive: she was more actively and openly involved in politics than any of her contemporaries, both through her role as *dogaressa*, the *doge's* official companion (a role usually filled by the doge's wife) from 1779 to 1789, and through publication of her six-volume *Origine delle feste veneziane* (1817–1827). She was also interested in a wide range of intellectual domains, studying chemistry, astronomy, optics, and physics, writing on botany, and translating Shakespeare in addition to her other literary and political activities.

Giustina Renier Michiel's correspondence and published works show how all of these elements are woven together, but they also do more, by demonstrating how these intellectual and political pursuits came into conflict with her role as wife and mother. Through her letters, we learn that while her husband expected her to be dependent, obedient, and reserved, her family integrated her into a world of elite sociability where she was expected to shine, offering herself, even in her husband's absence, as an example of republican gentility in both literary circles and political ones. In this chapter, I will study the conflicting pressures exerted on Renier Michiel by her husband, her family, and the more "worldly" sectors of Venetian society. The first section explores her experience as a young wife and mother, in which she was defined by obligations to her husband and her family. The second section explores her experience in a literary and political society that defined the norms of female behavior with reference to principles of civility and aesthetic theory. The nature of these diverse expectations and pressures helps us to understand how the continuing debate on gender norms in the Venetian Republic translated into real-life social tensions for patrician women intellectuals.

An Exemplary Wife and Daughter

From birth, Giustina Renier Michiel was well placed to succeed in Venetian society. Born to Andrea Renier and Cecilia Manin on October 14, 1755, she was a member of a leading family. Her paternal grandfather, Paolo Renier, was the penultimate doge of Venice, while her maternal uncle, Ludovico Manin, was the last to hold this post before the fall of the Republic. Even her godfather was an important political and literary figure: Marco Foscarini was the author of the much-admired *Della letteratura veneziana* (Manfrè, 1752), the head of conservative forces among the five *correttori delle leggi* responsible for proposing government reforms during the political crisis of 1761–1762, and doge from 1762 until his death in 1763. If it is true, as authors have suggested, that the patrician government functioned increasingly like the court from the sixteenth century onward,[6] Renier Michiel occupied its upper echelons. She was educated in the manner of most noble girls across Europe, having been sent to a Capuchin convent in Treviso from the age of three to nine, where she received instruction in English, French, music, and art. Subsequently, she studied with a French woman in Venice, although it is not clear exactly who this was or what material she covered.[7]

At the age of twenty, on October 25, 1775, Giustina married Marc'Antonio Michiel, who came from a prestigious ducal family. Her marriage was not destined to be a long or happy one, although there were not many indications of this during the first years of their union. In fact, to my knowledge, the first extant letter from Giustina to Marc'Antonio dates from 1772, when she was still only sixteen and seemed to possess the qualities which made their marriage last as long as it did: she expressed her obedience and appeared to have genuine affection for her future husband. She wrote in French—the fashion among educated women of the time—telling him that she had chosen to write rather than sleep, as everyone else in the house was doing, since, as she states, "I am permitted to do so, I do not want to let the opportunity pass without taking advantage of it."[8] The remainder of her correspondence with Marc'Antonio, even once her affection had dwindled, would be characterized by the same intimacy and spontaneity.

As a young woman and new bride, Renier Michiel's letters to her husband and her new mother-in-law in the first few years of her marriage show her to be principally defined by the same obliging nature. Shortly after her nuptials to Marc'Antonio, the couple moved to Rome for a year, accompanying Andrea Renier, Renier Michiel's father, to his post as Venetian ambassador to the court of Pope Pius VI. During their year in the papal city, Renier Michiel was well received. In her first letters to her mother-in-law, she recounted how she was introduced to the Pope, who subsequently offered her a 120-pound sturgeon as a gift. She wrote that she was the recipient of great politeness and that she was astounded by the warm welcome they had received from everyone. "Those who say that the nobility of Rome is proud are mistaken; I reply that they cannot be more affable."[9] Part of this success must be attributed to her father, who held the post of ambassador and was no doubt responsible for arranging the introduction both to the Pope and, more generally, Renier Michiel's introduction into society. She wrote that her father "cannot have more tenderness for me." He introduced her to the city by taking her on a tour.[10]

Nonetheless, Renier Michiel was also very conscious of thanking her mother-in-law, Elena Corner Michiel, for her social success. Throughout the year, Corner Michiel constantly sent her new daughter-in-law clothes and accessories and Renier Michiel diligently expressed her appreciation. For example, on February 10, 1776, Renier Michiel thanked her mother-in-law for the clothes and purses, asked her for a "*vesta di camera*," or house dress, and complimented her on her good taste.[11] Indeed, Renier Michiel wrote that the dresses she sent suited her perfectly, allowing her to cut the most beautiful figure among all the princesses, duchesses, marquises, and countesses.[12] The following February, Renier Michiel informed her mother-in-law that she planned to wear one of her new outfits to a lunch the following day at the home of Cardinal de Bernis (1715–1794), the French ambassador to Rome, where there were always many guests present. She wanted the dress to be admired and used the occasion to underline once again her gratitude for clothing in which she could display magnificence and good taste.[13] This sartorial splendor would reflect well not only on her but also on her family and her husband. In a society still very much defined by group identities, the privileges enjoyed by married women and minors—who were legally dependent on their husbands and parents—constituted a sign of the success and virtue of those charged with their well-being.[14]

Fashion, however, was not all that Corner Michiel provided to her daughter-in-law. She also gave her motherly advice and support in her marriage. During the year in Rome, Renier Michiel became pregnant. Very early on, she shared this news with her mother-in-law: "I can do no less than share with my dear mother my hope of being pregnant, making this confession to you, it being against my nature to keep secrets from those whom I truly love."[15] Subsequently, Renier Michiel continued to assure her mother-in-law of her good health, claiming that her pregnancy was causing her no problems, especially when she decided to be bled for the first time in her life during a difficult period in the month of April.[16] We may imagine that her expanding girth was the reason she asked for the aforementioned house dress. Near the end of her pregnancy, Elena Corner Michiel sent a wet nurse for the birth of her granddaughter, also named Elena, and often referred to as "Nene" in Renier Michiel's correspondence.[17]

For all this maternal attention, Renier Michiel expressed her sincere gratitude. These feelings were especially ardent around the time of the birth of her child. She was extremely grateful for all the trouble to which her mother-in-law went for her, asking her to forgive her lack of words, knowing the quality and quantity of her feelings.[18] Even when Renier Michiel was unhappy with her mother-in-law, she was careful about how she expressed her displeasure. Renier Michiel wrote on one occasion that she was a "little bit angry" with her because of a letter that she had written to Marc'Antonio, but "on this point I will remain silent, as I left the task of responding to him."[19] She curbed the impact of even this slight rebuke by preceding her confession with an affirmation that she always spoke well of Corner Michiel because she deserved it, diverting her mother-in-law's attention from even this mild criticism by filling the letter with news of her incipient pregnancy and reception by the Pope. Worrying, however, that her mother-in-law may have taken offense, she excused herself, writing that "More phlegmatically than last time, I report the continuation of my good health."[20] Her measured strategy seems to have been successful, as soon after gifts began to arrive and expressions of affection and esteem multiplied.

This deferral to others is characteristic of this period in Renier Michiel's life. When she grew tired of the novelty of Rome and wanted to return home, she succumbed to her father's desire that she remain with him.[21] Even after her return from Rome, she defined her happiness primarily in relationship to her life with her husband and children. During their marriage, Renier Michiel's husband often traveled; his frequent absences were a source of tension between the couple.[22] Consequently, while Renier Michiel found her husband adorable and professed a tender love for him at the beginning of their marriage,[23] just a few years later she was often angry that she did not hear from him. Her letters from this period underscore the fact that she, not he, was most often the one to initiate their correspondence.

Thus, in a letter dating from January 1788, Renier Michiel wrote that she was waiting to hear whether he would be staying in Dolo, a small town just east of Venice, for long. She then added, "I am responding to you first as I know that it will make you happy, but I assure you that in making you happy I do the same for myself."[24] After this gentle reprimand, she prompted him to tell her about the impression she made on his family the last time that she visited them. While her tone at this point was still generally affectionate, she told him that he need not explain himself at length as he had previously done, as she knew him well enough.[25] Ten months later, she was not so forgiving. Not only had Marc'Antonio not taken her with him on his most recent trip, but he had also neglected to say goodbye to her when he left. Renier Michiel's exasperation was apparent since she had waited for him to do so until one o'clock. She excused herself from rising to see him off, as she had just begun her first menstruation after having given birth, and her mother told her that she should remain quiet at this time. In a bittersweet conclusion, she told him that she awaited the next opportunity for an embrace upon his return.[26]

Increasingly during this period, Renier Michiel sought news of his activities, even from visitors in passing.[27] When none was forthcoming, her anger with her husband amplified. Increasingly she was less pleased at the fact that she always seemed to be taking the initiative in their relationship. "Although you have no interest in hearing from me, I do not feel the same toward you. And after having waited many days without receiving a reply which would have been much appreciated by me, I ask that you finally send me some news."[28] She even tried to use their children to chide him into responding or returning home. In addition to sending expressions of their affection, Renier Michiel stressed how much their children would like to see him: "Our little ones, all well and beautiful, ask for their father, who has run off."[29] In another letter, she wrote: "Our little ones are all well, but complain at not seeing their father."[30] Renier Michiel even resorted at times to quoting their own comments to her, including an episode in which her eldest, Elena (Nene), allegedly said, "Enough, enough; go to call Papà, such that he will come here to be with [me]."[31]

That Renier Michiel used her children's wishes to underline her own is not surprising. Although some authors writing on the subject of marriage in the eighteenth century stressed that a husband had certain duties towards his wife, and that there should be an exchange between the two, most asserted that the wife should be obedient towards her husband. But all agreed that each spouse had power in different domains, and that of the wife was raising their children.[32] Renier Michiel never adhered to these gender codes slavishly, as we shall see shortly. Like many women of her station, she had a wet nurse and sent her children to be educated elsewhere.[33] However, it is clear that she bore the greater responsibility in her marriage for raising them. Although she was occasionally away from them, she was generally the one who called on her husband to return; she sent him samples of Elena's reading and told him of their daughters' health and development.[34] In the most colorful of these descriptions, for example, she says that Elena is as beautiful as a flower and as healthy as a fish.[35] Even during this early period of her life, however, Renier Michiel never solely defined herself as wife and mother. As a member of an elite patrician family, she participated in social activities fitting to her station. As we have seen, while in Rome she was introduced to that city's social elite. Within a month of her arrival, Princess Rezzonico introduced her into several social gatherings, which she called "le Conversazioni."[36] In one night, she was introduced into three gatherings, which she enjoyed despite the elaborate etiquette that was expected.[37] Later in her stay, these social formalities started to wear on her nerves; she began to be bored by the conversations, being constrained to always repeat the same things: that she was well, that she was content with her situation, and that she wanted very much to embrace her dear mother.[38]

Luckily, there were other activities to keep her amused. Renier Michiel talked of attending the opera,[39] and during Carnival season she and her husband spent a few weeks considering what they would wear to the masquerades. Their task was rendered more difficult by the fact that everyone kept what they would be wearing secret, making it more difficult for Giustina and her husband to know how people dressed for these events in Rome.[40] They must have chosen well, as Renier Michiel claims that they were more magnificent and showed more taste than anyone; when they presented themselves in public, the crowd clapped their hands and shouted *Evviva!*[41] During Lent, activities calmed down considerably, and the best pastime to be had were visits to academies.[42] The year that Renier Michiel spent in Rome in the company of her husband and father served as an apt training ground for her adult life of intense sociability. In her literary portrait of Renier Michiel of 1833, Isabella Teotochi Albrizzi claimed that it was there that she acquired a love of fine arts and a "grandness of the soul" that she would never lose.[43]

By January 1778, Renier Michiel had returned to the Veneto where she kept up some of her former amusements. She went to the theater in Venice and in Padua.[44] She also continued to frequent intellectual circles. Having acquired the confidence that accompanied the social education of her year away, Renier Michiel now described herself as visiting a new academy "like a citizen of the world."[45] In Padua, Renier Michiel also strove to improve her mind by studying a number of subjects, including optics and astronomy.[46] She even tried her hand at chemistry, visiting Professor Marco Carburi (1731–1808), who showed her how to make musk essence.[47]

In addition to cultivating these interests, Renier Michiel participated in the larger public events of Venetian society. For example, when outside of the city with her daughter Chiara, she attended a series of balls and concerts, offering a critical judgment of them in her correspondence with her husband. While Morichelli (no doubt soprano Anna Bosello Morichelli, 1750/55–1800) pleased her very little, she wrote that Marchesini (probably the famous castrato, Luigi Marchesi, 1755–1829) surpassed himself; indeed it was to hear him that so many Venetians and foreigners had come.[48] Renier Michiel also made reference to a series of "amusements" in Padua that drew many people, although she felt she was there more out of duty than for her own pleasure.[49] This last comment, as well as the fact that Renier Michiel was away from her children, might indicate that her participation in these events formed part of her official function of dogaressa, a position she filled as of 1779, although the lack of dates and the vagueness of her comments make it difficult to determine this with certainty.

Renier Michiel became dogaressa not by marriage but because of her family's prominent role in the Venetian Republic. The dogaressa was the official consort of the doge of Venice, the elected head of government who served for the duration of his life. After the death of Alvise Mocenigo in December 1778, Renier Michiel's paternal grandfather, Paolo Renier, was elected to the post. Normally his wife, Margherita Dalmet, would have fulfilled this role, but she was not considered a viable choice. Because Dalmet was not a member of the Venetian patriciate, their marriage, which took place three years before the beginning of his tenure as doge, was not officially recognized or marked in the *Libro d'Oro* (the official registrar of the birth and marriages of all Venetian patricians).[50]

Although the doge was an elected official, he had an ambiguous role in the life of the Venetian Republic. Serving as symbolic head of the government, he was required to strike an uneasy balance between princely and republican attributes. On the one hand, his public actions were circumscribed to show that he was first and foremost a patrician like all others, simply the first among equals, and that true power emanated from the councils. On the other, his regal bearing and central role in processions and governance made him seem like a king.[51] The position of dogaressa and her role in public ceremonies added to this ambiguity. During the sixteenth century, the dogaressa, in a modified version of ducal rites, was honored in a coronation and funeral ceremony.[52] Like many European queens, she was accorded this position only by virtue of her marriage to the *doge*.

By the eighteenth century, much of the pomp surrounding the dogaressa had been curtailed. The coronation of the dogaressa was officially prohibited in 1645 because of concerns over the public display of luxury, although the dogaressa Elisabetta Querini Valier was crowned with the usual pageantry in 1694. After 1700, dogaresse were no longer even permitted to wear the ducal crown, the *corno*. Pisana Corner Mocenigo was the last to enjoy any official celebration of her entry into the post in 1763, when a procession of parade boats and *gondole* welcomed her along the Grand Canal. Upon her entry into the Ducal Palace, she was accompanied by the two *procuratori* of San Marco and fifteen patricians.[53] By contrast, Renier Michiel's assumption of this role in 1779 was not celebrated with any festivities. Still, she did participate in official ceremonies. Her grandfather, Paolo Renier, had been elected early in the year, and there is some indication that Renier Michiel assumed her own functions no later than the spring. In July 1779, she spoke of having to turn down numerous requests from visitors, male and female, who wished to see her in her newly official capacity and observed that her life had started to resume its normal rhythm.[54] Nine days later, she visited the Arsenal for the launching of a ship.[55]

Through her intellectual and political activities in the late 1770s, Renier Michiel began to develop a separate life that was independent of her husband's authority. Marc'Antonio Michiel would eventually react to this tendency by trying to regain control over her. Initially, however, his objections did not seem to be marked, and at certain points his attitude even seemed to be conciliatory. Through her letters, Renier Michiel shared her intellectual interests with her husband. She asked him to send her a volume of *Heroides* containing a letter by Louis Sébastien Mercier (1740–1814) and told him about her recent activities.[56] To some extent, this newfound intimacy brought the two of them closer, for a limited period, because they could share their intellectual passions at a distance. Marc'Antonio responded to her efforts by sending his wife his own composition, *Le conte*. Renier Michiel flattered him by responding that it was a work of genius, well written in a graceful and lively style. However, she could not resist observing that she wished that he would occupy himself with more joyful and pleasant things, suggesting that the contents were not uplifting.[57]

At other times, though, Marc'Antonio seemed uneasy with his wife's pastimes. On hearing of her attempts to learn Latin—Renier Michiel claimed that she had reached the point where she could understand perfectly well a lecture in experimental physics by Simone Stratico (1733–1824)—he laughed and called it a woman's fancy.[58] He also labelled her studies as an expression of pride, or "*amor proprio*."[59] Marc'Antonio's attitude toward her abilities underlines his more general skepticism regarding women's intellect. When Renier Michiel sent him a piece of writing by Giustiniana Wynne di Rosenberg,[60] he responded that while he enjoyed it and found it beyond reproach, he refused to believe that it was written by a woman.[61]

This generally conservative stance toward women's abilities later became a real source of tension between the two of them. During the period preceding their separation in 1784, Renier Michiel defended herself against her husband's criticism. She felt that he had misinterpreted her words and responded poorly to her actions for a while. And yet she wrote that her life in Venice should in no way displease her husband. She spent her days looking after their children and acquiring some useful notions, reserving only her evenings for seeing a few people, going for walks and attending the boring *casini*, the gathering places where nobles gambled and talked. She felt that he was more concerned with what others said, seeing evil where none existed, only to upset himself and deny her the simple pleasures of an innocent life. Renier Michiel was especially upset over his accusation that she preferred his absence. Given the fact that she constantly asked him to return home, though by the 1780s this may have been purely out of a sense of duty, she felt that she, and not he, was the aggrieved party.[62]

The difficulties in their marriage raise important issues about relations between the sexes in late eighteenth-century Venice, namely the question of separation and the problem of control. Renier Michiel's mounting participation in a wide range of public activities without her husband hurt both his pride and his feelings: people apparently talked about their situation and knew that she disobeyed his wishes. Marc'Antonio was increasingly distressed at the amount of time his wife spent away from Venice and evidently asked her to return. Renier Michiel told him that she would do so whenever he wanted. Nonetheless, she outlined her reasons for not wanting to comply. So far she had preferred Padua because it was an escape from Venice, which seemed, more and more, filled with the same gossip. Consequently, she wished to go to Ponte Casale, where his family had a villa, for a few days with her friend Santorini (possibly architect and inventor Giovanni Antonio Santorini, 1754–1817) to remove herself from all annoyances.[63] Michiel took her response as a personal rejection of his wishes; in response, Renier Michiel explained that her primary dissatisfaction was not with him but with the empty social obligations of a woman in her position in Venetian society. She enjoyed these activities up to a certain point, after which they bored and bothered her.[64]

These letters signaled the start of serious trouble in their relationship and precipitated an exchange that clearly laid out the couple's divergent viewpoints on women's proper behavior. For Renier Michiel, there was nothing wrong with her lifestyle; it harmed no one and brought her pleasure. Under his continued pressure to limit her activities, however, she announced that the situation had reached a point at which it required serious deliberation on her part about what was reasonable in a marriage. She could no longer bear his demands to renounce everything, even the daily pleasure of the theater. Instead, as we learn from later letters, she asked for his permission to go the countryside in the company of the Wynne family.[65]

Michiel did not react well to this request. His standards for his wife's behavior were very different from her own. In raising objections to her plan to leave Venice in the company of the Wynnes, he condemned both her sociability and her disobedience. First, he objected to the fact that she asked his permission only after her plans had been made and did so in company or through letters so that he could make no true objections and yet at the same time could not complain that he was not informed. Second, he was distraught that she planned to take their children with her. He saw himself in a comfortless marriage in which even his children had been taken from him. Third, he felt that she would be committing a breach of etiquette by receiving guests in the country without sufficient resources, having neither a carriage and horses nor enough money to pay for the meal she shared with them at the *locanda* every day. Through these actions, she would make the world think that he had abandoned her, dishonoring her own reputation and exposing him to scrutiny, misery, and discredit as well. He concluded by asking her to postpone her trip for two days so that he could raise the money she would need for an appropriate *villeggiatura* by pawning jewels.[66]

For Marc'Antonio Michiel, control of the couple's finances was intimately tied to his role as a husband. He believed that he was expected to give his wife enough funds to support her in the manner to which she was accustomed, and he was willing to incur debt to fulfill this social role. "Finances are not all that interests a gentleman," he told her, but nonetheless, he did show concern about her estate, the money that she had brought into the marriage and that he was duty bound to look after—in the same way, he observed, that as a citizen he had a duty toward his country. From his perspective, Renier Michiel had misunderstood his criticisms, which were signs of his affection and the fulfillment of his marital duties. He felt that she no longer loved him because he increasingly could not afford to pay for the various "pleasures" that she now considered to be her right.[67]

In addition to feeling hurt, misunderstood, and embarrassed, Marc'Antonio Michiel also found his wife's behavior unseemly. The question of disobedience was central to his view of her actions. In stating this position, he echoed the warnings of some Italian moralists about the danger of marrying a woman from an elevated social class. Early in the eighteenth century, for example, Francesco Beretta wrote that noblewomen made intractable wives because they were eager to devote themselves to "dissolute liberty." Rich women would respond petulantly to their husbands' reprimands and demand to exercise authority for which they are not qualified.[68] In summary, the question of misalliance lay at the heart of their strained relations.

While not belonging to the wealthiest sector of Venetian society, Renier Michiel's family occupied the echelon just below it.[69] Like other families of its class, the male members of Renier Michiel's were eligible for and elected to important political offices. As a woman, Renier Michiel could not hold office, but she benefited from her connections and occupied an essential public position in Venetian society. Through her father's appointment as Venetian ambassador to Rome in the 1770s, she had been introduced into court life and the cultural elements that accompanied it. This experience served as a training ground that made her the ideal candidate to fill the role of dogaressa for her grandfather two years after her return home, and following the birth of her children. Marc'Antonio's family was not at all poor, but he would never hold the positions that her father, uncle, and grandfather had held near the top of Venice's political and social hierarchy, a sign that his family was neither as wealthy nor as well-connected as hers.[70]

Serving as dogaressa for her grandfather only furthered Renier Michiel's sense of autonomy from her husband's wishes because it placed her in an unusual social situation. While her husband ostensibly had authority over her, her role within her family and the state increasingly came into conflict with these traditional social expectations.[71] In fulfilling the role of dogaressa for her grandfather, though, Renier Michiel benefited from a measure of independence from her husband that would not usually be afforded to women in this position, as most dogaresse would have also been the doge's wife.[72] Her familial and social connections also helped her in other ways in the later years of their marriage. Although many women were socially and financially dependent on their husbands, as Marc'Antonio intimated, Renier Michiel had other resources. She personally exhibited no concern about her ability to receive the Wynnes properly. Not only did she and the family share an intimate confidence and friendship, but she still had some money from her uncle's inheritance at her disposal.[73]

In the end, the quarrelsome couple finally reached an understanding on Renier Michiel's departure from the city. But they were ultimately unable to compromise on the larger issues that would have saved the marriage.[74] She suggested that no reunion was possible, and the two finally separated on August 4, 1784.[75] This was not an uncommon solution to matrimonial difficulties in Venice: twenty-five couples asked to have their marriages annulled or be allowed to separate in the same year as did Renier Michiel.[76] The separation did not lead to seriously acrimonious relations, despite Marc'Antonio's initial claims that he did not want to see his wife again.[77] The couple continued to write, mostly concerning the health and welfare of their children, and Marc'Antonio inherited her dowry at the time of her death.[78]

Renier Michiel, Civility, and Aesthetics

Giustina Renier Michiel's separation from her husband ultimately centered on gender issues. Marc'Antonio clearly felt ambivalent about women's intellectual abilities, but more problematic for him was his wife's extravagant socializing. What rendered her behavior particularly improper was her lack of deference to either his authority or his financial constraints. For Renier Michiel, however, the pleasures of intellectual society were too great to be forsaken, and she was fortunate enough to have the financial resources and support from her friends and family, which together enabled her to live independently from her husband. Unlike Marc'Antonio, many Venetians did not find anything wrong with Renier Michiel's lifestyle. In the 1760s numerous Venetian authors wrote about the "woman question," and some of them were favorable to women's active presence in society.[79] These texts indicate that Renier Michiel grew up in a world that validated, and even encouraged, her choices.

The presence of so many women in Venetian literary circles at the end of the eighteenth century would seem to support the assertion that at least some members of the city's literary elite were welcoming to women intellectuals. Renier Michiel hosted a literary salon and attended conversations hosted by others in the casini[80]; she attended the theater and the opera, and she frequented the *caffè*, from which she sometimes wrote to her husband[81]; finally, she formulated aesthetic judgments of art and literature in her literary correspondence and even published two works in her own name, both of which were edited by some of the century's most notable men of letters: Melchiorre Cesarotti helped her with her translation of and preface to Shakespeare's *Coriolanus* (1800) while Angelo Dalmistro, Saverio Bettinelli, and the poet Francesco Negri made stylistic corrections to her *Origine delle feste veneziane* (1817–1827).[82] In this world of sociability, it was Renier Michiel's writing, alongside that of her friends and collaborators Cesarotti and Bettinelli, that indicated how the norms of Venetian sociability and beliefs about women's nature influenced the role that they occupied in the city's literary society.

Venice's openness toward learned women can be explained in part by the Republic's particular cultural and political climate. Although republican thought in early modern Europe is generally perceived as excluding women from public life, Venice was an oligarchic republic that combined a certain notion of social equality with a very strict understanding of social hierarchy.

On the one hand, all patricians were supposed to be equal in status, and the Republic continuously took pains to erase any external distinctions within this group. On the other hand, as of 1297 the patriciate as a group constituted a political elite into which one was born. New laws created in the fifteenth and sixteenth centuries laid greater emphasis on these blood ties, paying closer attention to the social status of the mother. The effect was to define patrician status increasingly as a physical and moral heritage as time went on, a heritage transmitted by both men and women.[83] As members of an elite social group who inherited their right to govern over other portions of the population through birth, patricians were a kind of nobility who justified their monopoly on power with reference to their long-established families' patrician virtue.[84]

In the early modern period, patrician virtue was thought to be manifest in the group's refined behavior and noble bearing, constituent elements of *civility*. This was a humanistic conception of learned social interaction that was defined in a series of conduct books published in sixteenth-century Italy. One stream of civility, exemplified by Baldassare Castiglione's *Il libro del Cortigiano* (Venice, 1528), was adapted to the exigencies of courtly life. His book and the tradition of civility it inspired laid particular emphasis on love and beauty, assigning women a privileged place in conversation and intellectual society. Drawn to women through love, men would seek to emulate their delicacy and refinement in hopes of being loved in return. In this way, women were held to have a moderating influence on men's aggressive tendencies.[85] As the norms of civility spread across Europe in the seventeenth and eighteenth centuries,[86] they secured a place for women in literary society. The most visible evidence of this phenomenon was the establishment of literary salons in England, France, and Italy, building on women's reputation as a civilizing force with a talent for language.[87]

Although conduct books inspiring the concept of civility originated in Italy, by the eighteenth century many Europeans agreed that the French had best mastered its precepts.[88] Saverio Bettinelli, a man of letters from Mantua who, in addition to teaching across northern Italy (including the Veneto), was one of Renier Michiel's collaborators (as we have seen above), identified civility as specifically French, blaming the spread of French sociability for the introduction of French words into Italian. An integral part of this urbanity and courtesy, as he called it, was "free and amicable commerce between men and between the sexes."[89] According to Bettinelli, domestic factors also explained the visibility of women in Italian literary society, including the rise of *belle lettere*, a style of literature that prized an elegant and refined form. He thought this form of literature had "its seat in the heart"; because he believed it capable of "agitating the soul, . . . [and decorating] serious reason with the grace and sweetness of passion," it therefore had the effect of softening manners, spirits, and hearts. He also thought that women, upon whom nature had bestowed "elegance, delicacy, and a facility for thinking and expressing themselves," had a natural affinity for this type of literature. Because of their innate simplicity, Bettinelli claimed, they had "the merit of softening men of letters and rendering them more genteel in their conversations, as one sees more commonly in France."[90] For Bettinelli, this was not an entirely happy development; it led Italians away from a healthy and virtuous life and to a sedentary one rife with luxury.[91]

Women's place in intellectual society was not only limited to their role as a civilizing force; they also constituted a less educated audience that pushed philosophers and writers away from pendantry toward a simpler style that could be immediately understood by a wider public.[92] In addition, according to certain aesthetic theorists of the eighteenth century (some of whom worked in close collaboration with Giustina Renier Michiel), a lack of education did not forestall formulation of aesthetic judgments. More specifically, Melchiorre Cesarotti wrote an essay on the aesthetics of tragedies in response to David Hume, Anthony Ashley Cooper, the third Earl of Shaftesbury, and Jean-Baptiste Du Bos. This last writer, author of *Réflexions critiques sur la poésie et sur la peinture* (Paris, 1719), laid particular emphasis on the question of reception, and more specifically on the primacy of emotions over reason in aesthetic judgment. In brief, he theorized that the ability of a work of art to evoke pleasure and emotion, to move one's heart, was what marked it as good. Consequently, one did not need to be learned to be able to judge a work; one simply had to have a feeling heart. The emphasis on reception naturally raised the question of the identity and nature of the public, and in fact Du Bos, Hume, and Cesarotti acknowledged that reception would be affected by factors such as the audience's disposition, as well as its nationality and sex. Nonetheless, Cesarotti, citing Du Bos, reaffirmed the legitimacy of the general public's judgment: its members were neither too learned nor too ignorant, possessing natural taste and good sense. Cesarotti did specifically mention that those who were weak or who had a "feminine mind," among others, were excluded from this general public, although it is unclear as to whether or not he actually intended to exclude all women.[93]

Both Bettinelli and Cesarotti, then, betrayed a certain ambivalence toward "female" emotions and their place in literary society. On the one hand, sentiment was a key tool in matters of taste, giving women a clear advantage; on the other hand, those who showed too much emotion were thought of as weak and tending toward corruption. Renier Michiel showed a keen awareness of the strong association between women and sentiment in her correspondence to learned men. Despite the more negative implications, Renier Michiel in some sense bowed to conventional wisdom concerning women by continuously formulating her judgments with reference to the emotional responses art and literature provoked in her. Writing to Bettinelli, for example, Renier Michiel claimed, "Oh, how I will be forever grateful to you, my valued friend, for having provided such beautiful reading for me! Oh, I have read so many things that will remain engraved in my heart! What a contrast of different sensations did this awaken!"[94] Renier Michiel also thought that sentiment could reinforce a more reasoned judgment, as she made clear in her discussion of an unknown woman author's *Poemetto*:

> For many years, she has already given me the right to admire her, and I have also kept a manuscript of hers as a precious object, which publication has made no less precious to me; and since then, my appreciative heart has applauded my judgment. She did not have to renew my sentiment of gratitude now to reclaim the same effect; each of her works goes straight to the heart and to the mind, and spreads a sweetness there that attracts everyone towards the happy and skilful writer.[95]

The significance of emotion to Renier Michiel's intellectual endeavors, and to women more generally, becomes even clearer when one examines her published works. Renier Michiel began the preface to her translations of Shakespeare's *Othello, Macbeth*, and *Coriolanus* (1798, 1800)—the third volume, it should be noted, was revised by her friend Melchiorre Cesarotti—by writing that as a woman she wanted to repay Shakespeare for the multiplicity of tender and sweet female characters that he created in his plays.[96] Although she conceded that the translation would be a difficult enterprise, Renier Michiel wrote that she was pushed to undertake the task by her feeling, a force whose importance she made clear in the body of the piece. The great art of Shakespeare was his ability to make his audience's passions speak, almost in spite of themselves, whereas reactions to lesser playwrights depended on the predisposition of those who watched the plays. Her reflections on the matter of sentiment were warranted, as she claimed that this was the one domain on which women could make pronouncements without fearing the censure of men.[97] Renier Michiel evidently did fear some censure, however, as she also justified the decision to undertake her translations by claiming that she wanted to provide reading material for her daughters that would help them to "regulate their incipient passions."[98] She published the work anonymously.

Sentiment again played a key role in Renier Michiel's next publication, *Origine delle feste veneziane* (1817–1827), although on this occasion the sentiment she felt was no longer gratitude or maternal solicitude; rather, it was a form of patriotic longing inspired by her love of Venice's fallen Republic. This was the force that pushed her to write and the justification for producing a commemoration of the Republic's greatness through a description of its festivals.[99] The effect, she hoped, would be one of moral instruction. Just as government officials had organized festivals to excite civic virtue through enthusiasm, Renier Michiel sought to inspire Venetians to virtue and glory by recalling the celebrations to their minds.[100] Her mission was especially urgent given that the Republic no longer existed—Venice, we should recall, fell to French forces in 1797—and was thus in danger of disappearing from memory.[101] On this occasion, it was Bettinelli, among others, who helped her on questions of style.

In both works, Renier Michiel lays particular emphasis on the *embodiment* of beauty and morality in provoking the emotions upon which judgments were formed and from which lessons were learned. Festivals and monuments, she wrote in her *Origine delle feste veneziane*, were the teachers of philosophy and morality and were more persuasive than any arguments; similarly, Shakespeare's actors were the portrait of humanity, speaking and acting by the impulse of universal passions that were felt in all hearts. "Each one," she wrote, quoting Le Tourneur's preface, "is an individual and has his own existence, as do real individuals in society."[102] Renier Michiel often made this link between art and life, and thus aesthetics and civility, evaluating individuals and their art according to the same criteria. The art and the artist were even sometimes tied together, each functioning ideally as an expression of the other. For example, in reference to the monument Antonio Canova created in 1795 to honor Admiral Angelo Emo (1731–1792), Renier Michiel wrote, "and I remember well that while we were rapt by the charm of the art, we were brought to equally admire the modesty of the craftsman."[103] Conversely, Renier Michiel was unimpressed with Madame de Staël, as much for her lack of refinement in person as for the discrepancy between her beautiful writing and her physical presence.

> This Mme de Staël seems to be someone for whom there is a great contrast, although this is far from rare, between the person and the writer, which I absolutely detest. All that one reads of hers has a certain pathetic quality, a certain delicacy, a certain refinement, an insinuating sweetness, that forces one to love her respectfully. But then to see her, one is presented with an easy and militant step; her black eyes cast an impudent look; her fashionably curly hair seems like Medusa's serpents; her big lips, big shoulders, and large proportions should be more moderate and gentle.[104]

True beauty, then, was inextricably linked to morality in both life and in art, but only if it was sincere, transparent, and—of increasing importance in the late eighteenth century—natural.[105] Returning to the preface of Renier Michiel's Shakespeare, she thought that what set the bard apart from other literati was his lack of formal education, which caused him to eschew models and draw his material from within himself, thus (again quoting Le Tourneur) "becoming that for which Nature had destined him."[106] Similarly, women, being "closer to nature," as she says, could not remain unmoved by his work.[107]

The act of establishing a link among Shakespeare, nature, and women was a shrewd literary strategy, constituting an attempt to rehabilitate the value of women's contribution to literary society.[108] As we have seen above, Bettinelli expressed his uneasiness with women's social influence by tying them to the rise of belle lettere; in so doing, he was part of a wider movement in Italian literature that sought to transcend the precepts of Arcadia, an academy renowned for its openness to women, and its emphasis on strict imitation of the Ancients. Part and parcel of this shift away from adherence to established literary forms was a movement toward a more natural style, one that sought its origins in the aesthetics and morality of everyday life. In Venice, this turn was exemplified in theater by Goldoni, and in painting, according to Gasparo Gozzi, by Pietro Longhi, who painted a family portrait of Giustina Renier Michiel and her husband with their children and his sisters and mother[109] (Figure 3.1). More significant, however, was Giuseppe Baretti's identification of Shakespeare as a model of a natural genius who was "instructed" by emotions rather than formal learning.[110] Building on this tradition, Renier Michiel established emotion and nature as a common ground between Shakespeare and women, thus according women's literary talents a legitimacy that was distinct from the tradition of belle lettere.

Figure 3.1 Portrait of Giustina Renier Michiel and her husband with their children and his sisters and mother. Pietro Longhi, *The Michiel Family.* Galleria Querini Stampalia, Venice, Italy. Courtesy of Scala/Art Resource, New York.

Conclusion

Renier Michiel's correspondence and her published works after her separation show that her experience in literary society mirrored the delicate position she occupied as a young married woman of a prestigious patrician family. In both her youth and her adult life, it is possible to see the reflection of the ambiguities surrounding the status of elite women: they were simultaneously representatives who transmitted Venetian republican values and individual women whose authority was always questioned. Patrician status was a moral and physical inheritance based on birth and made visible in behavior and appearance. As such, women had a role to play in its survival, both legally and culturally. As a patrician woman, Renier Michiel could give birth to patrician children; she could display her family's virtue through sumptuous clothing; she could serve as dogaressa, representing the Republic for her grandfather; she could judge beauty through the effect it had on her emotions; and she could be a part of literary society that promoted the values of civility.

On the other hand, the essence of the republican government, the very foundation upon which the myth of the Venetian Republic was founded, was that of equality and the exercise of patriotic virtue that was inherently male. Only men were members of the Great Council, thereby leaving women no active role in government affairs. Furthermore, this male government was also supposed to hold sway in the home: the same men who occupied government posts were to be the uncontested heads of families, families in which the woman's role was that of obedient wife and mother. Men of letters were equally convinced of their superiority over women, whose reputed lack of reason was thought to undermine their intellectual endeavors and, in the end, their judgment. Under the influence of this line of thinking, Bettinelli was quick to point out the dangers of women's civilizing influence and celebrated the modest, maternal women of Italy's past; Marc'Antonio Michiel, meanwhile, rejected his wife's role as a representative of the patriciate, finding the lavishness of her "exhibitions" ridiculous.[111]

In addition to illustrating the ambiguity of gender norms, however, Renier Michiel's experience demonstrates the flexibility of these precepts. Just as elite women could live independently given sufficient economic resources, so intellectual women could test the boundaries of gender norms by attempting to redefine the import of women's "natural" talents. In short, ideas about gender always worked in concert with other concerns. The most notable demonstration of this was the presentation and and reception of Renier Michiel's *Origine delle feste veneziane*. I have already mentioned Renier Michiel's evocation of emotion as a means of justifying the publication of her work, a strategy she also employed in the preface to her translations of Shakespeare. Equally notable is the fact that, in contrast to her earlier publication, Renier Michiel did not refer to the peculiarity of her status as a woman author in the *Origine*. Moreover, the publication of her work does not seem to have attracted much criticism. On the contrary, aside from mild disapproval of Renier Michiel's choice to write in French and then supply an Italian translation in the first edition, this work was celebrated by men and women alike and was quickly identified as her most important contribution to Venetian society.[112]

In fact, when women reflected upon Renier Michiel's life, they referred to her "feminine" attributes more often than did men. Thus, Ginevra Canonici Fachini, who compiled a biographical dictionary of illustrious women published in 1824, wrote that Renier Michiel possessed a soul that was touched by the "sweetest sensations," a good heart, and a shrewd intellect "adorned" with vast historical knowledge and healthy criticism.[113] Similarly, after Renier Michiel's death in 1832, Isabella Teotochi Albrizzi began a literary portrait of her fellow salon hostess with a description of her simple and yet elegant dress of linen and a garland of fresh roses. She ended the piece by comparing Renier Michiel to a flower and describing her as Venice's most precious ornament.[114] For both women, though, as for others, Renier Michiel's most notable trait was the patriotic love that she displayed in writing her *Origine*.[115] Other eulogies, including this example, celebrated only her nationalism:

> Since the insolent victor usurped
>> The powers of the defenceless Adria betrayed,
>> She [Renier], awakening sleeping courage,
>> Suffered to live in her time no more;
> And burying herself completely in eras gone by,
>> In the accomplishments and pomp of her ancestral people,
>> She offered a well-devised history of their festivals,
>> As a splendid token of patriotic love;
> In living her days thus,
>> In her ancestors' company,
>> The memory of the empire lost almost left her,
> And her ancient spirit, generous and proud,
>> Released from earthly joy,
>> Was welcomed among the shadows of the Venetian Heroes.[116]

How does one explain that in life, Renier Michiel was dogged by gender norms—a woman first and a Venetian second—yet in death remembered primarily for her contributions to the Venetian Republic? One might first consider the gap between gender prescriptions and interpretations as well as the complexity of cultural notions of gender. Ideas concerning gender never existed in isolation, and sometimes other matters, in this case politics, outweighed even differences between the sexes. Consequently, although Renier Michiel's ability to independently represent her social order was contested during the era of the Venetian Republic, the constraints of gender norms relaxed for those actively seeking to keep its memory alive after its fall. Once subjected to the humiliation of foreign rule, Venetians' similarities seemed more important than their differences, and they readily celebrated anyone who would evoke their glorious past.

PART TWO

Women and Cultural Institutions

Revisiting Arcadia

Women and Academies in Eighteenth-Century Italy

ELISABETTA GRAZIOSI

Few Italian women had the opportunity to travel in the age of the Grand Tour. If they did, they were accompanied by husbands, sons, brothers, and parents. They were rarely alone. This was part of a more general impediment which kept women far from the loci of culture and from the means of procuring culture: books, travel, good instructors, and the frequenting of cultured persons in a manner not directly aimed at marriage, the objective normally allowed women who circulated in society.

The academies were certainly an important means of overcoming this handicap, because they were capable of furnishing the loci and also the means for a female acculturation which was a viable alternative to their widespread convent education. In order to understand the possibilities for women in eighteenth-century Italy, we need to investigate further the presence and the roles of women in the academies. This chapter intends to respond briefly to the questions: When were the academies opened to women in Italy? Why did this occur and why only then? Who (or which academies) took this initiative? What sort of woman was accepted (and

Translated by Matthew Sneider.

what sort was excluded)? What was the role of these women in the academies? Which female models were promulgated through their presence in the academies?

Eighteenth-Century Openings: Nothing Female about Her Except Her Sex

Widespread participation of women in the academies dates only to the eighteenth century in Italy and starting with Arcadia.[1] A few women had been admitted to various academies in the previous century, but they were generally singular cases incapable of officially establishing a norm. The laws of the academies did not provide a place or specific function for a female membership. At most, women were permitted to be part of the audience at official meetings or to be "exceptional" members. Even this limited and controlled participation, however, caused diffidence and at times internal opposition. Two examples will suffice to illustrate a widespread custom. At the beginning of the seventeenth century the Neapolitan poet Margherita Sarrocchi (1560–ca. 1618) was admitted to the academics of the Oziosi of Naples and the Ordinati of Rome. Satires and polemics, however, arose; the admission of females did not continue in these academies and Sarrocchi remained an isolated case. The seventeenth-century Accademia degli Scomposti of Fano, by contrast, admitted women only to its public sessions, but even this appeared too much for one censor who defined the academy "more as a dance-mistress than a mistress of erudition."[2] Many male academicians felt that the very presence of women gave rise to untoward incidents or distracted from the serious business of culture. In the eighteenth century real participation was still off-limits for academy women in certain institutions, as was the case for the academy of the Ereini and the Geniali in Palermo, who, despite their cautiously libertarian motto "that which pleases is licit" (*quod licet libet*) declared unequivocally: "Academy women shall not be present at the meetings."[3]

The case of the Venetian Elena Lucrezia Cornaro Piscopia (1646–1684) is exemplary. Piscopia was the world's first female university graduate (1678). Prior to her celebrated university degree, she was admitted in 1669 to the academy of the Ricovrati in Padua with a public ceremony that guaranteed her exceptional status as a female member (it was even said that there was "nothing female about her except her sex"; *in ea praeter sexum nihil muliebre*).[4] This was a theoretical privilege because Elena was a Benedictine oblate who lived a life of great retreat and participated only two times in meetings. She was therefore a "virtual" member of the academy—not frequenting meetings and more a banner than a real presence.[5] At her death, the members of the academy renewed the ritual of honor by publishing a collection of poetry; acclamation and death therefore became the only occasions for a female presence. Even with these limits, Piscopia's presence in the Ricovrati was nonetheless an important victory for the women of the seventeenth century—women enclosed in domestic "precincts," according to Spanish usage, whose names were not to leave the family circle. The recognition of exceptionality, which spread to other cities, prepared the ground for other efforts to celebrate and co-opt the fame of exceptional women. In fact, the Ricovrati's decision to admit Piscopia set off a mechanism of emulation, inspiring the academies of the Dodonei and the Pacifici of Venice, the Infecondi of Rome, the Erranti of Brescia, and the Intronati of Siena to concede an analogous privilege to the Venetian Minerva (as Piscopia was called). Having admitted one (very exceptional) woman, the Ricovrati now sought out others to admit to their academy; the "virtual" academy women thus became Madame Dacier, Madeleine de Scudéry, Madame des Houlières, the proto-feminist Antoinette de Salvan de Salié, and the Pisan Maria Selvaggia Borghini.[6]

The fact that the promoters and protectors of the academies were generally men explains their caution in admissions in a climate of restrictions imposed on all women. The Grandduchess Vittoria della Rovere, by contrast, was from 1654 the protector of an entirely female academy, the Assicurate of Siena, whose close relations with the more well-known Accademia degli Intronati in the same city—an academy sympathetic to women—led the two academies to meet together.[7] That these were not simple salon entertainments and informal conversations is proven by the seriousness of the undertaking, including the names attributed to the academy women and the literary exercises which also included "the composition of sonnets and madrigals." It was later the responsibility of Violante di Baviera, wife of Siena's governor, to continue this work. The academy of the Assicurate constituted a local tradition that, through its female members, spread its influence into the larger Roman Arcadia; many members of the Assicurate later became "shepherdesses" (*pastorelle*) of Arcadia. This explains not only the significant number of Sienese women poets and writers among the Arcadians during the course of the eighteenth century but also their important participation in the debate over study for women. In fact, we owe the *Apologia in favore degli studi delle donne* to a member of both the Assicurate and Arcadia academies, Aretafila Savini de' Rossi. This treatise was written at some point after the Accademia de' Ricovrati's original debate in 1723 and before the publication of an expanded edition of opinions on women's education in 1729. In a climate of backlash against the presence of women in academies, it claimed that females were as apt for study as males.[8]

From Exclusion to Presence

Elena Cornaro Piscopia owed her presence among the Ricovrati to questions of prestige—for her family and for the academy. Elena's father, Giovanni Battista Cornaro, used his daughter to reassert the prestige of his declining family while the Ricovrati used her name to relaunch their academy, arisen again after a long silence. It was a propaganda operation whose novelty lay in the fact that it was linked to the name of a woman, but this did not change the laws regulating access. The academy remained an "affair of men," men who did not propose the spreading of knowledge, even if they helped to bring to light the problem of women's education. The discourse of Giovan Tommaso di Colloredo in the meeting of 24 February 1675 sets out with clarity the dual problem of the social constraints on women's education and the positive role of women's presence in male society. The orator "defended women as being wrongly excluded from the sciences and showed that the presence of ladies is greatly stimulating to minds and of great advantage in the academies."[9] But neither the handful of foreign academy women nor the debate which arose about women's education was able to transform the minority status of women who were admitted to the academy only when they escaped, like Cornaro Piscopia, from the *imbecillitas sexus*, the weakness of their sex. Given the limited place allotted to women in the academy, it was better if they were physically absent—present only in image.

Many things were to change with the foundation of the Roman Arcadia. It was the first academy that accepted women, no longer as an exceptional concession to individuals but according to an explicit internal rule. Rome, in contrast to Padua—a stronghold of university studies from which women had always been excluded (Cornaro Piscopia's graduation had no sequel)—was, as the seat of a supranational court, better able to innovate and export fashions of socialization. This concession to female personages might seem strange in a papal city inhabited prevalently by male ecclesiastics. But it is a mistake to fall for the stereotypical view of the great center of the papacy as merely the capital of conservatism. The fact is that Rome had become in those years the city of international diplomacy, in which women (sisters, wives, sisters-in-law, and daughters) could set informal diplomatic contacts in motion in the salons with more discretion than men.[10] They could open or close channels of communication without provoking incidents for complicated reasons of etiquette that, in essence, privileged the informality of the salon over the formality of diplomacy. But alongside the social and political reasons for the strong growth in female rôles in Roman life, we must also consider other motives for women's increased presence, motives that flowed from Arcadia's most fundamental objectives. The function of the academy, as proposed in those years by its guardian general Giovan Mario Crescimbeni, was not that of seventeenth-century and elitist models of academy life—promotion of honor and fame—but rather diffusion of good taste. This was a pedagogical aim, which meant that Arcadia was also open to beginners and dilettantes—in short, to women intent upon learning (*dame*).

Founded in Rome in 1690, Arcadia spread throughout Italy by means of numerous colonies that exported the Roman model of the academy.[11] It does not seem, however, that opening the academy to women was a clear part of Arcadia's program from its foundation. The group of Arcadia's fourteen founders was composed of men alone, who in one day co-opted another six men in a meeting in which women were not even present. In the laws of Arcadia, drawn up in 1695 in an archaic Latin, there is no hint of the admission of women. In the learned oration (*Pro legibus arcadum*) pronounced the following year by Giovan Vincenzo Gravina, there are also no references to the admission of women. Even though the inclusion of women had already begun (the first was admitted in 1691) the problem had not yet been posed with clarity on the institutional level. There were women in the academy, but a normative declaration which might admit them legally was lacking.

The feminization of Arcadia has often been traced to the exceptional presence in Rome of Christina of Sweden. It cannot be denied that symbols are also important in increasing the value of female roles. In reality, not only was Christina already dead on the date of Arcadia's foundation, but she had resolutely kept ladies out of her private academy. In short the modernizing leap accomplished by Arcadia in opening itself to women is not explained with reference to the past but with reference to the future; it was not exceptional female patronage that motivated the move, but rather the growing importance of women in society.

The Roman Arcadia, a supple academy in transformation, both perceived and provoked this change by modifying itself in midcourse. Only in 1700 did Crescimbeni explicitly set out the requirements for the admission of women, which, like those for men, were a minimum age of twenty-four years (though this requirement could be waived); noble quality, "especially in customs"; and culture.[12] In reality, the age requirement selected a population of academy women that was different from that of men; this was because, according to the standards of the time, that age group generally included married women: wives, female heads of household, and potential salonnières. Cut out were (fortunately) child prodigies and girls seeking husbands; this meant that Arcadia was not made into an antechamber of matrimonial negotiation and a stage for precocious pupils. There were also a few differences with regard to cultural formation. While it was prescribed that a man "be known as an erudite in at least one of the principal sciences," "more" was required of women—"that they currently practice [professino] poetry." This asking for more was in reality asking for less, because erudition was a much more complex matter than training in poetic writing, which was almost an obligation in social life; but this was a sensible rule if it was agreed that poetry, as opposed to science, was an easier key for female access to culture.[13] There would have been very few learned women to admit if Arcadia had limited itself to them. Moreover, *professare* is a nuanced verb which means that neither active exercise nor even the publication of texts was necessary for women, but rather the practice of poetry (appreciation, manipulation, and reading)—which is required even today in the Italian schools. In other words, women did not have to produce new knowledge or culture to be admitted to Arcadia but needed only to be participants, in a more general sense, in the literary world then in formation.

Admitted only by secret vote, women were moreover excluded from the custom of acclamation reserved for "cardinals, great princes, viceroys, and ambassadors," begun in 1695. It was a norm which in practice excluded women from an important aspect of academy participation, whether honorary or real, but which at the beginning of the century responded to the presence in Rome of "important" women: the only women acclaimed for a long period were the two sovereign exiles in Rome, Christina of Sweden and Maria Casimira of Poland. No learned or literary women received a similar degree of public acclamation.

Civic Symbols and Family Honor

Let us now ask ourselves about the first women to enter Arcadia. One might imagine that they were women living permanently in Rome. But this is not the case. Precisely because of the growing importance of diplomacy, the first women accepted in 1691 came from outside the city.[14] There were two Neapolitan aristocrats: Anna Beatrice Spinelli Carafa (1691, Amaranta Eleusina) and Aurora Sanseverino (1691, Lucinda Coritesia); an Orvietan, Anna Giuditta Febei (1691, Erminda Alicea); and two Tuscans, Maria Selvaggia Borghini (1691, Filotima Innia) and Faustina degli Azzi (1691, Selvaggia Eurinomia). These women were supported by various groups capable of promoting their image as potential Arcadians even in the absence of publications, which, moreover, the academy did not explicitly require. On the one hand, there was the pressure of the Neapolitan salons, to which the Marquis del Carpio, viceroy of Naples, had attributed great importance in a general reform of social customs in the years right before the Arcadian reform.[15] On the other hand, there was the growth of a female patronage which promoted its clients: the patronage of the grandduchess of Tuscany and of Violante di Baviera, who were linked to Borghini and Faustina degli Azzi respectively.[16] It is more difficult to interpret the case of Febei, about whom very little is known.[17] Everything becomes clearer, however, when one notes that she was a niece on her mother's side of the erudite and consistorial lawyer Carlo Cartari, who was probably the go-between for the Orvietans Rosa Agnese Bruni Cheli (1695, Galatea Beleminia) and Virginia Rossi Alberici (1692, Acasta Cromonia), who were also among the first admitted.

Every region, every city, and every court wanted to show off its jewels, and the number of women in Arcadia multiplied through imitation or emulation.[18] The international community of relatives and eminent protectors with ties to Arcadia was set in motion, and they applied pressure to have a woman in the academy. Two Genoese entered in this manner: Marzia Imperiali Lercaro (1695, Mirzia Condileatide) and Pellegrina Maria Viali Rivarola (1695, Dafni Eurippea); such mechanisms also led to admission of the Sienese Maria Settimia Tolomei Marescotti (1696, Dorinda Parraside) and the Savoyard-Parisian Maria Brulart de Sillery Marquise Gontieri di Cavaglià (1695, Cidippe Dereia). Provincial localities also entered the competition: from Spello, Gaetana Passarini (1694, Silvia Licoatide) was admitted; from Bitetto, Teresa Nicolai Volpi (1699, Licori Tersilia); and so on. Often the women admitted did not have (and still do not have) well-known names. Traces of only a handful remain in the *Vite degli Arcadi*. It is possible to locate verses or letters from only a very few. Sometimes the date of their admission is the only trace that remains of these women. It is clear, however, that membership in Arcadia was not a poetic laurel but the means of entering a circuit where culture was produced and enjoyed. What appears literarily insignificant to us had a promotional value in a society that had long excluded women from socialization.

At the beginning of the eighteenth century there were already approximately twenty women Arcadians, out of 575 total, throughout Italy—that is to say, one woman for every twenty-five shepherds, or male Arcadians. This was a notable percentage when one compares it to the small number of "exceptional" learned women of the seventeenth century such as Cornaro Piscopia. Although very few of these women were able to attend the meetings of the Roman *bosco Parrasio*, their very admission to the Academy was extremely useful; it constituted a safe-conduct pass into the peripheral colonies that were forming and that might not otherwise have admitted them so readily. Indeed, according to the internal constitution of the academy, those who were admitted in Rome could enter a colony with the permission of the vice-guardian and participate as "foreigners" in the Arcadian meetings of any peripheral city.[19] There were already eight colonies in 1700, nineteen in 1705, and twenty in 1710; by the end of the century there were almost a hundred. Perhaps not all were still active, but they had established the mixing of sexes as a custom.

The new colonies had a smaller number of women than did the Roman Arcadia. In 1698 there were no women among the founders of the Renia colony in Bologna and the Animosi colony in Venice. No woman was to be found in the Eridania colony—founded in 1699 in Ferrara—and not even in the colony of the Fisiocritici established the following year in Siena. At the inauguration of the Augusta colony held in Perugia in February 1708, the only women were members of the audience. Among the members of a later colony such as the Trebbiense of Piacenza, launched in 1715, there was not a single female name.[20] After a few years these male colonies were nonetheless also obligated to receive the shepherdesses already admitted in Rome: hence Borghini was able to enter the Alfea colony, which had been founded in Pisa in 1700. Felicita Tassi (1704, Clori Leucianitide), the first Venetian woman to join Arcadia; and Matilde Bentivoglio Calcagnini (1703, Amarilli Tritonide), the first Ferrarese woman member, were both admitted in the Roman center rather than in their homelands. This was also true for the Sienese women Elisabetta Credi Fortini (1708, Alinda Panichia) and Maria Antonia Bizzarrini Tondi (1710, Urania Corintia). In Bologna not even Laura Bassi succeeded in joining the restrictive Renia colony; she was admitted in Rome directly by the guardian general (1737, Laurinda Olimpiache).[21] The colony of Verona showed itself more open; Clarina Rangoni di Castelbarco (1706, Idalia Elisiana) and Giulia Serego Pellegrini (1706, Erminia Meladia) were soon admitted while in Isaurica, and for the colony of Pesaro Lavina Gottifredi Abati Olivieri (1703, Elisa Oritiade) was among the group of founders which shortly thereafter also admitted Teodora Ondedei (1704, Fillide Erannia). The Udinese Elena Cavassi Archivolti (1704, Giulinda Calcidica) was among the founders of the Giulia colony.

Given the above information, we must conclude that few women had a hand in the foundation of colonies and none had leadership or consultative roles. There were no female guardians or vice-guardians, no female consultants or colleagues of Arcadia; offices remained a male perquisite. In the previous century the office of prince of Venice's academy of the Pacifici had gone to Cornaro Piscopia alone. It seems to me that this nomination was meant for show; to have a woman at the head of a prevalently male assembly was not possible then or later, not only within Arcadia but also outside of Arcadia. When Cristina Roccati (1743–1766, Aganice Aretusiana), an Arcadian and a university graduate like Cornaro and Bassi, was named "prince" of the Concordi of Rovigo in 1755, many members split off to form the new Accademia degli Allegri. This was true even though the members of the academy had publicly sung her praises in 1750, and even though Cristina delegated an advisor to represent her, "since her modesty did not permit her to be present at meetings."[22] In virtually every Italian academy the presence of women was always subject to cautions and limitations.

Women of Arcadia: The Included and the Excluded

Until the end of the seventeenth century, admission of women to the Roman Arcadia was primarily an honor conceded to nonresident, or only occasionally resident, patrician women. Something began to change when the academy more routinely admitted women who lived in Rome, who possessed prestigious residences, and who were part of powerful, local familial networks. These women were truly able to participate and offered the academy—which had neither an official protector nor its own building—meeting places for official and semiofficial gatherings. The first of

the Romans admitted to Arcadia, in May 1695, was Prudenza Gabrielli
Capizucchi (1695, Elettra Citeria), the niece and sister-in-law of cardinals,[23]
who in that year inaugurated a literary conversation in her palace in which
Giovan Battista Zappi and Vincenzo Leonio, two of the academy founders,
took part. Also important was the presence in Rome of the widowed queen
of Poland, Maria Casimira Sobieski (1699, Amirisca Telea), acclaimed Arcadian, who aspired to a role similar to that of Christina of Sweden, hosting Arcadia in her palace as though it were a little social court.[24] These were
the centers, halfway between academy and salon, by means of which the
female presence in the central and peripheral Arcadias was multiplied.

Maria Casimira and Capizucchi were hosts and organizers; they carried
out low-level patronage in the halls of their palaces, in the midst of networks
of solidarity. The same function belonged a few years later to Teresa Grillo
(1705, Irene Pamisia) who arrived from Genoa in 1704 as the wife of Prince
Camillo Pamphili and was immediately admitted to Arcadia. In other cases,
by contrast, the role of the women Arcadians admitted had an explicitly exemplary character, which might serve to model female comportment. It is
certainly not possible to follow the stories of all the women who belonged
to Arcadia. Two names and two representative stories will suffice. In 1703
Faustina Maratti Zappi (1679?–1745), the legitimized daughter of the painter
Carlo Maratti, endured an attempted kidnapping by the aristocrat Gian
Giorgio Cesarini Sforza.[25] Faustina resisted. A trial was held which concluded
in condemnation of the assailant. The next year Faustina was admitted to Arcadia with the name of Aglauro Cidonia. In 1705, with the protection of Cardinal Ottoboni, she married the consistorial lawyer Giovan Battista Zappi.
In short, marriage and entry into the academy were almost official compensation granted to her by the protection of the pope. At the same time they
recognized her morality—a morality that had been called into question.

The aristocrat Petronilla Paolini, on the other hand, was married at a
very young age, for reasons of family alliance, to the Marquis Francesco
Massimi, a military man thirty years her senior.[26] She had three sons by
him, but theirs was not a happy marriage. Rather than live with her husband, who was the castellan of Castel Sant'Angelo, Petronilla took refuge in
a convent which she could leave freely only after his death, which occurred
in 1707. Before this, however, she was admitted in 1698 to Arcadia thanks
to the protection of Pope Innocent XII Pignatelli. This occurred despite
legal conflicts with a husband (from whom she was separated) who accused
her of being too worldly. Entry into Arcadia was therefore a public recog-

nition of her virtue and compensation similar to that given to Faustina
Maratti. In both cases, Crescimbeni's Arcadia selected female figures for the
lessons they could teach, against the excesses of an abusive aristocracy and
in favor of a moderate appreciation of female virtues.

The two best women poets of the century, the Anglo-Florentine (and
half Bolognese) Cristina di Northumberland Paleotti (1640–1719) and the
Bolognese Teresa Zani Marescotti (1664–1732)—remained outside the academy.[27] Both paid a high price for this exclusion: almost total loss of their
verses and scarcity of information about them. This was even more grave in
an environment like Bologna where the Renia colony was not lavish in its
recognition of cultured women. Indeed, an institution such as the Arcadia
also served the function of putting texts in circulation and preserving the
memory of its members; those who did not become members were less able
to find their public and create for themselves an authorial identity. The exclusion of Northumberland Paleotti and Zani Marescotti was probably due
to the less-than-irreproachable behavior of the two women, or even merely
the gossip that they fueled in local society. One had a husband and diverse lovers with whom she consorted openly within and without the city's
walls. The other, less aristocratic and therefore less free to transgress, took a
second husband when she was no longer young; this rather displeased the
citizenry of Bologna, as well as her daughter (and also her lawyer son-in-
law), who wished to inherit from her. The academy required acquiescence
rather than rebellion, and a minimum of comportment acceptable by local
society. Women who transgressed these moral boundaries were unlikely to
be admitted, no matter their literary merits.

One of the most fascinating female figures of the late seventeenth century—the most famous of the famous nieces of Cardinal Mazarin, who was
loved by the young Louis XIV and for love put the Peace of the Pyrenees at
risk—also remained outside of Arcadia. After having fueled scandal in various
European cities, Maria Mancini returned to Italy upon the death of her husband Prince Lorenzo Onofrio Colonna, from whom she had lived separately
for years, just when the great academy began its admissions. She had sons
and grandchildren, a palace, and two celebrated surnames in Rome. But none
of these marks of distinction opened the doors of Arcadia for her. Hence a
woman who had had a good literary education in the Paris of the précieuses,
who loved not only the life of society but also theater, music, and literature,
had no venue in Rome to encourage her literary productions, whether they
were rhymes for occasional verse collections, letters, or musical libretti.[28] None

of these things were required for academy admission, but membership in Arcadia certainly encouraged women to produce verse to be sung at its meetings and to appear in the publications it promoted. Here was a lost opportunity for the tiny eighteenth-century female Olympus, which found in Arcadia access to culture and a range of aims that encouraged women's literary efforts.

The Domino Effect: Female Texts and Models in the First Arcadia

In short, Arcadia admitted but it also excluded. It selected and circulated female voices and models just as do modern systems of communication. Since one certainly cannot imagine that the shepherdesses, in the span of ten years, had suddenly begun to write poetry, one must grant it the merit of having begun a "domino" effect in other academies and other editorial enterprises. Reorganization of literary life under Arcadia created a literary circuit that fostered diffusion of poetry, which, until that moment, had remained within domestic walls or had been consigned to ephemeral publications. In the great Bolognese anthology promoted by Manfredi, published in Bologna in 1711, the majority of the living women poets who contributed verses were those admitted to Arcadia, who participated with a decorous "feminine" Petrarchism in line with the Muratorian idea of *Perfetta poesia*. Did the "very learned" Manfredi accept the taste of Crescimbeni, or did Crescimbeni represent the average taste of the epoch? Perhaps both are true. But it is certain that a champion of erudite good taste trained in the shadow of the *Alma Mater* included the women of Arcadia among his examples of renewed poetry, drawing their poems from the Roman reservoir.

By 1716, when the *Rime degli Arcadi* (a collection that had been described with great anticipation since the beginning of the century) first began to appear, other anthologies had already given space to poetry written by contemporary women: the anthology of Lucca in 1709, the anthology of the Neapolitan poets of the Acampora in 1701, and the anthology of the Ferrarese poets in 1713.[29] Above all, the first anthology composed entirely of poems by women authors came out at the same time. This was the work of the Arcadian shepherd Giovan Battista Recanati, who, in 1716, at the same time that the first three volumes of Crescimbeni's *Rime degli Arcadi* appeared, published the *Poesie italiane di rimatrici viventi* in Venice. He included a large group of women poets (thirty-five in number), among whom Tuscans and northerners were conspicuous.[30] They were not all Arcadians, but the title with which the author decorated himself on the frontispiece ("Teleste

Ciparissiano, shepherd of Arcadia") made the work a fruit of the Arcadian garden. This is all the more significant if we compare its contents to that of a strong and determined collection such as the *Poesie italiane di rimatori viventi*, which came out the following year with a dedication to the Innominati of Bra—an academy which competed strongly with the Roman Arcadia even in its attempt to expand beyond its place of origin.[31] The verses of sixty poets were included in this volume, and none of them were women.

The first seven volumes of the *Rime degli Arcadi*, which came out in two years (1716 and 1717), included the work of twenty women poets representing the various cultural centers of the Italian peninsula. Their percentage was high with respect to the men.[32] Whether this was due to chance (the poems were sent anonymously) or to calculation (which is more probable), it is clear that Crescimbeni aimed at making this female presence a banner, exporting to the colonies the model of a literary society in which women could be full members. In this progressive adjustment to a changed social situation the academy also revealed its flexibility. Born of an exclusively male conversation, Arcadia progressively opened itself to women, first practicing and then formalizing their admission, and finally receiving the recitations and printed texts of its shepherdesses. The general guardian had become increasingly convinced of female literary capabilities. Indeed, when he republished the *Bellezza della vulgar poesia* in 1712, he added an entire dialogue dedicated to the taste of the present century in which he pronounced himself also theoretically in favor of female studies and of the female propensity for poetry:

> Since the minds of women, and in particular those of high station, are neither diverted nor burdened with the many varieties of cares and thoughts, both public and private, which upset our minds, where they apply themselves to poetic studies they are fresher and more vigorous than the male mind in producing new and unusual fancies and rare and marvelous forms.[33]

One might imagine that after this kind of ideological beginning, the number of poems written by women—enriched by their presence in the new Arcadian colonies—would increase. But this was not the case. The eighth volume of the *Rime*, which came out in 1720, included no women authors, while the ninth, two years later, included only names already found in earlier volumes. The female Arcadia was marching in place. The vacuum of this Roman initiative was filled in Venice in 1726 by the anthology of the genre which still remains an indispensable source for the poems of many women poets of the seventeenth and eighteenth centuries, the *Componimenti poetici delle più illustri rimatrici d'ogni secolo.* In this book, Luisa Bergalli (1725, Irminda Partenide) collected the rhymes of more than fifty living women, both Arcadians and non-Arcadians.[34]

Between 1720 and 1728 only twelve women were admitted to Arcadia, fewer than in the first four years. Statistics are often of little value and can easily be manipulated; nonetheless, in this case comparison with the Arcadia of the early eighteenth century serves to confirm that space for women in the anthologies and in the academy was diminishing. Perhaps the colonies—whose duty it was to propose names—were partly responsible. The Veronese colony, in a state of disintegration, had not accepted any more women; the Milanese colony, even though it was held at the residence of Princess Trivulzio, did not take off; the presence of a woman in the colony of the Animosi provoked a fight which put the colony in a state of crisis.[35]

But it was above all the Roman center which, beginning in the 1720s, no longer encouraged new admissions. Key Arcadians, who in 1690 were a group of innovators in their thirties, now found themselves on the threshold of their sixties. In 1719 Crescimbeni became archpriest of Santa Maria in Cosmedin. Other founders drifted away, or died. But above all, the early female membership of the Roman Arcadia—those who had given life to the salons—had dispersed: Prudenza Gabrielli Capizucchi died in 1709 and Maria Casimira Sobieski returned to France in 1714. Faustina Maratti, widowed in 1719, lived a life of gallantry different from her heroines. Petronilla Paolini died in 1726. Teresa Grillo separated from her husband, Camillo Panfili.[36] Crescimbeni—who had always looked with a benevolent eye on these shepherdesses—died in 1728. His last two admissions were a pair of foreign women of some significance in the literary world of the eighteenth century: the Guastallese Gaetana Secchi Ronchi (1728, Erbistilla Argense), who would merit, fifty years later, an edition of Affò;[37] and the Neapolitan Giuseppa Eleonora Barbapiccola (1728, Mirista Acmena),[38] the translator of Descartes. The guardian general of the academy had maintained his promise, accepting women for whom poetry was an easier key, but not the only key with which to have access to literary society.

Gallant Arcadia: The Colony of Parma

The guardian general Lorenzini, who followed Crescimbeni, was not as diligent in cultivating a female membership. In the fifteen years of his guardianship, the number of women nominated (although the figure seems approximate) did not reach ten. There was no miscellany. The *bosco Parrasio* was closed. Lorenzini was not a man of society, nor was he a gallant; he cultivated Latin poetry and had made himself patron of a theater for young students, frequented by high ecclesiastics, in which Plautus and Terence were recited—where it is doubtful that women could participate. From his hand we have a mythological sonnet of accusation against love and against the female sex, one of the many reiterations of the Judgment of Paris and the fatal Trojan Helen. The sonnet's malevolent and slightly vulgar finale condemns all women ("the weak sex") "to mere generation and spinning."[39] This is an ideology opposed to that of the early Arcadia in which Petronilla Paolini, in a sonnet which pleased Guidi and which was published by Crescimbeni, proclaimed: "*So ben che i fati a noi guerra non fanno, / né i suoi doni contende a noi natura: / sol del nostro valor l'uomo è tiranno*" (I know well that the fates do not make war upon us / Nor does nature deny us her gifts / Only man is a tyrant of our worth).[40]

In this crisis of the Roman Arcadia the emerging colony was that of Parma, founded in 1738 with a special commission by Carlo Frugoni.[41] In the difficult years of passage from Farnese to Bourbon rule of the city, the foundation of this colony—one of whose vice-guardians was the statesman Jacopo Antonio Sanvitali—was an attempt to reunite the aristocracy in a period in which it appeared that the duchy would pass definitively to the Hapsburg Empire. After a decade disturbed by political events, the group formally emerged following the Peace of Aquisgrana and the arrival of don Philip de Bourbon and Louise Elisabeth de France who fixed their court at Parma. It is unnecessary to give more than a brief account of Frugoni's weakness for women. But the attraction of female poetry was evidently not an inconsequential part of his taste in love. One finds among his paramours the two women poets who were most representative of the first and second Arcadias: Faustina Maratti and Corilla Olimpica.

It was not only Frugoni but the atmosphere of a small, refined, and French-influenced court which gave its tone to the Arcadia of Parma, making it an island apart. Lorenzini had symbolically given possession of the entire island of Aegina to the colony of Parma, thus emphasizing its separateness. In fact the meetings were held on a little island in the ducal gardens: a sort of Arcadian microcosm where the nymphs, whether they were Arcadian shepherdesses or not, were guests and entertainers. In the young court of the Bourbons, female roles were strong and confident and poetry was a social practice made for communication and seduction—a practice of which women were the recipients, the crafters, and the dedicatees. Louise Elisabeth de Bourbon was an acclaimed Arcadian (1743–1766, Clorisbe Dircea); Anna Malaspina, chief lady-in-waiting at the court and lover of Du Tillot, was an Arcadian (Fiorilla Dejaneja),[42] as were Maria Trotti Gonzaga (1705, Eurilla Teutonia), Maria Ginevra Toruzzi Mellini (1743–1766, Nidalma Mellania), and Dorotea Del Bono (1743–1766, Dori Delfense), together with a lesser band of shepherdesses, wives, daughters, sisters, and sisters-in-law whose names sometimes do not even appear in the official lists of Arcadia but which recur in Frugoni's rhymes and in the miscellanies for occasions: Adelaide Malaspina Arrivabene (Amarillide), Maria Isabella Cenci Sanvitale (Licori), Caterina Scotti Landi (Crinatea), and Angela Pizzi (Mirtinda). In the 1769 celebrations of the marriage between Ferdinando de Bourbon and Maria Amalia of Austria, the Arcadian shepherdesses who recited and danced (together with the vice-guardian and the fellow shepherds of the court) had Arcadian names which were unknown in Rome. This did not mean, however, that they were outsiders at the entertainments of the colony, because an aristocratic name was enough to admit them to the society of the court: Cornelia Lampugnani (Doride), Teresa Malaspina (Aglauro), Enrichetta Meli Lupi (Eurilla), Luigia Sanvitale (Nigella), and Laura Tarasconi (Tirrena) were among the participants.[43]

Such women were not great, statuesque Arcadians like those of the Roman Arcadia. They did not narrate their life stories in the guise of Lucrezia or Vetturia, as did Maratti Zappi; nor did they paint themselves as victims of destiny like Paolini Massimi, nor were they chaste widows like Capizucchi, nor platonic lovers like Teresa Grillo Pamphili. They were as ready to exchange rhymes as they were little notes, jokes, thank-you cards, and compliments which left no trace in the editorial monuments of the *Rime degli Arcadi* (of which the last five volumes came out between 1747 and 1781). Some of these women became important symbolic emblems of the role of poetry in the royal courts, as literary works were dedicated to them. Anna Malaspina is one example. Monti dedicated one of the jewels of eighteenth-century publishing to her, the 1789 Bodoni edition of Tasso's *Aminta*.[44] Nearly all the women admitted to Arcadia during the Bourbon period received gallant compliments and poetry composed for weddings, births, masked balls, court celebrations, and theatrical performances. Frugoni was the lesser Anacreon of this sweet life, of which poetry was the means and the ornament; he was the soul of the band gathered together in the Malaspina house.[45] It is no surprise, then, to find in the volumes of his works not only rhymes written for the nymphs or in the name of Arcadian nymphs but also the compositions of his interlocutors—some dilettante compositions, some jokes, some duties of courtesy.[46] It was not the great patronage of cultural enterprises that ruled the occasions of poetry at the ducal court of Parma. Rather, it was a modest convivial patronage, of which women were an important part, the *melior pars.* The Arcadian disguise, which did not last for many years in Rome, served to narrate the stories of a miniaturized Olympus and to allow the women of Parma a sort of sweet participation in the mythology of the academy.

That this involved a casual—so to speak—management of admissions to the academy is understandable. The importance of the nearby court, and the distance of Roman Arcadia, made it impossible not to prevaricate. This was clear when Frugoni wanted to admit the ballerina Maria Rivière—who arrived in 1758 in Parma on tour—and asked two of Arcadia's friends to sponsor her, each without the knowledge of the other's role. The fascinating Rivière had, because of the distraction of the guardian and a subguardian (Morei and Pizzi), two admissions and a double pastoral name: Cleonice Corinatea and Doride Tespia.[47] "All of Arcadia laughed," commented one critic of the gallant eighteenth century.[48] And perhaps this was true. Frugoni had different ideas about the Arcadian shepherdesses than those that had guided Crescimbeni. He wished to honor women who had succeeded with the public in some fashion, further guaranteed by their academy membership, rather than selecting them on the basis of any particular literary ability. "This virtuous maiden," wrote Frugoni,

> infinitely pleases our court; she is pleasing in those qualities in which it is the highest honor of a beautiful and wise maiden to please. She has at one and the same time the applause and the approval of this public. She merits finding in Italy those who would recognize and distinguish her merit and I know not how better to distinguish and decorate her than to give her the name and the laurel of Arcadia.[49]

Female merit *par excellence,* according to Abbot Frugoni, was to please a public of which men were an important part.

I do not believe that female intermediation can in this case be called Arcadian "sisterhood" (as was partly the case later).[50] But certainly the double co-optation of Cleonice Corinatea / Doride Tespia is symptomatic of a change in selection of shepherdesses that was accomplished not by secret vote of the Arcadian college but by friends of friends, and female friends of male friends. Parma was an important center for this new image of a female Arcadia, shaped by public opinion rather than by a closed world of academicians.

New Arcadias and Other Female Models

The case of Rivière was not an isolated one. Indeed, under the leadership of Morei inclusion of women—intended to give luster to the academy and modernize the image of women in academies—began to increase again, encompassing a much broader geographic constituency. In 1758, with a touch of xenomania, Morei proclaimed Madame Du Boccage (Doriclea Parteniate)—the author of well-known poems that were translated in Italy (in the Milan of the Trasformati and the Venice of Bergalli)—as an acclaimed Arcadian. Du Boccage arrived in Rome for her admission, passing first through Parma and Bologna, where she was received among the few eminent women of the Academy of the Istituto delle Scienze.[51]

Once again, Arcadia probably represented the average taste and the cultural horizon of the various cities of Italy. Nonetheless, the nomination of a French woman, who wrote and published, but who also maintained a well-attended literary salon in Paris, was an important moment for the female history of the academy. Not only was her nomination successful, but it introduced new criteria of literary merit as a condition of her admission in order to glorify Arcadia to an even greater degree. A public ceremony was organized in honor of du Boccage, and in addition, a miscellany—illustrating her merits—was published for the occasion.[52] The compositions of another foreign shepherdess, equally celebrated but more aristocratic—Maria Antonia Walpurgis of Bavaria, wife of the elector of Saxony (1749, Ermelinda Talea)—were also recited (in her absence) on that occasion.[53] Present was the new Italian star of Arcadia, the very aristocratic and cultured Giacinta Orsini (1756, Euridice Ajacidense), admitted to Arcadia as a fifteen-year-old shortly before her marriage to Duke Antonio Boncompagni Ludovisi.[54]

The event, highly unusual in Arcadic tradition, was also celebrated with an important portrait of the new *pastorella* by Pompeo Batoni[55] that depicted Giacinta with a bust of Minerva, a lyre, and a crown of laurel leaves. After all, Giacinta was in a certain sense a "daughter of Arcadia." In 1742 her mother, Paola Erba Odescalchi, died before reaching the age of twenty and Giacinta was raised by relatives while her father, the prince Domenico

Orsini, embraced an ecclesiastical career and became a cardinal. An earlier portrait of Giacinta as a child depicts her among emblems of Diana in an Arcadian landscape beside her mother, who was portrayed as Latona, and her brother, in the guise of Apollo beneath the laurel tree, sacred symbol of the glory of poetry.[56]

In 1759 the twelfth volume of the *Rime degli Arcadi* included a sufficiently wide selection of Orsini's rhymes, already known from preceding miscellanies, together with a sample of the less representative verses by the Pisan Arcadian Marianna Lanfranchi Aulla (1743–1766, Euriclea Doriense). "*Misere!*" lamented the aristocratic Orsini Ludovisi in verses that contain a trace of feminism in contrast to the gallantry of Parma: "*usar dobbiam l'arti più fine / I sguardi a regular, gli atti, gli accenti / e a un vetro adulator comporre il crine*" (Unhappy women! We must use the finest skill / to rule our glances, our acts, our accents / and compose our locks before an adoring glass).[57] These were dignified verses sufficiently austere for a young woman, but the Arcadian name did not bring luck to the new Eurydice. The rhymes were already a commemoration, because the young duchess of Gravina, eighteen years old, had died in Rome a few months before. Arcadia therefore lost another of its exquisitely mannered models who might have repeated the role that had belonged to Capizucchi in Rome. Indeed, the foreign women who were members of Arcadia were inevitably passers-through and were destined to furnish models of poetic accomplishment without establishing any particular following.

The growing fashion for improvisation was an important variation in themes and language, superimposing its style to a certain degree on the more traditional and moralizing female Petrarchism, with which it ultimately came into conflict. This phenomenon was already foreshadowed in the 1760s. Morei, drafting the *Memorie istoriche dell'Adunanza degli Arcadi*, noted the extremely large audiences that crowded into Arcadia when there was improvisational singing.[58] Improvisation had always been highly valued in Arcadia because it was a source of entertainment and conformed well to the sociability of the period. Improvisation does not exist without an audience, and Arcadia was above all a potential audience. Pietro Metastasio was in a certain sense a model, because it was well known, as Morei sought to publicize, that he had begun his career in Arcadia as an improviser.

For this reason, many women Arcadians of the 1770s (improvisers or not) turned to Metastasio for advice, encouragement, and propaganda. In 1753 Maria Maddalena Morelli (1750, Corilla Olimpica), the most celebrated of the improvisers, only recently admitted to Arcadia, addressed a *capitolo* from Naples to the poet in Vienna.[59] The Tuscan improvising poet Maria Fortuna (1766, Isidea Egirena) probably aspired to a role like that of Metastasio at one of the German courts; in 1767 she dedicated certain *Rime* to the imperial poet and to Arcadia's new guardian, Giuseppe Brogi (Acamante Pallanzio), adding—as a final touch—a letter of praise which Metastasio himself had sent to her.[60] The twenty-one-year-old Eleonora Fonseca Pimentel (1768, Altidora Esperetusa) also wrote from Naples not only for literary advice but also for support at court[61]; she was still seeking to win a position in the household of Maria Carolina, daughter of the Hapsburg empress (she was named librarian in 1775). Through its networks of correspondence, Arcadia also served to save peripheral shepherdesses from isolation and attract readers for texts, which did not circulate widely.

But the change which had begun in the 1760s would occur decisively ten years later. Improviser, court poetess, show-woman, adventuress Corilla Olimpica, on the level of taste, represents the passage from the Arcadia of Metastasio (of whom she was an admirer and from whom she sought aid) to the philosophic and inspired Arcadia of the 1780s promoted by Pizzi and Golt.[62] On the level of literary custom, by contrast, Morelli was the first to launch with success a new image of the literate woman: not the dilettante lady or the pupil of erudite scholars, and not even the aristocratic salonnière, but the professional in improvisation connected to the world of politics and active culture. The background of this new type of poet was no longer the literary salon, with its idea of literature tied to light entertainment, but rather a stage where poetry was exhibited as spectacle.

It is not possible here to reconstruct the story of success and infamy which Corilla Olimpica—first crowned in Arcadia and in the Campidoglio with the laurels of poetry in 1776, and then forced to flee—encountered in Rome.[63] The coronation was the work of the Roman, Venetian, and Florentine protectors of the poet-improviser, who had a project of modernizing the academy, but it cannot be said that Corilla and the women of Arcadia played a purely passive role in these events. A large part of the improviser's success was owed to the many new women Arcadians whom Pizzi had admitted with an effective policy of admission or whom he had promoted by acclamation.[64] The Arcadia of the 1770s had again become a fashionable place, frequented by many male and female foreigners who found themselves in Italy for the Grand Tour. Since Italian women poets rarely traveled, the Academy became a simple means of establishing contacts and circulating ideas. The scope of the literary world of Arcadia grew ever wider, extending from Rome to Italy to Europe, such that the enlightened Roman salons truly began to function on an international level.[65]

In Arcadia the female models that the academy received during its long history were formed, conserved, and publicized. The very story of Corilla, the Arcadian crowned amid applause, would give rise thirty years later, in 1807, to *Corinne ou l'Italie*—the novel of that other great Arcadian Madame de Staël, in which the events of thirty years earlier flowed into the changed Romantic culture. The character of the protagonist—poet and dancer, rich in sensibility, gifted and passionate—reproduced the image of Corilla and other improvisers which was offered to the public of Arcadia. This eighteenth-century material, republicized by the texts, thus served to construct the biographical identity of women in the following century by analogy or by contrast, by sympathy or by aversion.[66] Arcadia had made itself the guarantor of the memory of female models by publishing the rhymes of the women poets, the *Vite* of the Arcadians, and the acts of the academy, in a constellation of women's texts, dedicated to women and approved by women who first made acceptable and then made possible the stories of real life which are also very often modeled on fiction.

But it is not only a question of models. In the network constructed by the first academy that accepted them fully, the women Arcadians introduced in Rome and in the colonies multiplied their contacts with each other and with the other sex through social interaction and through correspondence. Other shepherdesses, inspired by them, more easily opened the doors of other academies or informal groups in which they certainly found suitors, lovers, and cicisbei (for this, however, it was not necessary to be in Arcadia) and also friends, teachers, and masters to correct their rhymes and direct their reading. With Arcadia and by means of Arcadia, society was also changing. Women could, by participating in the lively climate of the salons, integrate their education. They could also, starting with a little success in the academies, survive matrimonial misfortune and social disapproval and participate as protagonists in political events, as occurred with Eleonora Fonseca Pimentel.[67] A wife separated from a violent husband, Eleonora moved progressively away from poetry to throw herself into the study of law and economics, in which she found as her guides cultured friends and companions of thought. This was a process of formation that induced her to participate in the political life of the Repubblica Partenopea, to the point of compiling its political newspaper *Il Monitore Napoletano*. When the Neapolitan Republic fell in June 1799, Fonseca Pimentel faced death courageously on the gallows, a punishment that awaited her and her political companions. In fact, a dispatch from the sovereign issued in September of the same year ratified this practice by decreeing that whoever denigrated the Royal House through the printed word would be condemned to death along with those accused of treason against the king because they had held key positions in the Parthenopean Republic or had taken up arms.[68] Thus, for women who could not hold political office or take part in conspiratorial plots, their writing and their intellectual work became the avenue through which they could be condemned to death—a grim juridical privilege that also acknowledged women's ability to leave their mark on history.

The case of Fonseca Pimentel demonstrates that admission to Arcadia (and more generally to the academies and the salons of the eighteenth century) truly permitted women to approach and diffuse new ideas, and take on new roles and new responsibilities. Participation in this literary world offered women a means to acquire a socialized culture that the convent education of the preceding century was not capable of giving. There are no new social roles without a new culture. From the visionary and inspired nun of the Baroque world to the femme salonnière, to the diva, the journalist, and the patriot of the eighteenth century—this is truly a modernizing leap of which we must take notice, and we must recognize its roots in the broadening of the academic cooptation of women. In the era of the Grand Tour, it was not the experience of travel which changed female models of life and culture in Italy, but the practice of a more varied society, where people found opportunities and were encouraged to gather in groups which were not exclusively familial. For this reason, then, admission to the academies represented for the women of the eighteenth century not only and not so much a recognition of literary merit already ascertained, or a reward for the development of talents that had long remained invisible to the majority of readers. It was also, and perhaps more important, an effective means of overcoming a handicap in a society in which opportunities for women remained scarce, an opportunity conceded by those who held greater power in society—then as now—in order to evade obstacles faced by the female sex while still maintaining their own privileges.

FIVE

"On Canvas and on the Page"

Women Shaping Culture in Eighteenth-Century Venice

CATHERINE M. SAMA

At first glance, it might seem unlikely that the daughters of a clerk, a small shopkeeper, and a gazetteer could have become forces in shaping literary and artistic culture in eighteenth-century Italy and Europe. And yet three Venetian girls with these humble beginnings did grow up to become, respectively, one of the most successful women painters in early eighteenth-century Europe (Rosalba Carriera, 1673[1]–1757); a poet, playwright, and editor of collections of Italian women's poetry (Luisa Bergalli Gozzi, 1703–1779); and one of Italy's first female journalist-publishers and the center of the most progressive Enlightenment influence in the Veneto region of Italy (Elisabetta Caminer Turra, 1751–1796). For nearly three hundred years before the three women were born, the Venetian Republic had been home to a remarkable number of women who made important contributions to literary and artistic culture; following in their footsteps, Carriera, Bergalli, and Caminer continued this tradition into and throughout Italy's eighteenth century.

I would like to gratefully acknowledge the support of the University of Rhode Island Center for the Humanities Jabour Family Faculty Sabbatical Fellowship which allowed me to conduct research in Venice for this chapter.

Carriera, Bergalli, and Caminer each successfully negotiated the risks and rewards of making a name for herself in a male-dominated profession. Yet their experiences differed in terms of the extent of professional success they achieved during their lifetime, the balance of support and criticism they received from contemporaries, and the strategies they used to negotiate the gendered boundaries of their society. In this chapter, I explore the connections between and among the three women and begin to reconstruct how they influenced each other and formed a network of personal and professional support. I examine what Carriera, Bergalli, and Caminer had in common and also what distinguished one from the other in terms of their professional achievements, their personal life choices, and their acceptance (or rejection) by contemporaries. In doing so, I begin to describe the strategies each woman used to make her way in public arenas usually reserved for men. Finally, I consider the degree to which the women participated in the debate on the condition of women and, in this context, whether or not she regarded herself as an "exceptional woman." Because the three women's lives span the whole of the eighteenth-century—from Carriera's birth in 1673 to Caminer's death in 1796—their stories are a venue for exploring shifting notions of femininity as well as women's actual experiences during the age of the Grand Tour. Examined together, their lives offer a veritable triptych of women shaping culture in eighteenth-century Venice and shed light on the larger context of women's contributions to literary, artistic, and scientific culture in Italy and Europe.

Rosalba Carriera (Figure 5.1) began her career as a miniaturist, painting in tempera or gouache on an ivory ground. She was the first artist to popularize miniature painting as an independent form of portraiture, separating it from the functionality of snuffbox lid decoration and the like. She quickly made an international reputation for herself. Her innovation and expertise were recognized in 1705 when, despite its regulations barring women from membership, the Accademia di San Luca in Rome admitted Carriera as an *accademica di merito*, or meritorious member—a status which recognized her fully as a professional artist. This status set her apart from the few women before her who had been admitted to the academy as *accademiche d'onore*, or honorary members, a category designed for amateurs, collectors, patrons, and connoisseurs.[2] She began working with pastels sometime in the first years of the eighteenth century, and she rapidly gained a wide range of patrons seeking to be portrayed by her hand—from foreign royalty and grand tourists to local patricians and members of the clergy. Within a decade or so, Carriera established herself as a premier portraitist in pastel, and she was much in demand by royalty from across Europe.[3] One admirer of her portraits warned her good-humoredly that her artistic talent reached heretical heights and would one day "lead [her] to the Inquisition:" "You assume the omnipotence that is the most reserved honor of God, and instead of imitating men you create them."[4]

Carriera established herself in a medium (pastel) and genres (miniatures and portraits) considered appropriate for women during the eighteenth century. Whether due to circumstance or inclination, such a choice would certainly have made her less threatening to her male colleagues than if she had attempted to assert herself in higher academic ranks as a history painter, for example.[5] On the other hand, Carriera's embrace of genres and materials commonly associated with women was anything but traditional; she quite literally transformed them. By removing miniature painting from the purely decorative realm of snuffbox lids, she raised it to the status of a fine art. She also heightened the academic value of her work generally by

Figure 5.1 Rosalba Carriera, *Self-Portrait* with portrait of her sister, ca. 1709 (pastel, 71 x 57 cm). Galleria degli Uffizi, Florence. Polo Museale Fiorentino.

painting allegories or by imbuing her portraits with historical or allegorical overtones.[6] Finally, and perhaps most dramatically, Carriera transformed the medium of pastel from something used for preliminary sketches to a vehicle for serious portraiture, thus significantly influencing development of the rococo style in Europe.[7]

In 1720 Carriera was invited to live and work in Paris, where she counted the young Louis XV and numerous French aristocrats and artists among her sitters. During this period Carriera was admitted to the Académie Royale, thus becoming the first non-French woman ever to receive this honor. She was also admitted to the Accademia Clementina in Bologna the same year. Upon her return to Venice in 1721, Carriera continued to receive copious commissions from abroad, and her studio was an important stop for tourists making their Grand Tour through Italy. Over the course of her long career, Carriera made three other important professional trips outside the Serenissima to accept commissions from, among other patrons, the Este court in Modena and the imperial court in Vienna.[8] Aside from these travels, Carriera maintained a highly successful business in Venice, inducing her many and diverse clients to come to her—in person or "by mail order"—rather than becoming beholden to a single patron or court.[9] Carriera enjoyed a vibrant career that sustained her and her family throughout her life. She worked into her seventies until her blindness—caused by cataracts, which, despite partially successful surgeries, could not be cured—forced her to stop.[10] She died at the age of eighty-four.

Luisa Bergalli Gozzi (Figure 5.2) was a poet, playwright, and translator of classical and French theater. She published her poetry in anthologies and in roughly fifty collections of occasional poetry. She translated Terence's comedies (1733, 1735), the works of Racine (1736), and Molière's *Misanthrope* (1745).[11] Bergalli's most important works are her original compositions for the theater and her editions of Italian women's poetry. The range of her original theatrical compositions is impressive, spanning such diverse genres as the melodrama, sacred works for music, tragedy, and comedy. Three of her compositions were set to music by the renowned musicians Tommaso Albinoni, Giovanni Porta, and Giuseppe Giovanni Bonno; they were also performed in at least two Venetian theaters as well as at the royal court in Vienna.[12] Her comedy *Le avventure del poeta* (The Adventures of the Poet, 1730), perhaps her finest theatrical composition, is a social satire of poets living in poverty and the ignorant whims of the aristocrats upon whom they rely for patronage.[13] By eliminating commedia dell'arte masks from

this play, and by highlighting the differences among the aristocratic, artisanal, and burgeoning professional writer classes, Bergalli anticipated some of
the reforms that Carlo Goldoni would undertake twenty years later in the
same Sant'Angelo theater.[14]

In fact, one of the most surprising and original aspects of Bergalli's career
was her one-year position as director / manager of the Sant'Angelo theater
in Venice (1747–48), which she assumed along with her husband, Gasparo
Gozzi. This was, to my knowledge, an unprecedented position for an Italian
woman. At this theater, some eighteen years after publishing *Le avventure
del poeta*, she was able to experiment with abolition of commedia dell'arte
masks on stage, rather than simply on the page. In this way she aspired to
accustom Venetian theatergoers to a more literary and morally instructive
theater.[15] The repertoire at the Sant'Angelo theater under the management
of Luisa and Gasparo included translations or adaptations from French playwrights Boursault and Destouches, and at least one original dramatic work
in verse written by Bergalli (or written in collaboration with her husband)
titled *La Bradamante*.[16] Unfortunately, the management of the theater did
not prove to be financially profitable, and the venture lasted only one year.

Figure 5.2 Rosalba Carriera, *Portrait of Luisa Bergalli* (formerly identified as a self-
portrait, pastel, 29 x 23 cm). Formerly at the Museo di Ca' Rezzonico. Image courtesy
of the Biblioteca del Museo Correr, Venice.

Bergalli's merit also lies in her important work in what today we would call textual recovery; she was a forerunner in collecting and publishing the works of past and contemporary Italian women poets. In 1726 she published a two-volume anthology, *Componimenti poetici delle più illustri rimatrici d'ogni secolo* (Poetic Compositions by the Most Illustrious Women Poets from Every Century), the most extensive anthology of Italian women poets ever published at the time, and the first edited by a woman. Bergalli included 253 poets from the thirteenth through the eighteenth centuries in the collection, placing herself and Rosalba Carriera's sister, Giovanna, among the contemporary poets.[17] The anthology functioned (and functions still) as a literary network of sorts, filled with poems as well as biographical profiles of the poets themselves. In a subsequent anthology, Bergalli led the way to a positive reevaluation of the sixteenth-century poet Gaspara Stampa by publishing a new edition of her work, *Rime di Madonna Gaspara Stampa* (1738).[18] Bergalli produced her major publications prior to her marriage and subsequent years of childrearing, though she continued to publish translations and write poetry for collections of occasional verse until the year before she died in 1779.[19]

Elisabetta Caminer Turra (Figure 5.3), the youngest of this trio of Venetian women shaping culture, spread Enlightenment ideas into Italy through her work in journalism, the theater, and the publishing industry. At age seventeen, she began collaborating with her father on his new literary periodical, the *Europa letteraria* (1768–1773). She went on to assume direction of the family periodical in 1777 (under its various titles, *Giornale enciclopedico*, 1774–1782; *Nuovo giornale enciclopedico*, 1782–1789; and *Nuovo giornale enciclopedico d'Italia*, 1790–1797). In this capacity she participated in and monitored contemporary debates on everything from the latest experiments in regeneration to the state of the Italian language and literature, to the effects of new fashion periodicals on women's status in society. She was outspoken about the condition of women in society, and women's right to a life of the mind was one of her most passionate convictions. Throughout her life she defended women's intellectual equality to men, decried their neglected education, and espoused their responsibility to work to change their own lot in life. Through her journalistic writing and her extensive correspondence with the most renowned men of letters and science of her day, Caminer promoted the reputation of accomplished women of the past as well as those who were her contemporaries.

Caminer was also an active presence in the vital theatrical debates of post-Goldoni Venice. She published more than fifty plays from across Europe in three collections of translations (1772–1794),[20] and—following in Bergalli's footsteps—she directed productions of her translations at the Sant'Angelo theater between 1769 and 1771. Through her translations and her stage direction, Caminer was largely responsible for introducing to Italy the controversial new French bourgeois drama. She became enmeshed in a protracted conflict with playwright Carlo Gozzi over this new theatrical genre and pitted the theatergoing public's approval of her work against his aristocratic and literary disdain. Caminer further promoted her ideas through the printing press she and her husband opened in their home in Vicenza; the Stamperia Turra was one of the most active presses in the Venetian Republic, and Caminer used it to publish numerous pedagogical, historical, literary, and botanical works between 1779 and 1795.

Figure 5.3 Portrait of Elisabetta Caminer Turra. Civica Raccolta delle Stampe "Achille Bertarelli," Milan.

During her lifetime, and especially early on in her career, Elisabetta Caminer's work in journalism and the theater led to published attacks against her. Most seriously, when she was nineteen years old a rival journalist publicly accused her of committing sexual improprieties with her mentor, the abbé Alberto Fortis.[21] Caminer's profession as a journalist, perhaps more so than Carriera's as a painter and Bergalli's as a playwright / poet, put her in a position that was both powerful and vulnerable. On the one hand, she exercised great influence in deciding which publications would be reviewed in her periodical and whether or not they would be promoted or criticized. On the other hand, her position as a journalist made her dependent upon public opinion, a force that was coming into its own for the first time during the second half of the eighteenth century. The periodicity of her medium meant that she maintained a week-to-week relationship with her reading public; her professional survival depended upon her ability to keep her finger on the pulse of public opinion. She could not have kept a low profile had she wanted to, and her very visible role as critic of the latest literary, scientific, and philosophical publications (by men, predominantly) was her greatest transgression in the eyes of many of her detractors. Caminer died of breast cancer at the age of forty-four, just over a century after Carriera was born, the year before the fall of the Venetian Republic in 1797.

Eighteenth-Century Venice as Crucible

The single most important factor that Carriera, Bergalli, and Caminer had in common was their Venetian birth. Living in the Republic of Venice during the eighteenth century offered the women a particular combination of opportunities they might not have encountered had they been born elsewhere.

Contrary to many nineteenth- and early-twentieth-century accounts that portray the Venetian Republic in the eighteenth century as a crumbling state of pure carnivalesque decadence, the Serenissima was a relatively wealthy and extremely culturally vibrant Republic. Venice remained one of the most important cultural centers in Europe, despite its conservative and politically recalcitrant system of government. It was still the area of the Italian peninsula most noted for its relative independence from papal influence, for in this Republic the church's power was submissive to the state's power. During the first half of the century, the incredible building and renovation boom that spread across the entire city was a testimony to the Serenissima's economic vibrancy. A great number of private palaces and churches were built, in addition to the seats of the Scuole Grandi and numerous villas on the mainland. For artists this building boom meant ongoing opportunities for work.[22] Furthermore, the Serenissima experienced a period of peace during the eighteenth century, roughly from the treaty of Passarowitz in 1718 until its final days in 1797 when Napoleonic troops occupied the city.[23] As a result, there was little social unrest, and living conditions in Venice compared favorably with the rest of Europe. For visiting royalty, ambassadors, and collectors, Venice's position of neutrality in the face of ongoing war elsewhere on the continent made the Lagoon city

> a haven of peace, still fantastically rich, where their entertainment was encouraged by a government only too anxious to win as many friends as possible; a city whose palaces were filled, as nowhere else in Europe, with easily appreciated masterpieces of sensuous beauty and whose courtesans were renowned for their charms. . . . they wished both city and women recorded for them to take back to their warring kingdoms in the North.[24]

Venice's status as an essential destination for royalty, artists, and aristocratic travelers making their Grand Tour in Italy was fundamental to the success of Rosalba Carriera's artistic career. The presence of these travelers from England, France, and the German States shaped the course of her career, both in terms of influence and exchange with fellow artists and in terms of royal and aristocratic patronage. Compared to the rest of the Italian peninsula, Venice reigned supreme in attracting royal patronage from the many courts in Northern Europe for its painting.[25] Not coincidentally, Carriera's most important patrons were from the German States, most notably Maximilian Prince Elector of Bavaria, Duke Christian Louis of Mecklenburg, the Elector Palatinate Johann Wilhelm von der Phalz, King Frederick IV of Denmark, and especially Frederick Augustus II, prince elector of Saxony (later known as Augustus III, king of Poland). Royalty as well as aristocrats sought the prestige of returning home with a portrait of themselves or of a Venetian beauty created by "the famous Rosalba" to hang in their private residences or cabinets.

Eighteenth-century Venice was also a major Italian center for journalism, the publishing industry, and the theater, and these facts made possible the literary careers of Luisa Bergalli and Elisabetta Caminer. Venice was the principal center of journalistic activity in all of Italy and ranked among the most important publishing centers in Europe.[26] The city boasted an exceptionally rich book market that fostered a vibrant intellectual climate for its middle and upper classes. According to historian Mario Infelise, "there existed no other city on the Italian peninsula where it was possible to earn a living from intellectual work, translating from the French, editing books, revising proofs, compiling newspapers."[27] Venice consistently had at least seven active public theaters throughout the century, which was more than either London or Paris could claim. The importance of theater in the daily lives of Venetians was in part due to its very accessibility: the price of entry was low, and the theater-going public in Venice was made up of all social classes. For Bergalli and Caminer, the constant access to publications from across Europe afforded by the publishing industries and the growing profession of journalism kept them abreast of new ideas and opened doors to venues for publishing their own writing. Venice's internationally famous and locally revered theatrical life offered the two women a number of stages and a diverse audience, consistently hungry for new plays, including those that Bergalli and Caminer wrote, translated, or directed.

All these factors—neutrality in the face of European conflicts, economic viability, richly decorated palazzi, lavish entertainment, vital theatrical and musical centers, important publishing houses and newspapers maintaining a steady influx of ideas into the city—helped make Venice a unique home for the literary and artistic ambitions of Carriera, Bergalli, and Caminer.

Historical Ties: Venetian Women of the Past

Venice was also a crucible for the dreams and talents of women such as Carriera, Bergalli, and Caminer because of its long history of producing accomplished women writers and artists. Many of these women had argued for improvement in the conditions of women's lives and by their very lives had defied the social, academic, and artistic restrictions generally placed on their sex.

During the fifteenth century the Serenissima was home to the humanists Isotta Nogarola (1418–1466), who wrote a literary dialogue on the relative responsibility of Adam and Eve for the fall of humankind; and Cassandra Fedele (1465–1558), whose orations and letters made her the best-known female scholar in Europe. During the sixteenth-century Venice produced the poet Veronica Franco (1546–1592), whose verses in *terza rima* and whose status as an honorable courtesan[28] earned her an international reputation, and Moderata Fonte (1555–1592), who composed a literary dialogue claiming women's superiority to men. The Republic also fostered the talents of the painters Irene di Spilimbergo (1540–1559), Marietta Robusti (ca. 1554–1590), and Chiara Varotari (1584–post-1663), as well as the commedia dell'arte actress Isabella Andreini (1562–1604). In the seventeenth century the Venetian Republic was home to painters Elisabetta Lazzarini (1662–1692), Margherita Caffi (ca.1647–1710), and Elisabetta Marchioni (second half seventeenth century) as well as the polemical nun Arcangela Tarabotti (1604–1652), author of fiery tracts decrying forced monarchization and women's subservient position in society. In the same century, the Venetian Republic produced the first woman ever to earn a university degree (*laurea*), Elena Cornaro Piscopia (1646–1684). During this period, Venice fostered the careers of the accomplished singer and composer Barbara Strozzi (ca. 1619–1664) as well as the talents of the girls and women who were rigorously trained in music at the *Ospedali grandi* by the likes of Antonio Vivaldi himself. During the late seventeenth century and throughout the eighteenth centuries, Carriera, Bergalli, and Caminer became part of this genealogy of talented and celebrated Venetian women who made important literary and artistic contributions to public culture.[29]

Carriera, Bergalli, and Caminer were certainly aware of this heritage, and the latter two wrote explicitly about some of these women and about their own places in this genealogy of women.[30] The very fact that Bergalli collected, edited, and published an anthology of poetry by "the most illustrious [Italian] women poets from every century" was paramount to challenging the established literary (male) canon; including herself in the anthology left no room for doubt about her own literary ambitions. In the Foreword to the anthology, Bergalli openly stated that her goal was "to pave the way" (*apro la strada)* to restoring glory to women poets past and present, and through doing so to acquire some merit for herself. She tells her readers that alongside the famous women poets in her anthology, she has included those worthy women who, "through great misfortune, are unknown to the Republic of Letters."[31] Bergalli highlights the presence of her compatriots by reminding her readers that "without looking beyond our own Venice for examples of valorous women who made their mark in even the most serious realms of study, we have a Cassandra Fedele . . . an Elena Cornaro Piscopia, and many others still, whose stories would take too long to tell."[32] In addition, Bergalli incorporates the opening stanzas of a canto written by "our own Moderata Fonte" into the Foreword; they constitute an explicit defense of the intellectual and literary talents that

"Nature has granted to women of every age."[33] Her use of Fonte's canto makes the latter a kind of *portavoce* or spokesperson for Bergalli's own desire for literary recognition as poet and compiler of the anthology.[34]

Elisabetta Caminer shared Bergalli's goal of redressing the wrongs committed against women from the past and of promoting the reputation of her contemporaries. Her medium for realizing this goal was primarily her periodical, where she published reviews of publications by, for, or about women. In 1769, at the age of eighteen, she wrote one of the lengthiest reviews ever published in the twenty-five-year history of the Caminer family's periodicals. In this review she chastises a French journalist for his review of a new historical dictionary of celebrated women.[35] She accuses him of having focused on the infamous women included in the volume and having passed over "that respectable number of women who distinguished themselves in the virtues, in letters, in the sciences, in the arts, and even in arms, many of whom deserve to be better known to the world than they are presently."[36] Like Bergalli, Caminer saw herself as part of this heritage of accomplished women and desired to help bring women the recognition they deserved:

> Moved by this blameless affection for her sex, a woman must think to speak up for [them] . . . choosing the names most deserving of celebrity, and most capable of exciting a praiseworthy emulation. Should any wily individual wish to believe that self-interest and gratification motivate on this occasion a pen which should be perfectly impartial, let him keep it to himself; there is no reason for us to hide ourselves, and in any case it is most reasonable that women find satisfaction at seeing themselves as good as men at everything.[37]

In her review, Caminer singled out the names of some of the Italian women included in the French dictionary, including the humanists Laura Cereta (1469–1499) and Cassandra Fedele, and the courtesan and poet Tullia d'Aragona (ca. 1510–1556), among others. She also reprimanded the dictionary's author for not having included more *contemporary* Italian women in his important work; by proudly extolling the merits of women such as experimental philosopher Laura Bassi (1711–1778) and mathematician Maria Gaetana Agnesi (1718–1799), Caminer virtually added them to the dictionary in a kind of journalistic appendix to the work. Among the important contemporary Italian women that she vindicated in this review was Luisa Bergalli herself.

Living Ties: A Female Network

Indeed, among the compelling reasons to examine Carriera, Bergalli, and Caminer together are their shared connections. Despite the differences in profession and age (Carriera was thirty years older than Bergalli; Bergalli was forty-eight years older than Caminer), they were to varying degrees each other's mentors, friends, and colleagues. Ties between Carriera and Bergalli are found in the extant letters from their correspondence, in the portrait Carriera made of Bergalli (see Figure 5.2),[38] and in some of the latter's published works. Direct links between Bergalli and Caminer are less easily traced, but their published works and their individual relationships to the Venetian playwright Carlo Gozzi (brother-in-law to Bergalli) reveal interesting connections. A careful perusal of archival sources and a general knowledge of literary and artistic figures in the Lagoon city during the women's lifetimes make it possible to trace documented connections among the women and to speculate further about the personal and professional relationships that Carriera, Bergalli, and Caminer may have shared with each other.

ROSALBA CARRIERA AND LUISA BERGALLI

The friendship between Rosalba Carriera and Luisa Bergalli brought both women personal and professional benefits and allows us a glimpse into the profitable intersection of literary and artistic circles in eighteenth-century Venice. Although it is not clear exactly how or when the two met, Bergalli was frequenting the Carriera household at least as early as 1723—the year she turned twenty—and Carriera had made a portrait of Bergalli by 1724 (the year the artist turned fifty-one).[39] The extant letters from their correspondence confirm that their friendship continued into the following two decades.[40] Throughout this period in her life, Carriera, who never married, was living in Venice with her mother and younger sister, Giovanna.[41] The Carriera home was of course also functioning as Rosalba's studio, and Giovanna and other female apprentices worked there as her assistants. In fact, the unconventional Carriera household was run entirely by women and financially maintained by Rosalba's profitable business. It was often filled with artists, progressive thinkers, writers, and grand-tourists, and it seems that Bergalli was a regular visitor there, together with her future husband, the count Gasparo Gozzi. Perhaps the Carriera sisters' home was a place where Bergalli could comfortably spend time with Gozzi during the long and unconventional courtship she enjoyed with him—a man ten years her junior—prior to their interclass marriage. In addition to her friendship with Rosalba, Luisa shared a passionate interest in poetry and literature with Giovanna, who, like her, was well versed in Latin and was an accomplished poet.

If the fact that the Carriera household was entirely made up of women is significant for our discussion of the development of friendship and professional networking among women, then it is important to consider what was perhaps the single most important factor contributing to the absence of men: Rosalba Carriera's decision not to marry. The artist's unmarried status has been much discussed in more than two centuries of biographical accounts, and the most common image of Carriera that emerges from these studies is that of a devout, austere, rather asexual woman who was so completely devoted to her mother, her sisters, and her art that she simply did not have room for suitors or a husband. In an often-cited letter among Carriera's papers, she rejects the attentions of a suitor by positing her dedication to her work as the central reason she must refute the very idea of marriage. But she also describes herself as having a "cold, withdrawing nature" which renders her unsuitable for marriage:

> My work, which keeps me too busy, and a natural coldness have always kept me far from suitors and thoughts of marriage. I would certainly make the world laugh if now, having already passed my youth, I entered into such things.[42]

Are we to read this description ingenuously, or should we view this "cold spinster" as a public persona Carriera was purposefully creating to ward off potential suitors—or in this case, to soften the blow of her rejection?[43]

Because most successful female artists prior to Carriera were related either by blood or marriage to professional male artists, a potential husband for Carriera would likely have been a professional artist himself. Carriera might have decided to remain single in order not to risk having her career subordinated to a husband's artistic career. Another factor that almost certainly contributed to Carriera's decision or ability to remain single was her financial success, since the independence it allowed her freed her from having to rely on a husband to support her financially.[44] Furthermore, since one of the primary eighteenth-century arguments against educating women or allowing women professional careers was the fear of their subsequent neglect of husband and children, Carriera may have consciously avoided that obstacle altogether by not marrying or having children.

Was Carriera for all intents and purposes "married" to her art or dedicated to her studio of young apprentices? A letter to the artist from Rosanna Pozzolo, one of her former pupils, may shed some light on these questions.[45] In 1739, Pozzolo wrote to her former mentor to tell her that, after great effort, she had secured work in the studio (*scuola*) of the painter Antonio Dei Pieri in Vicenza. In the same breath she lamented the fact that her "lack of merit" and her "misfortune" did not permit her to work for Carriera as she would have preferred. The most striking part of the letter is Pozzolo's bald description of her difficult circumstances and her claim that her art is primarily a means to achieve professional autonomy and the goal of personal freedom. In fact, she actually positions her desire to remain independent—free from husband and brother—above her art:

> Believe me, there is no other reason for my perseverance in drawing [*disigniare*], than my having decided that I do not want to marry; moreover, until now I have had such little good fortune that I do not know how I was able to maintain this opinion, but thinking about my station, [and] being of scant resources, I dedicated myself with all my might. . . .

The letter is illuminating for our discussion because of Pozzolo's absolute surety that Carriera would approve of her choice of career over marriage—or better, her use of a career to avoid marriage altogether. "I think that you will be pleased with my resolution, and will judge it excellent," she continues, "and [you will be pleased] to know that the love and goodness you have heretofore shown me, have given me the courage to notify you [of this]."[46] While I do not intend to extrapolate a direct parallel with Carriera's case, it is nevertheless clear that Pozzolo viewed the older artist as a role model when making these life choices and was confident that her mentor shared the same values. Her letter dramatizes the direct links between the limited personal and professional options available to women. In doing so, it may offer some perspective on Carriera's retort to a correspondent that there was "nothing in the world" she thought less about than men.[47] Although I do not intend to speculate about Carriera's sexual orientation in this chapter, one must also consider the possibility that she may simply have preferred not to make a life with a man.

It is worthwhile to keep Carriera's choices about marriage and career in mind when considering her friendship and professional collaboration with Bergalli. The two women's experiences make for a striking contrast between Carriera on the one hand as a financially successful, single artist and self-sufficient businesswoman, and Bergalli on the other, whose literary career was greatly diminished once she married and bore five children into a family that was in constant, serious financial difficulty.[48]

Prior to Bergalli's marriage, in addition to offering the writer access to an uncommon and intellectually stimulating environment, Carriera probably also taught her how to draw and paint in her studio. This aspect of the Carriera-Bergalli relationship merits further attention. The women's correspondence reveals that Carriera sent some pastels to Bergalli in 1741, after the latter was married and living in the Gozzi family residence outside Venice. Certainly, Bergalli had been an accomplished enough amateur some years earlier for the Emperor Charles VI's secretary, the Conte Antonio Rambaldo Collalto, to request that she send him a self-portrait. It is important to note that this was not to be a simple, straightforward portrait. Rather, Collalto, a keen admirer of Bergalli's, had requested that the portrait be "istoriato con idea pittoresca"—meaning with literary or allegorical elements—and that Bergalli should be depicted "in idealized poetic dress."[49] Such a request implies that Collalto believed not only that Bergalli was capable of the manual skill to produce a simple likeness (that is, directly imitate nature) but also that she had the intellectual and creative talent to invent a pleasing, allegorical composition. Perhaps Bergalli, who at the time of her 1741 letter to Carriera had been married for nearly three years and would soon be pregnant with her third child, wished to continue developing the skills her friend had taught her. She promises Carriera: "As soon as I can find a moment free from my familial occupations, I will put my desire to the test." With a nod of respect for her friend's immense talent, however, she hastens to add that she knows she will be utterly unable to adequately honor Carriera's kindness and attention in sending her the pastels, as such an endeavor is "beyond my abilities."[50]

Carriera's and Bergalli's friendship was also formed around the exchange of literary works. Even in a city as rich in books as Venice, most readers did not have the luxury of an extensive personal library, and such book-swapping was an essential mechanism in the circulation of new ideas during the eighteenth century. It is therefore important to regard any literary exchange between Carriera and Bergalli in the context of Bergalli's career as translator and playwright. A letter Bergalli wrote to Carriera in 1736 is illuminating in this regard. At the time she penned the letter to her friend, Bergalli had already published, among other works, four original theatrical compositions and a two-volume translation of Terence's comedies. In this letter, she thanks her friend for the loan of two volumes of French playwright Pierre Corneille's works, which she is now returning.[51] She also requests the subsequent two volumes from the collection.

Bergalli's interest in Corneille's works was not likely to have been casual; the very same year she wrote this letter—probably in the same months— Bergalli published her translation of the works of Corneille's peer and rival, Jean Racine. Furthermore, in the same letter Bergalli asked to borrow her friend's volumes of Molière's comedies, one of which, the *Misanthrope*, she would later translate and publish. For her part, Bergalli kept the Carriera sisters informed of where they might purchase more translations of French theatrical works: "these translations of French comedies and tragedies have already begun to come out and are selling at Lovisa's [bookshop] at the Rialto for 10 *soldi* each." Since it was in fact Domenico Lovisa who published Bergalli's translation of Racine's *Opere,* and since Bergalli's name as translator did not appear in the publication, this comment to Carriera may also exemplify a degree of self-promotion on her part.[52] In any case, Carriera had the financial resources and Bergalli the connections to the publishing world to make literary collaboration satisfying and successful.

Bergalli promoted the reputations of the three Carriera sisters and Rosalba's favored pupil, Felicita Sartori,[53] in her published works. When Luisa published her 1726 anthology of poetry by Italian women, for example, she included Giovanna Carriera among the contemporary poets. She also included a sonnet of her own that she dedicated to the three Carriera sisters. Bergalli's poem holds Rosalba and her sisters up as examples of the many Venetian women who "on canvas and on the page / give to others and to themselves eternal life." In an echo of her claims in the Foreword to the anthology, Bergalli again challenges those who "scorn the gentle sex" and claims that Venetian women are especially deserving of recognition, for she does not have to "seek out another more blessed City / in some distant clime" to find undeniable proof "of the talents which the Heavens grant to women."[54]

Literary and artistic collaboration between Bergalli and Carriera increased in subsequent years. A decade later, when Bergalli published the second edition of the collection of her translations of Terence's comedies, she dedicated one of the plays to Carriera. In the dedication, Bergalli says that she did so without forewarning her friend, because she knew that Rosalba would have protested. She extols Carriera's reputation which, "thanks to her beautiful Paintings, has penetrated everywhere." The poet writes that the artist has been welcomed and her work "magnificently collected by the most important Monarchs of Europe" whose galleries are not "complete . . . or ornate enough if they do not have the portraits of Princes done in [her] hand."[55] Bergalli also uses the dedication to praise Carriera's mother for having educated all three of her daughters so well "in Languages, the Arts, and the Sciences."[56] Perhaps she chose Terence's *The Brothers* among the other comedies she translated as the one to dedicate to Carriera because its subject was the education of children (albeit in reference to a father and his sons).

In 1736, Bergalli published a collection of poetry written by her recently deceased mentor and friend, Antonio Sforza, and she appended to this collection a group of poems written in Sforza's honor by friends and contemporaries.[57] She commissioned Carriera's pupil, Felicita Sartori, for the portrait of Sforza which appears in the volume's opening pages. It seems that Sartori had previously drawn Sforza's portrait, which she then engraved for this collection. In further promotion of the Carriera studio, Bergalli included in the collection a poem she wrote in praise of Sartori. Here the poet admires the talents the young artist already displays and speculates on the fame and recognition that await her as she will mature and gain wisdom: "It seems I already see your glory / rising, oh Woman. . . ."[58]

The following year, when Bergalli was preparing her anthology of Gaspara Stampa's poetry, she turned again to Carriera. She sent the artist portraits of Stampa and her companion the Conte Collaltino di Collalto, and asked Rosalba to convince Sartori to engrave them for her volume. Sartori, who had been reluctant to take on the project at Bergalli's request (perhaps out of excessive modesty, as Bergalli suggests in her letter to Carriera), accepted the commission only upon her mentor's urging. Sartori's engravings thus appear prominently in Bergalli's volume, which was published the following year in 1738 (Figure 5.4).[59] Through these collaborative efforts, Bergalli provided a venue for Sartori's work and for literary recognition of her artistic talent. In return, Bergalli's publications were enhanced by the portraits included in them. As these examples illustrate, Bergalli's and Carriera's friendship fostered and was fostered by profitable literary and artistic collaboration over the years.

LUISA BERGALLI AND ELISABETTA CAMINER

Luisa Bergalli and Elisabetta Caminer were two of the most important women writers of eighteenth-century Venice. Although it appears that

Figure 5.4 Felicita Sartori after Daniel Antonio Bertoli, *Portrait of Gaspara Stampa*, in *Rime di Madonna Gaspara Stampa* (Venezia: Francesco Piacentini, 1738). Biblioteca Nazionale Marciana, Venice.

they did not share the kind of friendship that Carriera and Bergalli enjoyed, they did have much in common. They were active in the theater, both as translators of literary works and as directors of theatrical productions on the Venetian stage—the latter an extraordinary if not unprecedented role for Italian women. Bergalli and Caminer were both passionate defenders of women's intellectual and literary abilities, and they both dedicated aspects of their careers to promoting the reputations and the work of past and contemporary women writers. In addition, through connections within the Venetian Republic of Letters, they certainly frequented the same circles, even if indirectly and primarily through correspondence networks.

In 1768–69, when Caminer was making her professional debut as journalist and theatrical translator, Bergalli's literary career was for all intents and purposes over. She had published original theatrical compositions and translations, anthologies of poetry by Italian women, collections of occasional poetry, and an almanac of illustrious women.[60] By the age of sixty-five, she had raised five children, endured the death of a son, directed productions at the Sant'Angelo theater for a year, and tried unsuccessfully to help manage the impoverished Gozzi family income. Her family life had not been conducive to sustained, independent literary work on Bergalli's part, although she did enjoy a remarkable degree of successful literary collaboration with her spouse over the years. She and her family had been obliged to change residences several times over the years in continual attempts to lower the cost of living, even though this meant they were forced to leave Venice for periods of time to reside in the Gozzi terraferma home in Visinale where the cost of living was much lower. Along with her husband, mother-in-law, and sisters-in-law, Bergalli was enmeshed for decades in at least eighty legal battles with her brother-in-law Carlo Gozzi over how to manage the family properties left to them at her father-in-law's death. Worsening financial pressures and endless familial conflict in the larger Gozzi family ultimately contributed to the dissolution of her marriage.

Nevertheless, Bergalli did remain active within the literary sphere until the final years of her life, and she was the most prominent Venetian woman of letters in the first half of the eighteenth century. It seems likely that Caminer would have viewed her in some way as a predecessor or even a role model of sorts; indeed, the young journalist's review of the French dictionary of illustrious women confirms this notion. As we mentioned earlier, in the review Caminer highlights Bergalli's presence among the important Italian women of the eighteenth century. She describes Bergalli as "the learned and most notable Venetian countess Bergalli Gozzi, who honors letters, and particularly fine poetry, with her excellent compositions. . . ." Caminer also claims that Bergalli should be admired for "the way she cultivated her own mind from the time she was a young girl."[61] It is important to note that when the eighteen-year-old Caminer penned those lines, she was struggling to educate herself, especially in matters of writing and translation. Her description of her own situation in a letter from this period echoes the words she had used to praise Bergalli; writing to the Florentine journalist and new acquaintance Giuseppe Bencivenni Pelli, Caminer complains that she is "at an age and in a situation that do not allow me to hope for mediocre knowledge, to say nothing of great learning, and yet I am full of desire to cultivate my mind."[62] Constrained to utilize whatever resources were available to her in a society that denied women access to a formal education, Caminer virtu-ally enlisted Pelli as her new mentor:

> Nor because prejudice would have women confined within unreasonable limits can I stop myself . . . from begging you for a favor that you must absolutely grant me. . . . I beg you to put into practice what you think, by alerting me "in a friendly manner" to my errors [in translating from the French], so that I might avoid them in the future. . . . Do not be amazed at this frankness of mine. I am not ashamed of it at all.[63]

Perhaps Caminer identified with what she imagined to have been Bergalli's efforts to develop her mind as an autodidact. Certainly the road for Caminer was much steeper, since Bergalli had benefited immensely from the men-torship and the extensive personal library of Apostolo Zeno, the librettist and court poet in Vienna during the first quarter of the eighteenth century (1718–1731).[64]

If Caminer looked to Bergalli in 1769 when writing a review of a diction-ary of illustrious women for her periodical, then four years later the seventy-year-old Bergalli did not forget the young Caminer when she published a collection of poetry in honor of the Venetian patrician Caterina Dolfin Tron.[65] Such *raccolte* of occasional verse—poetry written to commemorate births, weddings, deaths, veil takings, elections to governmental posts, and the like—were usually dedicated to aristocratic or politically prominent individuals.[66] They constituted a public forum for displaying one's poetic bravura; perhaps more important, they were essential tools for building pa-tronage networks among elite and literary society. Bergalli's *raccolta* was oc-casioned by Dolfin Tron's spouse's election to the position of *procuratore* of San Marco, one of the most important governmental posts in the Venetian Republic. However, the collection should also be viewed in the context of Bergalli's lifelong efforts to promote and honor accomplished women.

Bergalli's collection stands out for the fact that it was dedicated to Dolfin Tron and not to her husband, for the fact that all its contributors were women, and for its very title—*Rime di donne illustri a sua eccellenza Caterina Dolfina Tron cavaliera e procuratessa* (Poems by Illustrious Women for Her Excellency Caterina Dolfin Cavalaressa and Procuratessa Tron*)*—which places as much emphasis on the exceptional qualities of the contributors as on the woman who is subject of their praise. Indeed, this raccolta appears to be the last compilation of poetry by women that Bergalli ever published.[67] By inviting Caminer to participate in it, Bergalli was welcoming the young writer into the ranks of the more established female poets contributing to the collection, some of whom belonged to the Arcadian Academy, which Caminer did not.[68] In fact, perhaps as a special gesture of patronage toward the younger woman of letters, Bergalli added the title "illustrious" (*illustre*) to Caminer's name in the raccolta, something she did for only one of the eighteen other contributors to the collection.

By the same token, Caminer's contribution to the collection should be understood in the context of her own outspoken claims to women's intellectual equality with men. While her poem functions on one level as a requisite panegyric for Caterina Dolfin Tron and for Venice itself, we may also read it as an example of her continued participation in the debate on the condition of women. In the context of contemporary arguments about the biological inferiority of the female sex, Caminer consistently argued that society, not nature, was responsible for any apparent deficiencies in women's ability to learn, imagine, and think abstractly on a par with men. So long as women were denied access to a solid education, she believed, they would be unable to realize their full potential, intellectually or socially. When, in her contribution to the *Rime di donne illustri,* Caminer holds Dolfin Tron up as a "clear example of how much noble intelligence / And knowledge *Nature* has bestowed upon our sex,"[69] she refutes the notion that women's minds are in any way biologically inferior to those of men, however lyrically she phrases it here. Caminer's "proof" of her sex's natural intelligence was thus published in a collection which itself constituted a living network of women joining together in the life of the pen.[70]

It is impossible to discuss connections between Bergalli and Caminer without analyzing the women's histories with a shared personal and professional antagonist, the playwright Carlo Gozzi, brother-in-law to Luisa.[71] It is chiefly through Gozzi's caustic comments about Bergalli in his *Memorie inutili* (Useless Memoirs) that her reputation after her death was established.[72] As Adriana Chemello has pointed out, Gozzi's comments about Bergalli in his memoirs were reproduced and his misogynist tone was even amplified by scholars throughout the nineteenth century, thereby distorting Bergalli's reputation with the power of "a deforming mirror."[73] Gozzi dismisses Bergalli's literary career in a series of disparaging comments. He claims that her publications reveal "a poetess of fancy" among the shepherdesses of Arcadia; she is a woman "of fervent and soaring imagination" prone to "high poetic flights" with no ability to regulate domestic matters of everyday life thanks to her "Pindaric raptures."[74] Gozzi describes his sister-in-law's decision to direct the season at the Sant'Angelo theater as driven by her "usual poetic plotting" with her equally typical "vagueness in terms of planning and administration." He tried unsuccessfully to persuade "that hot-headed woman" to change her mind, and he deeply regretted that she succeeded in "seducing" his brother into taking on the venture with her.[75] And while Gozzi writes in detail about a sonnet of his that was included in the new edition of Gaspara Stampa's poetry (1738), he fails to mention that Bergalli was the editor of that volume.[76] In fact, it was Luisa who appended the collection of poems by her contemporaries, including Gozzi's sonnet and several of her own poems, to Stampa's poetry.

Yet Carlo Gozzi seems to have objected most strongly not to Bergalli's literary ambitions but to her power and influence within the Gozzi household. When he returned to the family residence in Visinale in 1744 after his three-year sojourn in Dalmatia, Carlo found that his father had suffered a serious stroke and remained an invalid. His sister-in-law,

> in close alliance with my mother, who doted on her as the consort of her fa-vored first-born, ruled all the affairs of the family, which were rapidly going from bad to worse. My father's authority as head of the house had ceased to be more than a mere instrument for carrying out what my sister-in-law advised and my mother sanctioned.[77]

Carlo felt he needed to take action in order to prevent his family from be-ing "plunged into an abyss of ruin" at the hands of this woman who was acting the part of a "prime minister," albeit "in a realm which only existed in her imagination" (*prima ministra d'uno stato immaginario*).[78] With the subsequent death of his father in 1745, Luisa's husband, Gasparo, legally became the head of family, but he was by disposition unwilling or unable to assume a leadership role within the family and therefore to take con-trol of its dire financial situation. As a result, within a year lengthy legal battles over who should control the crumbling family resources had begun, thereby pitting Carlo against Luisa and her rather ineffectual husband for years to come.

Whereas Bergalli spent much of the 1740s and 1750s engaged in legal conflict with Gozzi, Caminer spent the years between 1770 and 1774 en-gaged in literary battle with him. During the 1760s, Carlo Gozzi had be-come the dominant playwright in Venice with the introduction of his new *fiabe*, or fantastical plays, that combined elements of fables together with the use of commedia dell'arte masks. In 1769 Elisabetta Caminer—an avid supporter of Gozzi's former rival, playwright Carlo Goldoni—began introducing Venetian theatergoers to the latest trend in French theater, the *drame bourgeois*. This new theatrical genre featured the everyday lives of individuals from the middle classes rather than those of kings and princes. It had a decisively pedagogical intent: to inspire moral behavior in the general public by giving examples of both virtuous and vice-ridden characters with whom the audience could identify. For Caminer and supporters of the bourgeois drama, the emotional involvement of the audience was an effective means by which to educate the broader public. Caminer's translations of the most recent plays by Baculard d'Arnaud, Fénouillot de Falbaire, de Belloy, Mercier, and Saurin were published and performed on stages in Venice, Padua, Bologna, and probably elsewhere in Italy. These didactic dramas flew in the face of Gozzi's conviction that theatergoers wanted pure entertainment, not instruction on moral behavior. More important, he found the content of bourgeois drama to be anything but edifying; plays featuring interclass marriage or portraying a military deserter as a victim of unjust laws rather than a traitor to his king threatened the ancien régime traditions so fiercely embraced by the aristocratic Gozzi.

The Caminer-Gozzi polemic took place on the stage and on the page as the writers competed for the attention of the Venetian theatergoers. While Caminer was overseeing performances of her translations at the Sant'Angelo theater (1769–1771), Gozzi was directing productions of his plays at the San Salvatore theater during the same period. Between 1772 and 1774, they engaged in a volume-by-volume race to publish these works (her translations, his original works), just as they had directed their respective acting troupes in the performances of competing plays.[79] Bergalli would not have missed the fact that Caminer was operating out of the very theater that she herself had managed more than twenty years earlier, the only woman to follow in her footsteps. It is hard to imagine that Bergalli would not have read these plays or attended some of these performances. She might have done so in order to keep abreast of the latest theatrical trends, to get a closer look at this ambitious young woman of letters, or perhaps even to enjoy seeing her difficult brother-in-law challenged by Caminer. In fact, it was in the midst of the Caminer-Gozzi conflict that Bergalli invited Caminer to contribute to her collection of poetry in honor of Dolfin Tron.

Whereas Gozzi's attacks on Bergalli had been largely personal and were published after her death, his criticisms of Caminer were professional and were published throughout her career (as well as after her death). In 1772 he sarcastically described Caminer and her supporters as "blind enlightened ones," and "slaves of a most vile subjugation to foreign writers" who spend their talents "scratching like hens, sniffing like hounds, and translating as best they know how those French works."[80] Gozzi also criticized Caminer for her journalistic work, berating the "young girl" for not having been satisfied with becoming "an ornament" of society capable of rendering a felicitous translation. Instead, she had insisted on becoming the "Capitanessa of a newspaper entitled the *Europa letteraria*" where "she gives her opinions, condemns, praises, and absolves magisterially all writers and all books on all subjects."[81] Gozzi's published criticisms of Bergalli and Caminer directly affected their personal and professional reputations and reveal his (and by extension his society's) discomfort with their ambitions to power and influence, whether as a "prima ministra" in the domestic sphere or as a "Capitanessa" of literary Europe.

The lives and careers of Rosalba Carriera, Luisa Bergalli Gozzi, and Elisabetta Caminer Turra—three Venetian women from the middle classes— shed light on how women were actively making public contributions to literary and artistic culture in Venice during the eighteenth century. Rosalba Carriera pushed the boundaries of miniature and pastel painting and elevated the image of the female artist. Luisa Bergalli secured greater recognition for Italian women poets past and present and anticipated Carlo Goldoni's reform of the Italian theater with her original theatrical writing and direction of performances on the Venetian stage. Elisabetta Caminer spread Enlightenment ideas through her journalistic writing and her printing press, and she expanded upon Goldoni's reform of the Italian theater with her popularization of the new French drame bourgeois. Both Bergalli and Caminer contributed greatly to the debate on the condition of women, arguing for women's intellectual equality with men. All three women found ways to work within the patriarchal structures of their society even as they challenged the notions that upheld them. Future research may well offer further insight into how these women, and perhaps others like them, created informal female networks to support and promote each other's literary and artistic careers.

Luisa Bergalli's sonnet "To the Three Most Worthy Carriera Sisters" which she published in her anthology of *Componimenti poetici delle più illustri rimatrici d'ogni secolo* (Poetic Compositions by the Most Illustrious Women Poets from Every Century) is worth citing here in full for the way it forges a link between women writers and artists.[82] While Bergalli holds up the Carriera sisters as proof that "the Heavens" do not "condemn Women to the needle and to the spindle," she is also clearly linking and celebrating *all* talented Venetian women writers and artists:

> If, when I will have greater help from Apollo,
> Someone will hear me sing in scattered rhyme
> Of the talents which the Heavens grant to women,
> Let him not judge me an impertinent young woman.
>
> For, without having to seek out
> another more blessed City, in some distant clime,
> I will point to several who, on canvas or on the page,
> Give to others and to themselves eternal life.
>
> You who scorn the gentle sex,
> Come and admire the works of Angela, of Rosalba and of Giovanna,
> and then say what you have to say.
>
> And tell me if I lie, or if Passion blinds me,
> and tell me whether it is true that the Heavens condemn
> Women to the needle and to the spindle.

Bergalli uses the center of the sonnet to impress upon her readers that these talented women "give to others and to themselves eternal life" through the legacy of their creative work, whether it be "on canvas" or "on the page." In other words, she suggests to her readers, it is by producing and publishing their work—and by honoring each other's work in venues like this very sonnet and anthology—that women can assure themselves (and their female peers) of well-earned fame and recognition. Bergalli's sonnet thus functions as a synecdoche for her larger project of reclaiming recognition for women's achievements in the past, and for promoting those women currently shaping literary and artistic culture. The poem, dedicated to three Venetian women artists and sisters, and published in an anthology dedicated to many women writers, embodies the very notion of a network of women shaping culture in eighteenth-century Venice.

"The Residence of the Arts"

Angelica Kauffman's Place in Rome

WENDY WASSYNG ROWORTH

Angelica Kauffman (1741–1807) was one of the most popular artists in Rome at the end of the eighteenth century, and as one of few women painters to achieve such recognition she holds a special place in the history of art[1] (Figure 6.1). Kauffman, in turn, always held a special place in her heart for the city of Rome, where as a young artist she enjoyed her first success as a history painter and where she lived and worked almost continuously, except for several sojourns in Naples, from 1782 until her death in 1807, when she was finally laid to rest in the church of S. Andrea della Fratte in the heart of the city she loved. Before settling in Rome Kauffman had lived and worked in London from 1766 to 1781, where she achieved wealth and critical acclaim. Nevertheless, according to her Italian biographer Giovanni Gherardo De Rossi, Kauffman always longed to return to Rome, a view supported

I would like to gratefully acknowledge the support of the University of Rhode Island Center for the Humanities Tom Silvia and Shannon Chandley Fellowship which allowed me to conduct research in Rome during a sabbatical leave in 2004–05 and the Getty Research Institute for a Library Research Grant in 2003 to study the Kauffman inventory and other documents in their Special Collections.

Figure 6.1 Angelica Kauffman, *Self-Portrait*, 1787 (oil on canvas, 128 x 93.5 cm). Florence, Uffizi. Scala/Art Resource, New York.

by a poignant note he discovered among her personal papers in London: "*Roma mi è sempre in pensiero*" (Rome is ever in my thoughts).[2]

Despite these sentiments and the evidence of Kauffman's twenty-five-year residence in Rome, her work has been seen primarily within the context of English art rather than in relation to artistic developments in Italy. She is considered a member of the "British School," while at the same time both the Swiss and the Austrians claim her as one of their own because of her family origins. De Rossi, nevertheless, asserted that in spite of her birth in Switzerland to a Swiss mother and Austrian father, Kauffman should be considered "come d'Italiana pittrice" (as an Italian painter), for it was in Italy that her talent first took root and was cultivated.[3] As a rare female artist who did not belong to any single nationality or school, especially at a time when the concept of nationalism itself was evolving, Kauffman may best be understood within the international milieu of Rome, where she first launched her career and later practiced her profession. As the English traveler Joseph Forsyth wrote in his journal in 1802, "I have heard Angelica say that the water of Rome revived her powers, and gave her ideas."[4]

The artist's own wistful words, "Roma mi è sempre in pensiero," were adopted by art historian Anthony Morris Clark for the title of his 1968 essay on Kauffman and Rome.[5] He traced the development of her early Roman manner in the mid-1760s, identified artists who influenced her work—most notably Anton Raphael Mengs and Pompeo Batoni—and situated her later paintings within the context of new stylistic trends in the 1780s and 1790s. Clark's essay was significant for first calling attention to Kauffman's painting in relation to artists active in Rome, including Antonio Cavallucci, Tommaso Conca, Giuseppe Cades, Anton von Maron, Gaspare Landi, and Jacques Louis David, as well as major art projects such as the decoration of the Casino of the Villa Borghese and the new Museo Pio-Clementino built to house the papal collections. Though Clark's essay situated Kauffman within the Roman milieu, he focused almost exclusively on issues of artistic style, influence, and pictorial sources with little regard for Kauffman's life in Rome or her unique situation as a woman in a decidedly masculine profession. More recently, the art exhibitions *Il Settecento a Roma* (Palazzo Venezia, Rome, 2005–06), *Il Neoclassicismo in Italia da Tiepolo a Canova* (Palazzo Reale, Milan, 2002), *The Splendor of Eighteenth-Century Rome* (Philadelphia Art Museum / Museum of Fine Arts, Houston, 2000), and *Angelika Kauffman e Roma* (Accademia di San Luca, Rome, 1998) increased awareness of Kauffman's work and presence in that city.[6] The purpose of the present chapter is to reconsider Kauffman's place in Rome by focusing on her literal location—the house in which she lived and worked—as well as her symbolic place, especially in regard to her gender, within the history of art in that city.

Kauffman first visited Rome in 1763 when she and her artist father, Johann Joseph Kauffman, journeyed to the major art centers of Italy, including Milan, Venice, Bologna, Parma, Florence, Rome, and Naples, to further her artistic education through visits to public and private art collections. This working trip was standard practice for young painters—standard, that is, for men—who learned to emulate the best artists of the past by copying artworks and studying antique statuary. Copies of Old Master paintings were also a good source of income; they were in great demand by foreign Grand Tourists who wanted replicas of celebrated works by Raphael, Titian,

Correggio, Domenichino, and Guido Reni to decorate their homes and to serve as reminders of their travels abroad. As a member of the "gentle sex," she was granted the special privilege of working alone in a private room in the Uffizi and permitted to make copies in the royal collection at Capodimonte. In Naples many English tourists were captivated by this gifted and by all accounts charming young woman, and she made portraits of, among others, the celebrated actor David Garrick (Burghley House, Stamford), the Marquis of Exeter (Burghley House), and the British Consul Isaac Jamineau (Bregenz, Vorarlberger Landesmuseum). It was in Rome, however, under the inspiration of the German antiquarian Johann Joachim Winckelmann and the encouragement of resident British artists Gavin Hamilton and Nathaniel Dance that Kauffman advanced her aspiration to become a *history painter* of subjects from classical and modern history, literature, mythology, and scripture. In academic theory since the Renaissance, history painting was classified as the noblest and most difficult genre—the equivalent of the epic form in poetry—and a highly unusual choice for a woman artist. Most female painters in the seventeenth and eighteenth centuries, with a few noteworthy exceptions such as Artemisia Gentileschi, specialized in still life painting or portraiture, genres considered less demanding than history painting but also less prestigious. Because these "lower" genres were based on direct imitation of nature, their practitioners did not require knowledge of history or literature, extensive study of human anatomy, or the ability to portray complex multifigured actions in large-scale compositions. Thus they were thought to be more practical as well as appropriate for women, who for the most part were denied access to academic training and the freedom to travel. Angelica Kauffman was fortunate to have a father who recognized his daughter's considerable talent and was eager to exploit as well as encourage her ambition.[7] De Rossi praised Kauffman for her rationality, reflection, striving for the best, and her attempt to pursue the challenging career of history painter, the aim of her desires.[8]

With its rich artistic heritage, Rome was the ideal place for an aspiring history painter. The great collections of antiquities and exemplary works by Raphael, Michelangelo, Annibale Carracci, Guido Reni, and other outstanding painters in numerous palaces and churches served as inspiration and models. Painters and sculptors (though not women artists) could draw from living models in the Accademia del Nudo, founded by Pope Benedict XIV in 1754; the Accademia di San Luca, the Roman art academy, held annual competitions to spur artists on to higher achievement.[9] Kauffman gained membership in this prestigious academy in June 1765, with a reception piece which represented an allegory of Hope personified as a pensive young woman, a reference perhaps to her desire for a successful career.[10] She had already been granted memberships in the art academies of Florence (1762) and Bologna (1762) before she arrived in Rome, though despite such apparent acceptance her sex always set her apart from male colleagues, a difference which provided both positive attention as well as limited expectations.[11]

By 1765 Kauffman had several commissions for portraits and history paintings from British travelers, and her new English friends persuaded her to pursue her career in England, where, they assured her, she would find steadier employment than in Rome. In contrast to the British travelers, Italians apparently had less interest in portraits than in paintings of religious or classical subjects, a factor which helped to encourage her move to London.[12] She accepted the invitation of Lady Wentworth, wife of the British Resident in Venice John Murray, to accompany her to England, and soon after her arrival in London in June 1766 Kauffman received new commissions from Lady Spencer and the Marquis of Exeter, whom she had met in Italy. She was introduced to the influential painter Joshua Reynolds, who recognized her exceptional skill as a history painter as well as a portraitist and became one of her staunchest supporters. Within two years of her arrival in England, Kauffman was a Founding Member of the Royal Academy of Arts (1768)—one of only two women—and a fashionable, well-paid society artist with aristocratic patrons, including the Princess of Wales and the Duchess of Richmond.[13]

Despite her popularity and steady work in London, Kauffman continued to yearn for Italy. In 1772 she wrote to Giuseppe Beltramelli, an art dealer in Bergamo, about her triumphs in England and Ireland; yet, she confessed, Italy was in her heart and she hoped to return.[14] As De Rossi later declared, Angelica never forgot Rome, and even from her first days on the Thames the desire to return was fixed in her heart and never died.[15]

Though she seems to have contemplated a trip to Italy at least as early as 1779, it was not until July 1781 that Kauffman and her elderly father, who had joined her in London in 1767, were able to make the journey. In failing health, Johann Joseph Kauffman wished to revisit his old home and to spend his final years in the mild Italian climate, though his poor condition caused them to postpone the journey for many months.[16] When they finally left England they were accompanied by Angelica's new husband, the

Venetian artist Antonio Zucchi, another foreign resident in England. Her decision to marry the considerably older Zucchi at this time may have been prompted by her father's desire to ensure that after his death his daughter would have the male companionship, protection, and assistance he had provided her entire life, though Angelica seems to have been very attached to Zucchi, who had been the Kauffmans' good friend for many years.

I believe that Angelica Kauffman's return to Italy was motivated by more than a daughter's duty to her father. Under the papacy of Pius VI (1775–1799), Rome was an exciting center of artistic innovation and commerce, archeological discoveries, tourism, building projects, and new museums.[17] Though she made a good living in London, especially through collaborations with printmakers and publishers such as Francesco Bartolozzi and Josiah Boydell, Kauffman missed the ready access to great works of art and antiquities in Rome and the prospect of increased patronage for history paintings, including religious subjects for a Catholic clientele. Despite the academic ideal of history painting as the most elevated genre and the exhortations of Royal Academy President Sir Joshua Reynolds, the English remained generally uninterested in history paintings by contemporary artists. In addition, intense rivalry among portrait painters in London, internal politics in the Royal Academy (including resentment of foreign artists), competition for exhibition venues and advantageous hanging space in the annual exhibitions, and the contentious and often bitingly critical London press may all have contributed to Kauffman's desire to leave that city.[18] Though she was a popular success, she could not compete for the highest honors, royal favors, or most profitable commissions with more powerful male colleagues, especially Sir Joshua Reynolds and Benjamin West. Kauffman and West had met as equals—two young outsiders—during her first visit to Rome in 1763 before both artists pursued their careers in England. However, while West went on to win acclaim in London as an innovative painter of contemporary history, Royal Painter to George III, and eventually president of the Royal Academy of Arts, Kauffman was not able to fulfill her highest aspirations to produce significant large-scale history paintings or to fully participate in academic discourse.[19] In contrast, her situation in Rome was very different. As Joseph Forsyth reported after his visit to Italy, "This amiable woman is the idol of her invidious profession, the only artist beloved by all the rest."[20]

Furthermore, I suggest that Kauffman missed the informal relations and social interactions she had enjoyed with male artists, writers, and intellectuals, including Winckelmann, during her youthful years in Italy, as evidenced by her exclusively male portraits from this period and a sketchbook filled with male sitters, including the English author James Boswell, cicerone and art dealer James Byres, the eminent American doctor John Morgan, the Scottish Abbé Peter Grant, and artists Benjamin West, Nathaniel Dance, Johann Friedrich Reiffenstein, and Giovanni Battista Piranesi.[21] Comments by those who met her in Rome and Naples in the 1760s suggest that Angelica enjoyed the flattering attention as well as relative freedom to pursue her art. On her return to Rome she would have been delighted with the city's vibrant salon culture in which (as Maria Pia Donato argues in Chapter 2) women played a major role in conversazione with antiquarians, artists, and Arcadians. As a mature artist with an established reputation, Kauffman resumed her career with renewed enthusiasm and opportunity. She went to England to make money, but she returned to Rome for art and the receptive community in which to produce it.

Kauffman and Zucchi first considered establishing their residence in Naples with its mild climate; however, as De Rossi emphasized, Rome was Angelica's desired goal.[22] On their way to Italy they stayed with family for several weeks in Kauffman's native village of Schwarzenberg, followed by a visit with Zucchi's relatives in Venice. During the journey, Johann Joseph Kauffman's condition declined, and he died in Venice in January 1782. After a brief period of mourning, Angelica and Antonio Zucchi resumed their trip south in the spring. They stopped long enough in Rome to make arrangements for new living quarters before going to Naples, where they planned to spend the summer. The couple commissioned an agent, Gioacchino Prosperi, to locate and furnish a commodious house with about fifteen rooms, a stable, storerooms, and garden, as well as a couple of servants, including a cook, to be ready for their return from Naples.[23] According to Prosperi's memoir, he found a suitable place even before they left Rome, and when he took Kauffman to view the house she was delighted to see it had everything she desired.[24]

The queen of Naples, Maria Carolina, who already owned a large collection of engravings after Kauffman's paintings, invited her to remain in Naples as a member of the court. Kauffman humbly declined this great honor because she valued her freedom and had already decided to settle in Rome. Despite her disappointment, the queen commissioned a large group portrait of the royal family to include her husband, King Ferdinand IV, and their six children. Kauffman made portrait drawings of each family member and promised to return to Naples after she completed the painting in Rome.[25]

In anticipation of establishing her permanent residence in Rome, Kauffman wrote from Naples to her kinsman in Schwarzenberg, Joseph Anton
Metzler, in June 1782, admitting that Naples was very beautiful but "Rome
is the residence of the fine arts" (Rom ist der sitz der schönen Künsten)—
a sentiment she repeated two months later, once again calling Rome "*die
Residenz der schönen Künst.*"[26] She similarly described her agreeable stay in
Naples in a later letter to her friend Dr. William Fordyce in London, re-
porting that she was now completing the important royal portrait in "*Rome
the residence of the arts.*"[27] The emphasis is Kauffman's own, for she was delighted to return to the city where she found inspiration and could realize
her ambition to produce paintings on a scale she was not able to achieve
in London.

The huge portrait (approximately ten by fourteen feet) of King Ferdinand
IV and Queen Maria Carolina with their six children in an idyllic rustic setting was acclaimed by visitors who saw the work in progress in her Roman
studio (Figure 6.2). The poet Polidente Melpomenio (Ippolito Pindemonte,

Figure 6.2 Angelica Kauffman, *King Ferdinand IV and Queen Maria Carolina of Naples
with Their Children*, 1782–1784 (oil on canvas, 310 x 426 cm). Naples, Museo Nazionale
di Capodimonte. Scala/Art Resource, New York.

Perinto Sceo in Arcadia) composed verses in praise of the artist and singled out this portrait for particular admiration:[28]

> . . . You return, and Rome, difficult Rome,
> Spying in your sweet, sacred refuge
> the Parthenopean Deities and their
> Divine offspring reborn, thanks to your creator brush,
> and happily applauds. . . .

The poet's sentiments underscore the significance of her return to Rome and her talent for flattering portraits as well as capturing public attention. When the artist brought the finished work back to Naples in 1784, the queen repeated her invitation for Kauffman to become a member of the royal court as painter and instructor to the princesses; but, as De Rossi reported, Angelica always entertained "maggior passione per Roma" and was steadfast in her respectful refusal.[29]

Kauffman's letter to William Fordyce cited above continued: ". . . the air at Naples deed [sic] not so much agree with him [Zucchi], he is much better since we returned to Rome, where we are just fixing our selfs [sic] in winter quarter in one of the finest situations on Trinità del Monte. . . ."[30] They could not have chosen a more appropriate location, for in addition to its reputation as a salubrious site on the old Roman *collis hortulorum* on the Pincio hill above the Spanish Steps, the neighborhood was a traditional artists' district and preferred location for foreign artists since the sixteenth century.[31] She understood from her experience in London the importance of dwelling in a good neighborhood where, in addition to comfortable living quarters and a studio, there would be rooms for entertaining and displaying finished works and others in progress to potential clients.[32] The house their agent found was number 72, via Sistina, where they occupied the top two floors.[33] Prosperi furnished their home as directed, including luxurious silk hangings for the *stanza di conversazione*,[34] and he hired two male servants (one German and one Italian) along with two female domestics, who lived on the ground floor to attend to the couple's needs.[35]

The Casa Zucchi stood across the street from the Palazzo Zuccari at the intersection of the via Sistina and via Gregoriana. Originally built by Federico Zuccaro, founder of the Accademia di San Luca, the Palazzo Zuccari was home at various times to Kauffman's artist friends, including Johann Winckelmann, Johann Reiffenstein, and Johann Wilhelm Tischbein.[36] The two buildings were connected by a wooden arch over the via Sistina, the

"Arco della Regina," constructed early in the eighteenth century for the Polish queen Maria Casimira Sobieski to facilitate passage between the Palazzo Zuccari, where she lived, and the Villa Malta across the street on the hill behind the property that became the Kauffman-Zucchi garden. The Villa Malta served as temporary home for Duchess Anna Amalia of Sachsen-Weimar during her Roman sojourn in 1789, and at various times the villa housed other German visitors.[37] Angelica developed a warm friendship with Duchess Anna Amalia, and the two women visited each other frequently by walking through their adjacent gardens. Their mutual friend Goethe, who arranged the Duchess's stay in Rome, planted a palm tree at the Villa Malta and a pine tree in Kauffman's garden as a fond remembrance of his sojourn before he departed Rome in 1788.[38]

The Kauffman-Zucchi household, their active social life, and her professional work are well documented in correspondence and visitors' travel writings, including those of Hester Lynch Piozzi, who visited Rome in 1786, Johann Wolfgang von Goethe (1786–1788), Johann Gottfried Herder (1788–89), Count Leo Stolberg (1792), poet Fredrike Brun (1796), playwright August von Kotzebue (1805), and the amateur painter Marianne Kraus, who served as companion to Duchess Charlotte von Erbach on her tour of Italy in 1791. Kraus accompanied the Duchess on several visits to Kauffman and Zucchi and commented on Angelica's pretty flower garden, situated just a few steps from her painting studio.[39]

Their numerous guests included writers and artists as well as dignitaries such as Prince Stanislaus Poniatowski of Poland, King Gustav III of Sweden, and Emperor Joseph II of Austria. Kauffman's cousin Giovanni (Johann) Kauffmann from Schwarzenberg, who came to live with her around 1793, reported that at a conversazione in March 1794 more than eighty persons were in attendance, including a cardinal, a bishop, four prelates, several aristocrats, clergymen, and artists.[40] The agent Prosperi, who claimed to have become practically a member of the family, identified some of the celebrities who attended Kauffman and Zucchi's conversazioni, which sometimes lasted until three in the morning. He noted their particular friends in Rome as the printmakers Raffaello Morghen, Domenico Cunego, and Giovanni Volpato, the sculptor Antonio Canova, and the celebrated *improvvisatrici* Teresa Bandettini and Fortunata Sulgher Fantastici.[41] De Rossi confirms that Bandettini and Fantastici became Kauffman's friends when they were in Rome, that both performed exceptionally well in her house, and that she painted their portraits as gifts of friendship[42] (Figure 6.3).

Figure 6.3 Angelica Kauffman, *Portrait of Fortunata Sulgher Fantastici*, 1792 (oil on canvas, 96 x 80 cm). Florence, Galleria Palatina, Palazzo Pitti. Polo Museale Fiorentino.

Additional information about Kauffman's friends, house, and business in Rome may be gleaned from documentary sources, which include a descriptive list of her painting commissions, an account book, her will, and an inventory of the contents of the house made after her death. These sources, together with descriptions in letters and memoirs, contain information that makes it possible to imaginatively reconstruct how Kauffman lived and worked in Rome. The evidence suggests she made a conscious effort to fashion surroundings to showcase herself as a prosperous artist, discerning connoisseur, and stylish woman of good character and intellect.

Kauffman's *Memoria delle piture fatte* (sic) or memorandum of paintings, in which Zucchi and later the artist herself recorded commissions and payments from 1781 to 1798, attests to her numerous international patrons and variety of painting subjects as well as her demanding work schedule and considerable income.[43] As a complement to this evidence

of income, the Kauffman-Zucchi account book recorded purchases ranging from furniture, porcelain, silver, linens, wine, and chocolate to books,
paintings and prints, canvases, frames, brushes, and other tools of the
painter's trade.[44] This document reveals, for example, that after taking on
more than fifty commissions within two years, the couple hired workers in
October 1787 to build a new studio. In the following year, their account
book reveals costly purchases of a carriage, horses, and Renaissance paintings. In January 1788, they acquired a picture by the Venetian artist Paris
Bordone for the large sum of 1,290 *scudi*, and in the following month they
purchased Titian's *Holy Family with Saints Jerome and Mary Magdalen* for
the same amount.[45] Goethe noted Kauffman's acquisition of these impressive works of art in a letter of 9 February 1788[46]:

> Angelica has indulged herself by buying two paintings. One by Titian, the
> other by Paris Bordone. Both for a high price. Since she is so rich that she
> does not use up her investment income and earns an additional amount an-
> nually, it is commendable that she is acquiring something that delights her,
> moreover objects of a kind that increase her artistic zeal.

Kauffman's artworks and other possessions are corroborated by her last
will and testament of 1803, in which she cited "my small collection of paintings by old masters." This collection consisted largely of works by sixteenth-
and seventeenth-century artists, including Titian and Paris Bordone, cited
above, in addition to others attributed to Van Dyck, Veronese, and Leonardo
Da Vinci. Her bequests included other luxury items, including a pianoforte
she had brought from London, an English table clock made by the royal
clockmaker, a silver tea service, fine linens, and rare engravings, which confirm visitors' observations that Kauffman was a very wealthy woman.[47]

The most detailed source of information about the Kauffman-Zucchi
home is the inventory compiled by Filippo Romagnoli in January 1808,
within months of Angelica's death on 5 November 1807.[48] The inventory proceeds from room to room with brief descriptions and valuations of furniture
and household items in each room, including the kitchen, studios, storerooms, and the garden. In its current form the inventory is bound together
with the will and 1829 inventory of Kauffman's primary heir, her cousin
Giovanni (Johann) Kauffmann, who lived with her and took over management of her business interests after Zucchi's death in December 1795.

According to the inventory, one entered the Kauffman-Zucchi residence
from the landing above the ground floor into a corridor that also led to a

servant's room and the door out to the garden, which was accessed from the second floor because the house was built against the slope of the Pincio hill. The first of two reception rooms, referred to as the *camera del cantone*, occupied the corner of the house facing out toward the Piazza Barberini at the eastern end of the via Sistina. This room was decorated with green silk faille wall coverings and green striped drapes, rich furnishings confirmed by the agent Prosperi's remark that Kauffman ordered silk wall hangings for the stanza di conversazione. The paintings on the walls of this room were protected by silk curtains of the same color (*verdepomar*) to shield them from sunlight and smoke. Furniture in this room included a sofa with cushions upholstered in striped cotton, fourteen Indian cane chairs ornamented with gold with a matching sofa, a pianoforte—the instrument mentioned in her will—several small tables with carved and gilded legs, lamps, and a bookcase with glass doors containing various books. A gilt framed mirror over the marble fireplace and bisque figurines manufactured by Volpato on the mantel enhanced the décor. In addition to the valuable Old Master paintings, the room contained devotional images of Christ and the Virgin Mary, a Brussels tapestry, and two framed portraits, one of which was an unfinished portrait of Angelica Kauffman, the one described in her will as "by the late celebrated painter in London, the Knight Reynolds."[49] The lavish furnishings, including a pianoforte and a large number of chairs, suggest this was where Kauffman hosted conversazioni, poetry readings, and musical performances.

A second large salone showcased Kauffman and Zucchi's taste for the antique. The inventory lists six pedestals supporting plaster replicas of celebrated classical statues, including *Apollo Belvedere*, *Adonis*, and *Camillus* in the papal collection, *Apollino de Medici*, seated *Mercury*, and *Jove as an Eagle with Ganymede*.[50] The wall decorations continued the theme of classical antiquity with seven consoles holding portrait busts and ten framed prints of views, most likely the ten rare Cunego engravings of Rome and the vicinity of Naples cited in her will.[51] Two large bookcases held volumes of engravings of ancient buildings and works of art, such as the reliefs on the column of Trajan, the Arch of Constantine, and fresco paintings discovered in Herculaneum. Others contained prints by Giovanni Battista Piranesi and Giuseppe Vasi of ancient sites; engravings of works by Palladio, Titian, Raphael, Domenichino, Guercino, the Carracci frescoes in the Farnese Gallery in Rome, and Rubens's paintings in the Luxembourg Gallery in Paris; a series of etchings by Salvator Rosa and other unspecified books in Italian and German. These books and engravings represent a collection worthy of a discerning antiquarian and connoisseur as well as the resources of a well-educated academic artist.[52]

The German author August von Kotzebue, who visited Kauffman in 1805 just two years before her death, recorded his impression of these rooms in his travel diary: "By indefatigable industry and good fortune she has acquired a property of two hundred thousand *thaler.* . . . Her house exuded Art: from a large room quite full of statues and busts, one enters her sitting room where she has a small choice collection of old paintings kept properly protected beneath silk curtains."[53] Kauffman must have been very proud of her home and well-kept collections, for they revealed, as both Kotzebue and Goethe observed, not only her good taste but also her ability to purchase costly artworks as the result of her own labor.

Kotzebue noted several of Kauffman's own paintings displayed alongside the Old Masters in the salone. These were primarily examples of her later work and included *Three Girls Singing* (1796), *Portrait of a Scottish Gentleman* (1800), an unfinished portrait of *Antonio Canova* (ca. 1797), and history paintings of *The Prophet Nathan Reproaching David* (1797), *Hagar and Ishmael* (1793), and the *Departure of Coriolanus* (1802).[54] He also saw Angelica's portrait by Sir Joshua Reynolds (1777), the same picture cited in her inventory in the camera del cantone that was bequeathed to her cousin Giovanni, and which, Kotzebue remarked, was well known through Francesco Bartolozzi's engraving[55] (Figure 6.4). This portrait, he noted, was displayed among two fine heads by Rembrandt and Van Dyck. These portraits would likely have been two paintings mentioned in her will: Kauffman's own youthful copy (1762) of Rembrandt's 1633 self-portrait in Florence and a portrait of a man by the Flemish painter Van Dyck.[56] This arrangement appears to have been calculated to link Kauffman as both image and artist to that masculine world of great portrait painters of past and present. What we know of Kauffman's pictures, statuary, books, and fine furnishings suggests a suite of rooms designed as a suitable setting for a fashionable woman of intellectual and artistic pursuits. Her salone, described by another German visitor as a "Temple of the Muses," would have more than fulfilled expectations of potential clients who came to meet the celebrated painter.[57]

In addition to the two saloni, the apartment boasted a dining room also decorated with a number of paintings. These works included framed architectural views—most likely by Antonio Zucchi, who specialized in such compositions—and copies of Kauffman's portraits of her friends, which must have provoked particular pleasure when the subjects themselves were

Figure 6.4 Francesco Bartolozzi after Joshua Reynolds, *Portrait of Angelica Kauffman*, 1780 (stipple engraving, 34.9 x 27.3 cm). New Haven, Yale Center for British Art, Paul Mellon Collection B1977.14.12422.

present.[58] Practical evidence of Kauffman's profession could also be found in the dining room. A corner cupboard stored fabrics of silk and other materials which, a note in the inventory explained, were used to drape mannequins so the artist could study folds in cloth in order to depict the dress in her portraits. We know from both the inventory and account book that she owned several mannequins, including two life-size figures of a man and a woman made in France that could be set in various poses.[59] These draperies stowed among the table linens remind us that Kauffman was not only a gracious hostess but a serious working artist.

The scope of Kauffman's professional practice is further revealed by items documented in her studios and storage rooms, such as easels, picture frames, assorted plaster and terra cotta fragments of torsos, limbs, heads, and ancient statues. She owned casts of Ghiberti's bas-reliefs on the Florence

Baptistery doors that Michelangelo called "The Gates of Paradise." The *Studio Grande* and an adjoining studio contained, among many other things, a table loaded with brushes, paints, pastels, tin boxes of pens, stones for grinding pigments, and jars of oil. The drawers in her writing table were filled with letters, papers, and sketches. Other practical and luxury items included a brass scale, a lorgnette, a pocket lens of tortoise shell inlaid with silver, medallions, a modern gold repeating clock, and the antique English clock previously noted in her will. She owned at least four palettes, two easels, two sets of steps for reaching high canvases and several mirrored lamps to illuminate her work. A second studio housed Kauffman's finished and unfinished paintings, oil sketches, portrait studies, and copies of works made for various patrons or her own collection. Among these were portraits of the Prince of Bavaria, her father Johann Joseph Kauffman, the improvvisatrice Fortunata Sulgher Fantastici (Figure 6.3), the artist-dealer Johann Reiffenstein, and the unfinished portrait of Antonio Canova that Kotzebue had seen in her sitting room two years earlier. The inventory lists two large religious paintings by Kauffman of *Christ and the Samaritan Woman* and *The Prophet Nathan Reproaching David*, also cited by Kotzebue.[60]

Giovanni Gherardo De Rossi, the influential art critic, poet, painter, and Kauffman's biographer, was one of her closest friends and a frequent guest. Between 1785 and 1788, when Kauffman was at the height of her career, De Rossi published the journal *Memorie per le belle arti*.[61] In the first issue, he declared his intention to employ the journal to foster appreciation of the arts and as a vehicle for raising public awareness of artists worthy of support in Rome, and during the four years of its existence *Memorie per le belle arti* published news on exhibitions, discoveries of antiquities, restorations, engravings, plans for new buildings and monuments, treatises on art, and reviews of paintings and sculpture by contemporary artists, including the spectacular reception of David's *Oath of the Horatii* in August 1785, when it was on view in the artist's studio.[62] De Rossi praised artists he considered exemplary, most notably Anton Raphael Mengs and Pompeo Batoni, and promoted the careers of artists he admired, including Angelica Kauffman and Antonio Canova. He lamented that the best works of art produced in Rome were too often taken away beyond the mountains and over the seas by British, German, Russian, Swedish, and Polish visitors; he wished more fine works would remain in the city.[63]

De Rossi published two lengthy essays on some of Kauffman's history paintings in *Memorie per le belle arti*. In April 1785 he discussed a pair of moralizing Roman subjects, *Cornelia Mother of the Gracchi Showing Her Sons as Her Treasure* (Virginia Museum, Richmond) and *Virgil Writing His Own Epitaph at Brundisium* (private collection). Both pictures demonstrated Kauffman's Neoclassical style, based on her knowledge of Latin literature, antique sculpture, and the frescoes rediscovered at Herculaneum. She sent both paintings, which had been commissioned by her British patron George Bowles, to London for the 1786 annual exhibition at the Royal Academy. De Rossi employed language in his discussion of these works that he repeated virtually word for word in his biography of the artist more than twenty years later. After a lengthy description of both paintings and praise for the artist's invention and erudition, he stated: "the works of Signora Kauffman have a certain universality of beauty from which one can deduce that this woman, besides a vast and fertile genius, has received from Nature that most rare gift of the Graces. With these she adorns every part of her pictures, and she makes the physiognomies so elegant, the expressions so true and pleasing, the attitudes so gentle and effective, she produces great harmony in chiaroscuro and color."[64] Ironically, these paintings were at first rejected for inclusion in the London exhibition and criticized by some in the British press—the same press that had so often praised her when she resided in England—as unworthy of an artist working in Italy. It has been suggested they were rejected because they were submitted by a printmaker rather than directly by the artist herself. Whatever the actual reason, the rejection, subsequent acceptance, and mixed reviews reflect conflicted feelings of resentment at England's loss, jealousy of Italy's superior reputation for painting, and disparagement of a woman artist's work in a genre that not many male artists in England had taken up.[65]

Two years later, De Rossi reviewed a pair of heroic multifigured history paintings Kauffman completed in 1786 for Emperor Joseph II of Austria, *The Triumphant Return of Arminius (Herman) after the Defeat of Quintilius Varus*, from Friedrich Gottlieb Klopstock's epic poem *Hermanns Schlacht* (1769) and *Aeneas Mourning the Death of Pallas* from Virgil's *Aeneid* (XI, 60–80; Figure 6.5). He commended her invention, variety, and range of expressions, and lauded at great length the skill with which she portrayed contrasting passions, joy in one picture and sorrow in the other. De Rossi praised the "valorosa Pittrice" and reiterated his strong desire for Rome to possess public works from Angelica's brushes to promote the Fine Arts and to furnish exemplary originals for the edification of younger artists: "When previously we spoke of Signora Kauffman it was stated that we wished Rome

Figure 6.5 Angelica Kauffman, *Aeneas Mourning the Death of Pallas, Evander's Son (Aeneid XI, 60–80)*, 1785 (oil on canvas, 44.8 x 61.6 cm). Innsbruck, Tiroler Landesmuseum Ferdinandeum, Kunstgeschichtliche Sammlungen.

would have some public works from her brushes. Our wishes have not yet been fulfilled, but we hope that one day they will be. . . ." In a footnote he addressed the consequences of this loss: "Who would ever have believed that Rome would have to lose an entire series of works by one of the most celebrated Painters? Yet it has lost them with the gravest damage to the Arts, and the studious youth finds only poor copies in place of wonderful originals."[66]

De Rossi expressed his view that Angelica's art surpassed that of women artists of earlier generations in both his *Memorie per le belle arti* (1785, 1787) and his later biography of Kauffman (1810). Kauffman, he believed, brought glory to the modern era through her works, which demonstrated her fertile imagination, ideal beauty, and grace.[67] Her only teacher was her father, a provincial painter, De Rossi wrote, yet she was able to succeed through her own effort and natural genius. In contrast, he reminded the reader, women painters of preceding centuries, most notably Sofonisba Anguissola and the Bolognese painters Lavinia Fontana and Elisabetta Sirani, had the advantage of direct instruction from great Renaissance masters, including

Michelangelo, who gave guidance to Anguissola, and Guido Reni, who, it was believed, had been Sirani's teacher.[68] Thus, in De Rossi's estimation, Kauffman's original achievement was remarkable. In addition, his particular choice of words imbued Kauffman with positive qualities, such as "genius," "invention," "originality," and "power" (*ingegno, invenzione, originalità, forza*) which were traditionally reserved for male artists in contrast to the more diffident and derivative skills (*timidezza, diligenza*) attributed to women artists.[69]

De Rossi concluded his glowing tribute to Kauffman with reference to a famous allegorical drawing by the painter Carlo Maratti (1625–1713), an artist whose work exemplified classical academic theory at the turn of the eighteenth century. This drawing, which was widely known through engravings, had been highly praised by Giovanni Pietro Bellori (1613–1690), art theorist, antiquarian, and biographer of artists, for demonstrating pictorially the equal importance of theory and practice in the art of painting.[70] Maratti portrayed an ideal academy of painting in which artists and young pupils study anatomy from a human model as well as antique statuary represented by figures of Hercules, Venus, and Apollo. They also learn the rules of geometry and perspective represented as drawings on an easel with an admonitory inscription "Tanto che basti" (as much as necessary). The human model bears the same advice, in contrast to the study of the classical statues which are tagged "non mai abbastanza" (never enough). The Three Graces perched on a cloud gaze down at the artists under an inscription that states, "Senza di noi ogni fatica e vana" (without the gift of the Graces all work is in vain)—important counsel to aspiring artists, for, as Bellori and other academic theorists declared, the labor of perfecting manual skills must be tempered by that inspired grace which only the best artists possessed. De Rossi validated his favorable opinion of Kauffman by identifying her with the theoretical knowledge, skills, and inspired creativity of the greatest artists—implicitly great *male* artists—and by stressing her superiority over and difference from other female painters. Through reference to Maratti's composition and praise for Kauffman's classical history paintings, De Rossi was also able to advance his broader views on the enduring value of academic practice and theory based on classical ideals in the grand manner of Maratti, Bellori, and the Accademia di San Luca.

De Rossi's primary objective in publishing Kauffman's biography in 1810 was to commemorate a dear friend as well as a fine artist, but it also gave him an opportunity to promote his own ideas about the development of painting in Italy, which, in his view, culminated in the triumph of Neo-classicism in Rome.[71] He also wished to highlight Kauffman's role in that triumph by granting her explicit credit for her part in halting the decline of art after Carlo Maratti's death in 1713. De Rossi stated his intention to prove this assertion by interrupting his biographical narrative to present a brief overview of the history and current state of the arts in Rome.[72] His analysis began with the High Renaissance artists Raphael and Michelangelo, followed by the achievements of major seventeenth-century painters of the classic Bolognese school, including Annibale Carracci, Domenichino, Guido Reni, Andrea Sacchi, and Pietro da Cortona. He devoted several pages to the esteemed Maratti, blaming the artist's weak imitators for Painting's decline after his death and criticizing his followers' feeble versions of the master's style. He believed the gifted Pompeo Batoni improved the situation some-what; however, De Rossi noted—repeating his complaint—Batoni worked primarily for foreigners and was underappreciated in Rome. The modern hero of De Rossi's history was the German painter Anton Raphael Mengs, who, he wrote, lifted the yoke of servile imitation with his grand and sub-lime ideas, fought against the frigid mannerisms of other artists, and initi-ated a new path for artists by reminding them of the importance of studying the antique and the great old masters in practice together with theory.[73]

At this point in the text, De Rossi returned to his main subject, Angelica Kauffman, noting that she set up her studio in Rome just a few years after the death of Mengs (1779) and the publication of his ideas on art (1780).[74] Her graceful style, expression, invention, color, and imitation of nature, he wrote, met with universal approval in Rome, and Kauffman's understand-ing that art theory must be accompanied by good practice constituted an excellent model for younger artists. Angelica's painting, together with the theoretical writings of Mengs, according to De Rossi, served to promote the advancement of the arts.[75] Thus De Rossi not only gave credit to Kauffman for her role in halting the decline of painting in Rome but also characterized her as a virtual partner and heir to Mengs. In fact, though she never met Mengs (who had left Rome in 1760 before she arrived), Kauffman lived in the same house Mengs occupied from 1752 to 1757, and though neither her agent Prosperi nor De Rossi note this coincidence, she must have known and been delighted to establish herself as his successor.[76]

Kauffman shared De Rossi's views on art and reciprocated her friend's admiration. In a letter to Fortunata Sulgher Fantastici, she recounted an occasion at Maria Pizzelli's salon in 1792 when De Rossi delivered "a most beautiful discourse" on the subject of painting and sculpture in which he attempted to explain the difficulties that impede achievement of perfection in these arts. She characterized the discourse as very learned, filled with an infinite number of instructive ideas, and she begged him to publish it because it would be extremely useful for young students.[77]

While De Rossi had his own reasons for constructing Kauffman's biography to promote her role within the progressive development of Roman painting, Kauffman also endeavored to secure her place in the history of art by arranging her residence as a workplace to create paintings as well as a showcase to affirm and promote her professional status. Her home and studio on the site formerly occupied by Mengs, across from the historic Palazzo Zuccari and adjoining the garden of the Villa Malta, where so many eminent German travelers stayed while in Rome, was the perfect setting for this extraordinary woman. Kauffman's finely furnished and elegantly decorated house established her at the center of artistic activity in Rome, while De Rossi's artfully crafted essays and biography, with their emphasis on Kauffman's enthusiasm for Rome and her artistic descent from Maratti and Mengs, despite her status as a woman, served to secure her place in the history of art.

Angelica Kauffman's love for the city of Rome and her desire to establish herself in a setting suitable for both business and pleasure sheds light on her decision to leave a lucrative practice and friends in London to settle in the Eternal City. The moderate climate, the lively community of artists, great collections, a salon culture dominated by gifted women, and the city's importance as a major destination for art enthusiasts made Rome an ideal place for her. As a mature artist with an established reputation and few serious rivals in Rome, she could work, entertain friends, and receive flattering attention from eager patrons and visitors with more freedom and on a grander scale than in London. Her considerable talent, intelligence, personal charms, and fluency in several languages, in addition to her wealth and sex, allowed her to achieve her hard-earned place in the "Residence of the Arts."

PART THREE

Enlightened Sexualities

SEVEN

Strange Births and Surprising Kin

The Castrato's Tale

MARTHA FELDMAN

In a Settecento history of gender and sexuality, the castrato might well be cast at center stage. Castrati were first cultivated in the sixteenth century to supply north Italian and papal chapels with powerful high voices.[1] Pauline doctrine prohibited female speech in church, and falsettists' voices were not as rich and piercing as those of castrati. By the early seventeenth century they were singing throughout Italy and beyond, holding positions at innumerable courts and chapels, and by 1637 and thereafter they were circulating widely on public, commercial stages in Italy and eventually throughout much of Europe.[2] To simplify a long and complex story, suffice it to say that

My sincere thanks to Patricia Barber, Emily Bauman, Ellen T. Harris, Berthold Hoeckner, David J. Levin, and to participants in the conference "Italy's Eighteenth Century: Gender and Culture in the Age of the Grand Tour" for conversations that helped clarify the thoughts in this essay; and to Maria Di Salvo, Daniel Schlafly, and Christine Wunnicke for lively and informative exchanges about Balatri's life and manuscripts. I also wish to thank my audience at the Dent Lecture, Annual Conference of the Royal Musical Association, Glasgow (November 2002), and the inspiring participants in my seminar on the castrato (University of Chicago, spring 2002): Drew Edward Davies, Justin Flosi, Douglas Ipson, Karl Kügle, Hedy Law, Karen Pagani, and Courtney Quaintance. I am indebted to Drew Davies for his exemplary work as my research assistant and to Courtney Quaintance for helping to procure images and permissions.

essentially all the chapels of Italy eventually came to be staffed with castrati on high parts—not least the pope's chapel, the Cappella Sistina, which employed castrati from the later sixteenth century to 1913; and that castrati could be found in opera houses throughout almost all of Europe from 1607 until 1830.

Nonetheless the castrato was born on a bed of paradox. According to most interpretations of canon law, castrated men could not marry, a situation ratified by Pope Sixtus V in a papal brief *Cum frequenter* on 27 June 1587.[3] As such they were largely exiled from the patrilineal social order, which was fundamentally reproductive, and were deemed inferior de facto by prevailing medical theories of the time, which were overridingly Aristotelian and Galenic throughout the early modern period.[4] The castrato was a biological curiosity, a male made infertile by human intervention and one who sometimes seemed to partake of the feminine as a result.

Taboos and Myths

Meanwhile the actual act of castration, never sanctioned by the church, remained taboo as social praxis and discourse. In 1773 the music historian Charles Burney tried famously to discover where boys were being castrated at a time when hundreds must have existed, but reported that all of his interlocutors passed the buck:

> I enquired throughout Italy where boys were chiefly qualified for singing by castration, but could get no certain intelligence. I was told at Milan that it was at Venice; at Venice, that it was at Bologna; but at Bologna the fact was denied, and I was referred to Florence; from Florence to Rome, and from Rome I was sent to Naples. The operation most certainly is against the law in all these places, as well as against nature; and all the Italians are so much ashamed of it, that in every province they transfer it to some other.[5]

What struck Burney as persistent indirection had become more pronounced in the decades leading up to his Italian tours. The paradox in this is that while Renaissance boys may occasionally have been castrated primarily for medical reasons, following the Galenic belief that castration cured wounds to the testicles (among other things),[6] boys in the seventeenth and eighteenth centuries became cogs in the wheel of a mass market for high male voices. The climate of economic crisis that prevailed in the seventeenth century seems to have allowed protagonists to be blunter about such realities than they were in the rationalizing, moralizing climate of the eighteenth century. Yet to judge from the fragmentary evidence that survives, indirection always played its part. The famous castrato Baldassare Ferri of Perugia (1610–1670) was apparently so named because he had suffered a deadly wound. Charles Ancillon, in his *Traité des eunuques* of 1707, explained that the famed singer Marc'Antonio Pasqualini had used castration "to cure distemper."[7] A testimonial by a boy singer, Rinaldo Gherardini, in the 1670s or 1680s, was more transparent, telling the Mantuan authorities that he wanted to be castrated (an avowal required by law) "so that he could serve the Duke of Mantua, make progress [that is, as a singer], and give much better service both to Our Lord and to Your Highness" and adding that he wanted to become a priest since he had two brothers who were already married.[8] Eighteenth-century explanations—at least those few that have surfaced thus far—do not approach Rinaldi's level of ingenuousness. Invoked instead are blurry admixtures of medical convention, financial need, Catholic sacrifice, and folk wisdom.[9] Domenico Bruni (1758–1821) of Frata (now Umbertide) in Umbria was said to have been prescribed castration by doctors following an "accidental physical indisposition" by which means he always "maintained his enchanting soprano voice."[10] In 1784 Giovenale Sacchi, Farinelli's posthumous biographer, managed to procure reports that Farinelli had been castrated following a fall from a horse.[11] And in the early twentieth century, when the German doctor and singing teacher Franz Haböck interviewed castrati in the papal chapel, he was told by Domenico Mustafà that he had been castrated owing to a bite by a pig, by Vincenzo Sebastianelli that the bite had been from a "wild pig," and that the cause of Alessandro Moreschi's castration was a "never thoroughly understood childhood mishap."[12]

Aspects of these explanations resemble accounts found in other cultures in association with taboos that serve to forestall perils to maleness, or the perception of such perils. Their explanatory value arguably lies in providing castration with a narrative of ritual passage from a situation that purportedly threatens to make a boy uncivilized, unmale, or inhuman to one that guarantees civilization, maleness (if modified in form), humanness, and even life itself.[13] Perhaps it is not so surprising, then, that in eighteenth-century visual caricatures and literary satires of castrati, and occasionally in their own self-parodies, we find castrati elided with various animals, particularly the group of fowl that includes roosters, hens, or capons, but also pigs—all farm animals that sit at the margins of human domestic life and often mirror human conditions and anxieties. A characteristic elision done by the Venetian artist Anton Maria Zanetti in 1735 caricatures the soprano Antonio Bernacchi as he struts vainly cocklike, plumed by a great head-dress, with a capacious breast and belly propped up by a dwarfed servant (Figure 7.1).[14]

Zanetti's image makes a fascinating juxtaposition with a burlesque passage from an extraordinary autobiography in verse completed in the same year by a Pisan castrato named Filippo Balatri. The passage tells of Balatri's encounter with one of the great Tartar khans, Kalmyk Khan Ayuki of the Astrakhan khanate on the lower Volga, whom Balatri claims to have astounded with his singing when he visited as part of an embassy sent by Peter the Great in the spring of 1699, months after being lured to the Muscovite court from Tuscany as part of the czar's westernizing projects.[15] The khan reportedly became so enraptured by the virtuosic singing of the young

Figure 7.1 Anton Maria Zanetti, *Bolognese Castrato Antonio Bernacchi in Caricature*, 1735 (pen and ink). Venice, Fondazione Giorgio Cini, Raccolta bibliografica e artistica.

"ominessa" that he asked where he could get one of his own. At first Balatri stumbles in embarrassment, but then settles the vexed question of gender by producing a myth of origins for the castrato:

> He started by asking me / whether I was male or female, and where from; / Whether such people are born (or rain down) / with a voice and ability to sing. / I was all confused about how to answer: / If "male," I'm practically lying, / if "female," still less do I say what I am, / and if "neuter," I would blush. / But, screwing up my courage, I finally answer / that I'm a man, Tuscan, and that / cocks are found in my region who lay eggs, / from which sopranos come into the world; / That these cocks are called Norcini[16] / who go on brooding for many days among our people, / and once the capon is made, the eggs are festooned / with flattery, caresses, and money.[17]

With this tale Balatri invents a natural order in which *reproduction* is the work of males—specifically cocks, which have widely symbolized male sexual aggression and procreative power. In this sense the castrato reworks mythically the very matter that castration made moot, since historically what the rampant castration of Italian boys produced through the intervention of men was a caste of *non*reproductive males. But to do so, he also absorbs the castrato into an ancient comic tradition that cast selected stage and social actors as feathered creatures, often sexually exaggerated, deviant, inefficient, or transgressive.[18]

The prototype for this comic tradition most proximate to the castrato was the carnivalesque figure of Pulcinella. Famed for his long beaklike nose, Pulcinella was an obscene, comic tramp who could impersonate and fraternize with aristocrats and royals. He was an indefatigable but unsuccessful lover, as well as a man of transformations who easily became like a woman and who, though largely human, could fraternize with donkeys, birds, dogs, cats, and pigs. His nose made him a *pullus gallinaceus*—hence his name "Pulliciniello" and "Pulcinella" from the Italian *pulcino*, or chick. In one of his two main myths of origin, he is hatched from an egg.[19] A figure of irony, ambiguity, and liminality[20]—in early modern depictions, often musical and sometimes castratolike—Pulcinella's defining trait was an inherent inability to maintain clear boundaries between the sexes or between the human world and the world of beasts. An engraving called "Pulcinella, maestro di canto," by Filippo Vasconi after the Roman caricaturist Pierleone Ghezzi, gives further confirmation that this ensemble of traits produced as the symbolic equivalent to the capon—a screechy singing teacher.

Like that of the castrato, Pulcinella's peculiar nature was sometimes attributed to his having been generated by a male and was also elided with states or processes of castration. In the seventeenth century, for example, the librettist and poet Francesco Melosio penned a burlesque sonnet that explains Pulcinella's birth as the result of a hen having been impregnated by severed testicles that were cut off by a boy's own father:

> A guy from Salò castrated one of his sons / so he could tend better to his talent / by putting it to some use, / [so] he threw his testicles aside. / There was a broody hen at his house, and I don't know / how one of those testicles got up inside her; / but anyway it too was brooded from eggs, / and it too hatched in its time. / This is how the Marquis was born, who / grew up making it as an ass / so as not to betray his birth. / And on stages from that time on, / anybody who acts like an ass in our day / is called Pulcinella.[21]

Here the vain marquis and Pulcinella are one and the same, their shared origins linked to a castrated male (or at least his dismembered parts).[22] Note that after the hen's egg hatched—presumably with a castrato, if we assume that what issued forth resembled its father—the son produced gave the slip to the social order of class relations, much as his birth had given the slip to the natural orders of species and gender: he ended up passing himself off as a *nobleman* (a "marchese"), hiding his bestial origins by strutting on the stage like a "coglioncello" (an ass, in slang derived etymologically from "coglione"). But the tricksterish creature was forever marked as a half-human whose name signified the *pullus* at his origins.[23]

Melosio's story corresponds to a narrative complex that is dispersed in other accounts. In one version of the myth, for example, Pulcinella is hatched at the summit of Vesuvius from an eggshell that had appeared there by the will of Pluto, male sovereign of the underworld.[24] In a later eighteenth-century variant on the same, Domenico Tiepolo shows Pulcinella being birthed from the immense egg of a proud and powerful turkey, the supreme male game bird who swaggers here in the background.[25] Both the castrato and the clown sit at a nexus of maleness and births that are as prodigious in kind as they often are in number. One anonymous painting from the eighteenth century even shows a group of men feeding Pulcinella food that turns into little Pulcinellini whom he births through his anus.[26]

How these various strands connect with the castrato is a question I will take up here piece by piece, but several connections suggest themselves from the outset. Much as the androgyne clown was a hybrid who defied the social order during Carnival—a liminal time that privileged liminal creatures—the castrato (of mixed gender, if decidedly weighted male) would rule the stage during Carnival when the opera season was at its height. While the castrato could variously embody angels, heroes, or sovereigns, he too was the target of comic tropes. Thus like the clown, the castrato allowed viewers to identify with a distorted, malleable body, reminiscent in his sacrificial aspect of the effigy of a murdered man who was typically carried about at Carnival—a kind of pagan approximation of Christ. And like the clown, the castrato was both exalted and jeered before, in the last event, the patriarchal social order was reinstated.[27]

Balatri's writings are a goldmine because they are without parallel. Working largely in the relative quiet of a few prominent courts, theaters, and churches, he produced an enormous literary *oeuvre*, mostly autobiographical but all marked by a preternatural taste for the burlesque. Nevertheless, among castrati who alluded to bizarre forms of reproduction, he was not entirely alone. A letter by the great Farinelli, recently come to light, shows him indulging in some braggartly tongue-in-cheek in writing his rich patron-friend Count Sicinio Pepoli for help in marrying off his brother: "I do not claim that I was born from the third rib of Venus, nor that my father was Neptune. I am Neapolitan and the Duke of Andria held me at the baptismal font."[28] Here Farinelli calls attention to the idea of a divine, mythological, and thus exalted, patrilineage for the castrato, even as he disavows it to end by associating himself with noble origins. The protest admits as much as it denies: many *do* consider him divine and virtually noble (he wants Pepoli to remember), though he himself allows only noble connections to his birth.

Both Farinelli and Balatri were writing ironically. Irony allowed them to conjure up tales underscoring the magic and divinity of their kind through allusions to extraordinary origins, at the same time as they rejected them— a strategy in which castrati had support from the imagination of a mass audience that repeatedly heard in them supernatural powers.[29] Invoked strategically in autobiography and epistolary self-construction, these texts justify indirectly otherwise very different accounts of the remarkable, if sometimes ambivalent, acceptance some castrati found in the inner circles of nobles and sovereigns. They also make use of strange but wondrous births to rationalize the prodigious social ascent of some castrati and their assimilation into what were effectively new kinship groups.[30] Subjectively it was useful for them and their fans to make mythological origins and modes of reproduction into points of discursive reference. Doing so in the idiom of the joke allowed anxieties about the castrato's status to be diffused while accommodating the silence, obfuscation, and myth making that surrounded castration. Furthermore, in a strongly patrilineal society, repeating tropes about the necessity of castration doubtless had a certain propitiary force in warding off imagined evils of divine retribution for impeding procreation,[31] even as it foregrounded the agency of castrati in manipulating and mediating the status of the natural world, and of prevailing social hegemonies, helping to forge bonds of kinship between themselves and their allies.

We should note in this regard that all of the births I have cited are seemingly informed by a strange logic: not only do men castrate other men to generate nonreproductive males but mythically they even act as parturients themselves in ways that participate in the social and symbolic procreation of particular males. Much as Balatri's rooster hatches castrated boys and Melosio's hen (mated with a castrato's testicles) hatches a castratolike comic, so the surgeons, fathers, teachers, and princes who effected castrations in Italy were arbiters of the physical and social reproduction of a caste of castrated males. Clearly justifications for social "procreation" (literal and figurative) acted to help male castrators compensate for castrations that were not socially or legally sanctioned, and to help castrated males make up for deficiencies in their own ability as males to reproduce.

Indeed castrati were not merely reproduced by others but were themselves involved in extensive projects of social reproduction, as teachers, choirmasters, and mentors to other young males.[32] The symbolic repetitions echo on: as Pulcinella often played a gelded man or a quasi-capon, with a high, cackling voice and enlarged bosom, and was widely depicted as sexually feeble even while reproducing himself prodigiously,[33] castrati were widely satirized in the eighteenth century as capons and depicted as feminized men or human-animal hybrids, both figures manifesting to Settecento spectators what they themselves were not. In versions of myths associated with both neutered castrati who played princes (or princesses) and "castrated" clowns, bizarre forms of male palingenesis also took place in connection with the egg. The link is not surprising, since historically the egg has probably been the world's most widespread, versatile, and polyvalent symbol of reproduction, as well as a symbol of birth, fertility, and wealth long linked in the West with rebirth in connection with Passover and the Resurrection.[34]

Given these suggestive facts, why did castrati and their patrons and families typically suppress histories of their "reproduction" (in particular, their castration) or make recourse to unnatural or comic tales about it? And how was castration itself reworked as a primal moment of self-production—a birth in effect? Why too were these various stories of insemination and procreation advanced in ways that revised the orders of class and gender relations?

Such questions can lead through countless byways. Valeria Finucci reminds us that for many centuries, including the seventeenth and even eighteenth, generation was understood as "men's business," and that the reason Pope Sixtus V declared in 1588 that "eunuchs, castrati, and *spadones* [males who were deformed or mutilated] were not real men [was] because they could not offer intergenerational continuity."[35] Manhood was essentially defined by generative capacity, not by sexual preference, physiology, or sexual prowess.[36] Thus masculinity took on vital importance precisely where male generation was in question.[37]

How then could castration be justified? As Pietro Stella's research on familial strategies and sacred celibacy in early modern Italy suggests, castration from the seventeenth century onward was regarded as a particular form of celibacy. It was as such that castration marked the beginning of new, or hybridized, family structures for the males who underwent it.[38] Often referred to with the metonymic euphemism of "musico," the typical castrato was born into a home of poor or middle-class parents and was castrated as a boy singer sometime between the ages of about seven and thirteen. By that time he had often already been removed from the natal home and placed for training either in the home of a teacher, who acted *in loco parentis* in accordance with an apprenticeship contract signed with the boy's parents, or in a conservatory, church, or cathedral school, which served a similarly parental role.[39] If the boy had not yet been placed by the time he was castrated, then placing him as a live-in student (and virtual child) in a teacher's home or in a conservatory was the parents' next step. In fact the four famous conservatories of Naples were originally orphanages, which called their charges "sons," so their function *in loco parentis* was part of their founding and discursive infrastructure.

This removal from the natal home and adoption by a male teacher furnished the castrato with someone who was often the first in a series of surrogate fathers. (Indeed, more often than not, it was the teacher who was the prime catalyst for a boy's castration.) Boys at the conservatories were known as "figliuoli" (sons), or when dressed in white for choral vigils or processions—especially common in the case of castrati—were called "figliuoli angelini" (little angel-sons or angel-children).[40] Unlike other boys, castrati were typically favored "sons," pampered and sheltered but also held to severe standards of discipline and accomplishment. The singing master Nicola Porpora was famous for subjecting his many castrati-pupils to regimens that were harsher the more promising the students were.

In the continuous travels of a castrato who attained any kind of success on the eighteenth-century stage, a widespread network of secondary families usually developed. Castrati were often represented in biography, apprenticeship, and employment contracts as exemplary surrogate sons to teachers and patrons—a role they would realize theatrically by impersonating model sons in the form of heroes and princes onstage (if they were successful enough to attain the stage at all). In this sense they were the upwardly mobile, youthful, hereditary embodiments of a magical sovereignty and ubiquity, archetypical of absolutist monarchies in expressing themselves generationally in a dynamic familial order of authority and succession.

The remainder of this chapter explores how these issues relate to the often changing array of nonnatural father figures in the castrato's life and the band of "brothers"—and sometimes "mothers" and "sisters"—that castrati acquired throughout their lifetime as they formed ongoing, often shifting, networks of what we now call "invented" or "adopted" families, with peers, fellow courtiers, patrons, impresarios, and poets. I look at the two very different examples of Farinelli and Balatri to explore how castrati could conduct and explain their lives as a series of encounters and bondings through which they created successive, interconnected families in the context of old-order social structures, marked by the extreme hierarchy and stratification that supported that world until it began to crack in the later eighteenth century. I also tie the castrato's representation and self-representation back to a wider public sphere and to its developing social and political consciousness. In a heavily patriarchal society in which castrati were loosed from their natal families to represent the old order on stage and to interact with it offstage, the kinship networks they cultivated throughout their lives played a critical role, even as castrati also circulated contradictorily as a new type of commodity in the fast-developing world of capital. We will see that life-writings by and surrounding castrati can be read for views about kinship,[41] while also showing how their lives became projects of self-production, self-invention, and self-preservation, which ultimately stood in for natural reproduction (if problematically so). Yet as family ideologies changed in the later eighteenth century, the castrato's nonreproductive and hence "unnatural" status demanded that he eventually be distanced from the familial and sexual politics of the new social order.

"One God, One Farinelli"

Farinelli was the ultimate incarnation of the castrato as model son.[42] Born Carlo Broschi in 1705 to a small-time official working in Andria and later Barletta (in Apulia) and a Neapolitan mother, Farinelli moved to Naples with his parents at about age six. He was twelve when his father died, and in the same year he started private study under Porpora, the greatest bel canto teacher of the time. By age fifteen, he debuted in Naples and shortly thereafter Rome, seducing audiences in both male and female roles. When the Roman Pierleone Ghezzi caricatured him in drag in 1724, he had already become the heartthrob of various publics throughout Italy.[43]

Farinelli was an unflagging monarchist; hence—like his great friend Metastasio (the architect of absolutist opera), who once snarled "Io . . . non sono repubblichista"—he was a good son of the old order.[44] After an audience with the imperial monarchs at Vienna, now datable to March 1732 since the recent discovery of Farinelli's sixty-seven letters to Pepoli,[45] he wrote:

> VITTORIA VITTORIA, . . . thanks to heaven, I had the good fortune last Saturday to sing before the Augustissimi Patroni. . . . When reverences were made [to the empress], I started to tremble like a leaf [and when] thrown at the feet of the emperor [I declared], "Genuflecting at the most clement feet of Your Sacred Imperial Catholic Majesty is the most fortunate moment of my life."[46]

A month later he boasted that no one in his profession had ever had the grace of singing privately before the emperor and empress.[47] It was only five years afterward that his career culminated in nothing but audiences with royalty, which took place over twenty-two years at the Spanish court, to which Farinelli was drawn in 1737 at the age of thirty-two, ostensibly to alleviate with his enchanting voice the severe depression of King Philip V. Having spent three years on the London stage being idolized, parodied, and sickened by bad weather and overwork, Farinelli found a quiet but lonely contentment in his Spanish retirement from the stage. Seemingly unphased by Philip's frequent psychotic episodes, which left the king by turns catatonic, drooling, and howling, Farinelli remained devoted to his patrons.

After Philip's death in 1746, he continued to be showered with wealth and privilege by Ferdinand VI. He was handed extraordinary responsibilities not just in his capacity as superintendent of public entertainments but in top matters of state, which famously included such feats as redirecting the River Tagus in Aranjuez. With his knighting in the order of Calatrava in 1750, he was also made not just an extraordinary intimate of the royal family but a virtual sovereign in his own right. Portrayed in a now-famous portrait of 1755 by Corrado Giaquinto wearing the cross of the order, Farinelli appears with the royal couple hovering angelically in the background (Figure 7.2).

The most complete contemporaneous historical account of Farinelli's life was the *Vita* of Giovenale Sacchi, printed in 1784, which constructs itself as a posthumous celebration of Farinelli's capacity for fraternal and filial

Figure 7.2 Corrado Giaquinto, *Farinelli Wearing the Cross of the Order of Calatrava, with the King and Queen in the Background*, ca. 1755 (oil painting). Bologna, Museo e Biblioteca Internazionale della Musica.

loyalty at the same time as it extols his reputation as a kind of *pater familias*. Farinelli's powers of friendship are elaborated chiefly through his relationship with Metastasio, now preserved only in Metastasio's part of their correspondence.[48] Daniel Heartz has enlarged on the epithet of twinship that marked their friendship when Farinelli first sang Metastasio's words at their mutual debut in Naples in 1720, an epithet that stuck until both died sixty-two years later.[49] In 1747, at Farinelli's request for a portrait of Metastasio, the poet answered, "Who can resist the solicitations of a beloved twin brother? I shall undertake this business as a penitence for my sins, and try to indulge your longing. . . ."[50] There is sometimes an erotic tinge to their exchanges, as in 1749 when they corresponded about their mutual attraction for a beautiful singer named Teresa Castellini. "Tell her . . . that as a twin I can only receive the emotions of your heart at the rebound," Metastasio wrote; "that when I hear your name I feel a certain tingling sensation that incommodes me, and yet I have no wish that it be discontinued." In Jacopo Amigoni's group portrait, all three protagonists are pictured in familial harmony along with the artist and Farinelli's dog (Figure 7.3).

Figure 7.3 Jacopo Amigoni, *Group portrait of* (left to right) *Metastasio, Teresa Castellini, Farinelli, Jacopo Amigoni, and an Anonymous Young Man with Farinelli's Dog,* ca. 1750–1752 (oil painting). Melbourne, National Gallery of Victoria, Felton bequest.

Farinelli's sexual interests remain ambiguous; we don't know whether his own passions in any way answered the ones seemingly avowed by Metastasio, and we do learn from his earlier letters that he fell in love with a ballerina in 1733.[51] But neither his sexuality nor his cross-dressing on stage as a young man (a typical rite of passage for a successful operatic castrato) would have marked him as ambiguous in gender, nor would his sexual practices. The culturally determined category he occupied was decidedly male, however modified.[52] It was as male that he and other castrati were always described, whatever qualifiers accrued to them (or roles they played). In fact, although (as Gilbert Herdt reminds us) sexual desire, ideas about sexual categories, and sexual morphology are all quite different matters, it was precisely in the European enlightenment that ideologies of sexual dimorphism took root, arising hand-in-hand with ideologies that condemned same-sex desire, even as "third-sexed" persons and groups continued to threaten them.[53]

Certainly what mattered to Sacchi's *Vita*, for reasons that included Sacchi's continued devotion toward the end of the eighteenth century to an old-regime consciousness, were the constellations of friendship and kinship that Farinelli had sustained. In enlarging on these and other bonds of Farinelli's, Sacchi ends by eradicating any sexual overtones from accounts of Farinelli's friendships and puts the accent firmly on his acts of charity on behalf of father figures, peers, inferiors, and countrymen.

Farinelli's largesse included his permanent financial commitment to his first father figure, Porpora (characteristic of other singers and indeed generally required by contract and ultimately by social convention)—this despite the disaffection he harbored for aspects of Porpora's character.[54] But not long after Farinelli's apprenticeship, Porpora was replaced in affection when Farinelli was virtually adopted by Count Pepoli, who educated him in the ways of the world from the time of their meeting in 1727.[55] By then aged forty-three, Pepoli had evidently given up on the prospect of having his own natural male children.[56] A landed gentryman on a quasi-feudal model, he had a reputation for a demeanor of "sovereign nonchalance" which embodied the noble ideal castrati were expected to project on stage. According to Sacchi, his great "friend and patron" did "every last thing" for him, including seeing to the care of Farinelli's lavish retirement residence on the outskirts of Bologna in his absence but above all turning him into a graceful social actor capable of managing the highest echelons of society.[57]

Like a natural son, however, Farinelli was eventually constrained to establish his independence from Pepoli through a painful process of separation. Once the possessive royal couple of Spain claimed Farinelli, Pepoli had to watch him from afar being treated as "a son by the nobility as much as by the royal family."[58] The Count stopped writing him during the initial months of Farinelli's transition to Spain as he watched his protective powers slip away, failing to answer at least four of Farinelli's beseeching letters in 1737 and 1738. When they finally reconciled, Farinelli could finally thank God for being "worthy of receiving one of your letters, so dear to me" and cajole Pepoli into accepting the new form of their relationship ("Facciamo come gli amorosi: la gara lasciammola da parte di chi ha ragione").[59]

It was not so long afterwards that Farinelli recruited Pepoli into helping to build his own vertical kinship system. In 1740 he wrote to ask that Pepoli use his connections in the urgent project of finding a good wife for Farinelli's brother, the composer Riccardo Broschi, and thus help Farinelli avail himself of a natural legal heir for his extraordinary fortune.[60] And in the same letter he feigned modesty about his roots with an eye toward improving them.

> I would like it if my possessions could be enjoyed by a person who merits them. Ambition is far from me, nor does vanity drive my sense of duty. I would like to find a woman who springs neither from the heavens nor the valleys. Your Excellency, with your good heart and true friendship, could find someone suitable; above all, so that there might be some weeding out. My brother is presently enjoying a good position, given him by the grace of the King of Naples, which earns him [just] under a thousand ducats a year, a nobleman having occupied this position with great esteem before it fell to my brother. My sister is married to another gentleman, who now occupies the post of preceptor in the province of Salerno, which gives him 2,000 ducats a year. Your Excellency may see how my heart sits with respect to my relatives. *I do not claim that I was born from the third rib of Venus, nor that my father was Neptune. I am Neapolitan and the Duke of Andria held me at the baptismal font. That is enough to give you the idea that I'm the son of a good citizen and a gentleman.* It seems to me that up to now I've produced a good deal of honor for myself, my homeland, my family, and my profession. I would hope in light of such reflections that no good daughter would have to speak ill of such a match. . . . I myself cannot (as you know) marry, so I must think about my blood and look for a woman who can merit all that God has given me.[61]

Blood still mattered to Farinelli, and he hoped that money could enrich and perpetuate it.

By the time Farinelli had become equal to and independent enough of Pepoli to exploit his potential for securing an affinal alliance and hence

Farinelli's own line of descent, his position with respect to his king had also become more parental than filial, and such too was his posthumous renown in Sacchi's *Vita*. Sacchi repeatedly effuses over Farinelli's paternalism: his nickname of "Padre degli Italiani," his paternalistic aid to the musical retinue of a disfavored general,[62] to musicians displaced by the great Lisbon earthquake,[63] and to his many Spanish friends following his retirement to Italy.[64]

Whether cast as father or son, Farinelli's success at court depended not just on his vocal gifts but his viability within an adopted family of royals and courtiers. It depended on a skill at displaying modesty and charity while transcending his inherited inferiority through a meticulous exchange of graces and tributes. The most visible consequence of this skill was of course the astonishing fact of his being knighted by the king. Yet its fame dated much further back than that, certainly to the reception he received in Vienna,[65] when the emperor accompanied him at the keyboard and advised him to temper the marvelous artifice of his singing with a more humanly expressive style[66]—advice Farinelli evidently heeded, to judge from his subsequent repertory.

None of these adopted ties precluded Farinelli's relationship with his natural brother Riccardo, but rather complemented it. Throughout his life Farinelli continued to regard Riccardo uniquely as natural kin, performed his music, and maintained a continuous if sometimes pitiable and rather opaque relationship with him. In a larger jigsaw of kinship relations, Riccardo was the piece that could enable natural reproduction and thus patrimonial continuity, without replacing (or even equaling) the place of acquired kin cultivated through social exchange, shared circumstances and conditions, and the circulation of wealth.

Filippo Balatri, Buffone and "Virtuoso da Camera"

Much different from Farinelli, Balatri was a modest court singer and sometime opera singer, but in this sense he was far more representative of the caste. He was unique in being both castrato and autobiographer, far more prolifically so than heretofore realized. Author of the satiric verse autobiography *Frutti del Mondo* of 1735, some 698 pages long in manuscript (about half of which were published in 1924), Balatri also composed a barely known prose autobiography in 1725–1732 called *Vita e viaggi* (now in Moscow) that runs to more than 3,500 pages in manuscript, a satirical testament in 1737–38 of 220 pages, at least one sacred comedy, and a singing treatise (now lost).[67] Both autobiographies were based on diaries (also now lost) that he kept on order of his patron the Grand Duke of Tuscany Cosimo III,[68] who was ever "curious to have particular things from remote parts [of the world], such as plants for his garden, minerals, paintings, statues, and other objects for the Gallery and wild animals for his menagerie, without caring how much they cost."[69]

It will be useful to trace the outlines of the quixotic life that produced this explosion of writing before returning to our themes of reproduction and kinship. Balatri's *Frutti del Mondo*, addressed as a moralistic tale to his adversary "the World," explains that he was born to a "poor cittadino" of ancient Florentine stock who was secretary to the Grand Duke Cosimo III of Tuscany and a French mother who had been a lady-in-waiting to the Grand Duchess.[70] Cosimo had provided the parents with a spartan palace outside Pisa in exchange for loyal service. Yet Balatri begins the *Frutti* with a sentence of one lone word, "Nacqui," as if he had sprung like Athena from the head of Zeus. On the heels of it comes an address to the dark muse who follows him throughout his tale:

> I was born. And up to the age of awareness, you [World] left me in harsh silence. But hardly was I fifteen years old than you came / with your net and fished me forth, / making my natural Sovereign / ask—fortunately—that my father / send me to Moscow; and within a few hours / I was cast away into the North.

This was the moment late in 1698 when prince Pyotr Golitsyn, sent from Russia to collect western artists and intellectuals for Peter the Great, succeeded in convincing Cosimo to allow the young castrato to accompany him to Russia.[71] The negotiations leading up to the agreement reveal the power dynamics involved in such exchanges. Cosimo wanted to satisfy the czar and turned for the boy's release to Filippo's father, who initially resisted, but Golitsyn renewed his appeal and succeeded on the condition imposed by both patron and father that Filippo be treated "as a son." Significantly, though, it was Cosimo who ultimately "sent him" abroad; nor was there any difficulty breaking a three-year contract the father had signed with a local singing master.[72] Thus from the outset, Balatri, like so many other castrati, was caught in a triangulated relationship of authority and submission in which the monarch nominally directed his "requests" to the castrato's father and the two passed down orders to the boy.[73]

The precipitous move north explains why, by the second stanza, the *Frutti del Mondo* already launches a picaresque tale of adventure, displacement, and hardship from which the author, following a conventional autobiographical strategy, repeatedly emerges triumphant. With his transfer to Russia, the complex network of authority and hierarchy thickened. The czar temporarily assumed the position of patron / surrogate parent held in the long run by Cosimo, while prince Golitsyn, who had fetched him, ended up substituting for his natural father. In this sense, the move to Russia entailed not just a new beginning but new vectors of kinship. Once arrived, Balatri was to live and serve at Peter's court as part of the czar's reformist project of modernizing Russian education, technology, and art. In Berneschian satire, he tells of suffering humiliations at the hands of other servants, who found his condition and religion repugnant and bullied him for it. The conflicts grew bad enough that within weeks he was moved from the czar's residence to that of the prince and his wife princess Dar'ia. Hardly had he passed a month there, however, before he was sent off on the large embassy through the steppes of central Asia to meet the Tartar khan of Astrakhan. Balatri describes the way back as a near death-march from which he returned ragged and filthy but found his efforts well repaid by a private audience with the czar, who called him "son," and by a warm familial reception from the Golitsyns.

Balatri and the Golitsyns always referred to and addressed one another as "son," "mother," and "father." The castrato resided with them in Russia for at least two years, gaining intimate—and unheard-of—access to the sexually segregated, staunchly Orthodox female quarters of the household (the so-called *terem*), living hour after hour by the embroidery frames, where once the princess Golitsyna and her girls had a hilarious time dressing him in drag.[74]

Called home by Cosimo and Balatri's father,[75] the boy began making his way west in 1701 in the company of the prince and his family through Warsaw and Breslau (Wrøclaw) to Vienna, where he stayed with them for another two years and studied with the head contralto castrato of the Viennese Hofkapelle, Gaetano Orsini. For the scene of his leavetaking, Balatri stages a protracted episode of heartbreak and tears on all sides. This in turn initiates a cycle of migration, wretchedness, bonding, and triumph, followed by bitter disengagement that was to repeat itself several times in as many decades, though never with the same intensity and esprit.

Once back in Tuscany, Balatri shuttled between his natal home in Pisa (which now struck him as shockingly spare and provincial) and the lavish court of the Grand Duke, from which he was kept far more distant than he had been from the czar's court in Moscow. In fall 1703, now twenty-one years old, he debuted in Florence playing Silvio in Albinoni's *Aminta*[76] and sojourned at the court as interpreter for a visiting Russian ambassador,[77] but otherwise stayed in Pisa singing at the Chiesa dei Cavalieri di Santo Stefano. Only when both of his parents died around 1710 did he mobilize attempts at employment elsewhere, getting leave from Cosimo to try his fortune abroad.[78] Leaving his last living natural kin, a brother Ferrante, he traveled alone through southern France,[79] and on to Paris and Versailles, where a gold outfit given him by the khan won him an audience with Louis XIV. In 1713 he arrived in London, studied there with the famed Handel singer Nicolini Grimaldi,[80] made a good debut at the Haymarket as *primo uomo* Rodoaldo, King of Norway, in a revival of the pasticcio *Ernelinda*,[81] and sang at the royal residence at Kensington. But his chances of finding sustained private patronage in London were reportedly hurt when the queen died on August 1, 1714.[82]

Balatri then reentered the crucible of dashed hopes, patrons lost, and harsh journeys in a renewed quest for court patronage, this time accompanied by his older brother Ferrante, a tenor, who by then had joined him. After again donning his Tartar outfit and obtaining a letter from Cosimo's daughter at Düsseldorf, the Electress Maria Anna Luisa,[83] he proceeded to the music-loving Elector of Bavaria, Maximilian II Emanuel (married into the Medici family), from whom at last he won for himself and his brother a secure position in the court family—though to accept it, he had to first gain consent from his primary patron Cosimo.[84]

The singer stayed in Bavaria, with only temporary excursions to Italy and Vienna, from 1715 until his death in 1756, performing at court gatherings and some public operatic and church occasions before his retirement to a local cloister. We can see him in a painting by Peter Jacob Horemans performing at a casual court concert at Schloß Ismaning, an electoral residence ten kilometers outside Munich, where he is seated at the harpsichord probably playing a trio sonata—the perfect courtier, at home in the court (Figure 7.4).[85]

The sunny first years at the Munich court had not lasted. By the time Horemans painted Balatri in 1733, he had already been devastated by a succession of paternal deaths that took place between 1723 until about 1726: first, the Grand Duke Cosimo III; then the Bishop Schönborn of Würzburg, with whom he had become a favorite; and most especially, the Elector

Figure 7.4 Peter Jacob Horemans, *Hofkonzert im Schloss Ismaning*, 1733 (oil painting, detail). Munich, Bayerische Nationalmuseum.

Maximilian.[86] Two years later he was crushed by the death of his brother Ferrante, which he pictures as the loss of his last familial anchor and the final catalyst in a classic Augustinian conversion, by which his earlier life of worldliness, caprice, vanity, and ignorance turns through a sudden epiphany to one of asceticism, introspection, repentance, and enlightenment. Not unlike Farinelli, though in his own unique genre, Balatri presents the reader with a tale of familial networks created, adapted, and reshaped over time through his divine singing, and also of the intersection of his adoptive families with natural ones.

Yet narratively the loss of his brother virtually erased a life that had gradually built a familial edifice from fragments of adopted and natural kin. In the conversional account of his *Frutti del Mondo*, Balatri turns to thoughts of the world beyond and eventually opts for a cloistered life, singing in a Cistercian monastery at Fürstenfeld, outside Munich. At his investiture in 1739, he took the name of Teodor in recognition of his last patron, Johann

Teodor, prince bishop of Frisinga and Ratisbona, as he says "in memory of the maker of his vocation"—and by extension, in dedication to the ultimate father, God (Theodore, "gift of God") in an elision of ruler and God emblematic of the old order. In a sense, then, his turn to the cloister reproduced the pattern of acquiring adoptive fathers that had marked his whole career. Even as at last he ascended the old patriarchal order to the status of "father" himself, he could become father figure to other nonreproductive boys.[87]

Reproduction, Kinship, and the Demise of the Old Order

What, then, of the link between these kinship patterns and Balatri's status as a male subject? Revealing are the encounters with the *spalniks* (pages) at the lower end of the culture wars (retold in the *Frutti del Mondo* in the carnivalesque language of Berni, Ariosto, and Boccaccio),[88] who regard the castrato as untouchable. To them he is the polluted other, of wrong confession, whose food they refuse to eat and whom they refuse to eat with. But the axis of food and pollution is reversed when Balatri attains the position of subject / ego on encountering another who is still more "other" than he, the khan—more object and difference—and who disgusts but endears him by kindly offering him food from his own divinely ordained mouth. This reversal establishes another strategy that is perpetuated throughout Balatri's autobiographical odysseys and also in his will, a strategy of acknowledging the veracity of an abject self before resolving its torments and foibles into a superior (if always self-mocking) being, mediated through its transcendent contact with higher authorities of the court. At first he is unworthy as a commensal among fellow servants, who are other than he, but soon thereafter becomes the most intimate commensal of a still-more-other monarch. He goes off on the march to Tartary as a weakling and "capon," but, once "uncaged," returns cocky, a "real warrior."[89] Through this scheme of turning abjection from self to other and back, and through his persistent literary techniques of self-parody, invective, and mischief, he manipulates a constant tension between the abject self and the courtly one, at last affirming the courtly imperative that finally informed the life of any performing castrato, especially in the early eighteenth century when the order that supported that life was still well in place. This imperative was at once part of his pathos and a means to overcome it.

It is also advanced in the face of an incessant stream of satire that he directs at himself and his inability to reproduce or perform sexually—charges of which he is a target especially because he is also an "idol" of princes and nobles—an "Orpheus," as he calls himself.[90] But in a world of dynastic supremacies, a world order that cascaded downward from God the father to the sovereign to the various social orders successively poised beneath them, he is also harmless in his irreproducibility. So it is not surprising that Balatri's few flirtations with women (the czar's mistress Anna Mons, we are told, and later a Pisan nun) are hopeless bagatelles. Before long he forswears the female sex and at last jokes that he is writing his own testament because he does not want to be inspected by old women after his death: "As regards my body, I don't want . . . to be washed and handled by women, as is the custom in the country in which I find myself at present. And should I die, . . . besides the indecency that I see in this, I don't want them to be entertaining themselves by seeing how sopranos are made. . . ."[91]

In this way and others, Balatri again and again lampoons a lack. He is forever a castrato, a "castratino," "di gener misto," a "hic et hoc," a "castrone male," a "cappone," a "capponcino." Here and there he even spells out literally his lack of kind not as a castrato or "ermafrodito," but as a "cast . . . o," or "ermaf. . . ."[92]

Balatri might almost have penned his text to give form to Julia Kristeva's psychoanalytic poetics of the abject, as sketched in the opening of her *Powers of Horror*:

> There looms, with abjection, one of those violent, dark revolts of being, directed against a threat that seems to emanate from an exorbitant outside or inside, ejected beyond the scope of the possible, the tolerable, the thinkable. It lies there, quite close, but it cannot be assimilated. It beseeches, worries, fascinates desire, which nevertheless does not let itself be seduced. Apprehensive, desire turns aside; sickened, it rejects. A certainty . . . of which it is proud holds on to it. But simultaneously . . . that impetus, that spasm, that leap is drawn toward an elsewhere as tempting as it is condemned. Unflaggingly, like an inescapable boomerang, a vortex of summons and repulsion places the one haunted by it *literally beside itself*.[93]

Kristeva defines food loathing as the most elemental stimulus of this sensation, and one that initiates a cycle of revulsion-rejection-desire and then becoming the other. Death, concentrated in the corpse, is its *ultimate* stimulus. "It shows me what I permanently thrust aside in order to live," Kristeva writes—a kind of disintegration of the subject in the face of abjection but also a reintegration. By this logic, the castrato, epitomized by his corpse, can be thought of as indeed the ultimate stimulus of such a cycle, ultimate because desire, mixed even with envy, the increased heartbeat, spasms in the belly, what Kristeva calls "sight-clouding dizziness," is so terribly extreme and the fear it causes so great. Why else would that proudest and most desired of beings, Farinelli, have told Charles Burney in the 1770s that he was a "despicable being"? To be sure, his was a transposition of Kristeva's dynamic of the abject from the *self* in whom revulsion-desire begins in the eye of the *other/beholder,* who first perceives it as a state seemingly outside himself (and only thus experiences it). But it is nevertheless a bald acknowledgment of the abjection of the castrato, and one all the more striking for issuing from the proudest, most private, and most revered of them all.

The threads that wind together this sense of abjection and Balatri's own physical vulnerability with his laments over reproduction and kinship are brought together over the issue of death in the castrato's darkest text, the satirical, diffuse, literary, but nevertheless serious testament that Balatri wrote eighteen years before he died. Death here is a kind of unveiling that Balatri wants to avoid. It is the body grotesque, consumed by worms, reeking of stench, rotting away. Repeatedly over many pages he stages scenes of the castrato as a monstrous object of spectacle and gossip. In one scene he imagines what would happen were he to die on a visit to Italy, where his fetid corpse would be attended by a nun who trades horrors over it with a female curiosity-seeker:

> SISTER: I wouldn't know what to tell you, except that he's a foreigner, who came not long ago to stay in this city. Oh, how ugly he is, my Agatha, I tremble for fear of dreaming about him.
> AGATHA: I was thinking about that too, Sister, and to tell you truly I repented of my own curiosity . . . , since I share your fear.
> SISTER: Dear Agatha, I could spend three days not eating, he turns my stomach so much! . . .
> AGATHA: . . . Blessed Sister, don't you see that he has no beard yet, nor any sign of having had one? The illness must have been long and painful. . . .
> SISTER: He has no beard because he's a castrato. Nothing but dry figs.
> AGATHA: Oh, he was a castrato? Well, if that's the case, he will have left a lot of money. Does anyone know who he left it to?[94]

Money without blood relations: this is the castrato's dilemma. But note that the cycle of disgust-desire that marks Balatri's scene is three-pronged, mobilized because he is grotesque, because he is a foreigner, and because he is monied. In keeping with Farinelli's comment to Burney, what he stages is a meta-commentary on the self, not so much his own disgust-desire in the face of the abject as a recognition of his own abjection as the stimulus of disgust-desire in others.

In his mood of gross satire, Balatri explains money as the key element of the dilemma by making recourse to a life-and-death parable of the pig—like the chicken, a domestic animal and historically one of the most ambivalent of creatures for humans.[95]

> Were I a stubborn sort, I'd have cut the figure of a pig. The pig, so long as it lives, is deemed a vile animal. Every hole is fine for the pig. All the garbage is given to the pig. Is there anyone who caresses it, or keeps it close at hand? But as soon as it's dead, everybody runs to the larder and from its skin on in, there's not the minutest part that isn't prized. It's praised, it's tasted, it's the delight of everyone, because one can eat it.

Balatri's identification with the pig in life echoes traditional cultural uses of pigs as mediators of money, but also a spectrum of other conditions that render the subject stable—status, class, and gender. In the sixteenth century, for instance, Ambroise Paré dramatized the close but ambivalent relations of pigs to humans in telling of a girl who ran after a pig, jumped over a ditch, and became a boy.[96] Precisely because of this precarious association, Balatri on the brink of death feels not "prized," like a dead pig, but unloved and alone like a live one. Nor is he about to turn himself into a conceited ass, and let everyone who disdained him in life feed on his funeral and riches in death:

> Would you think me so foolish, having been a simple castrato, that I might then want to *turn my ass into a marquis*—that is, associate my body with money—when it goes to putrefy the earth? I have fed it fodder enough in life, without my thinking to distinguish it by embalming it, perfuming it, and flattering it after it's kicked the bucket.

No, he plans to shed his worldly ties and die a pauper and a pauper's friend:

> For, having been graced by the blessed sacraments, it suffices [to have] the distinction of going to a cemetery, or a church, which is the house of God. If a thousand, two thousand candles were to suffice to send the soul straight to its true center, oh I would like to fill my mug with my own fisticuffs had I not thought of making such an expenditure. But having considered that two thousand sighs of the poor, sent to God to obtain mercy for me, burn better (and at the same time put out that fire that burns without burning out), *I greatly prefer going to the burial as baron of the piazza than as marquis of the city.*[97]

For anyone who knows Ghezzi's cross-dressed caricature of Farinelli, the elision between the castrato and the pig may not seem entirely new. Giving Farinelli a ladylike dress and a porcine profile, Ghezzi fashioned a figure made still more "piggish" by contrast with his feminine vanity. Recall that the marquis and the ass who emerge from Balatri's tortured meditations on the pig were figures elided in Melosio's sonnet cited above, where the Pulcinella of castrated patrimony was a pompous, strutting fool—the marquis / ass hatched from an egg that had been fertilized by a pair of castrated testicles. By contrast with that vain marquis of the city, the "baron of the piazza" is a three-penny image in early-modern poetics. Balatri may no longer have any kin in this world, he says, but by going to the burial as baron of the open-air piazza through the stroke of a single bequest of his wealth to the nameless poor, he will acquire a whole family in the afterlife:

> Inasmuch as I . . . have no wife, children, or relatives, a lone friend (and even then, only if he wants to be), few acquaintances (mostly monks), no one who is beholden to me, and no one who cares if I live a hundred years or drop dead tonight, I wanted to marry some people I don't know, and get from them sons, brothers, relatives, friends, and others myself . . . and because of that I've resolved to make a testament conforming to what I'll state below.[98]

Between his many yarns and gags, *burle* and *facezie*, Balatri proceeds to make a bequest that is actually pointed in its practical instructions on how his assets should be liquidated and distributed.[99]

If Balatri's will feigned gladness at lacking natural offspring, his earlier texts had told a different story. Particularly striking is a passage from the first volume of his *Vita e viaggi,* in which he describes the motive, process, and consequence of his castration—the only such description by a castrato ever to come to light:

> It was established that my voice was of the finest metal, with a natural trill and good attack, outstanding fluency in passagework and a general taste for natural singing. The basis for this judgment was urgently arrived at by friends of my father's, crying out "Cut! Cut!" (and then, more than all the others, by my singing teacher) to advise my father; so that after the many cries of "Cut! Cut!" my father finally joined in too, and sent to Lucca for the surgeon Accoramboni, who was made to come to the house to stay for two months and engage me in a little gracious conversation.
>
> This chitter-chatter was so expensive that instead of the doctoral degree (which I would have been able to obtain one day) I was given a diploma to

pass as a "Frigidus et Maleficatus" [Cold and Injured Man] for the rest of my life, renouncing forever the sweet name that I would have heard given me one day of "Father."[100]

The paternal legacy Balatri sketches here is dark: his father capitulated to the pressure of peers, obstructed Balatri's higher education, bequeathed him a "cold," injured body (an obvious humoral reference to his loss of the vital male "heat" that was supposed to make men men), and made it impossible for his son to continue the paternal line or experience the joys of fatherhood. Small wonder that when it comes time to plan his funeral, Balatri shuns the ornate singing, with cadenzas, passaggi, and trills, that he had cultivated throughout his life. Unsuited to a stinking corpse and to a passage from earthly to celestial realms, he wants only monophonic singing.

> I don't want polyphonic music, but a mass in chant; and sung with devotion by four priests.
> Because I was a castrato of some distinction, perhaps a din of voices and instruments will come to me as if it were a wedding, to have no role except for people to say "let's go hear the funeral of so-and-so; hopefully it'll be nice, because all the music of the city will be there." And while I, closed in a coffin, warmed by candle lights and by the crowd, start to stink like a carrion, the musicians may go on extending *passaggi* and trills with cadenzas half an hour long, and with the auditor listening and applauding, perhaps not even singing me a "rest in peace."[101]

We might wonder if the twentieth-century apostle of castration theory was onto anything when he dreamt of a primeval world in which castration fantasies are an everyday part of family drama. In the scene Freud stages in *Totem and Taboo* as a kind of originary historical moment, a boy wants to kill his father because of his incestuous love for his mother. This Œdipal urge produces an overwhelming sense of guilt that generates the beginning of civilization. According to such a Freudian interpretation, the logic underlying the kinship structures of the castrati we have considered would understand the castrated boy as having seen his worst fear realized: that of having been castrated by an enraged father (or, phantasmatically, a totemic substitute), who, if we recast this as a kind of universal fantasy, the boy himself had had an urge to kill. Allowing that the fantasy is just that, but that in our case the castration itself is real, the substitution of alternate father figures, combined with the structural displacements from natal family required by prevailing patronage systems and the inaccessibility of the mother, could become intelligible, at least in theory, as characteristic features of the castrato's kinship system. So too the castrato's kinships with other castrati and theater people, as idealized in Amigoni's familial group scene (see Figure 7.3), which we might even understand as some distant realization of Freud's notion that a band of brothers shared the rebellious urge against their father.[102] Certainly, if we are fans of reality over fantasy we have plenty to chew on.

I am hardly prepared to argue that the narrative of Freud's Œdipus complex should be rehabilitated as an explanation for why many castrati had such hybridized kinship structures (natural and adopted), or why castration was taboo, though I'm not sure we can ignore it altogether either. Like it or not, psychoanalytic concepts have entered the critical discourse about castrati, where terms such as guilt, suppression, repressed desire, and substitution often appear unmarked and unremarked.[103] My own interest is to ground culture in history, in this case to entertain questions about how tales of birth and becoming that surround castrati link up with their patterns of kinship and with eighteenth-century patterns of the family generally; to explore how these are expressed in life-writing and wider discourses of praise and criticism that attach to castrati; and to ask how the unmanned man circumvents the hierarchical order in ways that speak to the status of that order.

A good place to return to these questions is Sacchi's life of Farinelli, which claims that his natural parents were noble.[104] Sacchi's terms are suspiciously generic, but they have the strategic advantage of allowing him to insist that Farinelli's castration was done out of necessity and not for profit: he was *not* "placed under the knife in childhood in order to preserve the tenderness of his voice, and thus sell it," Sacchi tells us, "but rather to preserve a life in grave danger as a result of his boyish liveliness in leaping over a horse, as a result of which he was also wounded on his front side."[105] The account, I have suggested, seemingly inverts Farinelli's own avowal to Pepoli that he was not of mythological but of quasi-noble lineage. Unlike Sacchi, Farinelli made the claim purely by association (with his godfather), but in the end both sustain the myth.

Writing in 1784, Sacchi was recasting mythologies of the castrato's birth in the face of charges that castrations were done out of meretricious motives, and in a cultural mood that had become less and less enamored of the castrato voice, more and more fearful of abjection and self-loss in its presence, and more and more intolerant of the practices that produced it. By the latter half of the century, the Englishman John Moore could write that

> the natural sweetness of the female voice is ill supplied by the artificial trills of wretched castratos; and the awkward sinewy fellows dressed in women's clothes, is a most deplorable substitution for the graceful movements of elegant female dancers. Is not the horrid practice which is encouraged by this manner of supplying the place of female singers a greater outrage on religion and morality, than can be produced by the evils which their prohibition is intended to prevent?[106]

In the second half of the eighteenth century, Moore's objections were shared by virtually all Italians who fancied themselves enlightened, and who could no more reconcile the disparities of gender, voice, and body signified by the castrato than a practice that seemed to them to contradict "nature."[107] Reading Sacchi's text against objections like Moore's, which were rampant by the later eighteenth century, dramatizes the critical historic juncture at which they were produced—a juncture of growing bourgeois embarrassment over the status of the nuclear family that worried a lot about the legitimacy of fathers and the morality of mothers, and that tried to improve the constitution and image of the nuclear family.[108] In his own suggestion of a noble lineage for himself, Farinelli proposed his natural place as a courtly one that could serve to mute the meretricious implications of his position and its sheer abasement. But by the later eighteenth century, to deny that the castrato was a mercantile being and a commodity became increasingly untenable in a time when he was radically commodified, and when his triumphs dangerously assumed the very supremacy that, in the court culture of old, had not belonged to the subject at all but to the sovereign.

EIGHT

Sex Without Sex

An Erotic Image of the Castrato Singer

ROGER FREITAS

In his 1702 comparison of French and Italian music, François Raguenet writes,

> these [castrato] voices, sweet as nightingales, are enchanting in the mouths of actors playing the part of a lover. Nothing is more touching than the expression of their pains uttered with that timbre of voice, so tender and impassioned. And the Italians have in this a great advantage over the lovers in our [French] theaters whose voices, heavy and virile, are consistently much less suitable to the sweet words they address to their mistresses.[1]

Essentially, Raguenet is suggesting that a castrated man is better suited to representing a lover than an intact one. Indeed, by the beginning of the eighteenth century, the castrato had become the overwhelming favorite to portray the young, amorous men—the *primi uomini*—who dominated the operatic stage. Of course today, such a preference seems, to put it mildly, strange: the original casting practices of early opera continue to exercise modern directors and critics of the genre. Recently, a number of writers have drawn attention away from this apparent problem by objectifying the castrato's voice, uncoupling his glorious sounds from his problematic body.[2]

Under the influence of such writers as Jacques Lacan and Roland Barthes, they often view the castrato body as a kind of blank, a vessel whose potency has been drained into the sole organ of the voice. Without taking time here to debate this tactic directly, I would like to suggest that if the castrati are viewed in their historical context—a context, I argue, that took shape over the course of the *seventeenth* century—the need for this additional, theoretical dismemberment vanishes. Indeed, as I shall try to show, the castrato represented not a neutral vessel for an exotic sound, but rather an alluring figure whose talent only augmented an innate desirability: castrati played amorous leading roles not in spite of their physical distinctiveness, but because of it. Or, to put it another way, as much as the taste for castrato singing may have produced emasculated protagonists, so also, I believe, did the taste for emasculated protagonists bolster the tradition of castrato singing.

A key to comprehending such an alien sensibility may be found in the conception of sexuality that characterized the early modern period. For this background, I am indebted primarily to the work of Thomas Laqueur, who, more than any other scholar, has traced the discontinuities in sexual attitudes between the early modern and post-Enlightenment periods.[3] He suggests that the most fundamental, and radically unfamiliar, element of the earlier viewpoint is its premise of a one-sex system. That is to say, instead of explaining male and female bodies as two distinct forms of the human species, the early modern tradition considered man to be the more perfect manifestation of the one body that both men and women shared.[4] The differences between the sexes lay not in the flesh itself, but in the higher phenomenon of vital heat. This insensible but fundamental energy of life not only determined the development of sexual organs in the womb but also influenced the balance of humors throughout life, and thus all aspects of a person's health, character, and intelligence.[5]

With respect to the castrato, the greatest significance of the one-sex model lies in its implication of a vertical, hierarchical continuum ranging from man down to woman. As Laqueur observes, woman was regarded in the seventeenth century and before as "a lesser version of man along a vertical axis of infinite gradations," while after the eighteenth century, she was considered "an altogether different creature along a horizontal axis whose middle ground was largely empty."[6] In the earlier period, difference in sex was a quantitative, not qualitative, matter, and a well-populated middle ground between the usual sexes was broadly acknowledged.[7]

Significantly, the most familiar inhabitant of this middle ground was the prepubescent child. Although in the womb differences in vital heat between male and female were considered great enough to determine genital formation, a man's full heat was not thought to develop until adolescence, when the bodies of boys and girls began to differentiate themselves.[8] Castrating a boy before puberty, then, did not throw his sex, in the modern sense, into question. It merely froze him within the middle ground of the hierarchy of sex: he never experienced the final burst of vital heat that would have taken him to full masculinity. Sexually speaking—and this is an essential point—the castrato would have been viewed as equivalent to the boy. In fact, he was an arrested boy: although his body would increase in size, his surgery ensured that his vital heat, and thus his physical characteristics, would remain at the less markedly masculine level of youth.

Lacking this vital heat, both castrati and young boys were described as *effeminate*, an important concept in this discussion.[9] Whereas today describing a man as effeminate might imply homosexual leanings, the same term in the seventeenth century connoted too great a taste for *women*.[10] Indeed, scholars such as Ann Jones and Peter Stallybrass have concluded that in this period "it is 'heterosexuality' itself which is effeminating for men."[11] Thus, a man who succumbed too much to the pleasures of the flesh, whose existence revolved too much around women, was considered in danger of losing his masculine nature and even physical strength.[12] By the same principle, a man who presented a rather feminine demeanor—like the boy or castrato—was considered predisposed to becoming ensnared in the womanish pursuits of love.

In fact, the erotically charged boy appears frequently in early modern literature and art, and I would like to pursue his representation briefly before turning to the castrato himself. As Winfried Schleiner observes, authors of Renaissance romances "had a predilection for very young heroes."[13] The central character of the paradigmatic *Amadis de Gaule*, for example, is described by his companion as "so young that you don't yet have any facial hair and have an appearance that will let you be taken for a beautiful girl."[14] Giambattista Marino's Adonis (from *L'Adone*, 1623) is obviously cut from the same cloth:

> Adonis was then at the age that feels
> the spark of love most vigorous and keen,
> and he was disposed to face
> the new bitterness, ill-timed to his years.
> Nor on the roses of his lovely cheeks
> had yet blossomed any bud of gold;

or if any shadow of hair had begun to show,
it seemed like a flower in the field or star in heaven.

In blond ringlets of pure shining gold
his hair writhed and curled,
under which there flowed the white line
of his ample forehead in smiling majesty.
A sweet vermilion, a sweet burning flame,
mingled with living milk and living frosts,
tinged his face with such a blush as
roses take on between dawn and daytime.

But who can paint the two stars, clear and bright,
of his twin brows?
Who can portray the lovely scarlet of his sweet lips,
rich and full of fiery treasure?
What whiteness of ivory or lily
can equal his throat, which raises and sustains,
like a column of adamant,
a heaven of marvels assembled in that lovely countenance?[15]

Far from the virile specimen the name Adonis popularly invokes today, Marino's paragon of male beauty is still waiting for puberty, with just the first hints of down on his face. The description of his long golden hair, white skin, blushing cheeks, ruby lips, clear eyes, and ivory neck could just as easily have been applied to a woman; but here, such traits portray a boy at the age "when the spark of love feels most vigorous and keen."

Of course, representations of Adonis and his youthful brethren also populate the visual arts. Annibale Carracci's *Venus and Adonis* (1588–89; Madrid, Museo del Prado; see Figure 8.1) shows a young hunter who almost seems the incarnation of Marino's hero, with his long golden hair, white body, and beardless, feminine face. Similarly, Domenichino's Rinaldo, lying in the lap of his Armida (ca. 1620–21; Paris, Louvre; see Figure 8.2), could almost be mistaken for the enchantress's handmaiden instead of her lover. Pietro da Cortona crowned his Sala di Venere (1641–42; Florence, Palazzo Pitti; see Figure 8.3) with an image of Minerva carrying off another of these youths from the sumptuous couch of a dismayed Venus and transporting him to the waiting arms of Hercules. The fresco, with its inscription "Pallas tears the adolescent away from Venus," clearly contends that lovemaking is an activity of boyhood and that mature men should strive for more heroic, manly deeds.[16] Luca Giordano's *Diana and Endimion* of the late

Figure 8.1 Annibale Carracci, *Venus and Adonis*, 1588–89. Madrid, Museo del Prado. Erich Lessing/Art Resource, New York.

Figure 8.2 Domenichino, *Rinaldo and Armida*, ca. 1620–21. Paris, Musée de Louvre. Erich Lessing/Art Resource, New York.

Figure 8.3 Pietro da Cortona, *Pallas Tears the Adolescent Away from Venus*, 1641–42. Florence, Palazzo Pitti. Alinari/Art Resource, New York.

1670s (Washington, D.C., National Gallery of Art) and Giovanni Battista Tiepolo's *Rinaldo Leaving Armida* of ca. 1756–57 (Florence, Galleria degli Uffizi) confirm the persistence of the ideal of the boyishly effeminate lover.

What is perhaps most surprising—and today disturbing—about the prevalence of the boyish lover in literature and art is that he also seems to have been the object of much real-life desire. That is, his evident effeminacy linked him to eroticism not only in theory but also in practice. One locus of this eroticization was the apparently widespread exercise of pederasty, for among men whose tastes included homosexual sodomy boys were the generally preferred partners.[17] In fact, in a society so misogynistic that some could view the purpose of sexual pleasure as "that which enables men to overcome their natural revulsion at the defectiveness of women," one is not surprised that in some circles pederastic sodomy was proposed as a more salubrious replacement for heterosexual sex.[18] Interestingly, one of the most important fora for this discourse was the Accademia degli Incogniti of Venice, an organization that played a central role in establishing the genre of opera.[19] The most extreme statement on the matter appears in *L'Alcibiade fanciullo a scola* (ca. 1651) by the "Incognito" Antonio Rocco.[20] In this treatise, a teacher tries to convince his student of the naturalness and indeed superiority of pederasty, citing the contaminating nature of sex with women. In Wendy Heller's assessment of Rocco's central point,

> [The boy] Alcibiade's perfection consists in his possession of female beauty in a male body. Boys are thus the ideal object for male love because they are superior to women both spiritually and physically. And the particular pleasure of boys is that they offer the possibility of enjoying feminine beauty without the necessity of congress with a woman.[21]

A boy partook of enough of the feminine to be attractive to a man, but not so much as to contaminate him.

For different reasons, presumably, such boys also seem to have been attractive to women. To be sure, discerning a true female perspective in the seventeenth and early eighteenth centuries is difficult: the many artworks depicting women with young boys all originate with men. Still, some of the earliest statements of preferences by women do focus on the softer, more effeminate male. Lady Anna Riggs Miller's *Letters from Italy* of 1776, for example, recounts the author's reaction to the famously brawny Farnese Hercules (Glykon, third century A.D.?; Naples, Museo Archeologico Nazionale):

> It may be very beautiful, and the most perfect model of a man in the world; but I am insensible enough to its charms to own, that if all mankind were so proportioned, I should think them very disagreeable and odious. The muscles of this Hercules . . . are like craggy rocks compared with the Belvideran Apollo.[22]

In fact, the latter, smooth-limbed and with "angelic sweetness," clearly represented Miller's ideal of male beauty (second century A.D.; Vatican City, Museo Pio-Clementino).[23] From this case and others, literary historian Chloe Chard generalizes, "grace and beauty are . . . qualities that are regularly identified in the eighteenth century as attributes of the female or effeminate body. They are also, however, defined as qualities to which women are particularly attracted."[24]

My central argument here is that, on the operatic stage, the castrato represented a theatrical imitation, characteristically exaggerated, of this erotically charged effeminate boy. Just as stage sets might idealize an architectural vista or the costumes aggrandize Roman armor, so too did the castrato magnify the familiar youth.

Support for this assertion comes from many quarters. Physically, of course, a castrato simply retained a number of his boyish qualities well into the years of adulthood: although he might grow in height (sometimes to unusual proportions), he retained the high voice, lack of beard, and soft body of the boy. The few known portraits of castrati also suggest that they retained their boyish round faces and full cheeks, probably a consequence of eunuchoid fat patterning (see Figure 8.4).[25] That this boyish appearance tended to affect the contemporary conception of these creatures is suggested by the frequent use, well into adulthood, of diminutive nicknames for them, such as Nicolino, Senesino, Marianino, and Pauluccio.[26] In addition, I have found evidence in the correspondence of the castrato Atto Melani (1626–1714) that he, at least, also sometimes thought of himself in boyish terms: at age thirty-five, for example, he lamented to one of his patrons that he was "le plus

Figure 8.4 Bartolomeo Nazzari, portrait of Carlo Broschi (Farinelli), 1734. London, Royal College of Music.

miserable garçon du monde."[27] For someone who was at the time serving as diplomat to the papal court to refer to himself as a "boy" in a letter to the French foreign minister surely hints at a peculiar contemporary mind-set.

A further indication of this mind-set is the similarity of sexual roles that adult men apparently expected of castrati and boys. Considering how much participants would have wanted to hide their activities, the number of documented liaisons between noblemen and castrati is surprising. Marc'Antonio Pasqualini's intimacy with Cardinal Antonio Barberini in the early 1640s is well known, and around fifty years later Grand Prince Ferdinando de' Medici carried on an even more open affair with the castrato Francesco (called Cecchino) de Castris, who himself replaced Ferdinando's previous castrato favorite, Petrillo.[28] Indeed, satirists treated such affairs as if they were the norm. In his poem on music, the painter and man of letters Salvator Rosa (1615–1673) complained of the special treatment castrati earned by their sexual services: "Miracles are so customary in palaces / that a beardless *musico*, with his charms, / [by being] ridden, unseats even the most wise."[29]

A well-known letter of Saint-Évremond from around 1685 emphasizes the connection between boys and castrati in a different way. The letter is addressed to a Monsieur Dery, a young page serving the Duchess Mazarin and known for his singing; Saint-Évremond's purpose is to convince the boy to submit to castration.

> I would say to you, in an entirely discreet way, that you must sweeten [*adoucir*] yourself by means of a mild operation that will assure the delicacy of your complexion for a long time and the beauty of your voice for your whole life. The money, the red coats, the little horses that you receive are not given to the son of Monsieur Dery because of his nobility; your face and your voice win them. In three or four years, alas!, you will lose the quality of both if you do not have the wisdom to provide for this eventuality, and the source of all these nice things will have dried up. . . . But you fear, you say, to be less loved by the ladies. Be rid of your apprehension: we are no longer living in the age of idiots. The merit that follows the operation is well recognized today, and for every mistress that Monsieur Dery would have in his natural state, the sweetened Monsieur Dery will have a hundred.[30]

Not only does this letter suggest that the operation will make the boy more (rather than less) attractive to women, but it also highlights the sense of *preservation* that surrounds the operation. The castrato is indeed viewed as a temporally extended boy. The effect—indeed, the purpose—of castration is to preserve the boy's attractions, his beautiful face and voice.

A number of artworks appear to corroborate the link between the physical appearance of the castrato and that of the boy. Having studied a number of paintings of castrati, art historian Franca Trinchieri Camiz describes Caravaggio's *Singer with Lute* (1595–96; New York, Private Collection)—apparently modeled after the castrato Pietro Montoya—as displaying the "androgynous and effeminate aspect characteristic of the representation of castrati."[31] Caravaggio's singer, however, exhibits all the same delicate qualities elsewhere used to depict the various youthful heroes of legend; to me, the singer's face particularly resembles that of Guido Reni's slightly later Hippomenes (1618–19; Madrid, Museo del Prado), clearly not intended to represent a castrato. Whether boys and castrati actually looked so much alike, the resemblance of artistic representations suggests how similarly they could be viewed.

That similarity seems particularly striking in a few works of Tiepolo. One of the visible physical distinctions of the castrati—besides the absence of facial hair—was a lack of proportion that frequently affected various elements of their bodies. Removal of the male sex glands had a secondary effect on the entire growth process; specifically, the larger bones of the body—primarily in the arms and legs—did not receive the chemical signal to stop growing at the appropriate time and so sometimes continued to abnormal lengths. Indeed, eighteenth-century caricaturists frequently exaggerate this feature (see Figure 8.5). Such cartoons also regularly emphasize the disproportion between the torso and head: again, the chest cavity seems to have expanded exceptionally while the head remained boyishly small. Even some serious portraits, such as that of Farinelli by Bartolomeo Nazzari (1734; London, Royal College of Music), register this latter incongruity (see again Figure 8.4).

Striking, then, is the appearance of that same incongruity in a number of Tiepolo's representations of heroes. In his *Family of Darius before Alexander* (1743–44, Montecchio Maggiore, Villa Cordellina; see Figure 8.6), for example, both Alexander and Hephaestion, at right, seem to have heads somewhat too small for their bodies; the same is true of the hero in the artist's *Rinaldo Leaving Armida* (mentioned above). While these small heads may be one more indicator of the youth (and resultant effeminacy) of these characters, the images so resemble the typical deformations of the castrati that I wonder if more is not implied. The sense of operatic spectacle may have so permeated the conceptions of this painter, working in the home city of the *dramma per musica*, that even the appearance of his heroes was sometimes affected by stage conventions.[32] For Tiepolo, it seems, the boyish ideal of male beauty has become imprinted with the castrato's peculiar features.

Figure 8.5 Antonio Maria Zanetti, caricature of Farinelli in *Catone in Utica*, 1729. Venice, Fondazione Giorgio Cini.

In this chapter, I have tried to suggest how a practice that at first seems paradoxical—castrated men portraying amorous heroes—can become at least comprehensible when viewed in context. If the convention today disconcerts, it is because it was rooted in a configuration of human sexuality that differs radically from current norms. The most significant distinctions are the equation of love with effeminacy and the link between psychology and physicality: to be not quite fully masculine, in body or manner, was to be especially susceptible to love. Indeed, the evidence from the period confirms that, whereas now masculine eroticism can be epitomized by firm muscles, a "healthy" tan, and perhaps even an unshaven face, the earlier period prized a soft body, pale skin, and smooth cheeks. The ideal male was simply younger, and so more androgynous, than is currently typical. When in the seventeenth century this youthful masculine ideal met the baroque penchant for exaggeration, the operatic castrato was the result. It was an age that valued artifice: the far-flung conceits of Marinistic poetry,

Figure 8.6 Giovanni Battista Tiepolo, *Family of Darius before Alexander*, 1743–44. Montecchio Maggiore (near Vicenza), Villa Cordellina.

the fantastic opulence of Jesuit church style, the extravagant rituals of court existence. Even in landscape design, as historian Franco Valsecchi writes, "it is artifice which dominates, the search for effect. . . . Nature is transformed, deformed; the vegetation is choked by art."[33] So too was the natural boy transformed by his deforming surgery into something deemed more compelling than Nature's own creations. When in the eighteenth century the taste for such exaggeration started to waver, the castrato tradition too began to be questioned. Within the protective conservatism of Italy and opera seria, the appreciation for artificially effeminate lovers survived the Age of

Enlightenment—latter-day representatives of an aesthetic that was under assault; the political and cultural changes of the nineteenth century, however, finally compelled their demise.[34] For the castrato was a quintessentially *baroque* figure. In that culture of hyperbole, which lived on in the opera houses of the eighteenth century, he represented not an asexual mechanism of vocal virtuosity, but rather the spectacular exaggeration of the "beardless boy," the idealized lover.

NINE

Anatomy of a Lesbian

*Medicine, Pornography, and Culture
in Eighteenth-Century Italy*

PAULA FINDLEN

In March 1751 a brief notice of a new book appeared in London's *Monthly
Review*. Titled *An Historical and Physical Dissertation on the Case of Catherine Vizzani* (London, 1751), it was written by an Italian anatomy professor,
Giovanni Bianchi, and freshly translated into English; interested readers
could purchase it for one shilling from W. Meyer in the May's Building
near St. Martin's Lane. The publisher of the *Monthly Review*, Ralph Griffiths, allowed the reviewer only the briefest notice of this treatise, remark-
ing: "We beg leave to decline any further mention of this article, for a
reason that our readers will easily guess at; and we are sure that the female
part of them will as easily pardon the omission."[1] The subtitle highlighted
the reason for Griffiths' discretion since the book purported to describe
"The Adventures of a young Woman, born at Rome, who for eight years
passed in the Habit of a Man, was killed for an Amour with a young Lady;
and being found, on Dissection, a true Virgin, narrowly escaped being

Thanks to Wendy Roworth and Cat Sama for their comments, to Katy Park and Gianna Pomata for
bibliographic suggestions, and to Clorinda Donato for her generosity in discussing our mutual fascination with Bianchi's little book.

treated as a Saint. With some Curious and Anatomic
Nature and Existence of the Hymen."[2] Despite the ac
of the first part of the title, the full description was
readers, presenting them with a tale of sex, violenc
that poked fun at the pretensions of Catholicism and delved into
tomical secrets of the female body. Only a publisher who had been arrested
for his role in distributing John Cleland's infamous *Memoirs of a Woman of
Pleasure* (1748–49) could exercise such moral restraint when faced with the
prospect of reviewing such a tempting subject.[3]

There was more to Griffiths' circumspection, however, than fear of offending the allegedly delicate sensibilities of his female readers. He knew
who the anonymous "English Editor" of Caterina Vizzani's life was: none
other than his friend and close associate Cleland (1710–1789).[4] Following
his release from debtors' prison in 1749 and the infamy of his novel about
the erotic life of Fanny Hill, Cleland embarked on a close and profitable
relationship with Griffiths for several years, writing numerous reviews for
the *Monthly Review,* including some which discussed his own publications.
He had recently finished his expurgation of *Memoirs of a Woman of Pleasure,*
printing a tamer version under the title of *Memoirs of Fanny Hill* (1750).[5] He
was in the midst of drafting his second novel, *Memoirs of a Coxcomb* (1751),
and had begun to consider the idea of devoting some portion of his literary
career to translation. *Catherine Vizzani* represented Cleland's first foray into
the potentially lucrative market for scandalous books from the continent.[6]
The choice of subject may also have reflected a growing interest in medicine since Cleland would later publish such works as *The Institutes of Health*
(1761) and *Phisiological Reveries* (1765). While it is still uncertain what role
Griffiths himself may have played in the appearance of this translation, neither he nor Cleland had any desire to draw undue attention to the fact that
they were still plying their trade in titillating tales of love and lust.

Despite the enticing subject, Cleland's translation of Bianchi's little treatise was not a rousing success. Since it is highly likely that he published the
book with the intention of making a profit—perhaps inspired by the recent
appearance of Henry Fielding's *The Female Husband* (1746), another true-life
tale of cross-dressing, same-sex desire, and crime that Terry Castle has aptly
described as "lesbian picaresque"[7]—he must have been sorely disappointed.
Memoirs of a Woman of Pleasure had already gone through at least three editions by 1750, but he did not have much to show for it beyond a dubious
reputation.[8] While we know very little about this other book's reception

.d distribution, a close examination of the second edition of 1755 suggests that it had languished in the publisher's stock of books for several years. In all likelihood, W. Meyer sold his remaining copies to W. Reeve of Fleet Street and C. Sympson "at the Bible-warehouse," who attempted to liven it up by changing the title and adding a frontispiece (Figure 9.1). *The True History and Adventures of Catherine Vizzani* (London, 1755) may have done better than its predecessor—though the fact that it still sold at one shilling suggests that it was purchased at a discount—but Cleland remained, to the end, an anonymous contributor to this obscure project.[9]

Hanoverian England was awash in a sea of lewd and erotic books, and Cleland was the master of this genre.[10] It was a society that eagerly consumed

Figure 9.1 Giovanni Bianchi, *The True History and Adventures of Catherine Vizzani,* trans. John Cleland, 2nd ed. (London, 1755). By permission of the British Library.

adventure stories, romances, and tales of true crime and reveled in a thriving popular medical literature that spilled forth the secrets of the body to willing readers. In this regard, the story of one of Cleland's failed publications tells us very little about the literary marketplace of the mideighteenth century because, unlike *Fanny Hill*, it was not a significant book that reached a wide audience. Yet it is nonetheless a work with an interesting history that offers a number of insights into the world of authorship, publishing, and translation. Most important, it affords us a fairly unique perspective on gender and sexuality in eighteenth-century Italy, as seen through the mirror of the Grand Tour.

A Physician's Lewd Little Book

Like John Cleland, the original author of the *Brief History of the Life of Caterina Vizzani, a Roman* (1744) was a man in search of opportunities to make his fortune in the Republic of Letters.[11] Giovanni Bianchi (1693–1775) of Rimini was one of the most prolific and polemical physicians of eighteenth-century Italy. After graduating from the University of Bologna in 1719, he honed his anatomical skills in further study with the physicians Giambattista Morgagni and Antonio Vallisneri in Padua and ultimately under the tutelage of the archbishop of Rimini's personal physician, Antonio Leprotti. Throughout the 1720s and 1730s, he self-consciously cultivated a reputation as a man of great literary style and scientific acuity. He became the secretary of archbishop Giovan Antonio Davia's academy, and in 1726 he opened a philosophical school for aristocratic pupils in his home that contemporaries described as "a public university of every sort of study."[12] At the same time, he traveled extensively throughout the Italian peninsula, establishing contacts with leading scholars and cultivating a vast correspondence. There was virtually no subject—medical, scientific, antiquarian, and literary—that did not interest Bianchi and virtually no academic controversy on which he did not voice his opinion. Having taken the pen name *Janus Plancus* in 1726 in order to distinguish himself from the physician Giovanni Bianchi of Turin who attacked his mentor Morgagni, Bianchi proceeded to publish an enormous number of works, many of them pseudonymous, to cement his reputation as a learned scholar.

At the beginning of the 1740s, Bianchi's career and reputation were well established. While failing to win a professorship in theoretical medicine at Padua, he succeeded in being appointed professor of anatomy at the University of Siena in fall 1741. From the start, he made it clear that he considered the Tuscan city a provincial backwater, spending as much time as possible in the academies, cafés, and publishing houses of Florence, debating the merits of vegetarianism with the great Florentine physician Antonio Cocchi, and visiting colleagues at the more distinguished University of Pisa. He lectured and dissected numerous cadavers during his three-year tenure there, greatly antagonizing his Sienese colleagues with his disdain for their own skills, which he jokingly called a form of paper anatomy (*anatomia cartacea*).[13] "They don't know how to hold a knife in their hands, let alone how to discern altered from healthy parts," he observed disparagingly after a group of young physicians dissected a female cadaver without his supervision in October 1742.[14] Bianchi evidently considered himself a modern-day Vesalius, fighting the battle for empirical knowledge at the dissector's table. He proudly declared that his teaching was based entirely on the "practice of dissection," in the tradition of his mentor Morgagni, who was in the process of making pathological anatomy a well-respected science. A signal feature of his lectures included the use of anatomical preparations, dried specimens taken from his personal collection of human body parts which he used to demonstrate his opinions about the body.[15]

By 1743 Bianchi's relations with the university were at an all-time low. He was in a struggle with university officials over payment of back salary. After the publication of his anonymous but thinly veiled autobiography, filled with comments praising his own knowledge and attacking the ignorance of the Sienese, relations with his colleagues and students further deteriorated. Publicly ridiculed for his learned pretensions during Carnival that year, he fled the city for the more hospitable climate of Florence and Pisa. The university superintendent Pompeo Neri was ultimately forced to publish an *Ordinance that the Insults against Bianchi Absolutely Cease* in March 1743 in order to entice the difficult anatomist back to his job.[16] He stayed in Siena for another year and a half before finally vacating his post, returning to Rimini in November 1744, less than two months after his *Brief History* appeared.

In the final conflicted months of Bianchi's tenure as anatomy professor, an unheralded opportunity to make his mark on its medical community came his way. In the early hours of 28 June 1743, twenty-four-year-old Giovanni Bordoni, a servant of the former governor of Anghiari, Francesco Maria Pucci of Montepulciano, died in his bed at the hospital of Santa Maria della Scala in Siena. Since June 16 he had been ailing from a gunshot wound in the thigh that he received while eloping with a priest's niece from Librafratta, where his master Pucci served as *podestà*. Shortly before his death, delirious and in pain from the infection that eventually caused his demise, Bordoni confided to a nun that "he" was actually a "female and virgin" who had dressed as a man for eight years.[17] The surgeons' assistants who removed the body from the bed immediately confirmed this fact because they "recognized her as a female, especially from the breasts." Amazed at their discovery—presumably the nun had exercised discretion—they asked some of the hospital personnel better versed in anatomy to examine the body to confirm their opinion. They pronounced Bordoni to be not only a woman but a virgin because her hymen was intact. Laid out in the church wearing the traditional white robes and flowered garland of a virgin, she was temporarily pronounced a saintly woman by the populace. By the end of the year, Bianchi would discover her real name and circumstances: Caterina Vizzani, the runaway daughter of a Roman carpenter.[18]

News of the presence of this "most beautiful hymen" in Santa Maria della Scala reached Bianchi later in the morning.[19] The physician, his surgical assistant Jacopo Berti, and his servant Giustiniani were all amazed at this discovery. As they later testified to the Ministry of Justice, they were personally acquainted with "Bordoni," having once lodged for six weeks at an inn in Florence where Pucci also resided; Giustiniani had even shared a bed briefly with the podestà's servants. They knew her as a man and had never suspected otherwise, though Bianchi, considering the matter more carefully, recalled two weeks later that while she was slim-hipped and had a pock-marked face and just enough downy facial hair on her chin and a mustache to shave occasionally, she was nonetheless "short in stature" and "fat more like women are."[20]

Eager to begin his inspection of the body, Bianchi rushed to the hospital after giving testimony. To his dismay, he discovered that the Sienese surgeons had already opened the belly, quite inexpertly in his opinion, to see if Vizzani was pregnant. He later complained that the "rummaging around that some young surgeons at the hospital in Siena secretly may have done" might be the cause of a small perforation of the hymen he observed which marred its perfection.[21] Fortunately, they had not ruined the reproductive organs, allowing Bianchi and Berti to dissect them thoroughly the following morning. Following the most current techniques of eighteenth-century anatomy, they did not simply observe them during the autopsy but transformed them into a set of specimens. As Bianchi reported, "I principally had the parts of generation separated from the body and then I had them brought to my home to observe them better and to dry them." He added Vizzani's hymen "with its adjacent parts" to his collection of hymens taken from the bodies of dead virgins, lamenting the fact that many of his best examples were still in Rimini.[22]

Like many other dissections he conducted before and after the appearance of the *Brief History*, Bianchi used Vizzani's body as a pretext to debate some of the more controversial questions of the human body. He confirmed that the cause of Vizzani's death was not the wound but subsequent infection, lamenting the fact that the poor quality of Italian surgery had made it impossible to save her life. He belittled those physicians who doubted that the presence of the hymen was proof of virginity, noting wryly that some of his colleagues in Siena were among the skeptics.[23] He dried and blew up the neck of the gall bladder in order to point out to observers that it was not a straight passageway but "somewhat folded over," more like a twisted funnel with many winding valves. Finally, he looked for "those canals called cysto-hepatic or hepatocystic" in the liver whose existence Bianchi had staunchly denied in print since 1726, considering them (erroneously as it turns out) to be a by-product of the perpetual confusion between human and animal anatomy because they were evident in dogs and oxen. According to his expert opinion, they were nowhere to be seen in Vizzani's cadaver. Invoking the thousands of bodies he had dissected, Bianchi reminded his readers that it was better "to see things in reality" than to simply accept the word of some authority.[24]

The physical reality of Vizzani's body also raised a number of vexed issues about human sexuality that Bianchi addressed summarily. As a woman who dressed as a man for love of other women, many people presumed that she would demonstrate evident signs of her sexual desire in the unusual nature of her reproductive anatomy. Bianchi carefully inspected her body with these concerns in mind. He noted that her left Fallopian tube, when dried and blown up, was three or four times the size of her right one and that her left ovary contained many tiny blisters. But otherwise he could discern no bodily pathology, a point he firmly underscored in his inspection of her clitoris:

> This young woman did not have a clitoris greater than others, as it was written from Rome that she had, and as they say that all those women whom the Greeks called Tribades, or who follow the custom of Sappho have. Rather,

it can be said that hers was very ordinary and should be placed among the small instead of the large or medium ones.[25]

With the stroke of his pen, Bianchi dismissed two centuries of anatomical lore about the size of the clitoris and its relation to female sexual desire. By contrast, Vizzani's own father Pietro reported that she had always been female, "but that at a very tender age, she had had in her feminine parts a protrusion like a strawberry and that thus she had always been inclined to love women."[26] Instead, Bianchi observed nothing of the kind. "All the parts of the cadaver of this woman supposed a man were entirely healthy," he told his former mentor Leprotti, who wielded considerable influence in the Italian medical community as papal physician to Benedict XIV. Several months later, he responded specifically to reports that she dressed as a man because she was a hermaphrodite. Not only did she lack "a long clitoris," making it impossible to believe that her own rather small one "grew much in female heat," but he was quite certain that "she did not have anything in the pudenda that seemed like a strawberry."[27]

Understanding the clitoris was one of the most vexed questions of medical sexology in the Enlightenment. Just a few years before Bianchi's dissection of Vizzani, the English physician James Parsons boldly denied the time-honored image of the enlarged clitoris as a female penis, exclaiming:

> How few there were, who (from the obscurity of the clitoris in females in a natural state), knew that any such part existed. It is not therefore much to be wondered at, that at the first sight of a large clitoris divers odd conjectures should arise, and supply the fancy of those unskilled in due knowledge of the part, with matter sufficient for the erection of a new doctrine.[28]

Medical interest in the clitoris first emerged during the midsixteenth century, when Italian anatomists, beginning with Realdo Colombo, identified it as the seat of desire. Within a few decades, physicians agreed that, under the right circumstances, it might grow large enough to make a woman a tribade, a woman attracted to other women, and possibly even transform her into a male. The midseventeenth century Danish physician Thomas Bartholin affirmed that in young girls attracted to ancient Sapphic practices "the Clitoris does first discover it self." However, he dismissed the idea that it could "grow as big as a Gooses neck," suggesting instead that a large clitoris at best resembled a young boy's penis.[29]

Bianchi's treatise appeared at a moment when anatomists were actively debating the nature of this singular female part. While his contemporary Parsons evidently agreed with Bianchi that female sexual behavior could not simply be explained by recourse to their anatomy, citing his "Collection of morbid uterine parts" as evidence, others persisted in believing that same-sex desire was a direct product of some reproductive irregularity, principally an excess of heat that caused the part in question to exceed its normal size.[30] In the same period when Bianchi composed his *Brief History*, the English physician Robert James described the story of a cross-dressing female soldier whose "masculine Turn of Mind" was revealed, upon examination by three midwives, to be the product of an overly long clitoris. He alerted readers of *A Medicinal Dictionary* (1743–1745) that the clitoris could grow so "shamefully large" that it might look "like the tail of some Animal."[31] But James, like many early modern medical authorities, reassured his readers that this phenomenon rarely occurred in Europe, since a large clitoris was commonly believed to be a result of the kind of overheated climate found predominantly in Africa or possibly the Indies.

In the late seventeenth and early eighteenth century, anatomists gradually scaled back their claims regarding the monstrous possibilities of the clitoris. Citing Bartholin and other new research, the ecclesiastical jurist Ludovico Maria Sinistrari declared in 1700 that a large clitoris wouldn't make you male since it was incapable of true ejaculation; he nonetheless felt that some women possessed of such a part were more likely to "run after other women, and especially girls." To contradict stories of tribades, he piously invoked the case of a Pavian nun whose "clitoris . . . suddenly burst out" in 1671. She resisted the temptation to succumb to such desires, eventually asking a surgeon to perform a clitoridectomy to safeguard her virtue. A few decades later, the German physician Martin Schurig preceded Parsons in stating that tribadism was not the same as hermaphroditism because the clitoris could never become a male penis. Yet he continued to describe the clitoris as a "female penis," writing that women in this condition could ejaculate though they could not procreate.[32] Despite a growing interest in the specific nature of sexual difference, anatomists were often reluctant to give up these older Galenic descriptions of female reproductive anatomy as a mirror of the male body.[33]

Bianchi's silence on these issues surely did not reflect any ignorance on his part regarding these differences of opinion. He prided himself on his extensive knowledge of the most current anatomical research, in Italy and elsewhere; it provided ripe fodder for his polemics about the body. Both his certainty in his own opinion—the clitoris simply did *not* explain Vizzani's behavior—and his strong sense of the constraints of genre informed his approach to this contentious issue. He had written a medical novella, a tale of Vizzani's life and her body designed to entertain as well as instruct, rather than a medical sex manual in the fashion of the French physician Nicolas Venette's best-selling *Portrait of Conjugal Love* (1696), the most popular sex manual of his day.[34] The *Brief History* was not a Latin scientific treatise written solely for scholars but an effort by Bianchi to stake his claim as a literary topographer of the body.[35] It was the only one of his well-known *novelle*, bawdy tales written in imitation of the great fourteenth-century Tuscan writer Giovanni Boccaccio, that he chose to publish.

Bianchi's interest in Vizzani, in other words, was not purely medical. He was fascinated by the narrative possibilities of the story of her life as well as the anatomical issues raised by the dissection of her body; his pamphlet sought to reconstruct both histories simultaneously. The fact that he composed the *Brief History* while still in Tuscany only made his choice of genre more appropriate. Among other things, Bianchi hoped to demonstrate not only that he understood the human body better than any Sienese physician but that he could write about it in perfect Tuscan, borrowing his words from the mouth of one the region's greatest writers. He had high ambitions for his lewd little book.

Evading the Censors

Bianchi's reputation in the eighteenth-century Republic of Letters was due to his literary endeavors as well as his anatomical acumen. He was repeatedly praised—and satirized[36]—for his Tuscan style, which he began to cultivate long before he became an anatomy professor in Siena. By the middle of the 1720s his Bolognese friends described him as "a most perfect imitator of Boccaccio," after reading the *novelle* that he typically composed and sent during Carnival.[37] While none of these early literary efforts seem to have survived, Bianchi's correspondence gives us a good sense of the effect he strove to create through circulation of his stories, primarily among readers in Bologna, Padua, and Modena. Billed as true tales of prominent individuals, Bianchi repeatedly underscored the select nature of his audience, heightening the impression that he was probing the most salacious gossip that his society offered by "speaking freely in them of true things and living persons, and sometimes of those of some distinction."[38] Friends and relatives sent him any gossip they considered to be worth a novella.[39] Bianchi invited them to help him perfect the stories. But he also reminded his readers not to copy or liberally distribute his novelle, frequently requesting that they be returned. In some instances, he told his audience to burn them.

The literary career that Bianchi developed around his novelle highlighted the reading and writing practices of a socially closed world. He cultivated a literary reputation without ever subjecting his work to the vicissitudes of public opinion and ecclesiastic censure. "Our living Boccaccio of Rimini," enthused Pier Jacopo Martello in 1729.[40] Bianchi's discerning audience might enjoy a good laugh at the expense of others, but they recognized the dangers of sharing such pleasurable pastimes with a less discriminating public. "The work of a storyteller . . . is very dangerous," counseled Domenico Maria Manni in his *History of the Decameron of Giovanni Boccaccio* (1742), "and can cause spiritual injury in readers. Therefore, I concede that it may not be placed in the hands of anyone who lacks maturity so that he may best reap its fruit." On one occasion, when Bianchi made the mistake of scandalizing Don Lorenzo Zanotti by reading two novelle to him at an inn in Faenza, he was reminded that not everyone enjoyed "that Boccaccesque freedom" (*quella libertà boccaccevole*) with which he wrote.[41] Presumably, however, the fact that the tales remained unpublished allowed him to escape the cleric's full censure. Yet the Neapolitan publisher Lorenzo Ciccarelli had disregarded the long-standing prohibition against printing the unexpurgated *Decameron* by producing an uncensored edition in 1719 that restored Boccaccio's tales to their bawdy, iconoclastic original form.[42] In the end, Bianchi was not exactly worried about the consequences of his literary pastime, even living in the Papal States.

In the 1740s Bianchi's appetite for writing his Carnival novelle subsided. He was increasingly preoccupied with his scholarly research and hard at work on an ever-growing number of medical and scientific publications. But the unmasking of Giovanni Bordoni right before his eyes gave him an unparalleled opportunity to display these literary skills in public. Vizzani, after all, was no exalted personage whose libertine pastimes could only be discussed in the salons *sotto voce*. She was a woman of low birth who had lived a picaresque life and created a public scandal with her deathbed confession. Briefly, she was a curiosity and a posthumous celebrity, with tales of her exploits circulating between Tuscany and the Papal States. As an eyewitness to her story and as the anatomist of her body, Bianchi considered it his duty—and his opportunity—to publish an account of her life.

It took Bianchi little more than a year to prepare the manuscript. Four days after completing the autopsy, a copy of his report was on its way to the papal physician Leprotti. His former mentor was so delighted with its particulars that he responded immediately on 6 July that the "case of the supposed Giovanni, who lived in a virginal state as a servant, being a true female, is memorable." Leprotti added that he had no disagreement with Bianchi's opinion of the ubiquity of the hymen in virgins.[43] Throughout the warm summer months, Bianchi plied his friend with juicy details, practicing how he might tell the story to others while he researched its missing parts. He recalled Vizzani's ability to sleep "between two men" without the least hint of temptation. He immediately collected accounts of Vizzani's behavior from associates who had known her as Bordoni in Anghiari, Montepulciano, and Librafratta. "She seemed a great whoremonger for spending all day behind the women, having received a neck wound over there," he heard from the citizens of Anghiari (where she had lived for three years), "and there she passed as a man who was well endowed in the instrument of generation."

Bianchi wasted no time getting to the bottom of the ultimate mystery of Vizzani's imposture: How had she convinced people of her masculinity? The current podestà of Anghiari, Guazzesi d'Arezzo, explained the origins of the rumors about her sexual prowess. When a washerwoman found Vizzani's shirt bloodied every month, she hid the fact of her menstruation by claiming that it was due to a bad case of gonorrhea; subsequently she visited the local surgeon on two occasions for a cure. Bianchi could not recall if he had offered Leprotti the final proof of the deliberate nature of Vizzani's deception: a description of the red leather cylinder "that she filled with rags and always kept tied above her groin."[44] The dildo had been mistaken by the surgeons' assistants in the hospital as a purse. He could not help but laugh at their disappointment regarding its contents after they ripped it open in search of a few coins.

Leprotti's interest emboldened Bianchi to ask for help in researching aspects of Vizzani's life that were not immediately accessible to him in Siena. In particular, he understood that she was Roman in origin. Leprotti promised to see what else he could find out through his friend Monsignor Giovanni Gaetano Bottari, personal librarian of the Corsini family, Vatican librarian since 1739, and canon of Santa Maria in Trastevere since 1741. Bottari had heard the Roman story of Vizzani from the previous canon, Giuseppe Lancisi, who had known her briefly when she took refuge in his church, already dressed as a man, before leaving for Tuscany. He helped Bianchi transform gossip into history.

The story Bottari told only increased Bianchi's desire to see Vizzani's life in print. He confirmed that she had initially fled Rome at age sixteen because of a romance with "another young girl," fearful of being prosecuted in the criminal court (*Tribunale del Governo*) by the angry father.[45] After her initial flight to Viterbo, she returned to Rome but did not think it prudent to stay with her family. Lancisi found her hiding in his church; he fully intended to return what he believed to be a misguided and apprehensive teenage boy to her parents when a gentleman en route to Tuscany took on "Bordoni" as a servant. Subsequent employment took her from Perugia to Arezzo and ultimately into the service of Pucci. News of Bordoni's disgraceful reputation in Anghiari reached Lancisi in Rome. He went in search of the father to discuss his alleged son's "bad conduct." Pietro Vizzani could not resist saying that his "son" had always been a womanizer (*donnaiolo*). When Lancisi persisted in his condemnation of the family's lax morality, the father finally told him in exasperation that Bordoni "was a girl and had always been one."[46] Neither Bottari nor Leprotti ever understood why Lancisi kept this information to himself, allowing Vizzani to continue her imposture. They suspected it was due to his embarrassment in helping her to secure employment; he had even recommended her to his own brothers after her first position ended.

By September 1743 the gossip in Siena and further material gathered in Florence produced new questions for Bianchi's contacts in Rome. Was Bordoni her brother-in-law's surname? Was her father a silversmith, or a carpenter? Why had she begun to dress as a man? One month later, after talking with her last employer, Pucci, Bianchi had further queries. Had her name been Giovanna? Had she already been a servant in Tuscany before Lancisi's encounter with her in the heart of Trastevere?[47] Bottari's absence from Rome slowed the flow of information, leading Leprotti to counsel patience while they awaited his return. Bianchi was increasingly anxious that his account of Vizzani's life meet the same standard of truthfulness as his autopsy of her body; the details did indeed matter in crafting this kind of story. He simply could not publish his history without ascertaining "the true family name of that woman who pretended to be a man." Bianchi finally received Leprotti's response in mid-December.[48] He now felt that he had enough information to write a good medical novella.

During the winter and spring of 1744, Bianchi polished his *Brief History*, worked on other projects, and continued to quarrel with the Sienese about his salary and position. In July the manuscript was complete and he began to consider what he should do with it. It already was affording entertaining after-dinner conversation in Florence. As Bianchi walked through the city, he continued to refine the narrative—between cups of the sinful chocolate for which Florentine cafés were quickly becoming famous and quarrels about which works of Boccaccio's were his most significant—by trying it out on his companions. Domenico Bracci heard the story on a stroll from the Ponte di Santa Trinità to the Palazzo Vecchio on the night of 12 July 1744, leaving Bianchi to retell the tale to the physician Cocchi when they parted. A few days later, he tried it out on another dinner companion, Tommaso Perelli, who approved it heartily, "declaring it most worthy of being printed," before they retired to his friend's palace to observe a series of air-pump experiments. Bianchi ordered the paper and began to make plans for its publication.[49] He could imagine no better place than Florence to print his Boccaccesque novella.

Ultimately, Bianchi published the *Brief History* in Florence, but not quite in the way that he expected. Problems with the ecclesiastical censors surfaced in the final week of July. He heard on 23 July that they were scandalized by two aspects of his manuscript in particular: the use of the word *piuolo*, Bianchi's word to describe the cylindrical leather dildo, and "the description that it has of the French disease that that woman said she had."[50] His printer Viviani was so concerned that he restored the manuscript to the author, washing his hands of the entire affair. A week later Bianchi found himself in the office of the *Vicario Criminale* headed by canon del Riccio, the cleric authorized by the archbishop of Florence to inspect and license books. Del Riccio assured him that both he and the archbishop considered the book "to be rather well written," but they could not risk publishing anything at this moment that might offend the Holy Office in Rome. Bianchi argued that both details were "a matter of fact and essential to the history and that they were neither contrary to religion nor to good manners."[51] Truth telling, the canon reminded him, was always a matter of selective omission. He was not convinced that Vizzani's life needed such salacious detail. Nonetheless, he consoled Bianchi by suggesting that he publish the book in Venice if he could obtain a license there. That evening after dinner, Bianchi began to make a second copy to send to La Serenissima.

Caught between the conflicting jurisdiction of church and state, Bianchi had no alternative. He was the victim of the Grand Duke Francis Stephen of Lorraine's decision to modernize Florentine censorship practices as of 23 March 1743, granting civil authorities the prerogative to license all books, save for those with religious content, without consulting the Catholic Church. The Holy Office responded by banning all Florentine books from entering the Papal States and threatened Florentine printers with excommunication if they did not comply with traditional censorship practices that required the approval of the Holy Office for any book to be licensed for publication.[52] Florence, in the eyes of Rome, had fulfilled its reputation for all manner of debauchery and permissiveness in its attempt to subvert their authority over the printed word. As a result, church officials in Florence found themselves in an awkward situation. They could not authorize any books that might incur the censure of the Holy Office. Written in imitation of Boccaccio's tales, Bianchi's *Brief History* recalled the well-known censorship and expurgation of the *Decameron* in the late sixteenth century, when its content had been so sanitized as to become, in the eyes of some critics, virtually unrecognizable.[53]

Still smarting from the Criminal Vicar's prudery over "certain ridiculous difficulties he had in reviewing certain facts that were very modestly and nobly described and that are essential to the story," Bianchi wrote Leprotti that he expected no such problems in Venice. "That history that I wrote in a Boccaccesque style will be printed easily in Venice," he boasted.[54] The papal physician, perhaps exercising a certain prudence that his friend lacked, did not respond. Bianchi expressed a somewhat more cautious view in a letter to the Venetian publisher Giambattista Pasquali about his novella "written in a Boccaccesque style, that is, in ancient Tuscan." While assuring Pasquali that the Revisors should have no difficulty with it, he suggested that if the printer thought otherwise, he would approve his decision to "print it with the date of another city, as is now the custom, putting Milan, Modena, or who knows what, but not Lucca since in Siena, where I reside, publications from Lucca already are not accepted."[55]

By August 8 the *Brief History* was in the hands of the Venetian Inquisition. One of its Revisors offered his opinion at the end of the month. He also objected to the piuolo, adding that he further disapproved of a passage describing some monks riding a bitch as unbecoming to their clerical dignity. In his view, it clearly violated the spirit of the prohibition against Boccaccio's *Decameron*, since the Roman Inquisition had placed it on the Index of Prohibited Books almost two centuries earlier for speaking scandalously of priests, monks, abbesses, nuns, and other religious matters.[56] Bianchi's erstwhile publisher in Venice, Pasquali, reassured him that all he needed to do was eliminate any mention of the dildo and change "monks" to "men" for it to be approved. Venice, in the end, was not in mortal combat with the Holy Office and had always held itself apart from the politics of the Papal States.[57] He was terribly sorry for the delay since he greatly admired Bianchi's literary style and wanted to add the *Brief History* to a collection of stories, *The Italian Short Storyteller*, that he was about to publish.[58] But he could do nothing without a license.

It was now September and Bianchi's lewd little book had yet to find a publisher. Contemporaries joked in the bookshops and cafés of Tuscany that one of Bianchi's problems was literary since he seemed to prefer the inelegant and erotic misogyny of Boccaccio's *Fiametta* to the tales from the *Decameron*.[59] He had already written to Rome, asking Leprotti to tell Pope Benedict XIV of his troubles with the Florentine censors and asking for his absolution.[60] But he was beginning to think that the only way to get the book published was to negotiate over the contentious passages. While sipping chocolate with the Grand Duke's minister Giulio Rucellai at the beginning of the fall, he mulled over the possibilities before him. They discussed the problem of the "leather instrument." Finally, Bianchi was ready to make certain concessions to ensure the book's appearance. If the Catholic Church truly felt that his book was in need of revision and if Rucellai really considered it an act of good will in the relations between church and state, he would remove the offending passages.

On September 16 Bianchi visited the papal *nuncio* in Florence to ask his advice before making a final decision. Upon discovering that monsignor Archinto had played no role whatsoever in the censure, which had been entirely at the behest of the Criminal Vicar who continued to insist on the changes, Bianchi changed his tactics. The problem, he now saw with some clarity, was not Rome but the ecclesiastical establishment in Florence. He rushed to Palazzo Riccardi on Via Ginori in search of his friend Giovanni Lami, the Riccardi librarian, scholar, publisher, and journalist who also worked as a Revisor under the new regime.[61] Lami told him they could resolve the matter instantly. After dinner, he introduced him to another printer, Andrea Bonducci, who had no fear of the church censors and a particular interest in scientific books. Bianchi gave him the manuscript. By the evening of September 19, he had printed (albeit typo-ridden) copies of the *Brief History* in his hands, with the false imprimatur of Venice.[62] There was a certain irony in this decision since Pasquali continued to write that he would love to publish Bianchi's book if only he would make those "two little changes."[63]

Reading about a Lesbian

Bianchi rushed his book into print not only because he feared it otherwise would never be published but also because he had finally decided to leave Tuscany for good and wished to conclude unfinished business there. He confided in his friends that he happily would have remained if opportunities had appeared in Florence or Pisa, but he made it clear that Siena "didn't do it for me, and I did quite a lot to stay there for three years."[64] Abandoning his professorship in Siena, he hoped that the appearance of two new publications might assist his efforts to find a new position.[65] Virtually the last thing he did before heading home to Rimini was to post a freshly printed copy of the *Brief History* to Leprotti from Florence. Two days after the book appeared, he stopped in Forlì to see his friend Morgagni. The physician's house was filled with ladies, but he wasn't at home. Bianchi eventually found Morgagni in town, "giving him the history of the woman and telling it to him briefly."[66] By nightfall, he was in Rimini; after unpacking, he sent a second copy of the book to Rome.

It was not long before Bianchi received a preliminary response to his *Brief History*. Some colleagues in Florence, including the minister of state Rucellai, who had urged him to comply with the censor's demands, were not exactly pleased at the appearance of an unauthorized version. Bianchi defended his decision by invoking the history of censorship of Boccaccio's *Decameron*. He tartly reminded them that piuolo was not one of the words expurgated by the Holy Office from the original novelle. "One finds it in the corrected Boccaccio in Rome, emended according to the order of the Holy Council of Trent." He referred them to page 503 of the 1573 Giunti edition. He observed that, contrary to what the Criminal Vicar del Riccio had implied, the papal nuncio had had nothing to do with this affair. He recalled that the civil Revisor and therefore the Grand Duke himself had approved the book's publication without emendation. Still smarting from his humiliation, he told another Florentine reader that he had been willing to "take out that *Piuolo*" and redo the parts dealing with the dildo's use until he discovered that the Criminal Vicar refused to let him allude to it in any way. Since he could not trust the ecclesiastical censor to leave the rest of the content alone, he resolved "to have it published as it was without any change, being ready to launch a defense." There was nothing in the book "against the Catholic Religion or against good customs."[67] Even the expurgated *Decameron* spoke of dildos.

Other than a handful of critics who saw it as their duty to uphold the Florentine censor's decision, few readers seem to have been shocked by what Bianchi had published. In the next few months Bianchi distributed the *Brief History* throughout the Italian peninsula. Cocchi received his copy in mid-October, responding that he had unsuccessfully tried to find a copy while treating a patient in Venice, through the publisher Simone Occhi, whose name appeared on the false Venetian imprimatur created by Bonducci. Occhi denied publishing the *Brief History*. Cocchi not only expressed his enjoyment of the book's content but also told Bianchi that he additionally admired "your power to overcome all obstacles."[68]

The collusion of his readers was exactly what Bianchi had hoped for. He wanted them to recognize how he had played the game of culture, bending the rules just enough to see his book in print. Bianchi sent copies to friends in Bologna and Padua who knew of his youthful pastime as an imitator of Boccaccio. His Bolognese mentor Jacopo Bartolomeo Beccari expressed his pleasure at the "very witty history of the girl Vizzani, clothed in your usual grace and learning." Morgagni distributed additional copies among their mutual friends in Padua, telling his former student how well it had been received.[69] Leprotti, too, was helpful in assisting Bianchi's efforts to publicize the book. He gave the *Brief History* to key figures in Rome, among them Benedict XIV's secretary of state and the Vatican librarian Bottari. The latter was the author of a recent lecture on the history of censoring Boccaccio that sought to prove that the fourteenth-century Tuscan was a good Christian author whose reputation had been much maligned. This openness toward a new reading of Boccaccio might possibly have made him appreciate Bianchi's own dialogue with Boccaccio, though unfortunately no response from him to this little book survives.[70] Bianchi felt certain that the book's recommendation by such well-placed ecclesiastical readers would greatly improve "the distribution of the history."[71]

In addition to donating copies to key readers, Bianchi also directed its commercial distribution. He asked the printer Bonducci to leave four hundred copies with Giovanni Lami at his Centaur Press in Florence. Thinking that the Sienese who had seen the final dramatic moments of Vizzani's life and death unfold before their eyes would want to read his *Brief History*, he subsequently consigned one hundred of them to the Sienese bookseller Vincenzo Pazzini Carli, with whom he had developed a good relationship during his tenure as an anatomy professor. Only ten days after the book was printed, he began to consider what sort of summary he would write of its contents for Lami's *Literary News*, one of the most popular Italian journals since its inception in 1740.[72] Bianchi was a regular contributor to this periodical and hoped to entice its more far-flung readership into buying a few copies. His self-review was ready by mid-October and appeared in the 30 October issue. Reminding readers that "his name is frequently praised in this *News*," Bianchi highlighted his skill at combining an account of "the adventures of the dead young woman" with an investigation of "a great many anatomical questions." He concluded by admiring his ability to both delight and instruct the public with such a strange tale, written in a "rather Boccaccesque Tuscan style."[73] Scholars who satirized Bianchi's predilection for quoting letters, books, and passages of the *Literary News* that praised his accomplishments in the bookstores of Siena surely knew who had written these laudatory words.[74]

A couple of weeks after the review appeared, Bianchi returned to Siena briefly to pack all his things for a final farewell to a city he thoroughly despised. In mid-November he read his book notice in the *Literary News* at the home of an acquaintance in Borgo San Sepulcro, writing Lami to inquire anxiously (and repeatedly) as to when his own copy would arrive. With the review out, he felt the time was ripe to sell the book publicly. He authorized Lami's associate Brazzini, who seems to have been in charge of distributing publications at the Centaur Press, to sell one hundred fifty copies of the *Brief History* at a half *paolo* apiece, reserving the other half of the Florentine consignment for later.[75]

What Bianchi most wanted, however, was Benedict XIV's approval. He was relieved to hear from Leprotti in late October 1744 that the pope absolved him of any guilt regarding his problems with the Florentine censor. But he expressed frustration over the fact that Leprotti had not yet given the pope his personal copy of the *Brief History*. "Regarding the presentation of the copy of the said life to His Holiness, I have exempted myself from this obligation," Leprotti explained. "I preferred to pass it into the hands of His Excellency, the Cardinal Secretary of State."[76] Upon receiving this letter, Bianchi rushed a second copy to Rome for Leprotti to give to the pope. He was quite sure that news of his brilliant dissection of the cross-dressing lesbian had already made its way into the audience halls of the Vatican. "Since it is a very curious and strange case, His Holiness easily could have heard it spoken of. Perhaps he is wondering why I have not presented it to him, as I have aspired to do with all my other things."[77] Marveling at the hubris and obtuseness of his friend, Leprotti kept silent. On November 1, Bianchi posted a third copy, this time without a cover, perhaps thinking that the pope might prefer to read a version that bore no traces of the illicit imprimatur. On December 17, he sent yet another, asking whether the pope had received one of the earlier copies. Finally, Leprotti responded. With the utmost tact and discretion, he informed Bianchi that he had received both the coverless version and the more recent copy. Being delighted to receive two exemplars in succession, he had decided to give one to Bottari.[78]

There were limits, in other words, to papal approval. Benedict XIV may well have been a man of letters who was fond of good jokes and belonged to the Bolognese circle Bianchi knew well, but he wore a mantle of authority that did not allow him to openly approve of such illicit publications from Florence, a city openly in conflict with the Holy Office.[79] Whether the pope hesitated on other grounds that concerned the content of the *Brief History* is hard to say, since he never expressed his personal opinion in any way that has come to light. But his physician and close confidant Leprotti was quite certain that Benedict neither would—nor should—publicly accept the gift of such a book.

Vizzani's behavior intrigued a number of readers who, not wearing the papal tiara, commented upon it more freely. Thanks to the brief notoriety of his book, Bianchi did indeed initiate a public conversation about sexuality that we might otherwise not know of. The actions of a Roman carpenter's daughter who boldly transformed herself into a Tuscan Casanova led him to consider key issues regarding the nature of human desire. What, in the end, did women want? How did they achieve it? Some of the most interesting responses to his questions came from prominent women who examined the *Brief History* in light of their own understanding of female sexual behavior. In such exchanges, we can see a spectrum of opinion about how sexual relations between women were understood and explained in eighteenth-century Italy.

The first female reader to receive a copy was Bianchi's former pupil, the Bolognese noblewoman Laura Bentivoglio Davia. She had attended his school in Rimini in the 1720s and remained a close friend. Bentivoglio Davia heard rumors of the appearance of his novella shortly after its hasty publication; in late September she received her personal exemplar of "the most pleasing adventure of the woman believed to be a man with your learned anatomical observation." After reading the *Brief History*, she offered a characteristically frank response regarding Vizzani's conduct:

> I would have advised this young woman to place herself in a female mon-astery where she could have been able to satisfy her inclination without

danger, and would have satisfied so many other women. The sanctity attributed to her by the monks made me laugh quite a bit."

Bentivoglio Davia considered it to be such a humorous example of Bianchi's Boccaccesque style, which she knew well from perusing his previous novelle, that she read it aloud to the Marchesa Angelelli, who was recuperating in bed from a leg ailment. She delighted in telling Bianchi that both the Marchesa and her servants absolutely adored his "way of writing."[80] None of them seemed the least bit perturbed about the idea of a woman who loved other women. If anything, they marveled at Vizzani's inability to imagine what the appropriate place for such behavior might be in their society—the convent rather than the dusty road leading from Librafatta to Siena. One can only wonder what they would have made of the story of sister Felice Alessandra Becchelli, who was expelled from the ancient Umbrian convent of Santa Chiara della Croce in Montefalco in March 1722 after a physician, a surgeon, and two midwives declared her a hermaphrodite rather than a woman.[81] If only Bianchi had known of this case, he might have written a second novella.

Throughout the fall, Bentivoglio Davia continued to amuse friends by telling and retelling the story of Vizzani's life. She was perhaps his best publicist and the reader who most appreciated the kind of lightly learned and libertine book he had composed. In contrast to his definitive opinions about Vizzani's anatomy, Bianchi deliberately offered no moral censure of her conduct. Instead, he preferred to sketch the details of her life, allowing his audience to draw their own conclusions. Conversation, in other words, completed the novella. In October, Bentivoglio Davia found herself at an evening salon with her younger contemporary, Bologna's equally learned professor and physicist Laura Bassi. She could not resist telling the tale to Bassi, who was open-mouthed with astonishment. "Truly curious and entirely unusual," was her judgment. As she later told Bianchi, "Here there has been quite a lot of discussion of such a strange fact."[82]

Unlike the aristocratic Bentivoglio Davia, whose own personal life had been quite a scandal in her youth, Bassi's reaction reflected more conventional attitudes toward the norms of female behavior.[83] She herself was happily married, with a growing brood of children. Her first thought was to imagine the vast difference between Vizzani's life and the common experience of most women. Recalling her conversation with Bentivoglio Davia, she told Bianchi: "We did not know how to understand the bizarre folly of a woman who wanted to live so difficultly and die so violently for a love entirely opposed to that which usual prevails in women."

Nonetheless, Bassi too did not entirely condemn Vizzani. As someone who had spent her own life in the public eye, due to the celebrity of her position as Bologna's only woman university graduate and professor, Bassi understood well the difficulties that women who chose an unusual path in her society might face. Prior to her marriage in 1738, her moral conduct had been repeatedly questioned by critics who could not understand how a single woman professor might spend so much time with male colleagues and still maintain her virtue. As a result, Bassi's primary response to Vizzani's life was to express her regret that such a woman had not found a better use for her native bravery and ingenuity. "This Amazon of our day could have employed her courageous constancy a little better, yet at least it's made her famous in some way. After all, she met a good end that comes from being described by your famous pen."[84] She understood, and to a certain degree appreciated, the desire to be different.

As a natural philosopher married to a physician, Bassi also savored the anatomical aspects of the *Brief History*. In this regard, her response was quite different from Bentivoglio Davia's since she immediately recognized the scientific significance of what he tried to accomplish with his dissection. She was especially pleased to see that Bianchi had, once and for all, concluded the endless controversy about the "cystohepatic ducts." Not coincidentally, she added that her husband, the physician Giuseppe Veratti, had also enjoyed the book.[85] While she conversed about Vizzani the woman with another female reader during one of Bologna's evening salons, she discussed Vizzani the cadaver at home with a spouse who had inspected—and dissected—many other bodies.

In the midst of conversations with his Florentine, Roman, and Bolognese readers, Bianchi received an appreciative letter from Ludovico Antonio Muratori, librarian to the Este dukes of Modena and one of the unofficial founding fathers of the Italian Republic of Letters. Muratori had sponsored Bianchi for his professorship in Siena; he continued to see himself as an intellectual mentor to this promising, if egotistical, young physician. He understood why Bianchi had published his *Brief History*. "Truly the case is curious and rare, and therefore it is very worthy of having your pen inform the public of it," he responded. "This little thing will do very well." At the same time, Muratori could not resist commenting on how Bianchi had discussed Vizzani's sexuality. In contrast to the censors in Florence and Venice, he applauded his colleague's prudence:

> You have wisely kept silent about the strange genius of that young girl, but one understands well enough that she loved those of her sex with the lasciviousness advertised by our theologians as most contrary to nature. Then how did she, talking and sleeping with men, never feel aroused by that other appetite which conforms to her same nature? Or perhaps she was aroused? It's hard to know how to take it.

Speculating about the nature of Vizzani's passion reminded Muratori of a story he knew of an aged sodomite who had finally married a widow, after many years of enjoying the company of men. "Not knowing the straight and narrow path, he began by walking backwards," he joked, "believing it to be licit. The wife, who was a widow, taught him the true road." Muratori added, however, that he could not really believe that women were truly ignorant of the alternatives to declaring a passion for their own sex. Surely, after all these centuries, women as well as men had learned "all the secrets of lust"?[86]

For a fleeting moment, Bianchi's *Brief History* engendered a public debate about sexuality in eighteenth-century Italy. The readers who responded directly to the appearance of his book seemed perfectly willing to accept his contention that sexual preference was not a product of anatomical difference but of "human appetites . . . in the facts of love."[87] They were enlightened Catholics who knew church doctrine on sodomitical practices, male and female, very well. Yet they did not necessarily believe that human behavior could be so easily classified as either "natural" or "unnatural."[88] To the extent that they wondered about anything, they seem to have asked themselves what else might be the cause of such unusual passions. Muratori's question was indeed the one of the moment: What exactly was the nature of Vizzani's desire?

To the extent that Bianchi offered any response to such queries, he did so by allusion to classical precedent. "Although she was born in Rome and died in Tuscany," he observed in a letter of 11 October 1744 to the poet Giambattista Passeri of Pesaro, "the vicissitudes of this woman don't have anything to do with the customs of the Romans and the Etruscans, but quite a bit to do with those of the Greeks, especially with those of Sappho and other young women of Lesbos, which conform a great deal to those of Pindar, although of the other persuasion."[89] He wrote these words knowing of Passeri's own imitation of the erotic poetry of the ancient Greeks. Bianchi's curiosity about these ancient precedents played no small role in his research in preparation for the composition of the *Brief History*. He was a great collector, after all, of erotic statuettes depicting ancient satyrs and the ever-erect god Priapus, and of "venereal conches"—all of which he allegedly enjoyed showing to the women of Siena along with his "box of female hymens."[90] Had Bianchi been an Englishman, he would surely have joined the Society of Dilettanti, populated by Italianate Englishmen who loved antiquities and debauchery and did their best to stimulate these twin passions while on the Grand Tour.

During a trip to Florence two weeks after his dissection of Vizzani, Bianchi noted with pleasure a Greek coin from the island of Lesbos, depicting "two women in an obscene act."[91] Whether he added it to his well-known collection of ancient erotica is unknown, but he alluded briefly to this way of understanding passion between women by describing Vizzani, in the opening pages of his book, as "a girl who ceded nothing to Sappho or the other young women of Lesbos in loving only those of the same sex."[92] His fondest desire had been to embellish the frontispiece of his *Brief Life* with "some medal of Sappho, if it can be found, or one of Lesbos or Mitilene that indicates something of that female poet, that island, or its cities in general." He hoped that his friend Cocchi, not only a physician but grand ducal antiquarian as of 1738 with access to the numismatic collections of the Uffizi gallery, might find just the right thing to convey the image of Vizzani as a modern-day Sappho. Cocchi replied that the Uffizi contained no images of Sappho but had a turreted cityscape of Mitilene.[93] Beneath the doctor's robe beat the heart of a libertine antiquarian who was deeply fascinated with the history of human sexuality.

Bianchi's goal was not exactly to become infamous but to advance his career as an anatomist with a literary flair for telling a good, sexy story. As he soon discovered, the literary marketplace of eighteenth-century Italy, alas, was not filled with readers eager to purchase his book.[94] Despite Bianchi's optimistic self-promotion and Muratori's predictions of good sales, the *Brief History* was not a rousing success. By January 1745 Bianchi had begun to wonder why copies were not selling as well as he thought they should. "I am not far from cutting a deal with foreign booksellers and even with those in Florence," he informed Lami, asking his friend if he would trade issues of the *Literary News* in return for copies of his books.[95] He felt that his absence from Tuscany had limited considerably his ability to promote his new publications.

At the end of the spring, Bianchi decided to collect all the remaining copies of the *Brief History*. He asked the Florentine booksellers who had them on consignment to send them to Rimini. Thirty-seven unbound copies of the book arrived at the beginning of June, soaking wet after falling into the Po somewhere on the road near Forlì. While drying them out, Bianchi noted that he was still missing another twenty-four that came with a frontispiece. Almost two months later, he still had no news from Florence as to what had happened to this final shipment.[96]

In retrospect, it is tempting to think that one of Bianchi's readers might have been a young Giacomo Casanova (1725–1798). In his autobiographic memoirs, Casanova recalled a singular episode in his amorous affairs that began in the winter of 1744, en route from Rome to Bologna. In an inn he heard a young castrato named Bellino sing and became utterly enamored of this "anomalous being." So certain was Casanova of his own heterosexuality that he could not believe the boy to be male. The boy insisted but Casanova pressed him further. The answer lay in an examination of the body. He felt Bellino's breasts and became more certain that he was a she. Bellino denied it even more strongly. While accompanying Bellino to sing in the opera in Rimini, Casanova's curiosity finally overwhelmed him and he attempted to touch his groin. To his horror, he believed that he saw a castrated penis. Doubts and desire assailed him. He had to *know* whether Bellino indeed was castrated or merely in possession of "a monstrous clitoris." During a long carriage ride Casanova begged him "to let me touch an object which cannot but fill me with disgust." Finally, they made love when they shared a bed at another inn in Sinigaglia.

At this point, Bellino allows Casanova to discover his sex. His instincts have been right all along since "he" was indeed a she, a girl of modest origins named Teresa whose father was employed by the Bologna Academy of Sciences and who had been taught by a castrato how to resemble one in her appearance. Casanova's question after hearing this revelation—"Good God! What has become of the monstrous clitoris I saw yesterday?"—is quickly answered. Teresa demonstrates the "little apparatus" her instructor had fashioned for her. Predictably, Casanova is so inflamed by the possibility of making love to a woman with a dildo that they return to bed.[97]

So many of the details of Casanova's love affair with a false castrato seem drawn from the world inhabited by Bianchi: the geographic terrain between Rome, Bologna, and Rimini; the ready-made intimacy of the inns; a young woman who no longer wishes to pass as a male, with a dildo so well made that it can fool men upon close inspection; and the passing reference to the scientific world of Bologna to which Bianchi was intimately connected, as a graduate of its university and a member of its scientific academy. While we might simply attribute all of these echoes of another story to coincidence, this explanation seems unlikely. Surely, Casanova had read the *Brief History*? His response may have been to imagine himself as a lover of Vizzani, now made stranger by associating her with the castrato he encountered in Rome and found very feminine.[98] While Casanova did not begin to compose his memoirs until 1789, many years after these events had transpired, it is none-theless striking that he recalled 1744 as the year he met a young girl dis-guised as a boy. His own story might well be described as a kind of retelling of the life of Caterina Vizzani and an homage to her biographer Bianchi.

The last we hear of the Italian edition of Bianchi's *Brief History* comes from a review in the *New Acts of the Learned*, published in Leipzig in May 1747. The anonymous reviewer paid special attention to Bianchi's resolution of the medical debates about the role of the hymen in proving virginity and the ab-sence of cystohepatic / hepatocystic ducts in humans.[99] Perhaps the notice had been written by Bianchi in an attempt to interest a foreign readership. Pos-sibly one of his sympathetic correspondents engineered this piece of publicity. By this point, Bianchi had returned fully to his life in Rimini. He accepted the post of town physician in the fall of 1744 and embarked on his dream of reestablishing the Accademia dei Lincei one year later. He continued to review for the *Literary News* and to write prolifically on a variety of subjects, earning the admiration of Voltaire for his thoughts on comedy and intriguing Rousseau with his critical analysis of vegetarianism. He never ceased to forget an insult or find reasons to quarrel with his colleagues. Years later, in 1769, his former pupil Clement XIV would make him an honorary papal physician as a tribute to his long-standing contributions to Italian medicine.[100] But no one asked him anymore to tell the story of the cross-dressing lesbian from Rome.

Shocking the English

Just as Bianchi's book disappeared into obscurity in the Italian peninsula, suffering the fate of the vast majority of publications in a highly competi-tive and expanding book market, it reemerged in a new guise for an entirely different audience. Sometime before or during 1751, a copy of the *Brief His-tory* found its way into John Cleland's hands. He read the little book and, undoubtedly at the urging of a printer, decided to translate it. Despite its commercial failure in Italy, someone thought it might be appealing to an English readership.[101]

We may never know exactly how Cleland got a copy; nor do we know how he developed his proficiency in Italian. To my knowledge, he did not go on the Grand Tour, having instead spent twelve years working for the East India Company in Bombay.[102] It is highly likely, as Clorinda Donato observes, that one of the members of the English residential community in Florence purchased or received a copy that he took home and circulated among his friends.[103] The possibilities abound since Bianchi, the printer Bonducci, and especially the physician Cocchi all knew Horace Walpole and the English resident Horace Mann. Perhaps Bianchi precipitated this transaction; he had considered the idea of bartering copies with foreign publishers in exchange for their books, and it is certainly possible that one of a smaller number of English travelers who passed through Rimini received the *Brief History* directly from his hands.

Bonducci might equally have seen it as a next step in his largely unsuccessful efforts to secure English patronage. In the years prior to the appearance of Bianchi's *Brief History* he had been actively courting Walpole with such projects as his Italian translation of Alexander Pope's *Rape of the Lock*, which he dedicated to Horace Walpole's cicisbea Elisabetta Capponi. After Walpole returned to England in 1741, Bonducci hoped that he might enlist Mann's friendship with Walpole to support his transfer to London as a librettist in the Italian Opera. Could he have seen this little publication as another gift to offer his English acquaintances? Years later Walpole vaguely recalled "his buffoonery" when discussing Florentine publications from the Stamperia Bonducciana with Mann.[104]

Cocchi had a much more intimate and long-lasting relationship with the English than either Bianchi or Bonducci, as their physician of choice in Florence and the imperial antiquarian who routinely educated young Englishmen in the pleasures of ancient coins.[105] He also had some personal experience of the ways in which Italian books found their way into English. Through Mann's graces, his own publications routinely made their way to Walpole in London via the English ships departing from Livorno. In one instance, the result was also an English translation. In January 1745, Walpole wrote to inquire whether Cocchi knew anything about an English edition of his defense of vegetarianism now advertised for sale in London. Mann responded in March that he did not, and then added: "He is vastly curious to know the author, and to see his performance."[106]

Finally, we might consider the possibility that one of the members of the Dilettanti Society who knew Cleland put the book in his hands. A libertine male society founded in London in 1732, with an interest in Graeco-Roman sexual practices, its members certainly made their appearance in Florence in the mid-1740s. Walpole famously remarked to Mann that the Dilettanti was "a club, for which the nominal qualification is having been in Italy, and the real one, being drunk."[107] Both the sexual and antiquarian dimensions of Bianchi's book would have interested this audience, fresh from their continental travels.

However it occurred, the *Brief History* left Florence and traveled to London, where it participated fleetingly in the enormous industry for news of Italy that the Grand Tour generated by the eighteenth century.[108] From the beginning of his translation, Cleland made it clear to his readers that he had a different perspective on Vizzani's life from that of her Italian biographer. Describing her actions as "a pregnant Example of the shocking Ebullition of human Passions," he exercised his role as editor to offer an extended commentary on the moral depravity of the Italians. Vizzani's precocious sexuality was not unusual in the Italian peninsula, he assured his readers, because her affair with Margherita had occurred when she was fourteen, "the Age of Love in our forward Climate."[109] Cleland put these words in Bianchi's mouth—they were nowhere to be found in the original—in order to suggest an agreement between the author and the editor regarding the image of Italy as a "torrid zone," a hot, steamy climate where love and passion could be found in superabundance.[110] In subsequent "Remarks Upon the Foregoing Dissertation" that appeared at the end of the volume, Cleland elaborated further on his image of Italy. "[I]n a warm Country like theirs, where Impurities of all Sorts are but too frequent, it may very well happen that such strange Accidents may, from Time to Time, arise as highly to excite both their Wonder and their Attention."[111] In retrospect, we might conclude that English readers were far more fascinated with same-sex behavior than the Italians, on the basis of the sheer quantity of English-language publications on this subject that appeared in the eighteenth century in contrast to their relative paucity in Italian. But at the time it seemed evident to Cleland that the reverse must be true.

The idea of Italy as an endless erotic landscape had long played a role in foreign perception of this region. The late sixteenth-century chronicler of the sexual scandals of the French court, Pierre Brantôme, made lesbianism an Italian predilection when he described it as *donna con donna*.[112] Sodomy, both male and female, was typically described outside the Italian peninsula as an Italian vice. In general, unnatural lust of any kind was associated with the Italians. Such ideas had a specific literary genesis, beginning with the widespread popularity of Pietro Aretino's infamous sonnets of 1527, written to accompany the engraver Marc'Antonio Raimondi's sixteen images depicting different sexual positions, and his subsequent *Dialogues* (1534–1536), in which Nanna, the oldest, lewdest whore in Rome, initiated young Pippa into a life of sexual debauchery at the behest of her mother.[113] By the late seventeenth century, the expanding market for erotic literature produced a steady stream of English books written in imitation of the Italian and French authors who had defined this genre for more than a century.[114] The eros of Italy had been cemented in print and circulated abroad long before many Englishmen set foot on its soil.

Contrasting Italian vice with English virtue became a favorite pastime of the English translators of Italian erotica. *The Whore's Rhetorick* (1683), a loosely adapted translation of Sforza Pallavicino's eponymous work of 1642, had one of the protagonists deny the necessity of Aretino's infamous postures for an English audience by stating with great wit that the English disdained such libertine practices: "They are calculated for a hot Region a little on this side of *Sodom*, and are not necessary to be seen in any Northern Clime." Italian examples of sexual excess were frequently invoked as a cautionary tale about the dangers of indulging in unnatural passions. One of the most popular English sexual advice books of the eighteenth century, for example, counseled its female readers against excessive masturbation by invoking the case of two Roman nuns who were expelled from their convent because they had "grown in such a manner as to have changed their Sex."[115] It is little wonder that by the time Cleland composed *Memoirs of a Woman of Pleasure*, he too was inclined to depict certain aspects of erotic experience as Italianate. He could not resist comparing the coloring of an open vagina to the vermillion reds of Guido Reni's paintings and jokingly referred to a young boy's buttocks as "the mount-pleasants of *Rome*."[116]

In the period just before the appearance of Cleland's translation of Bianchi's *Brief History*, the notion of Italy as "the *Mother* and *Nurse* of Sodomy" seems to have reached its apogee. The anonymous author of *The History of the Human Heart* (1749) was quite certain that Italian and French women were more likely to couple with female hermaphrodites—in other words, women with penises or penislike parts—because the warm Mediterranean climate incited them to pursue such monstrous pleasures. That same year, the equally anonymous *Satan's Harvest Home* (1749) argued that Italy was the root of all sexual debauchery since the French simply imitated the Italians in pursuing "*unnatural Vices*."[117] It portrayed Italy as a place that made men effeminate and women masculine, citing with great disapproval the importation of such customs to England. Vizzani, who embraced other girls "with all the Eagerness and Transport of a Male Lover" and whose life was an ever-escalating series of "unnatural Desires," was the perfect example of the Italian Sapphist for an English audience. It was Cleland, not Bianchi, who attributed such behavior to her "masculine Spirit, as well as masculine Desires."[118]

At the same time, Cleland could not resist inserting his own sense of the limits of an exclusively female sexuality into the conversation. His views were consistent with comments he previously had made in his popular novel. At the beginning of *Memoirs of a Woman of Pleasure* an older woman, Phoebe Ayres, sexually initiated Fanny Hill. Cleland made it clear from the start that this was not a form of tribadism or any other kind of persistent same-sex desire because neither woman exclusively preferred women. In fact, Fanny quickly decided that she didn't really like women at all. Once she lost her innocence and discovered her libido at the hands of her female tutor, she immediately craved "more solid food" and resolved to have nothing further to do with "this foolery from woman to woman."[119] Such attitudes reemerged in Cleland's translation of Vizzani's life: "[H]ere was Effrontery and Folly in the Abstract, to fall in Love with those of her own Sex; to amuse them with passionate Addresses; to kindle in them Desires, without the Power of Gratification."[120] While Bianchi reserved judgment regarding a woman's perspective on Vizzani's sexual attractions, Cleland was quite sure that, in the end, she failed to complete the transaction.

Ultimately, it was Bianchi's own attitude toward Vizzani's sexual behavior that most engaged and puzzled his English translator. He wanted readers to understand the Italian author's relationship to his subject. If Vizzani was an Italian Sapphist, then Bianchi was a sublime example of the kind of lax but learned Italian morality that allowed such women to flourish below the Alps. Cleland, for example, chose to omit only one passage from the original version: the initial description of the rag-filled dildo that she "displayed with a stealthy boldness to her companions."[121] Later in the narrative, he would have no difficulty translating Bianchi's detailed description of the use, placement, and appearance of the "leathern Machine."[122] But in this crucial description of her "delusive Impudicities," Cleland portrayed himself as a moral arbiter of Italian sexuality who felt certain that an English audience would find such bold expression too shocking for their eyes and ears. Since they were not his own words, he did not provide an asterisk, as he had done in his expurgated *Memoirs of Fanny Hill*, but instead chose to comment on what he would not translate. "The Doctor enters into a nauseous detail of her Impostures," he informed his readers,

> which is the more inexcusable, they not being essential to the main Scope of the Narrative. Those, if agreeable to the *Italian Goût*, would shock the Delicacy of our Nation, with whom I hope the following Lines will ever be in full Force, as the Standard of Criticism:
> *Immodest Words admit of no Defence;*
> *and Want of Decency is Want of Sense.*[123]

Cleland added, rather tongue in cheek, that the only reason he had not omitted all the offensive passages was because of his professional standards as a literary man. He did not wish to violate the "Laws of History"; nor did he want to "occasion too great a Chasm in a Translation."[124] Nonetheless, he confirmed his readers' prejudice that Italian conversation was far more libertine than anything English, filled with those "immodest words" that they should not say.

How strange to imagine the author of *Memoirs of a Woman of Pleasure* as the self-appointed censor of a book that was considerably less explicit than his own sexually saturated work, which the Bishop of London, Thomas Sherlock, had declared "the Lewdest thing I ever saw"—even after Cleland expurgated all the passages describing the endless litany of sexual arousals, orgasms, and anatomically voyeuristic views of genitalia in his far more sanitized and far less popular second edition, *Memoirs of Fanny Hill*.[125] The first edition of Cleland's infamous book set a new standard for the richness and variety of its sexual vocabulary, its lurid anatomical precision about the appearance of the clitoris—"the mark of the sex, the red-center'd cleft of flesh"[126]—and the possibilities for its arousal. The second edition discovered the beauty of the asterisk to omit anything that was best left to the imagination. Such experiences evidently shaped Cleland's understanding of his role as a translator of foreign erotica. In the years immediately prior to his encounter with Bianchi's *Brief History*, he reframed his own experiment in erotic writing to conform to a Janus-faced morality that imagined what Fanny Hill did without reading about it in any detail. On this occasion, Cleland reinvented himself yet again, becoming the innocent "English Editor" who found himself immersed in a world of foreign sexual behavior that was as novel as it was distasteful.

In his translation of Bianchi's *Brief History*, Cleland became the guardian of English virtue when confronted with Italian vice. Like his innocent Fanny, who fainted at the sight of a man engaged in the act of sodomy with a young boy and was perpetually shocked by (albeit curious about) all sorts of sexual behavior, Cleland chose to highlight the imaginative possibilities of desire by suggesting that Bianchi's Italian original was far more lurid than his translation. Whether this was actually the case or not didn't really matter. He promised an English audience that he would not tell them how a Roman girl had become a man—even though, in fact, he told them exactly how she did it a few pages later. Better to let them guess what she had done to prove her masculinity, or read the original to find out. He would not furnish English words for Italian deeds.

Cleland's omission at the beginning of *Catherine Vizzani* became the basis for subsequent additions to Bianchi's *Brief History*. In his "Remarks Upon the Foregoing Dissertation," Cleland chastised Bianchi for not offering any explanation of Vizzani's behavior. Such unnatural desires deserved a commentary—at least in the world that he inhabited. He reminded his readers that women loved other women for only two reasons: "from some Error in Nature, or from some Disorder or Perversion in the Imagination." Bianchi's description of Vizzani's clitoris—which Cleland further embellished by translating the author's words as "not pendulous, nor of any extraordinary size"—had ruled out the former. She was no tribade and certainly not a hermaphrodite. If the cause of "so odious and so unnatural a Vice" was not her body, then the fault must lie in her mind.[127]

This conclusion allowed Cleland to explore the question, What corrupts the mind of a young girl? It was a question that had already fascinated him, since *Memoirs of a Woman of Pleasure* explored in exquisite detail how Fanny reacted to everything she heard and saw. Readers of his translation were well aware of those practices that could corrupt her body; it was commonly believed by the mideighteenth century that excessive masturbation at a tender age would enlarge the clitoris.[128] If she had been a "Rubster," as one English medical book described this form of mutual masturbation, the dissection would have revealed signs of such activity.[129] Instead, deformation of mind occurred when the passions were inflamed at an early age by what one heard and read. Cleland presented Italy as a region that delighted in "obscene Tales" and encouraged "the Discourses of Women, who are generally too corrupt in that Country."[130] Raised in Rome—the imaginary home of Aretino's famous lewd whore Nanna, whose conversational initiation of a young woman into all manner of whoredom and debauchery defined the very idea of erotic corruption for generations of readers[131]— Vizzani became the living incarnation of the lusty, bawdy Italian woman who had fueled the English imagination since the sixteenth century. She heard tales of aristocratic amours and convent romances, and they emboldened her to embark upon her own adventures. Reading about Renaissance dildos inspired her to fashion a leather penis. This, at least, was Cleland's suggestion about the root cause of her sexual preferences, an explanation surely fashioned from his own reading of early modern Italian erotica. He allowed an unspoken question to form in the minds of his readers: Had it turned him, an anonymous and respectable Englishman, into an Italianate pornographer?

Cleland's image of Vizzani as the inevitable product of a world that read and talked about sexuality presents us with the paradox of his own identity as one of the best-read authors of the 1740s. John Cleland, author of *Memoirs of a Woman of Pleasure*, capitalized on the market for sexual conversation by transforming it into an art form. Cleland, the "English Editor" of Bianchi's *Brief History*, strove to profit from the unabated prurience of the self-same readership, but he also satisfied moral critics of this libertine world by reassuring them that English vice was really Italian in origin, an inevitable by-product of "our Desire to copy Foreigners in every Thing."[132] Possibly inspired by such works as *Satan's Harvest Home*, he became a critic of the effects of the Grand Tour on his society. What did one really learn in Italy, after all, amidst the pimps and prostitutes, the salons and the opera houses, the art galleries and the ruins? Without a trace of irony, he concluded that the sexually saturated climate of Italy wreaked havoc with English moral rectitude. Whether it explained why an English apothecary's wife had persuaded a gentlewoman to marry her—a story he invoked by comparison with Vizzani's tale in his "Remarks"—he left to the reader's own judgment.[133] Perhaps this brief insertion of a wholly English example of passion between women was a sly way of reminding readers that, in the end, such practices could also flourish on native soil, independent of foreign influence.

Cleland completed his commentary by offering three moral lessons for his English readership. First, "lewd or lax conversation" could only lead to increasingly unnatural forms of sexual behavior. Libertine words created libertine deeds. If society did not reform its conversational habits, then one could not blame authors for writing in a language that reflected what they heard. Second, he encouraged moral censors to redouble their efforts to suppress

> Those scandalous and flagitious Books, that are not only privately but publickly handed about for the worst Purposes, as well as Prints and Pictures calculated to inflame the Passions, to banish all sense of Shame, and to make the World, if possible, more corrupt and profligate than it is already.

It was a world of erotic words and images which Cleland knew well, both as an author and a consumer, since he inhabited the Grub Street of his day. Finally, he felt that society should be more vigilant in preventing women from publicly cross-dressing, yet another vice that allegedly emerged from the English fashion of imitating the Italians.[134]

Catherine Vizzani seems to have reached approximately the same audience as it did in Italy: a small portion of the market for stories of sexual misadventures and medical curiosities. Yet close examination of its content allows us to see Cleland reflecting on erotic literature, sexual behavior, and cultural translation in the age of the Grand Tour. Both Bianchi and Cleland shared the increasingly common view that sexual desire was a subjective aspect of the human psyche, though they evidently disagreed as to what exactly caused women to love other women. Reading Italian erotic and bawdy literature was important to both of them in the construction of Vizzani's life as an eighteenth-century example of a kind of story that had been told and retold since the Renaissance. For Bianchi, it was an act of cultural continuity that connected his own literary efforts to those of Boccaccio; for Cleland, the writings and imagery of Aretino and his successors—books that truly had been banned rather than simply expurgated by the Catholic Church—shaped his understanding of how to read what Bianchi had written. Long after Vizzani's life disappeared from the bookshops of London, the idea of taking an erotic Grand Tour of Italy persisted. Toward the end of the eighteenth century, the anonymous *A Sapphic Epistle* described the lesbian adventures of an Englishwoman which culminated in an allusion to how an Italian experience had unleashed her desires:

> May I not hope—dear, lovely Fair,
> Of you to have some little share?
>   For if report is right,

> The maids of warm Italia's Land,
> Have felt the pressure of your hand,
>   The pressure of delight.[135]

This imaginary English Sappho crossed the Channel in search of the sexual freedom that numerous authors promised their English readers when they wrote about Italy. Like most travelers, she found what she was looking for. Had she stopped at the English inn in Florence in 1750, she might have even been able to borrow a copy of Cleland's *Memoirs of a Woman of Pleasure* to read in bed, as the Margrave of Baden-Durlach Karl Friedrich did while nursing a cold.[136] Surely this was the epitome of the liberation that a voyage to Italy allowed.

As Who Dare Gaze the Sun

Anna Morandi Manzolini's Wax Anatomies of the Male Reproductive System and Genitalia

REBECCA MESSBARGER

The gaze of the female subject in the traditional anatomical scene was of three principal types: the humiliated, taciturn look of the anatomical Eve; the fixed, dead stare of the female cadaver; and the voluptuous, aroused trance of the anatomical Venus, produced in abundance in Florence at the end of the eighteenth century. The archetypal Eve sculpted by Bolognese wax modeler Ercole Lelli, who dominated the art of anatomical ceroplasty

I am grateful to a number of people without whose generous assistance I would never have completed this study. Dr. Adam Kibel, associate professor of urology at Washington University, permitted me to observe a surgery involving the organs of the lower abdomen, aided with the translation of Morandi's text, and explained the workings of the male urogenital system. Daniel Garrison, professor of classics at Northwestern University, generously provided copies of relevant excerpts of his translation-in-progress of Vesalius' *Fabrica*. My thanks to Sam Fiorello, Marta Cavazza, Tom Broman; members of Washington University's Eighteenth-Century Studies Salon; and members of Washington University's Medical Humanities and Social Sciences Working Group, especially Walt Schalick, for their helpful comments on drafts of this chapter. I appreciate Rishi Rattan's skilled technical and research assistance. I am grateful to Lilla Veckerdy and the staff of the Washington University Bernard Becker Rare Book Archive. My thanks go also to the capable editors of this volume, Wendy Wassyng Roworth, Catherine Sama, and Paula Findlen, for their hard work and encouragement. The chapter title is taken from Philip James Bailey, *Festus*.

during the first half of the eighteenth century, is shown in classic fashion with bowed head, downcast eyes, and a defective veil of flowing hair that cannot hide her shameful nakedness (Figure 10.1). She stands together with Adam at the head of a series of eight life-size anatomical figures progressively demonstrating the muscular and skeletal systems within an allegorical tableau of sin and mortality. The intact female figure, whose skeletal counterpart emblematically completes the series by brandishing an iron sickle (Figure 10.2), connotes both fallen femininity as well as moral recompense against the criminal body. The title page to Andreas Vesalius' *Fabrica* manifests even more starkly the debased position of woman standard to the Early Modern dissection scene, that of inert specimen beneath the scientist's deliberate touch and gaze (Figure 10.3). As Katharine Park has incisively observed, "Vesalius embodied his own vaunted reform of anatomy in a scene that shows him exposing the entrails of a female cadaver to an unruly band of male colleagues and students."[1]

Figure 10.1 Ercole Lelli, female nude, *Eve* (wax). Palazzo Poggi, Bologna. Courtesy of the Poggi Museums.

Figure 10.2 Ercole Lelli, female skeleton with sickle. Palazzo Poggi, Bologna. Courtesy of the Poggi Museums.

Figure 10.3 Andreas Vesalius, detail of title page of *De humani corporis fabrica*. Courtesy of Bernard Becker Rare Book Archive, Washington University.

Yet the marked ambition of the anatomist to take possession of, lay bare, and thereby discipline the *secretum mulieribus* exhibited in this canonical image, reached a hyperbolic intensity in the wax anatomical Venus. These popular figures, complete with romantic hair, glass eyes, and jewelry, offered both a vision of superficial feminine sexuality as well as access to the hidden depths of the female sex. Spectators were invited to behold successive removal of layer upon corporeal layer in the mode of an anatomical undressing: off came the breast plate, the superficial muscles, the deep muscles, and the lower abdominal organs (Figure 10.4). The climax arrived at the disclosure of the naked core, the gravid uterus with its tiny fetus in view. Rewarding far more than misogynist scopophilia, each separate anatomical component could be physically extracted and possessed.

Feminist theorists and historiographers Ludmilla Jordanova, Elaine Showalter, and Karen Newman have successively performed notable *analytical* dissections of the symbolic position and meaning of the Early Modern female anatomical subject, in particular that most verisimilar variety wrought in colored wax. Jordanova and Showalter have explicated the cultural and political connotations of the Florentine Venuses, while Newman has sought to show the link between current antiabortion obstetrical representation and the wax uterine models of the eighteenth-century Bolognese School of Obstetrics. In each case, the author retraces the poses and the naturalistic shades and contours of the wax models back to the commanding gaze of the scientist and that of his presumably male audience. This expectant male onlooker was, according to Jordanova, "intended to respond

Figure 10.4 Clemente Susini, *Venus*. Palazzo Poggi, Bologna. Courtesy of the Poggi Museums.

to the model as to a female body that delighted the sight and invited sexual thoughts."[2]

Building on Jordanova's critique, Showalter contrasts the fetishistic interest in the anatomized female body evidenced by the production of numerous wax Venuses with the absence of a complementary interest in male anatomy. Overlooking such widely circulated texts as Regnier de Graaf's *Tractatus de Virorum Organis Generationi Inservientibus* (1668),[3] as well as the male wax models displayed alongside their female counterparts in Bologna and Florence, not to mention the recumbent male wax figure with removable parts made in Florence for the University of Pavia,[4] Showalter avers that "there were few overt cultural fantasies about the insides of men's bodies, and opening up the man was not a popular image." She attributes this disparity to men's control over anatomical science as well as their gynophobia: "[men] open up a woman as a substitute for self-knowledge, both maintaining the illusion of their own invulnerability and destroying the terrifying female reminder of their impotence and uncertainty."[5] Karen Newman focuses her more recent study, *Fetal Positions: Individualism, Science, Visuality*, on the figures of the gravid uterus and female reproductive system created during the middle of the eighteenth century for the first Bolognese obstetrical school and museum.[6] Newman interprets these figures as a "series of disembodied wombs," separated and decontextualized from the female body, and thus as antithetical by design to the always male fetus "conceived of as preformed, a fully fashioned though tiny adult that simply grew in size." Newman's argument, while absorbing and provocative, falters on thin historiography. Her account of the historical and cultural context from which these waxes emerged both disregards the practical use of the models as teaching instruments for midwives and surgeons and fails to consider the models in the context of the extensive written and visual oeuvre of the artists who made them, one of whom is the subject of this chapter.

Each of the studies discussed above posits an unqualified dichotomy of the fully realized male subject (anatomist, spectator, and indeed fetus), his presumed agency and desire, and a conversely submissive and ontologically deficient female corporeal object. Each author views and defines woman's position in the anatomical theater solely through the lens of the authoritative male gaze. Yet in her discerning critique of predominant feminist interpretations of the symbolic and cultural significance of the wax Venuses, Mary Sheriff indicates the historical and theoretical insufficiency of only considering "men as they look at women's bodies." Sheriff points out that "women appear . . . only insofar as they are objects of the male gaze and are never considered looking themselves."[7]

Insufficient attention has been paid to the authority and subversive power of the female anatomist, scientist, artist, and spectator who gazed upon and at times possessed expert knowledge of the body, including the sexed body.[8] This chapter seeks to address this deficiency by examining the expansive visual and written study of the male reproductive system and genitalia by the eighteenth-century Bolognese anatomist and anatomical wax modeler Anna Morandi Manzolini (1714–1774).

In the new anatomical scene that Morandi constructed and occupied during the second half of the eighteenth century, woman is no longer the docile anatomical object of discovery, the vacant-eyed cadaver at the center of the thronging theater, splayed and rent by the master anatomist. Rather, as Morandi's wax self-portrait makes manifest, she is herself the master anatomist who directs her own knowing gaze on and inside the parts of the body she uncovers, including the brain, the sense organs, and indeed, the male sex (Figure 10.5).

At the height of her prestigious career as anatomist and anatomical modeler, when patrons of her meticulous, realistic anatomical models included Pope Benedict XIV, Catherine the Great, and the Royal Society of London, Morandi sculpted a comprehensive series demonstrating the male reproductive system and genitalia. Historians have virtually overlooked this focal point of her oeuvre, no doubt in part because of extensive gaps in the primary documentation. However, enduring disregard for Morandi's radical recasting of the gender roles standard to the anatomical dissection scene is also due to a narrow view of women's role in the realm of the body during the Early Modern age.

Gianna Pomata's recent analysis of midseventeenth-century reconceptualizations of human generative anatomy and the concomitant rise in interest in the question of sexual difference serves as a theoretical backdrop for my interpretation of Morandi's contributions in the sphere of reproductive anatomy.[9] Focusing on two interconnected innovations of the Scientific Revolution, the widely accepted redefinition of "female testicles" as ovaries and the discovery of spermatozoa by Antoni van Leeuwenhoek (1632–1723), Pomata argues that application of the experimental method to analysis of the organs and processes of human generation produced a decisively "anti-Aristotelian view of sexual difference."[10] Pomata's explication of seventeenth-century theories of reproduction bolsters mounting criticism of Thomas Laqueur's influential

Figure 10.5 Anna Morandi Manzolini, *Self-Portrait* (wax). Palazzo Poggi, Bologna. Courtesy of the Poggi Museums.

thesis that only in the eighteenth century did the monolithic "one-sex *male* model*,*" in relation to which woman was seen as essentially derivable and deficient, give way to a conception of the sexes as incommensurably different. Seventeenth-century ovist and spermist theories, notwithstanding their essential opposition, manifest a shift away from received notions of human generation and indicate the discrete reproductive functions of each sex.[11] Moreover, as a result of the distinct and crucial generative role attributed to ovaries, Early Modern medical writings frequently expressed the view that "both sexes are necessary to reproduction and that each is perfect in relation to its own function."[12] Pomata thus disputes Laqueur and feminist historiographers who argue with him that the "Scientific Revolution did not displace the dogma of male superiority nor shed light on the problem of sexual difference."[13] As will be seen, Anna Morandi Manzolini builds explicitly on the "new" theories and practices of seventeenth-century anatomists, through both her study of their work and her meticulous analysis of the parts and functions of the reproductive male body. She thereby contributes significantly to the discourse of sexual difference as it evolved during the eighteenth century. Indeed, Morandi unmistakably allied herself with those progressive Early Modern practitioners of the empirical method in the realm of the body to whom Pomata rightly calls attention. With Malpighi, de Graaf, Valsalva, Morgagni, and other anatomical empiricists whose work she studied, Morandi looked anew at the body and explored its deepest depths and microscopic elements literally first-hand in order to know and accurately convey its parts and design. However, notwithstanding the unmistakable merit of her analysis, Pomata's generalized critique of the feminist historiography of the age and her conclusions that "the assumption of male superiority . . . had become . . . an open problem" in seventeenth-century medical discourse to such a degree that this period gave rise to a "new positive perception of the female body"[14] elide the vast Early Modern cultural discourse on the subject of female inferiority, in particular the especially relevant body of literature Luciano Guerci so aptly designated "scientific misogyny."[15] As I aim to show, Morandi stood at the intersection of the two dominant scientific and discursive currents in contention in Pomata's analysis: the progressive empirical mode of scientific analysis of the body and sexual difference, and the age-old "dogma of male superiority," seemingly contrary dispositions that in fact often coexisted in the same *masterwork*.[16] Morandi's modern method and practice of anatomical science derives from and furthers the scientific re-visioning of the body that Pomata elucidates. However, Morandi's controversial position as woman anatomist, for which she came under explicit and implicit attack, as well as the tactical partiality of her visual and written account of human reproduction also serve to shed light on the staunch scientific misogyny that persisted and indeed thrived well into the Enlightenment.

Representing the Reproductive Body

Together with her husband Giovanni Manzolini, Morandi sculpted the original 20 of more than 170 models of the gravid uterus and the female reproductive system used by Giovanni Antonio Galli in Bologna's first School of Obstetrics, which he opened in his home ca. 1734. Galli first commissioned Giovanni Manzolini to "express in wax two placentas, one with its membranes, and the other showing the structure of that part that remains attached to the uterus," for a presentation Galli was to give before the Institute of Sciences in 1746.[17] Pleased with these first figures, Galli commissioned eighteen more tables illustrating the pelvis and gravid uterus for use in his practical instruction of midwives and surgeons in childbirth and delivery. These twenty figures along with the rest of Galli's collection became part of the permanent holdings of the institute in 1757 and were displayed in two rooms on the first floor designated for the study of obstetrics.[18]

After her husband's sudden death in 1755, Morandi sculpted some occasional anatomical models of the gravid uterus and female reproductive organs. However, unlike all other subjects she studied, she produced no written analysis of the reproductive female body.

She left the scientific explication of these particular facsimiles to such prominent (male) authorities as Galli, for whom and according to whose specific directives the greater part were created.[19] There are many possible explanations for her silence on the science of women's bodies, not the least probable of which was the expansive, often virulently misogynist contemporary discourse about the female anatomy.[20]

At the pinnacle of her career, Morandi was, in fact, a target of a notorious tract that proffered a fresh, "scientific" apology for the ancient axiom that women's intellectual inferiority was a natural effect of their reproductive function. In 1771, the Bolognese anatomist Petronio Ignazio Zecchini anonymously published *Genial Days: On the Dialectic of Women Reduced to Its True Principle*,[21] which included a malicious attack on several unnamed contemporary women renowned for their learning. It was clear he was referring to the Bolognese physicist Laura Bassi, the Milanese mathematician Maria Gaetana Agnesi, and most notably Anna Morandi, whom he plainly regarded as an interloper in his own field of scientific expertise.[22] The author proposed a series of unconventional arguments that contradicted the prevailing encephalocentrism (the philosophy of the brain) and culminated in the assertion that women and their intellects are subject to one "predominant organ," the everirritated and erratic uterus. In a tone of acid condescension, he addressed his female readers directly, ascribing to them a "thinking uterus" (*l'utero pensante*) that "is the absolute ruler of your thoughts . . . and . . . causes you to think the way it wants."[23] Plainly, Zecchini's thesis rearticulated ancient notions of the uterus as an itinerant, insatiable, and lustful creature,[24] while his conclusions also echoed the misogynist politics of his remote precursors. He ended his tract by commanding women: "willingly subject yourselves to men, who, by their counsel, can curb your instability and your concupiscence."[25]

In the face of Zecchini's offensive, and the potent misogyny that suffused his and the preponderance of contemporary arguments constituting the burgeoning (pseudo) Science of Women during the period, Morandi dared to carry out a comprehensive theoretical examination of the male reproductive system and genitalia both in wax works and in extensive writings. I would argue, however, that the male reproductive body may in fact have appeared relatively less risky for her to study. Her own ("thinking") uterus and its presumed physiological and psychological effects would undoubtedly be implicated in any written theories she set down on the female body. Whatever the reason, Morandi sought to establish her legacy and her distinction among (male) authorities in anatomy by staking her own claims to mastery of that most virile of the new sciences on the male reproductive body itself.

Anatomy Lessons

After the death of her husband, the forty-one-year-old *anatomica* and mother of two young sons assumed control of the household studio where the couple had worked side by side for the previous ten years dissecting cadavers, sculpting wax anatomical models, and instructing medical students and illustrious visitors to Bologna in the science and practice of human anatomy. Buoyed professionally and economically by papal patronage and a lifetime honorarium from the Bolognese Senate, the widow Manzolini undertook at this time her comprehensive anatomy of the male urogenital system. She delved deep beneath the fig leaf to uncover the intricate structures and corresponding functions of the "male generative parts" in direct defiance of the rules governing the art of anatomical design. Contemporary leaders of the Bolognese cultural establishment, such as the influential author and member of the Bolognese Academy of Science Francesco Algarotti, and the secretary of Bologna's Academy of Art Giampietro Zanotti, explicitly denounced the training of artists in anatomical science beyond what was necessary "for correctly representing the male nude."[26] They and other influential arbiters of Bologna's cultural standards publicly disparaged, in letters, tracts, and staged comedies, artisans who asserted an equal claim to chisel and scalpel the ideal exterior and the unruly interior of the body. Morandi thus transgressed the established borders between art and science no more egregiously than with her sculptures of the dissected male sex.[27]

Yet, while Morandi engaged this provocative subject to vie for a place in the society of illustrious anatomists, she allied herself with authors who sought to reconceive the human body and sexual difference through impartial hands and eyes. Following the method of such authentic practitioners of the "new" anatomy as de Graaf, Malpighi, and Morgagni, whose work she knew, cited, and in some cases even corrected, Morandi subordinated the authority of received knowledge to that of the dissection table.[28] These authors, as Pomata has adeptly shown, advanced the discourse on sexual difference by ascribing greater importance to women's distinct reproductive system and functions.[29] The Dutch anatomist Regnier de Graaf (1641–1673) substantiated William Harvey's claims of 1651 that "ex ovo omnia" (all living things come from eggs) by elaborating the function of ovaries,[30] identifying their follicles (which he erroneously believed were eggs), and mapping the passage of eggs through the fallopian tubes to the uterus. From his microscopic studies of chick embryos, Marcello Malpighi (1628–1694) identified, among other parts, the embryonic blastoderm, developing blood vessels, somites, and neural grooves. He also amended the theories of de Graaf, with whom he had an extensive correspondence, by distinguishing follicles from eggs.[31] Giovanni Battista Morgagni (1682–1771) conducted extensive anatomical demonstrations to arrive at his conclusions with de Graaf that female ovaries produce eggs from which, through fertilization by semen (which he and de Graaf incorrectly believed took place in the ovaries), offspring are produced.

It is necessary to point out, however, that while each of these authors emphasized the particular and indispensable organs and functions of the female body for human reproduction, each also adhered in varying themes and degrees to ancient concepts of female deficiency and male supremacy. De Graaf's strikingly expressive and often anecdotal account of the female reproductive system offers a colorful recapitulation of certain leitmotifs of the misogynist anatomical tradition, as when he describes the insatiable uterus with hymen intact of a pregnant fourteen-year-old girl: "When semen poured in between the lips of her pudendum, her uterus, greedy for this kind of food, drew it to itself, just as a stag attracts snakes out of deep holes with the breath of its nostrils."[32] In a series of lessons on human reproduction given at the University of Padua, Morgagni explicitly reiterates a core Aristotelian axiom that the female contributes the material cause of the fetus while the male contributes the nobler efficient, formal, and telic causes[33]:

> We observe that our theory admirably agrees with the hypothesis of Aristotle: the material of the fetus comes entirely from the mother, from the father, almost nothing, while exclusively from the paternal contribution obtains the principles of motion and energy.[34]

As regards Malpighi, Catherine Wilson observes in her incisive analysis of theories of generation among early modern microscopists that he believed "that females in general produce eggs and cast them off, and that these eggs, when fecundated by the male 'unfold into a new life.'"[35] In his analysis of the cause of sterility in a Lucchese couple, Malpighi provides a précis of his notions on conception, formed as they were from his knowledge of plant generation: "The generation of man is so obscure that it can be explained only by analogy with perfect animals and with plants. This is certain: Nature has constituted twin principles, an active and a passive, the latter producing the egg, which the other principle fecundates by moistening it with semen. Moreover, in order that [the egg] may grow like a plant, the semen must be committed to the uterus as to its proper soil, and when favorable colliquament emanates from the uterus, the parts of the animal become visible, grow, and are made strong."[36]

Anna Morandi's representation of the reproductive male body not only overcomes conventional masculinist bias regarding the reproductive body and sexual difference but also rejects the long-established *competitive* anatomy (male versus female). Morandi conceptualizes the reproductive male body both outside of the male-female binary while, at the same time, attributing to it a reproductive imperative parallel to that of the female body. By focusing on the specific generative functions of the components making up the male urogenital system, Morandi implicitly rejects difference as a requisite means for delineating the processes and final cause of human reproduction. As will be shown, she looks at the male anatomy in isolation, indexing its component parts and their distinct and collective form and function for human reproduction.

ANATOMICAL PREPARATION
OF THE MALE GENERATIVE PARTS
CONSTRUCTED BY ANNA MORANDI MANZOLINI,
BOLOGNESE CITIZEN, ANATOMIST,
and Honorary Academician in the Institute of Sciences of Bologna[37]

With this weighty heading identifying the subject of Morandi's investigation and her notable academic authority to perform such a study, she begins analysis of the parts of the male reproductive system. As in all of her anatomical studies, Morandi first exhibits the intact, animate body, in this case "the trunk of a man in its natural situation in which the integuments (coverings/membranes) in the lower abdomen are opened and all the viscera removed that would impede a clear vision of the generative parts of the male sex."[38] She proceeds systematically from the uppermost parts of the specimen to the lowest, and from exterior to interior. In the first table, she renders a whole, macrocosmic image of the male reproductive body from which will systematically follow anatomies of discrete, ever smaller, even microscopic, details of this composite form.

In accordance with the canon of modern, empirical anatomical design, Morandi's literal overview of the subject, from diaphragm to severed thighs, indexes the primary anatomical components of the urogenital system. The atlases and anatomical studies by Cowper, Vesalius, Vesling, Casseri, Morgagni, and numerous others that filled the shelves of her private archive served at most as archetypes and more narrowly as points of departure for Morandi's anatomical studies. Just as Morandi quoted illustrations in Cowper of intact, looking eyes and the octopuslike ocular muscles (Figures 10.6, 10.7), she doubtless modeled her sculptures of the male body to some extent on canonical illustrations.

Figure 10.6 Anna Morandi Manzolini, eyes. Palazzo Poggi, Bologna. Courtesy of the Poggi Museums.

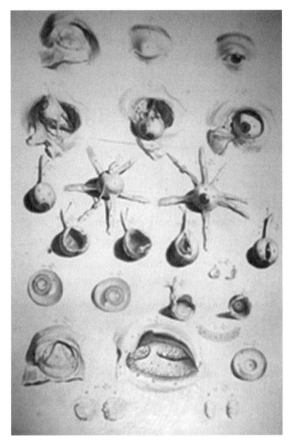

Figure 10.7 William Cowper, *Anatomia corporum humanorum*, Table 11. Courtesy of Bernard Becker Rare Book Archive, Washington University.

In the absence of her actual wax sculptures of the male reproductive system, it is therefore possible to approximate what the first figure and subsequent tables in the series looked like. Vesalius' *Fabrica*, whose illustrations were likewise imitated in the works of Valsalva, Casseri, and others, likely served as the principal font for her facsimiles. In her study of the male reproductive system, Morandi, like Vesalius, begins with the trunk of a man with organs of the lower abdomen exposed (Figure 10.8). Although Morandi's figure would have perhaps exhibited a less heroic posture and musculature than the Vesalian archetype, based as it was on the torso Belvedere, the general content appears to resemble that of her precursor. Apart from Vesalius' inclusion of the liver, which Morandi has extracted, the mode and general syntax of each author's expression of the male urogenital system are broadly analogous, having been based in both cases on dissection.[39]

Following this overview, Morandi subsequently isolates and details the key parts of the system, beginning with the passage of the urethra from the bladder to the tip of the glans penis. This is followed in order by tables demonstrating the anterior and posterior of the bladder opened to show the passage of the urethra; the prostate and the seminal collicles (more commonly known as the verumontanum); the penis with and without its coverings; the two spongy bodies of the corpus cavernosum that make up the penis; the seminal vesicles, their parts, and secretions; the seminal vesicles, the prostate, and the antiprostate (now known as Cowper's gland); the bladder distended with urine; the prostate shown to expose the passage of the bladder to the urethra; the scrotum shown with the testicles *in* and *extra situm*; various figures and sections of the testicles; a macerated testicle to show "the silken threads" of which it is composed; the integuments of the scrotum, testicles, and penis; the kidneys and their substances and "papillae radiating in the pelvis"; the sectioned kidney; the tiny blood vessels of the testicle shown by means of wax injections; the arterial, venal, and nervous vessels that "nourish the genital parts"; and finally the pelvic bones. Her visual and literary account thus simultaneously strives toward deeper and

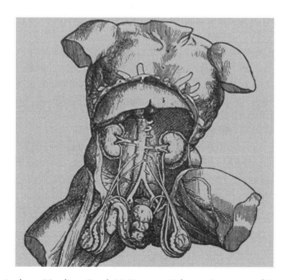

Figure 10.8 Andreas Vesalius, Book V, Fig. 22, *Fabrica.* Courtesy of Bernard Becker Rare Book Archive, Washington University.

deeper views, as well as the particular, the detail, of ever more minute components and substances within the larger reproductive system.

As this summary suggests, Morandi's bipartite visual and written study of the male urogenital system was fundamentally didactic. In the 250-page companion text to her wax anatomies, the anatomist methodically schools her student-spectators in the structure, organization, and function of the anatomical system on display. Her notes convey the didactic voice with which she likely addressed the many medical students, dilettantes, and tourists who visited her studio, the site of her anatomical practice from the beginning of her career in 1742 until the last six years of her life.[40] Here she dissected cadavers and body parts obtained from the city mortuary and the Hospital of Santa Maria della Morte, gave anatomy lessons to medical students and surgeons, created wax facsimiles of the anatomized body, and received countless tourists and visiting dignitaries to Bologna. From her extensive notes on the subject, it may be surmised that in her household studio she likewise demonstrated for medical practitioners and the curious the parts and the functions of the male reproductive system, a subject that comprised more than 20 percent of her complete oeuvre. For example, in her notes elucidating the components of the bladder that enable retention and expulsion of urine, she identifies the relevant parts as they appear during dissection, defines key anatomical terms, and maps the location and functional interrelation of the parts through her use of symbols inscribed on the wax models that correspond to the index and analysis in her notebook:

> The substance of the urinary bladder is composed of three membranes. The first is called *carnosa* [fleshy, muscular], the second *nervous*, and the third *villous*. The first membrane of the bladder is composed of three strata of variously woven fibers, the first marked with the symbol *E*. These are generally the straightest and are destined to attract the urine; the second, marked by *FF*, are oblique, and have the function of casting out the urine, the last marked *GGG*, are crossed at a sign near the neck of the bladder where they come to form an entire sphincter, which one can see in this figure, and these are destined by reason of their circulation, or sphincter-like form, to hold the urine in the bladder so that it does not escape without our consent, just as Galen and Vesalius thought.[41]

As Nancy Siraisi has observed, inherent to the tradition of modern dissection was not only itemization and analysis of the anatomical subject, the cadaver, or body part, but complementary dissection of the accuracy and relevance of master anatomical texts.[42] Adhering to this tradition, here

Morandi confirms the theories of Galen and Vesalius, while implicitly, but unmistakably, surpassing her forebears' anatomical precision.

The Purposive Design of the Male Anatomy

Beyond its didactic design, evident in Morandi's study of the male anatomy are essential teleological concerns. She adheres in this and select parts of her oeuvre to a tradition in anatomical science most explicitly articulated by Galen in his work *On the Usefulness of Parts*, which presumed the perfect utility and constitution of all parts and aspects of the body for realizing the functions of the soul as designated by what he termed the *demiurgos*.[43] As Siraisi has observed, Galen "followed Plato in ascribing conscious, purposeful design to a divine Craftsman."[44] Although decidedly more mechanistic in his anatomical expositions, Vesalius continued to advocate a teleological conceptualization of human anatomy and physiology, making explicit reference to their ideal design by that divine force he variably identified as the "Opifex," the "Founder of Things," the "Creator," and "God,"[45] while "Nature," for Vesalius, denoted God's handmaiden and intermediary in the physical world. As Siraisi points out, however, for Vesalius scientific accuracy in explicating the parts and functions of the body represented the supreme mode of venerating the original Anatomical Designer. Galen's failure to correctly describe and sufficiently detail the anatomical parts and structures revealed through dissection thus signified for Vesalius a corresponding failure to glorify the Creator.[46]

Seventeenth-century anatomists who influenced Morandi's illustration of the male reproductive body continued to venerate in their writings the perfect composition of human anatomy by God and Nature, the ordered actualization of divine will in the material world. In his anatomical tracts, de Graaf discovers the signs of "Almighty God," "the provident Maker of the universe," and "His marvelous wisdom" inscribed on the body and traces Nature's laws and ingenious design within the structure and processes of the anatomical subject: "The main reason why Nature did not make [the scrotum's] membrane a fatty one seems to us to have been to ensure that it did not grow excessively large and incapable of relaxing and wrinkling."[47] Morgagni similarly casts Nature as engineer of physiological processes.[48] His references to God, however, consistently indicate those mysteries that exceed the reach of science: "our proposition is not to discover objectively that same process known only to God, but simply to find among the many possibilities, the conjecture that is least improbable."[49] Malpighi is perhaps closest to Morandi in his evocation of "Nature," whose enigmatic rules and procedures the natural philosopher seeks to disclose through systematic, repeated, and direct experience. Comparing himself to an artist who, in order to complete a painting, must free the mind of the preliminary designs, he states that "in studying the tablets of Nature, infrequent but repeated investigations reveal more elegant mysteries after the old concepts that once possessed the citadel of Pallas have been banished."[50] Morandi's interpretation is also devoid of any reference to a divine Creator and, unlike myriad key terms in her anatomical notebook, without an uppercase acknowledgment of "nature's" exalted roles as architect and engineer of the human form.

Morandi's interdependent visual and literary interpretation of human anatomy attends to vital function as well as form by illustrating the purposive design of the body and its parts in the context of the performance of their ideal functions.[51] As I have said elsewhere, whether intact or dismembered her eyes look about, her hands feel, her ears hear.[52] In her illustrations of the male urogenital system, the male reproductive body is conceived in the act of becoming fecund for generation. Indeed, Morandi repeatedly invokes nature as author and agent of the body's ideal anatomical and physiological design in only two sections of her anatomical notebook, here on the male reproductive body and in her redolent study of the hand, the organ of touch. In each, the body's substance and form attain completion through experience.

Morandi makes repeated reference to the ideal composition of the male body by nature, which, for example, placed the testicles deliberately "outside of the lower abdomen . . . to modify the heat of the sperm or semen . . . [and] to maintain the tautness of their conduits by means of gravity."[53] In Table Three, she identifies the function of what she terms the "accelerator muscles of the urethra" (the bulbo cavernous muscle), which "are endowed by nature with peristaltic motion in order to render them able to thrust the semen with vigor into the uterine cavity."[54] In broad agreement with the anatomists she studied, Morandi thus conceives of nature as the ideal ordering and creative force operating on and within the constitutive material elements of the body.

In Via Perfectionis

As Morandi's visual and written study advances, the process of seminal "perfection," "completion," or "fermentation" becomes the focus of analysis and signifies an implicit final cause of the reproductive male body. The generative process, *in via perfectionis*, is both intricate and vast, permeating all parts and substances of the urogenital system, each of which contributes to the forward drive of male fecundity. By means of the technique of wax injection, Morandi shows in Table Twenty, for example, the "many tiny blood vessels"[55] that invisibly "communicate with the substance of the testicle through the tunica albuginea [whitish membrane that encases the spongy chambers inside the penis and helps to sustain erection by trapping blood in said chambers] . . . [and] likewise communicate with the liquor of the spermatic vessels through the fermentation of the semen."[56] The tubes or canals that store and transport the sperm from the testes, known as the vas deferens, likewise serve "to receive from the epididymis the semen, which this had already received from the testicles, and to transmit this and deposit it in the seminal vesicles as in a reservoir for the fecundation or generation of the offspring."[57]

The intensified attention to purposive design is accompanied in Morandi's notes by an increasingly suggestive commentary on the process of male fecundity, culminating in her description of the seminal vesicles, where she mistakenly believed semen collected as in an antechamber for finishing enrichment before ejaculation.[58] Straining the conventions of dispassionate scientific discourse, Morandi's schematic notes gradually transform into a miniepic of male fecundity. Her précis turns poesy as she narrates the long journey of the semen to the urethra. At each juncture, from the testicles through the epididymis to the vas deferens, the seminal vesicles, through the prostate and Cowper's gland and the ejaculatory ducts, the semen is enriched and its impulsive generative energy steadied by critical nutritive and congealing components. The odyssey of seminal completion culminates then in the seminal vesicles. She exposes in her wax facsimile this "reservoir for that balsamic liquor[59] called semen . . . in order to show those velvety or glandulous coves or chambers where the semen resides and continually perfects itself."

Of course there was nothing new in the notion that semen undergoes a process of perfection or, more accurately, completion, according to Latinate usage.[60] De Graaf and Morgagni too describe this procedure. However, unlike these near precursors Morandi did not revise such ancient notions of male generative potency as "pneuma," Aristotle's "vector of the soul," which, in the "modern" anatomies of de Graaf and Morgagni become invisible "animal spirits" carried by the nerves to the testicles where they mix with blood conveyed by the spermatic vessels and form the noble life force. According to de Graaf, these "spirits cause the ingredients to foam . . . and bestow final perfection upon them, a process we believe Hippocrates to have understood similarly to ourselves where he says that foam is the 'essence of semen.'"[61] Her very different emphasis on the process of becoming, of completing, of satisfying a reproductive imperative makes no reference to a point on the trajectory of male fecundity when seminal fluid is infused with an ennobling spirit, Hippocrates' "effervescent foam of life." In her schema, the urogenital system *in toto* serves the realization of male fecundity, which accrues in and along its numerous parts, pathways, and junctures.

The most distinctive aspect of Morandi's teleology of the male reproductive body is, however, the absence of a feminine foil. No corollary account of female difference or deficiency attends Morandi's explanation of the process of seminal completion and male fecundity.[62] Nor does Morandi assert with many of her precursors "the pre-eminence of the product formed by the male" for reproduction.[63] The male reproductive body is, for Morandi, ideally designed as a composite whole and in all of its parts for the generation of the species. Her schema is neither phallocentric nor fetishistic. She considers reproduction to be a systemic process to which the aggregate of organs and bodily elements contribute. She does not identify a predominant organ for male reproduction or a material point of origin for male ontological difference. She offers no "thinking penis" as complement or counterargument to Zecchini's "thinking uterus." At the same time, she ascribes to the male body a reproductive imperative both essential and integral. From the fascia and membranes to the arteries, veins, and vessels; from the kidneys to the bladder, blood, and chyle; from the integuments to the penis, testicles, and pubic bone—all parts serve the progressive processes of fertility and reproduction. Her conceptualization of the purposive design of the masculine body imputes traditional attributes neither of transcendence nor dominance. The male body is instead ideally formed, as a whole and in all of its parts, for the purpose of generation. Indeed, the symmetry of the male reproductive imperative with that of the female suggests a kind of teleological balance of the sexes.

As has been noted previously, Morandi's anatomy of the reproductive female body is without written gloss, and limited in scope primarily to her patron's commission. However, given the hundreds of extant wax figures and pages of scientific notes on myriad parts of the body created by Morandi, which steadfastly manifest her aim for maximum scientific accuracy as well as her consistent conceptualization of bodily components within the context of a vital, interdependent anatomical and physiological whole, it is fair to presume that her extensively elaborated poetics of anatomy would not have dissolved before the female body. Nor would Morandi, who in her written analyses boldly interrogated and often disputed the theories of such canonical authors as Galen, Vesalius, Valsalva, Malpighi, Rivinus, Winslow, and Adriaan van den Spiegel, have likely yielded to the misogynist tradition of representing the female anatomy. Indeed, the few occasional waxes of the female reproductive system that form part of her private collection are consistent with her written descriptions of her wax renderings of the reproductive male anatomy. Her illustration of the uterus and its realistic dimensions after labor and delivery shows the vital organ open, round, and distended with ligaments, muscle, and fascia attached. The expression of the tissues adjoining the uterus alludes to the larger context of the lower abdomen, just as Morandi's representation of a rippling swirl of placenta that seems to spill over the side of the wooden display table in her facsimile of the anatomy of a newborn child, indicates the origin and furious motion of that birth.

In the actual and ideal anatomical theater she occupied, Morandi's look upon the body does not demean or dehumanize. Nor does she conform to the canon of anatomical science and design by venerating the male body, its transcendent force and potential. She asserts her authority neither through a reiteration nor a reversal of the sexual imbalance. As with all the parts of the body under her scalpel and her gaze (Figure 10.9), Morandi seeks to demonstrate what is dispassionately revealed by experience in accordance with the modern method, while at the same time acknowledging the perfection of nature's complex design.

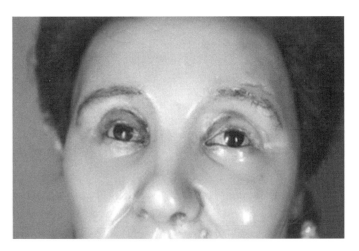

Figure 10.9 Anna Morandi Manzolini, detail, *Self-Portrait* (wax). Palazzo Poggi, Bologna. Courtesy of the Poggi Museums.

PART FOUR

The Spectacle of Gender

ELEVEN

Between Modesty and Spectacle

Women and Science in Eighteenth-Century Italy

MARTA CAVAZZA

A New "Literary Phenomenon"

Of the numerous travelers who crossed the Alps in the eighteenth century, Charles de Brosses was certainly one of the most acute observers of Italian customs. In his *Lettres d'Italie*, De Brosses noted a new phenomenon which stimulated his curiosity and imagination and at the same time took him off guard. In Milan, where he arrived in the summer of 1739, he was favorably impressed by the number of scholars crowding into the Biblioteca Ambrosiana, but he found it "singular to see a woman there, working amidst a pile of Latin books." This was Francesca Manzoni, who held the title "poet of the empress," and De Brosses warned his correspondent De Neully that she was only the first of a series: "You shall soon see that there are women still more erudite here." His diffidence toward learned women led him to ignore without regrets the invitations of Countess Clelia Grillo Borromeo, patron of philosophers and academies "who not only knows all the sciences and languages of Europe but also speaks Arabic like the Koran [*parle l'arabe*

Translated by Matthew Sneider.

comme l'Alcoran],*" and to manifest to one of his correspondents his scarce enthusiasm for the prospect of a meeting with the young Maria Gaetana Agnesi (Figure 11.1), "a walking polyglot" who, not content to know all the oriental languages, "even dares to defend theses against all comers on any science whatsoever, as did Pico della Mirandola."[1]

When, however, he arrived in the salon of don Pietro Agnesi, a rich bourgeois with aspirations of nobility, De Brosses did not escape the allure of his learned daughter. Amid another "thirty persons from all the nations of Europe seated in a circle," he witnessed "a sort of *action publique*" whose center was "Mademoiselle Agnesi, all alone with her younger sister, seated in an armchair." First the girl responded in perfect Latin to a discourse made by one of the sitters in the same language on the origin of springs and the cause of tides; then, pressed by the questions which De Brosses and the others were

Figure 11.1 Benigno Bossi, *Portrait of Maria Gaetana Agnesi* for the Accademia dei Trasformati Milan, Venerabile Biblioteca Ambrosiana.

invited to pose to her, she discussed in Latin and French the mechanisms of sensation and imagination, light and colors, the transparency of bodies, and the properties of certain geometric curves. In the general conversation which followed, the young woman continued to astonish, speaking with each of the guests in the language of his nation. The spectacle was capped by a concert by her sister Maria Teresa—almost as famous a musician as her sister was a philosopher—who played certain pieces by Rameau and others of her own composition on the harpsichord (Figure 11.2). In the letter he wrote that night, De Brosses confessed to his correspondent that the "species of literary phenomenon" which he had witnessed seemed "a more stupendous thing than the Duomo of Milan," but that "it almost caught me off guard" (*j'ai manqué en même temps d'y être pris sans vert*)—an expression which gives a sense of the phenomenon's novelty and of the perplexities it probably caused.[2]

Figure 11.2 Benigno Bossi, *Portrait of Maria Teresa Agnesi* for the Accademia dei Trasformati Milan, Venerabile Biblioteca Ambrosiana.

In mid-September of the same year, De Brosses arrived in Bologna, where he was able to make the acquaintance of another woman philosopher. In this case he was not surprised, because by then Laura Bassi's fame had long been secured in Europe by the resonance of her laurea (university degree) and the extraordinary honors given her in 1732 by the political and university authorities of the city. The French traveler was invited to one of the "philosophical conferences" which Bassi, married for a year to doctor Giuseppe Veratti, held in her house. He discussed with her the properties of magnets and "the singular attraction of electrical bodies." According to De Brosses, these discussions had the principal aim of showing off the learning of the lady of the house ("to show off the ability of she who responds"). They were therefore a kind of exhibition; they were not real philosophical disputations. These displays evidently impelled De Brosses to make the same comparisons that he did for singers: "The Signora Bassi has spirit, politeness, and doctrine; she expresses herself with ease; but even with all this I would not trade her for my young girl of Milan." Even the public lectures which the Bolognese *dottoressa* and chair in universal philosophy (*philosophia universa*) gave at the university while dressed in a toga and ermine were solemn occasions compared to the regular lectures of the other professors because, as De Brosses explained, "it was not thought decent for a woman to reveal every day, to all comers, the hidden things of nature."[3]

In his epistolary account of his visit to the only woman in the Europe of this period who had obtained, thanks to her studies, the public recognition elsewhere reserved exclusively for men, De Brosses emphasizes, as in the Milanese case the almost theatrical ostentation of female knowledge. Moreover, he notes the contradictions which this unusual overexposure entailed morally and socially. It was not acceptable for a woman to undertake a daily intellectual activity like public teaching at a university; yet the same woman was authorized to exhibit her philosophical culture in solemn ceremonies before an audience of nobles, ecclesiastics, and curious Italians and foreigners—an activity which granted her a visibility far more dramatic than that gained through teaching normal university classes.

In the opinion of De Brosses and other travelers who, before him but above all after him, included among their destinations a visit to one or another of these Italian women who were honored and made famous for their knowledge (particularly in Bologna), this "literary phenomenon" appeared to be thoroughly Italian. It was something very different from the French institution of the salon in which women played a fundamental role as promoters and animators but rarely made original contributions to the conversation or carried out scientific studies of their own.[4] In eighteenth-century Italy, Bassi and Agnesi—like Eleonora Barbapiccola, Faustina Pignatelli, Maria Angela Ardinghelli, Cristina Roccati, and Anna Morandi—not only played a more or less meaningful role in research, in teaching, or in the popularization of science but received recognition, honors, and in certain cases university degrees and teaching duties. This is a unique historical case which, until a short while ago, did not receive the attention it merited from scholars of the Italian Enlightenment and particularly from historians of science.

Only over the last two decades, thanks above all to research carried out by an ever larger group of women scholars (for the most part not Italian), the phenomenon of women of science in Enlightenment Italy has come into focus, with the result that we now know much more about individual figures—some of whom were literally rescued from the dust of archives and oblivion—and about the intellectual and social contexts from which they emerged and in which they interacted.[5] Nonetheless much remains to be done, especially on the second issue. In a political and social panorama as diverse as that of eighteenth-century Italy, I believe that research on the specific conditions that made women's pursuit of knowledge possible and on the inevitable contradictions with socially codified female roles should be intensified.[6] Even though the 1720s inaugurated a strong push toward change which reopened the debate over study for women—the fulcrum of the sixteenth-century *querelle des femmes*—the current ideas about the nature, rights, and most important the duties of women were still those that had been imposed in the seventeenth century—the misogynist century *par excellence*—by preachers and moralists who often considered ignorance to be the best guarantee of respect for the fundamental female virtues of obedience and decency.[7] Women's access to instruction was a new Pandora's box, the opening of which could cause a series of explosive consequences for power relations between the sexes in the family and in society.[8] The majority of participants in the debate over the role of and education of women which animated eighteenth-century Italy were more than conscious of this fact, from Antonio Volpi, who in 1723 argued against study for women in a famous meeting of the Academy of the Ricovrati of Padua, to Benvenuto Robbio of San Raffaele, who in 1793 pilloried women guilty of aspiring to cultivate the sciences while neglecting their duties as wives and mothers.[9]

We must therefore ask ourselves how public exaltation of female knowledge could have taken place, on many occasions, in such unfavorable circumstances. We must also ask ourselves about the meaning and the aims attributed to these public displays by their promoters. Once we have understood these things, we may ask these decisive questions: What role did these events play in the process of redefining gender identity in eighteenth-century Italy? What role did they play, that is, in modifying the commonly accepted representation of the nature and social role of women? Consequently, what importance did these episodes have in the evolution of female self-representation and in promoting the birth of an autonomous female subject, or at any rate a subject different from that imposed by the traditional patriarchal codification of female identity?[10]

"A Continual Spectacle of Herself"

I would like to suggest one way of responding to these questions, beginning with the phenomenon described by De Brosses: what we might call the "spectacularization" of female knowledge. The examples are numerous, span the entire century, and are more than sufficient to show that spectacularization was intrinsically connected to cases of young women celebrated for their knowledge in philosophical-scientific (and in two cases also legal) subjects, the same subjects that their male peers regularly studied without exciting clamor in the colleges and universities.

The first cases appeared in Bologna, a city characterized by a very peculiar political and cultural history. From the beginning of the sixteenth century, Bologna was part of the Papal States (it was the second city after Rome) and was governed by a representative of the pope, the cardinal legate, and by the Senate, the expression of the city's aristocracy. The lecturers and the doctoral colleges of the public university also exercised a notable influence on social and political life. Indeed Bologna was the seat of a prestigious university, which was thought to be the world's oldest; in the Middle Ages and the Renaissance it was a very active center for production of knowledge—in law, medicine, mathematics, astronomy, natural philosophy, and philology—capable of attracting teachers and students from all over Europe. In the seventeenth century an unstoppable process of decline did not prevent moments of excellence: Benvenuto Cavalieri in mathematics, Giandomenico Cassini in astronomy, and Marcello Malpighi in anatomy, to mention a few examples. With the foundation of the Istituto delle Scienze, a public institution focused on research and the teaching of modern experimental science, which came to stand beside the university, at the beginning of the eighteenth century the tendency toward provincialization diminished thanks to more continuous connections with other Italian and European scientific centers, in particular with the Royal Society of London and with the Académie des Sciences of Paris.[11] A final note, significant for our purposes, concerns the partly legendary tradition of a female presence in the fourteenth- and fifteenth-century University of Bologna. Some women, such as Bitisia Gozzadini (in the thirteenth century), were thought to have obtained a university degree in law, while others, such as Novella d'Andrea (in the fourteenth century) and Dorotea Bocchi (in the fifteenth century), were thought to have taught legal and philosophical subjects. In the eighteenth century, these medieval memories were often recalled and presented as an integral part of the Bolognese historical identity; they were used to legitimate requests and concessions of university degrees and lectureships to young women. False documentary evidence was even passed off as authentic; an ancient university calendar, for example, listed Gozzadini among the teachers, but it was in reality fabricated by the author of the work *De mulierum doctoratu* (1722).[12]

The first of the *exempla* to which I would like to draw the reader's attention dates back to the dawn of the eighteenth century, when the Bolognese could witness the home exhibitions of the now-forgotten Laura Danielli, the young daughter of a professor of medicine at the university, Stefano Danielli, known as the most faithful pupil of Giovanni Gerolamo Sbaraglia, the adversary of Malpighi. Laura's first master was her father, who made her "so learned in the philosophy and in the elements of Euclid that she was observed with the greatest admiration by the greatest virtuosi of that city as she defended conclusions publicly in her own house."[13]

The defense of a series of legal theses by the aristocratic Maria Vittoria Delfini Dosi had a very different resonance. This occurred in 1722 in the prestigious Collegio di Spagna in the presence of Queen Elisabetta Farnese and was immortalized in an engraving by Domenico Fratta, in which the young disputant appears supported by a figure identifiable as Felsina Minerva, the personification of wisdom and learned Bologna (Figure 11.3). The event was made even more spectacular by parades of carriages, lunches, and gifts for the people, not to mention publication of celebratory poems and a volume on the aforementioned precedent of Bitisia Gozzadini's university degree. The promoter and director was the Count Alfonso Delfini Dosi, father of Maria Vittoria, who fought (and lost) a strenuous battle to obtain from the College of Jurisprudence the concession of a university degree for

Figure 11.3 Domenico Maria Fratta, *Maria Vittoria Delfini Dosi Presents Her Legal Theses to Elisabetta Farnese, Queen of Spain*, 1722. Bologna, Biblioteca Universitaria, MS 775.

his daughter. His objectives were in reality exquisitely political: to reinforce the clientage ties of his important family with the Spanish monarchy and to reaffirm the autonomy of the Bolognese aristocracy—heir and guardian of the memory of the city's glories—from the Roman government.[14]

The spectacles organized by Count Delfini Dosi pale before the year-long series of events organized in 1732 not by a private person but by the highest Bolognese authorities, which were intended to give the greatest possible resonance to the case of Laura Bassi. A young Bolognese, Bassi was gifted with a capacity for learning considered so extraordinary in a woman that it justified the concession of a university degree in philosophy, entrance to the city's Academy of the Istituto delle Scienze, admission as an honorary member of the college of the doctors of philosophy, and, finally, assignment of a university lectureship. Her thesis defenses, the conferring of her doctorate, her first lecture, and other related events took place in the most prestigious halls of the Palazzo Pubblico or the Archiginnasio in the presence of the civic authorities, the Cardinal Legate and the Archbishop, not to mention so numerous an audience that fights and other moments of unrest marked the day. Everything—from the candidate's dress to the choice of two ladies as her escorts, to the succession of interventions, discourses, and thanks—was rigorously planned. Bassi—the university degree recipient, the dottoressa, the lecturer—was always at center stage, as we can see from the three official miniatures commissioned by the Senate, which memorialized the most important events of 1732 (Figure 11.4). An engraving by Domenico Fratta and the reverse of a silver medal comparing her in verse to Minerva helped to spread her image—with her crown of laurel and ermine on her shoulders.[15] It goes without saying that during this period of Arcadia's reign, there were also collections of poetry (at least three printed and others handwritten) with verses that—in Italian, in Latin, and even in Bolognese dialect—expressed admiration and marvel for her philosophical and scientific culture, so unusual in a woman.[16]

In 1732 and in the years following, Bassi was frequently called upon to give proof of her training and dialectic ability at receptions in certain patrician salons of the city and at the "academies" held in her house, where foreigners passing through and curious to meet her and to dispute with her were often present. The "philosophical dispute" organized at the end of 1739 by Filippo Aldrovandi Marescotti as part of the celebrations in honor of Frederick Christian, son of the king of Poland and prince elector of Saxony, had particular resonance. On this occasion, Bassi was called upon

Figure 11.4 Leonardo Sconzani, *Laura Bassi Defends Her Philosophical Thesis in the Palazzo Pubblico*, 1732 (miniature). Bologna, Archivio di Stato, Anziani Consoli, Insignia, vol. 13, c. 94. Ministero per i Beni e le Attività Culturali della Repubblica Italiana.

to undertake a discussion in Latin on metaphysics, natural philosophy, and mathematics with a number of the best-known university and Istituto professors. Among them were Iacopo Bartolomeo Beccari, with whom she spoke about the famous Bologna stone and the relative phenomena of luminescence,[17] and Francesco Maria Zanotti, who interrogated her on a problem of analytical geometry.

The prince appreciated the performance and gave to the protagonist a "golden tobacco holder of very elegant workmanship."[18] In February 1734, her participation as a disputant in the annual public anatomy lesson, which was already a spectacle in itself, made the event worthy of being celebrated with a new miniature in the *Insignia* of the Anziani (Figure 11.5).[19] In successive years, experiments in mechanics, hydrodynamics, electrical physics, and even physiology, carried out in the halls of the Istituto delle Scienze or in the laboratory set up in the Veratti-Bassi household, would be added to the disputations. Here was a tireless exhibition of scientific knowledge, experimental expertise, and dialectical and rhetorical ability which led Eustachio Manfredi, the famous astronomer and poet, to complain in 1737 that the young Bassi (of whom, moreover, he was a convinced admirer) had been forced from the beginning "to make an almost continual spectacle of herself to the city, becoming the target of the questions, the inquiries, and the objections of as many literati—Bolognese or foreign—as were admitted to her house."[20]

What was it that the young Agnesi offered to Milan if not a "continual spectacle"? She had one of her most dramatic successes in December of the same year in which De Brosses admired her, in the course of a magnificent reception offered by don Pietro in honor of the prince elector of Saxony. This was the same prince who, shortly thereafter in Bologna at the Istituto delle Scienze, demonstrated his appreciation for the precision of Bassi's experiments after having admired her culture and dialectical ability at Aldrovandi's house. Before the prince and "the most qualified and erudite"

Figure 11.5 Bernardino Sconzani, *The Public Anatomy in the Anatomic Theatre with Laura Bassi as a Disputant*, 1734 (miniature). Bologna, Archivio di Stato, Anziani Consoli, vol. 13, c. 105. Ministero per i Beni e le Attività Culturali della Repubblica Italiana.

nobility, Maria Gaetana, expressing herself in Latin, confuted the Cartesian explanation of the flux and reflux of the sea by opposing it with the Newtonian explanation based on the universal law of gravitation of matter. Then she illustrated Antonio Vallisneri's theory of the origin of springs and rivers. While she spoke, her sister Maria Teresa played music that she herself had composed at the harpsichord.[21]

One could continue with a list of examples, recounting episodes which occurred in Bologna in the second half of the century: the ceremonies for the laurea of Cristina Roccati (1751); the experiments of Bassi carried out before travelers and crowned heads among whom, apart from the aforementioned elector of Saxony, were the French poet Anne-Marie du Boccage (1757) and Emperor Joseph II (1769), who, on the same day, was also able to witness Anna Morandi's anatomical demonstrations in her museum of wax figures. But first it is necessary to stop and reflect on the social and cultural implications of these events.[22]

The Concealing of Knowledge: A Female Virtue

The visibility of women philosophers and "scientists" in eighteenth-century Italy—their presence at the center of the social scene—must have astonished foreign travelers not only for the originality of the phenomenon but also for the difficulty of reconciling it with the image of modesty and "seclusion" (*ritiratezza*) to which women were supposed to conform according to the behavioral codes and their associated values prevalent in Italy at the time. It is also true that the same travelers were witnesses—often scandalized witnesses—to another phenomenon, considered equally characteristic of Italy, which implied an ample freedom of movement for women and their release from many family duties, perhaps even from the obligation of conjugal fidelity: cicisbeismo. This was the custom by which married ladies were accompanied in all their social appearances by a cavalier servente or a cicisbeo who was not their husband—a husband who in his turn could be the cicisbeo of another lady.[23] De Brosses himself dedicates a highly interesting Roman letter to the issue.[24]

De Brosses, like others, underscored with restrained marvel the vivacity and the casualness of the Bolognese ladies and a certain freedom of association between the two sexes, made possible also by an institution like the *casino della nobiltà*, a sort of club which removed the nuisance and the expenses of private receptions. Such customs were certainly indicative of profound changes in forms of sociability and in relations between the sexes but regarded only the aristocracy (and certainly not all the aristocracy). Moreover, the difference in freedom and visibility among women of the upper, middle, and lower classes in Bologna was made immediately evident by the clothing each group wore: if aristocratic women would not wear "even a ribbon unless it came from Paris," women of the bourgeoisie wore black soutanes, jackets of the same color, mantles (probably black as well), long collars, and little knotted wigs. The women of the lower classes are described in the following manner by De Brosses: "The wives of the people [*peuple*], when they go out, cover themselves from the belt downward in a piece of black taffeta, and from the belt upwards—including the head—in a rude veil or scarf, of the same material, which hides their faces: a real populace of phantoms."[25] There are many reasons to think that the sober bourgeois women, almost indistinguishable in their black uniforms, and even the *popolane* or women of the lower classes, disturbingly invisible as phantoms, corresponded rather more to the "normal" feminine model advanced by preachers, moralists, and teachers than did the colored, bewigged, and Frenchified ladies of the aristocracy with their low-cut necklines.

At the end of the previous century, a preacher as famous as Padre Segneri exalted "holy rusticity" and "staying hidden" as manifestations of the most precious female virtues: "morality" and "seclusion." In 1711 the Jesuit Antonfrancesco Bellati, although recognizing that in the past it had been an exaggeration to force women "to live from morning to evening withdrawn in their houses," manifested his worries about the nascent usage of "mixed conversations," that is, the mixed company of men and women in salons. He lamented the consequent deplorable "freedom" of women "who, from being sheltered and secluded, have become more sociable [*usanti*] and loquacious than even men should be." Again in 1730, when the new form of sociability had already become popular, the Udinese Count Francesco Beretta, in a successful treatise on education for marriage, attacked "modern conversations," praising "withdrawal" and "seclusion" and proposing to girls what has been called "a pedagogy of reclusion and ignorance."[26]

As Luciano Guerci, the author of well-documented studies on the eighteenth-century debate over women, has observed, over the course of the eighteenth century the "ideal of feminine seclusion" weakened and softened but never disappeared. Even the authors most open to Enlightenment ideas and the new forms of sociability were careful to place limits, if only interior limits, on the social visibility of women. They did this by emphasizing the importance of the outstandingly female virtue of modesty. One could give many examples, but to convey how persistent and widespread this value was as the model of female comportment it is sufficient to record the ideas of one of the most intelligent and courageous representatives of the Enlightenment in Lombardy, Pietro Verri. His *Ricordi a mia figlia* (Advice to My Daughter), written in 1777, certainly reflect his modern and rational vision of life and society, but at many points they also seem to reinvent the traditional model of femininity for a secular readership. This is also revealed by his insistence on modesty, "one of the key words of the *Ricordi*."[27] Verri reminds his daughter that "the singular merit of woman is sweetness and modesty," and he advises her that "you can never be too modest." The reasons he adduces point, on the one hand, to the conviction that the "first gift" of women is their "passive reserve" (*passiva ritenutezza*) and, on the other, to the weight of "public opinion" in the social destiny of females.[28] They point, that is, to the model of female comportment outlined a few years earlier by Jean-Jacques Rousseau in his *Letter à D'Alembert sur les spectacles* (1758) and in the fifth book of *Emile* (1762), a model which took up the traditional demand for subordination of women and their segregation from men and inserted it into a new framework of family relations destined to dominate in the following century.[29]

If in Verri's *Ricordi* as in Rousseau's writing modesty was on the one hand associated with decency—and therefore with the sphere of sexual relations—it was also significantly connected to the question of female knowledge. If the most radical supporters of "seclusion" saw ignorance as a shield for the virtue of girls, others—and Verri was among them—were convinced that a certain level of education was necessary for women in the higher social classes; this was not only so that they might better govern their houses but also so that they might participate in social life and particularly in conversations. They considered it necessary, however, to set limits and to identify modalities in which it was preferable to manifest this education. Verri advised his daughter to avoid "the rash desire for public esteem" which impelled some women "to show off what they know." Instead, he reminded her that "the woman of true spirit keeps her knowledge to herself" and "modestly uses it when the occasion demands." If, for example, it is good that a mother read "the authors who discuss physical and moral education" to better raise and educate her children, she should not speak of them in conversation because she could be laughed at "as a know-it-all, a female philosopher [*filosofessa*], or an eccentric." A woman who shows off her learning places her social life at risk, because she might irritate and humiliate interlocutors of both sexes who are more ignorant than she is. Above all, she might diminish her chances of getting married "because the man is humiliated if his wife knows more than he does."[30]

Modesty was a corrective for a level of culture which exceeded that normally held by women, or, worse still, which exceeded even that of men. Modesty offered reassurance that knowledge would not be used to demand a less subordinate role or even a public role. In short, modesty was a guarantee that a cultured woman was still a woman. The association between female culture and modesty was certainly not new to the eighteenth century. It had already appeared in Baldassarre Castiglione's *Book of the Courtier*, a work emerging from that sixteenth-century courtly society in which debate on the theme of women and culture became central for the first time. In the third book, which traces the figure of the "female courtier" (the "woman of the palace") after discussing the "male courtier," Castiglione writes that "this woman" must have "knowledge of letters, of music, of painting," must know how to "dance and celebrate," and must accompany "the other instructions which have been taught to the male courtier with discrete modesty and by giving a good impression of herself."[31] Reference to qualities such as "discrete modesty" and preoccupation with the judgment of others set precise limits to the undoubtedly unconventional female image of a cultivated woman advanced by Castiglione. Moreover it was not expected that the female courtier receive a philosophical education which would make her an autonomously knowing subject, but only notions and abilities which make her apt, as Marina Zancan emphasizes, "to receive and reflect, in a harmoniously ordered image of unity, the discourse of another."[32]

The proximity between female knowledge and modesty (or also "moderation") and the aversion toward women who showed off their culture were widespread from the beginning to the end of the eighteenth century.[33] The greatest praise one could make of a cultured woman was that she knew how to hide her knowledge. A telling example is offered by Lazzaro Spallanzani, a naturalist immune from misogynist prejudice if for no other reason than that he learned physics from a woman: his "venerated teacher" Laura Bassi, to whom he dedicated his first work.[34] His third work was also dedicated to a woman, the Marquise Olimpia Agnelli Sessi, protector of the young abbé and herself a student of natural sciences. Sessi's scientific studies, as the author informs us, were appreciated "outside of Italy" "despite" the "noble moderation" of the marquise, who preferred to pass them off as fashionable pastimes rather than useful research. They fed "a happy, though modest, intelligence and a soul elevated above the ordinary, though it is firm in concealing its own greatness and its certainly not vulgar notions."[35] Speaking to the marquise, Spallanzani reaffirmed his admiration for what seemed a new virtue, the virtue of concealing knowledge—indeed, intelligence itself—a virtue which was certainly not masculine and was in particular not cultivated by the ambitious young scientist:

> To enter into the fullness of your praise, I would willingly let myself be taken by the same pleasure which I feel when I recognize in you, lady marquise, this so rare and so noble concealment of your intelligence and knowledge; so able and loveable are you, although you present yourself, in simple, varied, light, and happy ordinary conversation, as though there were nothing extraordinary about you.[36]

The attitude of the marquise, who disguised her serious scientific research as a salon pastime, like the attitude of her admirer, who implies that female knowledge is worthy of greater praise when it is elegantly minimized, are eloquent manifestations of the difficulties eighteenth-century Italian culture, even those aspects open to the values of the Enlightenment, had in making intellectual activity part of a socially acceptable female image.

In Italy during this period, there is also evidence for the growing acceptance of learned women in society, and an increased interest in study on the part of women themselves. This included study of "academic" disciplines such as mathematics, physics, and natural history, subjects which were not part of the knowledge considered useful for better governing one's house; nor were they among the "notions" which, according to the author of the *Cortegiano*, were necessary for the "woman of the palace." This new female interest in science and philosophy was both the cause and the effect of the diffusion of a popularizing scientific literature aimed at women. The works on optics and Newtonian cosmology, on electricity, and on the new chemistry of Lavoisier by Francesco Algarotti, Eusebio Sguario, and Giuseppe Compagnoni are the best known examples; they testify to the interest of the book market in the nascent female public.[37] On the other hand, the instruction of women threw into crisis the segregated and subordinated role assigned them in patriarchal society, especially when they moved from the role of passive consumers of knowledge to the role of producers or organizers of culture. The abundance of misogynist texts which, in verse or in prose, ridiculed the *filosofesse* and the *saputelle* (female know-it-alls) is indicative of a vast reaction rejecting the new gender identity which was emerging among women.[38] The very protagonists representing the new cultural position of women seemed at times to hesitate—especially when the role of a male mediator became less complicit—as if attracted by the security of domestic "withdrawal" and uncertain as to the legitimacy of an autonomous social life.

Let us examine the case of Bianca Laura Saibanti, who, along with her future husband, the musician Giuseppe Valeriano Vannetti, founded and presided over the Accademia degli Agiati of Rovereto (1750). The Accademia met in her house and exercised for a number of years a positive role in propelling the cultural life of the border city between Italy and the German world. Marriage and the birth of a son, with the consequent necessity of adapting herself to the role expected of mothers by social conventions, reduced her participation in the life of the academy. It was, however, the death of her husband in 1761 which induced her to reduce it to the point of definitive cessation.

In nine discourses from 1754 to 1761, Saibanti—one of the very few female voices—intervened in the lively Italian debate over the nature and the social role of women. Year after year, in erudite historical dissertations and dispassionate philosophical discourses, she advanced her reflections on the virtues and the defects of the female sex and on the prejudices and the social conditioning which prevented women's minds from developing freely. In her *Ragionamento intorno allo spirito delle donne*, read before the Academy in 1755, she did not hesitate to claim intellectual equality of the sexes and even the compatibility, for the "donna di spirito," of a life with both private duties and a public role. In this context it seems at the very least unexpected, if not incongruous, that in a meeting of the academy on 28 March 1758 Saibanti delivered a panegyric on the "seclusion of women" in order to defend her renunciation of social life and public appearances. She claimed that it was an act of freedom, of "dutiful seclusion," of voluntary distancing from the Republic of Letters whose character she implicitly but clearly affirmed as that of a male sodality.[39]

Women's hesitation to abandon the canonical model of femininity in order to fully embrace an intellectual identity appears to mirror the limits of male praise of female knowledge, which emphasized the need for such knowledge to be "veiled" and "concealed." There were, however, those who at least in literary fiction seemed to decisively reject the idea of an insuperable opposition among culture, femininity, and respectability. In his *Newtonianismo per le Dame*, for example, Francesco Algarotti concludes his portrait of the Marquise of E** with a vindication of visibility for "female knowledge":

> To the mind and to the gentlest imagination she joins a not ordinary solidity of intellect, and to the most delicate sentiments she joins a learned curiosity which awakens at the slightest word and which is sometimes not satisfied by long philosophical discussions. If necessary she knows how to speak of ribbons and bonnets; she is superior to other women without caring to show it; and no less does she know how to propose problems and listen to the responses, being more eager to know than impatient to speak. A natural insouciance and an unstudied and unaffected demeanor enhances each of her words and each of her most ingenious sayings. Her beauty, moreover, would provide her husband with a throng of friends were it not for her discretion and a certain manner of repulsion, which neither offends virtue nor feeds hope. Since her female knowledge is accompanied by such rare qualities, must she keep herself hidden for fear of not being received with applause by gentle persons?[40]

The author of *Newtonianismo per le dame* was proposing an image of women and of femininity that was freer and airier than what many of his contemporaries had in mind when they praised the severe seclusion of the virtuous woman or when they represented the filosofessa as a presumptuous ignoramus or a virago. Like Verri and other Italian Enlightenment figures, Algarotti perceived the inadequacy of the traditional discourse on women and the urgency of renegotiating the terms of gender relations in view of the growing female presence in the public sphere, in social spaces previously occupied exclusively by men. Nonetheless, the image of women that he proposed, although far from the traditional ideal of seclusion, ignorance, and obedience, was not one which subverted the male-centered vision of the gender hierarchy. It seems to me to confirm the judgment of Rebecca Messbarger: "the Italian *philosophes'* answer to the 'woman question' simultaneously contested and confirmed traditional construction of femininity."[41] Indeed, Algarotti felt the need to reassure the reader, setting the condition that "female knowledge" be protected by "discretion" and by "a certain manner of repulsion" against illegitimate male advances—"rare qualities" which were nothing more, when carefully examined, than a light and sociable version of the traditional feminine virtues of modesty and decency.

The Exhibition of Female Knowledge and Strategies of Power

There appears to be an element of contradiction in this spectacularization of female knowledge. Indeed, this contradiction was felt not only by the "spectators" witnessing learned women publicly displaying their erudition; it was also experienced by the female protagonists themselves and by those who functioned as the stage managers and directors of the women's performances. These demonstrations in no way involved manifestations of nonconformity; women were not rebelling against socially imposed gender roles. Rather, these public displays were initiatives designed and directed by political authorities or by male family members as a part of power strategies; in these schemes, the interested female figures played the role of pawns, though as we shall see, not always passive pawns. The motivation that impelled fathers, teachers, cardinals, and senators was not promotion of female education in general. On the contrary, these men highlighted the *exceptionality* of the young women who had a university-level education in philosophical or legal subjects; they pointed out that these women were gifted with an intelligence that was extraordinary for their sex. This rarity inspired marvel and procured fame; the family and the city therefore basked in the fame of the young Minervas and drew social and political prestige from them. This had already occurred in the preceding century when, in 1678, the University of Padua agreed to grant a university degree in philosophy to Elena Lucrezia (the daughter of the procurator of San Marco Giovanni Battista Cornaro Piscopia) who was a scholar of theology and philology. The European resonance of the event (well justified by the fact that it was the first university degree given to a woman in Europe and therefore in the world) reflected positively on the father of the graduate, allowing him and his family to regain in Venetian society that prestige which a dishonorable marriage and an accusation of corruption had previously obscured.[42]

The Venetian case was undoubtedly a necessary precedent for the aforementioned cases of exhibition of female knowledge in the eighteenth century. The choices of don Pietro Agnesi and above all of the Bolognese directors of the Bassi episode (and before them the father of Laura Danielli or Count Delfini Dosi) might also be linked to another model which is less close and less obvious: the sixteenth- and seventeenth-century collectors of natural and artificial *mirabilia*, so well studied by Paula Findlen, who has focused her attention on the two important Bolognese collections of Ulisse Aldrovandi and the Marquis Cospi.[43] It was the uniqueness or at least the rarity of the pieces possessed which defined the value of a collection and determined the prestige of its possessor and his chances of acquiring fame and establishing relations with socially authoritative personages. Among the most sought-after rarities were living humans; this was the case for the Museo Cospi, whose guardians were two dwarves, a brother and a sister "monstrous in that they were not generated by dwarves"; miniscule but well-proportioned, in particular the female "who in youth was rather gracious in aspect" and the object of amorous sentiments and sonnets on the part of an aristocratic poet.[44]

In my opinion, the expression often used to describe these women scientists and philosophers—"a marvel of her sex"—and the insistence on their singularity with respect to their sex make this comparison between unusual dwarves and extraordinary learned women less of a stretch. It is true that the social and intellectual context in which the two phenomena were located was very different. Eighteenth-century aristocratic society, both in Bologna and Milan, was different from that of preceding centuries. New forms of sociability had arisen. On the one hand, there were the salons, which were private forms of aggregation and political and cultural influence; on the other hand, there were the public institutions of culture—academies and museums—desired by and financed by a political power which had begun to consider the problem of the education and the consent of its subjects. This political power had become conscious of the prestige such institutions could win for the state, not only domestically but also abroad.[45] The predominant epistemology in the museums and laboratories of the Enlightenment was based on the search for and exhibition of order in nature; it rejected the baroque categories of rarity and marvel.

But despite the period's social and intellectual changes which should have rendered it obsolete, the model of propaganda and social promotion founded on the value of possessing and exhibiting rare marvels of nature and art—including, as we have seen, human monstra—continued to function in the eighteenth century. From this point of view, salons, academies, and universities were theaters for the propagandistic use—sometimes private and sometimes public—of female intelligence and culture, which were presented as extraordinary transgressions from the normal natural and social canon of femininity. They were therefore sources of marvel and fame, but thanks to their exceptionality they did not risk calling into question the commonly accepted gender hierarchies.

It should be pointed out, however, that the theatrical exhibition of culture was a part of both ancient and recent academic traditions of spectacularizing knowledge which had a necessarily masculine connotation. Some key examples include the public thesis defense which preceded the concession of a university degree or a chair and which in Bologna usually occurred in great churches in the presence of a large public; the public anatomies which from the end of the sixteenth century were organized everywhere in Europe as spectacular ceremonies with complex moral and religious meanings (in Bologna they were ambiguously near to Carnival and its masquerades) and which took place in anatomical theaters, edifices planned and constructed on the architectural model of the Roman amphitheater; and finally, the markedly theatrical bent which modern experimental science manifested from its very beginnings—indeed in European universities of the seventeenth and eighteenth centuries, anatomical theaters were soon joined by theaters of physics or even of chemistry.[46]

The publicity and the repeatability of experiments, which were the chief characteristics of experimental science, necessarily implied a public not only of readers but of veritable spectators to the experiments and witnesses to their success. From the very beginning, this public was formed not only of competent scholars in mathematical and natural science but also of amateurs and curious people who often belonged to the court aristocracy. It was in the age of Enlightenment, however, that this public expanded enormously, involving also strata of the population which had previously been excluded—in the first place, women. The "experiences" of pneumatics, of electrical physics and magnetism, the most popular sciences of the eighteenth century, began to be held not only in the academies but also in salons, in theaters, and even in public squares, often for a fee.[47]

Another novelty was that the women of eighteenth-century Italy did not limit themselves to being part of science's audience; some of them played roles on its stage. The examples are numerous, but the most important are once again the two very different cases of the Milanese Agnesi and the Bolognese Bassi. After her uncommon gifts of intelligence and learning were discovered, the former was instructed by the best teachers according to the wishes of her father, the rich and ambitious don Pietro Agnesi, a silk merchant who aspired to enter the ranks of the nobility. To acquire prestige, he thought up a strategy centered on protection of intellectuals and artists, to whom he offered hospitality and opportunities to meet in his salon, in hopes of making it a desirable destination for representatives of the most exclusive Milanese patriciate. The appeal of Maria Gaetana's erudition and intellect (together with her sister Maria Teresa's musical talent) naturally became a central aspect of this strategy.

At the beginning of the century, Milan and Lombardy were absorbed into the Hapsburg Empire after the long and oppressive Spanish domination; they entered a new phase of social, economic, and cultural dynamism and became, especially after the advent to the throne of Maria Teresa in 1740, the engine of Italian Enlightenment culture. It was in particular the educational institutions, and first among these the University of Pavia—until then not involved in the developments of modern philosophy and science—which profited from Maria Teresa's reforms. Another characteristic of Milan was the profound influence exercised on social structures and consciences by Catholicism, an influence which had its roots in the anti-Protestant reform—directed in the sixteenth and seventeenth centuries by such charismatic personages as Cardinals Carlo and Federico Borromeo—and which remained strong in the more secular eighteenth century. The education of youth was completely controlled by the religious orders (Jesuits, Barnabites, and Somaschi) through their colleges. Perhaps more than elsewhere in Italy, these priests or monks were not only theologians and moralists but also mathematicians and students of experimental physics. These were the teachers engaged by don Pietro to instruct his children, and in particular Maria Gaetana.

It is also noteworthy that an opinion favorable to female instruction had formed in the Milanese ecclesiastical environment—which from the time of the Catholic Reform had seen an active social apostolate and the example of ascetic sanctity on the part of numerous women—in the first decades of the eighteenth century; the Archbishop Erba Odescalchi (in office from 1712 to 1737) had placed the Ursuline order in charge of female instruction. His successor, Cardinal Pozzobonelli, attributed great importance to the education of women as part of a broad program of religious education inspired by the concept of "reasonable" religiosity founded on the connection between devotion and charity. Some of the tutors and spiritual directors of the young Agnesi shared this favorable attitude toward study by women and this severe idea of religiosity; their influence was probably in some way connected to her painful rebellion against the worldly designs of her father.[48]

Pozzobonelli, who greatly respected Agnesi's theological culture, was very near to the cautiously innovative positions of Benedict XIV, the protector both of Agnesi and of Bassi. The proximity of their views on women's education might establish a link between the two cases which would allow us to see both as manifestations of the Catholic Enlightenment. Nonetheless

the familial, social, and cultural context of the Bolognese case was, as we
have already seen, very different. The path along which Laura Bassi arrived
at knowledge and notoriety also diverged from that of Agnesi. The role of
her family was almost without influence, and the duty of secretly preparing
her to undertake public defenses of philosophical theses—first to obtain her
university degree and then to obtain a chair in the Bolognese *Studio*—was
assumed by a professor of philosophy and medicine, Gaetano Tacconi, who
was also the Bassi family doctor. He too was nonetheless partly deprived
of authority when his project became known and its management passed
directly into the hands of the Senate and the archbishop. It was they who
decided to give Bassi recognition in the form of the university degree and
the chair, normally reserved for men, in order to render the figure of the
young philosopher even more extraordinary, attracting to Bologna and its
university the attention of cultured Europe.

The function that the Bolognese authorities, at least initially, intended
for the young dottoressa was of a purely ornamental character: promotion
of learned Bologna, of which she became almost a symbolic personification. Her role as virgin Minerva and her promotion from on high weakened, but did not succeed entirely in quelling, the critical voices which
considered the presence of a nubile young woman in mixed environments
like salons, the university, and the Accademia delle Scienze unacceptable,
and which, when she decided to marry, decreed that "she would have done
better to remain a virgin in some retreat."[49] On the other hand, the worry
that study and honors might damage the dottoressa's image as a virtuous
girl respectful of her feminine duties was also felt by the members of the
Bolognese Senate who, in a meeting of 12 April 1732, put down in writing that the young woman, while she studied under the guidance of her
teacher, had continued to perform her domestic duties with diligence:

> she nonetheless knew how to hide such a worthy occupation which was, as
> much as possible, never disjoined from the usual female duties and ordinary
> domestic cares; she hid her intellect and knowledge with so much modera-
> tion and prudence. . . . [50]

The senators themselves would give her a "lectureship in philosophical subjects at the *Studio*" as just recognition for her "virtues" and her "doctrine,"

> on the condition, however, that she must not lecture in the public schools if
> not commanded either by the most excellent Legate or by the most illustri-
> ous *signor Confaloniere* and according to the aforesaid relation.[51]

This, according to the explanation heard seven years later by De Brosses, was done because it was not believed "decent for a woman to reveal every day, to all comers, the hidden things of nature."[52] It is unclear if the reference is to the secrets discovered by natural philosophy, the object of her teaching, or to the very body of the woman teacher.

Nothing was further from the intentions of the promoters of Laura Bassi and Maria Gaetana Agnesi than the idea of offering a model of the woman scientist for the emulation of other women. If some perceived Bassi and Agnesi this way, it was because the symbolic reading which other ambitious young women in Italy and Europe made of these figures was exactly opposed to the exaltation of rarity and uniqueness; they saw in them pioneers of the opening of education to women and therefore unprecedented possibilities for subjective realization. This alternate symbolic reading was possible because Bassi and Agnesi themselves were the first to refuse to be the passive instruments of others' designs and interests, seeking to construct an identity of their own as scholars and as women.[53]

From Passive Resistance to the Construction of New Female Subjects

It was not expected that the "seven-language oracle" of Milan or the "virgin dottoressa" of Bologna manifest a will of her own, yet this occurred in both cases. The manner in which it happened is of great interest because it reveals the difficulties that the situation of unusual public exposure created for the two adolescents' self-image and the differences in the paths taken by each, at a more mature age, to win an identity of her own choosing. The final outcome of Laura Bassi's reconstruction of her own image, which followed her refusal to play a purely ornamental role, was the unprecedented figure of a woman scientist who was authoritatively and (almost) equally a part of the contemporary scientific community. She succeeded in escaping from the symbolic identification with Minerva, virgin goddess of wisdom, and she realized the unheard-of idea that the duties of wife and mother might be compatible not only with study but with an intellectual profession. Bassi became a scientist conscious of her value and capable of struggling to obtain recognition of her right to a career similar to that of her male colleagues. Her singularity was nonetheless marked by the fact that, among other limitations impossible to recount here, she was always required to play her role as a cultural attraction of her city, almost as a form of public service, and to represent a source of its civic pride.[54] To construct and affirm her image as a successful and authoritative woman scientist, Laura Bassi not only had to refuse the models which were proposed to her from the outside but also had to overcome resistance due to her own assimilation of the traditional model of femininity.

Unfortunately, we almost completely lack autobiographical writings that might explicitly illuminate the manner in which these young women scholars experienced their exceptional condition and their role as cultural attractions. Nonetheless, contemporary biographies and other documents indicate their discomfort with the discrepancy between the behavior required of them and their concept of the role and destiny of women, an image which was inevitably shaped by the models of the day. When Laura Bassi's teacher, the doctor Gaetano Tacconi, believed that her preparation was complete and that the moment had arrived to "take this light out from under the bushel and show it to all the *patria*," the girl's initial reaction was one of refusal—a reaction which was thus described by her contemporary Giovanni Fantuzzi:

> But Laura's humility, her spirit which abhorred pomp, and a natural morality which made her reluctant to make a spectacle of herself before an entire people, as Tacconi and her friends were asking her to do—exposing herself before a gathered public—did not know how to adjust to this; and here it was that with resignation she had to discount all the pleasure that she had experienced up till then in her application to her studies.[55]

It was not study but "making a spectacle out of herself" that Laura, then little more than an adolescent, felt to be contrary to her "natural" female tendencies. In the end, "won over by coaxing and prayers," she consented to hold "a public defense in philosophy." The modalities of such a test, nonetheless, had to be different from those normally followed for males of her age: "the rarity of so much knowledge in a woman seemed to require that, in making public display of it, the particular manners and solemnities be different."[56] According to the judgment of a contemporary admirer, the Riminese physician Giovanni Bianchi, the young Bassi quickly succeeded in finding the proper balance between the manifestation of knowledge and feminine modesty:

> And then she must be infinitely praised for the modesty of her customs, as she always maintains a consistent noble reserve, and a female modesty without incivility, but with much conjoined docility. I also mention docility because I have observed that there is not in this maiden that vanity and presumption which is ordinarily found in all women who know, or who believe they know, something.[57]

For Bassi, famous throughout Europe for the public demonstration of her knowledge, the greatest praise that could be made of her was that if she did not conceal her knowledge, she showed it without showing off. Her brother-in-law Ferdinando Veratti, in a family diary which remains in manuscript form, spoke of the successes and of the debates undertaken by his celebrated sister-in-law. He affirmed that, despite her fame and knowledge, she never lost the fundamental female virtue of humility:

> To the sciences she always joined morals and holy Christian virtues, and always made stand out a singular humility, a merit which she preserved in the midst of so many lauds and honors, whose bestowal in this manner on a woman was unusual.[58]

A brief biographical manuscript, signed by her husband, Giuseppe Veratti, is notable for its insistence on the secondary place that studies occupied in the life of the adolescent Laura—only "that time which remained after her domestic duties." The account also emphasizes Bassi's reluctance to expose herself, as her teacher Tacconi desired, "to the ordeal of public dispute." According to Veratti, "this was hindered by the moral temperament of the young woman, very far from showiness not to mention from flaunting qualities so rare for her sex."[59]

In reality, it is difficult to establish the degree to which this insistence on modesty and humility reflects Bassi's real traits, or rather the need on the part of her admirers and biographers to render her dedication to study compatible with the canonical model of femininity. The image given to us by the striking appraisal of Bassi by a contemporary ("She fears no one") clearly diverges from this model. This judgment refers precisely to the fearless courage with which she faced dialectical debates.[60] Bassi's decision and the tenacity with which she conducted her battle (which in large part she won) to carry out an active role as a researcher and as a teacher in the Bolognese and Italian scientific community also diverge from the canonical model of femininity. Her inclusion in the new class of Benedictine academics in 1745 and her nomination as professor of experimental physics in the Istituto delle Scienze in 1778 represented two fundamental successes in the course of this lengthy struggle.[61]

Even more than Bassi, the young Agnesi seems to have sought an identity of her own choosing, a subject in which to identify herself. Her intolerance, verging on repugnance, for the reduction of her culture to a worldly spectacle manifested itself very early on, provoking the alarmed reaction of her father, who was already worried about his musician daughter's desire to get married. De Brosses himself heard Agnesi's confession about the discomfort that those exhibitions, carried out before a public largely indifferent to the questions debated, caused her. However, it was certainly not the vocation of Maria Gaetana, who had manifested on many occasions a lofty conception of the intellectual and moral dignity of women, to be the obedient wife of a husband perhaps more ignorant than she was.[62] De Brosses recounted, with enlightened astonishment, that he had heard it said that she intended to withdraw into a convent.[63] Indeed, it seems that at a young age, Agnesi had already formulated a radical rejection of the life to which she was bound by her class and the ambitions of her father, from whom she later succeeded in winning the concession of dressing modestly, of dedicating herself to devout practices, and of abstaining from social life. Hence she could concentrate in solitude on her mathematical studies which, platonically, seemed a means of elevating her intellect to the contemplation of truth, but of which she also appreciated the utility. Indeed, the final fruit of these studies was her famous manual of analytic geometry "for Italian youth," published in 1748.[64] The work won her a new wave of celebrity, the appreciation of the most important mathematicians and the Académie des Sciences of Paris, and even the offer of a chair in analytical geometry at the University of Bologna, proposed by Pope Benedict XIV himself.[65] It seemed that she might possibly follow a path similar to that of Laura Bassi, constructing for herself a career as a woman scientist and teacher.

However, once Agnesi had real control over her life—following the sudden death of her father in 1752—she decided differently and dedicated the rest of her existence (almost a half century) to religious meditation and assistance of the marginalized sick and poor who abounded in the large city of Milan. Numerous interpretations have been made of her choice, which surprised and disturbed many contemporaries. The most convincing are the ones that seek to understand her choice in the context of the Lombard church's currents of mystical and social spirituality, which were particularly widespread among clerics tied to the so-called Catholic Enlightenment, torn between acceptance of modern rationalism and refusal to admit the full autonomy of reason and science. The flight of Agnesi, who was effectively defined by Mazzotti as "both an anti-modern symbol of the Catholic faith and a celebrated figure of the Italian Enlightenment," from academic honors and from the pleasures of science may also have been inspired by the prevailing antimodern preoccupations.[66]

I wonder if it is also possible, alongside these explanations, to read Agnesi's choice in gender terms, as the final outcome of her search for an autonomous female identity. She had refused the role of woman prodigy and the exhibition of knowledge as an end in itself. She was not, however, interested in a career as a woman scientist; she was not, that is, interested in becoming like men, engaged in the search for knowledge and power in the world. She was even less attracted by marriage and consequent subordination to a husband. She found instead in the tradition of the great mystics and the mystical marriages with Christ a satisfying model. But she contextualized this model in a social, or I would even say maternal, idea of religiosity as an absolute dedication to one's neighbor and as a commitment to rational organization of assistance for indigent women. It is not difficult to sense the influence of Enlightenment reformism in Agnesi's choice.[67] Paradoxically, her flight from the world and from celebrity served only to guarantee her lasting fame. Indeed, the motto—drawn from Tacitus's *De vita Agricolae*—which surrounds her portrait on the first leaf of the biography published in 1799, the year of her death, by Anton Francesco Frisi, declares *Dissimulatione famae famam auxit* ("By the concealment of fame she increased her fame").[68]

Even if Maria Gaetana Agnesi's abandonment of scientific activity was not at all a retreat toward the traditional model of subordination and female "seclusion" (quite the opposite), she would be praised above all for having offered "the model of a heroic sacrifice of literary celebrity to intelligent women."[69] This was the conclusion of a book (*Disgrazie di donna Urania*, 1793) which at the end of the century resolved once again to convince readers, using old and new arguments, that female study was incompatible with the duties of wife and mother. It was one of the many signs[70] that the times were not yet ripe for affirmation of the new images and the new female roles (in particular those of scientist and teacher) which had begun to take form in eighteenth-century Italy, in part as an unforeseen and undesired result of the spectacular exhibitions of female knowledge which so struck travelers on the Grand Tour.

"Monsters of Talent"

Fame and Reputation of
Women Improvisers in Arcadia

PAOLA GIULI

> The talent of improvising, which may be called indig-
> enous to [Italy], gave celebrity to two or three female
> poets. . . . But women of such celebrity are rare in Italy
> and are looked upon not so much with respect as with
> wonder, as *monsters of talent.*
>
> —Ugo Foscolo, "The Women of Italy"

Although one can trace the history of Italian improvising, in all literary genres and in all milieus, back to the thirteenth century, the golden age of improvising, as several authors including Giulio Natali have noted, was the eighteenth century. Foreign travelers remarked on Italians' ability and excellence at improvising throughout the century, and it became a point of national pride. From Charles de Brosses and Joseph de Lalande, to Madame de Staël and Karl Fernow, foreign visitors and intellectuals marveled at the

I would like to thank the editors of this volume for their patience and their help. A special thanks to Catherine Sama for her thorough reading of the first draft of my paper. I also owe a debt of gratitude to all participants in the 2002 Clark workshop that inspired much of my research, and especially to Paula Findlen, Wendy Roworth, and Rebecca Messbarger. I am deeply thankful for the assistance of all the librarians of the Biblioteca Angelica in Rome, who let me consult their archives even on days when the library was closed to the public. A special thanks to Drs. Fano, Muratore, Scialanga, and Sciarra. Incredibly gracious and helpful were Mr. Savi and Dr. Dolfi of the Biblioteca Forteguerriana in Pistoia, as well as Dr. Pensauti of the Biblioteca Nazionale in Florence. I would be amiss if I did not mention my "assistant" in Rome, Mrs. Caterina Bruzzone (my dear mother), and my very patient husband, Christopher Smith. Last but not least, this paper was also made possible by a Summer Grant from Saint Joseph's University: to all my colleagues I owe my deepest thanks for their continuing support.

ability of the Italian genius. To take one example, in describing an improvisation by Orazio Arrighi Landini, Madame du Boccage wrote:

> Mr. Landini took his mandolin and, with changing melodies, according to his custom, sang well-rounded verses on any subject proposed to him. *This talent, unknown in our country, astounds us.* I am not sure if our language would lend itself to such an art.[1]

Likewise the *Encyclopédie*, after defining improvisation as "the talent of declaiming verse extemporaneously and on a subject given (by the public)," remarked that "some Italians are capable of this to an astonishing degree." Jean Jacques Rousseau, in his *Dictionnaire de musique*, wrote, "The word improvising is purely Italian." Not only were poetry, music, and comedy the subjects of improvisation; even painting was at times practiced extemporaneously. The Neapolitan Paolo De Matteis surprised his public with the rapidity with which he could give shape on canvas to the most bizarre thoughts.[2]

At the end of the nineteenth century, French writer Eugène Bouvy could still write that "Italy is truly the classical land of improvisation. Because of their tradition and of their temperament, Italians are improvisers."[3] The Italian literary establishment responded by acknowledging such *primato*, or preeminence; writer Giuseppe Baretti was among the first to mention Italians' unique improvising ability in his *Lettere famigliari*. Imperial poet Pietro Metastasio, in a famous letter to Francesco Algarotti, discussed improvising as the "phenomenal faculty that so much honors our nation." Ugo Foscolo and Carlo Goldoni, addressing the British and French public respectively, extolled the virtues of Italian improvisers (the former invoked Sgricci while the latter praised Perfetti), and improvised themselves. Many learned poets began their careers as improvisers, or improvised at some point in their life: Metastasio, Gian Battista Felice Zappi, Paolo Rolli, Tommaso Crudeli, Carlo Innocenzo Frugoni, Bartolomeo Lorenzi, Aurelio de' Giorgi Bertola, Giovanni de Rossi, Giovanni Pindemonte, and Vincenzo Monti, just to mention the most prominent figures.[4]

By the second half of the eighteenth century, women had become the most acclaimed and prominent improvisers in the Italian peninsula. Performing "solo" or in competition with other improvisers, women improvisers such as Maria Maddalena Morelli, Teresa Bandettini, and Fortunata Sulgher Fantastici were especially popular and successful.[5] At a time when many *savants* actively debated whether or not women had the same intellectual capabilities as men, and when a woman's literary activity was still considered immodest and imprudent, women improvisers were extolled as Italy's cultural treasures and literary sensations. Foreigners flocked to hear them perform; most Italian literary men paid them homage; famous painters, sculptors, and engravers celebrated them with their work; international as well as regional journals covered the main events of their life. The women improvisers were praised in literary circles and adored by the crowds who flocked to hear them. Most remarkably, *improvvisatrici* were often recognized as excelling in this art with respect to their male counterparts. Judging Corilla Olimpica's improvising competition with three male improvisers, Cristofano Amaduzzi (a professor of Greek and usually a rather reserved commentator) described the event in a letter as the "humiliation of virility" by "Sappho reincarnated," adding that he considered Corilla to be "a true prodigy."[6] Ugo Foscolo, one the most prominent Italian literati of the time, testified: "indeed it appears that the sweetness of women's voices, the mobility of their imagination, and the volubility of their tongues, would render extemporaneous poetry better fitted to them than to men."[7] The peak of the woman improviser's success was to be the crowning of Corilla Olimpica as poet laureate on the Roman Capitol in 1776 (Figure 12.1), in a ceremony of great pomp and magnificence. She was the first and last woman poet to receive such an honor.

This chapter explores the literary foundations of and cultural circumstances contributing to the emergence and success of women improvisers in eighteenth-century Arcadia and Italy, as well as how unexpressed gender assumptions about literary values eventually influenced the evaluation of improvisers and of the Arcadian academy that sponsored them. Little studied, improvisation was seen by twentieth-century critics as an aberrant expression of eighteenth-century superficiality and penchant for empty theatricality—the frivolous pastime of a frivolous and politically subjugated people. Benedetto Croce, for example, interpreted improvisation as a superficial form of expression and as the product of a decadent and academic Italian culture.[8] Carlo Dionisotti and Alessandra Di Ricco echo Croce's arguments. For Dionisotti, the improviser is just a manipulator of traditional and stereotyped literary materials.[9] Recently, Alessandra di Ricco, in her study of Teresa Bandettini's work, wrote:

> The myth of extemporaneous poetry, glory and scourge of our culture, largely contributed to the consolidation of an Italian "ethnic stereotype," that is, the stereotype of Italy as a country rich in artistic talent, but deficient as regards civic and philosophic virtues.[10]

Figure 12.1 Bartolomeo Pinelli, *Portrait of Corilla Olimpica, Based on the Portrait by Francesco Bartolozzi,* date unknown (etching, 253 x 158 mm). Raccolta dei disegni e delle stampe, Biblioteca Forteguerriana, Pistoia.

Unable to overlook the popularity of improvising and the praise lavished on improvisers by literary personalities of the time, these critics dismissed them as either insincere or naïve.[11] By showing that improvising was appreciated throughout the century as an expression of poetic virtuosity, this chapter challenges the generally accepted assumption that the eighteenth-century literary establishment saw improvisation as a second-rate, superficial form of entertainment, devoid of literary value. The improvisers' success in the eighteenth century was firmly grounded in Italian aesthetic and cultural values. By the end of the century, however, at a time of heightened nationalistic discourse, the fortunes of improvising were paradoxically undermined by the great success of women improvisers. Not only were women improvisers' own voices erased from literary history; improvising itself was doomed to neglect and scorn. Women's predominance in this medium induced critics, at the end of the eighteenth century and in subsequent generations, to dismiss the whole field as "effeminate" and therefore ipso facto marginal and inferior. It was women's success with this once highly regarded medium that determined patriarchal reappropriation by devaluation.

"*Cultura dell'improvviso*": The Social and Aesthetic Foundations of Improvising in Arcadia

The Accademia dell'Arcadia, the most representative Italian literary institution of the time, played a leading role in how women poets and improvisers achieved preeminence in eighteenth-century Italy. As Giulio Natali noted, in an era when improvised comedy was dying out, improvised poetry began to flourish thanks to the Arcadian academy's patronage. "Improvisers acquire historic relevance in a specific time and place, that is, in Italy in the eighteenth century and in Romantic Arcadia," wrote Croce.[12] Many of the most respected eighteenth-century poets belonged to Arcadia and improvised for the Academy (most notably, Metastasio and Vincenzo Monti, but also Gian Battista Zappi, Paolo Rolli, Domenico Petrosellini, and all the major women improvisers).[13] It was in Arcadia that the two most celebrated artists, Bernardino Perfetti and Corilla Olimpica, were awarded the Capitol laurel as a tribute to their excellence, in 1725 and 1776 respectively.

The prestige of improvising in the Arcadia academy's early years is well documented and was founded in Arcadia's classicist literary theory and in its courtly literary rituals. As Fabio Finotti remarks, Arcadia "fostered the humanist tradition that, since the thirteenth century, had recognized the preeminence of learned improvisation."[14] According to Giovan Maria Crescimbeni, Arcadia's influential director during the academy's fundamental first years (1690–1728), Arcadian improvisers participated in a literary tradition as old as Italian literature itself, with glorious antecedents in the Italian Renaissance, which was then acquiring an increasing following and reputation in Arcadian literary circles:

> Improvising has greatly increased its reputation in our times, since . . . we have noble personages and excellent literary men who often enjoy performing extemporaneously, not just in verse and in every kind of meter and style, but also in prose and in every scholarly and learned matter.[15]

In its criticism of baroque extravagance, Arcadia proposed a taste for classical simplicity. It called itself "Arcadia" after the name of the region that Virgil had consecrated to bucolic poetry. Crescimbeni wrote in his *Istoria della volgare poesia*, an erudite and encyclopedic study of Italian literature from the Middle Ages to the present, that Arcadians "by choosing the pastoral state [had the purpose of] beginning to moderate . . . the overwhelming turgidity of contemporary Italian poetic style with the simplicity and spontaneity of the Pastoral style."[16] The poet-shepherds of antiquity were symbols of a spontaneous creative power, unencumbered by artifice. Arcadia's ideal was that of producing, through masterful use of technique, the impression of the natural spontaneous poetry of a Virgilian golden age. Learned improvisations were seen by some as the expression, par excellence, of such poetry. They represented the balance between culture and inspiration, technique and spontaneity, nature and art that Arcadians aspired to achieve.

The best example of improvisation's privileged and emblematic status in Arcadia is probably to be found in chapter three of Crescimbeni's *Arcadia* (1708), a *sui generis* work at once historical and fictional devoted to celebration of the academy's modernizing spirit. A microcosm of the book as a whole, the chapter is largely devoted to description of the academy's encyclopedic interests, represented here by Monsignor Leone Strozzi's (Nitilo's) collection and study of various extraordinary objects, "marvels of nature and art" that encompassed everything from shells to marbles, from butterflies to medals, from crystals to porcelains, from paintings to "artistic rarities." The chapter fittingly culminates with the description of an improvising performance at a convivial Arcadian gathering. Countess Prudenza Gabrielli Capizzucchi (Elettra), the hostess of the dinner, asked Pompeo Figari (Montano) to improvise. Marchioness Petronilla Paolini Massimi (Fidalma) proposed "Nitilo's museum" as the topic; more precisely, she wanted to know whether one should admire more its natural or its artistic objects. After a cup of "generous *Chiaretto* wine," Montano, the modern *aedo*, started singing, accompanied by the gentle strumming of a guitar (*cetra*). A series of ten well-crafted octaves, his song praised the beauty of both nature and art and concluded that, at their best, the two are interdependent. Art imitates nature, and nature art: "ovunque io volga i lumi, grande il valore di entrambe a me s'addita / . . . Par che Natura opri con arte e che i pregi sol di quella emular questa si pregi" (everywhere I look, whatever I consider, the great value [of nature and art] is revealed to me / . . . It is as if nature followed an artful design, and as if art aspired only to imitate nature).[17]

It is not surprising that Crescimbeni had the poet improviser comment on the essence of beauty and the interdependence of nature and art. Introduced as "one of the greatest marvels of Arcadia," Montano's improvisation was the "fitting crowning" to a chapter devoted to Arcadia's aesthetic and scientific interests. Able to spontaneously produce technically accomplished and cultivated poetry, the learned poet improviser achieved the union of art and nature that was the highest expression of poetic virtuosity. Crescimbeni in fact postulated that the greatest of all marvels cultivated by Arcadians was the improviser's own *ingegno* (genius), since "he can produce extemporaneously what other poets can hardly produce with time and meditation [*comodo studio*]."[18] Arcadians believed in a classical notion of poetry as "mother of all sciences," and in poetic discourse as the philosophical discourse par excellence. With Arcadian poetry the greatness of Italian classical and Renaissance civilization—when nature produced art, and art imitated nature—would be renewed. In the humanist tradition, Crescimbeni saw learned improvising (*extemporanea oratio*) as the privileged moment in which erudition found spontaneous creative expression.[19] The genius of the poet improviser more than any other learned activity embodied the greatness to which Arcadia aspired: that of uniting the mastery of a long literary tradition and of a refined technique with the gift of spontaneous creation. Like the classical poet, the Arcadian poet improviser would be the cantor of his or her civilization.

Learned improvisation was not only the highest expression of poetic virtuosity; it was also the most prized and the most difficult of the intellectual games played by the Arcadian academicians. Improvising acquired popularity as intellectual entertainment in the context of conversazioni and in the spirit of the Arcadian courtly games. Competitions among poet improvisers as well as the Olympic poetic games—a competition held every four years to mark the end of an administrative cycle and to celebrate the academy's accomplishments—reenacted the poetic competitions of a pastoral golden age.[20] Although later in the century improvisation was romantically interpreted by some as a titanic creative act of a solitary genius, it was initially seen as a collegial and collective creative effort. Crescimbeni's *Istoria della volgare poesia* highlights the competitive and collective quality of improvisers' performances and compositions in early Arcadia:

> These past few years Cardinal Pietro Ottoboni . . . has held private literary academies in his palace on Monday nights . . . in which participants improvised learned speeches as well as poems of all kinds, weaving together,

with or without musical accompaniment, octaves, *capitoli*, chains of sonnets, *canzoni, canzonette*. These improvising sessions climaxed with the composition of perfect chains, with the improvisers *challenging each other* for four to six hours in a row.

A typical private academy at the house of cardinal Ottoboni included extemporaneous poetic competitions where the modern "shepherds" composed chains (*corone*) of poems. A corona, Crescimbeni explained in his *Commentarji*, was a series of sonnets or octaves, composed round-robin style according to the "unalterable law that each stanza should begin with the last word of the stanza that preceded it." Such a rule was added by the moderns, "so as . . . to prevent improvisers from declaiming poems they have previously memorized." A corona was particularly admired "not just for the difficulty of its composition, but also for its beauty and nobility." A group of Arcadians would therefore improvise poetry in turns, with each new song having to continue the rhyming scheme of the last stanza that preceded it. Crescimbeni's works provide several examples of improvised music academies as well as poetry improvisations, with or without music, but they do not offer examples of improvised corone.[21] Nevertheless a chapter of *Arcadia* entitled "Academy of Music" offers a unique description of the collective and competitive nature of an improvising performance and its effect on the public. Describing the improvisation of two arias by the famous poet Giovan Battista Zappi (Tirsi) and the universally renowned musician Antonio Scarpelli (Terpandro), Crescimbeni remarked:

> Everybody was overwhelmed in seeing how those two excellent maestri— one a musician and the other a poet—competed with each other. Their creative energy was such that no sooner would the poet finish declaiming the last verse of the new aria than the musician would be concluding the last line of his music.[22]

Their improvisation and the process of poetic creation are described as the result of a creative synergistic competition in which both men found inspiration in competing with each other.[23]

Even though improvisation was highly valued by Crescimbeni and most Arcadians, there was an active debate over the value of improvisation present from the beginning. From its very foundation, Arcadia had to defend itself against accusations of supporting a superficial poetics.[24] Aware that improvising could be seen by some as an example of this superficiality, Crescimbeni took pains to distinguish the popular and uncultivated improvising of itinerant performers from the learned improvisation practiced in Arcadia. The description of the poet Montano's improvisation offered Crescimbeni the opportunity to address these issues. According to Crescimbeni, when asked to perform Montano was initially hesitant. Crescimbeni explained Montano's behavior: since "simple and uncultured people" had started practicing it, improvising had acquired a dubious reputation. He commented that "it has become popular, abject, abused . . . by simple goat herders and country folk."[25]

Although improvising poetry had been very esteemed and renowned in Arcadia—the most learned and the most eminent Arcadians having made a name for themselves improvising not just in Italian but also in Latin—some early eighteenth-century Arcadians hesitated to practice improvisation, lest their art be misrepresented and misunderstood. Elettra understood Montano's concerns and dispelled his qualms by assuring him that she knew him to be as worthy an improviser as "in other times were our most renowned shepherds, who are no longer to be heard in public . . . as one of the greatest marvels of Arcadia."[26] The chapter ends by reassuring readers and Arcadia's critics: if uncultivated street performers have given improvisation a bad name, the improvisation practiced in Arcadia was by contrast highly crafted and learned as well as philosophical in the classical sense of the term.

The Emergence of the Woman Poet and Academician: Arcadia's Cultural Policies

Not only did the first groups of poet improvisers flourish in Arcadia, but this academy also fostered women poets throughout the eighteenth century. Unlike seventeenth-century Italian academies, which only exceptionally allowed women's active participation, Arcadia endeavored to be socially and culturally inclusive. Aspiring to set itself up as a cultural and intellectual model throughout the Italian peninsula, the academy initiated a vast program of cultural expansion. Founded in 1690 in Rome, Arcadia soon developed into a peninsulawide entity, with colonies and affiliations in every part of Italy. At a time when academies and salons were the center of cultural life, membership in Arcadia outnumbered the cumulative membership of all other Italian academies.[27]

Although some critics have pointed out that Arcadian egalitarian tendencies were exaggerated, most commentators agree with Mario Fubini that Arcadia fostered "under the aristocratic blazon, a more democratic literary manner."[28] As a few scholars have begun to outline (among them Elisabetta

Graziosi, Anna Teresa Cervone, and Amedeo Quondam), women's presence in Arcadia was unprecedented. Already in 1824 Ginevra Fachini, in the introduction to her bio-bibliography of Italian literary women, linked the foundation of Arcadia to the proliferation of women poets. A century later Croce wrote that

> Arcadia . . . again made literature available to women. . . . With Arcadia, ascetic seventeenth-century feminine literature came to an end; women devoted themselves also to science, and to debates on sociology, economy, and politics.

More recently, Cervone pointed out that Arcadia was the first Italian cultural movement after the Renaissance to give significant consideration to women: "The Academy granted women the chance to be subjects and not just objects of culture. . . . Women would participate in a process of renewal that had as its scope the restoration of good taste, and not just a change in rhetoric."[29]

Women's involvement in Arcadia developed from a merely honorific presence to active participation to a privileged position within the academy. Not unlike their male counterparts, women had to be at least twenty-four years old and reputable in order to be admitted. Yet, while men had to "be known for their erudition in at least one of the most important sciences," it was granted women need only "profess poetry or some other kind of literary pursuit."[30] Given the fact that women were generally not admitted to universities and rarely received a scientific education, this different requirement ensured the admittance of a larger number of literary women.

It is generally agreed that women's inclusion was part of Arcadia's effort to reform Italian taste, purging Italian literature of the excesses of the seventeenth century, and of an undue reliance on foreign (especially French) models. Although disagreeing profoundly in other matters—including the level of participation in academic life one should grant women—the two most influential literary men among Arcadia's founders, Vincenzo Gravina and Crescimbeni, agreed on the necessity of fostering women's knowledge and practice of Italian letters. In his "Regolamento degli studi di nobile e generosa donna" (1694–1699), Gravina insisted on the importance of cultivating the Italian language and Italian literary tradition. "One will learn foreign languages for practical reasons [i.e., commerce] but will cultivate Italian for . . . the glory of good conversation and good writing."[31] In his history of Italian letters, the *Istoria della volgare poesia* (1701), which enjoyed great editorial success and was reissued and revised several times, Crescimbeni defined his audience as a female readership that might otherwise be too devoted to foreign letters:

> We write especially for the sake of the Ladies, more inclined than other people to be subject to the above mentioned attraction. We exhort them to do justice to our language, as did all the literary women mentioned in our history, as well as many contemporary ones we could mention, such as, among those living in Rome, the marchioness Camilla Caprara Bentivogli, the marchioness Cleria Cavalieri Sacchetti, and the Countess Flavia Teodoli Bolognetti.[32]

By participating in Arcadia's activities, women would contribute to the reform of Italian letters. Yet any participation on their part beyond the most honorific form of membership could not be explained in this fashion. The extent of women's participation in Arcadia became the object of a power struggle waged within the academy in 1711.

There were also strategic reasons for women's emergence in Arcadia. Aristocratic women and women of important social standing in Rome afforded the fledgling academy much-needed financial and political support.[33] Most notably, influential Roman women were instrumental in obtaining regular meeting places for Arcadia. Private academies in the salons of Roman women (such as those held by Faustina Maratti Zappi, Petronilla Paolini Massimi, Teresa Grillo Pamphili, and Prudenza Capizzuchi) were as integral to the academy's life as those held at the court of cardinals Ottoboni and Pamphili or as the public winter academies held in the house of the custode Crescimbeni.[34] Public summer academies, held in a garden called Bosco Parrasio, changed venue six times in seventeen years, until Prudenza Gabrielli Capizzuchi, very active in the first years of the academy, was able to find a stabler home in the Esquilino gardens of her stepson, Francesco Maria Ruspoli.[35] Aristocratic Roman women were also instrumental in funding publication of Arcadian books; Crescimbeni's *Arcadia* testifies to their patronage, as both editions of his *Arcadia* were dedicated to Roman noblewomen. The 1708 dedication to Lady Ondedei Albani specified that "the main part [of the book] is the product of the talent and of the spirit of many among the most illustrious Italian ladies." Crescimbeni repeated this sentiment in the 1711 dedication to Maria Isabella Cesi Ruspoli, when he stated that *Arcadia* was

> founded, above all, on the conspicuous production of several literary ladies, and came out the first time under the patronage of a Princess who, in the greatest degree and with great partiality, looks upon the arts; it now wishes to find in you an equally munificent protector.[36]

Yet affiliation of influential women aristocrats with Arcadia was not the ultimate reason for Crescimbeni's inclusive policies. The first Arcadian women
came from very diverse cultural and social backgrounds. If Aurora San-
severini Gaetani (known in Arcadia as Lucinda, inducted in 1691), Anna
Beatrice Spinelli Carafa (Amaranta Eleusina, 1691), Giovanna Caracciolo
(Noside), and Prudenza Gabrielli Capizzucchi (Elettra, 1695) were noblewomen, Maria Selvaggia Borghini (Filotima, 1691) and Faustina Maratti
Zappi, for example, were not. Borghini was a learned woman who studied Latin, logics, mathematics, and Greek and published a translation of
Tertullian as well as poetry. Faustina Zappi was the natural daughter of the
well-known painter Carlo Maratti and an accomplished poet who had had a
troubled past, having been at the center of a notorious scandal involving the
powerful Cesarini Sforza family. She was among the first Roman women to
be admitted to the academy. Of about thirty women mentioned in the first
edition of Crescimbeni's *Arcadia*, only about half were noble.

Women's participation in Arcadia was more radical, more extensive, and
more contested than is usually acknowledged. Their inclusion in the academy was the result of a hotly contested political and ideological choice on
the part of Crescimbeni's administration of Arcadia, a decision based on the
principles of Christian egalitarianism espoused by him, Anton Maria Salvini,
and others. Women's participation was part of Crescimbeni's program for a
socially and culturally inclusive Republic of Letters, ideally open to all social
classes and all Italian cities, in an effort to foster Italian literary tradition,
especially in lyric, epic, and dramatic poetry, and to create a national forum
for propagation of scientific discoveries.[37] Women were to be equal partners
in this program of literary and intellectual reform.

From the very first years of his leadership, Crescimbeni and his supporters had to defend the academy against attacks on its credibility and on the
viability of its principles and customs. While initially the debate regarded
the literary value of pastoral poetry and the academic value of a pastoral
institution, by 1711 it had developed into a struggle over the definition of the
academy's role and membership that risked undermining its very existence.[38]
On that occasion, Gravina and a group of followers left the Academy in protest over its literary, cultural, and institutional direction. The ostensible reason for Gravina's well-known secession of 1711 was Crescimbeni's choice of
colleghi (a body of twelve prominent Arcadians, with legislative and executive
authority second only to the custode). Most histories of Arcadia have usually
seen it as merely a pretext for his separation. Yet given the colleghi's power

in deciding matters of membership (all new members had to be approved by them), it was in fact a fundamental reason for Gravina's displeasure with Crescimbeni's decision to privilege this group within the academy.[39] In the letters issued to explain his position, Gravina in fact focused especially on two issues: the Academy's perceived focus on love poems, to the detriment of tragedies in the Greek and Latin tradition; and its supposedly indiscriminate criteria for membership which, in his opinion, resulted in the admission of too many "semi-learned" members. Given the fact that Crescimbeni's publications, and *Arcadia* in particular, accord an unprecedented and probably unmatched stature to women, and given the fact that a few Arcadian women had excelled not just in the art of writing Petrarchan poetry but also in theorizing Platonic and Petrarchan love, Gravina's remarks suggest a growing concern about the place of women in Arcadia.

First published in 1708 and reissued at the time of the so-called great schism of 1711, Crescimbeni's *Arcadia* can be read as an apology for his inclusive cultural choices and institutional policies. While showcasing the academy's multifarious scientific and literary activities, complex organization, and liberal philosophy, the book gave voice to Arcadian women's claim to legitimacy and participation within the Republic of Letters. It highlighted women's capabilities and production, citing a great number of their works, and it exposed the ideological obstacles that women needed to overcome in order to be accepted as intellectual peers in the Academy and within the scholarly community at large. *Arcadia* is framed in the context of Arcadian women's search for legitimization and a voice. The very first chapter highlights the struggle to legitimate women's participation as the ultimate aim of the academy's history and consequently as a main policy concern of Crescimbeni's and of early Arcadia. The book is therefore not just the "narration of women's activities in favor of the academy" but, even more strongly, a manifesto of the Crescimbeni administration's favorable position regarding women's participation.[40]

Crescimbeni described the struggle for cultural authority allegorically. He imagined that after a stormy meeting, during which the most prominent female Arcadian poets (called "nymphs" in the text) voiced their grievances over their exclusion from the Arcadian Olympic games, they decided to undertake a trip through Arcadia to *Elide* (the seat of the games) in order to fight for their right to participate.[41] Until publication of the first collections of poetry and prose, in 1716 and 1718 respectively, the publication of the Olympic proceedings was one of the academy's most prominent venues for self-promotion. Allowing women to participate amounted to publicly recognizing their excellence—their being among the most accomplished and representative members of the Arcadian academy. It is not surprising, therefore, that the prospect of including women in the Arcadian Olympics encountered opposition; women were excluded until 1701.

During the first thirty-eight years of the organization's history, under the directorship of Giovanni Maria Crescimbeni, seventy-four women were admitted to Arcadia. Although women constituted just under 3 percent of the academy's membership, they were published in proportionally high numbers: of the 237 selected authors in the first eight volumes of the *Rime degli Arcadi* published between 1716 and 1722, 20 were women, that is to say, 8 percent of all selected authors, and 27 percent of all Arcadian women. The manuscript collections, containing works presented in Arcadia during public and private academies, reveal women's contribution and began no later than 1695.

My research not only confirms Amedeo Quondam's data about the quantitative preeminence given women poets' works in Arcadia's publications, but also offers evidence of the depth of accomplishment, the variety of interests, and the influence of these women poets. Women's participation was not just a matter of fashion and superficial curiosity, as some commentators have suggested.[42] Women played an active and influential role during this phase of the academy's life, as sponsors and patrons and also as poets and academicians. Aimed at divulging and showcasing the activities, the organization, and the philosophy of the academy in the face of mounting opposition, Crescimbeni's *Arcadia* is a tribute to women's literary contribution to the academy, and by extension to the Italian Republic of Letters. The 1708 dedication to Lady Ondedei Albani specifies that "the main part [of the book] is the product of the talent and the spirit of many among the most illustrious Italian ladies," a sentiment repeated in the 1711 dedication we have already mentioned. Arcadian women are presented as able to sustain a conversation on various challenging scientific subjects, and as accomplished poets and improvisers. On several occasions, Arcadian women are portrayed in the act of "lecturing" the assembled Arcadians on literary topics. Crescimbeni had them engage their hosts in conversations about medicine, anatomy, and botany (book 2); antiquarianism, archeology, and natural history (book 3); painting (book 4); mathematics (book 5); and philology (book 6). Far from assuming an acquiescent listening posture, the women of Arcadia in his vision actively contributed their knowledge of virtually every important subject to the academy's learned conversations.

Alternating narrative and poetry, in the manner of Jacopo Sannazaro's *Libro pastorale nominato Arcadia* (1504), which Crescimbeni recognizes as a model in his preface, Crescimbeni's work incorporates verbatim the most representative prose and verse production of the academy's first eighteen years. A good percentage of the poetic works introduced in *Arcadia* are by women. As we compare these works with those in manuscript and published collections, we find that Crescimbeni's *Arcadia* is quite representative of Arcadian women's production in these years. Indeed, my research in Arcadia's archives belies the notion that Arcadian women's production was secondary and ornamental.[43] Far from being limited to a few literary forms and subjects, the pastorelle wrote in a variety of poetic forms: madrigals, sonnets, eclogues, canzoni, cantate, elegies, and *settine*. In addition to Petrarchan and occasional poetry, women wrote poems about maternal love and the gentleness of nature, as well as philosophical poems on Platonic love, poems on religious topics, and proto-feminist and autobiographical poems. Less frequently, women also wrote about recent military and political victories, and later in the century about scientific phenomena and famous works of art. Arcadian pastorelle were competent in all types of versification, but their work displayed originality and a personal touch even when constrained by the prescribed limitations of form and content, as was the case with the compositions presented at the Olympic games.

While showcasing Arcadian women's intellectual virtues, Crescimbeni's *Arcadia* clearly foregrounds the objections to women's participation to the academy's life and exposes their bias. In the introductory first "Prose" (the first section of the volume), princess Giovanna Caracciolo sets the stage for the nymphs' voyage of discovery and self-affirmation when she asks:

> Why are women excluded from the greatest and most solemn ceremony in all of Greece? Is it because our sex is not worthy to contend with men? Yet the whole world is aware of the wonderful works of great ladies of every nation.[44]

In their answers, the nymphs list and undermine the arguments of those who oppose women's access to the study of science and the arts. Among the arguments against women's participation that the text rebuts were those based on the fear of its potentially subversive value: women's participation might unravel the very fabric of society. Although brave and worthy (*valorose*), women did not belong to the public sphere; they could not be allowed to compete with men in the public arena because, as the nymph

Daphne explains, "by distracting men with their presence, women might lessen men's resolve, thereby, in a way, feminizing them."[45]

Similar arguments were used in the 1720s by those opposing Maria Vittoria Delfini Dosi's graduation with a law degree from the University of Bologna, and again at the beginning of the nineteenth century by one of Italy's most enlightened and prominent literary personalities, Foscolo, in his famous essay on the "Women of Italy."[46] Yet here such arguments were opposed with much candor and force, in terms that discredited the criticisms that were subsequently made of Arcadia in the ensuing centuries. Crescimbeni acknowledged that, by including women, Arcadia opened itself up to be considered *feminized* by critics of women's participation. Given the fierce political and literary battle that Crescimbeni was waging at the time over control of the academy's cultural and literary policies, these words, appearing in the very first chapter of his *Arcadia*, amount to a defiant *prise de position* that cannot be ignored. They also call attention to the mixed fortunes of women's presence in Arcadia.

If Crescimbeni's Republic of Letters cannot be understood without women's participation, his inclusion of women as both the object and subject of literary and cultural reform fundamentally separated his Arcadia from his contemporary Ludovico Antonio Muratori's utopian literary Republic of Letters and from Antonio Magliabechi's even more actively misogynist epistolary network.[47] Thanks to Crescimbeni's model, the new figure of the woman poet and academician emerged into public prominence in the course of the eighteenth century. In this context, the improvvisatrice played an especially important role.

The Emergence of the Women Improvisers

The first canonization of women improvisers occurred in the *Dialogo pastorale di Eurasio Nonacride*, a pastoral dialogue published on the occasion of the 1754 Olympic Games, celebrating famous Arcadians of the past and present. Before midcentury, we have only one mention *en passant* of a woman improviser in Crescimbeni's *Arcadia* in relation to his discussion of several improvisations by male poets. No women are mentioned in his histories of improvisation; nor is there any mention of women in his lists of exemplary poet improvisers.[48] When we collate Crescimbeni's histories with later eighteenth-century sources, we find references to at least twelve prominent male improvisers in early Arcadia (1690–1728), among whom the better known are Metastasio (known as Artino in the Literary Academy Arcadia), Perfetti (Alauro), and Zappi (Tirsi); and to three women improvisers, about whom we have scant information: Faustina dagli Azzi Forti (known as Selvaggia, inducted in 1691), Emilia Ballati (Eurinda, 1712), and Maria Domenica Mazzetti Forster (Flora, 1725).[49]

By contrast, the *Dialogo pastorale* records the names of quite a few improvisers who are not usually remembered in histories; it testifies to a rather widespread practice of improvisation, offering evidence of both male and female improvisers' prestige in the second half of the century.[50] Eurasio, one of the two "shepherds," laments the loss of famous Arcadian poets, and especially the loss "of those prodigies who were heard among us / singing their quick extemporaneous song." The other shepherd Norinteo rebukes him; there is no reason to be sad, since these improvisers are among those "celebrated shepherds / who [are praised] in their time and beyond their time." In other words, according to the Arcadian aesthetic sensibilities that Norinteo represents, improvisers' prestige was to be considered eternal. Women played an important role in this new image of Arcadia's fame. As part of celebrating the superior abilities and eternal fame of Arcadian improvisers, past and present, the *Dialogo pastorale* mentions three *improvvisatrici* among the ten most famous Arcadian contemporary poets: Anna Maria Parisotti Beati from Roma (known as Efiria Corilea in Arcadia), Maria Maddalena Morelli from Pistoia (known as Corilla Olimpica), and Maria Domenica Mazzetti Forster from Firenze.[51]

At least fifteen women improvisers were well known during the eighteenth century and into the nineteenth.[52] While male improvisers came from all walks of life (Gaspare Mollo, for example, was a duke, and Francesco Gianni, a former tailor; both were admired in the salons of imperial Paris), the celebrated women improvisers of the second half of the century were almost exclusively from the professional middle class. They were able to emerge thanks to the patronage of prominent noblemen and noblewomen.[53] Given the more stringent rules of decorum for noblewomen, it was not considered appropriate for them to perform publicly, and yet one had to have access to a high level of education to compete in this learned terrain. Unlike their male counterparts, female poets did not begin to improvise in theaters and for monetary compensation until the end of the century.[54] But women such as Domenica Mazzetti Forster and Corilla had become court poets in Tuscany (in the 1720s and 1760s respectively) thanks to their improvising abilities. Thus, in an ancien regime context, these women were professional improvisers who used their poetic skills to carve a place for themselves within the social and cultural elite of the Italian peninsula.

There are cultural and aesthetic reasons for the success of women improvisers in the second half of the century. The same strategic reasons that had prompted Crescimbeni to open the academy's doors to women inspired Arcadian custodians Michele Morei and Gioacchino Pizzi to make women improvisers the centerpiece of their projects of literary and institutional reforms in the mideighteenth century. As Arcadia aspired to achieve international recognition and membership, improvisers ensured a large public in attendance, international attention, and prestige.

In his *Memorie istoriche* (1761), Morei, custodian and historian of Arcadia at the time, noticed the number of members in attendance when improvisers performed: "Popular attendance of Arcadian public academies is extraordinary when it is rumored that some of the most felicitous Arcadian poets are about to sing extemporaneously about any subject and in any meter proposed by the audience."[55] Morei's comments on Bernardino Perfetti's 1725 poetic laurels further reveal and specify the enduring political and strategic reasons for Arcadia's fostering of improvisation: improvising attracted the interest, the participation, and the patronage of Italian and "foreign" nobility. Noting that Arcadia was honored by Pope Benedict XIII's favors and Princess Violante's (Princess of Tuscany and Governess of Siena) benevolence as well as by the presence of a numerous audience of nobles, prelates, and literary personalities, he observed how beneficial such recognition was for the academy, describing the crowning of "Alauro Euroteo" (Perfetti) in the great hall of the Campidoglio as "one of the most clamorous occasions for the promotion of Arcadia."[56]

When a woman improviser who elicited the admiration of kings, queens, and literary personalities all over Europe finally emerged in the late eighteenth century, the Roman Arcadia took the opportunity to elevate her to the Capitol crown. Corilla Olimpica was the first woman improviser to achieve international fame and recognition; according to Giulio Perini (vice-secretary of the "Accademia fiorentina"), it was only with Corilla that the art of improvising began to deserve the title of "divine"[57] (Figure 12.2). Although several sources indicate that Corilla's fame and ascension to the status of poet laureate rested on both her published poetry and her improvisations,[58] most commentators ascribe the admiration of "cultured travelers, . . . sovereigns, . . . and the most prominent poets of Italy" to Corilla's astounding improvising abilities.[59] As the official acts of the ceremony put it, Corilla's "ease . . . in improvising elegantly in any meter and on any literary topic, had made her the object of universal wonder." Gian Battista Bodoni, the director of the Royal Press in Parma, a member of the Parma Academy of Fine Arts and a man known for his moderation, poignantly introduced the proceedings celebrating Corilla's crowning on the Capitol by quoting, and therefore affiliating her with, Petrarch.[60]

After 1776, Corilla's celebrity knew no bounds. Famous painters, sculptors, and engravers celebrated Corilla with their work,[61] collections of poems were printed in her honor,[62] and official literary documents identified her as the greatest poetic genius of her time. Especially remarkable among the tributes to Corilla in the proceedings published after her crowning was Luigi Godard's statement: "By combining philosophical study and insight with a warm and enthusiastic imagination," he wrote, ". . . [Corilla] is one of those few geniuses who produced real art."[63] Perhaps the most poignant

Figure 12.2 Francesco Bartolozzi, *Portrait of Corilla*, 1765 (etching after a painting by Anna Piattoli). From *In lode della sac. Maestà rea. app. di Maria Teresa . . .* (Venezia: Antonio Zatta, 1765). Biblioteca Forteguerriana, Pistoia.

praise of Corilla is to be found in private expressions of admiration in the letters of her contemporaries. Gioacchino Pizzi, custodian general of Arcadia, fervent admirer of Corilla's poetry, and staunch supporter of her crowning as poet laureate, thought Corilla belonged to the list of the most prominent eighteenth-century scientific and literary personalities, together with "Newton, Fontenelle, Voltaire, Polignac, Manfredi, Metastasio, and Frugoni." After first witnessing one of Corilla's moving improvisations during a weekly private seminar organized around Corilla's public performances in Arcadia, Cristofano Amaduzzi wrote: "I count among the most distinctive satisfactions of my life having had the fortune of witnessing the worth of this great woman, for whom our past has no peer."[64]

Travel books and memoirs give us a measure of Corilla's international reputation and prestige. By the 1760s the most prominent travelers sought Corilla's company—including Casanova, who, upon his arrival in Pisa in 1760, insisted on meeting with her. Unable to meet with Corilla on his 1765 tour of Italy when she was at the court of Vienna, the French astronomer Joseph de Lalande wrote that he "had found everywhere the traces of her reputation." The English musician Charles Burney, a regular visitor of Corilla's Florentine salon after 1766, wrote in his memoirs: "Every evening there were assemblies at Corilla's, attended especially by the foreigners and the men of letters living in Florence at the time. . . . Europe had known her success." The main events in Corilla's life were widely covered by the international as well as the national press.[65] Jean Baptiste Gaspard D'Ansse de Villoison (1750–1805), one of France's most prominent classicists of the time, published a Latin poem celebrating Corilla's crowning in Pierre-Sylvain Marechal's collection of love poems *Biblioteca degli amanti*. The poem was reported by the Parisian correspondent of the Florentine newspaper *Notizie dal mondo* on 9 April 1777.[66]

By the time Corilla went to Rome in January 1775, she was already internationally famous. Arcadian manuscript archives clearly portray the great expectations that preceded her performances. On 5 January 1775 one reads that, thanks to the performance of the improvisers Talassi, De Rossi, and Rocchetti, attendance at Arcadian academies had greatly increased, and the present event was "one of the most crowded because of the rumor that the famous improviser Corilla might attend." Corilla eventually did appear in Arcadia on 12 January 1775. After performing to a delirious audience, she was unanimously entered in the list of *pastorelle acclamate*, an honor previously reserved only for queens and princesses.

The years 1775 and 1776 saw a constant stream of Corilla's triumphal performances in Arcadia. The Arcadian archives record the presence of a vast public that waited for hours in order to be able to see one of her performances:

> the whole of the Roman nobility competed to show her their appreciation, and everybody was happy to hang on her every word with wonder and astonishment for four or five hours at a time, without minding the discomfort provoked by such a great crowd of people.

The public interest and attendance was such that armed guards had to be placed at the entrance of the *Serbatojo* (as Arcadians called their seat) when Corilla performed.[67]

Women Improvisers and the Cult of Spontaneity

To put Corilla's poetic apotheosis in historical perspective and understand the political, institutional, and aesthetic principles that contributed to her success, we need to look beyond the enlightened and democratic principles (as well as the pragmatic concerns) of the Arcadian academy, and consider how a poetics of enthusiasm played a major role in Corilla's literary rise to fame. The emergence of improvvisatrici in the second half of the century coincided with a change in the perception and evaluation of improvisation. The publication of Saverio Bettinelli's *Entusiasmo* (1763) reflected and at the same time codified this different taste and sensibility. Although performers still engaged in a social ritual, in the second half of the century improvisers also became the symbol of the performative and progressive poetic imagination, according to emerging pre-Romantic ideals. They were prized for their spontaneity and immediacy, and they were seen as the embodiment of the very process of poetic creation. Discussions of poetic improvisation increasingly exalted the poet's creative furor rather than simply appreciating his or her technical ability. The new mystique of the poet improviser, with its emphasis on divine inspiration, lent itself to a gendered interpretation that favored women's emergence, while at the same time undermining their agency, as we shall see.

To my knowledge, Eurasio Nonacride's (abbé Pier Francesco Versari) 1754 pastoral dialogue is the earliest Arcadian document that testifies to the emergence of this new poetics of enthusiasm. The poem presents what the author sees as two extreme interpretations of improvising. He explains that while some consider improvising to be just a rare gift of memory, since improvisers do nothing but recite poems they have previously memorized, others by contrast view it as "a spontaneous expression, a fanatic speech." Eurasio, one of the two pastors engaged in this fictional discussion, dissuades his readers from the former view, arguing that the notion that improvisers recite poems they have previously memorized is "bereft of the light of reason." Memory plays a role only in aiding the improviser in his creative effort by assisting him in "remembering the meter and the last syllable of the verse which he must use to make the connection and form a ring in the chain of poems that is being formed." Nor does he consider improvisation to be something purely instinctive and beyond the realm of reason, since in that case, the improviser would not be able to "weave with the appropriate meter and verse / with convincing reasoning and with surprising arguments / a story, a fable or some pastoral simile."[68] Still firmly grounded in the classicism and rationalism of early Arcadia, the fictional Eurasio refutes the image of the improviser as possessed by a sacred "furor" (or enthusiasm) that was to become the hallmark of pre-Romantic criticism in the second half of the century.

In contrast, Bettinelli's *Entusiasmo* provided just such a description of the poet's activity as creation. He spoke positively of the virtues of this approach:

> Enthusiasm creates . . . apparitions, spirits, deities, idols that only exist in the mind of the poet and because of him. He created a new Heaven, a new Hell. . . . Those who do not have enthusiasm, repeat, combine, imitate, and copy, but neither surprise nor enchant us; whereas inspiration that he found within himself, without prior example and without help, he drew from nothingness, and truly created it.[69]

For Bettinelli, therefore, enthusiasm was the creative energy of the original artist who shaped *ex nihilo* an artistic world with a strong emotional and intellectual impact on the listener.

After describing the characteristics of enthusiasm, and defining it as "an elevation of the soul that, rapidly seeing unusual and wonderful things, passionately feels them and is able to communicate this passion to others," Bettinelli affirmed that it was through the observation of a great improviser, the abbé Bartolomeo Lorenzi, that he was able to confirm the accuracy of his description of the character and stages of artistic creation.[70] In a very real way, the improviser's performance was considered by many as an almost sacred moment in which one could witness the creative energy and inspiration of genius take shape and come forth right before their eyes. In his description of what poetry is, and why Corilla was a great poet, Godard presented a poetics of enthusiasm very close to Bettinelli's—so much so that the latter remarked that he was flattered by Godard's appropriation of his idea. Godard described Corilla's performances as beginning in a low and subdued manner, then suddenly burning with progressive rapidity to their exhaustion, as they emotionally enveloped the poet and her audience. After a "languid and uncertain" beginning, Corilla would "suddenly ignite" with the sacred fire of inspiration, after which her poetry flew "like a torrent, surging immense and turgid with waters."[71]

The idea that Corilla's poetic improvisation was considered not simply the product of divine *inspiration* but as a consequence of divine *possession* suggests the framework within which we should understand the construction of women's literary authority in the eighteenth century. The woman improviser's unusual freedom lay in the fact that contemporaries could perceive her ability as an unself-conscious exhibition of divine genius. In such an interpretation, the concept of "enthusiasm" acquired a gendered connotation. While contemporary commentators and literary historians described the male improviser as a "prophet," they envisioned the female improviser as an instrument of another spirit; her originality and her contributions were ultimately not hers.

Bettinelli saw Lorenzi, a male improviser, *rise* to celestial inspiration. The academician Giovanni Cristofano Amaduzzi, by contrast, described Corilla as being *invaded* by the celestial fire: "At that moment," he observed, "the fast pace of her singing, the rapidity of her expressions . . . announced the heavenly fire that had descended on her and acted on her without any precise or reflective cooperation on her part." In Amaduzzi's definition, Corilla becomes a mere passive recipient, or a vessel, of the divine "fire." This concept is rendered more explicit by what Corilla herself is said to have claimed:

> She herself would realize that she pronounced things that presented themselves as new and unexpected to her imagination. She also would admit that she could hardly understand anything at the height of poetic frenzy; in fact, she never recognized as hers the vibrant and enthusiastic things she pronounced.[72]

Amaduzzi adduced as corroborating proof the fact that Corilla's bold, proud, and expressive way of speaking during her improvising performances was uncharacteristic of her personality.[73] Such a judgment is uncorroborated by the image Amaduzzi presents of Corilla elsewhere, and it is completely undermined by the image Corilla gives of herself and her art in her correspondence with the very same Amaduzzi.[74] Since Amaduzzi was familiar with Corilla's disregard for conventional language and behavior, as well as with her strong sense of her professional self, he could not have failed to see the correspondences between Corilla's controversial improvising moments and her outspoken character. The fact that he nevertheless described Corilla's poetic activity as unself-conscious and even impersonal in a document that could be construed as an official literary judgment, is to be ascribed to Amaduzzi's desire to legitimize his admiration of Corilla's poetical gifts according to an acceptable and traditional representation of a woman's enthusiasm: the Apollonian maenad, the "enthusiastic woman, with prophetic spirit."[75] The authority of the woman improviser was thus founded on the traditional permission accorded to religiously inspired women to make utterances as long as they were construed as involuntary. If the eighteenth-century male improviser owed his success to his poetic genius and stamina, contemporaries could still perceive the female improviser as owing hers to more traditional sources of inspiration that downplayed the originality and authorship of her own contributions.

No matter how highly they were praised in sonnets and odes, no matter how enthusiastically crowds of cultured and uneducated listeners alike reacted to their performances, the approbation of women improvisers—not unlike that of other literary women—was always gendered, limited, and conditional. While opinions regarding the value of improvising varied, what remained a constant was the hierarchal relationship between male and female improvisers. Even Corilla's crowning as poet laureate did not change this aspect of the literary dynamic of Arcadia.

Conclusions: Poetry, Gender, and the Definition of National Character

At the same time that Arcadia grew into a widely known academy with an international membership, improvisation became more and more popular. Christopher Johns' research offers strong evidence of the international dimension of Roman cultural life in the eighteenth century as the global reputation of the Eternal City as the cradle of Western civilization grew: "Increasingly, Settecento popes used culture and art patronage to appeal to the good opinion of Catholic and even Protestant Europe, promoting the role of the institution as a guardian of monuments and works of art that were almost universally regarded as fundamental to western traditions."[76] While it is easy to see how this strategy applies to restoration of Roman and Christian monuments, it also extended to preservation of a classical literary and cultural patrimony, of which Italy—and Rome in particular—considered itself the privileged keeper. The popes' support of Arcadia, among all other academies prospering at this time, was part of their effort to promote and preserve Roman and Italian cultural patrimony. The preservation, promotion, and reinterpretation of Italian classical patrimony was the main objective of Arcadia; it was also the main point of pride of the Italian literary establishment. Italian writers invoked this classical tradition when appealing for restoration of Italian letters and Italian cultural prestige. They encouraged improvisation as a poetic genre that captured the spirit of Italy's classical tradition. The success of the improvvisatori, both male and female, was firmly grounded in Italian aesthetic and cultural values. As improvisation acquired popularity with the cultured elites, improvisers began to be promoted in Arcadia also for the international interest and attention they could bring to the institution.

Yet with the Capitol crowning of an internationally famous woman improviser, Arcadia and Rome went too far in their quest for international attention to not provoke a critical response. As I have shown elsewhere, this ceremonial gesture unleashed a furious backlash against Corilla and her sponsors. Groups of Arcadians seceded from the academy; different academies were revived or newly founded to rival and oppose Arcadia; and the event became strongly identified in the eyes of Arcadia's detractors as the cause of its decline and "degeneration."[77] But the most important consequence of Corilla's crowning for our present study was, without a doubt, the feminization of improvisation. The image of Corilla as poet laureate had an enormous impact on the collective imagination; it inspired plays and novels for a century to come, and most important, it inspired generations of women poets.[78]

Two women in particular followed in Corilla's footsteps and became, by all accounts, the most famous improvisers of the last two decades of the century: Teresa Bandettini (1763–1837) and Fortunata Sulgher Fantastici (1755–1824). Improvisation came to be perceived more and more as a feminine occupation, as is made clear by an episode of Bandettini's autobiography. When her confessor discovered her knowledge and her secret love of poetry, he turned to her mother and said: "this young lady gives signs that she will be another Corilla."[79] From that moment on, according to her own testimony, Bandettini was allowed to pursue her interests unhindered; she became the toast of Arcadia, as well as of the most refined literary salons in Tuscany.

As the eighteenth century progressed, and Italian culture strove toward "virile" and "manly" intellectual pursuits, improvising increasingly lost the prestige it had enjoyed for most of the century. Fostered by both neoclassical and pre-Romantic culture, improvisation was to fall under the criticism of Enlightenment thinkers. By the end of the century, improvisation, and the Arcadian academy and poetics that had fostered it, were a major casualty of the Enlightenment effort to redefine Italian character. Enlightenment thinkers condemned Arcadian poetry in general and improvisation in particular for what they perceived as its "effeminate" and "unmanly" poetics. Italian philosophes criticized Arcadian poetry's lack of social commitment and originality. Giuseppe Baretti, in his very well-known editorials in the *Frusta letteraria*, called Arcadia a "very celebrated childish thing" and referred to its poetry as "unmanly little sonnets."[80] Whenever a critic felt the need to disparage the activities of the academy, or its poetics, he referred to them as nothing but *pastorellerie*, that is, works and activities pertaining to a pastorella (shepherdess), a female member of the academy. In this fashion, the female membership of Arcadia became the public faces of what were seen as its sterile and outdated poetic practices.

If the success of improvisation contributed to what has recently been called an "ethnic stereotype" of Italian poetry,[81] it was because of a cultural manipulation in which Italian literary personalities were at times complicit. At the end of the century, in an era of rising nationalist sentiment, Italians' unique talent for improvisation acquired a negative connotation. It fed the stereotype of Italians as great artists, poets, and musicians, but poor philosophers, scientists, and statesmen. European critics saw Italians' excellence at improvising as resulting not only from a peculiarly musical language, an especially versatile prosody, and a uniquely oral literary tradition but also from disadvantageous political circumstances. According to such interpretations, because of their political subjugation to foreign countries and despotic regimes, Italians were not free to practice "free research and thinking" and were compelled to devote themselves to supposedly less "serious" and "virile" subjects such as poetry and art. Motivated by a Protestant anti-Catholic bias, Karl Fernow (a professor of aesthetics at the University of Iéna), for example, presented Italians' excellence in poetry as the only outlet for a nation oppressed by the supposedly obscurantist papist education system:

> If, then, the Italian language is the favorable soil in which this artistic growth thrives more than anything else, one can consider the highly deficient, wrong, papist education which prevails in this country as the fertilizer. . . . In a country, the inhabitants of which are too educated not to feel actively the need for the nobler joys of the spirit, and who also have enough genius and taste to fulfill that need, but where for long centuries the free use of reason in their own concerns is a religious crime, . . . where therefore true scientific culture and the incumbent product of it, true enlightenment, can never flourish, because the underlying conditions for it—free research and thinking—are lacking. . . . In this country, poetry is an excellent diversion for the ever active drive of the mind for occupation.[82]

In other words, Italians' perceived preeminence as artists, poets, and musicians could be portrayed as the consequence of the escapist attitude of an emasculated people who, although endowed with great intellectual gifts, could not freely cultivate them because of their lack of political and civil freedoms.

Such an image found further justification in the most famous literary portrayal of the Italian culture of female improvisation, written by a Frenchwoman at the beginning of the nineteenth century. Germaine de Staël's *Corinne ou Italie* (1807) describes Italians as being almost universally artistic; common people are familiar with the arts and show their taste and preference by arguing over statues in the streets. Painting, monuments, and antiquities as well as a certain level of literary achievement are a national preoccupation—and yet, she observed in the wake of the Napoleonic invasion and occupation of much of the Italian peninsula, "without military strength and without freedom" Italy could not but be politically fragmented and intellectually weak. Corinne asks:

> How is it that under the Romans this was the most military of nations; among the medieval Republics, the most jealous of its freedoms; in the sixteenth century, the most illustrious in letters, science, and the arts? . . . And if she no longer has any, why not blame her political situation, since in other circumstances she proved so different from what she is today? . . . Throughout the ages, making this beautiful country a prey for their endless ambitions, foreigners have conquered and torn her to shreds! The Italians gave Europe the arts and sciences and now she turns their gifts against them, often contesting the last glory allowed nations without military strength and without freedom: the glory of science and the arts.[83]

Unable to produce great thinkers, or philosophers according to Fernow, or great statesmen, generals, and even scientists according to de Staël, Italians had to content themselves with the gift of poetry, improvising being its most admirable manifestation.

Gender assumptions inevitably informed the discourse on national character at the dawn of a new century. Literary endeavors devoid of a stringent philosophical motivation or of a civic mission were considered inherently sensual and unmanly. As Fernow wrote, in the absence of

> true Enlightenment . . . the enthusiasm of the noblest spirits . . . is enticed into the magic country of imagination in order to burn itself out in harmless bursts of poetic inspiration which . . . enervate reason and lull the spirit into that *indifferent sensual ease* from which nothing is to be expected or feared for the benefit of mankind.[84]

According to one stereotype that de Staël strives to undermine in her *Corinne ou Italie*, Italian men have "no strength of character nor any serious purpose in life. . . . [They] have the mildness and flexibility of women's character."[85] Because of its assumed focus on improvisation, poetry, and art, Italian culture could be stigmatized as sensual, disengaged, and effeminate.

THIRTEEN

Gender and Genre in the Religious Art of the Catholic Enlightenment

CHRISTOPHER M. S. JOHNS

Until relatively recently, many scholars considered the term *Catholic Enlightenment* to be oxymoronic, since such a notion flies in the face of the entrenched secularist narratives of modernism that depict the Catholic Church as monolithic, repressive, obscurantist, and a leading opponent of modernism per se. In the present context, one could add *misogynistic* to the list of pejorative adjectives describing the Universal Church. This intellectual prejudice is seen especially in Italian scholarship of the twentieth century, much inspired by the work of Benedetto Croce (1866–1952), who reacted strongly against the obstructionist activities of the Roman Catholic Church during the Risorgimento, the movement for Italian national unification that culminated with the annexation of Rome to the kingdom of Italy in 1870.[1] In addition, the anticlericalism of most Italian intellectuals of the last century was deeply rooted in the antiprogressive and antimodernist positions assumed by the papacy, not to mention its ultraconservative political and social agenda. It must also be said that non-Italian scholars have usually shared these prejudices, much to the detriment of a more balanced view of the Church in historical perspective. The eighteenth-century papal institution and its response to Enlightenment ideology, scrutinized through the lens of religious imagery—above all, representations of female saints—are the primary themes of this chapter.

While it is true that the post-Napoleonic papacy could with some justice be characterized by all the negative terms listed above, its Settecento counterpart had a very different world view. Relatively progressive in its legal and penal codes, social policies, and even spiritual governance, the eighteenth-century papacy had little reason to reject outright at least some of the reformist agenda of the European Enlightenment. Indeed, abolition of papal nepotism at the end of the seventeenth century, intense interest in the preservation of monuments, and protection and display of the cultural patrimony of Rome and the Papal States were all proactive responses to the social transformation of Europe at the dawn of the Enlightenment.[2] While conservative forces remained active and, like other institutions of privilege, the Church looked carefully after its own interests, the early modern papacy was perhaps never so liberal or so progressive as it was in the eighteenth century. In sum, there was indeed a Catholic Enlightenment, and it left no aspect of Catholic Europe untouched.

As an art historian, I am especially interested in the impact of the Catholic Enlightenment on forms of visual culture in eighteenth-century Rome, especially painting, although the trends I describe in due course also have major repercussions for sculpture, printmaking, architecture, urbanism, and material culture. In studying the evolution of religious art in Rome from the late Baroque to the age of the Grand Tour, I have identified one transformation that has gone virtually unnoticed by other scholars: a strong current in painting that moves away from the mystical, transcendent, and triumphalist aura so notable in Baroque sacred imagery toward a rationalistic, reportorial, genrelike approach that often excludes or at least remarkably underplays supernatural presence, reification of virtues, swarms of cherubs, celestial illuminations, and physical transport. Like all trends, it moved in fits and starts, and one can identify numerous exceptions to the general course of development. Moreover, certain types of religious imagery continued to be governed rigorously by tradition. Often, however, even when supernatural figures were deemed "necessary," they seem somehow disconnected to the earthbound context, self-consciously aware that they create visual hybridity and that they add a note of irrationality to the scene.

Pompeo Girolamo Batoni's (1708–1787) *Benedict XIV Presenting the Encyclical "Ex Omnibus" to the Comte de Stainville, Later Duc de Choiseul* of 1757 is a case in point (Figure 13.1).[3] Celebrating a diplomatic agreement

Figure 13.1 Pompeo Girolamo Batoni, *Pope Benedict XIV Presenting the Encyclical "Ex Omnibus" to the Comte de Stainville, Later Duc de Choiseul,* 1757 (oil on canvas). Minneapolis: Minneapolis Art Institute. Photo: Minneapolis Art Institute.

between Louis XV and the Holy See, the painting was ordered by Cardinal Domenico Orsini d'Aragona, a leading papal diplomat, to "document" his pivotal behind-the-scenes role in the negotiations.[4] Benedict XIV Lambertini (reigned 1740–1758), the century's most enlightened pontiff, is seated in full regalia, blessing the kneeling French diplomat with his right hand while he proffers the papal letter with the other. At left, Ecclesia and two playful cherubs seem comfortable enough, but note how the other reification, Divine Wisdom, touches the arm holding the encyclical with her scepter, indicating its supernal origin. Both compositionally and chromatically, she recedes into the background. Even more compositionally incongruous are the figures of Peter and Paul floating in on a cloud to witness the deed, accompanied by the dove of the Holy Spirit. While personifications of such abstract notions as virtues had long been visualized by artists as female figures, these two seem both more naturalistically rendered and less engaged in the painting's narrative than their saintly male counterparts. Tradition dies slowly, and Batoni must have felt that in such a narrative both virtues and the favored papal saints were *de rigueur.*

What these figures lack, however, is real pictorial conviction, and I would argue that the pastiche quality one immediately perceives is not due to a lack of artistic sophistication and ability but to a growing unease with such "unreasonable" inclusions. This seems an especially cogent observation when one considers the almost obsessively intricate details of lace, satin, feathers, and brocade that characterize the dress of both the pope and the French ambassador and that are at variance with the highly generalized draperies of the "unreal" presences. Acute painterly differentiation between such visual phenomena is generally associated with nineteenth-century religious images. Jean-Auguste-Dominique Ingres's *Vow of Louis XIII* comes immediately to mind. In this large historical painting, which created a sensation at the Salon of 1824, Ingres depicts a kneeling Louis XIII, resplendent in a blue coronation mantle lined with ermine and studded with golden fleur-de-lis. Above, painted in a much more ideal manner, the object of the monarch's gaze is revealed by a curtain to be the Madonna holding the Christ Child, an image inspired directly by Raphael's *Sistine Madonna*. Batoni's Baroque predecessors also explicitly visualized the gap between heaven and earth, but in decidedly different ways. In most seventeenth-century religious images of this type, one does not sense the disparity between the earthly and the supernatural in such an obvious manner. My point here is partly dependent on the fact that Batoni's picture represents a scene of contemporary history (the encyclical was issued in 1756). Modern narratives increasingly begged the question of modern treatment, and literal inclusion of the supernatural increasingly seemed inappropriate, although there are certainly precedents for this phenomenon in the religious art of earlier eras. What emerges from the more fundamental Settecento shift in artistic conception is a religious imagery that engages the here and now (note especially the absolutely convincing view of Saint Peter's in the right background), underscoring the profound connection between the divine and the diurnal.

It may also be instructive at this point to examine briefly a sacred image that fully embraces the new ideas of religious experience and modernity but without any overt reference to the issues of gender that will be my central focus. In 1746, to celebrate Benedict XIV's canonization of Camillo de Lellis (the Lambertini pontiff had beatified him in 1742), the Camillan Order commissioned Pierre Subleyras (1699–1749) to paint two scenes from the founder's life in order to present them to the Pope. *Saint Camillo de Lellis Saving the Sick of the Hospital of Spirito Santo from the Floodwaters of the Tiber* (Figure 13.2) was one of the pair.[5] Subleyras invented a scene utterly devoid

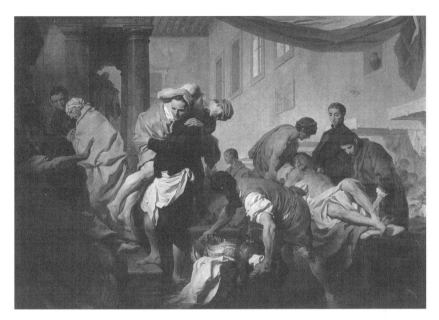

Figure 13.2 Pierre Subleyras, *Saint Camillo de Lellis Saving the Sick of the Hospital of Spirito Santo from the Floodwaters of the Tiber*, 1746 (oil on canvas). Rome: Museo di Roma. Photo: Museo di Roma.

of supernatural presence and in a highly naturalistic manner shows Camillo and his followers physically removing the patients from the lower floor of the hospital to safety above during an inundation of the Tiber River on the evening of 23–24 December 1598. Shortly after his heroic act, which was resisted by the hospital authorities, the flood swept through the area where the helpless sick people had been sleeping. Although the event occurred a century and a half before the artist executed the painting, its intense naturalism fully resonates with the contemporary world. The stunningly beautiful still life in the foreground is especially convincing as something palpably real. Spirituality is internalized in the quiet determination of Camillo de Lellis and his helpers; there is no need to visualize the supernatural. Although such a complete exclusion of "unreal" presence is not wholly unprecedented in sacred images, the emphatic rejection of earlier formulae for such representations is highly characteristic of the new approach to many modern religious subjects initiated in the middle decades of the eighteenth century.

Such a sea change in the nature of sacred art owes much to the reformist agenda of the early eighteenth-century papacy, *desiderata* that called for a return to the simplicity of the Early Church and a rejection of the personal corruption and political expediency of the recent past. Modernity in the abstract was to be understood as a type of Catholic Utopia, despite the compromises and growing secularism that were the eighteenth-century reality.[6] The Church increasingly wished to portray itself as both socially useful and divinely necessary, adapting itself to altered circumstances.

Issues of gender were crucial to this re-presentation of Catholicism to progressive opinion. The waxing awareness of the crucial relationship between women and official Church activities in the eighteenth century is seen with rare clarity in the case of the beatification in 1751 of Jeanne Françoise de Chantal (1572–1641) and the activities of her Order of the Visitation in Rome. Chantal was a wife and mother of four living in the secular world, unlike the vast majority of officially beatified or canonized holy women who were enclosed conventual nuns or working in the lay world in minor orders (like tertiaries). This pattern was also prevalent in the Settecento, so the case of Jeanne de Chantal stands in special relief.[7] Women undeniably assumed a more influential place in Church history and Catholic practice than they had previously occupied. Evaluating altered gender dynamics helps us understand better the new role that Rome wished to play in Enlightenment Europe.[8] Paintings of daily religious activities that foreground women and images associated with the beatifications and canonizations of new female saints will be my point of entry into this extremely complex phenomenon.

In about 1712, the celebrated Bolognese artist Giuseppe Maria Crespi (1665–1747) painted a series of seven small pictures representing the sacraments of the Roman Catholic Church for the eminent Cardinal Pietro Ottoboni (1667–1740). Such series are rare in the history of art. Nicolas Poussin (1594–1665) executed two separate series of sacraments in the mid-seventeenth century, but his attention was focused on historicist and archaeological interests he shared with his elite circle of patrons.[9] The use of an accurately rendered Roman lamp and the triclinium table at which Christ and his disciples recline in the *Last Supper* are typical inclusions in this classicizing series of images. Above all, Poussin's paintings were inspired by a scholarly interest in the culture of antiquity and not by the populist piety of their Settecento successor. For the father of the French classical tradition, the seven sacraments were an occasion to execute history paintings fully accessible only to the learned. Crespi's *Sacraments* are presented as genre scenes in which everyday people are doing the things required of them by a religion that was also the main feature of their daily lives, and in this emphasis on modernity Crespi is remarkable.[10]

As opposed to Poussin's paintings, Crespi's canvases do not visualize the sacraments by reference to biblical / historical prototypes; they are simply conceived as normal activities.[11] For example, in common practice the sacraments of baptism, marriage, and extreme unction were often performed at home, and Crespi's settings seem emphatically domestic. Only *Confession*, *Ordination*, and *Confirmation* take place in church, and this is more a logical inference than something the painter explicitly indicates. The *prie-dieu* seen in *Marriage* was commonly found in even humble residences, and priests often brought fonts and holy oil into the abodes of the faithful to perform baptisms and (necessarily) the last rites. In *Communion*, which was also often taken in private, the sole reference to an ecclesiastical setting is the candle in the upper left that may rest on an altar, but even this small detail is highly ambiguous. Placing the sacraments in the domestic sphere necessarily aids in the feminization of the sacred rites and helps to create an aura of tranquil sanctity. I believe that this is one of the major reasons some contemporaries undervalued and mocked Crespi's achievement, an idea to which I shall soon return. In sum, *entrée* into Crespi's narratives requires only knowledge of what the sacraments are and how they function in their modern form; the viewer is not called upon to determine the difference between a table and a triclinium.

In *Marriage*, an unidentified couple kneel at the prie-dieu while a priest conducts a simple service in the presence of a few lay witnesses and ecclesiastical attendants. Giampietro Zanotti and Luigi Crespi, Giuseppe Maria's earliest biographers, both mention the "fact" that the groom "appears to be about eighty years old, while the wife did not seem older than fourteen," an assertion that has been often repeated in scholarly literature that attempts to characterize the series as comic burlesques.[12] The younger Crespi could never have seen the paintings as an adult, and he relies on Zanotti's account, itself written more than thirty-five years after he had seen the paintings, if indeed he ever did. The age of the nuptial couple is uncertain, although it is safe to describe the man as middle-aged. Far from being an adolescent, the bride seems much older, an observation made more convincing by close scrutiny of the painting in the Gemäldegalerie in Dresden.

In *Baptism*, *Communion*, and *Marriage*, women are crucial participants, and the domestic naturalism of the style gives increased authority to their presence. This is not only an indication of the emphasis on religion in everyday life, in which women necessarily participate alongside men, but it is also a statement about ecclesiastical reforms of the early Settecento. Starting with Pope Clement XI (reigned 1700–1721), a renewed sense of the Church's mission at the familial and parochial level was zealously promoted. The role of women in catechistic instruction in the home and in setting the example of piety and attendance at Mass was both recognized and celebrated. Crespi's pictures are, in part, an acknowledgment of the fact.

In a similar manner, ecclesiastical hagiography in the eighteenth century redefined the role of religious women in the culture of Catholic Enlightenment. One of the major progressive critiques of Church activities and governance was that contemplative religious orders, male and female, had little part to play in the rational world of social utility increasingly demanded of all traditional institutions, including the Catholic monarchies. Contemplative orders, it was widely believed, performed few valuable social roles. Rather, they owned an enormous amount of untaxed land and other property acquired through centuries of mortmain and had little interest in deploying innovative technologies to promote greater agricultural productivity on their vast holdings. Such underdeveloped property was a major whipping boy for the physiocrats, among other enlightened progressives. The large number of people in the contemplative orders was also faulted for reducing the labor force and what we would today call the social talent pool. It is true that many quasi-clerical and even lay incomes ultimately derived from Church property administered by the contemplative orders; indeed, some of Rome's harshest critics were supported by ecclesiastical pensions. But the contemplatives were castigated by many, both inside and outside the Catholic Church, as parasites on the body politic. While unevenly successful in making reform work, the papacy did much to respond to such criticism because it believed it was in the Church's best interests to do so. The suppression of some unproductive houses of contemplatives and a relatively ardent promotion of socially useful orders, both established and new, were an important element of the Roman entry into the Age of Reason. The papacy's efforts were no more or less successful than those of the supposedly more enlightened Catholic countries that attempted to embrace reason and reform.[13]

Such rationalistic disapprobation was not brought to bear on the nursing and teaching orders. These institutions were frequently composed of small groups of nuns, above all tertiaries, who lived in the world and who worked sedulously for its amelioration. Even with the anticlerical initiatives of the French Revolution, the service orders were preserved much longer than the contemplative ones because they performed vital social functions.[14] There were many female and male teaching and nursing orders, and others who gave instruction to children, but as the century progressed such activities became more closely associated with women. Public preaching, elite education, and missionary work, on the other hand, became even more masculinized than they had been in the past. Although works of charity, instruction, and self-sacrifice had always been characteristic of the religious life, at least in theory, there is a remarkable pattern in eighteenth-century canonizations of saints that underscores the Church's greater valuing of the socially engaged religious orders. Pierre Subleyras' *Saint Camillo de Lellis Saving the Sick of the Hospital of Spirito Santo from the Floodwaters of the Tiber* commemorates the canonization of the founder of a major Catholic nursing order, the Lellians, as I have already observed. Saint Camillo, represented by Subleyras as a common laborer, became a prototype for the socially conscious Catholic Enlightenment saint.

It may reasonably be argued that the Church's more direct engagement with socially useful religious orders and active campaigns against certain forms of popular mysticism and "superstition" are seen with special clarity in the causes of female saints selected for canonization in the middle decades of the eighteenth century. The Settecento papacy actively discouraged such activities as flagellant processions and the ringing of church bells as protection against natural disasters, among many other popular practices. Trials for witchcraft, sorcery, and magic, never commonplace in Italy, largely died out all over the Catholic world, encouraged by resistance to such excesses coming from Rome. The attempt to rationalize faith while retaining its revelatory mystique was a chief goal of the innumerable preaching and teaching missions supported by the popes.[15] I would like to document this trend more thoroughly and in the context of the feminine by examining the cases of three women saints created at the zenith of the papacy's attempts to engage early Enlightenment critique.

The holy mystics and conventual contemplatives favored as candidates for sainthood during the sixteenth and seventeenth centuries, such as Teresa of Avila, were in large part replaced in the eighteenth century by the nurses, teachers, and ministers to the poor, although some of these women were also mystics.[16] In paintings created on the occasion of their beatifications and canonizations, one clearly sees how the utilitarian ideas about female sanctity and religious vocation permeated sacred art, emphasizing their socially beneficial activities while often downplaying their mystical transports and visions. Like Crespi's *Seven Sacraments*, artistic style is brought to bear to create a contemporary vision of the holy largely devoid of Baroque histrionics. Even in paintings of mystic vision and transport, there is sometimes tangible artistic unease. Works of art, however, became one of the primary instruments for the dissemination of the new ideas.

The Franciscan Tertiary Margaret of Cortona (1247–1297) was canonized by Pope Benedict XIII (reigned 1724–1730) in 1728, an event celebrated by the dedication of a chapel in the prominent Roman church of Santa Maria in Ara Coeli that was decorated with two large paintings of stories from the saint's life by Marco Benefial (1684–1764).[17] *St. Margaret of Cortona Discovering the Body of Her Lover* (Figure 13.3), one of the lateral altarpieces in the chapel, tells the story of how the Tuscan woman was led by her dog to where her murdered lover lay covered by brush. This shocking discovery inspired Margaret to reform her life and enter a Franciscan house, where she dedicated herself to reclaiming fallen women and nursing the indigent. Living with her illegitimate son in abject poverty and giving most of the alms and food she received to the needy, Margaret daily counseled young women about the perils of a libertine life. As a Franciscan Tertiary she founded the Poverelle, an order of nuns who established in Cortona the Ospedale di Santa Maria della Misericordia where the sisters nursed the sick. The funds for this hospital and others like it were raised by Margaret's appeals to the affluent businessmen of Cortona and nearby Italian towns.

What is aesthetically remarkable about Benefial's painting is the genrelike quality of the sacred scene, and in this feature it resembles the *Sacraments* by Giuseppe Maria Crespi.[18] As a *storiella* of a new saint, Baroque tradition would have suggested a more "decorous" presentation, but Benefial has presented us with an imminently natural tableau. Margaret's dress is very elegant because her aristocratic lover was rich. It is also historically accurate. Most notable, however, is the fact that there are no indications of the miraculous, at least in the Baroque sense. Even *Last Communion of Saint Margaret* (Figure 13.4) is visualized in an absolutely humble and ordinary way. Death comes to the saint in a spartan bedroom, and the palette is notably subdued and is composed almost exclusively of earth colors. No attempt at painterly bravura has been made, and only the presence of the priest and his few attendants suggests the last rites. There is an immediacy of belief that bridges the gap between the spectator and the spectacle that is not reliant on supernatural intervention. The painting encourages the faithful, above all those of the humbler classes, to identify with the saint as someone like them

Figure 13.3 Marco Benefial, *Saint Margaret of Cortona Discovering the Body of Her Lover*, 1729 (oil on canvas). Rome: Church of Santa Maria in Ara Coeli. Photo: author.

Figure 13.4 Marco Benefial, *Last Communion of Saint Margaret of Cortona*, 1729 (oil on canvas). Rome: Church of Santa Maria in Ara Coeli. Photo: author.

in earthly circumstances but who could also serve as a model of holiness and as a paradigm of the good death.

Eight years after the canonization of the nurse to the poor Margaret of Cortona, Pope Clement XII (reigned 1730–1740) declared Giuliana Falconieri (1270–1341) a saint. Giuliana was the founder of the Servite Tertiaries, a female order devoted primarily to the care of the sick, above all to plague victims, and to similar works of mercy and charity. In many ways Falconieri was an even better poster saint for the Catholic Enlightenment than Margaret of Cortona because she came from a noble Florentine family and gave up rank and wealth to serve the less fortunate. When one considers the elitist nature of both the broader Enlightenment and its Catholic counterpart—social and intellectual phenomena that assumed change could only be generated from above—the foregrounding of a woman like Giuliana Falconieri is highly logical.

To celebrate her canonization, the Falconieri family, who ardently campaigned for her sanctification, commissioned the prominent Roman painter Pier Leone Ghezzi (1674–1755) to execute an altarpiece for the new church of Santa Maria dell'Orazione e Morte depicting Giuliana's ordination as a nun (Figure 13.5).[19] The taking of the veil ceremony is conducted by San Filippo Benizi (1200–1310) in the Florentine church of SS. Annunziata in 1290 and is presented as a historical high-life genre scene. One of Giuliana's relatives, Sant'Alessio Falconieri, observes the ceremony in the upper right area of the composition. Ghezzi depicts him as a sturdy old man who was ninety at the time. The young woman, her hair recently shorn, kneels to receive the habit surrounded by friends and family in historically accurate dress. Ghezzi pays almost obsessive attention to details of costume accessories, textures of fabrics, and the fall of drapery. The only hint at the supernatural is the subtle halo around both saints' heads. In the past, representations of important saints (not necessarily the ones recently canonized) almost always included the ubiquitous cherubini, dazzling rays of celestial light, and sometimes even Christ or Mary smiling benignly onto the scene from a conveniently placed cloud. In the new sacred genre context, however, Ghezzi shows us a straightforward ecclesiastical ceremony that was commonplace in both the thirteenth and the eighteenth centuries. If we did not know which young lady of privilege was actually taking the veil, we would be hard pressed to guess.

Another female saint renowned for nursing and especially for her tender treatment of plague victims was Saint Catherine Fieschi Adorno of Genoa (1447–1510). She was canonized by Clement XII in 1737, having been beatified in 1675 by Clement X (reigned 1670–1676). Although a noted contemplative and mystic, Catherine was even more celebrated as a nurse in the city hospital of Genoa, an institution that was often filled with plague sufferers because of the city's position as a major international port. Memories of the catastrophic plague at Marseille in 1720 were still quite fresh in the minds of many when Catherine was canonized. A victim of domestic abuse and a noblewoman whose husband squandered her fortune, Catherine embraced the religious life and combined contemplation with keen competence in practical affairs. She eventually converted her wayward spouse to the cause of social melioration, and he joined her in the nursing vocation. He served

Figure 13.5 Pier Leone Ghezzi, *Saint Giuliana Falconieri Taking the Veil*, 1737 (oil on canvas). Rome: Church of Santa Maria dell'Orazione e Morte. Photo: author.

as her assistant when she became director of the Genoa plague hospital. Like Giuliana Falconieri, Catherine Fieschi Adorno was patrician and devoted her life to improving the lot of the sick and poor, a socially useful role for the privileged classes much encouraged by the Settecento papacy. Catherine of Genoa is still the patron saint of Italian hospitals.

One of the images created to celebrate the canonization of Catherine of Genoa is Marco Benefial's magnificent *Vision of Saint Catherine Fieschi Adorno* (Figure 13.6) of 1737.[20] Unlike the canonization paintings previously discussed, Benefial's picture narrates a mystical incident in Catherine's life in which she, during a visit to the convent where her sister was abbess, had a vision of the crucified Christ carrying his cross and bleeding profusely onto the floor. The visionary part of the picture is replete with the Baroque accessories typical of such mystical apparitions, but it should also be noted that the saint is rendered in carefully observed historical dress, kneeling on a convincingly painted cushion next to a footstool on which she has placed her cloak and missal. Through the curtain we see an ordinary feminine domestic space depicted in a highly naturalistic manner. The other women are unaware of the miracle transpiring in the next room. It is unclear who decided to illustrate this particular story from the saint's hagiography, which

Figure 13.6 Marco Benefial, *Vision of Saint Catherine Fieschi Adorno*, 1737 (oil on canvas). Rome: Palazzo Corsini. Photo: Alinari/Art Resource.

was the best known of her visions, but Benefial's juxtaposition of the miraculous with the everyday is noteworthy and visualizes Catherine's position as a contemplative visionary deeply engaged with socially useful works of charity and mercy. This image also demonstrates the strength of tradition in mystical imagery. Indeed, some stories simply could not be told without reference to the Baroque miraculous.

These three female saints and the images their sanctification engendered are important markers of a radically changed attitude toward the Church's role in revealed religion and modern society and also toward artistic depictions of sacred women in the eighteenth century. Moreover, they are typical of a much wider range of religious imagery in the middle decades of the Settecento. Stressing service to the underclass in the form of nursing, counseling, and teaching rather than the mystical experience of God through individualistic revelation as the sole qualities for sainthood, the Church revisited its traditional views as part of an enlightened response to new social realities. This is not to say that prayer, mystic vision, and divine union were no longer important; rather, such manifestations of holiness were no longer sufficient justificatory qualities for sainthood, above all for women.

Artists, as members of society, and patrons, as representatives of the privileged classes, were not slow to adapt to altered circumstances. In emphasizing good works like nursing and teaching as all but prerequisite for canonization, and in promoting a more reality-based approach in sacred imagery, women could not but benefit, both in terms of their more prominent role in ecclesiastical reform and in the conspicuous position they occupy in much religious art. The traditional womanly function of selfless service to family and society had always been of vital importance in Catholic culture, but it had only rarely been conspicuously acknowledged by the Church before the Catholic Enlightenment. As the public (however it may be defined) for art expanded during the Enlightenment, Baroque theatrics seemed increasingly dated and irrational. Religion had to be made relevant to the modern world, and a major current in Roman painting answered the call.

Notes

Notes to Introduction

1. Germaine de Staël, *Corinne, or Italy*, ed. and trans. Sylvia Raphael (Oxford: Oxford University Press, 1998), p. 99.

2. Abbé Gabriel-François Coyer, *Voyage d'Italie et de Hollande* (Paris, 1775), vol. 1, p. 4.

3. Hester Lynch Thrale Piozzi, *Observations and Reflections Made in the Course of a Journey Through France, Italy, and Germany*, ed. Herbert Barrows (Ann Arbor: University of Michigan Press, 1967), p. 86.

4. James Boswell, *Life of Johnson*, as quoted in Brian Moloney, *Florence and England: Essays on Cultural Relations in the Second Half of the Eighteenth Century* (Florence: Olschki, 1969), p. 5. On women and travel, see Brian Dolan, *Ladies of the Grand Tour: British Women in Pursuit of Enlightenment and Adventure in Eighteenth-Century Europe* (New York: HarperCollins, 2001).

5. Boswell, *Boswell on the Grand Tour: Italy, Corsica, and France 1765–1766*, ed. Frank Brady and Frederick A. Pottle (New York: McGraw-Hill, 1955), p. 28 (10 January 1765).

6. Tobias Smollett, *Travels through France and Italy*, ed. Thomas Seccumbe (Oxford: Oxford University Press, 1907), p. 231 (28 January 1765).

7. Boswell, *Boswell on the Grand Tour*, p. 81 (11 May 1765).

8. Ann Radcliffe, *The Italian*, ed. Robert Miles (London: Penguin, 2000), p. 5.

9. Robert Casillo, *The Empire of Stereotypes: Germaine de Staël and the Idea of Italy* (London: Palgrave Macmillan, 2006).

10. This issue is highlighted in Fabio Tongiorgi, "La Toscana dei viaggiatori: una tappa del *Grand Tour*," in Lucia Tongiorgi Tomasi, Alessandro Tosi, and Fabio Tongiorgi, *La Toscana descritta. Incisori e viaggiatori del '700* (Pisa: Pacini Editore, 1990), pp. 79–83.

11. Charles Burney, *An Eighteenth-Century Musical Tour in France and Italy*, ed. Percy A. Scholes (Oxford: Oxford University Press, 1959), pp. 147, 188.

12. Lady Anne Miller, *Letters from Italy* (Dublin, 1776), vol. 1, p. 205 (9 November 1770).

13. Readers who want to understand the effect of the Grand Tour on Italy should begin with Franco Venturi, "L'Italia fuori d'Italia," in *Storia d'Italia*, vol. 3: *Dal primo Settecento all'Unità* (Turin: Einaudi, 1973), pp. 985–1481, esp. pp. 985–1120; Cesare de Seta, *L'Italia del Grand Tour. Da Montaigne a Goethe* (Naples: Electa Napoli, 1992); Andrew Wilton and Ilaria Bignamini, eds., *The Grand Tour: The Lure of Italy in the Eighteenth Century* (London: Tate Gallery, 1996); Chloe Chard, *Pleasure and Guilt on the Grand Tour: Travel Writing and Imaginative Geography 1600–1830* (Manchester, U.K.: Manchester University Press, 1999); Clare Hornsby, ed., *The Impact of Italy: The Grand Tour and Beyond* (London: The British School at Rome, 2000); and Mirella Agorni, *Translating Italy for the Eighteenth Century: British Women, Translation and Travel Writing (1739–1797)* (Manchester, U.K.: St. Jerome Publishing, 2002). For a review of recent scholarship in this area, see Wendy Wassyng Roworth, "Rethinking Eighteenth-Century Rome," *Art Bulletin* 83 (2001), 135–144; John-Wilton Ely's review essay of fourteen recent books on the Grand Tour "'Classic Ground': Britain, Italy, and the Grand Tour," *Eighteenth-Century Life* 28:1 (Winter, 2004), 136–165; and Barbara Ann Naddeo, "Cultural Capitals and Cosmopolitanism in Eighteenth-Century Italy: The Historiography of Italy on the Grand Tour," *Journal of Modern Italian Studies* 10 (2005), 183–195.

14. Giuseppe Baretti, *An Account of the Manners and Customs of Italy; with Observations on the Mistakes of Some Travellers, with Regard to That Country* (London, 1768), vol. 1, pp. 28, 56. Baretti is a good example of the kind of figure described in Shearer West, ed., *Italian Culture in Northern Europe in the Eighteenth Century* (Cambridge, U.K.: Cambridge University Press, 1999), e.g. pp. 122–123. For a detailed account of his life, see Norbert Jonard, *Giuseppe Baretti (1719–1789): l'homme et l'oeuvre* (Clermont-Ferrand: G. de Bussac, 1963); Charles Marie Franzaro, *Baretti: gentiluomo piemontese a Londra* (Arpignana: Talone, 1965).

15. On the reputation of Italians, see Joseph Luzzi, "Italy without Italians: Literary Origins of a Romantic Myth," *Modern Language Notes* 117 (2002), 48-83; and Andrew M. Canepa, "From Degenerate Scoundrel to Noble Savage: Italian Stereotypes in Eighteenth-Century British Travel Literature," *English Miscellany* 22 (1971), 107–146.

16. On foreign artists in Italy, see Corlette Rossiter Walker, ed., *The Anglo-American Artist in Italy 1750–1820* (Santa Barbara, CA: University Arts Museum, 1982); John Ingamells, comp., *A Dictionary of British and Irish Travellers in Italy, 1701–1800, compiled from the Brinsley Ford Archive* (New Haven: Yale Univ. for the Paul Mellon Centre for Studies in British Art, 1997), Appendix 5, pp. 1061–1065; Nicola Figgis, "Irish Portrait and Subject Painters in Rome 1750–1800," *Irish Arts Review Yearbook*, 1988; Nancy L. Pressly, *The Fuseli Circle in Rome, Early Romantic Art of the 1770s* (New Haven: Yale Center for British Art, 1979); and many sources on individual artists.

17. Mary Wortley Montagu, *The Complete Letters of Lady Mary Wortley Montagu*, ed. Robert Halsband (Oxford: Clarendon Press, 1965–67), vol. 2, p. 177 (to Lady Pomfret, March 1740). See also Bruce Redford, *Venice and the Grand Tour* (New Haven: Yale University Press, 1996), p. 16.

18. Mary Wortley Montagu, *Selected Letters*, pp. 392–393 (Mary Wortley Montagu to Lady Bute, 10 October 1753).

19. See Marta Cavazza's Chapter 11 in this volume for further information on Agnesi.

20. Madame [Marie-Anne] du Boccage, *Letters Concerning England, Holland, and Italy* (London, 1770), vol. 1, p. 163.

21. Ibid., vol. 2, p. 114. See Françoise Waquet, *Le modèle français et l'Italie savante: conscience de soi et perception de l'autre dans la République des lettres, 1660–1750* (Paris: Ecole française de Rome, 1989).

22. Thomas Nugent, *The Grand Tour: or, a Journey through the Netherlands, Germany, Italy, and France*, 2nd ed. (London, 1778), vol. 3, p. 36. The larger political context for such statements is explored in Anthony Pagden, *Lords of All the World: Ideologies of Empire in Spain, Britain and France c. 1500–c. 1800* (New Haven: Yale University Press, 1995).

23. Marquis de Sade, *Voyage d'Italie*, ed. Maurice Lever (Paris: Fayard, 1995), p. 70.

24. Nelson Moe's *The View from Vesuvius: Italian Culture and the Southern Question* (Berkeley: University of California Press, 2002) offers a good model of how to combine these perceptions of Italy in this period. See also Larry Wolff, *Venice and the Slavs: The Discovery of Dalmatia in the Age of Enlightenment* (Stanford: Stanford University Press, 2001).

25. Ilaria Bignamini, "The Grand Tour: Open Issues," in Wilton and Bignamini, *The Grand Tour*, p. 33. This point is also made in West, *Italian Culture in Northern Europe*, esp. pp. 1–19.

26. The idea of exploring other narratives of the eighteenth century is also raised in West, ed., *Italian Culture in Northern Europe*, p. 17.

27. For an overall bibliography on women and gender in the eighteenth century as well as examples of recent work, see Sarah Knott and Barbara Taylor, eds., *Women, Gender and Enlightenment* (London: Palgrave, 2005). Many discussions of marriage and family in this period take works such as Lawrence Stone's *The Family, Sex, and Marriage in England 1500–1800* (London: Weidenfeld and Nicolson, 1977) as a point of departure, even while being highly critical of its findings. See also Randolph Trumbach, *The Rise of the Egalitarian Family: Aristocratic Kinship and Domestic Relations in Eighteenth-Century England* (New York: Academic Press, 1978); Lynn Hunt, *The Family Romance of the French Revolution* (Berkeley: University of California Press, 1992); and Suzanne Desan, *The Family on Trial in Revolutionary France* (Berkeley: University of California Press, 2004).

28. Recent work on eighteenth-century sexuality includes Robert Purks Maccubbin, ed., *`Tis Nature's Fault: Unauthorized Sexuality during the Enlightenment* (Cambridge, U.K.: Cambridge University Press, 1985); George Rousseau and Roy Porter, eds., *Sexual Underworlds of the Enlightenment* (Chapel Hill: University of North Carolina Press, 1988); Randolph Trumbach, *Sex and the Gender Revolution* (Chicago: University of Chicago Press, 1998); Thomas Laqueur, *Solitary Sex: A Cultural History of Masturbation* (New York: Zone Books, 2003); Karen Harvey,

Reading Sex in the Eighteenth Century: Bodies and Gender in English Erotic Culture (Cambridge, U.K.: Cambridge University Press, 2004); and Peter Cryle and Lisa O'Connell, eds., *Libertine Enlightenment: Sex, Liberty, and License in the Eighteenth Century* (New York: Palgrave, 2004). For an interesting example of a recent contribution to this subject that uses Italian materials, see Larry Wolff, "'Depraved Inclinations': Libertines and Children in Casanova's Venice," *Eighteenth-Century Studies* 38 (2005), 417–440.

29. Readers interested in the Italian scholarship in this field should begin with Anna Maria Mambelli, *Il Settecento è donna: indagine sulla condizione femminile* (Ravenna: Edizioni del Girasole, 1985); Luciano Guerci, *La discussione sulla donna nell'Italia del Settecento: aspetti e problemi* (Turin: Tirrenia, 1987); idem, *La sposa obbediente: donna e matrimonio nella discussione dell'Italia del Settecento* (Turin: Tirrenia, 1988); Adriana Chemello and Luisa Ricaldone, *Geografie e genealogie letterarie. Erudite, biografe, croniste, narratrici, épistolières, utopiste tra Settecento e Ottocento* (Padua: Il Poligrafo, 2000); Marzio Barbagli, *Sotto lo stesso tetto. Mutamenti della famiglia in Italia dal XV al XX secolo*, 2nd ed. (Bologna: Il Mulino, 2000), pp. 325–371; and three volumes edited by Silvana Seidel Menchi and Diego Quaglioni which contain interesting case studies of eighteenth-century marriage: *Coniugi nemici: la separazione in Italia dal XII al XVIII secolo* (Bologna: Il Mulino, 2000); *Matrimoni in dubbio: unioni controverse e nozze clandestine in Italia dal XIV al XVIII secolo* (Bologna: Il Mulino, 2001); and *Trasgressioni: seduzione, concubinato, adulterio, bigamia: (XIV–XVIII secolo)* (Bologna: Il Mulino, 2004). Recent works by contributors to this volume have begun to develop an account in English; see Rebecca Messbarger, *The Century of Women: Representations of Women in Eighteenth-Century Italian Public Discourse* (Toronto: University of Toronto Press, 2002); Susan Dalton, *Engendering the Republic of Letters: Reconnecting Public and Private Spheres in Eighteenth-Century Europe* (Montreal: McGill-Queens University Press, 2003); Catherine M. Sama, ed. and trans., *Selected Writings of an Eighteenth-Century Venetian Woman of Letters* (Chicago: University of Chicago Press, 2003); and Rebecca Messbarger and Paula Findlen, eds. and trans., *The Contest for Knowledge: Debates over Women's Learning in Eighteenth-Century Italy* (Chicago: University of Chicago Press, 2005). Further bibliography will be cited throughout this volume.

30. In addition to the chapter by Roberto Bizzocchi in this volume, see Luigi Valmaggi, *I cicisbei. Contributo alla storia del costume italiano nel secolo XVIII*, ed. Luigi Piccioni (Turin: Giovanni Chiantore, 1927); and Bizocchi's new book, which appeared after this volume was in press: *Cicisbei. Morale privata e identità nazionale in Italia* (Rome: Laterza, 2008). Roger Freitas and Martha Feldman both discuss castrati in this volume; see also Patrick Barbier, *The World of the Castrati: The History of an Extraordinary Operatic Phenomenon*, trans. Margaret Crosland (London: Souvenir Press, 1996). On sexuality, masculinity, and the Grand Tour, see Redford, *Venice and the Grand Tour*; Chard, *Pleasure and Guilt*; and especially Chard, "Effeminacy, Pleasure, and the Classical Body," in *Femininity and Masculinity in Eighteenth-Century Art and Culture*, ed. Gill Perry and Michael Rossington (Manchester: Manchester University Press, 1994), pp. 142–161.

31. For the contrasting trajectories of the Italian princely families, see Harold Acton, *The Last Medici*, 4th ed. (London: Thames and Hudson, 1980); and Geoffrey Symcox, *Victor Amadeus II: Absolutism in the Savoyard State 1675–1730* (Berkeley: University of California Press, 1983).

32. Acton, *The Bourbons of Naples (1734–1825)*, rev. ed. (London: Prion Books, 1998).

33. Mirella Mafrici, *Fascino e potere di una regina: Elisabetta Farnese sulla scena europea (1715–1759)* (Cava de' Tirreni: Avagliano, 1999); and Edward Armstrong, *Elisabeth Farnese, "The Termagant of Spain"* (London: Longman, Green, 1892).

34. [Certain banished Marquis], *Memoirs of Elizabeth Farnesio, the Present Queen Dowager of Spain . . . Translated from a Spanish Manuscript* (London, 1746), pp. 24, 94, 80.

35. Owen Chadwick, *The Popes and European Revolution* (Oxford: Clarendon Press, 1981); and Hanns Gross, *Rome in the Age of Enlightenment: The Post-Tridentine Syndrome and the Ancien Regime* (Cambridge, U.K.: Cambridge University Press, 1990).

36. Christopher Johns, *Papal Art and Cultural Politics: The Rome of Clement XI* (Cambridge, U.K.: Cambridge University Press, 1993), p. 5. See also Jeffrey Collins, *Papacy and Politics in Eighteenth-Century Rome: Pius VI and the Arts* (Cambridge, U.K.: Cambridge University Press, 2004).

37. See Mario Rosa, ed., *Cattolicismo e lumi nel Settecento italiano* (Rome: Herder, 1981); and idem, *Settecento religioso: politica della religione e ragione del cuore* (Venice: Marsilio Editore, 1999) as well as the work of Franco Venturi mentioned below. This subject lies at the heart of Johns' contribution to this volume.

38. Franco Venturi, *Settecento riformatori* (Turin: Einaudi, 1969–1990), 5 vols. Only three volumes have been translated so far: *The First Crisis*, trans. R. Burr Litchfield (Princeton: Princeton University Press, 1989); *The End of the Old Regime in Europe, 1768–1776*, trans. R. Burr Litchfield (Princeton: Princeton University Press, 1989); and *The End of the Old Regime in Europe, 1776–1789*, trans. R. Burr Litchfield (Princeton: Princeton University Press, 1991). See also his *Utopia and Reform in the Enlightenment* (Cambridge, U.K.: Cambridge University Press, 1971) and *Italy and the Enlightenment*, trans. Susan Corsi (London: Longman, 1972). For a critical appraisal of work on the Italian Enlightenment, see John Robertson, "Franco Venturi's Enlightenment," *Past and Present* 137 (1992), 183–206; and Marcello Verga, "Le XVIIIe siècle en Italie: le "Settecento" réformateur?" *Revue d'histoire moderne et contemporaine* 45 (1998), 89–116.

39. West, ed., *Italian Culture in Northern Europe*.

40. Implicitly, Spain and Portugal have also had secondary status in general accounts of the eighteenth century, though new scholarship on Iberia in this period is actively seeking to revise this standard interpretation. See, for example, Theresa Smith, *The Emerging Female Citizen: Gender and Enlightenment in Spain* (Berkeley: University of California Press, 2006).

41. For examples of recent studies of Goldoni that are directly relevant to this volume, see Maggie Günsberg, *Playing with Gender: The Comedies of Goldoni*

(Leeds, U.K.: Northern Universities Press, 2001); and Giuseppina Scognamiglio, *Ritratti di donna nel teatro di Carlo Goldoni* (Naples: Edizioni Scientifiche Italiane, 2002). The classic discussion of this subject can be found in the studies of Franco Fido such as his *Nuova guida a Goldoni. Teatro e società nel Settecento* (Turin: Einaudi, 2000), pp. 207–244.

42. On this subject, see especially Johns, *Papal Art*; and idem, *Antonio Canova and the Politics of Patronage in Revolutionary and Napoleonic Europe* (Berkeley: University of California Press, 1998). In addition to the exhibition catalogue of Wilton and Bignamini cited in note 13, there have been a number of interesting exhibits and publications in the past two decades highlighting the artistic culture of eighteenth-century Italy. See *The Golden Age of Naples: Art and Civilization Under the Bourbons, 1734–1805* (Detroit: Detroit Institute of Arts, 1981); Jane Martineau and Andrew Robison, eds., *The Glory of Venice: Art in the Eighteenth Century* (New Haven: Yale University Press, 1994); Edgar Peters Bowron and Joseph J. Rishel, eds., *Art in Rome in the Eighteenth Century* (London: Merrell, 2000); *Il Neoclassicismo in Italia da Tiepolo a Canova* (Milan: Palazzo Reale, 2002); Jeffrey Collins, *Papacy and Politics in Eighteenth-Century Rome: Pius VI and the Arts* (Cambridge University Press, 2004); and *Il Settecento a Roma* (Rome: Palazzo Venezia, 2005–06).

43. A good starting point on this subject is Daniel Heartz, *Music in European Capitals: The Galant Style, 1720–1780* (New York: Norton, 2003). See also Reinhard Strohm, *Dramma per musica: Italian Opera Seria of the Eighteenth Century* (New Haven: Yale University Press, 1997); idem, ed., *The Eighteenth-Century Diaspora of Italian Music and Musicians* (Turnhout: Brepols, 2000); and Martha Feldman, *Opera and Sovereignty: Transforming Myths in Eighteenth-Century Italy* (Chicago: University of Chicago Press, 2007). Thanks to Feldman for her bibliographic suggestions.

44. The most general studies of eighteenth-century Italian science are Vincenzo Ferrone, *The Intellectual Roots of the Italian Enlightenment: Newtonian Science, Religion, and Politics in the Early Eighteenth Century*, trans. Sue Brotherton (Atlantic Highlands, NJ: Humanities Press, 1995); Marta Cavazza, *Settecento inquieto: alle origini dell'Istituto delle Scienze di Bologna* (Bologna: Il Mulino, 1990); Brendan Dooley, *Science, Politics, and Society in Eighteenth-Century Italy: The "Giornale de' letterati d'Italia" and Its World* (New York: Garland, 1991); and Paola Bertucci, *Viaggio nel paese delle meraviglie. Scienza e curiosità nell'Italia del Settecento* (Turin: Bollati Boringhieri, 2007). For specific studies of individual figures, see, for example, John Stoye, *Marsigli's Europe: The Life and Times of Luigi Ferdinando Marsigli, Soldier and Virtuoso* (New Haven: Yale University Press, 1994); and Giuliano Pancaldi, *Volta: Science and Culture in the Age of Enlightenment* (Princeton: Princeton University Press, 2003). The bibliography on the role of women scientists in eighteenth-century Italy is cited extensively in the contributions by Marta Cavazza and Rebecca Messbarger (Chapters 10 and 11) in this volume.

45. Recent surveys of Italian history that discuss the eighteenth century with extensive bibliography to guide further reading include Jean Delumeau, *L'Italie de Botticelli à Bonaparte* (Paris: A. Colin, 1974); Stuart Woolf, *A History of Italy 1700–1860* (London: Methuen, 1979); Giuseppe Armani et al., *Storia della società italiana,*

vol. 12: *Il secolo dei lumi e delle riforme* (Milan: Teti Editore, 1989); Spencer Di Scala, *Italy from Revolution to Republic: 1700 to the Present* (Boulder, CO: Westview Press, 1995); Gregory Hanlon, *Early Modern Italy 1550–1800* (London: St. Martin's Press, 2000); and John Marino, ed., *Early Modern Italy: 1550–1796* (Oxford: Oxford University Press, 2002). The important work of Eric Cochrane played a foundational role in fostering interest in aspects of Italy's eighteenth century. See especially his *Tradition and Enlightenment in the Tuscan Academies 1690–1800* (Chicago: University of Chicago Press, 1961); and idem, *Florence in the Forgotten Centuries 1527–1800* (Chicago: University of Chicago Press, 1973).

46. In addition to the work of Venturi, other contributions to the study of eighteenth-century Italy available in translation include Maurice Vaussard, *Daily Life in Eighteenth-Century Italy*, trans. Michael Heron (London: George Allen and Unwin, 1962); Maurice Andrieux, *Daily Life in Papal Rome in the Eighteenth Century*, trans. Mary Fitton (New York: Macmillan, 1969); Dino Carpanetto and Giuseppe Ricuperati, *Italy in the Age of Reason 1685–1789*, trans. Caroline Higgitt (London: Longman, 1987); Vincenzo Ferrone, *The Intellectual Roots of the Italian Enlightenment: Newtonian Science, Religion, and Politics in the Early Eighteenth Century*, trans. Sue Brotherton (Atlantic Highlands, NJ: Humanities Press, 1995); Girolamo Imbruglia, ed., *Naples in the Eighteenth Century: The Birth and Death of a Nation State* (Cambridge, U.K.: Cambridge University Press, 2000); and Anna Maria Rao, "Enlightenment and Reform," in Marino, ed., *Early Modern Italy*, pp. 229–252.

47. The most recent effort to dissect this myth is Calogero Farinella, "La 'nobile servitù.' Donne e cicisbei nel salotto Genovese del Settecento," in *Salotti e ruolo femminile in Italia*, ed. Maria Luisa Betri and Elena Brambilla (Venice: Marsilio, 2004), pp. 97–123.

48. Mario Battaglini, ed., *Eleonora Fonseca Pimentel: il fascino di una donna impegnata fra letteratura e rivoluzione* (Naples: G. Procaccini, 1997); and Elena Urgnani, *La vicenda letteraria e politica di Eleonora de Fonseca Pimentel* (Naples: La città del sole: Istituto italiano per gli studi filosofici, 1998). Fonseca Pimentel is also the protagonist of an interesting historical novel: Enzo Striano, *Il resto di niente*, 2nd ed. (Milan: Rizzoli, 1998).

49. Amadeo Quondam, "L'istituzione Arcadia: sociologia e ideologia di un'accademia," *Quaderni storici* 23 (1973), 389–438; Elisabetta Graziosi, "Arcadia femminile: presenze e modelli," *Filologia e critica* 17 (1992), 321–358; and Susan M. Dixon, *Between the Real and the Ideal: The Accademia degli Arcadi and Its Garden in Eighteenth-Century Rome* (Newark: University of Delaware Press, 2006).

50. Muratori, *Primi disegni per la repubblica letteraria* (1703); Brendan Dooley, *Science, Politics, and Society in Eighteenth-Century Italy: The Giornale de' letterati d'Italia and Its World* (New York: Garland, 1991).

51. See, for example, Massimo Viglione, *Le insorgenze: rivoluzione e controrivoluzione in Italia, 1792–1815* (Milan: Ares, 1999); Carlo Capra, *L'età rivoluzionaria e napoleonica in Italia, 1796–1815* (Turin: Loescher, 1978); and Renzo De Felice, *Italia giacobina* (Naples: Edizioni scientifiche italiane, 1965).

52. Desmond Gregory, *Napoleon's Italy* (Madison, NJ: Fairleigh Dickinson

University Press, 2001); and Michael Broers, *The Napoleonic Empire in Italy: Cultural Imperialism in a European Context* (New York: Palgrave, 2005).

53. Gregory, *Napoleon's Italy*, pp. 180–182.

54. Alexander Drummond, *Travels through Different Cities of Germany, Italy, Greece, and Several Parts of Asia* (London, 1754), p. 42.

55. Baretti, *An Account of the Manners and Customs of Italy*, vol. 1, p. 88.

56. Lady Sydney Morgan, *Italy* (Paris, 1821), vol. 2, p. 20.

57. Burney, *An Eighteenth-Century Musical Tour*, p. 159 (27 August 1770). Marta Cavazza's Chapter 11 provides further information on Bassi.

58. The most detailed study of Piscopia is Francesco Ludovico Maschietto, *Elena Lucrezia Cornaro Piscopia, 1646–1684: prima donna laureata nel mondo* (Padua: Antenore, 1978).

59. Charles de Brosses, *Lettres d'Italie du Président de Brosses* (Paris: Mercure de France, 1986), vol. 1, p. 144. For his descriptions of other women, see pp. 131, 133, 267–268. Long neglected, Grillo Borromeo is now the subject of an interesting monograph: Anna M. Serralunga Bardazza, *Clelia Grillo Borromeo Arese: vicende private e pubbliche virtù di una celebre nobildonna nell'Italia del Settecento* (Biella: Eventi & Proietti, 2005). Cavazza's Chapter 11 in this volume has further information on Agnesi, though readers will also want to consult Massimo Mazzotti, *The World of Maria Gaetana Agnesi, Mathematician of God* (Baltimore: Johns Hopkins University Press, 2007).

60. Guerci, *La discussione sulla donna*; and Messbarger, *The Century of Women*. For a critical commentary and selected translation of the texts emanating from the Ricovrati debate, see Messbarger and Findlen, *The Contest for Knowledge*.

61. Chemello and Ricaldone, *Geografie e genealogie letterarie*, pp. 50–55; Susan M. Dixon, "Women in Arcadia," *Eighteenth-Century Studies* 32 (1999), 372.

62. Pietro Chiari, *Il secolo corrente* (Venice, 1783), as quoted in Messbarger, *The Century of Women*, p. 3. For an interesting comparison of Chiari and Goldoni's views of women, see Luisa Ricaldone, *La scrittura nascosta. Donne di lettere e loro immagini tra Arcadia e Restaurazione* (Paris: Honoré Champion Éditeur, 1996), esp. pp. 55–58, 101.

63. Giuseppe Baretti, *La frusta litteraria* 17 (1764), 461, as quoted in Ricaldone, *La scrittura nascosta*, p. 83.

64. Piozzi, *Observations*, p. 93. See Mirella Agorni's interesting commentary on this passage in *Translating Italy*, pp. 129–130. The Bolognese tradition of learned women is well described in *Alma mater studiorum. La presenza femminile dal XVIII al XX secolo* (Bologna: CLUEB, 1988); and Marta Cavazza, "'Dottrici' e lettrici nell'Università di Bologna nel Settecento," *Annali di storia delle università italiane* 1 (1997), 109–125.

65. See Rebecca Messbarger's Chapter 10 in this volume for more on Morandi Manzolini; Catherine Sama's article for a discussion of Caminer Turra and Carriera; and Wendy Wassyng Roworth's Chapter 6 for more on Kauffman. Faustina Maretti Zappi's life and work might be best understood in relation to the discussion of Roman literary and salon life in the essays by Elisabetta Graziosi and Maria Pia Donato

(Chapters 4 and 2); see also Bruno Maier, *Faustina Maratti Zappi: donna e rimatrice d'Arcadia* (Rome: Orlando, 1954); and Carla Cacciari and Giuliana Zanelli, *Faustina Maratti tra Roma ed Imola: imagine pubblica e tormenti private di una poetessa italiana del Settecento* (Imola: Editrice La Mandragora, 1995).

66. Giacomo Casanova, *History of My Life*, trans. Willard R. Trask (Baltimore: Johns Hopkins University Press, 1966), vol. II, p. 81. On Casanova's role in debates about the nature of women, see Marta Cavazza, "Women's Dialectics, or the Thinking Uterus: An Eighteenth-Century Controversy on Gender and Education," in *The Faces of Nature in Enlightenment Europe*, ed. Lorraine Daston and Gianna Pomata (Berlin: Berliner Wissenschafts-Verlag, 2003), pp. 237–257.

67. Boccage, *Letters*, vol. 2, p. 76 (8 October 1758), pp. 98–99 (25 October 1758).

68. Baretti, *Account*, vol. I, p. 91.

69. On Emma Hamilton, see Lori-Ann Touchette, "William Hamilton's 'Pantomime Mistress': Emma Hamilton and Her Attitudes"; and Chard, "Comedy, Antiquity, the Feminine and the Foreign: Emma Hamilton and Corinne," both in Hornsby, *The Impact of Italy*, pp. 123–169; and Ian Jenkins and Kim Sloan, *Vases and Volcanoes: Sir William Hamilton and His Collection* (London: British Museum, 1996). On Giustiniana Wynne, see Andrea di Robilant, *A Venetian Affair: A True Tale of Forbidden Love in the Eighteenth Century* (New York: Vintage, 2003). Paola Giuli's Chapter 12 in this volume has further information on Corilla Olimpica.

70. Thomas Watkins, *Travels* (London, 1792), vol. 2, p. 61, as quoted in Chard, *Pleasure and Guilt*, p. 92.

71. Brady and Pottle, eds., *Boswell on the Grand Tour*, p. 106 (Boswell to Alexandre Deleyre, 19 July 1765), p. 28 (Boswell to Rousseau, 11 January 1765).

72. Samuel Sharp, *Letters from Italy, Describing the Customs and Manners of That Country, in the Years 1765 and 1766* (London, 1766), pp. 8, 73, 257. For a short summary of the role of the cicisbeo in marriage, see Marzio Barbagli, *Sotto lo stesso tetto*, pp. 331–336.

73. For an early example of this kind of comedy, see Giovan Battista Fagiuoli, *Il cicisbeo sconsolato* (Venice, 1727). At the beginning of the twentieth century, Luigi Gramegna made the cicisbeo into an archetype of the eighteenth century in his fictional *Il cicisbeo. Racconto storico. 1747, la Battaglia dell'Assietta* (Turin: Andrea Viglongo e C. Editori, 2000; 1912).

74. Muratori, *Annali d'Italia* (1707), as quoted in Valmaggi, *I cicisbei*, p. 227. Valmaggi, however, considered it a largely Italian phenomenon (p. 239). For an interesting discussion of the political legacy of cicisbeismo in the early nineteenth century, see Silvana Patriarca "Indolence and Regeneration: Tropes and Tensions of Risorgimento Patriotism," *American Historical Review* 110 (2005), 380–408.

75. Johann Georg Keyssler, *Travels through Germany, Bohemia, Hungary, Italy, and Lorraine* (London, 1756–57), vol. I, p. 373.

76. Baretti, *Account*, vol. I, p. 101. The image of the cicisbeo as a woman's slave can be found in George Edward Ayscough, *Letters from an Officer in the Guards to His Friend in England: Containing Some Accounts of France and Italy* (London, 1738), pp. 99–102.

77. Brady and Pottle, eds., *Boswell on the Grand Tour*, p. 17 (Boswell to Rousseau, 3 October 1765); Sade, *Voyage d'Italie*, pp. 61, 72. Horace Mann complained, in fact, that British travelers were disrupting the system of cicisbeismo by trying to woo Florentine women; Moloney, *Florence and England*, p. 8.

78. W. S. Lewis, Warren Hunting Smith, and George L. Lam, eds., *Horace Walpole's Correspondence with Sir Horace Mann* (New Haven: Yale University Press, 1954–1971), vol. 2, p. 477 (Mann to Walpole, Florence, 21 July 1744). The actual Italian word is *cisbeatoi*, with thanks to Marta Cavazza for pointing this out.

79. Wortley Montagu, *Complete Letters*, vol. 1, p. 429 (28 August 1718).

80. Miller, *Letters from Italy*, vol. 3, pp. 208–210; Hester Lynch Thrale Piozzi, *Thraliana*, vol. 2, p. 622. These passages are also discussed in Barbagli, *Sotto lo stesso tetto*, pp. 333–334. Agorni, *Translating Italy*, pp. 126–127, also notes the favorable views of women travelers.

81. Coyer, *Voyage d'Italie*, p. 96 (27 October 1763).

82. Stael, *Corinne*, p. 97.

83. For an introduction to the work of two artists who have left behind ample documentation of these forms of male sociability, see Edward J. Olszewski, "The New World of Pier Leone Ghezzi," *Art Journal* 43 (1983), 325–330; and Rolf Bagemihl, "Pietro Longhi and Venetian Life," *Metropolitan Museum Journal* 23 (1988), 233–247.

84. Valmaggi, *I cicisbei*, pp. 2–3.

85. Sade, *Voyage d'Italie*, p. 68. See also John Rosselli, "The Castrati as a Professional Group and a Social Phenomenon, 1550–1850," *Acta Musicologica* 60, fasc. 2 (1988), 143–179; and Patrick Barbier, *The World of the Castrati: The History of an Extraordinary Operatic Phenomenon*, trans. Margaret Crosland (London: Souvenir Press, 1996).

86. [Anon.], *The Entertaining Travels and Adventures of Madamoiselle de Richelieu. Cousin to the Present Duke of That Name. Who Made the Tour of Europe, Dressed in Men's Clothes, Attended by Her Maid Lucy as Her Valet de Chambre* (London, 1740?), vol. 1, p. 3; vol. 3, p. 16 (see also pp. 8, 102–104).

87. See Paula Findlen's Chapter 9 in this volume.

88. As quoted in Redford, *Venice and the Grand Tour*, pp. 22, 24. See Amelia Rauser, "Hair, Authenticity, and the Self-Made Macaroni," *Eighteenth-Century Studies*, 38:1 (2004), 101–117.

89. Robert Hitchcock, *The Macaroni*, 2nd ed. (London, 1773), pp. 3, 70.

90. Trumbach, *Sex and the Gender Revolution*.

91. Moe, *The View from Vesuvius*, pp. 23-27. See Montesquieu, *The Spirit of the Laws*, esp. book 14. This image of Italy is also invoked in Felicity Nussbaum, *Torrid Zones: Maternity, Sexuality, and Empire in Eighteenth-Century English Narratives* (Baltimore: Johns Hopkins University Press, 1995).

92. Baretti, *Account*, vol. 1, p. 123; vol. 2, p. 327. On climate, see vol. 1, pp. 89, 296; vol. 2, pp. 257–276.

93. Joan Scott, "Gender: A Useful Category of Historical Analysis," *American Historical Review* 91 (1986), 1053–1075; Judith Butler, *Gender Trouble: Feminism and the Subversion of Identity* (New York: Routledge, 1999).

Notes to Chapter One

1. J. C. L. Sismondo Sismondi, *Storia delle repubbliche italiane dei secoli di mezzo*, tome 16 (Capolago: Tipografia Elvetica, 1832), pp. 197–200. Equally severe judgments were expressed some years later by the poet Ugo Foscolo, exile in London: "Le donne italiane" (1826), in *Opere*, Edizione Nazionale, vol. 12, ed. U. Limentani (Florence: Le Monnier, 1978), pp. 417–469.

2. S. Sharp, *Letters from Italy, describing the customs and manners of that country, in the year 1765, and 1766* (London: Henry Cave, 1766); G. Baretti, *An account of the manners and customs of Italy, with observations on the mistakes of some travellers with regard to that country* (London: Davies, 1768).

3. L. Valmaggi, *I cicisbei. Contributo alla storia del costume italiano nel secolo XVIII*, posthumous work with preface by and ed. L. Piccioni (Turin: Chiantore, 1927) (here are also cited the previous studies spoken of in the text).

4. L. Guerci, *La discussione sulla donna nell'Italia del Settecento. Aspetti e problemi*, (Turin: Tirrenia stampatori, 1988), pp. 77–121. Consonant and clear in its positive evaluation of the phenomenon as regards the liberation of women is the essay by C. Pellandra Cazzoli, "Dames et sigisbées: un début d'émancipation féminine?" in *Studies on Voltaire and Eighteenth Century*, 193 (1980), 2028–35. See also M. Mari, *Venere celeste e Venere terrestre. L'amore nella letteratura italiana del Settecento* (Modena: Mucchi, 1988), pp. 208–57.

5. R. Canosa, *La restaurazione sessuale. Per una storia della sessualità tra Cinquecento e Settecento* (Milan: Feltrinelli, 1993).

6. M. Barbagli, *Sotto lo stesso tetto. Mutamenti della famiglia in Italia dal XV al XX secolo*, 2nd ed. (Bologna: il Mulino, 1996), pp. 331–37.

7. Guerci, p. 81; Canosa, p. 99.

8. Barbagli, p. 333.

9. C. Cantù, *L'abate Parini e la Lombardia nel secolo passato* (Milan: Gnocchi, 1854), p. 124 and n. 7.

10. G. Carducci, *Storia del "Giorno" di Giuseppe Parini* (Bologna: Zanichelli, 1892), p. 45.

11. A. Neri, "I cicisbei a Genova," in *Costumanze e sollazzi*, ed. Neri (Genoa: Tipografia del R. Istituto Sordo-muti, 1883), p. 189; C. F. Gabba, *Della condizione giuridica delle donne*, 2nd ed. (Turin: Unione Tipografico-editrice, 1880), p. 610, n. 2.

12. D. Silvagni, *La corte e la società romana nei secoli XVIII e XIX*, vol. 2 (Rome: Forzani, 1883), p. 248.

13. P. Ungari, *Storia del diritto di famiglia in Italia (1796–1942)*, 2nd ed. (Bologna: il Mulino, 1974), pp. 78–9 (for the documentary appendices see the 1st ed., 1970, pp. 278, 293, 327–39).

14. J. Georgelin, *Venise au siècle des lumières* (Paris-La Haye: Mouton, 1978), p. 732 (italics by Georgelin).

15. G. B. Bronzini, *Vita tradizionale in Basilicata*, 2nd ed. (Matera: Montemurro, 1964), pp. 169–70.

16. S. Gabriele, "Usi e costumi della Sardegna," in *Archivio per lo studio delle tradizioni popolari*, 7 (1888), 468–74 (469).

17. A. Fine, *Parrains, marraines. La parenté spirituelle en Europe* (Paris: Fayard, 1994), p. 169.

18. C. Corrain and P. Zampini, *Altri documenti etnografici e folkloristici nei sinodi diocesani d'Italia. Considerazioni conclusive* (Rovigo: Istituto Padano di Arti Grafiche), s. d., p. 10 of the extract.

19. C. Corrain and P. Zampini, "Documenti etnografici e folkloristici nei Sinodi Diocesani dell'Italia meridionale (Abruzzo, Campania, Beneventano, Lucania-Salernitano, Puglia, Calabria)," *Palestra del Clero*, 45: (3–5) (1966), pp. 1–57 of the extract (44, 51).

20. S. D'Onofrio, "Amicizia ed eros nel comparatico siciliano. Prime considerazioni sull'incesto di terzo tipo e l'atomo di parentela spirituale," in *Forme di comparatico italiano*, ed. Italo Signorini, fasc.1 of *L'Uomo*, 11 (1987), pp. 93–135.

21. Fine, *Parrains et marraines*, op. cit., pp. 171–72.

22. Neri, *Costumanze e sollazzi*, op. cit., pp. 138–42.

23. Fine, *Parrains et marraines*, op. cit., pp. 176–77.

24. G. Pitré, *Usi e costumi credenze e pregiudizi del popolo siciliano*, 4 vols., vol. 2 (Palermo: Pedone Lauriel, 1889), pp. 278–79; Fine, *Parrains et marraines*, op. cit., pp. 169–70; E. Milano, *Dalla culla alla bara. Usi natalizi, nuziali e funerei nella provincia di Cuneo* (Borgo San Dalmazzo: Istituto Grafico Bertello e Compagnia, 1925), pp. 45–6.

25. A. van Gennep, *Manuel du folklore français*, tome 1, vol. 1 (Paris: Picard, 1943), pp. 291–93.

26. Valmaggi, *I cicisbei*, op. cit., pp. 150–52. For the court of the Savoy, Valmaggi depends on D. Perrero, "Memorie torinesi," in *Il Filotecnico*, 2 (1887), pp. 53 and 119, where, however, further information cannot be found. Of Galiani's brief *Orazione*, printed posthumously in 1788 and included in the 1825 collection of *Opuscoli*, I know the edition of the Stabilimento Poligrafico Coster, Napoli, 1842.

27. Archivio di Stato di Lucca, Archivio Arnolfini, 191, *Memoires ou Notices à l'usage de Louise Palma Mansi*, 4 vols. (1791–1823), vol. 1, pp. 5–6 (17 October 1791), p. 130 (2 June 1795); vol. II, p. 11 (4 July 1796), p. 54 (Spring 1798).

28. J. Pitt-Rivers, *The Fate of Shechem or the Politics of Sex. Essays in the Anthropology of the Mediterranean* (Cambridge: Cambridge University Press, 1977), especially pp. 40–7.

29. C. Dupaty, *Lettres sur l'Italie en 1785*, 2nd ed., tome 1 (Paris: chez les Libraires associés, 1796), p. 56. On Dupaty: W. Doyle, "Dupaty (1746–1788): a career in the late Enlightenment," in *Studies on Voltaire and Eighteenth Century*, 230 (1985), pp. 1–125 (on the *Lettres* see pp. 72–81). For an Italian view of the Italy of Dupaty: F. Venturi, "L'Italia fuori d'Italia," in *Storia d'Italia, 3. Dal primo Settecento all'Unità* (Turin: Einaudi, 1973), pp. 985–1481 (1115–16).

30. Cited in L. Sozzi, "*Petit-maître* e *Giovin signore*: affinità fra due registri satirici," in *Saggi e ricerche di letteratura francese*, n. s., 12 (1973), pp. 153–230 (197). There is a review, with further precious information, of Sozzi's essay in F. Fido, *Le metamorfosi del centauro. Studi e letture da Boccaccio a Parini* (Rome: Bulzoni, 1977), pp. 247–51.

31. For further information about this comedy, see the introduction of F. Deloffre to Marivaux, *Le petit-maître corrigé* (Genève and Lille: Droz e Giard, 1955), pp. 11–143 (81). See also the substantial monograph of P. Laroch, *Petits-maîtres et roués. Evolution de la notion de libertinage dans le roman français du XVIIIe siècle* (Québec: Les Presses de l'Université Laval, 1979), pp. 179–80.

32. L. A. Muratori, *Annali d'Italia dal principio dell'era volgare sino all'anno 1749*, vol. 12 (Milan: Pasquali, 1749), p. 49.

33. P. M. Doria, *Lettere e ragionamenti varj*, tome 2, part 1, s. i. t. (Perugia: 1741), p. 332.

34. The references are in R. Trumbach, *La nascita della famiglia egualitaria. Lignaggio e famiglia nell'aristocrazia del '700 inglese* (Bologna: il Mulino, 1982), pp. 163, 171-72.

35. W. Congreve, *The Way of the World*, ed. N. Neri (Bari: Adriatica Editrice, 1961), pp. 133-34.

36. Idem, p. 47, note 1.

37. C. Martín Gaite, *Usos amorosos del dieciocho en España* (Madrid: Siglo XXI de España Editores, 1972), especially pp. 1–20 (for the citation see p. 11), 60, 72.

38. P. Deacon, "El cortejo y Nicolás Fernández de Moratín," in *Boletín de la Biblioteca Menéndez Pelayo*, 55 (1979), 85–95 (especially 92–4). On p. 87 one also finds the evidence of doña Paula and Campomanes. Leandro's diary is published: Leandro Fernández de Moratín, *Diario (Mayo 1780–Marzo 1808)*, ed. René and Mirelle Andioc (Madrid: Editorial Castalia, 1968).

39. A review, inspired by a biting moralism against the "cynical and fun loving eighteenth century," may be found in the dissertation of M. Merlato, *Mariti e cavalier serventi nelle commedie del Goldoni* (Florence: Carnesecchi, 1906).

40. I refer to an essay which marked an important stage in Goldoni criticism: M. Baratto, "Mondo e Teatro nella poetica del Goldoni," in *Tre saggi sul teatro (Ruzante-Aretino-Goldoni)* (Vicenza: Neri Pozza, 1971), pp. 159–234.

41. C. Goldoni, *Mémoires*, ed. N. Jonard (Paris: Aubier, 1992), p. 288. The Italian translation is by C. Goldoni, *Memorie* (Turin: Einaudi, 1993), p. 288.

42. See the recently published book on the subject, Roberto Bizzocchi, *Cicisbei. Morale privata e identità nazionale in Italia*, Rome-Bari: Laterza, 2008.

43. The work was published and introduced by S. Rotta, *"Une aussi perfide nation. La Relation de l'Etat de Gênes di Jacques de Campredon (1737)*," in *Genova, 1746: una città di antico regime tra guerra e rivolta = Quaderni Franzoniani. Semestrale di bibliografia e cultura ligure*, XI, n. 2, July–December 1998, ed. C. Bitossi and C. Paolucci, pp. 609-708.

44. M. Wortley Montagu, *The Complete Letters*, vol. 1, ed. R. Halsband (Oxford: Clarendon Press, 1967), p. 429. Astute reflections on these themes may be found in the essay of E. Grendi, "Ipotesi per lo studio della sociabilità nobiliare genovese in età moderna," in *Quaderni Storici*, n. 102, anno 34 (1999), 733–747.

45. L. De Biase, *Amore di Stato. Venezia. Settecento* (Palermo: Sellerio, 1992); to this one may add the article of M. Manzatto, "La fiera delle opportunità: dame e

cavalieri serventi nel Settecento Veneto," in *Annali dell'Istituto storico italo-germanico in Trento*, 25 (1999), pp. 205–237.

46. P. and A. Verri, *Carteggio dal 1766 al 1797*, vol. 1, part 2 (Milan: Cogliati, 1911), pp. 32–33. As for the abundant bibliography, one might begin with the recent and fundamental book of C. Capra, *I progressi della ragione. Vita di Pietro Verri* (Bologna: il Mulino, 2002).

47. See note 27. The interest of this text as a source for the political history of Lucca is underlined by M. L. Trebiliani, "Diario di un'aristocratica lucchese," in *La presenza dimenticata. Il femminile nell'Italia moderna fra storia, letteratura, filosofia*, ed. G. Pagliano (Milan: Angeli, 1996), pp. 93–119. See also Roberto Bizzocchi, "Vita sociale, vita privata in un diario femminile fra Sette e Ottocento," in *Genesis. Rivista della Società Italiana delle Storiche* III, 2004, 125–167.

48. See the Chapters (8 and 7) by Roger Freitas and Martha Feldman in the present volume.

49. A lovely comparison between England and Italy may be found in the article of E. Brambilla, "La storia di Mie Mie. Spirito di famiglia e condizione della donna tra Antico Regime e Rivoluzione," in *Acme. Annali della Facoltà di Lettere e Filosofia dell'Università degli Studi di Milano*, 52 (1999), pp. 63–93.

50. L. Hunt, *The family romance of the French Revolution* (Berkeley-Los Angeles: University of California Press, 1992), especially pp. 151–191.

51. Stendhal, *Promenades dans Rome*, ed. A. Caraccio (Genève-Paris: Slatkine Reprints, 1986), p. 88. A review of places where Stendhal writes of cicisbei may be found in M. Crouzet, *Stendhal e il mito dell'Italia* (original edition Paris: Corti, 1982), (Bologna: il Mulino, 1991), pp. 314–16.

Notes to Chapter Two

1. For the problems of definition and comparison, see Peter Seibert, "*Der literarische Salon, ein Forschungsüberblick,*" Sonderheft 3, *Internationales Archiv für Sozialgeschichte der deutschen Literatur* (1993), 159–216.

2. For a synthetic overview, see Vittorio Emanuele Giuntella, *Roma nel Settecento* (Bologna: Cappelli, 1971). Less useful is Hanns Gross, *Rome in the Age of Enlightenment. The post-Tridentine Syndrome and the Ancien Regime* (Cambridge, U.K.: Cambridge University Press, 1990).

3. The expression is by John Brewer, *The Pleasures of the Imagination. British Culture in the Eighteenth Century* (London: Harper Collins, 1997).

4. I refer to the hypothesis of Dena Goodman, "Enlightenment Salons: The Convergence of Female and Philosophic Ambitions," *Eighteenth Century Studies* 22 (1989), 329–350. Historiography on this subject has recently been significantly updated by Antoine Lilti, *Le monde des salons. Sociabilité et mondanité à Paris au XVIIIe siècle* (Paris: Fayard, 2005).

5. Jerôme de La Lande, *Voyage d'un François en Italie, fait dans les années 1765–1766* (Geneva, 1790), vol. 5, p. 32. On the caution which must be adopted in using these sources see Peter Burke, *The Historical Anthropology of Early Modern Italy. Essays on Perception and Communication* (Cambridge: Cambridge University Press, 1987), pp. 15-24.

6. Louis Dutens, *Mémoires d'un voyageur qui se repose* (Paris, 1806), vol. 1, p. 289.

7. Johann Joachim Winckelmann, *Opere* (Prato, 1833), vol. 9, pp. 478 and 532.

8. Renata Ago, *Carriere e clientele nella Roma barocca* (Rome-Bari: Laterza, 1990); Irene Fosi and Maria Antonietta Visceglia, "Marriage and Politics at the Papal Court in the Sixteenth and Seventeenth Centuries," in *Marriage in Italy, 1300–1650*, ed. Trevor Dean and Kate J.P. Lowe (Cambridge: Cambridge University Press, 1998), pp. 197–224; Marina D'Amelia, "Nepotismo al femminile. Il caso di Olimpia Maidalchini Pamphilj," in *La nobiltà romana in età moderna. Profili istituzionali e pratiche sociali*, ed. Maria Antonietta Visceglia (Rome: Carocci, 2001), pp. 353–399.

9. Ago, "Socialità e salotti a Roma tra Sei e Settecento," in *Salotti e ruolo femminile in Italia tra fine Seicento e primo Novecento*, ed. Maria Luisa Betri and Elena Brambilla (Venice: Marsilio, 2004), pp. 177–188; Maria Pia Donato, "I salotti romani del Settecento: il ruolo femminile tra politica e cultura," ibid., pp. 189–212.

10. Elisabetta Graziosi, "Arcadia femminile: presenze e modelli," *Filologia e critica* 17 (1992), 321–358.

11. Donato, *Accademia romane. Una storia sociale (1671–1824)* (Naples: ESI, 2000). In general see Claudio Donati, "La Chiesa di Roma tra antico regime e riforme settecentesche (1675–1766)," in *Storia d'Italia, Annali 9, La Chiesa e il potere politico dal Medioevo all'età contemporanea*, ed. Giorgio Chittolini and Giovanni Miccoli (Turin: Einaudi, 1986), pp. 721–766.

12. Elisabeth and Jörg Garms, "Mito e realtà di Roma nella cultura europea. Viaggio e idea, immagine e immaginazione," in *Storia d'Italia. Annali 5. Il paesaggio*, ed. Cesare De Seta (Turin: Einaudi, 1982), pp. 561–662; Annalisa Di Nola, "Dal pellegrinaggio alla gita turistica: un'analisi quantitativa delle guide di Roma," *Dimensioni e problemi della ricerca storica* (1989), 1, 181–262; *Grand Tour. Il fascino dell'Italia nel XVIII secolo* (Milan: Skira, 1997); useful are the indices in Friedrich Noack, *Das Deutschtum in Rom seit dem Ausgang des Mittelalters* (Berlin-Leipzig: Deutsche Verlag, 1927); *A Dictionary of British and Irish Travellers in Italy 1701–1800*, ed. John Ingamells (New Haven: Yale University Press, 1997).

13. Charles de Brosses had already noted that the Cardinal Acquaviva d'Aragona, minister of Naples, was a magnificent host: *Lettres familières sur l'Italie*, ed. Yvonne Bezard (Paris: Didot, 1931), vol. 2, pp. 213–214. On two diplomats who were very active in Roman cultural life, see Carlo Corona Baratech, *José Nicolás de Azara. Un Embajador español en Roma* (Zaragoza: Institucion Fernando el Catolico, 1948); Jean-Paul Desprat, *Le Cardinal de Bernis: la belle ambition: 1715–1794* (Paris: Perrin, 2000); on the French residents, see Gilles Montegre, "François de Paule Latapie: un savant voyageur français au coeur de la Rome des Lumières (1775–1776)," *Mélanges de l'École française de Rome. Italie et Méditerranée*, 117:1 (2005), 371–422.

14. "They last a little more than two hours and are sometimes very brilliant . . . in these sorts of assemblies, where one must not believe that everyone is equally received, there reigns much liberty which, however, removes nothing of their decorum. One sees in them almost all the important persons of Rome . . . it is in them that one learns the news, and also where one is taken to make distinguished acquaintances."

Jérôme Richard, *Description historique et critique de l'Italie . . .* (Dijon, 1766), vol. 5, pp. 149–150.

15. De La Lande, *Voyage d'un François*, vol. 5, pp. 32–33.

16. Richard, *Description*, vol. 5, p. 155.

17. De La Lande, *Voyage d'un François*, vol. 5, p. 32.

18. On this topic see *La nobiltà romana in età moderna* and in particular the critical overview of the editor in the introduction.

19. *Diario Ordinario* 226 (1 March 1777), 940 (3 January 1784), 942 (10 January 1784), 1926 (15 June 1793). Traces of this social activity are to be found in the Archivio di Stato di Roma (hereafter ASR), Fondo Santacroce, b. 1126.

20. Richard, *Description*, vol. 5, p. 154.

21. See for example Nicola Molinari, *Il Cosmofilo, ovvero delle conversazioni. Dialoghi* (Rome, 1766).

22. Carlo Bandini, *Roma e la nobiltà romana nel tramonto del secolo XVIII. Aspetti e figure* (Città di Castello: Lapi, 1914); Donato, *Accademie romane*, p. 120 et passim; Mirabelle Madignier, "Conversazioni, salons et sociabilités intellectuelles informelles à Rome et à Florence au XVIIIe siècle," in *Naples, Rome, Florence. Une histoire comparée des milieux intellectuels italiens (XVIIe–XVIIIe siècles)*, ed. Jean Boutier, Brigitte Marin, Antonella Romano (Rome: École française de Rome, 2005), pp. 575-598.

23. *Carteggio di Pietro e di Alessandro Verri dal 1766 al 1796*, ed. Francesco Novati, Emanuele Greppi and Alessandro Giulini (Milan: Cogliati, 1919–1942), vol. 1, I, pp. 379–380.

24. Ibid., pp. 385–386.

25. Giuseppe Gorani, *Mémoires secrets et critiques des cours, du gouvernement et des moeurs des principaux états d'Italie* (Paris, 1793), p. 148.

26. De La Lande, *Voyage d'un François*, vol. 5, p. 144.

27. *Choiseul à Rome. Lettres et mémoires inédits, 1754–1757*, ed. Maurice Boutry (Paris: Lévy, 1895), p. 302; in general, see *Court and Politics in Papal Rome 1492–1700*, ed. Gianvittorio Signorotto and Maria Antonietta Visceglia (Cambridge: Cambridge University Press, 2002).

28. Archives du Ministère des Affaires Étrangères (Paris), Mémoires et documents, Rome, 72, ff. 273–274. According to Richard, *Description*, vol. 5, p. 157, there was no one at Rome "more mixed up in intrigues than that woman, who had a part in almost all the principal affairs."

29. *Choiseul à Rome*, p. 304.

30. See for example *Diario Ordinario* 1934 (13 July 1793). Travelers emphasized this link. See Gorani, *Mémoires secrets*, p. 150, who recalls that her conversation was as gay and brilliant as the Parisian salons. More caustic was the judgment of Paul-Louis Courier, who called her a "very beautiful woman, a woman known by all those who have wanted to get to know her, [a woman] much below her reputation, at least as far as spirit goes." *Lettres écrites de France et d'Italie (1787 à 1812)* (Paris: Bibliothèque Nationale, undated), p. 12. On the role of this princess who, during the Roman Republic of 1798–99, hosted a political circle, see also David Armando, Massimo Cattaneo, and Maria Pia Donato, *Una <<rivoluzione>> difficile: la Repub-*

blica Romana del 1798–1799 (Pisa-Rome: IEPI, 2000); Marina Caffiero, "Questioni di salotto? Sfera pubblica e ruoli femminili nel Settecento," *Salotti e ruolo femminile,* pp. 527–537.

31. As de Bernis advised his friend Santacroce in *Lettres inédites du Cardinal de Bernis à la Princesse de Sainte-Croix,* ed. Maurice Mignon and Henri Buriot-Darsiles (Rome: Desclé, 1921), pp. 17, 27.

32. De La Lande, *Voyage d'un François,* vol. 5, p. 28 et passim. See Roberto Bizzocchi, "Cicisbei. La morale italiana," *Storica* 9 (1997), 63–90.

33. *Carteggio di Pietro e di Alessandro Verri,* vols. 1, 2, pp. 54–56.

34. I cite from Marina Pieretti, "Margherita Sparapani Gentili Boccapaduli. Ritratto di una gentildonna romana (1735–1826)," *Rivista Storica del Lazio* 8–9 (2000–01), 81–133, p. 84, since I was unable to consult the document conserved in ASR, Fondo Del Drago, despite repeated attempts.

35. *Carteggio di Pietro e di Alessandro Verri,* vol. 3, p. 421.

36. Ibid., p. 18.

37. G. C. Amaduzzi to G. Fontana, Biblioteca Apostolica Vaticana (hereafter BAV), Patetta 1836, f. 136v. On this personage see Marina Caffiero, "Cultura e religione nel Settecento italiano: Giovanni Cristofano Amaduzzi e Scipione de' Ricci," *Rivista di Storia della Chiesa in Italia* 28 (1974) 1, 94–126; 2, 405–410.

38. "See then that you do not leave Rome without having yourself presented at the house of the Marquise de Bocca-Paduli; her côterie is the most agreeable and the best chosen in Rome; among other persons of merit you will meet there Count de Verri, a Milanese *cavaliere,* who is full of politeness, talent and taste: the lady of the house will please you infinitely, for she is as full of spirit, as well made and as lovable as a French woman"; Martin Sherlock, *Lettres d'un voyageur anglois* (London, 1779), p. 110; Dutens, *Mémoires,* vol. 1, p. 291.

39. "Much natural spirit, obliging by nature and education, well born, she is an adorable being and is worthy of being happy at all moments. And yet she was not always known. She had a reputation for 'coquetry' since she had not attached herself to certain louts of the city who presented themselves with great pretension. But now it seems to me that the city generally renders her justice"; *Carteggio di Pietro e di Alessandro Verri,* vol. 3, p. 421.

40. ASR, Fondo Del Drago, b. 215, b. 387; *Carteggio di Pietro e Alessandro Verri,* vol. 4, p. 289; Giuseppe Gorani, *Mémoires secrets,* p. 386.

41. *Carteggio di Pietro e di Alessandro Verri,* vol. 3, p. 57.

42. Like the "Lettera . . . sulle antichità cimbriche" of Ippolito Pindemonte, *Antologia Romana* 9 (1782), 235–37; or *Il Socrate. Componimento drammatico* by the former Jesuit Antonino Galfo (Rome, 1780), which touched off a furious literary war. On this see Leone Vicchi, *Vincenzo Monti, le lettere e la politica in Italia dal 1750 al 1830* (Rome: Forzani, 1879–1887), vol. 2, p. 333 et passim.

43. Pieretti, "Margherita Sparapani," p. 89, but I have corrected what seems to be an error in transcription (Serassi, not Serafri). On the literati cited, see the entry in *Biografia degli Italiani Illustri nelle scienze, lettere ed arti del secolo XVIII, e de' contemporanei,* ed. Emilio de Tipaldo Pretendieri (Venice: 1834–1845).

44. *Carteggio di Pietro e di Alessandro Verri*, vol. 3, p. 188.

45. Ibid., p. 200.

46. Charles Burney, *The Present State of Music in France and Italy, or the Journal of a Tour . . . Undertaken to Collect Materials for a General History of Music* (London, 1771), vol. 2, p. 257 et passim.

47. Raimondo Cunich, *Epigrammata nunc primum in lucem edita* (Ragusa, 1827), p. 291 et passim.

48. Giovanni Gherardo De Rossi, "Lettera . . . sulla morte della celebre Maria Pizzelli," *Giornale Pisano* 8:22 (1807), 72. See Luigi Rava, *Un salotto romano del Settecento: Maria Pizzelli* (Rome: Fondazione Marco Besso, 1926).

49. *Accademia poetica in sette lingue per la morte di Maria Pizzelli nata Cuccovilla fra i poeti Lida insigne letterata romana* (Rome, 1808), p. 4.

50. Friedrich Münter, *Aus den Tagebüchern*, ed. Ø. Andreasen (København–Leipzig: Haase Søn-Harrasowitz, 1937), vol. 1, p. 281.

51. "Everywhere I go I find many people who know you, and who consequently esteem you; this is no little relief to my soul, which is as restored by domestic harmony as it is discouraged by the backwardness of my homeland. I found, therefore, in Pavia, where I passed 10 delicious days, the Marquis Luigi Malaspina, the Marquise Belcredi, and professor Cremani, three persons who are entirely yours, just as I am yours, just as all are yours. The first sends you as a gift a little work of his; the second (O! The loveable woman!) twice sends you her greetings; the third prays you to remember him, all three would like to be in Rome, or would like you to be in Pavia: I would like all four of you to be in Alessandria" wrote her on 3 October 1787 F. C. Guasco from Alessandria (BAV, Autografi Ferrajoli, Raccolta Visconti, ff. 3460–61).

52. De Rossi, "Lettera . . . sulla morte della celebre Maria Pizzelli," p. 72.

53. "Taught by pedants she only knows how to quibble and not to discuss, and she has not enough good sense to feel that ignorance is a thousand times more tolerable than an erudition without taste and without tact. . . . She sits at the back of a vast salon, she sits collectedly, very straight, very rigid, she presides over the assembly ranged on either side like a church ceremony. Everything in her house is methodical, is measured"; Gorani, *Mémoires secrets*, vol. 2, p. 322.

54. Pierre d'Hesinivy d'Auribeau, in *Accademia Poetica*, p. 54.

55. Dutens, *Mémoires*, vol. 1, p. 291.

56. Cesare Stasi, "Elogio," in *Accademia poetica*, p. 14.

57. Johann Wolfgang Goethe, *Viaggio in Italia*, trans. Emilio Castellani (Milan: Mondadori, 1983), pp. 156–57; Dionigi Strocchi, *Lettere edite ed inedite*, ed. Giuseppe Ghinassi (Faenza: Conti, 1868), vol. 1, p. 14.

58. Vittorio Alfieri, *Vita*, ed. Marco Cerruti (Milan: Rizzoli, 1987), p. 225. On the representation of *Antigone* by ambassador Grimaldi, see Ezio Raimondi, "Alfieri 1782: un teatro <<terribile>>," in *Orfeo in Arcadia. Studi sul teatro a Roma nel Settecento*, ed. Giorgio Petrocchi (Rome: Istituto della Enciclopedia Italiana, 1984), pp. 73–103. Jürgen Habermas has already suggested that the debut often took place in the salon; *Storia e critica dell' opinione pubblica* (Bari: Laterza, 1971), p. 49. See Maria Iolanda Palazzolo, "Leggere in salotto: le funzioni della lettura nei ricevimenti

mondani tra Sette e Ottocento," in *Salotti e ruolo femminile*, pp. 19–28; for a differ-ent appraisal, but referring to France, see Lilti, *Le monde des salons*, pp. 249–260.

59. The expression is that of the *custode* of Arcadia Gioacchino Pizzi, Biblioteca Angelica Roma, ms. arcadico 31, f. 85, and refers to the Maestro di Sacro Palazzo who had control over publishing in Rome.

60. *Lettere inedite di Vincenzo Monti, d'Ippolito Pindemonte, di Luigi Biondi, di Urbano Lampredi, di Tommaso Gargallo, di Gian Gherardo De Rossi e di altri*, ed. Enrico Castreca Brunetti (Rome, 1846), p. 187.

61. Among her works: *Breve istruzione de' principali successi del vecchio e nuovo testamento ai fanciulli cristiani . . .* (Rome, 1797); *Aristobolo. Tragedia . . .* (Rome, 1805); *Raccolta di n. 100 soggetti li più rimarchevoli dell'Istoria Greca . . . incisi da Bartolomeo Pinelli* (Rome, 1821). During the Roman Republic, Bertocchi presented to the National Institute a "Project for a national theater" (ASR, Miscellanea di carte politiche e riservate, n. 914). See also Ubaldo Solustri, *Fulvia Maria Bertocchi, Pensieri* (Rome: tipografia delle scienze matematiche e fisiche, undated).

62. Bettina Baumgärtel, *Angelika Kauffmann (1741–1807). Bedingungen weibli-cher Kreativität in der Malerei des 18. Jahrhunderts* (Weinheim-Basel: Beltz, 1990); Olivier Michel, *Vivre et peindre à Rome au XVIIIe siècle* (Rome: École française de Rome, 1996); *La città degli artisti nell'età di Pio VI*, ed. Liliana Barroero and Stefano Susinno, *Roma moderna e contemporanea* 10 (2002), 1–2; *Art in Rome in the Eigh-teenth Century*, ed. Edgar Peters Bowron and Joseph J. Rishel (London: Merrell & Philadelphia Museum of Art, 2000).

63. See Wendy Wassyng Roworth's Chapter 6 in this volume.

64. Giovanni Gherardo De Rossi, *Vita di Angelica Kauffmann pittrice* (Florence, 1810), pp. 74–75.

65. Ibid.

66. Goethe, *Viaggio in Italia*, p. 182 et passim.

67. Elisabeth Vigée Le Brun, *Ricordi dall'Italia*, ed. Marina Premoli (Palermo: Sellerio, 1990), pp. 56–57.

68. De Rossi, *Vita di Angelica Kauffmann*, p. 75. On the career of the two, see Alessandra Di Ricco, *L'inutile e maraviglioso mestiere. Poeti improvvisatori di fine Settecento* (Milan: Angeli, 1990).

69. For example, Friedrike Brun, *Römisches Leben* (Leipzig, 1833).

70. Diego Angeli, *Il salotto di Marianna Dionigi*, in idem, *Roma romantica* (Mi-lan: Treves, 1935), pp. 196–203; Nicola Marcone, *Marianna Dionigi e le sue opere* (Rome, press not specified, 1896).

71. Juan Andrés, *Cartas familiares . . . a su hermano d. Carlos Andrés dandole noti-cia del viage que hizo à varias ciudades de Italia en el año 1785* (Madrid, 1791), p. 70.

72. See the letters of Esteban Arteaga published by Miguel Batllori, *La cultura hispano-italiana de los Jesuitas expulsos españoles, hispano-americanos, filipinos, 1767–1814* (Madrid: Gredos, 1966).

73. Donato, *Accademie romane*; Marina Caffiero, Maria Pia Donato, and An-tonella Romano, "De la Catholicité post-tridentine à la République Romaine. Splendeurs et misères des intellectuels courtesans," in *Naples, Rome, Florence,*

pp. 171–208. An emblematic case is described in Daniela Gallo, "I Visconti, una famiglia romana a servizio di papi, della Repubblica e di Napoleone," *Roma moderna e contemporanea* 2 (1994), 77–90.

74. Self-portrait of the improviser Francesco Gianni, *Raccolta delle Poesie* (Milan, 1807–1808), vol. 1, p. 6.

75. Francesco Fortunati, *Avvenimenti*, BAV, Vat. lat. 10730–10731; Agostino Chigi, *Memorabilia pubblica e privata*, BAV, Archivio Chigi 3966 bis; for Cagliostro's attempt to found a "lodge of ladies" see *Raccolta di scritture legali riguardanti il processo di Alessandro Cagliostro e di p. Francesco Giuseppe di S. Maurizio innanzi al S. Uffizio*, Biblioteca Nazionale Centrale Roma, ms. Vittorio Emanuele 245, and Archivio della Congregazione per la Dottrina della Fede, Rome, Sant'Offizio, St.St. S3g.

76. Claudio Todeschi, *Lettere filosofiche dirette alla Nobil Donna la signora baronessa Laura Astalli Piccolomini sotto il nome di Clori* (Rome, 1783), p. 4. For the evolution of this debate in Italy see Rebecca Messbarger, *The Century of Women. Representations of Women in Eighteenth-Century Italian Public Discourse* (Toronto: University of Toronto Press, 2002).

77. Antonio Scarpelli, *L'Anti-eroismo o sia della superficialità* (undated but after 1781), p. 7.

78. As emerges from the "Regolamento degli studi di nobile e valorosa donna" which Gian Vincenzo Gravina wrote for Isabella Vecchiarelli Santacroce and for ladies "like those who, having to guard a great treasure, which is shame and virtue, in the midst of civil commerce, have need of greater light . . . particularly in our times in which custom permits noble women to frequent and converse with men; the which practice and familiarity, if not nourished by sublime discourses, ends up being nourished by conversations which are either low, or slanderous or unspeakable" (*Scritti critici e teorici*, ed. Amedeo Quondam, Rome-Bari: Laterza, 1973), pp. 177–194.

79. Antonio Scarpelli, *Sdegni* (Lausanne, undated), p. 64. Scarpelli, after a scandal, fled to Naples, where he published the *Giornale delle dame italiane* (1782–1783).

80. Scarpelli, *L'anti-eroismo*, p. 71.

81. *Antologia Romana* 9 (1783), 100. See also the little anonymous satirical poem *Il Simonide, ovvero della prima formazione delle donne* (1796).

82. Rosa Califronia (pseudonym), *Breve difesa dei diritti delle donne* (Assisi, 1794). Certain subjects announce the successive strategy of feminizing Catholicism. See Marina Caffiero, *Religione e modernità in Italia (secoli XVII–XIX)* (Rome-Pisa: IEPI, 2000).

Notes to Chapter Three

1. "[...]Giustina Renier Michiel ha il dolore immenso di assistere alla caduta della Repubblica di San Marco. Caduta? Non diciamolo più. La troppo vecchia Repubblica morì perchè doveva morire." Mario Vianello-Chiodo, "Giustina Renier Michiel e molte sue lettere inedite," *Ateneo veneto* 127: 3–4 (1940), pp. 61–76. All translations

are my own. When citing eighteenth-century letters, I have rendered the Italian as it is found in the original manuscripts, except for modernizing the script.

2. See Bruce Redford, *Venice and the Grand Tour* (New Haven: Yale University Press, 1996); Jeremy Black, *Italy and the Grand Tour* (New Haven: Yale University Press, 2003).

3. Luigi Carrer, *Anello di sette gemme* (Venice, 1838); Agostino Verona, *Le donne illustri d'Italia* (Milan: Colombo, 1864); Oscar Greco, *Bibliografia femminile italiana del XIX secolo* (Venice: Issoglio, 1875); Carlo Villani, *Stelle femminile. Dizionario bio-bibliografico nuova ed ampliata, reveduta e corretta* (Naples: Società editrice Dante Alighieri, 1915); Ginevra Canonici Fachini, *Prospetto biografico delle donne italiane rinomate in letteratura dal secolo decimoquarto fino a' giorni nostri* (Venice: Alvi Sopoli, 1924); Vittorio Turri, *Dizionario storico manuale della letteratura italiana (1000–1900) con un'appendice bibliografica*, 2nd edition (Turin: Paravia, 1900); Giulio Natali, *Storia letteraria d'Italia. Il Settecento* (Milan: Dr. Francesco Vallardi, 1929).

4. Antonia Arslan, Adriana Chenello, and Gilberto Pizzamiglio, eds., *Le stanze ritrovate: Antologia di scrittrici venete dal Quattrocento al Novecento* (Venice: Editrice Eidos, 1991); Bernardina Sani, ed., *Rosalba Carriera, 1675–1757* (Turin: U. Allemandi, 1988); Shearer West, "Gender and Internationalism: The Case of Rosalba Carriera," in *Italian Culture in Northern Europe in the Eighteenth Century,* ed. Shearer West (Cambridge: Cambridge University Press, 1999), pp. 46–66; Cinzia Giorgietti, *Ritratto di Isabella: Studi e documenti su Isabella Teotochi Albrizzi* (Florence: Le Lettere, 1992); Rita Unfer Lukoschik, ed. *Elisabetta Caminer Turra (1751–1796). Una letterata veneta verso l'Europa* (Verona: Essedue, 1998); Elisabetta Caminer Turra, *Selected Writings of an Eighteenth-Century Venetian Woman of Letters*, ed. and trans. Catherine M. Sama (Chicago: University of Chicago Press, 2003); Andrea di Robilant, *A Venetian Affair: A True Story of Impossible Love in the Eighteenth Century* (New York: Albert A. Knopf, 2003).

5. Gino Damerini, *Settecento veneziano. La vita, i tempi, gli amori, i nemici di Caterina Dolfin Tron* (Milan: A. Mondadori, 1939), pp. 54–55, 68–69, 76; Volker Hunecke, *Il patriziato veneziano alla fine della Repubblica, 1646–1797. Demografia, famiglia, ménage*, trans. Benedetta Heinemann Campana (Rome: Jouvence, 1997), p. 162; Lina Urban Padoan, "Isabella Teotochi Albrizzi tra ridotti e dimore di campagna del suo tempo," in *Canova e gli Albrizzi tra ridotti e dimore di campagna del tempo,* ed. Elena Bassi and Lina Urban Padoan (Milan: Libri Scheiwiller, 1989), pp. 73–157.

6. Edward Muir, *Civic Ritual in Renaissance Venice* (Princeton: Princeton University Press, 1981), pp. 253–261.

7. Regarding the details of Giustina Renier Michiel's life, see Vianello-Chido, "Giustina Renier Michiel," p. 62; Maria Bandini Buti, "Renier Michiel, Giustina," *Poetesse e Scrittrici*, V. 6/2: *Enciclopedia biografica e bibliografica italiana* (Rome: EBBI, 1942), p. 171; Lina Urban, "Giustina Renier Michiel (Venezia 1755–1832)," in *Le stanze ritrovate: Antologia di scrittrici venete dal Quattrocento al Novecento*, ed. Antonia Arslan, Adriana Chenello, and Gilberto Pizzamiglio (Venice: Editrice Eidos, 1991), pp. 163–167.

8. Italy. Venice. Museo Civico Correr, *Collezione P.D.* (hereafter *Col. P.D.*), 1442/3, letter 60, to M. A. Michiel, July 19, 1772, in Dolo.

9. "Hanno un gran torto chi dicono che la nobiltà Romana è altera, replico non può essere più affabile." *Col. P.D.* 1442/2, ibid., letter 23, to Elena Corner Michiel, December 9, 1775, from Rome. Regarding Romans' great politeness, see ibid., letter 3, to Elena Corner Michiel, December 16, 1776, from Rome. Regarding Renier Michiel's contact with the Pope, see ibid., letter 4, to Elena Corner Michiel, n.d. [from Rome]; ibid., letter 3, to Elena Corner Michiel, December 16, 1775, from Rome.

10. *Col. P.D.* 1442/2, letter 3, to Elena Corner Michiel, December 16, 1775, from Rome.

11. *Col. P.D.* 1442/2, letter 18, to Elena Corner Michiel, February 10, 1776, from Rome; ibid., letter 62, to Elena Corner Michiel, June 15, 1776.

12. *Col. P.D.* 1442/2, letter 1, to Elena Corner Michiel, December 30, 1775, from Rome.

13. *Col. P.D.* 1442/2, letter 20, to Elena Corner Michiel, February 20, 1776, from Rome.

14. On the role of clothing as a sign of social success, see Marcello Fantoni, "Le corti e i 'modi' del vestire," in *Storia d'Italia*, vol. 19: *La moda*, ed. Carlo Marco Befanti and Fabio Giusberti (Turin: Giulio Einaudi editore, 2003), pp. 749, 751.

15. "Non posso fare a meno di partecipare alla mia Cara Mamma la mia speranza che ho di essere incinta, nemica essendo de' nascondigli con chi amo da vero." *Col. P.D.* 1442/2, letter 2, to Elena Corner Michiel, n.d. [from Rome].

16. *Col P.D.* 1442/2, letter 9, to Elena Renier Michiel, April 20, 1776, from Rome. See also ibid., letter 10, to Elena Corner Michiel, May 18, 1776, from Rome.

17. *Col. P.D.* 1442/2, letter 5, to Elena Corner Michiel, August 3, 1776, from Rome.

18. *Col. P.D.* 1442/2, letter 4, to Elena Corner Michiel, n.d. [from Rome].

19. "Mi abbia fato andare un poco in colera in un periodo della lettera che scrisse a Marc'Antonio, ma sopra tal punto taccio poichè lasciai a lui l'oncombenza della risposta." *Col. P.D.* 1442/2, letter 2, to Elena Corner Michiel, n.d. [from Rome].

20. "Con un poca più di flema dell'altra volta la raguaglio della continuazione della mia buona salute." *Col. P.D.* 1442/2, letter 3, to Elena Corner Michiel, December 16, 1775, from Rome.

21. *Col. P.D.* 1442/2, letter 14, to Elena Corner Michiel, March 23, 1776, from Rome.

22. Francesco Schröder, "Michiel," *Repertorio genealogico delle famiglie confermati nobili e dei nobili esistensi nelle province venete* (Venice: Tipografia di Alvisipoli, 1830), vol. 2, p. 13. This may be the period that he occupies the post of *savio di terraferma*, one of five men responsible for military affairs on the mainland. Schröder does not indicate the dates that Michiel held this position.

23. *Col. P.D.* 1442/2, letter 1, to Elena Corner Michiel, December 30, 1775, from Rome.

24. "Je croyez que vous alliez a Ponte Casal, mais a ce que je voi vous restez au

Dolo, vous me fairez bien de la grace a me sçavoir dire si vous-y restez long tems. Je vous repond d'abord sçachans de vous faire plaisir, mais je vous assure qu'en vous satisfesans, je me satisfais moi-même." *Col. P.D.* 1442/3, letter 56, to Marc'Antonio Michiel, January 15, 1778, n.p.

25. Ibid.

26. *Col. P.D.* 1442/3, letter 1, to Marc'Antonio Michiel, October 8, 1778, from Venice.

27. *Col. P.D.* 1442/3, letter 11, to Marc'Antonio Michiel, n.d., to Palma; see also ibid., letter 2, to Marc'Antonio Michiel, n.d., n.p.

28. "A voi per niente interessa di sapere di mè, io non sono così verso di voi; e dopo avere atteso per molti giorni qualche riscontro il quale mi sarebbe riuscito molto grato, ve ne prego finalmente di farmi avere qualche avviso." *Col. P.D.* 1442/3, letter 3, to Marc'Antonio Michiel, n.d., n.p.

29. "le picenine tutte sane e belle dimandono del Papà, ch'è scappato." *Col. P.D.* 1442/3, letter 2, to Marc'Antonio Michiel, n.d., n.p.

30. "Le nostre picenine stanno tutte bene, ma si lamentano di non vedere il suo [sic] Papà." *Col. P.D.* 1442/3, letter 3, to Marc'Antonio Michiel, n.d., n.p.

31. "Basta, basta, andelo a chimar el Papà, ch'el vegna quà con [mì]." The last word is unclear. *Col. P.D.* 1442/3, letter 6, to Marc'Antonio Michiel, July 2, 1779, from Ponte Casale.

32. Luciano Guerci, *La sposa obbediente. Donna e matrimonio nella discussione dell'Italia del Settecento* (Turin: Tirrenia Stampatori, 1987), pp. 24, 36, 117, 223.

33. Vianello-Chiodo, "Giustina Renier Michiel," p. 67; Guerci, *La sposa obbediente*, p. 216; *Col. P.D.* 1442/2, letter 5, to Elena Corner Michiel, August 3, 1776, from Rome.

34. In one letter, she has Chiara with her, but tells her husband to embrace her other two daughters. *Col. P.D.* 1442/3, letter 9, to Marc'Antonio Michiel, n.d., n.p. Regarding Nene's reading, see *Col. P.D.* 1442/3, letter 64, to Marc'Antonio Michiel, n.d., n.p.

35. *Col. P.D.* 1442/3, letter 6, to Marc'Antonio Michiel, July 2, 1779, from Ponte Casale.

36. *Col. P.D.* 1442/2, letter 3, to Elena Corner Michiel, December 16, 1775, from Rome. Here Renier Michiel is no doubt referring to Faustina Savorgnan Rezzonico, wife of Ludovico Rezzonico, nephew of Pope Clement XIII. Pompeo Molmenti, *La storia di Venezia nella vita privata* (Bergamo: Istituto Italiano d'Arti Grafiche, 1889), vol. 2, pp. 446, 472.

37. *Col. P.D.* 1442/2, letter 23, to Elena Corner Michiel, n.d. [from Rome].

38. *Col. P.D.* 1442/2, letter 16, to Elena Corner Michiel, March 3, 1776, from Rome; ibid., letter 11, to Elena Corner Michiel, April 27, 1776, from Rome.

39. *Col. P.D.* 1442/2, letter 19, to Elena Corner Michiel, February 3, 1776, from Rome.

40. *Col. P.D.* 1442/2, letter 20, to Elena Corner Michiel, January 20, 1776, from Rome.

41. "Abbiamo la compiacenza di avere riportato sopra di tutti il buon gusto, e la

magnificenza, e tanto fù grande il Compatimento di tutti, che quando ci vedevano, Nobiltà, e Plebe, battevano Palma a Palma, gridando Eviva." *Col. P.D.* 1442/2, letter 17, to Elena Corner Michiel, February 23, 1776, from Rome.

42. *Col. P.D.* 1442/2, letter 15, to Elena Corner Michiel, March 9, 1776, from Rome.

43. Isabella Teotochi Albrizzi, *Ritratto di Giustina Renier Michiel* (s.l., 1833), p. 4. For more on the intellectual and cultural life in Rome, see Maria Pia Donato, *Accademie romane. Una storia sociale, 1671–1824* (Naples: Edizione scientifiche italiane, 2000).

44. *Col. P.D.* 1442/3, letter 1, to Marc'Antonio Michiel, October 8, 1778, from Venice; *Col. P.D.* 1442/3, letter 42, to Marc'Antonio Michiel, n.d. [from Padua].

45. *Col. P.D.* 1442/3, letter 25, to Marc'Antonio Michiel, n.d., n.p.

46. *Col. P.D.* 1442/3, letter 45, to Marc'Antonio Michiel, n.d. [from Padua].

47. "Fui oggi dal Professor Carburi, egli deve apprendermi a fare lo spirito di muschio, immaginatevi il mio piacere." *Col. P.D.* 1442/3, letter 65, to Marc'Antonio Michiel (1781–1784) [from Padua]. Given that Renier Michiel speaks of sending her husband copies of her Elena's reading in an earlier letter from the same set, I estimate the date to be the early 1780s. Marco Carburi was named to occupy the newly created chair in experimental chemistry at the University of Padua in 1759 and began organizing the creation of a chemistry institute and laboratory in 1764 or 1768. U. Baldini, "Carburi, Marco," in *Dizionario biografico degli italiani*, ed. Alberto M. Ghisalberti (Rome: Istituto dell'Enciclopedia Italiana, 1976 [1960–]), vol. 19, pp. 723–725.

48. *Col. P.D.* 1442/3, letter 9, to Marc'Antonio Michiel, n.d., n.p.

49. *Col. P.D.* 1442/3, letter 7, to Marc'Antonio Michiel, n.d., n.p.

50. Vianello-Chiodo, "Giustina Renier Michiel," p. 62; Hunecke, *Il patriziato veneziano*, p. 242.

51. Muir, *Civic Ritual*, pp. 253–261.

52. Muir, *Civic Ritual*, pp. 289–290.

53. Lina Urban, *Processioni e feste dogali* (Venice: Neri Pozza Editore, 1998), pp. 214–15; Bronwen Wilson, "Il bel sesso, e l'austero Senato: The Coronation of Dogaressa Morosina Morosini Grimani," *Renaissance Quarterly* 52:1 (Spring, 1999), pp. 78–79.

54. *Col. P.D.* 1442/3, letter 2, to Marc'Antonio Michiel, July 2, 1779, from Ponte Casale.

55. *Col. P.D.* 1442/3, letter 26, to Marc'Antonio Michiel, July 11, 1779, from Venice.

56. Renier Michiel may be referring to Mercier's *Canacé à Macarée et Hypermnestre à Lyncée, héroïdes nouvelles par l'auteur d' "Hécube,"* 1762. *Col. P.D.* 1442/3, letter 44, to Marc'Antonio Michiel, n.d., n.p. Regarding other activities, see notes 38–41.

57. *Col. P.D.* 1442/3, letter 43, to Marc'Antonio Michiel, n.d., n.p. I have been unable to consult Marc'Antonio's composition.

58. *Col. P.D.* 1442/3, letter 20, to Marc'Antonio Michiel, n.d., n.p.

59. *Col. P.D.* 1442/3, letter 67, to Marc'Antonio Michiel, n.d., n.p.

60. Giustiniana Wynne, contessa di Rosenberg (1737–1791), was the wife of the count of Rosenberg, an Austrian minister living in Venice. When he died, she began a relationship with Bartolomeo Benincasa (1745–1816), with whom she co-published *Alticchiero* (Padua, 1787), although a previous edition was published in Geneva, probably in 1786. Wynne di Rosenberg also penned *Pièces morales et sentimentales* (London, 1785) and *Les Morlasques* (Venice, 1788). Luisa Ricaldone in Elisabetta Mosconi Contarini, *Al mio caro ed incomparibile amico*, ed. Luisa Ricaldone, with commentary by Marco Cerruti (Padua: Editoriale Programma, 1995), pp. 60–61, note 2.

61. *Col. P.D.* 1442/3, letter 5, to Marc'Antonio Michiel, n.d., n.p. This letter was most likely written in the early 1780s, as Renier Michiel makes reference to an anonymous German book that was reissued with an Imperial licence concerning the Pope. No doubt this is Johann Nikolaus von Hontheim's *De statu Ecclesiae et legitima potestate Romani Pontificis liber singularis, ad reuniendos dissidentes in religione christianos compositus* (Bullioni, 1763), whose work was recalled in 1778, but whose author issued a new defense of his thoughts in 1781, prior to the visit by Pope Pius VI to Joseph II in Vienna in 1782 to protest against the latter's religious reforms. If this is the case, then Renier Michiel is perhaps referring here to Wynne di Rosenberg's *Du séjour des comtes du Nord à Venise en janvier MDCCLXXXII*, 1782, also published in Italian the same year. For more on Wynne, see Di Robilant, *A Venetian Affair*.

62. *Col. P.D.* 1442/3, letter 38, to Marc'Antonio Michiel, n.d. [from Padova].

63. *Col. P.D.* 1442/3, letter 46, to Marc'Antonio Michiel, n.d. [from Padova].

64. *Col. P.D.* 1442/3, letter 38, to Marc'Antonio Michiel, n.d. [from Padova].

65. *Col. P.D.* 1442/3, letter 48, to Marc'Antonio Michiel, n.d. [from Venice]; *Col. P.D.* 1442/3, letter 51, to Marc'Antonio Michiel, n.d. [from Venice].

66. *Col. P.D.* 1442/3, letter 50, to Giustina Renier Michiel, n.d. [from Venice].

67. *Col. P.D.* 1442/3, letter 50, to Giustina Renier Michiel, n.d. [from Venice].

68. Guerci, *La sposa obbediente*, p. 51.

69. Hunecke, *Il patriziato veneziano*, pp. 63–64, 419. According to Volker Hunecke's slightly modified version of Giacomo Nani's classification for Venetian patrician families created in 1750, Renier Michiel's father and grandfather were a class two family out of five groups ranked in terms of wealth and status. Class one included the richest families (8.3 percent of the patrician population), while class two families had more than enough money to meet their needs (11.3 percent of the patrician population).

70. Marc'Antonio would eventually become a senator. Schröder, "Michiel," p. 13.

71. For example, more traditional mores were promoted by Jesuit Antonfrancesco Bellati and Francesco Beretta. Guerci, *La sposa obbediente*, pp. 32, 50.

72. Michiel himself perhaps remarks on this opposition when stating that Renier Michiel was burdened with public duties, thus tearing the soul from him who would soon no longer have reason to complain and whom she would not miss. *Col. P.D.* 1442/3, letter 52, to Giustina Renier Michiel, n.d. [from Venice].

73. *Col. P.D.* 1442/3, letter 51, to Marc'Antonio Michiel, n.d. [from Venice].

74. *Col. P.D.* 1442/3, letter 53 and letter 54, to Marc'Antonio Michiel, n.d. [from Venice].

75. *Col. P.D.* 1442/3, letter 49, to Marc'Antonio Michiel, n.d. [from Venice].

76. Gaetano Cozzi, "Note e documenti sulla questione del 'divorzio' a Venezia (1782–1788)," *Annali dell'Istituto storico italo-germanico in Trento* 7 (1981), 327. For more on marriage in Venice in an earlier period, see Joanne M. Ferraro, *Marriage Wars in Late Renaissance Venice* (New York: Oxford University Press, 2001); and Silvana Seidel Menchi and Diego Quaglioni, eds., *La separazione in Italia dal XII al XVIII secolo* (Bologna: Il Mulino, 2000).

77. *Col. P.D.* 1442/3, letter 52, to Giustina Renier Michiel, n.d. [from Venice].

78. *Col. P.D.* 1442/3, letter 57, to Marc'Antonio Michiel, n.d., to Carpenedo.

79. Guerci, *La sposa obbediente*, pp. 125–126.

80. *Col. P.D.* 1442/3, letter 38, to M.A. Michiel, n.d., to Venice; ibid., letter 13, May 6 [1785].

81. *Col. P.D.* 1442/3, letter 46, to M.A. Michiel, n.d., n.p.; letter 66, to M.A. Michiel, n.d., n.p.

82. Vittorio Malamani, "Giustina Renier Michiel: I suoi amici, il suo tempo," *Archivio Veneto* 75 (1889), pp. 48, 81; Vianello-Chido, "Giustina Renier Michiel," p. 70; Antonia Arslan and Andrea Molesini, "'Macbeth,' 'Macbetto,' 'Macbeth,': dalla proposta del 1798 al trionfo mancato del 1830," *Rivista italiana di drammaturgia* 14 (1979), p. 76, note 42.

83. Stanley Chojnacki, "Kinship Ties and Young Patricians," in *Women and Men in Renaissance Venice: Twelve Essays on Patrician Society* (Baltimore: The Johns Hopkins University Press, 2000), pp. 224–226.

84. New families were occasionally admitted into the patriciate after 1297, as a reward for the exercise of patriotic virtue in war, to meet the expenses of the indebted Venetian government, or as a remedy for the demographic crisis in the patriciate. As a rule the most well-established families were also those who occupied the most prestigious government posts. See Piero Del Negro, "La distribuzione del potere all'interno del patriziato veneziano del settecento," in *I ceti dirigenti in Italia in età moderna e contemporanea. Atti del Convegno Cividale del Friuli, 10–12 settembre 1983,* ed. Amelio Tagliaferri (Udine: Del Bianco Editore, 1984). Regarding the "nobility" of the Venetian patriciate, see Claudio Donati, *L'idea di nobiltà in Italia. Secoli XIV–XVIII* (Bari: Editori Laterza, 1995), pp. 58, 61, 71, 74.

85. Jacques Revel, "Les usages de la civilité," in *Histoire de la vie privée*, vol. 3: *De la Renaissance aux Lumières,* ed. Roger Chartier (Paris: Le Seuil, 1986), p. 194; Roger Baillet, "Codes de comportement et communication dans le *Cortegiano*," in *Traités de savoir-vivre en Italie*, ed. Alain Montandon (Clermont-Ferrand: Association des Publications de la Faculté des Lettres et Sciences Humaines de Clermont-Ferrand, 1993), pp. 166–167; J. R. Woodhouse, "Il trattato di cortesia in Italia: tra idealismo e realtà," in *Traités de savoir-vivre en Italie*, ed. Alain Montandon (Clermont-Ferrand: Association des Publications de la Faculté des Lettre et Sciences Humaines de Clermont-Ferrand, 1993), p. 217.

86. Alain Montandon, "Pour une histoire des traités de savoir-vivre italiens. Esquisse bibliographique," in *Traités de savoir-vivre en Italie*, ed. Alain Montandon (Clermont-Ferrand: Association des Publications de la Faculté des Lettre et Sciences Humaines de Clermont-Ferrand, 1993), pp. 309–334; Peter Burke, *The Fortunes of the Courtier: The European Reception of Castiglione's "Cortegiano"* (Cambridge: Polity Press, 1995); Giorgio Patrizi, "La 'Civil Conversatione' libro europeo," in *Stefano Guazzo e la Civil Conversazione* (Rome: Bulzoni editore, 1990), pp. 9–23; Inge Botteri, *Galateo e Galatei: La creanza e l'instituzione della società nella trattatistica italiana tra antico regime e stato liberale* (Rome: Bulzoni editore, 1999), pp. 43–163.

87. See Dena Goodman, *The Republic of Letters: A Cultural History of the French Enlightenment* (Ithaca, NY: Cornell University Press, 1994); Sylvia Harcstark Myers, *The Bluestocking Circle: Women, Friendship, and the Life of the Mind in Eighteenth-Century England* (New York: Oxford University Press, 1990); Susan Dalton, *Engendering the Republic of Letters: Reconnecting Public and Private Spheres in Eighteenth-Century Europe* (Montreal: McGill-Queen's University Press, 2003); Maria Luisa Betri and Elena Brambilla, *Salotti e ruolo femminile in Italia tra fine Seicento e primo Novecento* (Venice: Marsilio Editori, 2004).

88. See Goodman, *The Republic of Letters*, p. 4.

89. "L'urbanità in oltre e la cortesia, che in Francia dicesi pulitezza, fece colà universale una libera ed amichevole conversazione tra gli uomini e i sessi." Saverio Bettinelli, "Da 'Il Risorgimento d'Italia negli studi, nelle arti e ne' costumi dopo il mille,'" in *Illuministi italiani*, vol. 2: *Opere di Franceso Algarotti e di Saverio Bettinelli*, ed. Ettore Bonora, coll. *Letteratura italiana. Storia e testi*, v. 46, t. 2 (Milan: R. Ricciardi, 1969), p. 929.

90. "Quindi ognun sa che han lor sede nel cuore"; "In contrario le belle lettere agitando l'anima tutta, . . . ornano in fine la seria ragione delle grazie e delle dolcezze della passione"; "Pur sempre è vero che la natura ha dato all'uomo la saldezza e la profondità per l'opere laboriose e lunghe e sublimi, come alle donne ha concessa l'eleganza, la delicatezza, la facilità nel pensare e nell'esprimersi"; "Quindi hanno esse il merito di addolcire e ingentilire i letterati conversando, come in Francia si vede più comunemente." Ibid., pp. 936–938.

91. Ibid., p. 986.

92. Paula Findlen, "Translating the New Science: Women and the Circulation of Knowledge in Enlightenment Italy," *Configurations* 2 (1995), 169; Daniel Gordon, *Citizens without Sovereignty: Equality and Sociability in French Thought, 1670–1789* (Princeton: Princeton University Press, 1994), p. 192.

93. Melchiorre Cesarotti, "Ragionamento sopra il diletto della tragedia," in *Dal Muratori al Cesarotti*, vol. 4: *Critici e storici della poesia e delle arti nel secondo settecento*, ed. Emilio Bigi, coll. *Letteratura italiana. Storia e testi*, v. 44, t. 4 (Milan: Riccardo Ricciardi Editore, 1960), p. 53. On the legitimacy of popular judgment, see also Francesco Algarotti, "Saggio sopra la pittura," in *Illuministi italiani*, vol. 2: *Opere di Franceso Algarotti e di Saverio Bettinelli*, ed. Ettore Bonora, coll. *Letteratura italiana. Storia e testi*, v. 46, t. 2 (Milan: R. Ricciardi 1969), pp. 410–411; Pietro Verri proclaimed the legitimacy of public opinion regarding painting, music,

and dramatic arts, areas in which judgment could be founded on sentiment alone. Pietro Verri, "I giudizi popolari," *Opere varie*, ed. Nino Valeri, v. 1 (Florence: Felice le Monnier, 1947), pp. 88–89. Regarding the increasing importance of the wider public in eighteenth-century Italy, including women, see Andrea Battistini and Ezio Raimondi, "Retoriche e poetiche dominanti," in *Letteratura italiana*, vol. 3: *Le forme del testo I. Teoria e poesia*, ed. Alberto Asor Rosa (Turin: Giulio Einaudi editore, 1984), pp. 131–133. On the importance of Du Bos for European aesthetics, see Elio Franzini, *L'estetica del Settecento* (Bologna: Il Mulino, 1995), pp. 403, 418.

94. "Oh quanto mai vi sono grate, mio pregiato amico, di avermi procurato una sì bella lettura! Oh, quante cose io lessi che mi resteranno scolpite nel cuore! Qual contrasto però di sensazioni differenti essa mi destò!" Letter to S. Bettinelli, May 13, 1807, from Venice. Giustina Renier Michiel, *Lettere inedite della N.D. Giustina Renier Michiel e dell'Abbate [sic] Saverio Bettinelli tratte dagli autografi* (Venice: Tipografia del commercio, 1857), p. 10.

95. "Ella già fin da vari anni mi ha dato il dritto di ammirarla, e conservo pur anco come cosa preziosa un suo manoscritto, che la stampa non mi rese men caro; e fin d'allora il mio cuore riconoscente festeggiò il mio giudizio. Ella non avea bisogno di rinovare adesso il mio sentimento di gratitudine per richiamare un medessimo effetto; ogni sua produzione và dritta al cuore e alla mente, e vi sparge quel dolce che attrae ognuno verso il felice e valente scrittore." Italy. Bassano del Grappa. Biblioteca Civica Bassano del Grappa. *Epistolario raccolto da Bartolomeo Gamba*, XVI, A.24, document 2515. Letter to Urbano Pagani-Cesa, October 1, 1803, from Venice, to Belluno.

96. Renier Michiel in fact translated from Pierre Le Tourneur's French translation of Shakespeare; certain elements of her preface, notably the detailed discussion of aesthetic questions, are drawn directly from the French author's text. Sections near the beginning and at the end of the preface, dealing with gender questions, are Renier Michiel's own. Therefore, Renier Michiel's claim that Shakespeare could make passions speak was drawn from Le Tourneur, whereas her discussion of her own feelings, women, and her daughters (see also notes 97 and 98) was her original contribution. Giustina Renier Michiel, "Prefazione della traduttrice," *Opere dramatiche di Shakspeare (sic) volgarizzate da una dama veneta*, v. 1 (Venice: Eredi Costantini, 1798), pp. 5, 10; Malamani, "Giustina Renier Michiel," 75, p. 50; Pierre Le Tourneur, *Préface du Shakespeare traduit de l'Anglois*, ed. Jacques Gury (Geneva: Librairie Droz, 1990 [1776]).

97. Ibid., pp. 9–10.

98. Ibid., p. 24.

99. Renier Michiel had been commissioned to offer a physical and moral description of the city by the French government after control of the area was transferred from Austria in the Treaty of Pressburg in December 1805. The resulting work was Renier Michiel's *Saggio delle feste nazionali venete. Il Redentore e S. Marta (Essai des fêtes nationales vénitiennes. Le rédempteur et Sainte Marthe)* (Venice: Per Francesco Andreola Stampatore della Reale Marina Italiana, e Dipertimentale, 1810), a sixty-seven-page document written in French and Italian. It was upon this basis that

Renier Michiel wrote her *Origine delle Feste Veneziane* (Venice: dalla tipografia Alvisopoli, 1817–1827), which in its first edition was also written in French and Italian. The 1829 edition is in Italian only.

100. Giustina Renier Michiel, "Prefazione," *Origine delle Feste Veneziane*, v. 1 (Milan, 1829), pp. xi–xiv.

101. Renier Michiel, "Prefazione," pp. xxiii–xxiv.

102. Renier Michiel, "Prefazione," p. xvi; "ciascheduno di essi è un originale che ha un'esistenza sua propria, come i reali individui della Società." Renier Michiel, "Prefazione della traduttrice," p. 12.

103. "[E] ben mi ricordo che mentre eravamo rapiti dell'incanto dell'arte, eravamo sedotti ad ammirar egualmente la modestia dell'artifice." Italy. Bassano del Grappa. Biblioteca Civica Bassano del Grappa. *Carteggio Canoviano*, vi-661, document 3916, letter to Antonio Canova, April 26, 1809, from Venice to Rome.

104. "Questa mad. de Stael mi porse uno di que' contrasti, pur troppo non rari, fra la persona e lo scrittore, ch'io poi assolutamente detesto. Tuttociò che si legge di lei ha un certo patetico, un certo delicato, un certo fino, dolce insinuante, che sforza ad amarla rispettosamente. Nel vederla poi essa si presenta con un passo molto sciolto e marziale; l'occhio nero getta uno sguardo ardito; i capelli inanellati alla modo sembrano i serpenti di Medusa; gran bocca, grandi spalle, grosse proporzioni, quelle pure che si vogliono più moderate e gentili." Letter to S. Bettinelli, June 20, 1807, from Venice. Renier Michiel, *Lettere inedite della N.D.*, p. 12.

105. Roger Chartier, "From Texts to Manners: A Concept and Its Books: *Civilité* between Aristocratic Distinction and Popular Appropriation," in *The Cultural Uses of Print in Early Modern France*, trans. Lydia G. Cochrane (Princeton: Princeton University Press, 1987), pp. 71–109; Revel, "Les usages de la civilité," pp. 169–209.

106. Renier Michiel, "Prefazione della traduttrice," p. 16.

107. Ibid., p. 6. On the increasing importance of natural characters in theater, see a brief discussion of Goldoni in Battistini and Raimondi, "Retoriche e poetiche dominanti," p. 132. On the influx of Shakespeare into Italy in the eighteenth century, see Siro Ferrone and Teresa Megale, "Il teatro," *Storia della letteratura italiana*, vol. 6: *Il Settecento*, ed. Enrico Malato (Rome: Salerno editrice, 1998), p. 865.

108. In this passage, also, Renier Michiel reworked a passage by Le Tourneur based on a verse recited David Garrick at the Shakespeare Jubilee in 1769. See Le Tourneur, *Préface du Shakespeare*, p. xvi.

109. See Pietro Longhi, *La famiglia Michiel*, 1780.

110. Mario Fubini, *Dal Muratori al Baretti. Studi sulla critica e sulla cultura del Séttecento* (Bari: Laterza, 1975), pp. 255, 281, 284, 361–362, 410–411.

111. Bettinelli, "Da 'Il Risorgimento,'" p. 984; "Io sono egualmente avezzo alla generosità delle vostre esebizioni come sono documentato a non prevalermene. Siete impegnata con il pubblico lacerate pure l'anima di chi presto forse non potrà più lagnarsene. ma non mancate! ed esponete pure il decoro di una Famiglia, e di un infelisce che odiate soltanto perchè in lui diventa vizio l'onestà guardarvi da quel ridicolo che voi acenate, e vedete, ed io non comprendo." *Col. P.D.* 1442/3, letter 52, to Giustina Renier Michiel, n.d. [from Venice].

112. See note 99 on the reasons behind this choice and a review of the first volume of the 1817–1827 Venetian edition of the *Origine* in *Giornale dell'italiana letteratura compilato da una società di letterati italiani* 44 (January–February 1817), 135–136. In her *Saggio delle feste nazionali venete*, 1810, however, Renier Michiel did use gender codes to justify her work.

113. "Il leggiadro pensiero poteva essere creato che . . . da un animo pieghevole alle sensazioni le più soavi, da un cuor buono, da un intelletto ornato di vaste cognizioni storiche, di sana critica, di fino accorgimento." Ginevra Canonici Fachini, *Prospetto biografico delle donne italiane rinomate in letteratura dal secolo decimoquarto fino a' giorni nostri* (Venice: Tipografia di Alvisopoli, 1824), p. 251.

114. Isabella Teotochi Albrizzi, *Ritratto di Giustina Renier Michiel* (s.l., 1833), p. 12.

115. Teotochi Albrizzi, *Ritratto*, pp. 5–6; Canonici Fachini, *Prospetto*, p. 251. Both women also mentioned an earlier manifestation of this patriotism, contained in Renier Michiel's response to François René Chateaubriand's criticisms of Venice published in 1806. See her *Risposta alla lettera del signor Chateaubriand sopra Venezia*, (Venice, 1806). Luigi Carrer also referred to her feminine attributes but insisted much more on her sharp intellect. Luigi Carrer, "Giustina Renier Michiel," in *Vite e ritratti delle donne celebri d'ogni paese. Opera della Duchessa d'Abrantès*, vol. 3 (Milan, 1837), pp. 230–242.

116.   Poichè insolente vincitor sovverse
   Il soglio della inerme Adria tradita
   Costei svegliando la virtù sopita
   Viver ne' suoi di più non sofferse;
E nelle andate età tutta s'immerse
   Tra l'opre e i fasti della gente avita,
   E delle feste lor la storia ordita
   Di patrio amor splendido pegno offerse
Così degli avi nel consorzio intero
   Traendo il giorno, quasi le fu tolto
   Il sovvenirsi del perduto impero;
Quindi dal suo terren gaudio disciolto
   Lo spirito antico generoso e altero
   Fu de' Veneti eroi fra l'ombre accolto.

Francesco Maria Franceschinis, cited in Vittorio Malamani, "Giustina Renier Michiel: i suoi amici, il suo tempo," *Archivio Veneto* 76 (1889), 364–365. Malamani published a number of other eulogies in the same article.

Notes to Chapter Four

1. See Elisabetta Graziosi, "Arcadia femminile: presenze e modelli," *Filologia e critica* 17 (1992), 321–58; Idem, "Presenze femminili: fuori e dentro l' Arcadia," in *Salotti e ruolo femminile in Italia. Tra fine Seicento e primo Novecento*, ed. Maria Luisa Betri and Elena Brambilla (Venice: Marsilio, 2004), pp. 67–96; William Spaggiari, "Lesbia nel Bosco Parrasio": poetesse in Arcadia, in *1782. Studi di italianistica* (Reggio Emilia: Edizioni Diabasis, 2004), pp. 13–33. More recently, for an important

example among female Arcadian figures, see Elisabetta Graziosi, "Ritratto d'Arcadia in un salotto: la sconosciuta e benemerita duchessa di Limatola," *Genesis* 2 (2005), 159–82.

2. See Michele Maylender, *Storia delle Accademie d' Italia* (Bologna: Cappelli, 1926–30), vol. 4, pp. 140, 185; vol. 5, p. 134. The problem of women in the academies of the seventeenth century has aroused scarce interest. See, for example, Lovanio Rossi, "Seicento, Accademie del," in *Dizionario critico della letteratura italiana*, ed. Vittore Branca (Turin: UTET, 1986), vol. 4, pp. 156–59. For the sixteenth century see Conor Fahy, "Women and Italian Cinquecento Literary Academies," in *Women in Italian Renaissance Culture and Society*, ed. Letizia Panizza (Oxford: European Humanities Research Centre, 2000), pp. 438–52.

3. Cited in Enrica Malcovati, "Le donne nelle Accademie," in *Atti del 1° Convegno nazionale delle Accademie di scienze e di lettere in occasione del 150° anniversario di fondazione dei due Istituti* (Milan-Venice: Istituto lombardo di Scienze e Lettere-Istituto veneto di Scienze, Lettere ed Arti, 1954), p. 104. For the Ereini see Silvia Parigi, "La 'biddizza' e il 'sapiri': il dialogo poetico-filosofico tra Girolama Lorefice Grimaldi and Tommaso Campailla," in *Donne, filosofia e cultura nel Seicento*, ed. Pina Totaro (Rome: Consiglio Nazionale delle Ricerche, 1999), pp. 143–54.

4. See Patricia H. Labalme, "Women's Roles in Early Modern Venice: An Exceptional Case," in *Beyond Their Sex. Learned Women of the European Past*, ed. Patricia H. Labalme (New York and London: New York University Press, 1984) pp. 128–52; Renzo Derosas, entry in *Dizionario biografico degli Italiani* (Rome: Istituto della Enciclopedia Italiana, 1983), vol. 29, pp. 174–79 (hereafter DBI); Lino Lazzarini, "La vita accademica dei 'Ricovrati' di Padova dal 1668 al 1684 e Elena Cornaro Piscopia," in *Atti e memorie dell' Accademia patavina di Scienze, Lettere ed Arti già Accademia dei Ricovrati. Memorie della Classe di Scienze morali, Lettere ed Arti* 94 (1981–82), pp. I, 50–109.

5. For the cloister spirituality of Piscopia see Giorgio Fedalto, "Elena Lucrezia Cornaro Piscopia (1646–1684). Tra spiritualità claustrale e secolare nella Venezia del Seicento," *Archivio veneto* 110 (1979), 55–69.

6. See Attilio Maggiolo, *Soci dell' Accademia patavina dalla sua fondazione (1599)* (Padua: Accademia patavina, 1983); Sandra Olivieri Secchi, "Immagini di donna e donne nell' Accademia dei Ricovrati (sec. XVII)," in *Dall' Accademia dei Ricoverati all' Accademia galileiana. Atti del Convegno storico per il IV centenario della fondazione (1559–1999)*, ed. Ezio Riondato (Padua: Accademia Galileiana, 2001), pp. 375–91.

7. See the information collected by Carolina M. Scaglioso, *Un' Accademia femminile. Le Assicurate di Siena* (Città di Castello: Gruppo Editoriale Marcon, 1995).

8. On the Paduan dispute see Luciano Guerci, *La discussione sulla donna nell' Italia del Settecento. Aspetti e problemi* (Turin: Tirrenia, 1988), pp. 149–50; Idem, *La sposa obbediente. Donna e matrimonio nella discussione dell' Italia del Settecento* (Turin: Tirrenia, 1988), pp. 245–46. Aretafila Savini de' Rossi's contribution has recently been translated into English in *The Contest for Knowledge: Debates over Women's*

Learning in Eighteenth-Century Italy, ed. and trans. Rebecca Messbarger and Paula Findlen (Chicago: The University of Chicago Press, 2004), pp. 102–16.

9. See *Giornale della gloriosissima Accademia Ricovrata. A. Verbali delle adunanze accademiche dal 1599 al 1694*, ed. Antonio Gamba and Lucia Rossetti (Padua: Edizioni LINT, 1999), pp. 333–34.

10. Renata Ago, *Carriere e clientele nella Roma barocca* (Rome-Bari: Laterza, 1990), pp. 65–70. See also Maria Pia Donato's contribution to this volume, Chapter 2.

11. A recent profile is in Maria Teresa Acquaro Graziosi, *L'Arcadia. Trecento anni di storia* (Rome: Palombi, 1991). Important is the general frame of reference offered by Maria Pia Donato, *Accademie romane. Una storia sociale (1671–1824)* (Naples: Edizioni Scientifiche Italiane, 2000).

12. Giovan Mario Crescimbeni, *La bellezza della volgar poesia* (Rome, 1700), pp. 217–22.

13. That Arcadia was (or was considered) an erudite academy instituted for the "cultivation of all the sciences" is explicit in a declaration by Crescimbeni which dates to the years of the Gravinian scission and is cited in Antonio Cipriani, "Contributo per una storia politica dell'Arcadia settecentesca," *Arcadia, Accademia, Letteraria Italiana. Atti e memorie* 5 (1971), 109. On the long exclusion of women from the sciences, see David F. Noble, *Un mondo senza donne e la scienza occidentale* (Turin: Bollati Boringhieri, 1994 and originally 1992).

14. For the admissions I refer the reader to the literature already cited in Elisabetta Graziosi, "Arcadia femminile: presenze e modelli," *Filologia e critica* 17 (1992), 321–58. I note in parentheses the Arcadian name and the year, or the guardianship, of admission according to data in Anna Maria Giorgetti Vichi, *Gli Arcadi dal 1690 al 1800. Onomasticon* (Rome: Arcadia. Accademia letteraria italiana, 1977), with some correction as indicated.

15. Fausto Nicolini, *Aspetti della vita italo-spagnuola nel Cinque e Seicento* (Naples: Guida, 1934), pp. 284–85.

16. On Borghini see the entry by Gianni Ballistreri in DBI, vol. 12, pp. 676–77. Recent detailed information may be found in *Il Canzoniere di Maria Selvaggia Borghini*, ed. Agostino Agostini and Alessandro Panajia, with an essay by Elisabetta Benucci (Pisa: Edizioni ETS, 2001). For more in general on the entire group of Tuscan Arcadians, see Antonella Giordano, *Letterate toscane del Settecento: un regesto*, with an essay on Corilla Olimpica and Teresa Ciamagnini Pelli Fabbroni by Luciana Morelli, preface by Riccardo Bruscagli and Simonetta Soldani (Florence: All'insegna del Giglio, 1994).

17. Scarce is the information on Febei, which may be drawn from "Notizie di scrittori orvietani per il sig. conte Mazzucchelli di Brescia estese dal sig. abate Gio. Battista Febei nel 1751," *Archivio storico per le Marche e per l' Umbria* 3 (1886), 378–79.

18. The figure given by Jane Stevenson in *Women Latin Poets: Language, Gender and Authority, from Antiquity to the Eighteenth Century* (Oxford: Oxford University Press, 2005), p. 313, is therefore incorrect. She mentions only five Arcadians and underestimates the importance of the Arcadian innovation compared to the limited, "ornamental" presence of women in the academies of the preceding cen-

tury—a subject treated in my essay "Arcadia femminile: presenze e modelli," which Stevenson quotes only secondhand.

19. For the Arcadian rules (until now not sufficiently studied) see Michele Giuseppe Morei, *Memorie istoriche dell' adunanza degli Arcadi* (Rome, 1761), p. 187.

20. I generally reconstruct presences in the colonies by the data regarding admission. Moreover, for the Renia colony see *La Colonia Renia. Profilo documentario e critico dell' Arcadia bolognese*, ed. Mario Saccenti, 2 vols. (Modena: Mucchi, 1988); for the Animosa colony see Antonio Franceschetti, "L' Arcadia veneta," in *Storia della cultura veneta*, vol. V/1: *Il Settecento* (Vicenza: Neri Pozza, 1985), pp. 132–70; for the colony of Verona see Antonio Spagnolo, *L' Arcadia veronese* (Rome: Tip. sociale Polizzi e Valentini, 1906); for the Augusta colony see Paola Pimpinelli, *I riti della poesia nell' Arcadia perugina* (Perugia: Volumnia, 2000); for the Trebbia colony see Francesco Picco, "Nei paesi d' Arcadia. La Colonia trebbiense," in *Bollettino Storico Piacentino*, 1907.

21. The diploma is found in the Biblioteca Bolognese dell' Archiginnasio, Fondo Bassi, cart. 6.3 (I owe the reference to Marta Cavazza). On Laura Bassi see the entry in DBI, vol. 7, 1965, pp. 145–47 (lacking in Giorgetti Vichi).

22. See Giuseppe Pietropoli, *L' Accademia dei Concordi nella vita rodigina dalla seconda metà del sedicesimo secolo alla fine della dominazione austriaca* (Padua: Signum, 1986), pp. 50–51.

23. On Gabrielli Capizucchi see the entry by Lucinda Spera in DBI, vol. 51, 1998, pp. 114–15.

24. See Morei, *Memorie istoriche*, pp. 236, 238. See also Gaetano Platania, *Gli ultimi Sobieski e Roma. Fasti e miserie di una famiglia reale polacca tra Sei e Settecento (1699–1715)* (Rome: Vecchiarelli, 1989).

25. There is no current biography of Maratti Zappi. For a recent profile see Antonio Franceschetti, "Faustina Maratti Zappi (1679?–1745)," in *Italian Women Writers. A Bio-Bibliographical Sourcebook*, ed. Rinaldina Russell (Westport, CT, and London: Greenwood Press, 1994), pp. 226–33. Some information may be found in Carla Cacciari and Giuliana Zanelli, *Faustina Maratti. Tra Roma ed Imola: immagine pubblica e tormenti privati di una poetessa italiana del Settecento* (Imola: La Mandragora, 1995).

26. Information about this vicissitude may be found in Prospero Colonna, *Francesco Massimi e i suoi tempi (1635–1707). Memorie e notizie storiche raccolte nell' Archivio dei Massimo all' Aracoeli* (Rome: Tipografia cooperativa sociale, 1911). A current biography of Petronilla Paolini Massimi is also lacking. Little information may be drawn from Ileana Tozzi, *Petronilla Paolini Massimi: una donna in Arcadia*, Nota di Marirì Martinengo (Pescara: Editrice Nova Italica, 1991).

27. On these not well-known women poets, I refer the reader to Elisabetta Graziosi, *Avventuriere a Bologna. Due storie esemplari* (Modena: Mucchi, 1998).

28. On the biographical vicissitudes of Maria Mancini Colonna, see Claude Dulong, *Marie Mancini. La première passion de Louis XIV* (Paris: Perrin, 1993). For the missing literary production, see Elisabetta Graziosi, "Lettere da un matrimonio fallito: Maria Mancini al marito Lorenzo Onofrio Colonna," in *Per lettera.*

La scrittura femminile tra archivio e tipografia, secoli XV–XVII, ed. Gabriella Zarri (Rome: Viella, 1999), pp. 535–84.

29. They are cited in this order: *Scelta di sonetti e canzoni de' più eccellenti rimatori d' ogni secolo* (Bologna, 1709–1711), 4 vols.; *Rime scelte di poeti illustri de' nostri tempi* (Lucca, 1709–1719), 2 vols.; *Raccolta di rime di poeti napoletani non più ancora stampate* (Naples, 1701); *Rime scelte de' poeti ferraresi antichi e moderni* (Ferrara, 1713).

30. *Poesie italiane di rimatrici viventi raccolte da Teleste Ciparissiano pastore arcade* (Venice, 1716).

31. *Poesie italiane di rimatori viventi non mai per l' addietro stampate. Agl' illustrissimi signori principe ed assistenti dell' illustrissima accademia de' signori Innominati di Bra'* (Venice, 1717). On this collection see Giampaolo Marchi, "Veronesi a Bra in una raccolta poetica del 1717," in *L' Arcadia e l' Accademia degli Innominati di Bra*, ed. Alfredo Mango (Milan: Angeli, 2007), pp. 153–82.

32. See Amedeo Quondam, "L' istituzione Arcadia. Sociologia e ideologia di un' Accademia," *Quaderni storici* 8 (1973), 412–13 (he does not, however, distinguish between the various phases of Arcadia in relation to the various guardianships).

33. Giovan Mario Crescimbeni, *La bellezza della volgar poesia, corretta e accresciuta del nono dialogo* (Rome, 1712), p. 203.

34. *Componimenti poetici delle più illustri rimatrici d' ogni secolo raccolti da Luisa Bergalli* (Venice, 1726), 2 vols. For a study of this work, which included 248 women poets from the thirteenth through the eighteenth centuries, see Adriana Chemello, "Le ricerche erudite di Luisa Bergalli," in Adriana Chemello and Luisa Ricaldone, *Geografie e genealogie letterarie. Erudite, biografe, croniste, narratrici, 'épistolières,' utopiste tra Settecento e Ottocento* (Padua: Il Poligrafo, 2000), pp. 49–88. See also Catherine M. Sama's Chapter 5 in this volume.

35. See Gino Benzoni, "La vita intellettuale," in *Storia di Venezia dalle origini alla caduta della Serenissima*, VII, *La Venezia barocca*, ed. Gino Benzoni and Gaetano Cozzi (Rome: Istituto per la Enciclopedia italiana, 1997) p. 880.

36. Information about this separation may be found in Benedetta Borello, "Annodare e sciogliere. Reti di relazioni femminili e separazioni a Roma (XVII–XVIII secolo)," *Quaderni storici* 37 (2002), 617–48.

37. *Rime di Gaetana Secchi Ronchi gentildonna guastallese* (Guastalla, 1776).

38. For the date of admission, see Giorgetti Vichi (but 1728 is the date of the second name given to her—Acmena—because Giuseppa Eleonora was already an Arcadian in 1722 with the name of Mirista). On Barbapiccola see the entry by Enzo Grillo in DBI, vol. 6, 1964, p. 39; Paula Findlen, "Translating the New Science: Women and the Circulation of Knowledge in Enlightenment Italy," *Configuration* 2 (1995), 167–206; Manuela Sanna, "Un' amicizia alla luce del cartesianesimo: Giuseppa Eleonora Barbapiccola e Luisa Vico," in *Donne, filosofia e cultura nel Seicento*, ed. Pina Totaro (Rome: Consiglio Nazionale delle Ricerche, 1999), pp. 173–78.

39. It may be read in *Tutte le opere* of Metastasio, ed. Bruno Brunelli (Milan: Mondadori, 1965), vol. 2, p. 1352 (Metastasio's response is on p. 953).

40. I cite from *Lirici del Settecento*, ed. Bruno Maier with the collaboration of

Mario Fubini, Dante Isella, Giorgio Piccitto. Introduction of Mario Fubini (Milan-Naples: Ricciardi, 1959), p. 49.

41. It can be found in Maylender, op. cit., vol. 4, pp. 209–11. On Parma in those years, the most complete treatment is still that offered by Henri Bédarida, *Parma e la Francia (1748–1789)*, ed. Andrea Calzolari and Armando Marchi, introduction by Giorgio Cusatelli, iconographic research by Marzio Dall' Acqua (Milan: Franco Maria Ricci, 1985 and originally 1928). For the presence of Du Tillot e Condillac, see now the volume of Carminella Biondi, *La Francia a Parma nel secondo Settecento* (Bologna: Clueb, 2003).

42. Missing in Giorgetti Vichi. On her see Marcello Turchi, "Ritratto di Anna Malaspina 'ispiratrice di poesia,'" *Aurea Parma* 60 (1976), 3–11. For other information and her Arcadian name see Pompeo Litta, s.v. "Malaspina" table XXII, in *Famiglie celebri italiane* (Milan, 1819–1874), 10 vols.; and Vincenzo Monti, *Poesie*, ed. Alfonso Bertoldi (Florence: Sansoni, 1904), pp. 60–61.

43. *Le pastorelle d' Arcadia. Festa campestre nelle augustissime nozze delle altezze reali del reale infante di Spagna don Ferdinando di Borbone duca di Parma . . . e della reale arciduchessa d' Austria Maria Amalia* (Parma, 1769) (all the names are missing in Giorgetti Vichi).

44. Gennaro Barbarisi, "L' Epistola del Monti alla Malaspina," in *Atti del Convegno sul Settecento parmense nel 2° centenario della morte di C.I. Frugoni* (Parma: Deputazione di Storia patria, 1969), pp. 223–40.

45. See Carlo Calcaterra, *La brigata frugoniana di casa Malaspina*, in *Barocco in Arcadia e altri scritti sul Settecento* (Bologna: Zanichelli, 1950), pp. 99–113.

46. See for example the three epistolary sonnets with the responses of Costanza Ravanetti, "Arcadian Shepherdess," in Carlo Innocenzo Frugoni, *Opere poetiche* (Parma, 1779), vol. 8, pp. 606–11 (but traces of women who composed verses in epistolary dialogue may be found everywhere).

47. The two intermediaries were Maria Ginevra Toruzzi Mellini (Nidalma Mellania) and Maria Maddalena Trotti Bevilacqua (Climene Teutonica, and not Teutonia as in Giorgetti Vichi). See the story at ivi., vol. 10, p. 510.

48. See Guido Mazzoni, *Abati, soldati, autori, attori del Settecento* (Bologna: Zanichelli, 1924), pp. 23–40.

49. See *L' Epistolario ossia scelta di lettere inedite, famigliari, curiose, erudite, storiche, galanti . . . di donne e d' uomini celebri morti o viventi nel secolo XVIII o nel MDCC* (Venice, 1795), p. 242; Adolfo Equini, *C.I. Frugoni alle corti dei Farnesi e dei Borboni di Parma* (Milan, Palermo etc.: Sandron, 1920–21), vol. 1.

50. See Tatiana Crivelli, "La 'sorellanza' nella poesia arcadica femminile tra Sette e Ottocento," *Filologia e critica* 26 (2001), 321–49.

51. See Marta Cavazza, "Les femmes à l' Académie: le cas de Bologne," in *Académies et sociétés savantes en Europe (1650–1800)*, ed. Daniel-Odon Hurel and Gérard Laudin (Paris: Champion, 2000), pp. 161–75.

52. *Componimenti recitati nell' adunanza d' Arcadia in lode dell' inclita ed erudita madama du Boccage* (Rome, 1758).

53. Walpurgis—composer, harpsichordist, poetess, and painter—also signed her

compositions with the Arcadian name of Ermelinda Talea; see the entry in *Dizionario enciclopedico universale della musica e dei musicisti* (Turin: UTET, 1985–1988), vol. 5, pp. 662–63. On her presence in the realm of international politics, see Cecilia Campa, *Il mondo musicale di Maria Antonia Walpurgis elettrice di Sassonia,* in *Regine e sovrane. Il potere, la politica, la vita privata,* ed. Giovanna Motta (Milan: Angeli, 2002), pp. 165–78.

54. *Adunanze degli Arcadi pubblicate nelle nozze di sua eccellenza la signora d. Giacinta Orsini de' duchi di Gravina con sua eccellenza il signor don Antonio Boncompagno Ludovisi duca d'Arce dei principi di Piombino* (Rome, 1757).

55. See Serenella Rolfi, catalog entry for the portrait of the Principessa Giacinta Orsini Boncompagni Ludovisi duchessa di Arce by Pompeo Batoni, in *Il Neoclassicismo in Italia da Tiepolo a Canova* (Milan: Skira, 2002), pp. 462–63 (illustrated on p. 198).

56. See *La donna nella pittura italiana del Seicento e Settecento. Il genio e la grazia,* ed. Alberto Cottino (Turin, London etc.: Umberto Allemandi & C., 2003), fig. 20 and p. 174.

57. *Rime degli Arcadi* (Rome, 1759), vol. 12, p. 79.

58. Morei, *Memorie istoriche,* op. cit., pp. 84–85. See Paola Giuli's contribution to this volume (Chapter 12) for a more detailed discussion of female improvisers.

59. See *Saggio di poesie scelte filosofiche ed eroiche o sia sonetti, ed altri componimenti poetici filosofici ed eroici in parte finora inediti e per la prima volta insieme raccolti di diversi illustri autori molti de' quali ancora vivono* (Florence, 1753).

60. *Rime di Maria Fortuna fra gli Arcadi Isidea Egirena al chiarissimo signor abate Pietro Metastasio poeta cesareo* (Rome, 1767). For the biography see the entry of Valentina Coen, in DBI, vol. 39, 1997, pp. 221–22.

61. See the letter of Metastasio of 6 September 1773 (but contact had already been established in 1770) in *Tutte le opere,* op. cit., vol. 5, pp. 254–55.

62. See *Corilla Olimpica e la poesia del Settecento europeo,* ed. Moreno Fabbri (Pistoia: Maschietto editore, 2002), and in the same volume Paola Giuli, "Corilla Olimpica improvvisatrice: A Reappraisal," pp. 155–72.

63. It was reconstructed at the end of the nineteenth century in a lovely book rich with erudition; see Alessandro Ademollo, *Corilla Olimpica* (Florence: C. Ademollo e C., 1887). See also the more recent work of Giuli, Chapter 12 in this volume.

64. One example: Maria Antonia Walpurgis, an Arcadian since 1749 and acclaimed in 1772. *Adunanza . . . ad onore di sua Altezza reale Maria Antonia Walpurga di Baviera elettrice vedova di Sassonia fra le pastorelle acclamate Ermelinda Talea* (Rome, 1772).

65. See Donato's Chapter 2 on Roman salons in this volume.

66. See Gualtiero De Santi, "Madame de Staël e la letteratura italiana. L'esempio di Corinne," in *Miscellanea di studi in onore di Claudio Varese,* ed. Giorgio Cerboni Baiardi (Rome: Vecchiarelli, 2001), pp. 299–313.

67. On Fonseca Pimentel see Cinzia Cassani, in DBI, vol. 48, 1997, pp. 595–600; Elena Urgnani, *La vicenda letteraria e politica di Eleonora Fonseca Pimentel,* preface

of Luisa Muraro (Naples: La città del sole, 1998). Eleonora Fonseca Pimentel is lacking in Giorgetti Vichi.

68. The sovereign's dispatch is published in Alfonso Sansone, *Gli avvenimenti del 1799 nelle Due Sicilie. Nuovi documenti* (Palermo: Era Nova, 1901), pp. 114–18.

Notes to Chapter Five

1. Although 1675 continues to be erroneously cited as the year of Carriera's birth, Franca Zava Boccazzi proved that the artist was born on 12 January 1673. See Franca Zava Boccazzi, "Il vero atto battesimale di Rosalba Carriera," in *Arte Veneta*, 49 (1996), 93–95.

2. Christopher M. S. Johns, "'An Ornament of Italy and the Premier Female Painter of Europe': Rosalba Carriera and the Roman Academy," in Melissa Hyde and Jennifer Milam, eds., *Women, Art and the Politics of Identity in Eighteenth-Century Europe* (Hants, England: Ashgate, 2003), 20. See also W. W. Roworth, M. Sheriff, and A. L. Lindberg, "Academies of Art," in *Dictionary of Women Artists*, ed. Delia Gaze, I, 43–55.

3. Carriera received her first major commissions from Frederick IV of Denmark and the Elector Palatine Johann Wilhelm von der Platz, who was a collector of Rococo painting. One of Carriera's major patrons was Frederick Augustus II, prince elector of Saxony (later, Augustus III, king of Poland) who sat for his portrait in 1713. At his court in Dresden, Augustus III amassed an extensive collection of Rosalba's paintings—157 of her pastels—which he kept in a gallery dedicated to her works. See Bernardina Sani, ed., *Rosalba Carriera, Lettere, Diari, Frammenti* (Florence: Olschki, 1985), 1–41. A catalog of Carriera's pastels from the Dresden collection has recently been published; it includes reproductions of the 73 works still present in the museum from the complete original collection, as well as photographs of 21 works that went missing at the end of the Second World War. See *"Das Kabinett der Rosalba." Rosalba Carriera und die Pastelle der Dresdner Gemäldegalerie Alte Meister*, ed. Andreas Hemming and Harald Marx (Munich-Berlin: Deutscher Kunstverlag, 2007).

4. In a letter from Ferdinando Maria Nicoli to Rosalba Carriera, 26 June 1703: "Signora Rosalba, io temo assai che la vostr'arte eccelsa vi conduca un giorno all'Inquisizione per un'accusa di cui niun eresiarca è mai stato incolpato. Voi vi assumete l'onnipotenza, che è il più riserbato pregio di Dio ed in vece d'imitar gli uomini, li create." This and all translations are mine, unless otherwise noted. Sani, ed., *Rosalba Carriera, Lettere, Diari, Frammenti*, 67.

5. Mary D. Sheriff describes vividly the criticism that the French artist Elisabeth Vigée Lebrun (1755–1842) experienced for this very "transgression" in *The Exceptional Woman. Elisabeth Vigée-Lebrun and the Cultural Politics of Art* (Chicago: University of Chicago Press, 1996). See also Roworth's Chapter 6 in this volume, note 7.

6. Johns, "'An Ornament of Italy . . . ,'" 14–15.

7. One sign of Carriera's success with her pastel portraits was the number of prominent artists from across Europe who copied her and often openly described

her influence on their own work, including Vleughels, Watteau, Federico Tiepolo, and others. During and subsequent to the writing of this chapter, two catalogs celebrating Carriera were published in honor of the 250th anniversary of her death. Bernardina Sani published a second edition of her catalog of Carriera's works, *Rosalba Carriera*, a cura di Bernardina Sani (Torino: Umberto Allemandi & Co., 2007), and the Fondazione Cini organized an exhibit in Venice, Galleria di Palazzo Cini a Sani Vio, 1 September–28 October 2007, publishing its catalog *Rosalba Carriera "prima pittrice de l'Europa,"* a cura di Giuseppe Pavanello (Venice: Marsilio Editori, 2007).

8. In 1723 she traveled to Modena to paint the daughters of Rinaldo d'Este; in 1728 she traveled to Gorizia during the visit of Emperor Charles VI and painted the portraits of Count Paar and the Princes of Schwarzenberg and of Diedrichstein; and in 1730 she traveled to the Imperial Court in Vienna. On the importance of not overstating Carriera's "domesticity," see Shearer West, "Gender and Internationalism: The Case of Rosalba Carriera," in Shearer West, ed., *Italian Culture in Northern Europe in the Eighteenth Century* (Cambridge: Cambridge University Press, 1999), 46–66.

9. On Carriera's shrewd strategies as a businesswoman, see West, "Gender and Internationalism"; and Johns, "'An Ornament of Italy. . . .'"

10. In a 23 August 1749 letter to Pierre Jean Mariette, Carriera writes that she has been blind ("priva di vista") for three years but that after a recent surgery on her cataracts, she has regained a very limited degree of sight, which, "confused" as it is, is nevertheless "a great good for one who has experienced the great evil of blindness." Sani, ed., *Rosalba Carriera. Lettere, Diari, Frammenti*, 719. Carriera was correct not to hold much hope for the future in this letter, however, as her newly regained sight did not last for long.

11. *Le commedie di Terenzio tradotte in verso sciolto da Luisa Bergalli fra gli Arcadi Irminda Partenide* (Venice: Cristoforo Zane, 1733), and again in a revised edition in 1735 (but 1735–1738); prior to these collections Bergalli had published the comedies individually between 1727–1731; *Le Opere di M. Racine tradotte* (Venice: Domenico Lovisa, 1736); and *Il Misantropo, Commedia tratta dal Molière e messa in versi da Irminda Partenide* (Venice: Pasquali, 1745).

12. According to some scholars, Bergalli was the first woman to write libretti for melodramas. In 1725, she wrote the libretto for *Agide re di Sparta*, which was set to music by Giovanni Porta and was well received at the San Moisè theater in Venice. In 1730, she composed the libretto for *Elenia*, which was set to music by Tommaso Albinoni and performed at the Sant'Angelo theater in Venice. Bergalli's talent was also appreciated beyond Venice and in other genres; she wrote an oratorio, *Eleazaro*, which was set to music by Giuseppe Giovanni Bonno, sung at the court in Vienna, and published there in 1739.

13. *Le avventure del poeta. Commedia di Luisa Bergalli fra gli Arcadi Irminda Partenide* (Venezia: Cristoforo Zane, 1730). Another twelve original compositions as yet unpublished are also attributed to Bergalli. See Luisa Ricaldone, ed., and Paola Serra (Nota biografica e bibliografica), Luisa Bergalli, *Le avventure del poeta* (Man-

ziana RM: Vecchiarelli Editore, 1997), 5–14, 87–105. On Bergalli's theatrical works, see Pamela D. Stewart, "Eroine della dissimulazione, Il teatro di Luisa Bergalli," in *Quaderni veneti* 19 (1994), 73–91.

14. In his brilliant 1750–51 season at the Sant'Angelo theater, playwright Carlo Goldoni composed the famous sixteen new comedies for the Medebach troupe which helped move the Italian theater away from masks and stock characters toward scripted plays and protagonists from the middle classes.

15. C. De Michelis, *Letterati e lettori nel Settecento veneziano* (Florence: Olschki, 1989), 133–35.

16. Fabio Soldini, ed., Gasparo Gozzi, *Lettere*, XXXV.

17. *Componimenti poetici delle più illustri rimatrici d'ogni secolo. Raccolti da Luisa Bergalli* (Venice: Antonio Mora, 1726). It should be noted that there are several poems by authors to whom Bergalli refers as *incerte*, or anonymous; it is possible therefore, that some of these *incerte* may in fact be the same individual. Adriana Chemello has recently published an anastatic reprint of this work: Luisa Bergalli, *Componimenti poetici delle più illustri rimatrici d'ogni secolo*, con nota critica e bio-bibliografica di Adriana Chemello (Milan-Venice: Eidos, 2006).

18. *Rime di Madonna Gaspara Stampa; con alcune altre di Collaltino, e di Vinci-guerra Conti di Collalto; e di Baldassare Stampa. Giuntovi diversi componimenti di varj Autori in lode della medesima* (Venice: Francesco Piacentini, 1738). On Bergalli's collections of Italian women's poetry, see Adriana Chemello's illuminating essay, "Le ricerche erudite di Luisa Bergalli," in Adriana Chemello and Luisa Ricaldone, *Geografie e genealogie letterarie. Erudite, biografe, croniste, narratrici, "epistolières," utopiste tra Settecento e Ottocento* (Padua: Il Poligrafo, 2000), 49–88.

19. For the most recent collection of scholarly essays on Bergalli, see *Luisa Bergalli poetessa drammaturga traduttrice critica letteraria*, ed. Adriana Chemello (Milan-Venice: Eidos, 2008). See also Francesca Savoia's excellent article "Una storia tutta da raccontare: Luisa Bergalli Gozzi (1703–1779)," in *Essays in Honor of Marga Cottina-Jones*, ed. Laura Sanguinetti White, Andrea Baldi, and Kristin Philips (Fiesole [Florence]: Edizioni Cadmo, 2003), 109–22.

20. *Composizioni teatrali moderne tradotte da Elisabetta Caminer* (Venezia: Savioni and distributed by Paolo Colombani, 1772); 2nd ed. 1774; *Nuova raccolta di composizioni teatrali tradotte da Elisabetta Caminer Turra* (Venezia: Pietro Savoni, 1774–1776); *Drammi trasportati dal francese idioma ad uso del teatro italiano da Elisabetta Caminer Turra: Per servire di proseguimento al corpo delle traduzioni teatrali pubblicato dalla medesima qualche anno fa* (Venice: Albrizzi, 1794).

21. A network of male supporters rushed to Caminer's defense, and her father took successful legal action against the accusing journalist. For this and other episodes of attack and support from Caminer's early career, see Catherine M. Sama, "Becoming Visible: A Biography of Elisabetta Caminer Turra (1751–96) During Her Formative Years," *Studi veneziani* N.S. LXIII (2002), 349–88.

22. This intense construction activity was an especially important fact for artists decorating these buildings. Filippo Pedrocco notes that, just along the Grand Canal, several family palaces (Diedo, Civran, Corner, Marcello, Venier, Grassi, and Smith)

and all the churches facing the Canal (San Simeone Piccolo, San Marcuola, San Stae, San Geremia) were entirely built during the eighteenth century. An impressive number of buildings within the city were also built or renovated. Pedrocco, *Visions of Venice. Paintings of the 18th Century* (London: Tauris Parke Books, 2002), 23–24.

23. Ibid., pp. 17–18.

24. Francis Haskell, *Patrons and Painters. Art and Society in Baroque Italy* (New Haven: Yale University Press, 1980), 277. See also West, "Gender and Internationalism."

25. Christopher Becker, Axel Burkhardt, and August Bernhard Rave, "The International Taste for Venetian Art—The Hapsburg Empire," in *The Glory of Venice. Art in the Eighteenth Century*. Exhibition Catalog. Royal Academy of Arts, London, 1994, National Gallery of Art, Washington, 1995 (New Haven: Yale University Press, 1994), 46.

26. Alberto Postigliola and Nadia Boccara, eds., *Periodici italiani d'antico regime* (Rome: Società Italiana di Studi sul secolo XVIII, 1986).

27. Mario Infelise, "Gazzette e lettori nella Repubblica veneta dopo l'ottantanove," in *L'eredità dell'Ottantanove e l'Italia*, ed. Renzo Zorzi (Florence: Olschki Editore, 1992), 310.

28. Venice was well known for its courtesans. The state taxed all prostitutes, and the *cortigiana onesta* occupied the highest rank in terms of income and prestige in the city's hierarchy of prostitutes. Franco is the most famous of these "honorable courtesans," an elite group of women who were educated in literature and music and who were paid vast sums for their intelligent conversation and cultured companionship as well as for their sexual services. Their clients were men from the wealthiest, most prestigious levels of Venetian society.

29. For more on the concept of a "genealogy" of Italian women writers, see Adriana Chemello and Luisa Ricaldone, *Geografie e genealogie letterarie*.

30. While Carriera surely had strong opinions about the condition of women in society, we cannot claim as her own the interesting and passionate text found among her papers which discusses the relationship between the sexes, because the author of this text refers to the situation "especially here in England" (*qui specialmente in Inghilterra*). Since Carriera never traveled to England, this must be something written by someone else—perhaps part of a letter—which Carriera then copied in her own hand. Certainly, we must take note that Carriera considered it important and interesting enough to transcribe and keep among her papers and letters. This text was published, along with other *appunti* or "notes" found among Carriera's papers in Sani, *Rosalba Carriera. Lettere, Diari, Frammenti*, 738–39; a section of it was also published in English translation in *The Voices of Women Artists*, ed. Wendy Slatkin (Englewood Cliffs, NJ: Prentice Hall, 1993), 18–19.

31. From the Foreword, *A chi legge* (pages not numbered), in Luisa Bergalli, *Componimenti poetici delle più illustri rimatrici d'ogni secolo* (Venice: Antonio Mora, 1726), parte 1: " . . . tant'altre di famose, e tant'altre degne di esserlo, né so per qual loro mala sorte poco meno, che incognite alla Repubblica letteraria; desiderio mi prese di voler io tale onorata fatica intraprendere; per due cagioni in questo appagando me stessa, l'una perché così apro la strada, onde ritornar possa Gloria, ed

onore alle men conosciute, l'altra perché mi lusingo di acquistare a me ancora un qualche compatimento. . . ." Part of this Foreword was published in the original Italian in Chemello, "Le ricerche erudite di Luisa Bergalli," in Chemello and Ricaldone, *Geografie e geneologie letterarie*, 69–71.

32. From the same Foreword: "senza partirci dalla nostra Venezia per esempi di Valorose Donne, anche negli studj più gravi riuscite, abbiamo una Cassandra Fedele . . . un'Elena Cornaro Piscopia, e tant'altre ancora delle quali troppo lungo sarebbe il farne racconto."

33. Here Bergalli is quoting from Fonte's *Tredici Canti del Floridorio* (Venice, 1581): "Le Donne in ogni età fur da Natura / Di gran giudicio, e d'animo dotate."

34. Perhaps Bergalli had seen the Venetian writer Arcangela Tarabotti employ the same strategy the previous century when she concluded her defense of women, *Che le donne siano della specie degli uomini* (1651), by quoting verse directly from another of Moderata Fonte's works, *The Merit of Women* (1600).

35. Jean François De Lacroix, *Dictionnaire historique portative des femmes célèbres* (Paris: L. Cellot, 1769). Caminer reviewed the dictionary in *Europa letteraria*, November 1769, 79–94. The entire review is published in English translation in Sama, ed., *Selected Writings* (Chicago: University of Chicago Press, 2003), 167–83. Sections of this journalistic entry and of many others in the Caminer periodicals were published in the original Italian by Mariagabriella di Giacomo in *L'illuminismo e le donne. Gli scritti di Elisabetta Caminer. "Utilità" e "piacere": ovvero la coscienza di essere letterata* (Rome: Università degli studi Roma "La Sapienza," 2002).

36. Ibid., 167–68.

37. Ibid., 168.

38. This portrait was originally thought to be a self-portrait by Carriera, but Bernardina Sani posited correctly that it was indeed a portrait of Bergalli in "Alcune precisioni sugli Autoritratti di Rosalba Carriera," in *Per Maria Cionini Visani. Scritti di amici* (Torino: G. Canale e Co., 1977), 122–25. Unfortunately, the portrait is no longer available to the viewing public as it is has gone missing from the Ca' Rezzonico Museum in Venice.

39. In a 9 October 1723 letter to Bergalli, playwright Apostolo Zeno, writing from his post as court poet in Vienna, asked Luisa to send his greetings to "the incomparable Signora Rosalba" and to everyone in the Carriera household the very next time she would see them. See *Lettere di Apostolo Zeno. Cittadino veneziano. Istorico e poeta cesareo* (Venezia: Sansoni, 1785), vol. 3, 389–91. In a 30 September 1724 letter to Bergalli, Zeno mentioned Carriera's portrait of Bergalli; this letter is located in the Biblioteca del Museo Correr in Venice, Cicogna 3229 bis.

40. The nine extant letters between Carriera and Bergalli date from c. 1736–1742. They are located in the Biblioteca Laurenziana in Florence and were first published by Carlotta Egle Tassistro, in *Luisa Bergalli Gozzi. La vita e l'opera sua nel suo tempo* (Rome: Tipografia Nazionale Bertero, 1919), 197–204, and then by Bernardina Sani in her scholarly edition of Carriera's correspondence in *Rosalba Carriera. Lettere, Diari, Frammenti*, 617–18, 625–26, 631–33, 665–66, 676–77, 680–82.

41. Rosalba's sister Angela—who had also worked in the studio as her assistant—

was no longer living in the Carriera household because she had married the artist Antonio Pellegrini and was traveling with him. Rosalba's father was absent; he died in 1719.

42. "Il mio impiego, che troppo m'occupa ed un naturale assai fredo, m'han sempre tenuto lontana dagli amori e pensieri di matrimonio. Farei ben ridere il mondo, s'hora, ch'ho già passata la gioventù, entrassi in questi." Cited in Sani, ed., *Rosalba Carriera. Lettere, Diari, Frammenti*, 753. The letter is undated, but it must have been written before or during 1737, the year of her sister Giovanna's death.

43. See West, "Gender and Internationalism," for her insightful discussion about Carriera's exploitation of her image as spinster artist and her virginal, saintlike status.

44. Johns, "'An Ornament of Italy . . . ,'" 7.

45. Rosa o Rosanna Pozzolo or Pozzola (1704–1781) was the daughter of painter Giuseppe Pozzolo (1678–1753). On Pozzolo, see Margaret Binotto, "Rosa Pozzolo," in *Le tele svelate. Pittrici venete dal Cinquecento al Novecento* (Milan-Venice: Eïdos, 1996), 166–75.

46. "[P]rendo la libertà di incomodarla con questa mia e farli sapere che è da tre mesi circa che sono alla scuola del sig.r Antonio Dei Pieri pitore, già che il mio demerito e la mia cativa sorte, non [h]a voluto che venchgi soto di V.S. Ill.ma, mi son forzata di far tutto il posible di andar almeno soto a questo Signor. Mi chreda che non è stato altro motivo, che son stata perseverante nel disigniare, che haver fisato di non volermi maritare, per altro, [h]o avuto, sin ad ora, tanta poca fortuna, che non so come mi sii mantenuta in questa opinione, ma pensando al mio stato, esendo di povere fortune, mi son data con tuto il sforzo posibile, se poso far tanto di procaciarmi il merito, senza bramarlo dal fratelo, avendo imparato per esperienza, che, col lungo tempo, tutti si viene a stufar, ben che sii frateli. Chredo che lei averà piacere di questa mia risuluzione e la aproverà per otima, il saper l'amore e la bontà, che a autto sino adora per me, mi a dato il coragio di notificarli questa casa." Cited in Sani, ed., *Rosalba Carriera, Lettere, Diari, Frammenti*, 648. Nearly ten years later, Pozzolo's maestro Antonio Dei Pieri expressed great affection for her in his will; he left his *scolara* most of the supplies in his studio, as well as his books on painting.

47. From Carriera's letter to Giorgio Maria Rapparini, dated November 1710: " . . . in quanto agli huomeni, creda questa gran verità che non v'è cosa al mondo che meno mi dia pensiero." Cited in Sani, ed., *Rosalba Carriera, Lettere, Diari, Frammenti*, 171. Shearer West published part of this letter in "Gender and Internationalism," 48.

48. Further research is necessary, however, to determine more accurately the full extent of Bergalli's writing and translating activities.

49. " . . . con vestimenti ideali poetici." This request was made in a letter from the Conte Collalto to Apostolo Zeno, who shared the information with Bergalli in a 1724 letter to her. Collalto preferred that Bergalli make the portrait herself, but if she would not, he requested that it be done "in the hand of the famous Rosalba or that of the old Bellucci, her friend." Cited in Sani, ed., *Rosalba Carriera. Lettere, diari, frammenti*, 802–3. Luisa Ricaldone describes the context for this letter and Bergalli's correspondence with Collalto prior to her relationship with Gasparo Gozzi

in Ricaldone, *La scrittura nascosta. Donne di lettere e loro immagini tra Arcadia e Restaurazione* (Paris: Honoré Champion/Fiesole: Edizioni Cadmo, 1996), 200–201.

50. In fact, although Bergalli does not reveal anything about this to Carriera in the letter, she had just miscarried three days earlier, at nearly three months' term. On the miscarriage, see Fabio Soldini, ed., Gasparo Gozzi, *Lettere*, 82. Bergalli's letter to Carriera is dated 24 February 1741: "In questo punto mi capitano . . . le pastelle . . . di che le rendo le più vive grazie ch'io posso. Tosto che mi vegga avanzar qualche momento dalle mie famigliari occupazioni, farò prova del mio ardire; ma non ispero di far il menomo onere alla sua cortesia ed alla sua attenzione e conosco già di esser quella un'impresa che supera le forze mie." Sani, ed., *Rosalba Carriera, Lettere, Diari, Frammenti*, 665. While Bergalli may have been an accomplished amateur artist, no evidence has come to light to support some scholars' claims that she made portraits of Venetian doges.

51. In this instance, the loan had originally come from Rosalba's sister, Giovanna. Bergalli, though not yet officially married to Gasparo Gozzi, was writing from the Gozzi terraferma home in Visinale. Letter dated 22 September 1736, published in Sani, ed., *Rosalba Carriera, Lettere, Diari, Frammenti*, 617–18.

52. It is also worth noting that Domenico Lovisa was an editor who published illustrated books for which he employed major Venetian artists (Sani, ed., *Rosalba Carriera, Lettere, Diari, Frammenti*, 618). Perhaps Bergalli passed on this information in case it could be of interest to the Carriera studio. Bergalli herself collaborated with the Carriera studio for illustrations in at least two of her literary publications, as we shall see.

53. In 1728 the young Sartori (1715–1760) came to Venice (along with her sister Angioletta) to live in the Carriera household and work in the Carriera studio, where under Rosalba's guidance she became an accomplished pastel painter and miniaturist. She also became a skilled engraver. She remained with her mentor until 1741, when she left Venice to marry Franz Joseph Hoffmann, a counselor at the court of Augustus III in Dresden—a marriage which Carriera helped arrange. On Sartori, see Caterina Furlan, "Pittura al femminile a Dresda: Rosalba Carriera e Felicita Sartori Hoffmann," in *Arte per i re: Capolavori del settecento dalla Galleria Statale di Dresda*, ed. Harald Marx (Udine: Arti grafiche friulane, 2004), 104–14; and Sani, ed., *Rosalba Carriera, Lettere, Diari, Frammenti*, 497, 818.

54. " . . . Che senza ricercar, qual più fiorita / Cittade ha grido in questa, o in quella parte, / Tali ne mostrerò, che in tele e in carte / Danno ad altri e a lor stesse eterna vita." In Luisa Bergalli, ed., *Componimenti poetici delle più illustri rimatrici d'ogni secolo* (Venice: Antonio Mora, 1726), parte 2, p. 238. The poem was published in the original Italian in Sani, ed., *Rosalba Carriera, Lettere, Diari, Frammenti*, 833, and in Chemello and Ricaldone, *Geografie e genealogie letterarie*, 35. Bergalli also included poetry by artist Giulia Lama, an Arcadian poet, in both the *Componimenti* and the Stampa collections of poetry.

55. From the 1736 dedication to "I Due Fratelli" published in the second edition of Bergalli's *Le comedie di Terenzio tradotte in verso sciolto* (Venice: Cristoforo Zane, 1735 [but 1735–1738]; pages are not numbered): "Ho pensato per lo meglio recarlavi

senza dirvene cosa alcuna innanzi, perché così appagherò quel mio desiderio di of-
ferirvi qualcosa senza che voi lo mi contrastiate. . . . Voi, il cui Nome, mercè le belle
e artifiziose Pitture, è penetrato in ogni luogo, sicché foste desiderata, e magnifica-
mente raccolta dai maggiori Monarchi dell'Europa. Sembra oggimai, che non sieno
compiute del tutto, e bastevolmente ornate le loro Gallerie, se non hanno i Ritratti
de' Principi colorati dalle vostre mani."

56. Ibid.: " . . . si vede con qual cura ed amore [la madre di Carriera] si sia adoprata
coltivandole [le tre figlie] negli studj delle Lingue, nelle Arti, e nelle Scienze. . . ."

57. Luisa Bergalli, *Rime di Antonio Sforza. Giuntovi altri Componimenti di Diversi in morte del medesimo, e varie notizie della sua vita* (Venice: Pietro Marchesan,
1736).

58. "Parmi di già veder la gloria vostra / Levarsi o Donna. . . ." Ibid., 195. Bergalli also included in the collection two poems honoring Rosalba Carriera, one she
wrote herself and one written by Antonio Sforza.

59. Sartori made her engraving of Stampa's portrait after a drawing by Daniele
Antonio Bertoli (whose portrait Carriera had made in Vienna in 1730). Her engraving of the Conte Collaltino di Collalto (an ancestor of Count Antonio Rambaldo
Collalto, Bergalli's admirer) was made after a portrait by Jeremias Jakob Sedelmayr.
Literary exchanges served to foster the friendship between Carriera and Bergalli
on a more personal level as well. In this same letter, for example, Luisa enclosed a
poem she had written to comfort Rosalba upon the devastating loss of her beloved
sister, Giovanna. The poem was found among Carriera's surviving papers and was
published by Sani along with Bergalli's accompanying letter. Sani, ed., *Rosalba Carriera, Lettere, Diari, Frammenti*, 631–32.

60. Luisa Bergalli, *Almanaco sacro, e profano per l'anno santo MDCCL in difesa
delle donne. Aggiuntevi la Nascita de' Principi, Cardinali, Vescovi, ec.* (Venice:
Modesto Fenzo, 1750). Tiziana Plebani published a modern edition of the anonymous almanac with an introductory essay in which she identifies Bergalli as the
author; *L'Almanacco delle donne* (Venice: Ippocampo, 1991). Plebani notes that the
only other contemporary Venetian woman included in the almanac besides Bergalli
herself is Rosalba Carriera.

61. Sama, ed., *Selected Writings*, 182. Interestingly, Caminer does not mention
Carriera or any of the host of Italian women artists who were not included in the
dictionary.

62. Ibid., 107.

63. Ibid., 104. Caminer is quoting Pelli here. Caminer's extant letters have recently been published in the original Italian in Rita Unfer Lukoschik, ed., *Lettere
di Elisabetta Caminer Turra (1751–96). Organizzatrice Culturale* (Conselve: Edizioni
Think ADV, 2006).

64. Zeno's personal library was one of the richest in eighteenth-century Venice.
In 1724, he estimated that the number of volumes he possessed had reached ten
thousand. See his 25 March 1724 letter to Lorenzo Patarol in *Lettere di Apostolo Zeno*,
425–26. Bergalli's acquaintance with Zeno may possibly have originated through a
connection to her aristocratic godparents, Luigi Mocenigo and Pisana Cornaro.

65. *Rime di donne illustri a sua eccellenza Caterina Dolfina cavaliera e procuratessa Tron nel gloriosissimo ingresso alla dignità di procuratore per merito di San Marco di sua eccellenza cavaliere Andrea Tron* (Venice: Pietro Valvasense, 1773).

66. On these poetic compilations, see Alberta Pettoello, *Libri illustrati veneziani del settecento. Le pubblicazioni d'occasione* (Venice: Istituto Veneto di Scienze, Lettere ed Arti, 2005).

67. That we may view this raccolta as another of Bergalli's collections of poetry by *women* is supported by the contrast it offers with another collection of poetry for Andrea Tron's promotion to procuratore of San Marco to which Bergalli contributed that year: *Poesie pel solenne ingresso di Sua Eccellenza il signor Andrea Tron Kavaliere alla dignità di Procuratore di S. Marco per merito* (Venice: Carlo Palese, 1773), organized by her husband, Gasparo Gozzi. Significantly, this collection reflected the traditional formula for such raccolte in that all its contributors were men (aside from Bergalli), and it was dedicated to Andrea Tron himself (although a handful of its poems were also dedicated to Caterina Dolfin).

68. The most famous of these contributors was Cristina Roccati, the esteemed professor of physics from Rovigo. On Roccati (1732–1797), see Paula Findlen, "A Forgotten Newtonian: Women and Sciences in the Italian Provinces," in *The Sciences in Enlightened Europe*, ed. William Clark, Jan Golinski, and Simon Schaffer (Chicago: University of Chicago Press, 1999), 331–49.

69. My emphasis. In *Rime di donne illustri*, 20–21: ". . . chiaro esempio sei / Di quanto abbia natura al nostro sesso / Nobile ingegno, alto saper concesso." The poem was translated and published in Sama, ed., *Selected Writings*, 183–84.

70. This literary network extended to the pages of Caminer's literary periodical, as Caterina Dolfin Tron was a reader of the *Europa letteraria*. Interestingly, we know of this only through the correspondence between Dolfin Tron and Bergalli's husband, Gasparo Gozzi, who in 1772 was procuring copies of Caminer's periodical for Dolfin Tron. See the letter in Fabio Soldini, ed., Gasparo Gozzi, *Lettere*, 181.

71. Fabio Soldini has greatly enriched our knowledge of Gozzi with his scholarly edition of the playwright's letters: Carlo Gozzi, *Lettere* (Venice: Marsilio, 2004). He has also made possible continued study of Gozzi (and family) by bringing to the attention of the Marciana library in Venice a previously unexamined collection of Gozzi family papers. He also edited the catalog of the Marciana library's exhibition celebrating the bicentennial of Gozzi's death: *Carlo Gozzi (1720–1806). Stravaganze sceniche, letterarie battaglie* (Venice: Marsilio, 2006). The catalog includes a detailed description of the library's new collection of Gozzi papers.

72. Gozzi published these memoirs in three volumes, *Memorie inutili della vita di Carlo Gozzi scritte da lui medesimo e pubblicate per umiltà* (Venice: Palese, 1797); the third volume was actually published in 1798. Giuseppe Prezzolini published a two-volume edition of the *Memorie inutili* in 1910 (Bari: Laterza e figli). The first complete and scholarly edition of Gozzi's memoirs has recently been published by Paolo Bosisio (with the collaboration of Valentina Garavaglia) in two volumes, based on the only complete extant manuscript of the work (which slightly predates the manuscript of the Palese edition, which is lost to us). In extensive philologi-

cal notes, Bosisio also corrects the typographical errors in the Palese edition and therefore offers scholars a comparison of two manuscript editions of Gozzi's memoirs. See Carlo Gozzi, *Memorie inutili*. Edizione critica a cura di Paolo Bosisio con la collaborazione di Valentina Garavaglia (Milan: Edizioni Universitarie di Lettere Economia Diritto, 2006); hereafter, Bosisio, ed., Carlo Gozzi, *Memorie inutili*. An abridged version of Gozzi's memoirs was translated into English by John Addington Symonds, edited, revised, and abridged by Philip Horne and with an introduction by Harold Acton: *Useless Memoirs of Carlo Gozzi* (London: Oxford University Press, 1962); hereafter, Gozzi, *Useless Memoirs*. I will use Symonds' translation in this essay except where I find it to be unsatisfying, or where he has abridged the original text, in which case I will use my own and indicate it as such.

73. Chemello, "Le ricerche erudite di Luisa Bergalli," in Chemello and Ricaldone, *Geografie e geneologie letterarie,* 52.

74. My translation. Bosisio, ed., Carlo Gozzi, *Memorie inutili*, 215–16: ". . . tra le Pastorelle d'Arcadia . . . Poetessa di fantasia. . . . Questa femmina di fervida, e volante immaginazione, e per ciò abilissima a' poetici rapimenti, volle . . . inoltrarsi a regolare le cose domestiche disordinate, ma i suoi progetti . . . non poterono uscire da' ratti romanzeschi, e pindarici."

75. My translation. Bosisio, ed., Carlo Gozzi, *Memorie inutili*, 321–22: ". . . la Moglie di mio Fratello, sempre progettante poetica, e sempre vaga di maneggi e d'amministrare, aveva sedotto il povero mio Fratello, facendogli credere, e vedere mentalmente delle montagne d'utilità a firmare la Scrittura della condotta del teatro Sant'Angelo in Venezia. . . . e [io] compiansi il Fratello. . . . Tentai . . . di far disuadere quella femmina rovente sopra una tale impresa."

76. Bosisio, ed., Carlo Gozzi, *Memorie inutili*, 212–14.

77. Gozzi, *Useless Memoirs*, 64. In his memoirs, Carlo writes openly of his jealousy regarding his older brother Gasparo's favored position in their mother's heart, claiming that his eldest brother "earned more of her love than she bestowed on all her other eight children" (ibid., 64). The fact that Bergalli enjoyed a warm, affectionate relationship with both his mother and father further exacerbated Carlo's feelings of neglect.

78. Ibid., 65.

79. For a detailed discussion of the Caminer-Gozzi polemic, see Sama, "Verso un teatro moderno: La polemica tra Elisabetta Caminer e Carlo Gozzi," in Rita Unfer Lukoschik, ed., *Elisabetta Caminer Turra. Una letterata veneta verso l'Europa* (Verona: essedue edizioni, 1998), 63–79.

80. Carlo Gozzi, "Prefazione del Traduttore," in *Il Fajel. Tragedia del Sig. Baculard d'Arnaud, tradotto in versi sciolti dal Co: Carlo Gozzi* (Venezia: Colombani, 1772). The expression "ciechi illuminati" is found on page 32; the quotation "schiavi d'una vilissima soggezione degli'esteri scrittori a segno di essersi ridotti a confinare i talenti loro unicamente a razzolare come galline, a fiutare come brachetti, e a tradurre, come sanno, quelle opere de' francesi" is found on page 20.

81. From Gozzi's 25 September 1777 letter to Giuseppe Barretti: "Una giovinetta . . . [che] prometteva di potersi ridurre un adornamento delle nostre società, fu

eccitata a non contentarsi . . . del rendersi capace di una buona traduzione, ma a divenire Capitanessa d'un Giornale intitolato: L'Europa letteraria . . . a dar pareri, a condannare, a lodare, ad assolvere magistralmente, tutti i Scrittori, e tutti i libri di tutte le materie." Cited in Carlo Gozzi, *Lettere*, ed. Fabio Soldini (Venice: Marsilio, 2004), 120.

82. My translation, with thanks to Anthony Oldcorn for his generous assistance. Original Italian: "Se quando avrò maggior da Febo aita, / Talun alzar udrammi in rime sparte / I pregi, che a noi donne il Ciel comparte / Non prezzi me, qual femminella ardita, / Che senza ricercar, qual più fiorita / Cittade ha grido in questa, o in quella parte, / Tali ne mostrerò, che in tele, e in carte / Danno ad altri, e a lor stesse eterna vita. / Voi, che spregiate il gentil sesso, voi / D'Angela, di Rosalba, e di Giovanna / Venite a mirar l'opre, e dite poi, / Dite pur s'io mentisco; e se m'inganna / La passione e dite pur se noi / Donne all'ago, ed al fuso il Ciel condanna," in *Componimenti poetici delle più illustri rimatrici d'ogni secolo. Raccolti da Luisa Bergalli* (Venice: Antonio Mora, 1726), parte 2, 238. The sonnet was published in Sani, ed., *Rosalba Carriera. Lettere, Diari, Frammenti*, 833, and Chemello, "Le ricerche erudite di Luisa Bergalli," 71.

Notes to Chapter Six

1. For general background on Kauffman's life and career, see Wendy Wassyng Roworth, ed., *Angelica Kauffman: A Continental Artist in Georgian England* (Brighton and London: Reaktion Books and Brighton Art Gallery and Museums, 1992); Roworth, "Angelica Kauffman," in *Dictionary of Women Artists*, ed. Delia Gaze, (London and Chicago: Fitzroy Dearborn, 1997), II, 764–70; Bettina Baumgärtel, ed., *Angelika Kauffmann, Retrospektive,* exh. cat., Kunstmuseum, Düsseldorf (Düsseldorf: Hatje, 1998); and Angela Rosenthal, *Angelica Kauffman: Art and Sensibility* (New Haven and London: Yale University Press, 2006), especially on Kauffman's self-portraits and self image.

2. Giovanni Gherardo De Rossi, *Vita di Angelika Kauffman pittrice* (Florence, 1810), 26. Information about Kauffman's early life and years in England was based on a 1788 manuscript biography written by Kauffman's brother-in-law, Giuseppe Carlo Zucchi, in 1788. This is published in Helmut Swozilek, ed. and trans., *Memoria istoriche di Maria Angelica Kauffmann Zucchi riguardanti l'arte della pittura da lei professata scritte da G.C.Z. (Giuseppe Carlo Zucchi) Venezia MDCCLXXXVIII, Schriften des Vorarlberger Landesmuseums*, Series B, 2 (1999).

3. De Rossi, 3.

4. Joseph Forsyth, *Remarks on antiquities, arts, and letters during an excursion in Italy, in the years 1802 and 1803*, ed. Keith Crook (Newark: University of Delaware Press; London: Associated University Presses, 2001), 134.

5. A. M. Clark, "Roma mi è sempre in pensiero," *Angelika Kauffmann und ihre Zeitgenossen*, exh. cat., ed. Oscar Sandner (Bregenz and Vienna, 1968), 5–17 (in German); reprinted in English in E. P. Bowron, ed., *Studies in Eighteenth-Century Painting*, 1981, 123–38.

6. *Il Settecento a Roma* (Rome: Palazzo Venezia, 2005–06), *Il Neoclassicismo in*

Italia da Tiepolo a Canova (Milan: Palazzo Reale, 2002); E. P. Bowron and J. J. Rishel, curators, *The Splendor of Eighteenth-Century Rome* (Philadelphia Art Museum / Museum of Fine Arts, Houston, 2000); Oscar Sandner, curator, *Angelika Kauffmann e Roma*, Accademia Nazionale di San Luca / Istituto Nazionale della Grafica / Calcografia (Rome: Edizione De Luca, 1998).

7. On Kauffman's early training see De Rossi, 5–8. For background on women artists' training in Italy in the sixteenth and seventeenth centuries and issues surrounding painting genres, see Whitney Chadwick, *Women, Art, and Society* (London and New York: Fourth Edition, 2007), 87–113; Catherine King, "What Women Can Make," and Gill Perry, "Gender, Genres and Academic Art in the Eighteenth Century," in *Gender and Art*, ed. G. Perry (New Haven and London: Yale University Press, 1999), 61–107; Roworth, "Anatomy is Destiny: Regarding the body in the art of Angelica Kauffman," in *Femininity and Masculinity in Eighteenth-Century Art and Culture*, ed. G. Perry and M. Rossington (Manchester University Press / St. Martin's Press, 1994), 41–62.

8. De Rossi, 14: ". . . suo stile di operar sempre con raziocino, con riflessione, con ricerca del meglio, le faceva strada tentare la gran carriera della pittura storica, che era la meta de' suoi desiderj."

9. See exhibition catalogues cited in note 6, especially Christopher Johns' essay "The Entrepôt of Europe," in Bowron and Rishel, *Art in Rome in the Eighteenth Century* (London and Philadelphia: Merrell and Philadelphia Museum of Art, 2000), 17–45.

10. *Angelica Kauffman e Roma,* C. Petrangeli et al., *L'Accademia Nazionale di San Luca*, Rome, 1974.

11. She later joined academies of art in London (Founding Member, 1768) and Venice (1782). See W. W. Roworth, M. Sheriff, and A. L. Lindberg, "Academies of Art," in *Dictionary of Women Artists*, ed. Delia Gaze, I, 43–55.

12. John Moore, *A View of Society and Manners in Italy*, 1781, II, 62. See Brian Allen, "Die Grand Tour der Briten: Künstler und Reisende in Rome in der Mitte des 18. Jahrhunderts," in *Angelika Kauffman, Retrospektive*, 47–51.

13. The other woman academician was Mary Moser, an artist primarily known as a flower painter, who produced many works for Queen Charlotte. See Marcia Pointon, "Working, Earning, Bequeathing: Mary Grace and Mary Moser," in *Strategies for Showing, Women, Possession, and Representation in English Visual Culture 1665–1800* (1997), 131–71.

14. W. Maierhofer, ed., *Angelica Kauffman, "Mit traümte vor ein paar Nächetenich hätte Briefe von Ihnen empfangen," Gesammelte Briefe . . .* (Bottighofen, 2001), 32: ". . . ma confesso il vero, l'Italia mi sta a cuore—e spero ritornarei [sic]. . . ." This quotation follows Maiherhofer's transcription. I have not seen the original letter, which is in the Museo Correr, Civici Musei Veneziani d'arte e di storia, Venice.

15. De Rossi, 50. "Angelica non avea mai dimenticata Roma, e quel desiderio, che nutriva, di ritornarvi, e che fino dai primi giorni del suo arrivo sul Tamigi erale fisso nel cuore, col corso degli anni non erasi estinto."

16. G.C. Zucchi's manuscript cites concern for her family and her father's health

as the primary reason for the trip; manuscript p. 32, in Swozilek, 58. Letters to her friend Henrietta Fordyce and others also note this delay. See Maierhofer, *Gesammelte Briefe*, 48–50.

17. See Jeffrey Collins, *Papacy and Politics in Eighteenth-Century Rome: Pius VI and the Arts* (Cambridge University Press, 2004); Susanne Adina Meyer, "Le esposizioni di arte contemporanea a Roma durante il pontificato di Pio VI: il pubblico, la critica, il mercato artistico," *Incontri* 17:2 (2002), issue title *De Grand Tour in Italië en de reizen van Gerard (1722–1771 en Johan (1753–1815) Meerman in de achttiende eeuw*, 153–68.

18. See David H. Solkin, *Painting for Money: The Visual Arts and the Public Sphere in Eighteenth-Century England* (New Haven and London: Yale University Press, 1993); Shearer West, "Xenophobia and Xenomania: Italians and the English Royal Academy," in *Italian Culture in Northern Europe in the Eighteenth Century*, ed. Shearer West (Cambridge University Press, 1999), 116–39; and Mark Hallett, "'The Business of Criticism': The Press and the Royal Academy Exhibition in Eighteenth-Century London," in *Art on the Line, The Royal Academy Exhibitions at Somerset House 1780–1836*, ed. D. Solkin (New Haven and London: Yale University Press, 2001), 65–76.

19. On West, see H. van Erffa and A. Staley, *The Paintings of Benjamin West* (New Haven and London: Yale University Press, 1986).

20. Forsyth, *Remarks . . .* (as in note 4 above), 134.

21. The sketchbook is in the Victoria and Albert Museum, London; Peter Walch, "An Early Neoclassical Sketchbook by Angelica Kauffman," *Burlington Magazine*, 109 (1977), 98–111.

22. De Rossi, 56.

23. G. Prosperi, *Ricordi di famiglia*, ms., in Archivio Gesuitico, Rome; excerpts are published in G. Castellani, "Gli ultimi 26 anni di Angelica Kauffmann in Roma, 1781–1807," in *Strenna dei romanisti* (Rome, 1966), vol. 27, 75–79.

24. Prosperi / Castellani, 77.

25. See Baumgärtel, *Angelika Kauffmann, Retrospektive*, 276–285 for several preparatory drawings and *modelli* for this portrait, which is now in the collection of the Capodimonte, Naples.

26. Maierhofer, *Gesammelte Briefe*, 58 (Naples, 18 June 1782), p. 62; Kauffman to Johann Anton Metzler in Schwarzenberg, Rome, 23 September 1782: "Ich und mein libster finden unds Gott sey danck ganz wohl und vor 8 tagen wieder Glücklich in Rom angelangt alwo wier uns setzen werden. dan dieses ist die Residenz der schönen Künsten." See also a second letter to Metzler, 162 (Rome, 18 June 1791).

27. 28 December 1782; Maierhofer, *Gesammelte Briefe* 68–69.

28. "Alla Signora Angelica Kauffmann dipintrice celeberrima," *Versi di Polidente Melpomenio* (Bassano: Remondini, 1784), 99–105: ". . . Tornasti; e Roma, la difficil Roma, / Spiando il dolce tuo sacro ricetto, / Vede I Partonopèi Numi, e la Diva / Prole, mercè tuo creator pennello, / Nascere un'altra volta, e lieta applaude. . . ." The "sweet sacred refuge" refers to Kauffman's studio. See *Il Neoclassicismo in Italia da Tiepolo a Canova* (as in note 6 above), 483–84, on the *modello* Kauffman made for this painting, which is now in Vaduz, Sammlungen des Fürsten von Liechtenstein

(inv. G2070), and the connection with Pindemonte's poem; *Angelika Kauffmann, Retrospektive*, 278.

29. De Rossi, 68.

30. Maierhofer, *Gesammelte Briefen*, 69.

31. On artists' living quarters in eighteenth-century Rome, see Olivier Michel, "La vie quotidienne des peintres à Rome au dix-huitième siècle," *Vivre et peindre à Rome au XVIIIe siècle*, Ecole Française de Rome, Palais Farnèse (Rome, 1996), 41–47; and by the same author "Rome capitale artistique et village de peintres. Un programme informatique pour étudier la population romaine à partir des 'Stati delle Animae,'" *Roma Moderna e Contemporanea* IV:I (Jan.–Apr. 1996), 217–25. See also R. Assunto, *Specchio Vivente del Mondo, Artisti Stranieri in Roma, 1600–1800* (Rome, DeLuca, 1978); Friedrich Noack, *Deutsches Leben in Rom, 1700 bis 1900* (Berlin, 1907; Bern, 1971); and G.J. Hoogewerff, *Via Margutta centro di vita artistica* (Rome, 1953).

32. See A. Rosenthal, "Kauffman and Portraiture," in *Angelica Kauffman, A Continental Artist in Georgian England* (London and Brighton, 1992), 9–10; and W.W. Roworth, "Painting for Profit and Pleasure: Angelica Kauffman and the Art Business in Rome," *Eighteenth-Century Studies* 29:2 (Winter 1995–96), 225–28.

33. Noack, 367, n. 17 and 74–77.

34. Prosperi / Castellani, 77.

35. *Stati di anime*, San Andrea delle Fratte, Rome, cited in Noack, p. 367, n. 17. After 1785 they also employed a coachman.

36. In the 1750s Gavin Hamilton and Joshua Reynolds also lived in Palazzo Zuccari, which now houses the Bibliotheca Hertziana, Max-Planck-Institut für Kunstgeschichte.

37. Giovanni Caprile, *Villa Malta dall'antica Roma a "Civiltà Cattolica"* (Rome, 1999), 29–38.

38. Johann Wolfgang von Goethe, *Italian Journey*, ed. T.P. Saine and J.L. Sammons, trans. R.R. Heitner, *The Collected Works*, vol. 6 (Princeton University Press, 1989), 442.

39. Marianne Kraus, *Für mich gemerkt auf meiner Reise nach Italien im Jahre 1791, Reisetagebuch der Malerin und Erbacher Hofdame*, ed. Helmut Brosch (Verein Bezirksmuseum e. V. Buchen, 1996), 77.

40. Letter from Giovanni Kauffman to his cousin Joseph Anton Metzler, 7 March 1794 (Bregenz: Vorarlberger Landesarchiv), cited in Claudia Helbok, *Miss Angel. Angelika Kauffmann—Eine Biographie* (Vienna, 1968), 206.

41. Prosperi / Castellani, 78. See also Assunto, as in note 31 above, 50–7.

42. De Rossi, 76. On their friends and portraiture see Baumgärtel, *Angelika Kauffmann Retrospektive*, 320–32.

43. *Memoria delle piture fatte d'Angelica Kauffman dopo suo ritorno d'Inghilterra che fù nel mese d'otobre 1781, che si trovò a Venezia* (London: Royal Academy of Art). See Carlo Knight, ed., *La "Memoria delle piture" di Angelica Kauffman* (Rome, 1998); and W.W. Roworth, "Angelica Kauffman's Memorandum of Paintings," *Burlington Magazine* CXXVI (1984), 629–30. A somewhat inaccurate but still useful English

translation of the *Memorie* by Stella Vitelleschi was published by Lady Victoria Manners and G.C. Williamson, *Angelica Kauffmann, R.A., Her Life and Works* (1924).

44. *Memoria di spese fatta cominciando dalli 8 novembre 1782* (British Museum, Eg. Ms. 2169).

45. The Paris Bordone painting, an allegory of a woman with a mirror between two men, purchased on 23 January 1788 for 1,290 scudi from Pietro Concola (*Memoria di spese*, verso 15) and the Titian on 2 February 1788 for 1,290 scudi (*Memoria di spese*, 16).

46. Goethe, *Italian Journey*, 416.

47. C. von Lützow, "Das Testament der Angelica Kauffmann," *Zeitschrift für Bildende Kunst* 24 (1889), 294–300; an abstract in English is published in V. Manners and G.C. Williamson, *Angelica Kauffmann, R.A., Her Life and Times* (New York, 1924), 241–46. An Italian copy of her will (20 June 1803) with an English translation (undated), proved 5 July 1805, is in the Public Record Office, London, PROB 1/76.

48. *Descrizione di tutto ciò che vi è rinvenuto nell' Abitazione ritenuta dalla defonta Angelica Kauffman*, Getty Research Institute Special Collections, Filippo Romagnoli papers, 90–A136. The inventory is bound together with the will and inventory of her cousin and primary heir Giovanni (Johann) Kauffman, who died in Rome in 1829.

49. Manners and Williamson, 243. The painting (1777/78?), now in a private collection, was bequeathed to her cousin Giovanni (Johann) Kauffman.

50. On these canonical works, see Francis Haskell and Nicholas Penny, *Taste and the Antique, The Lure of Classical Sculpture 1500–1900* (New Haven and London: Yale University Press, 1981), 146–51, 167–69, 267–69.

51. Domenico Cunego (1727–1794), Kauffman and Zucchi's friend, was a well-known engraver active in Verona and Rome.

52. See Maria Iolanda Palazzolo, "Il libri di un artista nella Roma Neoclassica," *Roma Moderna e Contemporanea*, rivista interdisciplinare di storia, IV:3, Sept.–Dec. 1996), 637–60, for a discussion of the library of another artist, Giovanni Pikler (d. 1791). Kauffman and Pikler owned many of the same popular books and prints, such as Charles Rollin's sixteen-volume *Storia Romana*, engravings after Rubens, works by Ovid, Boccaccio, Metastasio, Fénélon's *Télemaque*, and Tasso's *Gerusalemme Liberata*.

53. August von Kotzebue, *Erinnerungen von einer Reise aus Liefland nach Rom und Neapel* (Berlin, 1805), II, 400–402, published in English in 1806.

54. One of two versions of *Three Girls Singing* is now in Bündner Kunstmuseum, Chur, Switzerland, the other in a private collection; *The Prophet Nathan Reproaching David* (Bregenz: VLM) was one of two large religious pictures—the other was *Christ and the Samaritan Woman*—carried in her funeral procession. See Sandner, *Angelika Kauffmann e Roma*, 51–54, and Baumgärtel, *Angelika Kauffmann, Retrospektive*, 269–70, 430. The portrait of Canova may be the one now in a private collection, Rome. See G. Pavanello, *Antonio Canova*, exh. cat. Correr Museum, Venice and Gipsoteca, Possagno (Venice: Marsilio, 1992), 92–93, and Angela Rosenthal,

Angelica Kauffman, Art and Sensibility (London and New Haven, 2006), 216–17. The Scottish gentleman was one of two full-length portraits of either Archibald Lord Montgomerie, later the Earl of Eglinton (private coll., Ayrshire), or Alistair Ranaldson Macdonell, Fifteenth Chief of Glengarry (private coll., on loan to National Museums of Scotland). See De Rossi, 90. *Hagar and Ishmael* (location unknown) was painted 1792–93 for Marchesa di Prie of Turin (*Memoria delle piture*, 203), and *Coriolanus* (now missing) is cited in G.C. Zucchi's index to the second part of his unfinished biography, 2, in Swozilek, 266; and De Rossi, 92, 97.

55. Several versions of the Reynolds portrait exist, including one in the Accademia di San Luca, Rome, and another copy, said to be by Kauffman herself (1794), in a private collection. The original Reynolds is in a private collection in the United States. See Sandner, *Angelika Kauffmann e Roma*, 49, 124; and David Mannings, *Sir Joshua Reynolds. A Complete Catalogue of His Paintings* (New Haven and London: Yale University Press, 2000), cat. 1026, 284–85, fig. 1251. Reynolds' painting was left unfinished, primarily the lower portion, arms, and hands in which she holds a blank sheet of paper. The Bartolozzi stipple engraving after Reynolds' painting was published 3 Sept. 1780 by John Boydell, London. The engraved composition was completed to include an image on the paper in her hand: a winged figure with a trumpet that may be understood as both the personification of Fame and an Angel as a pictorial play on her name. Bartolozzi must have consulted with Reynolds on how to finish the composition. See Barbara Jatta, ed., *Francesco Bartolozzi, Incisore delle Grazie*, exh. cat. Villa Farnesina, Rome, and Museu Nacional de Arte Antiga, Lisbon (Rome: Istituto Nazionale della Grafica), 1996), 55, 140–41.

56. Kotzebue, II, 400ff. The original Rembrandt now in the Uffizi was in the Gerini collection when Kauffman saw it in Florence in 1762. Her drawing of this portrait is in her sketchbook (1762–65) in the Victoria and Albert Museum, London. Another possibility is that the "Rembrandt" was actually a different portrait she owned, by Michiel Miereveld (or Mierevelt, 1567–1641), that Kotzebue misidentified as the work of the more famous Dutch artist. Kauffman's will describes these portraits as "A very beautiful head by VanDyke, another by Mierevelt, both painted with extraordinary skill." Manners and Williamson, 244.

57. J. J. Gerning, *Reise durch Österreich und Italien* (Frankfurt, 1802), III, 141.

58. Kauffman made portraits of numerous friends as gifts or replicas, usually of just head and shoulders in oval format, which she kept for herself. On the basis of the observations of visitors, together with evidence in her will, the inventory, and identified pictures, one may surmise that the dining room portraits included, among others, Goethe, Herder, Duchess Anna Amalia, Canova, Fantastici, Bandettini, English author Cornelia Knight, artists Johann Reiffenstein and Jakob Phillip Hackert, Giovanni Volpato, and Giuseppe and Francesco Zucchi, who were Antonio's brother and nephew. On eighteenth-century friendship portraits and Kauffman's in particular, see Baumgärtel, *Angelika Kauffmann, Retrospektive*, 320–31.

59. *Memoria di spese*, 20 (3 January 1791): ". . . due manichini uomo e donna di grandezza al naturalle" which cost, including packing and transport from Paris to Rome, 241 scudi. These were later bequeathed to Giovanni (Johann) Kauffmann.

60. The paintings inherited by Giovanni Kauffman appear in the inventory of his possessions (Rome, 24 August 1829), Getty Special Collections, 90–A136. The two religious pictures carried in Kauffman's funeral procession were noted above. See De Rossi, 104–5.

61. Giovanni Gherardo De Rossi and Onofrio Boni, *Memorie per le belle arti* (Rome, 1785–88). See L. Barroero, "Periodici storico-artistici romani in età neoclassica: 'Le Memorie per le Belle Arti' e il 'Giornale delle Belle Arti'" in *Roma "Il tempo del vero gusto." La pittura del Settecento romano e la sua diffusione a Venezia e Napoli*, Atti del Convegno, a cura di E. Borsellino e V. Casale (Ravello, 26–27 June 1997), 91–99.

62. *Memorie per le belle arti*, September 1785, cxxxv–cxli.

63. *Memorie per le belle arti*, August 1785, cxx; April 1787, lxxvii; March 1788, xliii.

64. *Memorie per le belle arti*, April 1785, li–liv: "Le opere della Signora Kauffman hanno una certa universalità di bellezze, dalle quali si deduce, che questa donna oltre un ingegno vasto, e fertile ha avuto dalla Natura il dono rarissimo delle Grazie. Di queste essa adorna ogni parte delle sue pitture, nelle quali perciò si veggono fisonomie tanto eleganti, espressioni così vere, e felici, atteggiamenti tanto gentili, ed effetto, ed accordo così nel chiaroscuro, e nel colorito."

65. *Morning Chronicle*, 3 May 1786: "Angelica has lost something, and has got nothing by her trip to Italy—the Cornelia and the Younger Pliny are neither warm nor delicate. . . ." This is a reference to a third painting she submitted, depicting *Pliny the Younger and His Mother at the Eruption of Vesuvius*. Another reviewer in the *Public Advertiser* (22 May 1786) wrote: ". . . . they do not appear to be either so beautifully conceived, or so tasty in their execution, as to drawing, characters, or colour, as those she painted in England. They seem to be done from memory of her former works, and no new beauties have been added to her style by her late tour to Italy. . . ."

66. *Memorie per le belle arti*, April 1787, lxxiv–lxxvii: "Quando altra volta parlammo della Sig. Kauffmann si disse, che desideravammo, che Roma avesse qualche opera publiche de' suoi pennelli. I nostri voti non sono stati ancora adempiti, ma speriamo che un giorno lo siano. . . ." Footnote: "Chi avrebbe mai creduto che Roma dovesse perdere una intera serie di opere di uno de' più celebri Pittori? Eppure l'ha perduta con danno per le Arti gravissimo, e la studiosa gioventù al luogo di quegli stupendi originali non trova ora che deboli copie." The two paintings, both signed and dated 1786, 154 x 216 cm., were destroyed in 1945 in Berlin, where they had been brought from Vienna by Hitler's order in 1944. One smaller surviving oil sketch is illustrated. See Kauffman's *Memoria delle piture*, numbers 122–23, in Knight, 37–38: "Rome, Settembre 1786, Per Sua Maestà Giuseppe Secondo Imperatore, Due quadri. . . . Con molte figure . . . rappresentanti li seguenti soggetti: La disfatta di Quintillio Varro, cioé Erminio vitorioso che fa ritorno alle sue selve ove viene rincontratto dalla sua moglie ed altre donzele qualli esultano di gioja le spargono da fiori d'inanzi all'Eroe vitorioso che viene seguito da suoi soldatti che portano le spoglie di Varro e le insegne delle acquile Romane. . . . L'altro compagno Rappresenta il Giovane Palante morto in bataglia, viene portato su una bara di fronde—Enea lo piange—e lo ricopre con una rica veste la quale ebbe da Didone

e le invoglie il capo d'un rico vello. . . ." There is more extensive description, much of which De Rossi seems to have followed in his own discussion of the pictures.

67. *Memorie per le belle arti*, April 1785, li–lii; De Rossi, *Angelica Kauffman*, 2–3. For further discussion of these passages see Wendy Wassyng Roworth, "Biography, Criticism, Art History: Angelica Kauffman in Context," in F. Keener and S. Lorsch, eds. *Eighteenth-Century Women and the Arts* (New York, 1988), 209–23; and "Matrons and Patrons: Angelica Kauffman's Classical History Paintings," in M. Hyde and J. Milam, eds., *Women, Art and the Politics of Identity in Eighteenth-Century Europe* (Aldershot: Ashgate), 2003, 188–210.

68. Sofonisba Anguissola (Cremona, 1532–1625), Lavinia Fontana (1552–1614), Elisabetta Sirani (1638–1665). See Chadwick, as in note 7.

69. For discussion of this language, see Roworth, "Biography, Criticism, Art History: Angelica Kauffman in Context . . ." (cited in note 67), 210–12, and more generally on the sixteenth and seventeenth centuries, see Frederika H. Jacobs, *Defining the Renaissance Virtuosa: Women Artists and the Language of Art History and Criticism* (Cambridge University Press, 1997).

70. G. P. Bellori, *Vite de' pittori, scultori ed architetti moderni* (Rome: Per il succeso, al Mascardi, 1672, 1731 edition). The drawing survives in the collection at Chatsworth, but the image was widely known through the engraving by Nicolas Dorigny, 1728. See *L'Idea del Bello. Viaggio per Roma nel Seicento con Giovan Pietro Bellori*, exh. cat. (Rome: Edizione De Luca), 2000, II, 456–58. Carlo Maratti was the father of the well-known poet Faustina Maratti Zappi (1680–1745).

71. See Ronald Lightbown, introduction, G.G. De Rossi, *Vita di Angelica Kauffmann, pittrice* (Pisa, 1811; London: Cornmarket Press, 1971), 16–23.

72. De Rossi, 58.

73. De Rossi, 64–65.

74. De Rossi, 65; Giuseppe Nicolo d'Azara, ed., *Opere di Antonio Raffaello Mengs primo Pittore del re Cattolico Carlo III* (Parma: Bodoni, 1780).

75. De Rossi, 66.

76. See Noack, *Deutsches Leben in Rome*, 74.

77. Letter to Fortunata Fantastici in Florence, from Rome, 22 September 1792, in Maierhofer, *Gesammelte Briefe*, 175. Maierhofer's transcription with Kauffman's spelling (I have not seen the original): " . . . in casa della Sig.a Maria Pizelli ove egli lesse un bellissimo discorso da lui scritto sopra la pittura e la scultura. Le difficultà che si opongano per arrivare alla perfezzione in queste due arte sono da lui molt ben spegate. Vi sono un infinità di cose molto <istruttive>. È di grande erudizione, . . . vi prego questo nostro comune amico di darlo al publico—che potrà molto giovare alla gioventù studiosa."

Notes to Chapter Seven

1. Most at first were Spanish; see the excellent archival and interpretative work of Giuseppe Gerbino on the Renaissance phase of this history, "The Quest for the Soprano Voice: Castrati in Renaissance Italy," *Studi musicali* 33 (2004), 303–57. The best overall introduction to the history of castrati in Italy is John Rosselli,

"The Castrati as a Professional Group and as a Social Phenomenon, 1550–1850," *Acta musicologica* 60 (1988), 143–79. Anthony Newcomb shows that castrati were hired for the chapel of the Duke of Ferrara in the late 1550s; see *The Madrigal at Ferrara, 1579–1597*, 2 vols. (Princeton: Princeton University Press, 1980), 1:30–31. The Duke of Mantua was looking for castrati slightly later; see Iain Fenlon, *Music and Patronage in Sixteenth-century Mantua*, 2 vols. (Cambridge: Cambridge University Press, 1980), 1:110; and Richard Sherr, "Guglielmo Gonzaga and the Castrati," *Renaissance Quarterly* 33 (1980), 33–56. Castrati at the papal chapel were dealt with in the early twentieth century by Enrico Celani, *I cantori della cappella pontificia nei secoli XVI. à XVIII* (Turin: Bocca, 1909); cf. Anthony Milner, "The Sacred Capons," *Musical Times* 114 (1973), 250–52. Until 1599 they were listed as "falsetti" but thereafter began to be listed as "eunuchi."

2.   Other basic works on the castrato include most importantly Franz Haböck, *Die Kastraten und ihre Gesangskunst: Eine gesangsphysiologische, kultur- und musik-historische Studie* (Berlin and Leipzig: Deutsche Verlags-Anstalt Stuttgart, 1927); as well as Gino Monaldi, *Cantanti evirati celebri del teatro italiano* (Rome: Ansonia, 1920); Anton Giulio Bragaglia, *Degli 'evirati cantori': contributo alla storia del teatro* (Florence: Sansoni Antiquiriato, 1959); and Hans Fritz, *Kastratengesang: Hormonelle, Konstitutionelle und Pädagogische Aspekte* (Tutzing: Hans Schenider, 1994). More popular or broader are the anecdotal Angus Heriot, *The Castrati in Opera* (London: Caldar and Boyars, 1956); Patrick Barber, *The World of the Castrati: The History of an Extraordinary Operatic Phenomenon*, trans. Margaret Crosland (1989; London: Souvenir Press, 1996); Hubert Ortkemper, *Engel wider Willen: Die Welt der Kastraten* (Berlin: Henschel Verlag, 1993); Sylvie Mamy, *Les grands castrats napolitains à Venise au XVIIIe siécle*, Musique-musicologie (Liège: Mardaga, 1994). Most recent and closest to my themes here is Valeria Finucci, *The Manly Masquerade: Masculinity, Paternity, and Castration in the Italian Renaissance* (Durham: Duke University Press, 2003), Chap. 6, which appeared in print just as this chapter was in final editing.

3.   Gerbino, "The Quest for the Soprano Voice," 334–39; Rosselli, "The Castrati," 146–48; Milner, "The Sacred Capons"; Finucci, *The Manly Masquerade*, 35, 263–64.

4.   See Thomas Laqueur, *Making Sex: Body and Gender from the Greeks to Freud* (Cambridge, MA: Harvard University Press, 1990); Rosselli, "The Castrati," 151.

5.   Charles Burney, *An Eighteenth-Century Musical Tour in France and Italy*, ed. Percy A. Scholes (London: Oxford University Press), 247. The Frenchman Jérôme Joseph Le François Lalande reported that castrati were mostly made in Naples, but he seems to have been repeating the speculations others made on grounds that so many were trained there; *Voyage en Italie*, 7 vols. (Venice and Paris, 1769; 3rd ed. Geneva, 1790), 5, 436–37.

6.   Gerbino, "The Quest for the Soprano Voice," 340, 348–57, argues from analysis of medical history that originally the "castrato was the creation of Renaissance medicine" (352).

7.   Charles Ancillon, *Traité des eunuques* (Berlin, 1707), 40; translated into English as *Eunichism Display'd, Describing the Different Sorts of Eunuchs* (London: E. Curil, 1718).

8. The document in question, and others concerning castration, was discovered by the late historian John Rosselli, *Singers of Italian Opera: The History of a Profession* (Cambridge: Cambridge University Press, 1992), 225 nn. 21 and 31.

9. Often parents acted in coordination with teachers, patrons, conservatories, princes, or relatives, though our concrete documentation is frequently limited by the taboo that surrounded castration.

10. Giovanni Battista Rossi Scotti, *Della vita e delle opere del cavalier Francesco Morlacchi* (Perugia, 1860), XLVI–XLVII; quoted in Nicola Lucarelli, *Domenico Bruni (1758–1821): biografia di un cantante evirato* (Città di Castello: Grafiche 2GF/Comune di Umbertide, 1992), 7; see also 16–19.

11. Giovenale Sacchi, *Vita del cavaliere Don Carlo Broschi* (Venice, 1874), 7–8.

12. Haböck, *Die Kastraten*, 203, 204; and on Moreschi see also Nicholas Clapton, *Moreschi: The Last Castrato* (London: Haus, 2004), 32–34.

13. "Eggs, Hens, Coops, and Castrati: Carnival and Sacrifice in Eighteenth-century Opera," paper delivered at the Clark Library conference Baroque Authority; revised versions given at the Annual Meeting of the American Musicological Society, Atlanta (Nov. 2001); Yale University, Department of Music (Nov. 2001); and Belgrade, Center for Music Information (Nov. 2002). This material has formed part of the first of my six Bloch Lectures, "The Castrato in Nature," Music Department, University of California at Berkeley, fall 2007, forthcoming from the University of California Press.

14. See *Caricature di Anton Maria Zanetti*, ed. Antonio Bettagno, intro. Giuseppe Fiocco (Venice: Neri Pozza, 1996), 100, plate 300. The Roman caricaturist Pierleone Ghezzi made a drawing of Bernacchi (now in the Vatican Library) in a remarkably similar posture, reproduced in Fritz, *Kastratengesang*, 87. On depictions of Renaissance men with plumes, in swaggering postures and with stiff protruding weapons, see Finucci, *The Manly Masquerade*, 4.

15. "Frutti del mondo esperimentati da F.B. nativo dell'Alfea, in Toscana," 2 vols., MS Munich, Bayerische Staatsbibliothek, cod. it. 39, vol. 1, fols. 36'–37. About half of the manuscript is published as *Frutti del mondo: autobiografia di Filippo Balatri da Pisa (1676–1756)*, ed. Mark Vossler (Milan: Remo Sandron, 1924), with connecting paraphrases of excised portions supplied by the editor. Recent literature on Balatri (1682–1756) by Slavicists includes Daniel L. Schlafly, Jr., "Filippo Balatri in Peter the Great's Russia," *Jahrbüchen für Geschichte ostereuropas* 45 (1997), 181–98; idem, "A Muscovite Boiarynia Faces Peter the Great's Reforms: Dar'ia Golitsyna between Two Worlds," *Canadian-American Slavic Studies* 31 (1997), 249–68; and Maria Di Salvo, "*Vita e viaggi* di Filippo Balatri (preliminari all'edizione del testo)," *Russica Romana* 6 (1999), 37–57, whose complete critical edition of the prose version of Balatri's autobiography is currently nearing completion. A popular biography of Balatri by German novelist Christine Wunnicke has recently appeared as *Die Nachtigall des Zaren: Das Leben des Filippo Balatri* (Munich: Claassen, 2001), who kindly corresponded with me about her research. Earlier Russian sources on Balatri are listed by Schlafly and Di Salvo (see esp. Di Salvo, "*Vita e viaggi*," nn. 5, 6, 9, and 11).

16. That is, surgeons who hail from the little Tuscan town of Norcia. In this, Balatri's tale draws on the traditional understanding that castrators commonly came from Norcia, which is still known today as a place of butchery owing to its famous sausages. Tommaso Garzoni's *Piazza Universale* (Venice, 1585; rev. 1587) notes that castrators "son comunemente i Norsini." A sixteenth-century comic poem by Francesco Berni alludes to the castrators of Norcia, and the famous Neapolitan castrato Caffarelli was said to have been castrated at Norcia by a Luccan, according to his will (Balatri, *Frutti del mondo*, ed. Vossler, 70 n. 1). See also Nelli, "Si chiama quel norcin castraporcelli, che fece l'operazione a quel musico"(14–2–2), quoted in *Grande dizionario della lingua italiana*, ed. Salvatore Battaglia, vol. 2 (Turin: Unione Tipografico-Editrice, 1962), 863, col. 1. In fact, castrations were performed in many places in Italy, commonly, for example, the province of Emilia-Romagna, and especially in Bologna, and elsewhere; see Gino Monaldi, *Cantanti evirati celebri* (Rome: Ansonia, 1920), 15 and 68. But Norcia was the provenance of many itinerant surgeons who performed castrations along with other surgeries; see David Gentilcore, *Medical Charlatanism in Early Modern Italy* (Oxford: Oxford University Press, 2006), 181–88, esp. 184–85; and for their late-medieval ancestors Katharine Park, "Stones, Bones, and Hernias: Specialists in Fourteenth- and Fifteenth-Century Italy," in *Medicine from the Black Death to the French Disease*, ed. R. French et al. (Aldershot: Ashgate, 1998), 110–30.

17. "Incomincia dal farmi domandare / se maschio son o femmina e da dove, / se nasce tale gente (ovvero piove) / con voce e abilitate per cantare. / Resto imbrogliato allor per dar risposta. / Se maschio, dico quasi una bugia, / femmina, men che men dirò ch'io sia, / e dir che son neutral, rossore costa. / Pure, fatto coraggio, al fin rispondo / che son maschio, Toscano, e che si trova / galli nelle mie parti che fanno uova, / dalle quali i soprani son al mondo; / Che li galli si nomano *Norcini*, / ch'a noi le fan covar per molti giorni / e che, fatto il cappon, son gli uovi adorni / da lusinghe, carezze e da quattrini." Balatri, *Frutti del mondo* 1:36'–37.

18. On Pulcinella, see most importantly the monumental work of Domenico Scafoglio and M. Luigi Lombardi Satriani, *Pulcinella: il mito e la storia* (Milan: Leonardo, 1990). A concise essayistic version of their thesis was extrapolated for the *1000 Lire* series as Domenico Scafoglio, *Pulcinella*, Napoli Tascabile, 30, ed. Romualdo Marrone (Rome: Tascabili Economici Newton, 1996). Among many fascinating images pictured, there is a drawing from an ancient Greek vase done in 1897, which shows a warrior with his equerry, the latter short, thin, and knobby-kneed but heavily beset with a feathered headdress and with a protruding belly and long pendulous testicles (Plate 150). Other eighteenth- and nineteenth-century drawings from Greek gems and herms show creatures who are half-human and half-fowl with exaggerated phalluses, often comic in kind (e.g., plates 152–54). See also the marvelous collection of essays in *Pulcinella: Una maschera tra gli specchi*, ed. Franco Carmelo Greco (Naples: Edizioni Scientifiche Italiane, 1990).

19. "Eggs, Hens, Coops, and Castrati." Scafoglio and Lombardi Satriani, *Pulcinella*, 426–46, demonstrate Pulcinella's relation to motifs of castration and to capons and chickens. See also Roberto De Simone and Annabella Rossi, *Carnevale*

si chiamava Vincenzo: rituali di Carnevale in Campania (Rome: De Luca, 1977), 183–221, on elisions between sexuality, chickens, Carnival, and Pulcinella in modern-day Campania.

20. One could look to other archetypal figures associated with the *commedia dell'arte* for affinities with the castrato: Harlequin, Zanni, and other tricksters. I discuss Pulcinella because he was the supreme instantiation of the archetype and shares with the castrato a strong association with Naples.

21. "Castrò un suo Figlio un dì quel di Salò / Perche meglio attendesse alla virtù / Per applicarlo, a qualche servitù; / Ed incauto i testicoli [g]ettò. / Hà in casa una chiocca, & io non sò, / Come di quei coglion si cacciò sù, / Basta con gli ovi anche ei covato fu, / Era suo tempo angli [anch'] egli pululò. / Quindi nacque il Marchese il qual così: / Per non far torto alla natività, / Cresciuto un coglioncello riuscì. / E in sù le scene da quel tempo in quà, / Un che faccia il coglione à nostri dì, / Pulcinella nominar si fa." (*Poesie e prose di Francesco Melosio da città della Pieve, aggiuntovi in questa nova impressione altre spiritose, erudite, e bizarre compositioni dello stesso auttore. Consacrate all'Illustriss. & Eccellentiss. Sig. Gio: Alberto di Ferschen* [Venice, 1695], 324.) "Chiocca" is a variant of "chioccia." Lines 5–7 might also be translated, "And I don't know how she threw herself on them, but this one was also brooded from eggs." In other editions line 8 reads "Ed a suo tempo anch'egli pullulò." Cf. the anonymous poetry quoted in Heriot, *The Castrati in Opera*, 56.

22. Sometimes the marquis is elided with Harlequin, including by Balatri.

23. Ángel Medina writes about the Spanish counterpart to the Italian history I trace out here, connecting singing castrati, capons, and comic characters; see *Los atributos del capón: Imagen histórica de los cantores castrados en España* (Madrid: Instituto Complutense de Ciensias Musicales, 2001), esp. chaps. 5 through 9.

24. Scafoglio and Lombardi Satriani, *Pulcinella*, 23–24. The original source is an anonymous Neapolitan comedy called *Gl'incanti delle Maghe per la nascita di Pulcinella dalle viscere del Monte Vesuvio* (Naples, 1802), but has its genesis in much earlier traditions.

25. Image reproduced in Adriano Mariuz, *Giandomenico Tiepolo*, preface by Antonio Morassi (Venice: Alfieri, 1971), plate 31.

26. In the painting a group of Pulcinella-styled men look on as a mannish midwife clasps her hands in joy; reproduced in Scafoglio and Lombardi Satriani, *Pulcinella*, plate 21. In another painting from the same group, Pulcinella gives birth through his back (ibid., plate 20).

27. Reports of heckling in eighteenth-century Italian theaters are notorious and include many performances of opera seria in which castrati reigned. See my "Magic Mirrors and the *Seria* Stage: Thoughts toward a Ritual View," *Journal of the American Musicological Society* 48 (1995), 423–84, and idem, *Opera and Sovereignty: Transforming Myths in Eighteenth-Century Italy* (Chicago: University of Chicago Press, 2007), esp. chaps. 1 and 4.

28. Carlo Broschi Farinelli, *La solitudine amica: lettere al conte Sicinio Pepoli*, ed. Carlo Vitali, with introductory note by Roberto Pagano and preface by Francesca Boris (Palermo: Sellerio, 2000), 164; letter to Count Sicinio Pepoli of 8 September

1740. The letters in the edition are based on Farinelli's correspondence with Sicinio Pepoli, preserved in Bologna, Archivio di Stato, Fondo Pepoli, Carteggi del conte Sicinio, busta 11 bis.

29. See my "Magic Mirrors and the *Seria* Stage," and the many references in my *Opera and Sovereignty*, esp. in chaps. 1 and 2.

30. I am indebted to Ellen T. Harris for encouraging me to think more extensively about the logic of reproduction that winds through these various tales. See her excellent contribution "Farinelli," *New Grove Dictionary of Music and Musicians*, 2nd ed., 29 vols., ed. Stanley Sadie and John Tyrrell (London and New York: Macmillan, 2001), 8:565–69.

31. They might also remind us of the quasi-mythical stories of genesis, ethnic roots, or early childhood that have bound together members of certain marginalized groups in recent times, for instance black men and women of the 1960s and 1970s, who reached back to their African roots and to Islamic traditions to establish distinct kinship structures, practices, shared histories, and forms of celebration; or gay men and women who share archetypal moments of youthful self-discovery or coming out and who draw on such moments in elaborating and solidifying alternative families. See Cornel West, "Malcolm X and Black Rage," in *Race Matters* (New York: Random House, 1993), 135–51; and Kath Weston, *Families We Choose: Lesbians, Gays, Kinship* (New York: Columbia University Press, 1991).

32. This is elaborated in my *The Castrato*, forthcoming.

33. In an anonymous eighteenth-century drawing, a Carnival chariot shows Pulcinella along with his own transformations into half-human Pulcinellini and Pulcinella-asses, pulling their Pulcinella-masters like rickshaw drivers (Scafoglio and Lombardi Satriani, *Pulcinella*, plate 34). On Pulcinella's castratolike voice, see ibid., 426–31.

34. Among many other writings, see Jean Chevalier and Alain Gheerbrant, *The Penguin Dictionary of Symbols*, trans. John Buchanan-Brown (2nd ed. 1982; London: Penguin, 1996), 337–41.

35. Valeria Finucci, "Introduction" to *Generation and Degeneration: Tropes of Reproduction in Literature and History from Antiquity to Early Modern Europe*, ed. Valeria Finucci and Kevin Brownlee (Durham and London: Duke University Press, 2001), 1.

36. Finucci, *The Manly Masquerade*; and Laqueur, *Making Sex*. It is well to remember here that for most of the eighteenth century medical views of sexuality were still Galenic, and in a Galenic view blood had to matter more than uterine ties because it restored youth and promoted vitality.

37. Of related importance in the English sphere is the vast satiric literature; see Thomas McGeary, "Verse Epistles on Italian Opera Singers, 1724–1736," *R.M.A. Research Chronicle* 33 (2000), 29–88; and Xavier Cervantes and Thomas McGeary, "From Farinelli to Monticelli: An Opera Satire of 1742 Re-examined," *The Burlington Magazine* 141:1154 (May 1999), 287–89.

38. Pietro Stella, "Strategie familiari e celibato sacro in Italia tra '600 e '700," *Salesianum* 41:1 (1979), 73–109. "Celibacy" here is unrelated to actual sexual practice,

of course. Castrati often did have sexual lives. See Roger Freitas's Chapter 8 in this volume, plus the many cases cited in Barbier, *The World of the Castrati*, 141–48; Finucci, *The Manly Masquerade*, 260–71; and Heriot, *The Castrati in Opera*, passim. The number of heterosexual accounts rises in the eighteenth century compared with the sixteenth and seventeenth, probably because by then castrati as opera singers were more prominent public personae, and moreover because the eighteenth century made nonheterosexual practices taboo and thus closeted.

39. John Rosselli, "L'apprendistato del cantante italiano: rapporti contrattuali fra allievi e insegnanti dal cinquecento al novecento," *Rivista italiana di musicologia* 23 (1988), 157–81.

40. Di Giacomo, *Il conservatorio.*

41. I use the term "life-writing" here to encompass a variety of genres: biography and autobiography, letters, diaries, etc. It should be noted that the only castrato ever known to have written an autobiography—in this case, two—is Filippo Balatri. Thus recourse to other genres is a necessity.

42. The phrase "one God, one Farinelli" appears in Hogarth's second engraving based on his own paintings picturing *The Rake's Progress*. The engraving shows a scroll rolling down the floor in back of a keyboardist behind whom appear the figures of Tom Rakewell, a dancing master, and others. At the bottom of the scroll is an image showing Farinelli raised on a pedestal before a burning altar, in front of which several women are falling forward in reverence. One of them has a tribune issuing from her mouth bearing the blasphemous words. A Lady Rich is reported to have shouted the phrase to Farinelli at one of his London performances in 1735. See Daniel Heartz, "Farinelli Revisited," *Early Music* (August 1990), 438–39 and n. 18.

43. On Farinelli, see, in addition to Sacchi's eighteenth-century *Vita*, Franz Haböck, *Die Gesangskunst der Kastraten, Erster Notenband: A, Die Kunst des Cavaliere Carlo Broschi Farinelli. B. Farinellis berümte Arien* (Vienna: Universal, 1923); Patrick Barbier, *Farinelli: Le castrat des lumières* (Paris: B. Grasset, 1994); Sandro Cappelletto, *La voce perduta: vita di Farinelli, evirato cantore* (Turin: EDT, 1995); and Vega De Martini and Jose M. Morilla Alcàzar, *Farinelli: arte e spettacolo alla corte spagnuolo del Settecento* (Rome: Artemide, 2001). For Ghezzi's caricature of Farinelli in a female role, see Ortkemper, *Engel wider Willen*, 87.

44. *Tutte le opere di Pietro Metastasio*, 5 vols., ed. Bruno Brunelli (Milan: Mondadori, 1954), 4:437, letter of 29 Jan 1766 to Francesco Giovanni di Chastellux.

45. Farinelli, *La solitudine amica*; see n. 22 above.

46. Farinelli, *La solitudine amica*, 98.

47. Farinelli, *La solitudine amica*, 100, letter of 26 April 1732.

48. Before Sacchi published his biography there had already been some partial editions of Metastasio's letters published in 1782 and 1783, *Opere di Pietro Metastasio*, ed. Giovanni Tommaso Masi (London, sold in Livorno: Gio. Tomaso Masi e Compagnia, 1782–83); and *Lettere del signor' abate Pietro Trapassi Metastasio, poeta cesareo* (Assisi: O. Sgariglia, 1783).

49. Metastasio spelled this out publicly in the dedication to a 1756 print of *La Nitteti*, where he spoke of "the affectionate name of twin (*gemello*) used between

Cavaliere Broschi and the author" since the time of their joint debut. See Daniel Heartz, "Farinelli and Metastasio: Rival Twins of Public Favour," *Early Music* 12 (1984), 358–66; passage quoted on 358–59, n. 6.

50. Metastasio, *Opere*, 3:314, letter of 26 August 1747.

51. Farinelli gave his infatuation a literary twist: "Cupido ancora mi tien legato e Iddio sa quando sarò slegato, poiché dall'una e l'altra parte, si soffre, si tace, si pena, e pure vien gradita tale dolcissima catena; viva la mia fedeltà, e la costanza di quella gioina" (*La solitudine amica*, 124). The passage has the romance and lovely rhythmic lilt of contemporaneous poetry for opera.

52. Here I would agree with Laqueur, *Making Sex*.

53. Indeed, the term *third sex* de facto presupposes a dimorphic model of sexuality, problematically so in many historic and ethnographic domains that are not predicated on two-sex models.

54. "Gli spedì più volte soccorso di danaro, a Londra, a Vienna, a Napoli; non però amava d'averlo vicino per la sua imprudente, e molto ardita loquacità" (he didn't like to have him nearby because of his imprudence and excessive loquaciousness). Sacchi, *Vita*, 38. In these strategies, Sacchi's text is more than a biography or even an encomium. As my students Courtney Quaintance and Justin Flosi have pointed out, it is formally a saint's life, a virtual hagiography displaying an exemplary life in order to demonstrate how its subject's memory can inspire the reader to self-doubt and hence self-betterment.

55. He first got to know Farinelli in 1727 through Roman relatives of the Colonna family: his cousin Don Fabrizio, *conestabile* (constable) of Rome and prince of Pagliano, and his wife Eleanora's uncle, cardinal Carlo.

56. Farinelli, *La solitudine amica*, 54.

57. See Sacchi, *Vita*, 40; and Vitali in Farinelli, *La solitudine amica*, 51.

58. Letter nos. 49–50ff.; quoted from Vitali in Farinelli, *La solitudine amica*, 54.

59. *La solitudine amica*, letter no. 51, 150.

60. On Riccardo Broschi, see Michael F. Robinson and Ellen T. Harris, "Broschi, Riccardo," *New Grove*, 2nd ed., 4:430–31.

61. *La solitudine amica*, letter 55, 163–64: "Vorrei che la robba mia potesse goderla persona che lo merita. L'ambizione da me sta molto lontana, né vanità trasporta la mio dovere. Vorrei trovare una signora né che sia esposta alle stelle, né tampoco alle valli. Potrebbe Vostra Eccellenza col suo bel cuore e vera amicizia trovarne cosa a proposito; sopra tutto, che ci sia ancora qualche epulenza. Mio fratello presentamente gode un buon officio, datogli dalla benignità del Re di Napoli, che ci rende sotto mille ducati l'anno, avendo esercitato questo impiego un Cavallier di molta stima prima che cadesse a mio fratello. La mia sorella sia maritata con un altro galant'uomo, che ora esercita la carica di percettore nella provincia di Salerno, che gli dà 2000 docati l'anno: veda Vostra Eccellenza quando ha fatto il mio core per i miei parenti. Io non dico esser nato dalla terza costa di Venere, né tampoco aver per padre Nettuno. Son napolitano; il Duca d'Andria mi tenne al fonte, questo basta per dar saggio d'esser un figlio di buon cittadino e galantuomo. Mi pare che io fin al presente d'aver prodotto molto onore a me stesso, alla mia patria, alla mia famiglia,

ed alla mia professione. Spererei a tale riflessioni che nessuna buona figlia doverebbe sputare a questo incontro: . . . Io non posso (come sa) maritarmi, dunque devo penzare al mio sangue e cercare una donna che possa meritare tutto quello che Iddio mi ha dato." Emphasis mine.

62. When a general coming from Italy fell from the good graces of the Spanish king just before his arrival, Farinelli allegedly procured employment for every single musician in the general's large entourage.

63. Sacchi, *Vita*, 47. In the years after the great earthquake many of the Lisbon musicians can be found at the Spanish court, as Drew Edward Davies has pointed out to me; see Manuel Carlos De Brito, *Opera in Portugal in the Eighteenth Century* (Cambridge: Cambridge University Press, 1989). Sacchi's portrait also finds corroboration in some other eighteenth-century evidence. For example, the composer Giuseppe Farinelli (1769–1836) allegedly so named himself in gratitude to the singer for protection and aid during his studies; see Giovanni Carli Ballola, "Farinelli, Giuseppe," *New Grove*, 2nd ed., 8:569.

64. Sacchi, *Vita*, 58.

65. Farinelli, *La solitudine amica*, 100.

66. See Sacchi, *Vita*, 38–39; Farinelli, *La solitudine amica*, letter 18, 98–100.

67. Balatri's manuscripts include, in addition to the *Frutti del Mondo*, *Vita e viaggi di F. B., nativo di Pisa*, Moscow, Russian State Library, F. 218, no. 1247 (1–9), in 9 vols., though undoubtedly lacking one volume (cf. Di Salvo, "*Vita e viaggi*," 41); *Testamento, o sia ultima volontà, di F.B., nativo Alfeo*, Munich, Bayerische Staatsbibliothek, cod. It. 329, dated 27 November 1737–8 January 1738; and the spiritual play *Santa Margherita* (see n. 70 below), dating from 1741. The treatise on singing, mentioned in Balatri's testament as *Istruzione di un giovane musico*, has not been found. Balatri has been almost totally ignored in musical scholarship, and there is not even an entry for him in the *New Grove Dictionary of Music and Musicians*, 2nd ed. The only musical discussions (even minimal ones) of the *Frutti del Mondo* (and that only at very minimal length) are Andrea della Corte, *Satire e grottesche di musiche e musicisti d'ogni tempo* (Turin: Unione Tipografico-Editrice Torinese, 1946), 160–68; Heriot, *The Castrati in Opera*, chap. 6; Enid Rhodes Peschel and Richard Peschel, "Medicine and Music: The Castrati in Opera," *Opera Quarterly* 4:4 (1986–87), 21–38; and Barbier, *The World of the Castrati*, 175–78.

68. In the *Vita e viaggi* Balatri writes, "The said memoirs that I kept in writing were developed by me through use of a travel diary, having had an express command to do so by the Grand Duke Cosimo III from the time that he sent me forth from my homeland" ("Le dette Memorie ch'io conservai in scritto furono damme distese ad uso di Giornale in viaggiando, avendo io avuto dal G. Duca Cosimo Terzo di Toscana un'espresso commando di ciò fare allorche mi mandò fuori di Patria"); *Vita e viaggi*, 1:4.

69. "Era altresì curioso di aver' dà remote Parti cose particolari, cioè Piante per il suo Giardino, minerali, Pitture, Statue et altro per la Galleria, et Animali feroci per il Serraglio; senza guardare a spesa che si fosse." Balatri continues by suggesting a set of political ramifications: "Quando venivano in Fiorenza Prencipi oltremontani, o

Signori di sfera di qualunque sia Parte, gli trattava con tale Distinzione che si rese Celebre dappertutto et amato dattutte le nazzioni." *Vita e viaggi*, 1:19–20.

70. *Frutti del Mondo*, 2:44. In the preface to the edition, Vossler gives the date of Balatri's birth as 1676. Divo Falossi and Maria Angela Mazzei revised it to 1672 in their edition: Dionisio Filippo Balatri, *Santa Margherita da Cortona: Istoria sacra da rappresentarsi* (Cortona: Calosci, 1982), 15, on the basis of a baptismal certificate found in Pisa. Their findings conflict with the evidence of printed opera libretti, as well as dates of journeys, residencies, and performances mentioned in Balatri's manuscripts. The printed libretti currently known to cite him as a performer number twelve, ranging chronologically from 1703 to 1737 and including performances in Florence, London, Munich, and Rome; see Claudio Sartori, *I libretti italiani a stampa dalle origini al 1800: catalogo analitico con 16 indici*, 7 vols. (Cuneo: Bertola & Locatelli, 1990–1994), passim. (We also know that he performed in Vienna with Faustina Bordoni on 28 August 1724 for the nameday of the Empress, but I have yet to locate a libretto for the occasion.) Balatri declared in his will, at the beginning of 1738, that he was then fifty. Vossler questioned this (*Frutti del Mondo*, 18) on the basis of a note found in an unedited chronicle of the monastery of Fürstenfeld by the abbot Gerhard (Munich, Bayerische Staatsbibliothek, cod. Germ. 3920, pp. 299–291, year 1741), which notes that Balatri was sixty-three on 15 July 1739 when his investiture took place there. In the *Frutti del Mondo* 2:44', Balatri claims that he was not yet twenty-five when the Russian ambassador Naryshkin came to Florence. The dates Balatri gives correspond generally with the dates of his performances given in printed libretti, and the various conundra have now been solved by the archival work of Di Salvo, "Vita e viaggi."

71. *Frutti del mondo*, 1:9'.

72. *Vita e viaggi*, 3:62'; 1:20, and 1:24–30.

73. The pattern crystallizes in a passage from the *Frutti del Mondo* describing the contractual negotiations: "My father is a man of the pen, and is protected / by his sovereign . . . / I was already made into a mixed gender, / that is a soprano, and was quite young. / I apply myself to singing in the most human style, / doing so with industry and a good vocation. / My patron sets his eyes on me / and thinks about putting me in the hands of the said prince. / So he has him listen to me and then says that if all the czar wants is to hear the singing / of Italian castrati, / one of them will satisfy him as well as two." *Frutti del mondo*, 1:9'.

74. Schlafly, "A Muscovite Boiaryarina," esp. 196. Note that the girls never knew their friend was a castrato.

75. See Falossi and Mazzei, *Santa Margherita*, 16 n. 17; and Di Salvo, "Vita e viaggi," no. 6, 54.

76. *Aminta. Drama regio-pastorale per musica da rappresentarsi in Firenze nell'autunno del 1703. Dedicato all'altezza sereniss. Di Viol.te Beatrice di Baviera gran principessa di Tosc. Firenze. Vincenzo Vangelisti.* The libretto was dedicated by Apostolo Zeno and dated 15 October 1703. See Sartori, *I libretti italiani*, 1:133.

77. The man was a cousin of Peter the Great named Alexandr Lvovich Naryshkin, who taxed Balatri with his ebullient curiosity and energies, especially when Balatri was forced to house him briefly at the family's ill-appointed palace.

78. London had recently seen the first raging success and counterreaction of Italian opera (and its singers) with Handel's *Rinaldo* of 1711.

79. There is a funny and revealing episode about the collision of Italian bel canto with French recitative-styled singing reported by Balatri from his stop in Lyons; see *Frutti del Mondo*, 2:63–72'; a partial reprint and commentary on the relevant excerpt appear in Andrea Della Corte, *Satire e grotteschi*, 160–68.

80. He made good connections with several well-placed nobles, including Lady Burlington of the Duchy of Devonshire, for whom he performed, and a field-marshal at the king's court.

81. *Ernelinda. Opera da rappresentarsi nel Reggio Teatro d'Hay-Market* (London: J. Tonson); see Sartori, *I libretti italiani*, 3:56. It is roughly based on the libretto *Ricimero, re di Goti*, by Silvani, with music by Gasparini, Orlandini, Bononcini, and Mancini. The dedication of the printed libretto to the baron Lowther of Lowther framed the event as a matter of national pride in the reigning competition of London with Italian opera: " . . . we may retrieve the Reputation of our Affairs; and in a short time Rival the Stage of Italy. . . ." The article on "Gasparini" in the *New Grove Dictionary of Opera* gives the date of 26 February 1713 as the premiere of this work; Sartori, *I libretti italiani*, gives 1713. Winton Dean in his article on the female lead Diana Vico gives the date as 1714 (*New Grove Dictionary of Opera*). The pasticcio was originally done at the San Bartolomeo in Naples in 1704, albeit in a different version.

82. Presumably he had an agile technique and fine artistry but probably lacked the necessary physique, power, and charisma (indeed by his own confession he was intimidated when ten years later he had to sing in Vienna opposite the illustrious Handelian soprano Faustina Bordoni).

83. She had married the Elector Palatinate Johann Wilhelm of the house of Neuberg.

84. He went through Cologne, Frankfurt, and the Black Forest, the so-called route of the assassins, where he greatly feared piracy, since it was the time of roadside terrorism; see Uwe Danker, *Die Geschichte der Raüber und Gauner* (Düsseldorf: Artemis & Winkler, 2001). My thanks to Drew Edward Davies for the reference. Filippo's brother Ferrante had a more minor appointment at a considerably lower salary.

85. Reproduced in Heriot, *The Castrati in Opera*, fig. 10, and as endpapers in Wunnicke, *Die Nachtigall des Zaren*.

86. The Grand Duke Cosimo III died on 31 October 1723; the Bishop Schönborn of Würzburg, of whom he had become a favorite, on 18 August 1724; and finally, and most especially, the Elector Maximilian on 26 February 1726.

87. I do not know how many of them may have been castrati, but many were surely destined for life as celibates, if they had not already pledged themselves to it.

88. Justin Flosi has written an innovative critical assessment of the web of genres that informs the *Frutti del Mondo*: "Strange Fruit: Genre in Balatri's *Frutti del Mondo*," paper delivered at the miniconference Castrati and Eunuchs, University of Chicago, May 2002.

89. *Frutti del Mondo*, 1:46'; 54'–55.

90. *Vita e viaggi*, 2:96'.

91. "Circa quanto riguarda il Corpo; Io non voglio . . . esser lavato e maneggiato da Donne, come si costuma nel Paese in cui alpresente mi trovo, et in caso ch'io morissi; poiche oltre l'indecenza che vi vedo, non vuò che si vadino divertendo in esaminare il come sia 'fatti i soprani'"; *Testamento*, fol. 16.

92. Paoluccio joked to Charles Ancillon that though he was a man, "si manca qualche cosa." Farinelli was parodied extensively in London for his "lack." A satirical play by Fielding from the time has a group of ladies swooning over Farinelli's performance of the previous night and punning on his assets and deficits. One Lady remarks to others, "Sure he is the Charmingest Creature," to which another answers "He's everything one could wish," and a third quips "Almost everything one could wish." See Daniel Heartz, "Farinelli Revisited," *Early Music* (August 1990), 441. The castrato Tenducci married, but his marriage was later annulled. Sara Goudar pretends to relate a conversation between Tenducci and his wife on learning she was pregnant, which ends with the castrato stressing that he can't give what he doesn't have: "Cara Consorte, lui-dit le Soprano, questa non me l'aspettavo. Nulladimeno ajouta-t-il, si vede oggi tante cose straordinarie ne' Matrimoni, che si puol vedere anche questa. Tuttavia, ajoute-t-il, se partorirete un maschio, che sia Eunuco, l'adotterò per mio figlio. Elle acoucha d'un mâle qui n'étoit pas Eunuque. Fedelissima Sposa, lui-dit alors le musicien, voi vedete bene, che non è mio, perché non posso dare a un altro quel che io non ho." From Sara Goudar, *Supplement au supplement de la musicque et de la danse ou lettres de M.r G—a Milord Pembroke* (Venice, 1774), 40. The suggestion is that generation can only occur from one kind to a like kind. Earlier she writes, "C'est ce même Tenducci qui s'engagea dans l'himen sans en avoir la valeur. Il devint Epoux par l'endroit que les hommes cessent de l'être. Si les Eunuques se marioient, il y auroit un double viude dans la propagation; car outre qu'ils n'auroient point d'enfans, ils empécheroient les femmes d'en voir" (ibid., 39–40).

93. Julia Kristeva, *Powers of Horror: An Essay on Abjection*, trans. Leon S. Roudiez (1980; New York: Columbia University Press, 1982), 1. My thanks to David J. Levin for pressing me to think here about Kristeva's text.

94. "Io non saprei dirvi altro sennon', ch'è un Forastiero, il qual' dà poco tempo è venuto a stare in questa Città. Uh come'è brutto (Agata mia) io tremo di spavento di sognarmelo. Lo consideravo ancor'io sorella, e per dirvela sinceramente mi son pentita della mia curiosità . . . ; poichè hò l'istesso vostro timore. Et io Agata cara son' capace di star'tre dì senza mangiare, tanto mi fà stomaco. . . .

Sorella benedetta, non vedete che non hà ancor'messo barbar, nè viè segno di'essergli mai stata fatta! La Malattia sarà stata lunga e penosa. . . . Ei non hà barba perchè è Musico; altro che fichi secchi.

Ah era musico eh? O s'è così, egli averà lasciato di gran denaro; Si sà nulla à chi habbia testàto?" Balatri, *Testamento*, fols. 29–30.

95. Edmund Leach, "Verbal Abuse and Animal Categories," in *New Directions in the Study of Language*, ed. Eric H. Lenneberg (Cambridge, MA: MIT Press, 1964),

23–63; Peter Stallybrass and Allon White, *The Politics and Poetics of Transgression* (Ithaca: Cornell University Press, 1986), 44–59 and passim; and the brilliant analysis in connection with early modern anti-Semitism in Jud Newborn, "'Work Makes Free': The Hidden Cultural Meaning of the Holocaust," 4 vols. (Ph.D. dissertation, University of Chicago, 1994), 1:72–78 and passim.

96. Ambroise Paré, *On Monsters and Marvels*, trans. Janis Pallister (1573; Chicago: University of Chicago Press, 1982), chap. 7.

97. "Se io fossi stato un'uomo tenace, averei fatto la figura del Porco. Il Porco (finche vive) è stimato il più vile Animale; ogni buco, è buono per il Porco; tutte l'immondizzie si diano al Porco. Chi v'hà che lo carezzi, ò sel tenga attorno? Morto però ch'egl'è, tutti corrono al lardo; e, dal pelo inpoi, non v'è minuta parte che non s'apprezzi. Si loda, si sapora, et è delizzia d'ognuno; perchè si fa mangiare. Mi crederesti forse sì stolto, che essendo stato un'semplice musico, io volessi far' poi marchese il mio Asino allorche và à inputridire la terra? Ei m'hà mangiato biada abbastanza in vita, senza ch'io penso à distinguerlo, inbalsamarlo, profumarlo, e carezzarlo doppo crepàto. Per esser'stato grazziato dei S.S. Sagramenti gli basti la distintione di andare in un' Cimitèro, ò imezzo di una Chiesa, ch'è la casa di Dio. Se mille, duemila ceri, bastassero à mandar' subito l'Anima al suo vero Centro, oh vorrei empirmi io stesso il muso di pugni se non avessi pensato a tale spesa, ma avendo considerato, che due mila sospiri di Povero, inviàti a Dio per ottonermi Misericordia, ardono meglio (e spengono nel tempo istesso quel fuoco che arde senza consumo) amo piu l'andare alla sepoltura dà barone di Piazza, che da marchese di Città." Balatri, *Testamento*, fols. 90–91. Emphasis mine.

98. "Coméche . . . io non hò moglie, figli, parenti, hò un' sol Amico (e anche s'il vuol essere), pochi conoscenti (tutti di cappello), niun' riconoscente, e niun'che si curì ch'io viva Cent'Anni ò crepi stasera, così voluto sposare alcuni che non conosco, e trarne figli, fratelli, parenti, amici, et altri me stessi (Conforme è l'obbligo che ne stringe tutti) e che perciò hò resoluto testare conforme dirò inseguito." Balatri, *Testamento*, fols. 14'–15.

99. "Dal Denaro che mi si troverà, fra scrigno, e tasche degl'ultimi calzoni che m'averò cavato per entrar' per l'ultima volta in letto . . . sen' estragghino le sudette spese dà farsi; e del restante, tutto, ne sia fatta elemosina ai Poveri subito, et avanti ch'io sia posto sotterra.

Non voglio che si Arbitrii, con darli tutti ad un Bisognoso, ò inpiegarli per terminàr' una Fabbrica di luogo Pio, ò altro con il dir' tutt'è Limosina;

So ancor'io che tutt'è profittevole all'Anima, ma io voglio che sian' dispensàti ai Poveri di Strada, quelli che cercan' la carità per le chiese, per le vie, e che dicono alto, un poca d'elemosina per l'amor di Dio;

Quando però vi fosse necessità di fare un' Letto ad una Creatura miserabile ammalata; ad una povera Parturiente che dovesse partorir' perterra sulla paglia; o à qualche Famiglia che per miseria dovessero dormir' moglie e marito con figli e figlie tutta in una stanza, et ammontàte sei ò otto persone in due letti; . . . voglio, anziche Supplico, che non sol' sia dato un'Letto à tali creature, ma cinque, sei, e otto. . . .

Lascio dunque tutta la moneta che misi troverà, per elemosine. . . . Indi con un' solo Item, lascio Biancarie, Abiti, e quanto si troverà fin all'ultima Bagattella dà cavarne un'Quattrino, tutto da vendersi e distribuirsi ai Poveri di Cristo." Balatri, *Testamento*, fol. 34'–36:

The above-said money should be taken from what's found on me, around my desk and in the pockets of the last pair of pants I'll have . . . to enter my bed for the last time . . . , and alms for the poor made immediately from all the rest, before I've been placed underground.

I want no disputes about whether to give it to a needy person or use it to finish work on a place of worship, or anything else, by saying: 'Everything is charity.'

I know everything is profitable for the soul, but I want [my money] to be dispersed to the poor on the street—those who seek charity at churches, on sidewalks, and who cry out 'A little charity for the love of God.'

But should there be need to have a bed made for a miserable sick creature, for a poor parturient who has to give birth on hay on the ground, or some family who, because of poverty, has to sleep wife with husband and sons and daughters all in one room, and six or eight persons heaped up on two beds; . . . I want, nay beg that not just one bed be given to such creatures, but five, six, and eight. . . .

I therefore leave then all the money that will be found on me as alms. . . . Hence with a single Item, I leave bank credits, clothing, and whatever else is found up to the last bagatelle to carve out a coin, all to sell and distribute to the Poor of Christ.

100.   Balatri, *Vita e viaggi*, 1:14–15: "La voce fu trovata d'un buonissimo metallo, il trillo naturale è ben battuto, agilità ben grande nei passaggi, e gusto naturale nel cantare, onde che di più potea bramarsi per farne un'buon cantòre! Tutte le dette cose cominciorno a sollecitare gl'Amici di mio Padre a dirgli *taglia, taglia* (et il Maestro poi più di tutti di essi[)] a consigliarlo onde doppo le molte . . . taglia, taglia (et il Maestro poi più di tutti di essi[)] a consigliarlo onde doppo le molte, taglia taglia disse anch'egli; e spedito à Lucca per il Cerusico Accoramboni, il fè venire in Casa, per restare per due Mesi a tenermi un pochetto di gratissima Conversazzione.

Fu sì cara quella Conversazzioncina, che invece della Laurea Dottorale (ch'avrei possuto un' dì ottonere) mi diè la Patente di passar' per un' de frigidis et maleficiatis, per tutt'il restante della vita mia, rinunziando per sempre al dolce nome che m'avrei sentito dar' un giorno di Signor Padre."

101.   "Non voglio Musica; ma una Messa in Cantofermo; e cantata con Divozzione da numero quattro Sacerdoti.

(Per esser'io stato Musico diqualche poca di Distinzione, forse misi verrà à far' un frastuòno di voci e strumenti come se fosse un' Sposalizzio, e che non serve ch'a dire, *andiamo à sentire l'esequie del Tale; caspita sarranno belle, poichè vi è tutta la Musica della Città*; et intanto che io, racchiuso in quella Cassa, scaldato dai lumi e dal Concorso, comincio a puzzare come una Carogna, vadino i Musici stendendo Passaggi e trilli con cadenze di mezz'ora, e l'uditorio ascoltando et applaudendo, senza forse dirmi alcun' di loro *Riposa in Pace*." Balatri, *Testamento*, 20–20'.

102.   By what may be a remarkable coincidence, a boy described by Freud who is pathologically attached to a totem animal has a fowl as his totemic object. His attachment takes the form of a love-hate relationship, and he is also obsessed with

the sexual life of the hens and cocks who live in his midst. See Sigmund Freud, *Totem and Taboo: Some Points of Agreement between the Mental Lives of Savages and Neurotics*, Standard Edition, trans. James Strachey, with biographical introduction by Peter Gay (1989; New York: W. W. Norton, 1950), esp. 164–92.

An engaging critical history of castration and castration theories has appeared recently by Gary Taylor, *Castration: An Abbreviated History of Western Manhood* (New York and London: Routledge, 2000).

103. Katherine Bergeron, "The Castrato as History," *Cambridge Opera Journal* 8 (1996), 167–84, engages Freudian-styled language for the castrato and tacitly analyzes Freudianism in Corbiau's 1994 film *Farinelli*. Cf. Michel Poizat, *The Angel's Cry: Beyond the Pleasure Principle in Opera*, trans. Arthur Denner (1986; Ithaca and London: Cornell University Press, 1992), for an explicit Lacanian view.

104. "nacque . . . da Salvatore Broscho, e Caterina Barese Napolitani, e della qualità della sua schiatta non plebea, ma nobile, e generosa"; Sacchi, *Vita*, 33.

105. " . . . al taglio nella puerizia per conservar la mollezza della voce, e così venderla a maggior prezzo; ma bensì conservare la vita in un grave pericolo corso per la sua fanciullesca vivacità, saltando sopra un cavallo, onde cadde, e fu anche offeso nella fronte"; Sacchi, *Vita*, 33.

106. John Moore, *A View of Society and Manners in Italy*, 4th ed., 2 vols. (1779; London, 1787), 2:89–90. Moore's attitude was shared by, among many others, Lalande, *Voyage en Italie*, 5:437–38; and the Irishwoman Sara Goudar, *Relation historique des divertissements du Carneval de Naples ou Lettre de Madame Goudar sur ce sujet À Monsieur le Général Alexis Orlow* (Lucca, 1774), 9, who gendered the view ("je ne sais si c'est parceque je suis femme, mais je n'aime point les Eunuques").

107. See Rosselli, "The Castrati," 178–79; and Barbier, *The World of the Castrati*, chap. 10.

108. On the family in eighteenth-century Italy, see Marzio Bargagli, *Sotto lo stesso tetto: mutamenti della famiglia in Italia del XV al XX secolo* (1984; Bologna: Il Mulino, 2000). On the relationships between family and the institution of opera seria, see my essay "The Absent Mother in Opera Seria," in *Siren Songs: Representations of Gender and Sexuality in Opera*, ed. Mary Ann Smart (Princeton: Princeton University Press, 2000), 29–46, 254–59.

Notes to Chapter Eight

1. François Raguenet, *Paralele des Italiens et des François, en ce qui regarde la musique et les opera* (Paris: Jean Moreau, 1702), 79–81: "ces voix [de *Castrati*] douces & rossignolantes sont enchantées dans la bouche des Acteurs qui font le personnage d'amant; rien n'est plus touchant que l'expression de leurs peines formée avec ces sons de voix si tendres & si passionnez; & les Italiens ont, en cela, un grand avantage sur les Amans de nos Théâtres, dont la voix grosse & mâle est constamment bien moins propre aux douceurs qu'ils disent à leurs Maîtresses."

2. For instance, in Michel Poizat, *The Angel's Cry: Beyond the Pleasure Principle in Opera*, trans. Arthur Denner (Ithaca, N.Y.: Cornell Univ. Press, 1992), 113–19; trans. of *L'opéra, ou Le cri de l'ange: Essai sur la jouissance de l'amateur d'opéra* (Paris:

Éditions A. M. Métailié, 1986); and Margaret Reynolds, "Ruggiero's Deceptions, Cherubino's Distractions," in *En travesti: Women, Gender Subversion, Opera*, ed. Corinne E. Blackmer and Patricia Juliana Smith, *Between Men—Between Women: Lesbian and Gay Studies* (New York: Columbia Univ. Press, 1995), 132–51. In this approach, these recent writers are actually echoing a long tradition of ignoring the castrato's body on stage, a tradition well articulated in Dorothy Keyser, "Cross-Sexual Casting in Baroque Opera: Musical and Theatrical Conventions," *Opera Quarterly* 5 (1988), 47: "Italian baroque opera assumes that the audience will not be disturbed by contradictions between the sexual identity of the character being portrayed and either the actual gender of the performer or the voice register of the musical part."

3. Thomas Laqueur, *Making Sex: Body and Gender from the Greeks to Freud* (Cambridge, Mass.: Harvard Univ. Press, 1990).

4. Laqueur (ibid.) examines this view in detail throughout the first four chapters of his book (1–148), but the idea receives a clear statement at 124. Laqueur's emphasis on the "one-sex system" has been criticized as an oversimplification, a privileging of the Galenic/Hippocratic model of sex over a competing Aristotelian account; see, for example, Lorraine Datson and Katharine Park, "The Hermaphrodite and the Orders of Nature: Sexual Ambiguity in Early Modern France," in *Premodern Sexualities*, ed. Louise Fradenburg and Carla Freccero (New York: Routledge, 1996), 118–19. But even these authors suggest that the Galenic/Hippocratic view seems to have predominated from the second half of the sixteenth through at least the seventeenth centuries (121–22).

5. Laqueur, *Making Sex*, 4.

6. Ibid., 148.

7. Ibid., 106, 126–30.

8. Stephen Greenblatt, *Shakespearean Negotiations: The Circulation of Social Energy in Renaissance England*, The New Historicism: Studies in Cultural Poetics, vol. 4 (Berkeley: Univ. of California Press, 1988), 91. Laqueur too notes that only with puberty would there appear signs of "the vital heat that arose in adolescence and distinguished [men] finally from women" (*Making Sex*, 101).

9. For example, "Eunuchs . . . seeme to have degenerated into a womanish nature, by deficiency of heate; their smooth body and soft and shirle [i.e., shrill] voyce doe very much assimulate weomen." Ambroise Paré, *The Workes of Ambrose Parey*, trans. Thomas Johnson (London, 1634), 27; as cited in Ann Rosalind Jones and Peter Stallybrass, "Fetishizing Gender: Constructing the Hermaphrodite in Renaissance Europe," in *Body Guards: The Cultural Politics of Gender Ambiguity*, ed. Julia Epstein and Kristina Straub (New York: Routledge, 1991), 83.

10. See Laqueur, *Making Sex*, 123–24.

11. Jones and Stallybrass, "Fetishizing Gender," 97.

12. From the *Vocabolario degli Accademici della Crusca* (Venice, 1612), s.v. "*femminacciolo*," we find the attestation, "Sapeva ben lo'ngegnoso huomo, che'l male dilettamento fa gli huomini femminaccioli, e assottiglia il corpo soggetto a carnalità." Further, as an example for the seventeenth-century use of the French word *efféminé*,

Le Grand Robert offers this passage from the writings of Fénélon, demonstrating again the conflation of femininity and addiction to pleasure: "Il y avait à Tyr un jeune Lydien nommé Malachon, d'une merveilleuse beauté, mais mou, efféminé, noyé dans les plaisirs."

13. Winfried Schleiner, "Male Cross-Dressing and Transvestism in Renaissance Romances," *Sixteenth Century Journal* 19 (1988), 618.

14. Le huitiesme livre d'Amadis de Gaule (Lyon, 1575), 525; as cited and translated by Schleiner, "Male Cross-Dressing," 608. The first known version of *Amadís de Gaula* is by Garci Ordóñez de Montalvo in 1508, but evidence suggests the material was in circulation from the late thirteenth or early fourteenth century. The work became particularly popular in the sixteenth century, especially in France, where it served as a model for deportment and writing style and was expanded and continued by other writers.

15. Canto 1, stanzas 41–43: "Era Adon ne l'età che la facella / Sente d'Amor più vigorosa e viva, / Ed avea dispostezza a la novella / Acerbità de gli anni intempestiva. / Nè su le rose de la guancia bella / Alcun germoglio ancor d'oro fioriva; / O, se pur vi spuntava ombra di pelo, / Era qual fiore in prato o stella in cielo. // In bionde anella di fin or lucente / Tutto si torce e si rincrespa il crine; / De l'ampia fronte in maestà ridente / Sotto gli sorge il candido confine. / Un dolce minio, un dolce foco ardente / Sparso tra vivo latte e vive brine / Gli tinge il viso in quel rossor, che suole / Prender la rosa infra l'aurora e' sole. // Ma chi ritrar de l'uno e l'altro ciglio / Può le due stelle lucide serene? / Chi de le dolci labra il bel vermiglio / Che di vivi tesor son ricche e piene? / O qual candor d'avorio, o qual di giglio / La gola pareggiar ch'erge e sostiene, / Quasi colonna adamantina, accolto / Un ciel di meraviglie in quel bel volto?" Translation adapted from Harold Martin Priest, trans. and intro., *Adonis: Selections from* L'Adone *of Giambattista Marino* (Ithaca, N.Y.: Cornell Univ. Press, 1967), 11–12.

16. The Latin inscription reads "ADOLESCENTIAM PALLAS A VENERE AVELLIT," as reported in Malcolm Campbell, *Pietro da Cortona at the Pitti Palace: A Study of the Planetary Rooms and Related Projects*, Princeton Monographs in Art and Archaeology, no. 41 (Princeton: Princeton Univ. Press, 1977), 93. This discussion of the painting is based on Campbell, 92–93, 99.

17. Criminal records of the period abound with reports of such transgressions, still a capital offense even in this comparatively tolerant era. See Luciano Marcello, "Società maschile e sodomia: Dal declino della 'polis' al principato," *Archivio storico italiano* 150 (1992), 115–38; and Gabriele Martini, *Il "vitio nefando" nella Venezia del Seicento: Aspetti sociali e repressione di giustizia*, Collana della Facoltà di Lettere e Filosofia dell'Università di Venezia in San Sebastiano, sezione di studi storici 2, Materiali e Ricerche, n.s. 4 (Rome: Jouvence, 1988). Also, Michael Rocke, *Forbidden Friendships: Homosexuality and Male Culture in Renaissance Florence*, Studies in the History of Sexuality (New York: Oxford Univ. Press, 1996). The norm of the pederastic model is established generally throughout Rocke's third chapter, 87–111.

18. The quotation is from Greenblatt, *Shakespearean Negotiations*, 83.

19. See Wendy Heller, *Emblems of Eloquence: Opera and Women's Voices in*

Seventeenth-Century Venice (Berkeley: Univ. of California Press, 2003), passim, but especially 48–81; Martini, *Il "vitio nefando,"* 106.

20. Antonio Rocco, *L'Alcibiade fanciullo a scola*, ed. and intro. Laura Coci, in *Omikron*, no. 27 (Rome: Salerno, 1988).

21. Heller, *Emblems of Eloquence*, 75.

22. Anna Riggs Miller, *Letters from Italy, describing the manners, customs, antiquities, paintings, &c. of that country, in the years MDCCLXX and MDCCLXXI, to a friend residing in France* (Dublin: W. Watson et al., 1776), 3:64. I was directed to Miller's book by Chloe Chard, "Effeminacy, Pleasure and the Classical Body," in *Femininity and Masculinity in Eighteenth-Century Art and Culture*, ed. Gill Perry and Michael Rossington (Manchester: Manchester Univ. Press, 1994), 142–61. Chard offers a fascinating consideration of the discourse surrounding the Farnese Hercules and several other famous classical sculptures during the latter eighteenth century.

23. Miller, *Letters from Italy*, 3:51–2.

24. Chard, "Effeminacy," 157.

25. On the full range of the physical effects resulting from castration, see Enid Rhodes Peschel and Richard E. Peschel, "Medical Insights into the Castrati in Opera," *American Scientist* 75 (1987), 578–83; or Peschel and Peschel, "Medicine and Music: The Castrati in Opera," *Opera Quarterly* 4:4 (1987), 21–38.

26. Nicolino is Nicolò Grimaldi (1673–1732); the best known Senesino is Francesco Bernardi (d. 1759), but at least two others were known by that nickname: Andrea Martini (1761–1819) and Giusto Ferdinando Tenducci (1735–1790). Giuseppino's identity is unknown, although he is documented in connection with the singer Anna Maria Sardelli; Marianino is Mariano Nicolini (fl. 1731–1758); Pauluccio is mentioned in Charles Ancillon, *Eunuchism Display'd* (London: E. Curll, 1718), 30, originally published as (and slightly altered from) *Traité des eunuques* (Paris: n.p., 1707), but I have been unable to discover anything further about his identity. Other diminutive nicknames for castrati include Annibalino (Domenico Annibali, c. 1704–c. 1779), Appianino (Giuseppe Appiani, 1712–c. 1742), Cusanino (Giovanni Carestini, c. 1704–1760), Gizziello (Gioacchino Conti, 1714–1761), and Matteuccio (Matteo Sassani, c. 1667–1737).

27. Letter of 31 October 1661 to Hugues de Lionne from Rome (Paris, Archives de la Ministères des Affaires Étrangères, Correspondance politique, Rome, 142, f. 227).

28. Evidence for these relationships appears in Harold Acton, *The Last Medici* (London: Faber and Faber, 1932), 175–76, 186, 199, and 215; and Warren Kirkendale, *The Court Musicians in Florence During the Principate of the Medici: With a Reconstruction of the Artistic Establishment*, "Historiae musicae cultores" biblioteca, no. 61 (Florence: Olschki, 1993), 437–46 (including several contemporary sources that he cites).

29. Rosa, "La musica," in *Poesie e lettere edite e inedite di Salvator Rosa*, vol. 1, ed. G. A. Cesareo (Naples: R. Accademia di Archeologia, Lettere e Belle Arti, 1892), 173: "Son miracoli usati entro à i palaggi, / Che un Musico sbarbato co i suoi vezzi / Cavalcato scavalchi anche i più saggi."

30. [Charles de Marguerel de Saint-Denis, seigneur de] Saint-Évremond, *Lettres,*

ed. René Ternois, Société des Textes Français Modernes (Paris: Librairie Marcel Didier, 1968), 2:49–50: "je vous dirai avec tous termes d'insinuation, qu'il faut vous faire adoucir par une operation legere, qui assûrera la délicatesse de vôtre teint pour long-temps, et la beauté de vôtre voix pour toute la vie. Ces guinées, ces habits rouges, ces petits chevaux qui vous viennent, ne sont pas donnez au fils de Monsieur Dery pour sa noblesse; vôtre visage et vôtre voix les attirent. Dans trois ou quatre ans, helas! vous perdrez le mérite d l'un et de l'autre, si vous n'avez la sagesse d'y pourvoir; et la source de tous ces agrémens sera tarie. . . . Mais vous craignez, dites-vous, d'étre moins aimé des Dames. Perdez vôtre appréhension: nous ne sommes plus au tems des imbeciles; le mérite qui suit l'operation est aujourd'hui assez reconnu, et pour une Maîtresse qu'auroit Monsieur Dery dans son naturel, Monsieur Dery adouci en aura cent." Clearly, Saint-Évremond refers here to two different people with the title "Monsieur Dery": first, he means the boy's father, and later, the boy himself.

31. For her general work on castrati, see Camiz, "The Castrato Singer: From Informal to Formal Portraiture," *Artibus et historiae* 18 (1988), 171–86; "Putti, eunuchi, belle cantatrici: L'iconographie des chanteurs en Italie," in *Musique, Images, Instruments* 2 (1996), 8–17; and "17th Century Mirrors of Musical Vogues in Rome," *Musikalische Ikonographie*, ed. Harald Heckmann, Monika Holl, and Hans Joachim Marx, vol. 12 of *Hamburger Jahrbuch für Musikwissenschaft* (Laaber: Laaber-Verlag, 1994), 53–64. This quotation comes from Camiz, "Putti," 14: "aspect androgyne et efféminé caractéristique de la représentation des castrats"; "une idéalisation qui fait bien comprendre quels pouvaient être le pouvoir de séduction et la fascination exercés par ces personnages."

32. Indeed, a leading scholar of Tiepolo's work, Michael Levey, comes close to this observation—without necessarily recognizing the characteristic castrato deformity—in his criticism of the *Family of Darius*: "Alexander . . . with his rigid bearing and distinctly unimpressive physique, might be the castrato of this *opera seria*: assertive, even arrogant but slightly ludicrous amid the firmly characterized, robust, bearded baritones and the impressive range of sopranos who yet all depend on him." Michael Levey, *Giambattista Tiepolo: His Life and Art* (New Haven: Yale Univ. Press, 1986), 124.

33. Franco Valsecchi, *L'Italia nel Seicento e nel Settecento*, vol. 6 of *Società e costume: Panorama di storia sociale e tecnologica* (Turin: U.T.E.T., 1967), 23–4: "È l'artificio, che domina, la ricerca dell'effetto. . . . La natura è trasformata, deformata; la vegetazione è soffocata dall'arte."

34. That castrati continued to be employed in the hyperconservative environment of the papal chapel only strengthens this point.

Notes to Chapter Nine

1. Entry XXXVIII, *Monthly Review* 4 (November 1750–May 1751), 379.

2. All of this information is provided on the title page of Giovanni Bianchi, *An Historical and Physical Dissertation on the Case of Catherine Vizzani, containing The Adventures of a young Woman, born at Rome, who for eight years passed in the Habit*

of a Man, was killed for an Amour with a young Lady; and being found, on Dissection, a true Virgin, narrowly escaped being treated as a Saint. With some Curious and Anatomical Remarks on the Nature and Existence of the Hymen. By Giovanni Bianchi, Professor of Anatomy at Sienna, the Surgeon who dissected her. To which are added, certain needful Remarks by the English Editor, trans. John Cleland (London: printed for W. Meyer, in May's Building, near St. Martin's Lane, 1751).

3. Thomas Parker printed 750 copies of Cleland's book for the publisher Fenton Griffiths to sell from his shop in the Exeter Exchange on the Strand. Ralph Griffiths was arrested with Cleland and Park in November 1749. See David Foxon, *Libertine Literature in England 1660–1745* (New Hyde Park, NY: University Books, 1965), pp. 52–63; William H. Epstein, *John Cleland: Images of a Life* (New York: Columbia University Press, 1974), p. 4; and John Cleland, *Memoirs of a Woman of Pleasure*, ed. Peter Sabor (Oxford: Oxford University Press, 1985), pp. ix–x.

4. Roger Londale, "New Attributions to John Cleland," *Review of English Studies* n. s. 30 (1979), 277.

5. Peter Sabor, "The Censor Censured: Expurgating *Memoirs of a Woman of Pleasure*," in *'Tis Nature's Fault: Unauthorized Sexuality during the Enlightenment* (Cambridge, U.K.: Cambridge University Press, 1985), pp. 192–201.

6. Cleland subsequently translated Charles Pinot Duclos' *Memoirs Illustrating the Manners of the Present Age* (1752) and J. F. Dreux du Radier's *The Dictionary of Love* (1753), and wrote a play, *Titus Vespasian: A Tragedy* (1755), derived from one by the great Italian poet Pietro Metastasio.

7. Sheridan Baker, "Henry Fielding's *The Female Husband*: Fact and Fiction," *Publications of the Modern Language Association* 74 (1959), 213–24; and Terry Castle, *The Female Thermometer: Eighteenth-Century Culture and the Invention of the Uncanny* (Oxford: Oxford University Press, 1995), pp. 67–81 (quote on p. 70).

8. Londale, "New Attributions," pp. 276–80; Epstein, *John Cleland*, p. 4.

9. Giovanni Bianchi, *The True History and Adventures of Catherine Vizzani, . . . With curious Anatomical Remarks on the Nature and Existence of the Hymen. With a curious Frontispiece* (London: Printed for W. Reeve, Fleet-street, and C. Sympson, at the Bible-warehouse, Chancery-lane, 1755).

10. Peter Naumann, *Keyhole und Candle: John Clelands Memoirs of a Woman of Pleasure und die Entstehung des pornographischen Romans in England* (Heidelberg: Winter, 1976); Peter Wagner, *Eros Revived: Erotica of the Enlightenment in England and America* (London: Secker and Warburg, 1988); and Karen Harvery, *Reading Sex in the Eighteenth Century: Bodies and Gender in English Erotic Culture* (Cambridge, U.K.: Cambridge University Press, 2004). For a good introduction to this period, see John Brewer, *The Pleasures of the Imagination: English Culture in the Eighteenth Century* (New York: Farrar, Straus and Giroux, 1997).

11. The only discussions of the Italian history of Bianchi's *Brief Life* to appear to date can be found in Giovanni Rimondini, "Il caso clinico di Teresa Vizzani," in his *Carne romagnola. Storia dei costumi sessuali in Romagna dai Malatest alle stagioni balneari* (Rimini: Maggioli, 1986), pp. 71–89; and Stefano De Carolis and Angelo Turchini, *Giovanni Bianchi: medico primario di Rimini ed archiatra pontificio*

(Verucchio: Pazzini, 1999), pp. 52–57. Clorinda Donato's "Public and Private Negotiations of Gender in Eighteenth-Century England and Italy," *British Journal for Eighteenth-Century Studies* 29 (2006), 169–89, appeared shortly after completion of this essay and offers a complementary account of these events.

12. Giampaolo Giovenardi, *Orazion funerale in lode di Monsig[nor] Giovanni Bianchi nobile riminese* (Venice, 1777), p. 27. Less reliable but equally informative is his anonymous autobiography, [Giovanni Bianchi], "Ioannes Blancus, seu Ianus Planchus," in Giovanni Lami, *Memorabilia italorum eruditione praestantium* (Florence, 1742), vol. 1, pp. 353–407. While a comprehensive study of Bianchi's life and work has yet to appear, the most useful modern biographies are A. Fabri, "Giovanni Bianchi," *Dizionario biografico degli italiani* (Rome: Enciclopedia Italiana, 1960-), vol. 10, pp. 104–12 (hereafter *DBI*); Antonio Montari, *La Spetiaria del Sole. Iano Planco giovane tra debiti e buffonerie* (Rimini: Raffaelli Editore, 1994); and especially De Carolis and Turchini, *Giovanni Bianchi*.

13. At one point, Bianchi reputedly dissected two hundred cadavers in seven months. Guglielmo Bilancioni, ed., *Carteggio inedito di G. B. Morgagni con Giovanni Bianchi* (Bari: Società Tipografica Editrice Barese, 1914), p. 164 n. 2; and *DBI*, vol. 10, p. 106 (s.v. Bianchi, Giovanni).

14. Biblioteca Gambalunga, Rimini (hereafter BGR), Sc. Ms. 968, f. 290r (Giovanni Bianchi to abbé Raymondo Niccoli, Siena, 8 October 1742). Bianchi's stay in Siena has been carefully discussed in Vincenzo Mazzi, "Giovanni Battista Bianchi 'IANUS PLANCHUS' ed i suoi rapporti con l'Università e la cittadinanza di Siena," in Baccio Baccetti et al., *Documenti per una storia della scienza senese* (Siena: Accademia dei Fisiocritici, 1985), pp. 141–81.

15. BGR, *Fondo Gambetti, Misc. riminese*, fasc. 310, as cited in De Carolis and Turchini, *Giovanni Bianchi*, p. 22; Mazzi, "Giovanni Battista Bianchi," p. 148.

16. [Bianchi], "Ioannes Blanchus," pp. 394–98; Mazzi, "Giovanni Battista Bianchi," pp. 151–52.

17. Giovanni Bianchi, *Breve storia della vita di Caterina Vizzani romana che per ott'anni vestì abito di huom in qualità di Servidore la quale dopo vari casi essendo in fine stata uccisa fu trovata Pulcella nella sezzione del suo Cadavero* (Venice [Florence]: Per Simone Occhi, 1744), p. 18. The fascination with cross-dressing during this period has been explored in such studies as Rudolf M. Dekker and Lotte C. van de Pol, *The Tradition of Female Transvestism in Early Modern Europe* (New York: St. Martin's Press, 1989); Vern Bullough and Bonnie Bullough, *Cross Dressing, Sex, and Gender* (Philadelphia: University of Pennsylvania Press, 1993); Gary Kates, *Monsieur d'Eon Is a Woman: A Tale of Political Intrigue and Sexual Masquerade* (New York: Basic Books, 1995); and Sylvie Steinberg, *La confusion des sexes. Le travestissement de la Renaissance à la Révolution* (Paris: Fayard, 2001). The case of Vizzani is mentioned very briefly in Dekker and van de Pol (p. 114 n. 2) and Bullough and Bullough (pp. 124–25).

18. BGR, *Fondo Gambetti. Lettere autografe al Dott[ore] Giovanni Bianchi. Posizione*: Leprotti (Rome, Antonio Leprotti to Bianchi, 7 December 1743). I have chosen to standardize the spelling from "Catterina" to "Caterina," to conform to the more common spelling of her first name.

19. Bianchi, *Breve storia*, p. 20.

20. BGR, Sc. Ms. 963, f. 523v (Bianchi to Leprotti, Siena, 10 July 1743).

21. Ibid., f. 573r (Florence, 14 July 1744).

22. Bianchi, *Breve storia*, p. 23. Readers can compare Bianchi's published account of his dissection with his 3 July 1743 letter to Leprotti; BGR, Sc. Ms. 963, ff. 522r–v. I have incorporated some of the comments in this manuscript account into my summary. While Donato raises the question of whether Bianchi actually performed the autopsy, I see no reason to doubt it in light of his comments about the body's appearance in correspondence; Donato, "Public and Private Negotiations of Gender," p. 171.

23. For a contemporary opinion contradicting Bianchi's judgment of the hymen, see Martin Schurig, *Parthenologia historia medica, hoc est, virginitatis consideratio* (Dresden and Leipzig, 1729), pp. 299–301.

24. Bianchi, *Breve storia*, pp. 24–28 (quotes on pp. 25, 27). Bianchi's earlier opinion on the *canali cisto-epatici*, opposing the views of Bianchi of Turin and Gaetano Tacconi of Bologna, first appeared in 1726 and was reprinted at the end of Giambattista Morgagni's *Epistolae anatomicae duae novas observationes et animadversiones complectentes* (Leiden, 1728), pp. 299–308. In modern terminology, Bianchi was debating the nature of the common bile duct and the role of the cystic and hepatic ducts in carrying bile from the liver. His point of reference was the Parisian medical professor Jacques-Bénigne Winslow's *Exposition anatomique de la structure du corps humain* (Paris, 1732), translated into Italian in Bologna, 1743–44.

25. Bianchi, *Breve storia*, p. 24.

26. BGR, *Fondo Gambetti. Lettere autografe al Dott[ore] Giovanni Bianchi. Posizione*: Leprotti (Leprotti to Bianchi, Rome, 7 September 1743).

27. BGR, Sc. Ms. 963, ff. 522r–v (Bianchi to Leprotti, Siena, 3 July 1743), f. 539r (Florence, 17 September 1743). Leprotti is yet another understudied medical and scientific figure who deserves a modern biographer; see Ernesto Setti, *Elogio storico di Monsignore Antonio Leprotti* (Carpi, 1806).

28. James Parsons, *A Mechanical and Critical Enquiry into the Nature of Hermaphrodites* (London, 1741), p. 9.

29. Realdo Colombo, *De re anatomica* (Venice, 1559), p. 243; and Thomas Bartholin, *Bartholinus Anatomy: Made from the Precepts of his Father, And from the Observations of all Modern Anatomists, together with his own*, English trans. (London, 1668), pp. 76–77. See Valerie Traub, "The Psychomorphology of the Clitoris," *Gay and Lesbian Quarterly* 2 (1995), 81–113; Katharine Park, "The Rediscovery of the Clitoris: French Medicine and the Tribade, 1570–1620," in *The Body in Parts: Fantasies of Corporeality in Early Modern Europe*, ed. David Hillman and Carla Mazzio (New York: Routledge, 1997), pp. 171–93; Gianna Pomata, "Menstruating Men: Similarity and Difference of the Sexes in Early Modern Medicine," in *Generation and Regeneration: Tropes of Reproduction in Literature and History*, ed. Valeria Finucci and Kevin Brownlee (Durham: Duke University Press, 2001), pp. 109–52; and Bettina Mathes, "As Long as a Swan's Neck? The Significance of the 'Enlarged' Clitoris for Early Modern Anatomy," in *Sensible Flesh: On Touch in Early Modern*

Culture (Philadelphia: University of Pennsylvania Press, 2003), pp. 103–24. Thanks to Gianna Pomata and Katharine Park for their bibliographic suggestions for this part of the chapter.

30. Parsons, *A Mechanical and Critical Enquiry*, p. 138.

31. Robert James, *A Medicinal Dictionary* (London, 1743–1745), vol. 3, part 2, n.p. (s.v. "Tribades" and "Clitoris"). By contrast, a medical inspection of the stocking-maker Catharina Margaretha Lincken, ca. 1721, revealed that she was entirely female; Brigitte Eriksson, "A Lesbian Execution in Germany, 1721," *Journal of Homosexuality* 6 (1980–81), 33, 37–38.

32. Ludovico Maria Sinistrari, *De delictis et poenis Tracatus Absolutissimus* (Rome, 1754; 1700), p. 235. Readers can also consult the English translation: *Peccatum Mutum (The Mute Sin, alias Sodomy)*, ed. and trans. Montague Summers (Paris: Isidore Liseux, 1893), pp. 17, 20. Martin Schurig, *Muliebra historica-medica, hoc est, partium genitalium muliebrium consideratio physico-medico-forensis* (Dresden and Leipzig, 1729), pp. 74–127 (quote on p. 110); see also his *Gynaecologia historico-medica hoc est Congressus muliebris consideratio physico-medico-forensis* (Dresden and Leipzig, 1730).

33. On this subject, see especially Michel Delon, "Le prétexte anatomique," *Dix-huitième siècle* 12 (1980), 35–48; Londa Schiebinger, "Skeletons in the Closet: The First Illustrations of the Female Skeleton in Eighteenth-Century Anatomy," *Representations* 14 (1986), 42–82; and Thomas Laqueur, *Making Sex: Body and Gender from the Greeks to Freud* (Cambridge, MA: Harvard University Press, 1990); and Elisabeth Wahl, *Invisible Relations: Representations of Female Intimacy in the Age of Enlightenment* (Stanford: Stanford University Press, 1999), pp. 28–36. More recently, the chronology and significance of discussions of anatomical difference has been debated; see Michael Stolberg, "A Woman Down to Her Bones: The Anatomy of Sexual Difference in the Sixteenth and Early Seventeenth Centuries," *Isis* 94 (2003), 279–99, with responses by Schiebinger and Laqueur (pp. 300–13).

34. Roy Porter, "Spreading Carnal Knowledge or Selling Dirt Cheap? Nicolas Venette's *Tableau de l'Amour Conjugal* in Eighteenth Century England," *Journal of European Studies* 14 (1984), 234–55.

35. Bianchi also published several learned treatises on human anatomy, including *De monstris ac monstrosis ad Josephum Puteum Sanctissimi D. N. Benedicti XIV Pontificis Maximi Archiatrum Extra Ordinem et Academiae Instituti Bononiensis Praesidem epistola* (Venice, 1749); and "Dissertatio varias cadaveram sectiones continens," *Nuova raccolta d'opuscoli scientifici e filologici* 5 (1759), vii–xix. He also wrote a number of other vernacular accounts of his dissections and interpretations of other anatomists' postmortems. Many are cited in *DBI*, vol. 10 (s.v. Bianchi, Giovanni).

36. For a good example, see Biblioteca Lancisiana, Rome, *Fondo Leprotti* LXXVII. I. 14 (281), ff. 177–90, esp. f. 180.

37. Maria D. Collina, *Il carteggio letterario di uno scienziato del Settecento (Janus Plancus)* (Florence: Olschki, 1957), p. 145 (Fernando Antonio Ghedini to Bianchi, Bologna, 6 June 1725). Collina provides the most extensive discussion of this aspect of Bianchi's career (pp. 137–54), and my comments on this subject are based primar-

ily on her research. See also Bianchi's own assessment of his early literary efforts in [Bianchi], "Ioannes Blancus," pp. 362–63.

38. Collina, *Il carteggio letterario*, p. 142 (Bianchi to Sebastiano Rocco, Rimini, 15 July 1724).

39. Montanari, *La Spetiaria del Sole*, pp. 41–44.

40. Collina, *Il carteggio letterario*, p. 146 (Pier Jacopo Martello to Bianchi, Bologna, 4 July 1729). For further discussion of the literary community in Bologna that read Bianchi's novelle, see Ilaria Magnani Campanacci, *Un Bolognese nella repubblica delle lettere: Pier Jacopo Martello* (Modena: Mucchi, 1994).

41. Domenico Maria Manni, *Istoria del Decameron di Giovanni Boccaccio* (Florence, 1742), p. xxii; Collina, *Il carteggio letterario*, p. 153 (Bianchi to Ghedini?, n. d.).

42. Mario Infelise, *I libri proibiti* (Rome: Laterza, 1999), p. 99. The early eighteenth-century history of publishing Boccaccio is discussed briefly in Manni, *Istoria del Decameron*, p. 663.

43. BGR, *Fondo Gambetti. Lettere autografe al Dott[ore] Giovanni Bianchi. Posizione*: Leprotti (Rome, 6 July 1743).

44. BGR, Sc. Ms. 963, ff. 524r–v (Bianchi to Leprotti, Siena, 10 July 1743). Catharina Margaretha Lincken fashioned a similar dildo, creating the penis out of stuffed leather and the testicles from a pig's bladder, and tying it to her pubic region; the deliberate nature of her deception was a decisive factor in the judges' decision to condemn her to death for her false marriage. See Eriksson, "A Lesbian Execution," pp. 31, 40.

45. My research to date has found no evidence that criminal proceedings ever took place against Vizzani for her teenage love of this Roman Margherita. The special file on sodomy in the Tribunale del Governo lists only instances of male sodomy between the midsixteenth and eighteenth centuries; Archivio di Stato, Rome, *Tribunale del Governo. Atti di Cancelleria* b. 105 [*Curiosità criminale*], fasc. 161. I thank Libby Cohen for her advice on using this archive. For further discussion of the criminal consequences of such activities, see Louis Crompton, "The Myth of Lesbian Impunity: Capital Laws from 1270 to 1791," *Journal of Homosexuality* 6 (1980–81), 11–25; Eriksson, "A Lesbian Execution"; Theo van der Meer, "Tribades on Trial: Female Same-Sex Offenders in Late Eighteenth-Century Amsterdam," *Journal of the History of Sexuality* 1 (1991), 424–45; and Wahl, *Invisible Relations*, pp. 20, 23.

46. BGR, *Fondo Gambetti. Lettere autografe al Dott[ore] Giovanni Bianchi. Posizione*: Leprotti (Rome, 7 September 1743).

47. BGR, Sc. Ms. 963, ff. 536r–39r (Bianchi to Leprotti, Florence, 17 September and 15 October 1743).

48. BGR, *Fondo Gambetti. Lettere autografe al Dott[ore] Giovanni Bianchi. Posizione*: Leprotti (Rome, 19 October, 9 November, and 7 December 1743); BGR, Sc. Ms. 963, ff. 5 BGR, Sc. Ms. 963, ff. 540r–39r (Bianchi to Leprotti, Florence, 5 November and 16 December 1743). Quote from letter of 5 November.

49. BGR, Sc. Ms. 973 (Giovanni Bianchi, *Viaggi*, 1740–1774), cc. 237v–38r (12 July 1744), cc. 241r–v (17 July 1744).

50. Ibid., c. 244v (23 July 1744).

51. Ibid., c. 251r–v (30 July 1744).

52. On Florentine publishing and censorship, see especially Renato Pasta, *Editoria e cultura nel Settecento* (Florence: Olschki, 1997); and Sandro Landi, *Il governo delle opinioni. Censura e formazione del consenso nella Toscana del Settecento* (Bologna: Il Mulino, 2000); see also, Eric Cochrane, *Florence in the Forgotten Centuries 1527–1800* (Chicago: University of Chicago Press, 1973), pp. 361–62; and Infelise, *I libri proibiti*, pp. 99–100. The impact of this law on Bianchi's book is also discussed in De Carolis and Turchini, *Giovanni Bianchi*, p. 55.

53. The condemnation of Boccaccio and its bowdlerization by Vincenzo Borghini in 1573 and Lionardo Salviati in 1582 is discussed in Manni, *Istoria del Decameron*, pp. 652–57; Raul Mordenti, "Le due censure: la collazione dei testi del Decameron 'rassettati,'" in *Le pouvoir et la plume. Incitation, contrôle et répression dans l'Italie du XVIe siècle* (Paris: Université de la Sorbonne Nouvelle, 1982), pp. 253–74; Giuseppe Chiecchi and Luciano Troisio, *Il Decameron sequestrato. Le tre edizioni censurate nel Cinquecento* (Milan: UNICOOPLI, 1984); and Infelise, *I libri proibiti*, pp. 46–47.

54. BGR, Sc. Ms. 963, f. 575r (Florence, 4 August 1744).

55. BGR, Sc. Ms. 969, f. 352r (Bianchi to Pasquali, Florence, 1 August 1744). A "Revisor" was one of the individuals authorized to review books prior to publication.

56. Bianchi, *Breve storia*, pp. 8, 19. The specific wording of this prohibition against Boccaccio is reproduced in Infelise, *I libri proibiti*, pp. 46–47.

57. On Venetian publishing and censorship, see Mario Infelise, *L'Editoria veneziana nel '700* (Milan: Franco Angeli, 1989); and, for an earlier period, Paul Grendler, *The Roman Inquisition and the Venetian Press, 1540–1605* (Princeton: Princeton University Press, 1977).

58. BGR, *Fondo Gambetti. Lettere autografe al Dott[ore] Giovanni Bianchi. Posizione*: Pasquali, Giambattista (Venice, 8 and 29 August 1744). Pasquali's *Del novelliero italiano* appeared in 1754.

59. Biblioteca Lancisiana, Rome, *Fondo Leprotti*, ms. LXXVII.1.14 (281), f. 180.

60. BGR, Sc. Ms. 963, f. 577r–v (Siena, 23 August 1744).

61. Infelise, *I libri proibiti*, p. 101. The most accessible account of Lami's significance to Florentine cultural life is Cochrane, *Florence*, pp. 315–96. See also Françoise Waquet, "Les registres de Giovanni Lami (1742–1760): De l'érudition au commerce du livre dans l'Italie du XVIIIe siècle," *Critica storica* 17 (1980), 435–56.

62. BGR, Sc. Ms. 973 (Bianchi, *Viaggi*, 1740–1774), c. 272v (13 September 1744), cc. 274r–v (16 September 1744). See also De Carolis and Turchini, *Giovanni Bianchi*, pp. 56–57. For more on Bonducci's activities, see Maria August Morelli Timpani, *Per una storia di Andrea Bonducci (Firenze, 1715–1766). Lo stampatore, gli amici, le loro esperienze culturali e massoniche* (Rome: Istituto Storico Italiano per l'Età Moderna e Contemporanea, 1996). Bianchi's response to the systems of censorship in place in Tuscany and Venice can be fruitfully situated in a recent survey of this subject in general; see Lodovica Braida, "Censure et circulation du livre en Italie au XVIIIe siècle," *Journal of Modern European History* 3 (2005), 81–99. Thanks to Norman Naimark for bringing this to my attention.

63. BGR, *Fondo Gambetti. Lettere autografe al Dott[ore] Giovanni Bianchi.*

Posizione: Pasquali (Venice, 5 September and 12 December 1744). Quote from 5 September.

64. Biblioteca Riccardiana, Florence (hereafter Ricc.), ms. 3707 (*Lettere originali a Giovanni Lami*, vol. 9), letter 34 (Bianchi to Giovanni Lami, Rimini, 5 December 1744).

65. The other book in question was Bianchi's edition of the early seventeenth-century Neapolitan naturalist Fabio Colonna's *Phytobasanos*, published in Florence in 1744 shortly before the *Brief Life* appeared. It reflected Bianchi's significant work as a naturalist as well as his desire to revive the academic projects of Federico Cesi's Accademia dei Lincei (1603–1630). Upon his return to Rimini, Bianchi reestablished this famous academy in 1745.

66. BGR, Sc. Ms. 963, f. 579r (Bianchi to Leprotti, Rimini, 24 September 1744); BGR, Sc. Ms. 973 (Giovanni Bianchi, *Viaggi*, 1740–1774), c. 276v (21 September 1744). For Morgagni's copy of the *Brief History*, see Elisabetta Barile and Rosalba Suriano, eds., *Il "catalogo di libri" di Giambattista Morgagni* (Trieste: Edizioni LINT, 1983), p. 27 (book # 533).

67. BGR, Sc. Ms. 969, f. 360v (Bianchi to Giulio Rucellai and Raimondo Niccoli, Rimini, 28 September 1744), f. 361r (Bianchi to abbé Marchese Antonio Niccolini, Rimini, 3 October 1744).

68. De Carolis, Conti, and Lippi, "Un carteggio inedito," p. 630 (Cocchi to Bianchi, Venice, 17 October 1744).

69. Alessandro Simili, *Carteggio inedito di illustri bolognesi con Giovanni Bianchi riminese* (Bologna: Azzoguidi, 1964), p. 30 (Beccari to Bianchi, Bologna, 14 October 1744); Bilancioni, ed., *Carteggio inedito*, pp. 168–71 (Morgagni to Bianchi, Padua, 21 July and 9 September 1745; and n.d.).

70. Bottari anonymously published his "Lezioni due sopra il Boccaccio" as part of Manni's *Istoria del Decameron*, pp. 433–53. He was also a consultor for the Index as of 1741; see *DBI*, vol. 13, pp. 409–18 (s.v. Bottari, Giovanni Gaetano). In my research to date in the Bottari correspondence in the Biblioteca Corsiniana, Rome, I have so far been unable to find any discussion of this book.

71. BGR, Sc. Ms. 963, f. 585v (Bianchi to Leprotti, Rimini, 1 November 1744).

72. Ricc., ms. 3707 (*Lettere originali a Giovanni Lami*, vol. 9), letter 29 (Bianchi to Lami, Rimini, 29 September 1744); ms. 3746 (*Lettere originali a Giovanni Lami*, vol. 48), letter 6 (Vincenzo Pazzini Carli to Lami, Siena, 5 November 1744). It is unclear from the documents how many copies were printed in total, though the fact that Bianchi had requested 750 copies in his negotiations with the Venetian publisher Pasquali makes this a possible number; BGR, Sc. Ms. 969, f. 352f (Bianchi to Giambattista Pasquali, Florence, 1 August 1744). The four hundred copies that Bianchi asked Borducci to leave with Lami may also have been the total, though the fact that this number was mentioned after he mailed several and had left Siena makes me think that it was not.

73. *Novelle letterarie* 5 (30 October 1744), coll. 692–93. The review appeared anonymously as a notice of new publications from Venice.

74. Mazzi, "Giovanni Battista Bianchi," p. 149.

75. Ricc., ms. 3707, letters 32–35 (Bianchi to Lami, Siena, 19 November 1744; Rimini, 1 December, 5 December, and 12 December 1744). By point of comparison, a yearlong subscription to the *Novelle letterarie* cost 15 paoli; Cochrane, *Florence*, p. 320.

76. BGR, *Fondo Gambetti. Lettere autografe al Dott[ore] Giovanni Bianchi. Posizione*: Leprotti (Rome, 21 October 1744).

77. BGR, Sc. Ms. 963, f. 583r (Bianchi to Leprotti, Rimini, 25 October 1744).

78. BGR, Sc. Ms. 963, f. 585v (Bianchi to Leprotti, Rimini, 1 November 1744); BGR, Sc. Ms. 969, f. 365v (Bianchi to Leprotti, Rimini, 17 December 1744); BGR, *Fondo Gambetti. Lettere autografe al Dott[ore] Giovanni Bianchi. Posizione*: Leprotti (Rome, 30 December 1744).

79. Renée Haynes, *The Philosopher King: The Humanist Pope Benedict XIV* (London: Weidenfeld & Nicolson, 1970); and Marco Cecchelli, ed., *Benedetto XIV (Prospero Lambertini): Convegno internazionale di studi storici sotto il patroncinio dell'Archidiocese di Bologna: Cento 6–9 dicembre 1979* (Cento: Centro studi "Girolamo Baruffaldi," 1981–82), 2 vols.

80. BGR, *Fondo Gambetti. Lettere autografe al Dott[ore] Giovanni Bianchi. Posizione*: Davia Bentivoglio, Laura (Bologna, 30 September 1744). The kind of same-sex behavior that Bentivoglio Davia had in mind has received its fullest treatment in Judith C. Brown, *Immodest Acts: The Life of a Lesbian Nun in Renaissance Italy* (Oxford: Oxford University Press, 1986); and, in a more literary guise, in Denis Diderot's anti-clerical *La religieuse*, written in 1760 and published in 1780.

81. Anne Jacobson Schutte, "'Perfetta donna o ermafrodita?' Fisiologia e 'gender' in un monastero settecentesco," *Studi storici* 43 (2002), 235–46.

82. BGR, *Fondo Gambetti. Lettere autografe al Dott[ore] Giovanni Bianchi. Posizione*: Bassi Veratti, Laura (Bologna, 28 October 1744). A printed version of this letter can be consulted in Beate Ceranski, "Il carteggio tra Giovanni Bianchi e Laura Bassi, 1733–45," *Nuncius* 9 (1994), 229.

83. For further discussion of Bentivoglio Davia's life, see Paula Findlen, "Women on the Verge of Science: Aristocratic Women and Knowledge in Early Eighteenth-Century Italy," in *Women, Equality and Enlightenment*, ed. Sarah Knott and Barbara Taylor (London: Palgrave Press, 2005), pp. 265–87.

84. BGR, *Fondo Gambetti. Lettere autografe al Dott[ore] Giovanni Bianchi. Posizione*: Bassi Veratti (Bologna, 28 October 1744). This specific aspect of Bassi's career is discussed in Findlen, "The Scientist's Body: The Nature of a Woman Philosopher in Enlightenment Italy," in *The Faces of Nature in Enlightenment Europe*, ed. Gianna Pomata and Lorraine Daston (Berlin: Berliner Wissenschafts-Verlag, 2003), pp. 211–36, which also contains further bibliography on Bassi's life and work.

85. BGR, *Fondo Gambetti. Lettere autografe al Dott[ore] Giovanni Bianchi. Posizione*: Bassi Veratti (Bologna, 28 October 1744).

86. *Epistolario di Ludovico Antonio Muratori*, ed. Matteo Campori (Modena: Società Tipografica Modenese, 1906), vol. 10, p. 4665 (Muratori to Bianchi, Spezzano, 4 October 1744). This passage is also discussed in Rimondini, *Carne romagnola*, pp. 85–86.

87. Bianchi, *Breve storia*, p. 3.

88. See Pierre Horteau, "Catholic Moral Discourse on Male Sodomy and Masturbation in the Seventeenth and Eighteenth Centuries," *Journal of the History of Sexuality* 4 (1993), 1–26, esp. pp. 12–14.

89. BGR, Sc. Ms. 969, f. 362r (Bianchi to Giambattista Passeri, Rimini, 11 October 1744).

90. Girolamo Carli, *Intorno a varie toscane e latine operette del dottore Paolo Simone Bianchi da Rimini, che si fa nominare Giano Planco ed in lode di sè medesimo* (Florence, 1749), as quoted in Mazzi, "Giovanni Battista Bianchi," p. 149; Biblioteca Lancisiana, Rome, *Fondo Leprotti*, ms. LXXVII.1.14 (281), ff. 181–82.

91. BGR, Sc. Ms. 973, c. 239v (Bianchi, *Viaggi*, Florence, 15 July 1744). This passage of Bianchi's travel diary is discussed in De Carolis and Turchini, *Giovanni Bianchi*, p. 53.

92. Bianchi, *Breve storia*, p. 3.

93. Stefano De Carolis, Andrea A. Conti, and Donatella Lippi, "Un carteggio inedito tra Antonio Cocchi e Giovanni Bianchi," *Nuncius* 18 (2003), 627 (Bianchi to Cocchi, Siena, 25 May 1744); 628 (Cocchi to Bianchi, Florence, 2 June 1744).

94. For a preliminary exploration of the relative absence of erotic and pornographic publications in Italy, see Armando Marchi, "Obscene Literature in Eighteenth-Century Italy: An Historical and Bibliographic Note," in *'Tis Nature's Fault: Unauthorized Sexuality during the Enlightenment*, ed. Robert Purks Maccubin (Cambridge, U.K.: Cambridge University Press, 1985), pp. 244–60.

95. Ricc., ms. 3707, letter 39 (Bianchi to Lami, Rimini, 2 January 1745).

96. Ibid., letters 46, 48, 52, and 58 (Bianchi to Lami, Rimini, 1 May, 7 June, 3 July, and 20 July 1745).

97. Giacomo Casanova, *History of My Life*, trans. Willard R. Trask (Baltimore: Johns Hopkins University Press, 1997; 1966), vol. 2, pp. 5, 18, 20, 25, 28.

98. On this episode, see Casanova, *History*, vol. 1, p. 266. In a caffè on Via Condotta he sees a famous castrato, Beppino della Mamma. Casanova's response: "His hips and thighs make me think him a girl in disguise." Beppino boldly replied "that if I will spend the night with him he will serve me as a boy or a girl, whichever I choose."

99. *Nova acta eruditorum* (May 1747), 265–66.

100. *DBI*, vol. 10, pp. 106–7 (s.v. Bianchi, Giovanni).

101. Cleland's translation of Bianchi's *Breve storia* has received somewhat more scholarly attention than the Italian original; see Lonsdale, "New Attributions," pp. 277–80; Emma Donoghue, *Passions between Women: British Lesbian Culture 1668–1801*, 2nd ed. (New York: Harper Perennial, 1995), pp. 80–85; Felicity A. Nussbaum, *Torrid Zones: Maternity, Sexuality, and Empire in Eighteenth-Century English Narratives* (Baltimore: Johns Hopkins University Press, 1995), p. 142; Randolph Trumbach, "London's Sapphists: From Three Sexes to Four Genders in the Making of Modern Culture," in *Third Sex, Third Gender: Beyond Sexual Dimorphism in Culture and History* (New York: Zone, 1996), pp. 121, 129–30; and Wahl, *Invisible Relations*, pp. 236–43.

102. Cleland returned from Bombay to London in 1741. His biographers have commented that we know virtually nothing about his life from then until his incarceration in debtors' prison in February 1748. As a result, it is certainly possible that he did indeed travel to Italy during the very years that Bianchi wrote his *Brief History*. See Epstein, *John Cleland*, pp. 7–8, 52–53, 61. However, he does not appear in John Ingamells' *A Dictionary of British and Irish Travelers in Italy 1701–1800* (New Haven: Paul Mellon Centre for Studies in British Art/Yale University Press, 1997).

103. Donato, "Public and Private Negotiations of Gender," pp. 172, 178–81. The growing English community in Florence during this period deserved to be much better studied, but see Cochrane, *Florence*, pp. 365, 378; and Fabia Borroni Salvadori, "Personaggi inglesi inseriti nella vita fiorentina del '700: Lady Walpole e il suo ambiente," *Mitteilungen des Kunsthistorischen Institutes in Florenz* 27 (1983), 83–124.

104. W. S. Lewis, Warren Hunting Smith, and George L. Lam, eds., *Horace Walpole's Correspondence with Sir Horace Mann* (New Haven: Yale University Press, 1954–1971), vol. 1, p. 64; vol. 2, pp. 198, 210; vol. 9, p. 508 (quote). See Morelli Timpanaro, *Per una storia di Andrea Bonducci*.

105. For recent work on Cocchi, see especially Luigi Guerrini, *Antonio Cocchi naturalista e filosofo* (Florence: Polistampa, 2002); and Miriam Fileti, *Antonio Cocchi: primo antiquario della galleria fiorentina, 1738–1758* (Modena: F. C. Panini, 1996).

106. Lewis, Smith, and Lam, eds., *Horace Walpole's Correspondence with Sir Horace Mann*, vol. 2, pp. 477, 496, 567; vol. 3, pp. 14–15 (quote). The book in question, *Del vitto pitagorico per uso della medicina* (Florence, 1743), appeared as *The Pythagorean diet, of vegetables only, conducive to the preservation of health, and the cure of diseases* (London, 1745).

107. Lewis, Smith, and Lam, eds., *Horace Walpole's Correspondence with Sir Horace Mann*, vol. 2, p. 211. On the Dilettanti Society, see Trumbach, "Erotic Fantasy and Male Libertinism in Enlightenment England," in *The Invention of Pornography: Obscenity and the Origins of Modernity, 1500–1800*, ed. Lynn Hunt (New York: Zone, 1993), p. 273; and especially Bruce Redford, *Dilettanti: The Antic and the Antique in Eighteenth-Century England* (Los Angeles: J. Paul Getty Research Institute, forthcoming).

108. See my introductory essay to this volume for the bibliography on the Grand Tour.

109. Bianchi, *Historical and Physical Dissertation*, pp. 2–3.

110. Nussbaum, *Torrid Zones*, esp. pp. 10, 142, 147–48. See also Chloe Chard, *Pleasure and Guilt on the Grand Tour: Travel Writing and Imaginative Geography 1600–1830* (Manchester, U.K.: Manchester University Press, 1999), pp. 37, 60, 120.

111. Bianchi, *Historical and Physical Dissertation*, pp. 51–52.

112. Lillian Faderman, *Surpassing the Love of Men: Romantic Friendship and Love between Women from the Renaissance to the Present* (New York: William Morrow, 1981), p. 24; Wahl, *Invisible Relations*, p. 45.

113. On the fortunes of Aretino, see David O. Frantz, *Festum Voluptatis: A Study of Renaissance Erotica* (Columbus: Ohio State University Press, 1989); Findlen, "Humanism, Politics, and Pornography in Renaissance Italy," in Hunt, ed., *The*

Invention of Pornography, pp. 49–108; and Bette Talvacchia, *Taking Positions: On the Erotic in Renaissance Culture* (Princeton: Princeton University Press, 1999).

114. David Foxon, *Libertine Literature in England 1660–1745* (New Hyde Park, NY: University Books, 1965); Roger Thompson, *Unfit for Modest Ears: A Study of Pornographic, Obscene and Bawdy Works Written or Published in England in the Second Half of the Seventeenth Century* (Totowa, NJ: Rowman & Littlefield, 1979); Ian Frederick Moulton, *Before Pornography: Erotic Writing in Early Modern England* (Oxford: Oxford University Press, 2000); and James Grantham Turner, *Schooling Sex: Libertine Literature and Erotic Education in Italy, France, and England 1534–1685* (Oxford: Oxford University Press, 2003).

115. Ferrante Pallavicino, *The Whore's Rhetorick* (London, 1683), p. 171; and *The Supplement to the Onania* (ca. 1710?), as quoted in Donoghue, *Passions between Women*, pp. 40–41.

116. Cleland, *Memoirs*, pp. 30, 158. Cleland also used one Italian word, *enamorato*, to suggest the importance of having an Italian erotic vocabulary (p. 155).

117. Anon., *Satan's Harvest Home: Or the Present State of Whorecraft, Adultery, Fornication, Procuring, Pimping, Sodomy, and the Game of Flatts* (London, 1749), pp. 51–52. On the content of *The History of the Human Heart*, see Trumbach, "London's Sapphists," p. 117.

118. Bianchi, *Historical and Physical Dissertation*, pp. 3, 20, 28.

119. Cleland, *Memoirs*, p. 34.

120. Bianchi, *Historical and Physical Dissertation*, p. 36.

121. Bianchi, *Breve storia*, p. 8.

122. Bianchi, *Historical and Physical Dissertation*, pp. 34, 37 (quote on p. 37).

123. Ibid., pp. 8-9.

124. Ibid., p. 9.

125. Sabor, "The Censor Censured," pp. 192, 195.

126. Cleland, *Memoirs*, p. 30. See also pp. 11, 24, 76–79, 115, 116.

127. Bianchi, *Historical and Physical Dissertation*, pp. 43, 53, 54.

128. The classic work in this genre for the eighteenth century was *Onania, or, The Heinous Sin of Self-Pollution, and All Its Frightful Consequences in Both Sexes* (London, 1708/09), which was expanded and reedited nineteen times by 1759. See Wagner, *Eros Revived*, pp. 16–19; and Thomas Laqueur, *Solitary Sex: A Cultural History of Masturbation* (New York: Zone, 2003).

129. Bartholin, *Bartholinus Anatomy*, p. 76.

130. Bianchi, *Historical and Physical Dissertation*, pp. 54–55.

131. I have borrowed the phrase "erotic corruption" from Moulton, *Before Pornography*, p. 31.

132. Bianchi, *Historical and Physical Dissertation*, p. 66.

133. Ibid., pp. 55–61. The inclusion of this story makes it all the more likely that he saw himself as capitalizing on the notoriety of Fielding's *The Female Husband*, which told a similar story. See note 7.

134. Ibid., pp. 63–65. Cross-dressing was at times described as an Italian fashion imported to England at the beginning of the early eighteenth century to enliven

masquerade balls. See Castle, *Masquerade and Civilization: The Carnivalesque in Eighteenth-Century English Culture and Fiction* (Stanford: Stanford University Press, 1986); Kates, *Monsieur d'Eon Is a Woman*, p. 180.

135. Anonymous, *A Sapphic Epistle from Jack Cavendish to the Honourable and most beautiful Mrs. D****, 2nd ed. (London, 1778), p. 20. I owe this reference to Peter Wagner, "The Discourse on Sex—or Sex as Discourse: Eighteenth-Century Medical and Paramedical Erotica," in *Sexual Underworlds of the Enlightenment* (Manchester: Manchester University Press, 1982), p. 59.

136. Lewis, Smith, and Lam, eds., *Horace Walpole's Correspondence with Sir Horace Mann*, vol. 4, p. 149.

Notes to Chapter Ten

1. Katharine Park, "Dissecting the Female Body: From Women's Secrets to the Secrets of Nature," in *Crossing Boundaries: Attending to Early Modern Women*, eds. Jane Donawerth and Adele Seef (Newark: University of Delaware Press, 2000), 29.

2. Ludmilla Jordanova, *Sexual Visions: Images of Gender in Science and Medicine between the Eighteenth and Twentieth Centuries* (Madison: University of Wisconsin Press, 1989), 55.

3. Regnier de Graaf, *On the Human Reproductive Organs*, edited and translated by H. D. Jocelyn and B. P. Setchell (Oxford: Blackwell Scientific Publications, 1972).

4. On this figure, see Fabio Bevilacqua, Lidia Falomo, and Carla Garbarino, *Musei e collezioni dell'Università di Pavia* (Milan: Ulrico Hoepli, 2003), 22–30. My thanks to Fausto Barbagli for information about this figure.

5. Elaine Showalter, "The Woman's Case," in *Sexual Anarchy: Gender and Culture at the Fin de Siècle* (New York: Penguin Books, 1990), 127–43.

6. Karen Newman, *Fetal Positions: Individualism, Science, Visuality* (Stanford: Stanford University Press, 1996).

7. Mary Sheriff, *The Exceptional Woman* (Chicago: University of Chicago Press, 1996), 31.

8. It is important to note that visits by countless women—local and foreign, highborn and common—to the Specola anatomical waxworks are recorded in the registry of the Museum. Institute and Museum of the History of Science, Florence, "Giornale del Reale Museo, o Libro in cui vien registrato tutte le persone che vengono a vedere il R. Museo, 1783–1788."

9. Gianna Pomata, "Donne e Rivoluzione Scientifica: verso un nuovo bilancio," in *Corpi e storia: Donne e uomini dal mondo antico all'età contemporanea* (Rome: Viella, 2002), 165–191; and "Perché l'uomo è un mammifero: Crisi del paradigma maschile nella medicina di età moderna," in *Genere e mascolinità: Uno sguardo storico* (Rome: Bulzoni, 2000), 133–52.

10. Ibid., 172.

11. Ibid., 174. In her positive valuation of Antoni van Leeuwenhoek's discovery of seminal animalcoli for advancement of conceptualizations of sexual difference, Pomata does not consider how this "discovery" exceeds even Aristotelian theories in rendering woman irrelevant to human generation except as nutritive matter.

12. Pomata, "Donne e rivoluzione," 173.

13. Pomata, "Donne e Rivoluzione," 167.

14. Ibid., 180.

15. Luciano Guerci, *La discussione sulla donna nell'Italia del Settecento* (Turin: Tirrenia Stampatori, 1987), 130.

16. Early modern and contemporary debates over the emergence of sexually differentiated anatomy are strikingly represented in the arguments and counter-arguments expressed by Michael Stolberg, "A Woman Down to Her Bones: The Anatomy of Sexual Difference in the Sixteenth and Early Seventeenth Centuries"; Thomas Laqueur, "Sex in the Flesh"; and Londa Schiebinger, "Skelettestreit," in *Isis* (2003), 94: 274–99, 300–306, 307–13.

17. Michele Medici, "Elogio di Giovanni Manzolini e Anna Morandi, coniugi Manzolini," in *Memorie dell'Accademia delle Scienze dell'Istituto di Bologna*, VIII, 1857, 6, cited in *Le cere anatomiche bolognesi del Settecento* (Bologna: 1981), 54.

18. On Galli's obstetrical practice and museum, see *Ars Obstetricia Bononiensis: Catalogo ed inventario del Museo Ostetrico Giovann Antonio Galli* (Bologna: CLUEB, 1988).

19. In the commission he contracted with Morandi and her husband, Galli stipulated the parts to be demonstrated and required that these be modeled on the illustrations in obstetrical treatises by Deventer and Mauriceau. See *Ars obstetricia Bononiensis: Catalogo ed inventario del Museo Ostetrico Giovan Antonio Galli* (Bologna: CLUEB, 1988).

20. For an adroit summary overview of ancient to early modern theories of the structure and function of the uterus, see Londa Schiebinger, "Skeletons in the Closet: The First Illustrations of the Female Skeleton in Eighteenth-Century Anatomy," in *The Making of the Modern Body*, ed. Catherine Gallagher and Thomas Laqueur (Los Angeles: University of California Press, 1987), 42–82.

21. Petronio Ignazio Zecchini, *Di geniali: Della dialettica delle donne ridotta al suo vero principio* (Bologna: A. S. Tommaso d'Aquino, 1771). Instrumental for my summary and analysis is the excellent study of the tract by Marta Cavazza, "Women's Dialectics, or the Thinking Uterus: An Eighteenth-Century Controversy on Gender and Education," in *The Faces of Nature in Enlightenment Europe*, ed. Gianna Pomata and Lorraine Daston (Berlin: BWV-Berliner Wissenschafts-Verlag, 2003), 237–57.

22. Cavazza, "Women's Dialectics," 6–9.

23. Zecchini, *Di geniali*, 102. Zecchini rejects the brain as the organ of intellection and theorizes that the mind occupies the entire nervous system and can thus "receive impressions from any innervated part of the body to form its ideas." *Di geniali*, 92.

24. On theories of the wandering uterus, see Lana Thompson, *The Wandering Womb: A Cultural History of Outrageous Beliefs About Women* (Amherst: Prometheus Books, 1999).

25. Zecchini, *Di geniali*, 114–15.

26. Their directives, in fact, formed part of a contentious contemporary debate

about the parameters and purpose of wax anatomical design, which I discuss at length in Messbarger, "Re-membering a Body of Work: Re-constructing the Life-work of Anatomist Anna Morandi Manzolini," *Studies in Eighteenth-Century Culture* 32 (2003), 123–54. Francesco Algarotti, *Saggio sopra la pittura* (Leghorn: Marco Coltellini, 1763). Giampietro Zanotti is cited by Massimo Ferretti in "Il notomista e il canonico: Significato della polemica sulle cere anatomiche di Ercole Lelli," in *I materiali dell'Istituto delle Scienza* (Bologna: CLUEB, 1979), 102.

27. This, and other key subjects of her oeuvre, as well as her scientific method of discovery and representation, served to justify the title of "Anatomica" (woman anatomist) that she repeatedly claimed for herself in her writings, in frank opposition to the sanctioned title given her by Bolognese civic and academic leaders of "artefice straordinaria," extraordinary artisan. For a full account of Morandi's marginal status as artist or modeler within the Bolognese academic world, see Messbarger, "Re-membering a Body of Work," especially pages 123–36.

28. Although Morandi does not cite de Graaf directly, she clearly knew his theories from extensive references to them in the works of Malpighi and Morgagni, whom she does cite explicitly.

29. Pomata, "Donne e Rivoluzione Scientifica," 165–91; and "Perché l'uomo è un mammifero" (Rome: Bulzoni, 2000), 133–52. I analyze at greater length these studies by Pomata in the chapter devoted to Morandi's anatomies of the male reproductive system in my forthcoming book *The Lady Anatomist: Anna Morandi Manzolini 1714–1774* (Chicago: University of Chicago Press).

30. "The common function of the female 'testicles' is to generate eggs, foster them and bring them to maturity. Thus, in women, they perform the same task as do the ovaries of birds. Hence they should be called women's 'ovaries' rather than 'testicles,' especially as they bear no similarity either in shape or content to the male testicles properly so-called." Regnier de Graaf, *Tractus de mulierum organis generationi inservientibus* (1668), trans. H. D. Jocelyn and B. P. Setchell (Oxford: Blackwell Scientific Publications, 1972), 135.

31. On de Graaf, Malpighi, and other sixteenth- to eighteenth-century theorists who expounded on the female reproductive organs, especially the ovaries, see R.H.F. Hunter, *Physiology of the Graafian Follicle and Ovulation* (Cambridge: Cambridge University Press, 2003), 3–16.

32. Regnier de Graaf, *Tractatus de mulierum organis generationi inservientibus*, trans. H. D. Jocelyn and B. P. Setchell (Oxford: Blackwell Scientific Publications, 1972), 100.

33. Maryanne Cline Horowitz, "Aristotle and Woman," *Journal of the History of Biology* 9:2 (1976), 183–213.

34. Giovanni Battista Morgagni, *La Generazione nel concetto di G. B. Morgagni*, ed. and trans. Renato Minghetti, Tommaso Mola (Rome: Istituto di Storia della Medicina dell'Università di Roma, 1963), 29–30.

35. Catherine Wilson, *The Invisible World: Early Modern Philosophy and the Invention of the Microscope* (Princeton: Princeton University Press, 1995), 122. Here Wilson cites Malpighi's letter to Spon.

36. Marcello Malpighi, *consulto*, 15 April 1693, cited in note I, Howard Adelmann, *Marcello Malpighi and the Evolution of Embryology* (Ithaca: Cornell University Press, 1966), 862–64.

37. Biblioteca Universitaria, Bologna, Ms. 2193. Anna Morandi Manzolini, Anatomical Notebook (n.d.), fol. 96r.

38. Ibid., fol. 96v.

39. Vesling and especially Morgagni, both of who wrote extensively on the male reproductive system and whose works Morandi owned, may also have influenced her studies. However, despite her familiarity with Cowper's atlas, the graphic depictions of the dead and putrefying male and female reproductive bodies he includes represent a point of view antithetical to Morandi's always vital body images.

40. During the final years of her life, from 1769 to 1774, Morandi moved her home and her anatomical practice to a palace apartment given to her along with £16,000 by Senator Count Girolamo Ranuzzi in exchange for her complete collection. The Senate bought the collection from Ranuzzi and installed it in the Institute of Sciences in 1776, two years after Morandi's death.

41. Morandi, *Notebook*, fol. 100v. Galen states: "The so-called neck of the bladder is muscular and the lower end of the rectum is held shut by circular muscles surrounding it [sphincter ani, externus and internus]. This is the reason, I suppose, why some have called it the sphincter. For all the muscles, being instruments of voluntary motion, do not allow the residues to be evacuated except at the command of reason, and here at the two outlets for the residues is the only instance in this whole long course of the physical (natural) instruments [alimentary tract and urinary organs] where there is an instrument of the psychic soul. If in some individuals these muscles are relaxed or impaired in any other way ever so slightly the residues flow out involuntarily and inopportunely, showing clearly how shameful and gross would be our life if from the beginning Nature had not planned something better." Galen, *On the Usefulness of the Parts of the Body*, trans. Margaret Tallmadge May (Ithaca: Cornell University Press, 1968), 241. In Chapter 49 of Book II of the *Fabrica* (page 326, numbered 226), Vesalius identifies in his Figure I "Muscle [m. sphincter urethrae externus] of the neck of the bladder, preventing urine from flowing down against our will." Translated by Daniel Garrison, 532.

42. Nancy Siraisi, *Medicine and the Italian Universities 1250–1600* (Leiden, Netherlands: Brill, 2001), 254.

43. For an astute analysis of ancient and early modern teleological anatomy, see Siraisi, *Medicine and the Italian Universities*, 253–86.

44. Ibid., 256.

45. Ibid., 266–69.

46. Ibid., 266–75.

47. De Graaf, *The Generative Organs of Man*, 14.

48. Morgagni, *La generazione nel concetto di G. B. Morgagni*, 200.

49. Ibid., 208.

50. Marcello Malpighi, *Repeated and Additional Observations on the Incubated Egg*, in Adelmann, *Marcello Malpighi*, 984–85.

51. Nancy Siraisi's interpretation of the teleology at work in Galen and Vesalius was instrumental for my analysis of Morandi's teleological concerns. *Medicine and the Italian Universities*, 254–85.

52. Messbarger, "Waxing Poetic: The Anatomical Wax Sculptures of Anna Morandi Manzolini," *Configurations* 9 (2001): 80–92.

53. It is important to observe that Morandi was by no means the first to make these observations about the positioning of the testicles.

54. Morandi, *Notebook*, fol. 98v. Indeed, she was quite accurate in her description of this part of the male anatomy.

55. Here she means wax injections, not an uncommon practice among anatomists by this point in time.

56. Morandi, *Notebook*, fol. 117r.

57. Morandi, *Notebook*, fol. 117r–v. Here again, Morandi misunderstood the role of the seminal vesicles, through which semen does not pass, but from which semen receives a necessary nutrient.

58. Semen resides in the epididymis prior to ejaculation and bypasses the seminal vesicles. My thanks to Dr. Kibel for his explanation of this process.

59. It was not uncommon in early modern anatomical texts to describe semen as, among other things, "genital liquor," "humor genitalis," and "men's milk." Its balsamic quality is repeatedly referenced in Antonio Vallisneri's long tract of 1724 on human generation, with which Morandi was very likely familiar. According to Robley Dunglison, M.D., *Medical Lexicon: A New Dictionary of Medical Science* (Philadelphia: Lea and Blanchard, 1839): "Sperm has been defined as: spermatic fluid or liquor, seminal fluid, seed, semen, s. virile seu masculinum genitale, humor genitalis seu seminalis, urina genitalis, genitura, sperma, s. virile, thoré, Thoros, lac maris, male's milk. Propagatory or genital liquor, vitale virus, vital or quickening venum. A whitish viscid fluid of a peculiar smell, secreted by the testicles, whence it is carried by the vas deferentia to the vesiculae seminales to be thrown into the vagina during coition, through ejaculatory ducts and the urethra. It is a fecundating fluid and must come into actual contact with the germ of the female."

60. On medieval accounts of this process, see Danielle Jacquart and Claude Thomasset, *Sexuality and Medicine in the Middle Ages* (Princeton: Princeton University Press, 1985), 52–70.

61. De Graaf, *The Generative Organs of Men*, 32, 113. Morgagni held that "the testicles produce sperm" and that the seminal vesicles, the prostate, Cowper's glands, etc., produce "materie" that are useful for said sperm. *La generazione nel concetto di G. B. Morgagni*, 114–49.

62. Absent from her account are any theories remotely similar to Galen's that, although "all the parts that men have, women have too," "of course the female must have smaller, less perfect testes, and the semen generated in them must be scantier, colder," and thus "incapable of generating an animal." Galen, *On the Usefulness of the Parts*, vol. 2, 630, 631. Like Galen, Vesalius viewed female semen as inferior to the male although necessary for reproduction.

63. Jacquart and Thomasset, *Sexuality and Medicine in the Middle Ages*, 60.

Notes to Chapter Eleven

1. Charles De Brosses, *Lettres d'Italie du Président De Brosses*, ed. Frédéric d'Agay, (Paris: Mercure de France, 1986), 2 vols., I, p. 131 (letter 8). On Francesca Manzoni (1710–1743), poet and translator of Ovid and on the relevant and meager bibliography, see Giulio Natali, *Il Settecento. Parte prima*, 5th ed. (Milan: Vallardi, 1960), I, pp. 149–51 and p. 176. On Clelia Grillo Borromeo, first-rate protagonist of the cultural and political life of Milan (1684–1777), see ibid., pp. 128 and 170; Giuliana Parabiago, "Clelia Borromeo del Grillo," *Correnti* 1 (1998), 36–60; and Anna M. Serralunga Bardazza, *Clelia Grillo Borromeo Arese. Vicende private e pubbliche virtù di una celebre nobildonna nell'Italia del Settecento* (Biella: Eventi & Progetti Editore, 2005).

2. Ibid., pp. 144–46 (letter 10 to M. le Président Bouhier).

3. Ibid., pp. 267–68 (letter 20 to M. de Neuilly).

4. For the role of women in the French salons, see Dena Goodman, *The Republic of Letters: A Cultural History of the French Enlightenment* (Ithaca and London: Cornell University Press, 1994).

5. Paula Findlen, "Science as a Career in Enlightenment Italy: The Strategies of Laura Bassi," *Isis* 84 (1993), 441–69; Eadem, "Translating the New Science: Women and the Circulation of Knowledge in Enlightened Italy," *Configurations* 2 (1995), 167–206; Eadem, "A Forgotten Newtonian: Women and Science in the Italian Provinces," in *The Sciences in Enlightened Europe*, ed. William Clark, Jan Golinski, and Simon Schaffer (Chicago: University of Chicago Press, 1999), pp. 313–49; Gabriella Berti Logan, "The Desire to Contribute: An Eighteenth Century Italian Woman of Science," *American Historical Review* 99 (1994), 785–812; Beate Ceranski, *"Und sie fürchtet sich vor niemanden." Über die Physikerin Laura Bassi (1711–1778)* (Frankfurt and New York: Campus, 1996); Marta Cavazza, "Laura Bassi e il suo gabinetto di fisica sperimentale: realtà e mito," *Nuncius* 10 (1995), 715–53; Eadem, "'Dottrici' e lettrici nell'Università di Bologna nel Settecento," *Annali di storia delle università italiane* 1 (1997), 109–25; Eadem, "Laura Bassi «maestra» di Spallanzani," in *Il cerchio della vita. Materiali di ricerca del Centro Studi Lazzaro Spallanzani di Scandiano sulla storia della scienza del Settecento*, ed. W. Bernardi and P. Manzini (Florence: Olschki, 1999), pp. 185–202; Eadem, "Les femmes à l'académie: le cas de Bologne," in *Académies et sociétés savantes en Europe (1650–1800)*, ed. Daniel-Odon Hurel and Gérard Laudin (Paris: Honoré Champion, 2000), pp. 161–76; Maria Laura Soppelsa and Eva Viani, "Dal newtonianismo per le dame al newtonianismo delle dame. Cristina Roccati una 'savante' del Settecento," in *Donne Filosofia e Cultura nel Seicento*, ed. Pina Totaro (Rome: Consiglio Nazionale delle Ricerche, 1999), pp. 211–40; Rita Unfer Lukoschik, ed., *Elisabetta Caminer Turra (1751–1796). Una letterata veneta verso l'Europa* (Verona: Essedue edizioni, 1998); Eadem, "L'educatrice delle donne. Elisabetta Caminer Turra e la Querelle des Femmes negli spazi veneti di fine Settecento," in *L'educazione dell'uomo e della donna nella cultura illuministica*, ed. Lionello Sozzi (Turin: Accademia delle scienze, 2000), pp. 249–63; Rebecca Messbarger, "Waxing Poetic: Anna Morandi Manzolini's Anatomical Sculptures,"

Configurations 9 (2001), 65–97; Eadem, *"The Century of Women." Representations of Women in Eighteenth-Century Italian Public Discourse* (Toronto: University of Toronto Press, 2002); and Massimo Mazzotti, *The World of Maria Gaetana Agnesi, Mathematician of God* (Baltimore: Johns Hopkins University Press, 2007).

6. An important step in this direction is the essay by Paula Findlen, "The Scientist's Body: The Nature of a Woman Philosopher," in *The Faces of Nature in Enlightenment Europe,* ed. Gianna Pomata and Lorraine Daston (BWV. Berliner Wissenschafts-Verlag, 2003), pp. 211–36.

7. For a well-documented overview of seventeenth- and eighteenth-century conceptions of gender roles and the debate over study for women, fervent in eighteenth-century Italy, see the two volumes of Luciano Guerci, *La discussione sulla donna nell'Italia del Settecento,* 2nd ed. (Turin: Tirrenia Stampatori, 1988) and *La sposa obbediente. Donna e matrimonio nella discussione dell'Italia del Settecento* (Turin: Tirrenia Stampatori, 1988).

8. On the myth of Pandora, by means of which Hesiod (*Theogony,* vv. 570–612; *Works and Days,* vv. 63–67) explains the separation of the sexes and the appearance of the first woman, bearer of life but also of all evils to mankind, see Giulia Sissa, *La verginità in Grecia* (Rome: Laterza, 1992), p. 144. Because of the connection between the woman's body and the box unluckily opened by Pandora, Sissa sees in this myth a foundational episode in the significance the Greeks attributed to female virginity. See also Giovanni Giorgini, *I doni di Pandora. Filosofia, politica e storia nella Grecia antica* (Bologna: Libreria Bonomo, 2001), pp. 195–207.

9. Giovanni Antonio Volpi, "Che non debbono ammettersi le Donne allo Studio delle Scienze, e delle belle Arti. Discorso accademico," in *Discorsi accademici di varj autori viventi intorno gli Studj delle Donne, la maggior parte recitati nell'Accademia de' Ricovrati di Padova* (Padua, 1729), pp. 23–45, now translated in English in Maria Gaetana Agnesi et al., *The Contest for Knowledge: Debates over Women's Learning in Eighteenth Century Italy,* ed. Rebecca Messbarger and Paula Findlen (Chicago and London: University of Chicago Press, 2005), pp. 67–101; Benvenuto Robbio di San Raffaele, *Disgrazie di Donna Urania ovvero Degli studi femminili* (Parma, 1793).

10. For a synthesis of the most recent studies on gender identity in the eighteenth century, see Dorinda Outram, *The Enlightenment* (Cambridge: Cambridge University Press, 1995), pp. 80–95.

11. On relations between the university and the Istituto delle Scienze and on the ties between the scientific circles of Bologna and the academies of Europe, see Marta Cavazza, *Settecento inquieto. Alle origini dell'Istituto delle scienze di Bologna* (Bologna: Il Mulino, 1990); on relations between the Istituto delle Scienze and the Royal Society see Eadem, "The Institute of Science of Bologna and the Royal Society in the Eighteenth Century," *Notes and Records of the Royal Society of London* 56 (2002), 3–25.

12. Carlo Antonio Macchiavelli, *Bitisia Gozzadini seu de Mulierum Doctoratu* (Bologna, 1722). In reality the author of the work seems to have been the lawyer Alessandro Macchiavelli, brother of the Abbot Carlo Antonio. On this episode see Marta Cavazza, "'Dottrici' e lettrici," pp. 109–10. On A. Macchiavelli's biography,

see the corresponding entry by Marta Cavazza in *Dizionario biografico degli Italiani*, vol. 67 (Rome: Istituto dell'Enciclopedia Italiana, 2006), pp. 24–28.

13. Domenico Golinelli, *Memorie istoriche antiche e moderne di Budrio* (Bologna, 1720), p. 210. Further information on Laura Danielli Landi may be found in the preface *Al leggitore* of the manuscript *Delle donne bolognesi per letteratura e disegno illustri dell'avv. Alessandro Macchiavelli*, in Biblioteca Comunale dell'Archiginnasio di Bologna (BCAB), Raccolta Malvezzi, vol. 326, pp. 1–8 not numbered. Her teacher of philosophy seems to have been the "public lecturer" Bartolomeo Aldrovandi, who prepared her to defend "philosophical conclusions . . . to great applause." She knew Latin well and was "versed in many foreign or almost barbaric languages." On Stefano Danielli and his role in the diatribe between "malpighians" and "sbaraglists," see Marta Cavazza, "The Uselessness of Anatomy. Mini and Sbaraglia versus Malpighi," in *Marcello Malpighi Anatomist and Physician*, ed. Domenico Bertoloni Meli (Florence: Olschki, 1997), pp. 129–45.

14. On the Delfini Dosi affair, see Lucia Toschi Traversi, "Verso l'inserimento delle donne nel mondo accademico," in *Alma Mater Studiorum. La presenza femminile dal XVIII al XX secolo. Ricerche sul rapporto Donne / Cultura universitaria nell'Ateneo bolognese* (Bologna: CLUEB, 1988), pp. 15–37; Marta Cavazza, "'Dottrici' e lettrici," pp. 111–13.

15. Archivio di Stato di Bologna (ASB), Anziani Consoli, Insignia, vol. 13, cc. 94, 95, 98; Biblioteca Comunale dell'Archiginnasio di Bologna (BCAB), Fondo Bassi-Veratti, cart. 6.9, 1732 medal in honor of Laura Bassi by Antonio Lazzari; Idem, Gabinetto delle stampe, Collezione dei ritratti, A/5, cart. 30, n. 3, Portrait of Laura Bassi (design of Domenico Maria Fratta, engraving of Ludovico Mattioli, 1732). These images and others equally connected to the laurea of Laura Bassi can be seen in the Web pages dedicated to her in the series *Bologna Science Classics on Line: Laura Bassi, Miscellanea 1732*, ed. Marta Cavazza and Paola Bertucci, with an *Introduction* of M. Cavazza, at http://www.cis.unibo.it/cis13b/bsco3/intro_opera .asp?id_opera=31.

16. *Rime in lode della Signora Laura Maria Cattarina Bassi / cittadina Bolognese / Aggregata all'Accademia dell'Istituto delle Scienze di Bologna / Prendendo la Laurea Dottorale in Filosofia* (Bologna, 1732); *Rime per la Conclusione filosofica / Nello Studio Pubblico di Bologna / Tenuta / Dall'Illustrissima, ed Eccellentissima Signora / Laura Maria Cattarina Bassi / cittadina Bolognese / Dottorata in Filosofia, ed Aggregata al Collegio* (Bologna, 1732); *Rime / per la famosa laureazione / ed acclamatissima aggregazione / Al Collegio Filosofico / Della Illustrissima ed Eccellentissima / Signora / Laura Maria Catterina / Bassi / Accademica nell'Instituto delle Scienze / e Cittadina Bolognese* (Bologna, 1732).

17. See Susana Gomez, "The Bologna Stone and the Nature of Light: The Sciences Academy of Bologna," *Nuncius* 6 (1992), 3–32.

18. There exists a detailed account of this event drawn up by Laura's husband, Giuseppe Veratti, in BCAB, Fondo Bassi-Veratti, cart. 6.1,4 (cc. 1–2).

19. ASB, Anziani Consoli, Insignia, vol. 13, c. 105; Giovanna Ferrari, "Public Anatomy Lessons and the Carnival: The Anatomy Theatre of Bologna," *Past and Present* 117 (1987): 50–106.

20. See the synthetic biography in the form of a letter written by Eustachio Manfredi and published in Italian and German in a "weekly of numismatic amusement of Nuremberg," in an edition dedicated to the medal in honor of Bassi coined in 1732 in Bologna: *Der Wöchentlichen Historischen Münz-Belustigung*, 9 Stück, 27 February 1737, pp. 69–72.

21. The information is reported in the *Gazzetta di Milano* of 2 December 1739, cited by Giovanna Tilche, *Maria Gaetana Agnesi, la scienziata santa del Settecento* (Milan: Rizzoli, 1984), pp. 57–58.

22. Cavazza, "'Dottrici' e lettrici," pp. 119–20; Eadem, "Lesbia e Laura. Donne spettatrici e donne sperimentatrici nell'Italia del Settecento," in *Lorenzo Mascheroni. Scienza e letteratura nell'età dei Lumi*, ed. Matilde Dillon Wanke and Duccio Tongiorgi (Bergamo: Bergamo University Press, 2004). To the Bolognese episodes we must at least add the ceremonies for the laurea in law conferred on 26 June 1777 by the University of Pavia to Maria Pellegrina Amoretti. For Amoretti, see Maria Carla Zorzoli, *Le tesi legali all'Università di Pavia nell'età delle riforme, 1771–1796* (Milan: Istituto Editoriale Cisalpino-La Goliardica, 1981); and for a summary of the literary production occasioned by Amoretti's laurea, *Cultura e vita universitaria nelle miscellanee Belcredi, Giardini, Ticinensia*, ed. Alessandra Ferraresi, Alberta Mosconi Grassano, Antonia Pasi Testa (Milan: Istituto Editoriale Cisalpino-La Goliardica, 1986).

23. For a recent review of the historiographical interpretations of the phenomenon, see Roberto Bizzocchi, "Cicisbei. La morale italiana," *Storica* 9 (1997), 62–90. See also his Chapter 1 in this volume. For an examination of eighteenth-century discussions on cicisbei and on mixed conversazioni, see Luciano Guerci, *La discussione sulla donna nell'Italia del Settecento*, pp. 77–121. For interesting considerations on female freedom and cicisbeismo, see the chapter "Compensazioni galanti (il cicisbeismo)," in Carla Pellandra, *Seicento francese e strategie di compensazione* (Pisa: Editrice Libreria goliardica, 1983), pp. 181–96. This was a custom which had different connotations in the various cities: in Genoa, for example, where it emerged at the beginning of the century, it corresponded to the real power of the women in the aristocratic élite and seems to have been encouraged by the government of the Republic as a means of "domesticating" riotous young nobles by means of the civilizing influence of women. See Calogero Farinella, "Donne e cicisbei nel salotto settecentesco: il caso genovese," in *Salotti e ruolo femminile in Italia tra fine Seicento e primo Novecento*, ed. Maria Luisa Betri and Elena Brambilla (Venice: Marsilio, 2004), pp. 97–123. The author bases the analysis on a document published by Salvatore Rotta, "'Une aussi perfide nation,'" La *Relation de l'Etat de Gênes* di Jacques de Campredon (1737)," in *Genova 1746: una città d'antico regime tra guerra e rivolta*, ed. Carlo Bitossi and Claudio Paolocci (Genoa: Archivio di Stato di Genova, 1988), pp. 609–708. The institutional character of cicisbeismo in Genoa is also confirmed by a letter of Lady Montagu to Lady Mar of 28 August 1718, published in an appendix by Paolo Bernardini, "'The Genoese are esteem'd estreamly Cunning': relazioni diplomatiche, mercantili e culturali tra Genova e Inghilterra alla metà del XVIII secolo," idem, pp. 709, 725, 724–25.

24. De Brosses, *Lettres d'Italie*, II, pp. 169–89 (letter 45 to Mme Cortois).

25. Idem, I, pp. 268–74. On the common meeting place of the nobility and on the nonchalance and spirit of Bolognese women of high society, see the appreciation of Charles Louis de Montesquieu, *Voyages de Montesquieu publiés par le baron Albert de Montesquieu* (Bordeaux: G. Gounonilhon, 1894–1896), 2 vols., II, pp. 82–95 (1729). See, however, also the scandalized reaction of Ange Goudar, *L'espion chinois ou l'envoyé secret de la cour de Pekin pour examiner l'état présent de l'Europe* (Cologne, 1764, III). On the "*cendalo*" or "*zendalo*" that covered the women of the people, see also the observations of Joseph-Jérôme Lefrançais de Lalande, *Voyage en Italie* (Paris, 1786), I, p. 53.

26. The citations of Segneri, Bellati, and Beretta are drawn from Luciano Guerci, *La sposa obbediente*, pp. 17–58.

27. Idem, pp. 105–11.

28. Pietro Verri, "Ricordi a mia figlia," in *Illuministi settentrionali*, ed. Sergio Romagnoli (Milan: Rizzoli, 1962), pp. 149–211 and in particular pp. 158, 161, 166, 188. On the figure of Pietro Verri, see Carlo Capra, *I programmi della ragione: vita di Pietro Verri* (Bologna: Il Mulino, 2002).

29. On the importance of the female virtue of modesty for Rousseau, see Michèle Sajous D'Oria, "'Les bornes de la modestie': est-il bon ou mauvais que les femmes assistent au spectacle?" in *L'educazione dell'uomo e della donna nella cultura illuministica*, pp. 219–29. On the political implications of Rousseau's ideal of femininity, see Sarah Kofman, *Le respect des femmes. Kant et Rousseau* (Paris: Galilée, 1982). On the importance attributed to shame and modesty in eighteenth-century discussions on the nature and the role of women, see Londa Schiebinger, *Nature's Body. Sexual Politics and the Making of Modern Science* (London: Pandora, 1994), pp. 99–106; Marta Cavazza, "Women Dialectics or the Thinking Uterus. An Eighteenth-Century Controversy on Gender and Education," in *The Faces of Nature in Enlightenment Europe*, pp. 237–57.

30. Verri, *Ricordi a mia figlia*, pp. 161–63 and 205.

31. Baldassarre Castiglione, *Il libro del Cortegiano*, in *Opere di Baldassarre Castiglione, Giovanni Della Casa, Benvenuto Cellini*, ed. C. Cordié (Milan and Naples: Ricciardi, 1960), p. 214.

32. Marina Zancan, "La donna," in *Letteratura italiana. V. Le Questioni* (Turin: Einaudi, 1986), pp. 765–827: 792.

33. Guerci, *La sposa obbediente*, pp. 252–53; and also, for the end of the century and with particular attention to Southern Italy, Annamaria Rao, "Il sapere velato. L'educazione delle donne nel dibattito italiano di fine Settecento," in *Misoginia. La donna vista e malvista nella cultura occidentale*, ed. Andrea Milano (Rome: Edizioni Dehoniane, 1992), pp. 243–310.

34. Lazzaro Spallanzani, *De lapidibus ab aqua resilientibus*, in *Dissertazioni due dell'abate Lazzaro Spallanzani* (Modena: Eredi B. Soliani, 1765). On the relations between Spallanzani and Laura Bassi, see Marta Cavazza, "Laura Bassi 'maestra' di Spallanzani," in *Il cerchio della vita*, ed. W. Bernardi and P. Manzini (Florence: Olschki, 1999), pp. 185–202.

35. Lazzaro Spallanzani, *Dell'azione del cuore ne' vasi sanguigni* (Modena: G. Montanari, 1768). On the relations between the naturalist and Olimpia Sessi, see Marta Cavazza, "Laura Bassi 'maestra' di Spallanzani," pp. 199–202.

36. Ibid.

37. Paola Govoni, *Un pubblico per la scienza. La divulgazione scientifica nell'Italia in formazione* (Rome: Carocci, 2002), pp. 56–72.

38. Some examples: Giovanni de Cataneo, *Il filosofismo delle belle* (Venice, 1753); Petronio Zecchini, *Dì geniali. Della dialettica delle donne ridotta al suo vero principio* (Bologna, 1771); Giovanni Pirani, *Le convulsioni delle signore di bello spirito, di quelle che affettan letteratura, e delle altre attaccate dalla dolce passione d'amore malattia di questo secolo. Con l'anatomia di alcuni cuori e cervelli di esse* (Venice, 1789); Benvenuto Robbio di San Raffaele, *Disgrazie di Donna Urania* (Parma, 1793).

39. On Maria Laura Saibanti, see Gian Paolo Romagnani, "Dal salotto di casa Saibanti all'Accademia Roveretana degli Agiati: l'avventura intellettuale di una donna nella Rovereto settecentesca," in *Salotti e ruolo femminile in Italia*, pp. 213–35.

40. Francesco Algarotti, *Il Newtonianismo per le Dame, ovvero Dialoghi sopra la luce i colori, e l'attrazione* (Naples, 1739), p. 3.

41. Rebecca Messbarger, *The Century of Women*, pp. 86–103: 86. The text analyzed by the author and considered paradigmatic is the *Difesa delle donne*, which appeared anonymously in the Enlightenment newspaper *Il Caffè* and which was in reality written by Carlo Sebastiano Franci under the supervision of Pietro Verri.

42. On Cornaro Piscopia, see Lodovico Maschietto, *Elena Lucrezia Cornaro Piscopia (1646–1684), prima donna laureata nel mondo* (Padua: Antenore, 1978); Patricia H. Labalme, "Women's Roles in Early Modern Venice: An Exceptional Case," in *Beyond Their Sex: Learned Women of the European Past*, ed. P. H. Labalme (New York and London: New York University Press, 1984), pp. 129–52; Paul Kristeller, "Learned Women of Early Modern Italy," idem, pp. 91–116.

43. Paula Findlen, *Possessing Nature: Museums, Collecting, and Scientific Culture in Early Modern Italy* (Berkeley, Los Angeles and London: University of California Press, 1984).

44. The catalogue of the Museo Cospi speaks of the portraits of Angelica and Sebastiano Biavati and their story; Lorenzo Legati, *Museo Cospiano, annesso a quello del famoso Ulisse Aldrovandi e donato alla sua Patria dall'Illustrissimo Signor Ferdinando Cospi patrizio di Bologna e senatore* (Bologna, 1677), pp. 6–7.

45. On the development of collecting and natural history museums from the Renaissance to the Enlightenment, see Giuseppe Olmi, *L'inventario del mondo. Catalogazione della natura e luoghi del sapere nella prima età moderna* (Bologna: Il Mulino, 1992), pp. 165–209.

46. Th. H. Lunsingh Scheurleer, "Un amphithéâtre d'anatomie moralisée," in *Leiden University in the Seventeenth Century. An Exchange of Learning*, ed. Th. H. Lunsingh Scheurleer, Guillaume Henri Marie Posthumus Meyjes, A. G. H. Bachrach (Leyden: E. J. Brill, 1975), pp. 216–77; Giovanna Ferrari, "Public Anatomy Lessons and the Carnival," pp. 53–66; Jonathan Sawday, *The Body Emblazoned: Dissection and the Human Body in Renaissance Culture* (London, etc.: Routledge, 1995).

47. Simon Schaffer, "Natural Philosophy and Public Spectacle in the Eighteenth Century," *History of Sciences* 21 (1983), 1–43; for Italy, see Paola Bertucci, "Back from Wonderland: Jean Antoine Nollet's Italian Tour (1749)," in R.J.W. Evans, Alexander Marr, eds., *Curiosity and Wonders from the Renaissance to the Enlightenment* (Aldershot: Ashgate, 2006); idem, *Viaggio nel paese delle meraviglie. Scienza e curiosità nell'Italia del Settecento* (Turin: Bollati Boringhieri, 2007); and Bernardette Bensaude-Vincent and Christine Blondel, eds., *Science and Spectacle in the European Enlightenment* (Aldershot: Ashgate, 2008).

48. On Agnesi and the social, religious, and scientific context in which she was formed and worked, see the recent book *The World of Maria Gaetana Agnesi*, cit., and other important contributions of Massimo Mazzotti, "Maria Gaetana Agnesi: Mathematics and the Making of the Catholic Enlightenment," *Isis* 92 (2001), 657–83; "Scienza, fede e carità. Il cattolicesimo illuminato di Maria Gaetana Agnesi," in *Scienza a due voci*, ed. Raffaella Simili (Florence: Olschki, 2006), pp. 13–37. Fundamental, in the literature on the Milanese mathematician, remain Anton Francesco Frisi, *Elogio storico di Donna Maria Gaetana Agnesi* (Milan, 1799), and Maria Luisa Anzoletti, *Maria Gaetana Agnesi* (Milan: Cogliati, 1901).

49. Giovanni Giacomo Amadei, *Libro delle cose che vanno accadendo in Bologna specialmente quelle che spettano al governo sì civile sì ecclesiastico*, Biblioteca Comunale dell'Archiginnasio di Bologna, ms. B 517. For an original and suggestive interpretation of the difficulties posed to the culture and the society of the time in defining the very gender, and therefore the nature, of a woman who like Bassi was not only a philosopher but also a "doctor" and a "lecturer," see Findlen, "The Scientist's Body"; see also Marta Cavazza, "Una donna nella Repubblica degli scienziati. Laura Bassi e i suoi colleghi," in *Scienza a due voci*, pp. 61–85.

50. ASB, Senato, *Diario 1714–41*, cc. 13–132: *Relazione della disputazione in palazzo pubblico del XII aprile 1732*.

51. ASB, Senato, *Vacchettoni*, registro 60, ff. 203–4.

52. De Brosses, *Lettres d'Italie*, I, pp. 267–68.

53. For Bassi, see Marta Cavazza, "Minerva e Pigmalione. Carriere femminili nell'Italia del Settecento," *The Italianist* 17 (1997), 5–17.

54. The strategies (and the battles) employed by Bassi to win a scientific and professional role comparable to that of her male colleagues are amply described and analyzed in the works of Findlen, Berti Logan, Ceranski, and Cavazza cited in the preceding notes.

55. Giovanni Fantuzzi, *Notizie degli scrittori bolognesi*, II, the entry *Bassi Laura Maria Catterina* (Bologna, 1782), pp. 384–91 (the text is the same as the *Elogio di Laura Bassi* published by the same author in 1778, again by the Stamperia di S. Tommaso d'Aquino).

56. Ibid.

57. Letter of Giovanni Bianchi to Antonio Leprotti dated Rimini 12 February 1733, in Gian Ludovico Masetti, "Laura Bassi (1711–1778). Testimonianze e carteggi inediti," *Strenna storica bolognese* 29 (1979), 231–33.

58. BCAB, Fondo Bassi-Veratti, cart. 5.3, pp. 100–108. Cited in Giovanni

Battista Comelli, *Laura Bassi e il suo primo trionfo* (Bologna: Cooperativa tipografica Azzoguidi, 1912), p. 54.

59. BCAB, Fondo Bassi-Veratti, cart. 6.1, 4, cc. 4–10 fasc. 1d, reproduced in the appendix of Beate Ceranski, *"Und sie fürchtet sich vor niemandem,"* pp. 271–72.

60. Letter of Giampietro Zanotti to father Giampietro Riva, 9 April 1732, BCAB, ms. B 382, on which see Beate Ceranski, *"Und sie fürchtet sich vor niemandem,"* pp. 45–46.

61. See note 54.

62. Apart from the Latin oration in defense of study for women recited when she was nine years old and inserted as her own work (although in reality it was composed by a tutor) in *Discorsi accademici*, pp. 91–105, the merits of women in intellectual matters are vindicated in a passage of the *Propositiones philosophicae, quas crebris disputationibus domi habitus coram clarissimis viris explicabat extempore, et ab objectis vindicabat Maria Cajetana de Agnesiis mediolanensis* (Milan, 1738), and above all in the dedication to the Empress Maria Teresa of Austria of her *Istituzioni analitiche ad uso della gioventù italiana* (Milan, 1748). The Latin oration in defense of study for women which Agnesi recited at age nine has been translated into English by Paula Findlen and Rachel Trotter Chaney: "Academic Oration in Which It Is Demonstrated That the Studies of the Liberal Arts by the Female Sex Are by No Means Inappropriate," in Agnesi et al., *The Contest for Knowledge*, pp. 117–40.

63. De Brosses, *Lettres d'Italie*, I, p. 146.

64. See note 62. On Agnesi's approach to mathematical disciplines and on the location of her work with respect to the Newtonian and the Leibnizian traditions of analysis, an article which offers interesting perspectives is that of Massimo Mazzotti, "Maria Gaetana Agnesi" (see in particular pp. 669–79).

65. See Carla Vettori Sandor, "L'opera scientifica e umanitaria di Maria Gaetana Agnesi," in *Alma Mater Studiorum*, pp. 105–18, which includes in its appendix *l'Extrait des registres de l'Académie royale des sciences du 6 Décembre 1749*, containing the positive judgment of the Paris academics on Agnesi's book (pp. 114–17).

66. Massimo Mazzotti, "Maria Gaetana Agnesi," pp. 658 and 681.

67. Idem, p. 663.

68. See note 48.

69. Benvenuto Robbio di San Raffaele, *Ragionamento sopra gli studi delle donne*, in idem, *Disgrazie di Donna Urania*, pp. 58–131: 131.

70. Other episodes of resistance on the part of the culture and society of eighteenth-century Italy to the idea of women's access to high culture are in Luciano Guerci, *La discussione sulla donna*; Marta Cavazza, "Women's Dialectics or the Thinking Uterus"; and Anna Maria Rao, "Il sapere velato."

Notes to Chapter Twelve

1. My emphasis. Mme du Boccage's letter from Venice, June 1, 1757, quoted in Natali, *Il settecento* (Milano: Vallardi, 1929), vol. I: 101. All translations from French and Italian are mine. I am indebted to Johanna Smith for her help with the German translations.

2. The *Encyclopédie* is quoted in Françoise Waquet, *Rhétorique et Poétique Chrétiennes. Bernardino Perfetti et la poésie improvisée* (Firenze: Olschki, 1992), 52. For musical improvisation, see P. Santucci *L'improvvisazione nella musica* (Bologna: Cappella Musicale S. Maria de' Servi, 1982). For improvised painting: B. De' Dominici, *Vite de' pittori, scultori ed architetti napoletani* (Napoli: Ricciardo, 1742), 529, 532–33, 540, 543. Charles de Brosses comments on Bernardino Perfetti in his *Lettres familières sur l'Italie* (Paris: Firmin-Didot, 1931), 1: 384–85; Joseph Jérôme de Lalande writes about Bartolomeo Lorenzi, Giovanni De Rossi, and Luigi Serio in his *Voyage* (Yverdon, 1769), 2:16, 3:123, 7:240; Mme. de Staël pays tribute to Corilla Olimpica in her *Corinne*, ed. Simone Balayé (Paris: Gallimard, 1985); and Karl Fernow to all improvisers in his theoretical essay "Über die Improvisatoren," in *Römischen Studien,*" vol. 2 (Zürich: Bei H Gessner, 1806–1808), 295–416.

3. Eugène Bouvy, "L'improvisation poétique en Italie," *Bulletin Italien* 6 (1906), 2.

4. Giuseppe Marco Antonio Baretti, *Lettere famigliari,* quoted in Giulio Natali, *Il Settecento*, vol. 2. (Milan: Vallardi, 1929), 130n; Pietro Metastasio, *Lettere*, ed. Bruno Brunelli, vols. 3–5 of *Tutte le opere di Pietro Metastasio*, 5 vols. (Milan: Mondadori, 1954); Carlo Goldoni, *Memorie*, transl. E. Levi (Turin, 1967), 218. See Natali, *Il settecento*, I:101; on Goldoni as an improvising *commedia dell'arte* actor. Ugo Foscolo, "Al tragico tuo carme," in U. Viviani, *Un genio aretino, Tommaso Sgricci, poeta tragico improvvisatore* (Arezzo, 1928), 188. The poem is quoted at length in Bruno Gentili, "Cultura dell'Improvviso. Poesia orale colta nel settecento italiano e poesia greca dell'età arcaica e classica," *Strumenti critici* 39 (1979), 258. According to Adele Vitagliano, Foscolo improvised in English to show that it was not the language used that made a difference, but the talent of the artist using it. Unfortunately, she does not provide any bibliographical reference. See Adele Vitagliano, *Storia della poesia estemporanea nella letteratura italiana dalle origini ai nostri giorni* (Rome: Ermanno Loescher, 1905), 178.

5. About Morelli, see below. Monti, an improviser himself according to Michele Maylender, wrote an ode in honor of Bandettini, which Vitagliano reproduces in part; Alfieri, Parini, and Mazza wrote sonnets for her. See Michele Maylender, *Storia delle Accademie d'Italia*, vol. I (Bologna: Licinio Cappelli, 1926–1930), 272; Adele Vitagliano, *Storia della poesia estemporanea*, 105–6. The latest and most comprehensive study on Bandettini is Alessandra Di Ricco's *L'Inutile e meraviglioso mestiere. Poeti improvvisatori di fine settecento* (Milan: Franco Angeli, 1990). Fortunata Sulgher Fantastici (Florence, 1755–1824) was praised by Vincenzo Monti, of whom she became a friend after 1792, and by Mme. de Staël. In 1792 she was in Rome, where she became acquainted with the British poet Cornelia Knight (to whom Corilla also dedicated a sonnet) and Angelica Kauffman, who portrayed her in the act of improvising verse. See G.V. Dentoni *Elogio della celebre poetessa Fortunata Sulgher Fantastici* (Parma, 1824); L. A. Ferrai, "Lettere inedite di Vincenzo Monti a Fortunata Sulgher Fantastici," *Giornale storico della letteratura italiana* 5 (1885), 370–82; C. Giommi, *Elogio di Fortunata Sulgher Fantastici Marchesini* (Florence, 1824). Several of Angelica Kauffman's letters to Fantastici are to be found in the volume "*Mir träumte vor ein paar Nächten, ich*

hätte Briefe von Ihnen empfangen": gesammelte Briefe in den Originalsprachen, ed. Waltraud Maierhofer (Lengwil: Libelle, 2001). Recall also the portrait of Fantastici in Chapter 6 (Figure 6.3).

6. Giovanni Cristofano Amaduzzi, letter of 28 January 1775, quoted in Alessandro Ademollo, *Corilla Olimpica* (Florence, 1887), 165. The names of the male improvisers who performed with Corilla are not mentioned in this letter, but we know from an Arcadian official protocol of the time that Corilla had recently performed a "polivocal" improvising together with Angelo Talassi, Giovanni de Rossi, and Giuseppe Giordani. See Atti Arcadia 5. Ms. Accademia Letteraria Arcadia, Biblioteca Angelica, Rome, 71.

7. Foscolo, "The Women of Italy," in *Opere,* vol. 12 (Florence: Le Monnier, 1958), 436.

8. Benedetto Croce, *Conversazioni critiche,* vol. 2 (Bari: Laterza, 1918), 220.

9. Carlo Dionisotti, *Geografia e storia della letteratura italiana* (Turin: Einaudi, 1967), 86.

10. Alessandra Di Ricco, *L'Inutile e meraviglioso mestiere,* 9.

11. See Alessandra Di Ricco, *L'Inutile e meraviglioso mestiere,* 189.

12. Giulio Natali, *Il Settecento,* vol. 2, 98. Benedetto Croce, "Gli improvvisatori," *Letteratura italiana del settecento* (Bari: Laterza, 1949), 299.

13. See Michele Maylender, *Storia delle Accademie d'Italia,* vol. 1, 272.

14. Fabio Finotti, "Il canto delle Muse: improvvisazione e poetica della voce," in *Corilla Olimpica e la poesia del settecento europeo,* ed. Moreno Fabbi (Pistoia: Artout, 2002), 32. See Finotti's well-documented article for several examples of Renaissance theories and practice of extemporaneous poetry.

15. In his *Istoria della volgare poesia,* Crescimbeni wrote: "We believe that improvising in the Tuscan tongue can be traced back to the very birth of our [national] poetry. Yet, because of the scarcity of information on this first period, we are forced to date its first documented examples to the sixteenth century, at a time in which, as Ruscelli writes, it was very widely practiced." The text continues with an account of the most important Renaissance improvisers (all male) as well as of the style, meter, and topics of their work, as recorded by Ruscelli. Giovan Maria Crescimbeni, *Istoria della volgar poesia,* vol. 6. (Venice: Basegio, 1730), 330.

16. Ibid.

17. Giovan Maria Crescimbeni, *Arcadia* (Rome: De Rossi, 1708), 117. Poetic improvisations could be either declaimed (as was Tirsi's in the example we mentioned above) or sung. Perfetti famously sang all his improvisations. Later in the century, declaiming became more and more used. In the case of Montano's poetic improvisation, music functions as mere background accompaniment.

18. Crescimbeni, *Arcadia,* 289.

19. See also Finotti, "Il canto delle Muse," 32.

20. Finotti, "Il canto delle Muse," 31.

21. Giovan Mario Crescimbeni, *Comentarj intorno all'istoria della poesia italiana,* 5 vols. (Rome: Chracas, 1702–1711). I used T.J. Mathias' edition: vol. 2 (London: T. Becket, 1803), 69 and 51 respectively. See also *Comentarj,* vol. 2, 65–68, for exam-

ples of recited corone composed in honor of prominent personalities, most notably, Pope Clement XI. The examples of improvisations Crescimbeni gives in *Arcadia* are not corone but arias, a "*canzonetta*," and a poem in octaves.

22. Crescimbeni, *Arcadia*, 293.

23. Ibid.

24. Criticism of improvisation and of Arcadian poetry, as well as of Arcadian intellectual pursuits in general, were initially motivated by a literal interpretation of Arcadia's pastoral symbolism and rituals. See "Ragionamento di Uranio," in Crescimbeni, *Arcadia*, 235–44; published also in *Prose degli Arcadi,* vol. 1 (Rome: De Rossi, 1718), Prosa XXI.

25. Crescimbeni, *Arcadia*, 116.

26. Crescimbeni, *Arcadia*, 116–17.

27. Maylender, *Storia delle Accademie d'Italia*, 270. For this reason Natali called Arcadia the first national academy, and the first cultural phenomenon to unify Italy. Natali also wrote that "Arcadia contributed to . . . diminishing the differences among the various social classes, which were all considered equal in front of poetry." Natali, *Il settecento*, vol. 2, 648.

28. Mario Fubini, "Arcadia e Illuminismo," in *Questioni e Correnti di storia letteraria.* (Milan: Marzorati 1973), 503–95. Scholars have been traditionally divided in their judgment of the intellectual import of this institution: see my articles "The Poetics of Seconda Arcadia and Literary History," *NEMLA Italian Studies* 19 (1995), 51–68, and "Women Poets and Improvisers: Cultural Assumptions and Literary Values in Arcadia," *Studies in Eighteenth-Century Culture*, 32 (2003), 69–92, for studies of the influence of gender values in the evaluation of the academy. See Antonio Piromalli's *L'Arcadia* (Palermo: Palumbo, 1975) for a thorough presentation of the academy's most prominent critics. On Arcadia as democratic see also Teresa Acquaro Graziosi, *L'Arcadia. Trecento Anni di Storia* (Rome: Fratelli Palombi, 1991); on the opposite view, Amedeo Quondam, "L'istituzione Arcadia. Sociologia e ideologia di un'accademia," *Quaderni storici* 23 (1973), 412–13.

29. Elisabetta Graziosi, "Arcadia femminile: presenze e modelli," *Terzo centenario d'Arcadia* (Roma: Arcadia, 1991), 249–73; Ginevra Canonici Fachini *Prospetto biografico delle donne italiane rinomate in letteratura* (Venice, 1824) 51; Benedetto Croce, "Donne letterate nel seicento," in *Nuovi saggi della letteratura italiana del seicento* (Bari: Laterza, 1931), 171; Anna Teresa Romano Cervone, "Presenze femminili nella prima Arcadia romana: per una teoria dei modelli," in *Tre secoli di storia dell'Arcadia* (Rome: Ministero per i Beni Culturali, 1991) 47.

30. Giovan Mario Crescimbeni, *Breve notizia dello stato antico e moderno dell'Adunanza degli Arcadi* (Rome: De Rossi, 1712); reprinted as part of volume 6 of *Istoria della volgar poesi*a (Venice: Basegio, 1730), 311.

31. Gian Vincenzo Gravina, "Regolamento degli studi di nobile e valorosa donna," *Di Gian-Vincenzo Gravina, Giureconsulto, Opere Italiane* (Naples: Stamperia di Giuseppe Raimondi, 1757), 249. The "Regolamento" was published posthumously. See Amedeo Quondam's edition of Gravina's *Scritti critici e teorici* (Bari: Laterza, 1973), 637–38, for information about its dating.

32. *Commentarj di G. Mario de'Crescimbeni intorno alla sua istoria della vulgar poesia*, vol. I (Roma: De Rossi 1701), 309; quoted in Elisabetta Graziosi, "Arcadia femminile: presenze e modelli," 252.

33. See Elisabetta Graziosi's Chapter 4 in this volume for women's diplomatic role in Arcadia. See also Maria Pia Donato, *Accademie romane. Una storia sociale: 1671–1824* (Rome: Edizioni Scientifiche Italiane, 2000) for the political and diplomatic functions of Roman academies. Finally, for the Arcadian academy's 1726 diplomatic dealings with the King of Portugal see Paola Ferraris, "L'Arcadia nella diplomazia internazionale," *Arcadia. Accademia Letteraria Italiana. Atti e Memorie* 8:4 (1987), 227–68.

34. From its foundation, the academy had to count on the generosity of Roman nobility and intelligentsia for both its private and its public gatherings. See Giovan Mario Crescimbeni, *Breve notizia dello stato antico e moderno dell'Adunanza degli Arcadi* (Rome: De Rossi, 1712); reprinted as part of volume 6 of *Istoria della volgar poesia* (Venice: Basegio, 1730), 305–28. See also Crescimbeni, *Arcadia*, 264.

35. G.M. Crescimbeni, *Notizie istoriche degli Arcadi morti* (Roma: De Rossi, 1721), 3:17. As of 1760 winter academies were still held in the custode's house for lack of a better place. See Michele Morei, *Memorie istoriche dell'Adunanza degli Aracadi* (Rome: De Rossi, 1761), 79.

36. Crescimbeni, "A Madama Ondedei Albani Cognata di N.S. Papa Clemente XI," *Arcadia*, 1708, no page number; "All'Illustrissima, ed Eccellentissima Signora, La Signora D. Maria Isabella Cesi Ruspoli Pricipessa di Cerveteri &c. [sic]," *Arcadia*, 1711, no page number.,

37. For Crescimbeni's program of literary reforms, see his *Istoria della volgare poesia* and his *Bellezza della volgare poesia* (Rome, 1700).

38. Amedeo Quondam reported most of the salient documents pertaining to the 1711 crisis in "Nuovi documenti sulla crisi dell'Arcadia nel 1711," *Arcadia. Accademia Letteraria Italiana. Atti e Memorie* 6 (1973), 105–228.

39. Crescimbeni, "Breve notizia," 310.

40. Anna Teresa Romano Cervone, "Presenze femminili nella prima Arcadia romana: per una teoria dei modelli," in *Tre secoli di storia dell'Arcadia* (Rome: Ministero per i Beni Culturali, 1991), 49. Maybe because of the ambiguity created by Crescimbeni's mixing of genres (history and fiction), *Arcadia*'s framework, i.e. Arcadian women's quest for inclusion in Arcadian activities, is not given historical legitimation by commentators. Teresa Cervone and Amedeo Quondam (author of several milestone articles on this period) read the framework as totally fictitious, although representative of the "feminine" nature of the academy. For Quondam the essence of Arcadian culture at this stage is epitomized by the scene of the nymphs who spy on Magliabechi from a peep hole: it is an attitude of superficial curiosity. See his "Gioco e società letteraria nell'Arcadia del Crescimbeni. L'ideologia dell'istituzione," *Arcadia. Atti e memorie* 6 (1975–1976), 176. Cervone does acknowledge that the text showcases women's participation, but does not address its conflictual status and its import in the genesis of the text: Anna Teresa Romano Cervone, "Presenze femminili nella prima Arcadia romana: per una teoria dei modelli," in *Tre secoli di storia dell'Arcadia* (Roma: Ministero per i Beni Culturali, 1991), 47–58.

The meeting among the most prominent Arcadian women poets portrayed at the beginning of the book may be fictional, yet not only does the introduction clearly specify the historical aspects of the narration ("L'Autore a chi legge"), but a note reveals that indeed women had been excluded from the Olympic games until 1701: Crescimbeni, *Arcadia*, 265.

41. The Olympic games were especially important in this first phase of the academy's life. As professor Acquaro Graziosi, today's custodian of Arcadia, confirmed during our recent conversation in Rome, the Olympic games were a competition in which only the best, the most representative, and the most prominent Arcadians were supposed to participate.

42. Quondam, "Gioco e società letteraria," 176.

43. Cf. Quondam, "L'istituzione Arcadia. Sociologia e ideologia di un'accademia," 412–13; and Susan Dixon, "Women in Arcadia," *Eighteenth-Century Studies* 32 (1999), 371–90.

44. Crescimbeni, *Arcadia*, 2.

45. Crescimbeni, *Arcadia*, 2. If women were admitted to philosophical studies, Giovanni Antonio Volpi, for example, argued at Padua's Accademia de' Ricovrati, they would give up marriage and the labors of procreation. Moreover, women's presence in schools would distract men from their studies. Giovanni Antonio Volpi, *Discorsi accademici*, quoted in Luciano Guerci, *La discussione sulla donna nell'Italia del settecento* (Turin: Tirrenia, 1987), 172.

46. Ugo Foscolo, "The Women of Italy," in *Opere*, vol. 12. (Florence: le Monnier, 1958), 424–66. On Maria Vittoria Delfini Dosi, see Antonio Francesco Ghiselli, *Esatta relazione della funzione fatta dalla Contessa Maria Vittoria Delfini Dosi nel tenere le sue pubbliche Conclusioni di Legge in Bologna nell'Almo Real Collegio Maggiore di San Clemente*, ms. 775, Biblioteca Universitaria di Bologna.

47. On Magliabechi, see Joseph Spence, *A Parallel in the Manner of Plutarch Between a Most Celebrated Man of Florence, and One, Scarce Ever Heard of, in England* (London: Printed and sold by Messieurs Dodsley . . . for the benefit of Mr. Hill, 1759); Amedeo Quondam and Michele Rak, *Lettere dal Regno ad Antonio Magliabechi* (Naples: Guida, 1978–79); Manuela Doni Garfagnini, *Lettere e carte Magliabechi: inventario cronologico Roma: Istituto storico italiano per l'età moderna e contemporanea* (Rome: Istituto storico italiano per l'età moderna e contemporanea, 1988); M. Mannelli Goggioli, *La Biblioteca Magliabechiana. Libri, uomini, idee per la prima biblioteca pubblica a Firenze* (Florence, 2000). On Muratori, see *Edizione nazionale del carteggio di L. A. Muratori* (Florence: L. S. Olschki, 1900); Michele Monaco, *La vita, le opere, il pensiero di L. A. Muratori e la sua concezione della pubblica felicità* (Lecce: Milella, 1977); Ezio Raimondi, *I Lumi dell'erudizione: saggi sul settecento italiano* (Milan: Vita e Pensiero, 1989); Gian Paolo Romagnani, *"Sotto la bandiera dell'istoria": eruditi e uomini di lettere nell'Italia del Settecento: Maffei, Muratori, Tartarotti* (Verona: Cierre, 1999).

48. Crescimbeni, *Arcadia*, 231. Faustina degli Azzi Forti (Selvaggia, 1691) was the first woman to be granted the honor (which she modestly declined) of founding an Arcadian "colony" (or branch): the "Forzosa" in Arezzo. Among the other Arcadian

poet improvisers listed by Crescimbeni are the abbé Francesco Cavoni, Francesco del Teglia, Fabio Ferrante da Valmontone, Giulio Cesare Grazini; Abate Pompeo Figari, Domenico Petrosellini, Paolo Rolli, and Paolo Vannini. See *Arcadia*, 116, and *Comentarj*, 73.

49. We have scant information on these poets. For Faustina dagli Azzi Forti, see previous note; we have a few poems by Emilia Ballati in *Rime degli Arcadi*, vol. 6 (Rome, 1716); Maria Domenica Mazzetti Forster (Flora, 1725) was at the service of the Grand Duchess of Tuscany, Beatrice Violante of Bavaria, and improvised with Perfetti in Rome in 1725. She presumably had a long and productive life, if a poem in honor of Corilla Olimpica's 1776 crowning found in *Atti della solenne coronazione fatta in Campidoglio della insigne poetessa Maria Maddalena Morelli, pistoiese, tra gli Arcadi Corilla Olimpica* (Parma, 1779), 195, can be considered hers. Hereafter this work will be referred to as *Atti della solenne coronazione fatta in Campidoglio* (1779).

50. Abate Pier Francesco Versari (Eurasio Nonacride), "Dialogo pastorale," *I giuochi olimpici celebrati in Arcadia nell'ingresso dell'Olimpiade DCXXXIII in onore degli Arcadi illustri defunti* (Rome: Monaldini, 1754), 47.

51. Versari, "Dialogo pastorale," 47.

52. Corilla Olimpica, crowned poet laureate on the Roman Capitol in 1776, is certainly the best known among these women improvisers. We shall write extensively about her below. Besides the three greatest (Corilla, Fortunata Fantastici, and Teresa Bandettini), Natali mentioned briefly another two: Emilia Ballati Orlandini (1683–1757) and Livia Accarigi (1719–1786). Jolanda De Blasi mentions also Maria Domenica Mazzetti Forster, "poetessa della serenissima Governatrice di Siena . . . Livia Sarchi, la Gazzeri, la Landi Mazzei e la Bacchini," but without supplying a single line of comment about them: *Le scrittrici italiane dalle origini al 1800.* (Florence: Nemi, 1930), 271. Several poems by Efiria Corilea are available in collections published between 1744 and 1764.

53. Corilla Olimpica was the daughter of a violinist; Teresa Bandettini Landucci declared she was born of "honest and comfortable citizens" ("Autobiografia," 229). Biographers simply refer to her parents as "poor." After the death of her father, Bandettini supported herself as a dancer. Of Fortunata Sulgher Fantastici we know only that she was born of a "modest family." Their success was made possible by prominent mentors who fostered their talents early in life; Corilla studied first under the patronage of cavalier Francesco Baldinotti, and then of Princess Pignatelli di Colubrano. Fantastici was able to further her studies (including ancient Greek) under the patronage of Marquis Viviani. Count Lodovico Savioli introduced Bandettini to the Bologna literary establishment and also financed publication of her narrative poem *La morte di Adone* (Parma, 1790).

54. Ademollo, *Corilla Olimpica*, xiv.

55. Michele Morei, *Memorie istoriche*, 84–85.

56. According to Morei, Pontiff Benedict XIII honored Arcadia by entrusting it with Perfetti's literary examination and with the administration of the poetic laurels; and Violante, Grand Duchess of Tuscany, by showing great benevolence toward the Arcadian examiners. Furthermore, the custodian Alfesibeo (Crescimbeni)

was honored by the Roman Senate by being granted a seating position of equal status to theirs; while Cardinal Alessandro Albani (Crisalgo Acianteo) renewed his patronage, as he "contributed to taking care of the academy's obligations," which I take to indicate that he contributed to the expenses. Morei, *Memorie istoriche*, 242–243.

57. See Natali, *Settecento* I, 157, on Corilla being the first woman improviser to achieve fame and recognition. Perini is quoted in Ademollo, *Corilla Olimpica*, xi. By the 1760s Corilla is celebrated in Arcadia. She tells us herself in her sonnet "Dopo tre lustri alfin" improvised on her return in 1775, and we find it confirmed by Morei's history: *Memorie istoriche*, 84–85.

58. See Pizzi in *Atti della solenne coronazione fatta in Campidoglio* (1779), 5–6. Among Corilla's panegyrists in official documents, abate Ceruti praised Corilla for her improvisations and her published work. In his preface to the proceedings of Corilla's solemn celebration in Arcadia, abate Ceruti wrote: "[Corilla is a] great woman, reputed to be not just exceptional, but indeed unique with respect to her poetical gifts, for which she is superior to all praises, . . . and the greatest of honors [*e primo vero onore*] for Arcadia, happy Tuscany, and all of beautiful Italy"; *Adunanza tenuta dagli Arcadi per la coronazione della celebre pastorella Corilla Olimpica* (Rome, 1775), xxx–xxxi.

59. In the context of Corilla's fame and reputation during her lifetime, it is appropriate to mention that it was her published occasional poetry in honor of queens and empresses that won her financial security and distinctions. A poem in honor of Maria Teresa of Austria won Corilla an invitation to the court of Vienna and eventually secured her financial stability with a post as court poet for Leopold II of Tuscany. Another poem in honor of Catherine the Great of Russia (now lost) won her an invitation to that court and a monetary compensation, in spite of Corilla's declining the invitation to court.

60. Bodoni admired Corilla, an "inimitable improviser, divinely inspired," for her "insight and keen intellect" so much that he wished he could build a monument to her on the Capitol, with the dedication "Sacred to Corilla, the Tenth Muse"; *Atti della solenne coronazione fatta in Campidoglio* (1779), X. Petrarch had often been invoked by Corilla's enemies to make comparisons unflattering to her. Bodoni quotes Petrarch's line "there is nothing in the world poetry cannot achieve"; ibid., ii.

61. On the occasion of Corilla's Arcadian crowning, the British sculptor Christopher Hewston donated to Arcadia a marble bust of Corilla. Her portrait can be found in *In lode della sac. Maesta` rea. app. di Maria Teresa* (Venezia: Antonio Zatta, 1765), 135–36. At the entrance of Biblioteca Angelica in Rome is a beautiful oil portrait of her. The famous Florentine coin maker Zanobi Weber forged a medal bearing her image in August 1779.

62. Besides the collections that we mentioned above, poems in honor of Corilla were published by literary personalities throughout the century. We mentioned a few names, but we only found a few of the actual poems, some in the proceedings of Corilla's Arcadian and Capitol-crowning, some others in collections. Ademollo reports a few, by Frugoni, Pagnini, and Pietro Belli.

63. Luigi Godard, "Ragionamento," in *Atti della solenne coronazione fatta in Campidoglio* (1779), 46–47.

64. Gioacchino Pizzi, quoted in Antonio Cipriani, "Contributo per una storia politica dell'Arcadia settecentesca," *Accademia degli Arcadi: Atti e Memorie* 5 (1969), 137. Amaduzzi quoted in Ademollo, *Corilla Olimpica*, 172.

65. Charles Burney, quoted in Ademollo, *Corilla Olimpica*, 129. A manuscript document written to protest Arcadian celebrations of Corilla complained that printed proceedings of the Arcadian crowning (*Adunanza*) were read widely abroad ("Supplica ai conservatori," quoted in Ademollo, 455–56). The *Atti della solenne coronazione fatta in Campidoglio* (1779) proclaimed that "the most credited European gazettes competed with each other to inform the public of the wonderful event [of Corilla's Capitol-crowning]" (2).

66. De Villoison, quoted in Carlo Grigioni, "Sedici anni della vita di Corilla Olimpica in un carteggio inedito (1776–1792)," *La Romagna* (1928), 272.

67. See *Atti della solenne coronazione fatta in Campidoglio* (1779), 6–7. This information is also reported by David Silvagni, *La corte e la società romana nei secoli XVIII e XIX* (Rome, 1885), 231; and by Clelia Bettini Attilj, "La donna in Arcadia" in *Secondo Centenario d'Arcadia* (Rome, 1891), 322. We have reports of the number of people in attendance at Corilla's precrowning "experiments": by the third evening there were so many people attending that the room chosen was not enough to contain them all, and some listeners had to content themselves with sitting in an adjacent one. Among the many nobles, there were a growing number of women: on the third night, "eighteen ladies and several princesses." Three hundred people attended the reception following the last performance. *Atti della solenne coronazione fatta in Campidoglio* (1779), 21, 23, 26.

68. Versari, "Dialogo pastorale," 48.

69. Saverio Bettinelli, quoted in Giandomenico Falcone, "Poetica e letteratura della seconda Arcadia," *La rassegna della letteratura italiana* 80 (1976), 95.

70. Bettinelli, *Dell'entusiasmo delle belle arti*, in *Opere* (Venice, 1780–1782), vol. 3, 33.

71. *Atti della solenne coronazione fatta in Campidoglio* (1779), 48.

72. Cristofano Amaduzzi, letter of 29 April 1777 to Aurelio de' Giorgi Bertola, in Grigioni, *Sedici anni della vita di Corilla Olimpica*, 287–88.

73. Ibid.

74. Corilla's letters to Amaduzzi reveal that Corilla cared little for formalities (she rebuked Amaduzzi for defending Gonzaga, and others for not being adamant; she felt free to criticize and censure) and was impatient with societal restrictions of women. See letters to Amaduzzi of 22 and 27 April 1777, *Il carteggio tra Amaduzzi e Corilla Olimpica 1775–1792*, ed. Luciana Morelli (Florence: Olschki, 2000).

75. Amaduzzi's letter of April 29, 1777 to Aurelio de' Giorgi Bertola, in Grigioni, *Sedici anni della vita di Corilla Olimpica*, 286.

76. Christopher M. Johns, "The Entrepôt of Europe: Rome in the Eighteenth Century," *Art in Rome in the Eighteenth Century* (Philadelphia: Philadelphia Museum of Art, 2000), 20.

77. Paola Giuli, "Women Poets and Improvisers: Cultural Assumptions and Literary Values in Arcadia," *Studies in Eighteenth-Century Culture* 32 (2003), 69–92.

78. Corilla Olimpica's life inspired the work of generations of women poets and was the object of innumerable historical and fictionalized studies and dramatizations until the end of the nineteenth century. The work of literary critics Ellen Moers, Madelyn Gutwirth, and Angela Leighton testifies to the fact that, through the mediation of de Staël's work, Corilla's literary career and especially her Capitol crowning inspired generations of British and American women writers. See Ellen Moers, "Performing Heroinism: The Myth of Corinne," in her *Literary Women, The Great Writers* (Garden City: Doubleday, 1976), 173–210; Madelyn Gutwirth, *Madame de Staël, Novelist: The Emergence of the Artist as Woman* (Urbana: University of Illinois Press, 1978); Angela Leighton, *Victorian Women Poets* (New York: Harvester Wheatsheaf, 1992). In Italy Corilla's story and work inspired poems, novels, and dramas. Corilla's biographer, Ademollo, commented: "Who can remember all the works with some reference to Corilla? By the middle of the nineteenth century Corilla had surged to legendary status." See *Corilla Olimpica*, xxi, for a list of these works. A few proud poems by Arcadian women in Corilla's honor can be found in *Atti della solenne coronazione fatta in Campidoglio* (1779), as well as in Anna Soderini, "Corilla Olimpica," in *Secondo centenario d'Arcadia* (Rome, 1891), 101–2. They testify that Corilla's story was inspirational to Italian women also.

79. "Autobiografia di Teresa Bandettini," Biblioteca statale di Lucca, Ms. 638, in Di Ricco,"*L'inutile e meraviglioso mestiere,*" 234.

80. Giuseppe Baretti, *Frusta letteraria,* 1763. According to Arcadian procedures, members pretended to be shepherds (pastori) and shepherdesses (pastorelle; notice how a diminutive suffix is used to create the feminine). Writing to Mme de Staël during her 1805 stay in Rome, Vincenzo Monti, for example, criticized Arcadian activities and poetry as *pastorellerie*; see his *Epistolario,* ed. Alfonso Bertoldi (Firenze: LeMonnier), I, 79. See also Schippisi in Piromalli, *L'Arcadia* (Palermo: Palumbo, 1975), 96–97.

81. See note 10.

82. Fernow, "Über die Improvisatoren," 414.

83. De Staël, *Corinne, or Italy,* 98–99.

84. Fernow, "Über die Improvisatoren," 414–16.

85. De Staël, *Corinne, or Italy,* 98–99, 26, 37, for more on this topic.

Notes to Chapter Thirteen

1. Croce was the most influential Italian philosopher and intellectual historian of modern Italy. His list of publications is vast. Numerous scholarly works assessing his intellectual legacy have been published in recent years. In reference to the Italian anticlerical tradition, see especially Leo Valiani, *Fra Croce e Omodeo: Storia e storiografia nella lotta per la libertà, Quaderni di storia,* 68 (Florence: Le Monnier, 1984); Jack D'Amico, ed., *The Legacy of Benedetto Croce: Contemporary Critical Reviews* (Toronto: University of Toronto Press, 1999); and Massimo Verdicchio,

Naming Things: Aesthetics, Philosophy and History in Benedetto Croce, Il pensiero e la storia, 64 (Naples: La città del sole, 2000). Each has copious bibliographical references to more specialized literature. I thank Anthony Grafton and Maria Conforti for discussing Croce's impact on Italian historiography with me and for suggesting pertinent bibliography.

2. Suppression of nepotism and the progressive cultural activities of the early eighteenth-century papacy are discussed at length in Christopher M. S. Johns, *Papal Art and Cultural Politics: Rome in the Age of Clement XI* (Cambridge and New York: Cambridge University Press, 1993), especially chapter two, pp. 22–38, with additional bibliography.

3. Anthony Morris Clark, ed. Edgar Peters Bowron, *Pompeo Batoni: A Complete Catalogue of His Works with an Introductory Text* (New York: New York University Press, 1985), p. 269; Edgar Peters Bowron, "Pompeo Batoni: Pope Benedict XIV presenting the Encyclical 'Ex Omnibus' to the Comte de Choiseul," in Joseph J. Rishel and Edgar Peters Bowron, eds., *Art in Rome in the Eighteenth Century*, exhibition catalogue (Philadelphia and London: Merrell Publishers, 2000), p. 312, with additional bibliography.

4. The papal encyclical *Ex Omnibus* was addressed to the French bishops, hoping to clarify papal doctrinal positions on a number of issues that were causing friction in the French church. These included tiresome Gallican claims counter to those of the Roman Curia, persisting Jansenist tendencies that had earlier been addressed by Clement XI Albani's bull *Unigenitus* of 1713, and resistance from the *parlements* to royal attempts to impose religious uniformity. The encyclical was issued by Benedict at the urging of Louis XV. See Dale K. Van Kley, *The Religious Origins of the French Revolution: From Calvin to the Civil Constitution, 1560–1791* (New Haven and London: Yale University Press, 1996), pp. 148–51, with additional bibliography.

5. Olivier Michel and Pierre Rosenberg, eds., *Subleyras (1699–1749)*, exhibition catalogue (Paris and Rome: Editions de la Réunion des musées nationaux, 1987), pp. 307–13. For a stimulating discussion of Subleyras' painting in the context of canonization pictures, see Andreas Schalhorn, *Historienmalerei und Heiligsprechung: Pierre Subleyras (1699–1749) und das Bild für den Papst im 17. und 18. Jahrhundert* (Munich: Scaneg Verlag, 2000), pp. 11–23.

6. For the Catholic Enlightenment in European context, see especially Mario Rosa, *Settecento religioso: Politica della ragione e religione del cuore* (Venice: Marsilio, 1999), with additional bibliography. My ideas about the visual culture of the Catholic Enlightenment owe a profound debt to Rosa's pioneering work.

7. See Stefania Nanni, *Roma religiosa nel Settecento: Spazi e linguaggi dell'identità cristiana* (Rome: Carocci, 2000), pp. 23–49, with copious bibliography. See also R. Po-Chia Hsia, *The World of Catholic Renewal, 1540–1770* (Cambridge: Cambridge University Press, 1998), pp. 138–51.

8. For a useful and intelligent introduction to the Enlightenment's attitudes to gender differences, both biological and social, see Dorinda Outram, *The Enlightenment* (Cambridge: Cambridge University Press, 1995; reprint 1999), pp. 80–95, with additional bibliography.

9. For a brief introduction to Poussin's *Seven Sacraments*, see Hugh Brigstocke, "Poussin and Cassiano dal Pozzo: A Study of the Seven Sacraments," *Apollo* 114 (1981), 373–77, with additional bibliography. The paintings of the sacraments have figured heavily in the vast recent literature on the Baroque polymath Cassiano dal Pozzo (1588–1657), scholarship that rightly emphasizes the archaeological and philological aspects of the scenes. See Ingo Herklotz, *Cassiano dal Pozzo und die Archäologie des 17. Jahrhunderts* (Munich: Hirmer Verlag, 1999), with additional bibliography.

10. The highly moralizing reforms of the early eighteenth-century papacy, above all in the context of the Early Christian revival, are discussed in Johns, *Papal Art and Cultural Politics*, pp. 195–200. For Roman popular religion of the period, see the breezy but engaging account in Maurice Andrieux, *Daily Life in Papal Rome in the Eighteenth Century*, trans. Mary Fitton (London: George Allen and Unwin Ltd., 1968), pp. 118–35. This study must be read with caution, however, since it often perpetuates outdated stereotypes of the popular classes.

11. The *Seven Sacraments* are discussed intelligently in John T. Spike et al., *Giuseppe Maria Crespi and the Emergence of Genre Painting in Italy*, exhibition catalogue (Fort Worth and Florence: Centro Di, 1986), pp. 132–36. Spike rightly rejects an eighteenth-century view of the paintings as comic, even burlesque, understanding the academic prejudices of the writers who found difficulty accepting "ignoble" treatment of such elevated subjects. The descriptions of the paintings in the early sources do not jive well with what we actually see and may, I believe, be safely dismissed. See Giovanni Pietro Zanotti, *Storia dell'Accademia Clementina di Bologna*, 2 vols. (Bologna, 1739), II:53–54; and Luigi Crespi, *Vite de' pittori bolognesi non descritte nella Felsina pittrice* (Rome: M. Pagliarini, 1769), pp. 212–13. The latter account, penned by the painter's son, is torn between the goal of establishing his father's primacy in the early eighteenth-century Bolognese school of painting while trying to downplay the elder Crespi's decided antiacademic and naturalistic tendencies, which were very much at variance with his own. From all we know of Ottoboni's combination of urbanity and piety, the idea that the Crespi *Sacraments* could be mockeries of the participants is, in my opinion, exceedingly far-fetched. Both primary texts are quoted in Spike, *Crespi*, pp. 132–33. For Ottoboni, see Francis Haskell, *Patrons and Painters: Art and Society in Baroque Italy* (New York: Harper and Row, 1980; originally published 1963), pp. 164–66; and Edward J. Olszewski, *The Inventory of Paintings of Cardinal Pietro Ottoboni, 1667–1740* (New York and Vienna: Peter Lang, 2004).

12. A recent example of uncritically buying into the early accounts is Harald Marx and Gregor J. M. Weber, eds., *Dresden in the Ages of Splendor and Enlightenment: Eighteenth-Century Paintings from the Old Masters Picture Gallery*, trans. Russell Stockman, exhibition catalogue (Columbus, OH: Columbus Museum of Art, 1999), pp. 207–10.

13. It would be hard to overemphasize the importance of the official condemnation of papal nepotism at the end of the seventeenth century to the development of an institutional mechanism that enabled the pontifical government to respond

to Enlightenment critique. See Christopher M. S. Johns, "The Entrepôt of Europe: Rome in the Eighteenth Century," in Joseph J. Rishel and Edgar Peters Bowron, eds., *Art in Rome in the Eighteenth Century*, exhibition catalogue (Philadelphia and London: Merrell Publishers, 2000), pp. 22–29, with additional bibliography. See also A. D. Wright, *The Early Modern Papacy from the Council of Trent to the French Revolution* (Harlow, England: Pearson Education Ltd., 2000), especially pp. 253–60. For a useful overview of monks and nuns in ancien régime Europe, see Owen Chadwick, *The Popes and European Revolution* (Oxford: Oxford University Press, 1981), pp. 210–52, with additional bibliography.

14. The National Assembly did not abolish binding monastic vows until 1790, and even then leaving monasteries and convents was voluntary. The services in nursing and teaching rendered by the religious continued to be funded by the government, at least in theory, after the suppression of tithes and mass confiscations of ecclesiastical property. See François Furet, *The French Revolution, 1770–1814*, trans. Antonia Nevill (Oxford: Blackwell, 1996), pp. 80–85. It was only the radicalization of the Revolution in 1792–93 that led to suppression, persecution, and attempted dechristianization. See Michel Vovelle, *The Revolution against the Church: From Reason to the Supreme Being*, trans. Alan José (Columbus: Ohio State University Press, 1991), pp. 12–24.

15. See W. R. Ward, *Christianity under the Ancien Régime, 1648–1789* (Cambridge: Cambridge University Press, 1999), pp. 39–52.

16. See especially the engaging discussion of the struggles of female conventual mystics and patriarchal Church authority in Hsia, pp. 138–51.

17. The best introduction to the ceremonies and imagery surrounding the creation of new saints is Vittorio Casale, "Gloria ai beati e ai santi: Le feste di beatificazione e di canonizzazione," in *La Festa a Roma dal Rinascimento al 1870*, ed. Marcello Fagiolo, 2 vols., exhibition catalogue (Rome: Umberto Allemandi, 1997), I: 124–41, with additional bibliography. I have benefited greatly from reading Professor Casale's myriad publications, too numerous to list here. For the processes and politics surrounding beatification and canonization in the eighteenth century, see the appropriate volumes in Ludwig von Pastor, *The History of the Popes from the Close of the Middle Ages*, 40 vols. (London: Kegan Paul, 1938–1961). Benedict XIV, while still archbishop of Bologna, authored a guide to canonization that is still in use. He argued for a slower and more reasoned approach to miracles, resistance to popular demands for sanctification, and the need for irrefutable evidence of divine intervention, to be determined by ecclesiastical authority. Above all, he wanted to rationalize the process by distancing it from local enthusiasm and establishing Rome as the only arbiter for canonization on the basis of established procedures.

18. Benefial was a maverick painter who was frequently at odds with the Accademia di San Luca, the pontifical artists' institution that wielded considerable cultural power, and it would not be inaccurate to describe his style as antiacademic in the tradition of Crespi. Although this is a factor in the decided naturalism of his paintings for Santa Maria in Ara Coeli, many other artists were pursuing similar paths without conflict with the Academy. See Italo Faldi, "Marco Benefial: Storia di

S. Margherita da Cortona," *Bollettino d'Arte* 41 (1956), 373–75; and Giorgio Falcidia, "Per una definizione del 'caso' Benefial," *Paragone Arte* 29 (1978), 24–51, who stresses the outsider status of the painter and, in my view, greatly overemphasizes its impact on the artist's stylistic choices. For Benefial's place in Roman eighteenth-century painting, see the overview by Lilliana Barroero, "La pittura a Roma nel Settecento," in *La pittura in Italia: Il Settecento*, ed. Giuliano Briganti, 2 vols. (Milan: Electa, 1990), II:353–427, with additional bibliography. This essay is the best survey of Roman eighteenth-century painting available.

19. Anna Lo Bianco, "Pier Leone Ghezzi: 'The Investiture of Saint Giuliana Falconieri between Saint Philip Benizi and Saint Alessio Falconieri,'" in Joseph J. Rishel and Edgar Peters Bowron, eds., *Art in Rome in the Eighteenth Century*, exhibition catalogue (Philadelphia and London: Merrell Publishers, 2000), 371–72. For Ghezzi's career and close connections to the Falconieri family, see idem, *Pier Leone Ghezzi: Settecento alla moda*, exhibition catalogue (Venice: Marsilio Editore, 1999), with extensive bibliography. Around 1710, Ghezzi painted *The Death of Saint Giuliana Falconieri* replete with lambent lighting, cherubs, angels, garlands, and clouds. The quasi-documentary mode seen in *Giuliana Falconieri Taking the Veil* may indicate study of works by Marco Benefial and other naturalistic painters.

20. Lilliana Barroero, "Marco Benefial: 'Vision of Saint Catherine Fieschi Adorno of Genoa,'" in Joseph J. Rishel and Edgar Peters Bowron, eds., *Art in Rome in the Eighteenth Century*, exhibition catalogue (Philadelphia and London: Merrell Publishers, 2000), pp. 323–24. For an overview of Benefial's career, see idem, *Benefial* (Milan: 5 Continents Editions, 2005), with bibliography.

Contributors

ROBERTO BIZZOCCHI is Professor of Modern History at the University of Pisa. His books include *Chiesa e potere nella Toscana del Quattrocento* (Bologna: Il Mulino, 1987), *Genealogie incredibili. Scritti di storia nell'Europa moderna* (Bologna: Il Mulino, 1995), and *In famiglia. Storie di interessi e affetti nell'Italia moderna* (Roma-Bari: Laterza, 2001).

MARTA CAVAZZA is Associate Professor of History of Science at the University of Bologna. Her research focuses on scientific institutions—the university and academies—in seventeenth- and eighteenth-century Italy, especially in Bologna and Emilia. Her books include *Settecento inquieto. Alle origini dell'Istituto delle Scienze* (Il Mulino, 1990), *La corrispondenza di Pietro Mengoli* (with Gabriele Baroncini; Olschki, 1986), and numerous essays in recent years on gender in eighteenth-century Italy, in particular the presence of women in the scientific academies and universities.

SUSAN DALTON is Associate Professor of History at the Université de Montréal and author of *Engendering the Republic of Letters: Reconnecting Public and Private Spheres in Eighteenth-Century Europe* (McGill-Queens University Press, 2003). She works in the field of late-eighteenth-century French and Venetian cultural history.

MARIA PIA DONATO is a Lecturer at the University of Cagliari. She is the author of *Accademie romane. Una storia sociale, 1671–1824* (Napoli, 2000) and, with D. Armando and M. Cattaneo, *Una 'rivoluzione' difficile: la Repubblica Romana del 1798–1799* (Pisa and Rome, 2000), as well as numerous essays on the political, social, and cultural history of early modern Rome.

MARTHA FELDMAN is Professor of Music and in the College at the University of Chicago. She is the author of *City Culture and the Madrigal at Venice* (University of California Press, 1995) and *Opera and Sovereignty: Transforming Myths in Eighteenth-Century Italy* (University of Chicago Press, 2007), as well as co-editor of *The Courtesan's Arts: Cross-cultural Perspectives* (Oxford University Press, 2006). Her current work involves issues of life-writing, myth, symbolic economies, and the body in connection with the castrato. She is a recipient of the Dent Medal of the Royal Musical Association (2001), and she gave the Bloch Lectures at the University of California, Berkeley, in 2007.

PAULA FINDLEN is Ubaldo Pierotti Professor in Italian History at Stanford University. She is the author of *Possessing Nature: Museums, Collecting, and Scientific Culture in Early Modern Italy* (University of California Press, 1994) and the editor of many other books, including *Athanasius Kircher: The Last Man Who Knew Everything* (Routledge, 2004) and (with Rebecca Messbarger, editors and translators) *The Contest for Knowledge: Debates about Women's Education in Eighteenth-Century Italy* (University of Chicago Press, 2005). She has recently finished *A Fragmentary Past: The Making of Museums in Late Renaissance Italy* and is completing *In the Shadow of Newton: Laura Bassi and Her World*.

ROGER FREITAS is Associate Professor of Musicology at the Eastman School of Music, University of Rochester. He has published on the Italian cantata, the castrato, and nineteenth-century vocal performance practice. His most recent publication is an edition of the complete extant cantatas of the seventeenth-century castrato Atto Melani (A-R Editions, Middleton, Wisconsin). His book-length study of the same singer—*Portrait of a Castrato: Politics, Patronage, and Music in the Life of Atto Melani*—is forthcoming from Cambridge University Press. He has been awarded fellowships by the American Academy in Rome (2003–04) and the National Endowment for the Humanities (2000–01). He received his Ph.D. in music history from Yale University in 1998.

PAOLA GIULI is Associate Professor of Italian and Director of the Italian program at Saint Joseph's University. Her publications include articles on Cristina Belgioioso, Anna Banti, literary improvisation, and the poetics of Arcadia. Her forthcoming book, *The Feminization of Italian Culture (1690–1776): Enlightenment, Arcadia and Corilla*, analyzes the cultural and epistemological conditions that allowed the emergence of an Italian female intellectual in the eighteenth century, and it exposes the gender values that shaped her representation in literary history.

ELISABETTA GRAZIOSI teaches Italian literature in the Facoltà di Lingue e Letterature Straniere of the University of Bologna. Her research focuses on women's writing, cultural geography, and the persistence of literary models. Her books include *Avventuriere a Bologna: due storie esemplari* (Mucchi Editore, 1998), *Aminta, 1573–1580: amore e matrimonio in casa d'Este* (M. Pacini Fazzi, 2001), *Questioni di lessico: l'ingegno, le passioni, il linguaggio* (Mucchi Editore, 2004), and *Lancio ed eclissi di una capitale barocca. Genova 1630–1660* (Mucchi Editore, 2006).

CHRISTOPHER M. S. JOHNS is Norman L. and Roselea J. Goldberg Professor of the History of Art at Vanderbilt University. He is the author of *Papal Art and Cultural Politics: Rome in the Age of Clement XI* (Cambridge University Press, 1993), *Antonio Canova and the Politics of Patronage in Revolutionary and Napoleonic Europe* (University of California Press, 1998), and many essays on art and society in eighteenth-century Italy. He is working on a book entitled *Visual Culture of the Catholic Enlightenment* and is a Fellow of the American Academy in Rome.

REBECCA MESSBARGER is Associate Professor of Italian at Washington University. Her research interests center on the role of women in Italian Enlightenment culture and intellectual discourse. Her publications include *The Century of Women: Representations of Women in Eighteenth-Century Italian Public Discourse* (University of Toronto Press, 2002) and *The Contest for Knowledge: Debates over Women's Learning in Eighteenth-Century Italy*, edited and translated with Paula Findlen (University of Chicago Press, 2005). Her chapter in this volume is from her forthcoming book with University of Chicago Press, *The Lady Anatomist: Anna Morandi Manzolini (1714–1774)*. She is the recipient of fellowships from the National Endowment for the Humanities, the American Philosophical Society, and the Mellon Foundation.

WENDY WASSYNG ROWORTH is Professor of Art History and Women's Studies at the University of Rhode Island. She curated the exhibition *Angelica Kauffman: A Continental Artist in Georgian England* (Brighton and York) and edited the accompanying book (Reaktion Books, 1992). Her recent publications include "Pulling Parrhasius's Curtain: Trickery and Fakery in the Roman Art World," in *Regarding Romantic Rome*, edited by Richard Wrigley (Peter Lang, 2007) and "Angelica in Love: Gossip, Rumor, Romance, and Scandal," in *Angelica Kauffman: A Woman of Immense Talent,* edited by Tobias G. Natter (Hatje-Cantz, 2007). She has held fellowships from the National Endowment for the Humanities and served as Scholar in Residence at the National Museum for Women in the Arts in Washington, D.C.

CATHERINE M. SAMA is associate professor of Italian and film media at the University of Rhode Island. She is the editor and translator of Elisabetta Caminer Turra, *Selected Writings of an Eighteenth-Century Venetian Woman of Letters* (University of Chicago Press, 2003) and several essays on the Venetian journalist Elisabetta Caminer Turra, including "Liberty, Equality, Frivolity! An Italian Critique of Fashion Periodicals" (*Eighteenth-Century Studies*, 37:3, 2004).

Index

Page numbers *in italics* indicate illustrations.
For Entries referring to people, names in parentheses, unless otherwise marked, signify Arcadian names.